Days of Conflict, Days of Glory

Ernie Macatuno

About the Author

Ernie Macatuno is a journalist who shifted to literature and music with works like the novels *Simon's Sanctuary, Gabriel's Legacy* and *Days of Conflict, Days of Glory,* a composite of his writings, particularly of his novels, *Ardor Left* and *Leandro's Odyssey. Here and There* is a compilation of his journalistic writings, a poem and two short stories. *The Son of God—Jesus Christ in the eyes of his disciples* is his biographical work on the life and teaching of Jesus Christ. Based on it is his play, *The Light of Goodness.* A self-taught pianist and composer, he has written *Fisherman's Wharf,* a musical about San Francisco's popular tourist spot.

He is known in certain journalism circles for his sparkling and incisive style of writing. He was an associate editor in *Sunday Times Magazine* and a political writer in *The Philippines Free Press.* He was editor of a number of community publications in California where his editorials and feature articles were read avidly for their depth, range and analytical writing.

He finished elementary school in Manila Cathedral School, high school in Letran College and a Bachelor of Arts degree in University of Santo Tomas where he taught journalism and literature as well in De LaSalle University.

Any similarity of the characters in this book to any person, living or dead, except for the historical figures, is purely coincidental.

TXu 2-316-567—United States Copyright Office,
Library of Congress

Copyright 2021 by Ernie Macatuno

Published by Bay Beacon Press, Stockton, California

This book is available in Amazon.com and Amazon Kindle.

$18.50 per copy

Part One

Chapter One

It was getting dark in San Francisco when Dick McCall stepped out to Market Street, the sign of *The San Francisco Sun* blurry with the fog now descending there.

He walked fast after a cable car as it was moving toward California Street. He was with one jump inside there and holding on to its handrail. Held in his other hand was his briefcase crammed with a book, magazines and newspaper clippings, he borrowed from the newspaper library.

He smiled, his topcoat flapping with the wind, thrilled by his assignment of covering a war taking place in the Philippines, at the other side of the Pacific Ocean.

The cable car moved on, past people on the sidewalk, the grand hotel, the magnificent cathedral, the Victorian mansions, the cozy homes at the side of the street. He was storing up in his mind those lovely sights in San Francisco, this city of his birth, he may not see again in a long time.

He was writing a news story, a few hours ago in the editorial room of *The San Francisco Sun,* when the copy boy rushed by his desk. A telegram held high in his hand, he was shouting about a great American naval victory in Manila Bay. He entered the glass-paneled office of Warren Davenport, the editor, and gave him the telegram.

Davenport's office was soon full of the newspaper's staff members. They cheered, right after he had finished reading the telegram.

Dick was at the edge of the crowd, just outside the room. He was likewise thrilled by that great American naval victory in Manila Bay. Here is the chance to do something great, he has been aiming at since he joined the newspaper, three years ago. He missed the chance to cover the war in Cuba which was assigned to another reporter. He now has another chance in this war in the Philippines, at the other side of Pacific Ocean.

He came in when everyone there had left the room and made his case with Davenport.

"You don't have the experience for this kind of assignment," Davenport said to him.

"Neither does the guy who is covering Cuba and I have one thing in my favor, I have been to the Philippines."

"A few days' visit there did not make you an expert on that Spanish colony."

"But I know it more than anyone here. I also speak Spanish, the language spoken by its rulers and the educated class there."

"Very well," Davenport then said, "you will cover the war there."

He smiled, he won his case and he thanked Davenport for the assignment.

"Bone up on that place," Davenport said to him.

"I will, right now."

The fog was thicker by the time Dick got off from the cable car, the street lamps' yellowish light guiding him in the fog.

He arrived home to a familiar domestic scene there.

Harry, his father, was seated on his armchair, reading a magazine. Gina, his ten-year-old sister, was playing house with her doll while Monica, his half-Hispanic mother, was in the kitchen, preparing their dinner.

He laid his briefcase on a table there, removed his topcoat and put it on a hanger there.

"Guess what, Dad," he said to Harry. "We won a great naval victory in Manila Bay."

"Why, that is great! How did it happen?"

He relayed the news, he picked up in the office.

"That should remind everyone, not to pick a fight with us," Harry said. "So, our navy is now operating in the far corners of the world, sinking the Spanish fleet in Manila Bay, of all places."

"Have you not been there before?" Gina asked Dick. "Where is it located?"

"It is at the other side of the Pacific Ocean."

Gina looked blankly at Dick.

"The street in front of our house leads to the sea, you know that," he said to Gina. "That is the start of the Pacific Ocean from our side here in America. If you will go straight and then bend down a little, just a little, you will get to the Philippines, sooner or later."

Gina nodded, satisfied with his explanation and returned to her doll.

"Hi, Mom," Dick said as he was approaching his mother.

Monica looked up at Dick who towered over her, at his brown, wavy hair and keen, grey eyes and boyish grin that made him look younger than his age of twenty-two years.

"Why," she said, "are you so excited about a naval battle that took place in that faraway place?"

"I am going to cover the war there, Mom."

"I'm afraid of that."

"Don't worry about me, Mom. I can take care of myself."

The frown in Monica's face showed Dick, she was opposed to him in going to the war there. He was about to reassure her about his safety, but then she said, "Call your Dad and Gina to the dining table before the food gets cold."

Dinner was usually a cheerful time for the McCall family, but Dick's impending departure for the Philippines had dampened their enthusiasm for small talk there.

"When are you leaving?" Harry asked Dick, finally breaking the silence there.

"I'll be leaving in a few days or weeks, Dad. It depends on the berth I can get in a troopship going there."

Monica did not want to hear about it. She stood up and returned to the kitchen.

"What sort of a place, is it?" Harry asked Dick. "You did not tell us much about it after you returned from your trip there."

"I did not tell you much about it because you were more interested about China and Japan which I also visited. But from what I have seen there, which was not much, and what I have read about it, the people there have absorbed what the Spaniards have taken the trouble of teaching them."

"Like what?"

"Like religion. Except for a few areas where the Muslims and the pagan tribes live, the Philippines is a Christian colony of Spain."

"That is something good that can be said about it."

"They have an educational system that has a number of schools, ran by the religious orders there. They have boarding schools for women, ran by nuns."

"How about the people, what are they like?"

"They are mostly simple folks, kept poor and ignorant by their Spanish rulers although they have a small privileged class of native people, some of them even educated in Europe. The colony's social, political life is dominated by the Spanish rulers and the Spanish mestizos, called the *Ilustrados*. The economy is in the hands of the Chinese merchants, the Ilustrados and some British trading firms."

"How about the country, what is it like?"

"It is believed to have extensive mineral, forestry, fisheries and agricultural resources. It is worth the trouble of taking that colony."

"Are we taking it?"

"I see that as the only reason, our navy fought and defeated the Spanish naval fleet there and why our army is going there."

"I don't see any reason too why we should be involved there," Monica said as she was returning to her seat at the dining table. "I don't see any reason, why you should go there."

"It is my job, Mom."

"Your job," Monica said, frowning. "You should have taken some other kind of work. You should have been a doctor, a lawyer or whatever line of work that would have kept you here. You could marry that girl Rosanna and join her family's fishing business."

"I like her. She is a very nice, beautiful girl, but I cannot imagine myself spending the rest of my life, fishing with her in San Francisco Bay. I want to see the world and write about people, places and events."

Monica looked away, so disappointed and saw Gina, who was listening idly as she was making circles with her spoon in her bowl of soup.

"Stop that and finish your soup," Monica said to Gina.

Dick, after their dinner, went down to his fingertip-size garden and vineyard at the back of their house, lovely with flowers and grapes.

He shook his head as he was looking at them. He will be gone by the time they will be in full bloom.

He was, later in his room, spending hours in reading the book, the magazines and newspaper clippings on Cuba and the Philippines. He learned from reading them why the United States became involved in Cuba as it is now involved in the Philippines. It was sympathy for the Cubans in their quest for independence from Spain, like what they did with England.

He read on:

"The United States could have kept out of Cuba since it had no business getting involved in what was Spain's internal affair with its Cuban subjects. It was not in the character though of the Americans to look away and do nothing while the Cubans were treated so badly by their Spanish rulers. The terrible condition in the Spanish concentration camps in Cuba, made worse by the yellow fever epidemic raging there, sent to their death nearly half a million Cubans in what was the most glaring example of how badly Spain was treating Cuba.

"It remained just that, a strong sympathy for the Cubans despite some newspapers' frenzied calls for direct American involvement there. It finally came about, following the explosion and the sinking in the harbor in Havana on February 15, 1898 of the American battleship *Maine*. It was sent there to protect American citizens and interests in

Cuba. Spain was blamed for it although who caused the explosion and the sinking of the *Maine* was never firmly established.

"Two months later, on April 20, 1898, President William McKinley signed a joint congressional resolution calling for Spain's withdrawal from Cuba. Spain responded by breaking diplomatic relations with the United States. Both sides then declared war. The Philippines is a prime target since it is also a Spanish colony."

All of those that he read added to what he had learned about the Philippines from a short visit he made there, two years ago. A revolution broke out there, a few days after he left it. The Spanish-American War has reached that distant Spanish colony in the Pacific Ocean and he will soon be going back there.

"So, Dick McCall," he said as he was looking at himself in the bathroom mirror, "sharpen your pen, your mind, your eyes and your ears for this tough, important assignment you are now facing."

He did not go to work, the following morning. He went instead to San Francisco's military base in Presidio about getting a berth in a troopship going to the Philippines. He had just left the base headquarters where he got a berth in a troopship when he heard his name called.

He looked back and saw Bill Shay. He was surprised to see him in military uniform, a captain.

"So, you are going back to the Philippines," Bill said smiling to Dick.

"So are you, I suppose," Dick replied likewise smiling.

He met Bill two years ago at the bar in Hotel de Oriente, Manila's finest hotel. He learned, after a few drinks there, that they had a common purpose of seeing what the Spanish colony was like, he as a newspaperman and not known to him then, Bill as a military agent.

They took in just like the ordinary tourists, the sights in Manila and in the towns nearby, sometimes on foot, as what they did in the Spanish enclave in Intramuros, in Escolta and in Rosario, the city's two principal shopping streets, but mostly in hired horse-drawn cabs.

A boat they hired, took them around Manila Bay with Bill taking a close look at the shore batteries in Fort Santiago in Manila and in the Spanish naval base in Sangley Point in Cavite. Their boat also plied the Pasig River, where they watched the ships in the port there and, not far from there, Malacanang Palace, the Spanish governor-general's riverside retreat. They managed, with the help of a Spanish banker they befriended in the bar in Hotel de Oriente, to get an invitation to a party held there.

"So," Dick said to Bill, "you are going back to the Philippines, not to tour the place, but to fight the Spaniards there."

"I went there before as I am going back there, never as a tourist, but as a military agent sent there to look around at their military capability."

"What did you find there?"

"Not much can be said about that."

"A few days after I left, a revolution broke out there."

"I know."

"Did you have a hand in it?"

"I wish I had."

"We will have a very busy time there, now that there will soon be a lot of fighting there."

"Let us start it, right here, right now with a few drinks."

They proceeded to a bar, not far from the Presidio.

Dick was, two weeks later, on the deck of a troopship with Captain Bill Shay. He was watching his family, smiling and waving at him in good-bye when he was surprised to see with them, Rosanna, who was also smiling and waving at him. He smiled and waved back at her although he knew she would be out of his mind, once the troopship was out at sea.

Chapter 2

It was early evening in Masakao when Paulo Palanas rode in the town's deserted road with his uncle Lukas who was seated beside him in their horse-drawn cab. The homes near the road looked lovely even at night with their flowering plants, palm and fruit trees.

The pleasant sight and the scent of the flowers eased up somehow the fear Paulo felt that they might run afoul of the law with this ride they were taking across the town to Manuel Mulawin's house. Masakao will be, within a short while, under a dusk-to-dawn curfew. They might end up in jail if the Civil Guard will catch them, out there on the road by that time.

His uncle Lukas seemed not too concerned about it, though. He was looking at the clouds hanging low in the dark sky. Rain was about to fall. It will be a welcome relief to the town from its warm, humid weather, the air there smelling faintly of hay and the fragrance of the flowers there.

He had the horse turning right at an intersection of the road and was, after a short distance, about to turn left toward the road to the town bridge when he suddenly pulled the rein. The horse stopped abruptly.

A spot of light from a lantern hanging in the bridge showed two Civil Guard sentries keeping watch there. They were talking and smoking and seemed to have noticed nothing to alert them. The shrubs and the trees with their overhanging branches at the side of the road gave their cab, the cover from the sentries.

"The sentries are too early. We should have left the house earlier," Lukas said, his voice kept low.

They cannot cross the bridge with the sentries there now.

He asked his uncle, his voice also kept low, "What do we do now? Do we turn back?"

"No. The meeting with Mulawin and the others is very important."

"Why don't we try the other route in San Martin?"

"It will take too long and we will be so late for the meeting. San Martin could also be under a curfew."

"What do we do now?"

"We'll think of something. We'll wait in the meantime. Something might turn up."

Paulo looked ahead, doubtful of that something that would enable them to cross the bridge. He nodded. They could hitch the horse near the river, cross its shallow part and walk the rest of the way to Mulawin's house. It was an absurd idea, he dismissed with a frown. There was nothing they could do but wait.

He looked around. The town square at the right side of the road was dark except for the checkpoint at the bridge. The roofed bandstand in the middle of the town square was barely visible.

The town church at the left side of the road, its two belfries pointed to the sky, stood dark and brooding over its churchyard fenced with adobe and iron grill. The municipal building stood near the narrow road that branched out from the road to the bridge and ended at the entrance to the town fort.

He watched the sentries with growing impatience. They will never leave their post even if he and his uncle will watch them and wait there, the whole night. They are waiting for nothing. This ride they are taking to Mulawin's house is not worth the risk of getting caught in the curfew. Mayor Echeverria imposed it on the town at the instigation of Lieutenant Zatayde, the new commander of the town fort.

A few drops of rain began to fall on the cab's tin roof. Lukas looked up at the dark clouds in the sky. Rain was about to fall.

"There is the answer to your question," he said to Paulo in a low, but confident tone of voice. "The rain will send the sentries running for shelter in the bandstand. We will then make a run for the bridge."

"They will shoot us once they will see us."

"We'll have to take that risk, but don't worry, we'll make it safely. We'll wait until they are at some distance from the bridge before we will make a run for it."

Paulo looked away, doubtful of his uncle's assurances. What they were about to do was nothing short of suicidal! But then, a lifetime habit of obedience to his uncle took hold of him and he made ready with the whip, he took out from its holder. Not a word passed between them as they waited for the rain to fall.

It did in a short while, heavily with claps of thunder and streaks of lightning in the sky as the wind and the rain swept through their cab.

They watched the sentries. One of them had removed the lantern from the bridge as they then ran for shelter in the roofed bandstand, their gas lantern swinging in the dark.

"Now, go!" Lukas said when they saw the sentries were now more than halfway to the bandstand.

The horse, at the crack of Paulo's whip, broke into a gallop. The rain was sweeping through him and his uncle as the horse was running on.

He glanced at his uncle who was looking intently ahead, his hand holding on to the cab's roof post.

He was jolted when he looked back and saw one of the sentries had turned around. The sentry had seen them. Fear cold as ice swept up in his spine, his body turned rigid with fear when he saw the sentry, now taking aim at him with his rifle. Any moment now, to the crack of a rifle shot, a bullet will hit him. All that he heard though was of the rain falling on the cab's tin roof as he then lashed the horse repeatedly with the whip, sending it running much faster toward the bridge.

He looked back and saw the sentry was stopped from shooting him by the rain pelting his face, he was wiping away with the back of his hand. The sentry fired and hit the rear compartment of the cab.

The horse ran on and had crossed the bridge when he looked back and saw nothing, but darkness. The horse stopped running when he pulled the rein. They were now out of danger. He bent down and took, out of relief, a deep breath.

"We made it safely," Lukas said as he tapped Paulo on his shoulders.

"Well, uncle," Paulo said, "the meeting in Mulawin's house should be worth the risk we just took of getting shot by the sentry."

"It is. I will tell you why, but we better move on. We're so late."

Paulo returned the whip to its holder and flicked the horse with the rein. It ran on leisurely, its hoofs splashing the puddles of rainwater that had collected on the road.

The horse had run only a short distance when the rain stopped as suddenly as it started. The sky cleared and a sprinkling of stars had appeared there. The air was now fresh and cool. A bank of dark clouds in the horizon showed more rain, far ahead.

They were now passing by an area in the town where the road was bound on both sides by rice fields.

It stretched from the left side of the road, westward toward the Central Plain of Luzon.

Rice fields were also at the right side of the road. They extended by more than a mile to a range of low-lying hills that ascended into the mountain range of Sierra Madre.

The flat expanse of land was relieved only by an occasional nipa hut, standing near palm and fruit trees. The light cast by a gas lamp was framed up by the window in a hut there.

"Keep to yourself everything that I will tell you," Lukas said, his forehead furrowed, as he gazed at Paulo.

His deep-set eyes and his dark hair made him look older than his age of twenty years. Their family has a serious facial expression and it likewise made Paulo look much older than his age.

He nodded as his uncle then said, "You asked me a few times why I often went to see Manuel Mulawin. I told you nothing then. We often met to discuss our plans for the Katipunan. It is a secret society founded in Manila, four years ago by Andres Bonifacio. He is a simple company messenger and warehouseman of limited formal education, but with an exceptionally strong will and organizational ability. The Katipunan now has thousands of members, all over the islands. Manuel and I, along with a few other men, organized a chapter here in Masakao. We now have more than a hundred members."

"What are you after?"

"Our freedom. Since Spain will never give it to us, we will then mount a revolution, for it is only with the use of force that we can get it."

He was so jolted by what his uncle said, it was as if a fist had hit his jaw. He swung his head back, the rein he abruptly pulled back.

The sudden stop, the horse then made might have thrown them out of the cab had they not managed to hold on to the cab's roof posts.

"That will be so terrible," he said.

"What is so terrible about it?"

"How else should I call that which will lead to fighting, to death and destruction? Why should we let that happen here?"

"Would you rather then that we remain, the Spaniards' slaves, we have been for more than three hundred years?"

"There are other ways to make changes."

"We will discuss that later on, not now. Let us move on."

He had the horse, running again with a flick of the rein.

He said at the same time, "Things are not so bad, we have to resort to something so violent, dangerous and destructive as in a revolution."

"You just don't want our plan for you to take up law in Spain upset by any disturbance here, but you must also think of our country. Change is in order here, but then it seems, you prefer for things to stay the way they are, here in our country."

"No, I don't, but there are a lot of other ways to make those necessary changes here."

"Like what Jose Rizal and Marcelo del Pilar did in Spain?"

"That is one."

"That is an admirable thing that they did, but you know very well that the reforms they sought in Spain came to nothing. Rizal, our foremost reformist, is exiled by the Spaniards in Dapitan while del Pilar is dead from tuberculosis. The situation in our country today is not any better than it was, ten years ago, when they started their reform movement in Spain."

"There are other ways to make changes."

"Like what?"

"One is by improving ourselves."

"What good can we get from that?"

"Our Spanish rulers treat us for what most of us are: poor, slavish and ignorant. They will treat us better if we can rise above all of that."

"You know that will never happen, for as long as they rule us."

"Have we not decided that I, for example, should study law in Spain so I can be as good as, if not better than the Spaniards?"

"I know that. That is why I wanted you to pursue your law studies there, but Paulo we are among the few exceptions. Our town itself is an exception. You, yourself said that most of our countrymen are held down in poverty, slavery and ignorance. The Spaniards will never allow us to be on equal terms with them. They will always be our masters while we will always be their slaves."

"We can, if we will try hard enough."

"Why do you keep insisting on that? Have you forgotten how your own father was so mistreated by the Spaniards?"

Paulo was jolted by what his uncle said. It opened an old wound from the past. His father was a victim of Spanish oppression. He shook his head at how he had all but forgotten that. He was so preoccupied with his future that he turned his back to the past, the past of sadness and suffering in their country, in their own family. His uncle was right about the unjust treatment they bear too willingly from their Spanish masters.

"I will never forget that to the day, I die," he said, his anger turned to the horse as he flicked it with the rein.

"We are past reforms. We must have our freedom and justice for your parents. We will seek them, no longer by argument and persuasion as Rizal, del Pilar and the other reformists had tried to do in Spain, but with our knives and spears as Bonifacio wants us to do, right here in our country."

"There is then no point for me to leave for Spain with the coming revolution. The Spaniards may already know about it."

"What made you say that?"

"Chemari told me one time in Lateran about a rumor he heard in the barracks in Fort Santiago, something about a secret, subversive society. He even kidded me about it. When you told me about the Katipunan, the secret, subversive society they were talking about could be the Katipunan."

"If you are right about that, it could mean we have lost our big advantage of secrecy and surprise. We should have been more careful."

Paulo shook his head. He will also worry over the discovery of the Katipunan. His uncle said it is a secret, subversive society. Every member must have taken a vow of secrecy, but words said carelessly, here and there, when put together, told of an impending uprising. The rumor had reached the College of Saint John of Lateran where he learned about it from his friend and classmate, Chemari Achutegui. If the soldiers had talked about it, Chemari's father, Colonel Vidal Achutegui, the deputy commander of the Civil Guard, certainly knew about it. The rumor had sent panic in Intramuros and spread to the rest of the colony. That could be the reason the curfew was imposed in Masakao recently.

"Whether the Spaniards know about it or not, the revolution will come anytime soon," Lukas said. "We are going to Manuel Mulawin's house to discuss the preparations in our town."

Paulo said nothing, his eyes turned to the road. So many things were happening in their country and here he was, blissfully unaware that it was about to blow up in a revolution.

"Why," he asked his uncle, "was I kept from all of that?"

"I told you nothing then because I did not want you distracted from your studies. I told you nothing about the Katipunan before we left the house so that in case we are detained by the Civil Guard, there is nothing they could pry out from you because you knew nothing then."

"Thank you for that, uncle."

"I only did what your father would have done for you."

He was stunned by what his uncle said. It was as if he said it at the behest of someone watching over him, someone sweeping evil away, like the spirit of his father. He was then gripped with longing for his father and his mother. He never knew them. He looked on sadly at the road.

What Lukas saw in Paulo's face reminded him about something sad and terrible that happened in the past. He saw that look in Paulo's face, many years ago, in the face of his brother Marko, Paulo's father. Paulo looked very much like his father. He has Marko's deep-set eyes, pale cheeks and an ascetic look that masked an intense and sometimes impulsive spirit. He has a slim build he inherited from his mother, Leticia. Paulo's life, like that of his father, will now be changed forever by events overtaking it. Paulo is his only family. He grew up under his care as if he is his own son. He never married after he lost an early love. He thought of his plans for Paulo, whose studies in Spain will now have to be put off.

He thought bitterly of how Marko's life had made such a fateful turn, twenty-one years ago. Marko was arrested, four years after the Filipino sailors' mutiny in Sangley Point Naval Base in Cavite in 1872. The Spanish friars, in connivance with the civil and military authorities, used the mutiny as a way of putting away the troublesome reformist Filipino priests.

It was a bad time for the Catholic Church in the Philippines when the much fewer Filipino priests were agitating for a change in the way the Catholic Church, dominated by the Spanish friars, viewed itself and the Filipinos.

The Filipino priests wanted the Catholic Church to see itself, not as an instrument of Spanish colonial rule, but as the Christian faith's missionary outpost in the Orient. They wanted the Catholic Church to see the Filipinos, less as subjects of Spanish rule and more as a flock of Jesus Christ. They also agitated for a better treatment of the Filipino priests, as in the parish assignments. The rich parishes in Manila and the big towns were assigned to the Spanish friars, the poorest and the remotest to the Filipino priests. If they were assigned at all to the rich parishes, the highest position they got was that of associate pastors.

The Filipino priests' reform movement died when its three leaders, Fathers Jose Burgos, Mariano Gomez and Jacinto Zamora were falsely implicated in the mutiny in the Cavite naval base. They were, in a mock trial held by their Spanish rulers, sentenced to death by the garrote.

The Spanish authorities made a show of their executions before a hushed and horrified crowd.

The priests were brought up, one at a time, to a platform. Mercifully for the old Father Zamora, he lost his mind before his execution. He never knew what was going on when he was strapped to a seat, a black hood put over his head and an iron collar, put around his neck. He died of strangulation when the executioner tightened the screw at the back of the iron collar. It was more painful for Fathers Burgos and Gomez, whose bodies twisted and jerked as the iron collar also strangulated them to their death.

Marko quit his job of a scribe in the parish in Santa Ana. He changed his mind about becoming a priest for what their Spanish rulers had done to the three reformist Filipino priests. He left Manila and returned to Masakao. He settled down to a country life where he rekindled an old love for Leticia, a town maiden. They were married and were so happy at the prospect of becoming parents when Leticia became big and heavy with their child in her womb.

Their lives were completely altered when a rumor of another uprising swept the colony. Their Spanish rulers reacted swiftly. They presumed this to be a part of a continuing conspiracy that began with the mutiny of the Filipino sailors in the naval base in Sangley Point. They arrested those who worked for or who openly sympathized with the three reformist Filipino priests.

Marko was among those arrested. He was taken to the prison in Fort Santiago. Leticia was not fit to travel and it was he, as Marko's younger brother, who was allowed to visit Marko in the prison.

He found Marko's disposition, the first time he was allowed to visit him, as gloomy as the prison's dark and bare visiting room. Marko despaired of ever getting out of the prison, alive. Memory of what the Spaniards did to the three Filipino priests troubled him. He was certain about their innocence, but that did not spare them from the garrote.

He saw in the following month, when he was allowed to visit Marko again, a marked change in his appearance and disposition. No longer unkempt and despairing, he was heartened by the talk making the rounds in the prison cells in Fort Santiago. It was like a ray of light in the dark, underground prison.

"I heard Madrid did not approve of the mass arrests and that the authorities are looking for a way out without losing face," Marko said to Lukas. "I doubt it, if the authorities will do to me, what they did to the three priests or else the governor-general might then find himself brought back to Spain to explain himself."

Rain, a week later, fell continuously for three days in Manila. Pasig River, which coursed through the northern side of the fort, rose at high tide and through a crack in the fort wall, sent a great amount of water into the underground prison.

A guard, the following morning, was stopped from going down to the prison cells by the floodwater that had reached near the top two steps of the stone staircase. The guard probed the cells with a gas lantern. He was shocked to find the prisoners there, holding on to the iron bars and pleading for help, their heads barely above the floodwater.

When the cells were drained, Marko was among those found dead.

He was covered with mud and his face and arms were bruised in a vain struggle from drowning. He died curled up on the stone floor, like a baby in a womb. His body was brought back to Masakao.

Leticia was so saddened and weakened by Marko's death she died right after she gave birth to Paulo. She was buried beside Marko.

He stayed behind after their burial. He bowed as he then stood at the foot of their graves that they would be served with justice. So too for everyone else, once they have succeeded in their revolution.

His mind keen in anticipation of the revolution that will come soon, he said to Paulo, "Give the horse another lashing to make it run faster. We are so late for the meeting."

Chapter Three

Cipriano, Mulawin's manservant, stood up quickly from his stool when he saw a horse-drawn cab coming on the road. He was the lookout, waiting for Lukas, the only one expected at their meeting who has not arrived yet.

He recognized Lukas, once the cab was near enough to him. He opened the wooden gate quickly, waited until the cab had passed through and closed the gate again. He walked quickly toward the cab, took the rein from Paulo and tied it to a post there.

Paulo and Lukas got off from the cab and followed Cipriano who then led them to the back of the house.

Mulawin's house, unlike the bamboo huts and wooden houses of most of the town residents, was big and built of stone and wood and roofed with tile. A big yard planted to fruit and palm trees and ornamental plants set it apart from its neighbors and kept it partly hidden from the road. Mulawin's house was built in the boom in international trade that followed the opening of the Suez Canal in 1869. He prospered in agriculture and in trade in rice and hemp. He owned, along with Lukas and their other friends as his minority partners, the town's lone rice mill.

They followed Cipriano as they went up in the stone staircase at the back of the house. Cipriano knocked lightly on the door and stepped back when it was opened a short while later by Narcisa, Mulawin's wife. Lukas said good evening to her. She smiled and nodded in response to his greeting.

"I'm sorry, you have to come in by the back door," she said to them. "Manuel did not want our neighbors, most of all a Civil Guard patrol, to see visitors coming to our house during the curfew."

Lukas replied that he did not mind it at all. He and Paulo followed her as she led them through a hallway, the light there provided by a lamp on a wall. They descended another staircase which led to a room. She knocked lightly on the door. The voices they heard coming from inside the room ceased immediately, followed by the opening of the door.

Mulawin appeared smiling and said to Lukas, "What took you so long? Everyone here is waiting for you."

He raised his eyes in surprise at Paulo who was standing beside Lukas and Narcisa. He glanced at Lukas.

"It is about time for Paulo to know what we are doing," Lukas said to Mulawin. "I told him about the Katipunan on our way here. Considering the situation, I thought I should dispense with the formalities in taking in a new member to our group. I trust my nephew, more than anyone else."

"Quite right, quite right," Mulawin said to Lukas. He turned to Paulo and said to him, "I'm sure, you will play a great part in our cause."

Paulo smiled and nodded, flattered by what Mulawin and his uncle had said about him.

"I am tired and sleepy. I'm going to bed," Narcisa said to Mulawin as they were about to enter the room.

He asked her, "How about the food?"

"It is ready. Call the servants when you want it brought in."

Mulawin smiled at Narcisa as she was leaving them.

Paulo followed Lukas and Mulawin to the room. It was Mulawin's library. It was cast in a soft, golden light from two gas lamps hanging above a table in the middle of the room.

"You all know my nephew, Paulo," Lukas said to the six men seated there.

They looked on at Paulo who nodded in deference to them, the town's leading residents.

Lukas pointed to Paulo, a chair in a corner of the room, near a closed window.

He crossed the room and sat down on a chair there. He is there only to observe the meeting.

He swept with his eyes, Mulawin's library. Bookshelves lined a wall. A desk near the window was cluttered with a book, a pen holder, a note pad with something written on it, receipts and crumpled paper. The clutter on the table gave him the impression of the work there, left unfinished. Nailed to a wall there were framed photographs and a diploma from the Dominican university in Manila. Mulawin and his uncle had studied there. He himself had finished there, his Bachelor of Arts degree.

He watched his uncle who had sat down at a corner of the table, at the left side of Mulawin who had sat down at the head of the table.

"You are late," Alfredo Masinop said to Lukas as he was seating down at his right side..

"We are lucky to be here, at all," Lukas said to Masinop.

"Why? What happened?" Mulawin asked Lukas.

He watched them, their eyes large from shock when his uncle then told them about the Civil Guard sentry who fired at them as they were rushing in their horse-drawn cab toward the town bridge.

"A good thing the sentry was a poor shot," Menardo Gayuman said to Lukas from across the table.

"I dread what would have happened to you, had the sentry been a good shooter," Mulawin said.

"And I will be the first person to miss you, if the sentry did not miss," Gayuman said smiling to Lukas.

Paulo smiled while the others laughed. He was not surprised Gayuman had cracked a joke over his and his uncle's close brush with death. Gayuman has a humorous turn of mind, his face often wreathed with a warm, friendly smile. He also has a way with people. He had talked Mayor Echeverria, with the help of a large amount of grease money, into granting him the license to mine the iron deposits in Alkayag. It will take, though, a lot of work and money before Gayuman could make the mine operational. It was in rough, mountainous terrain. Only a trail connected it to the town. Just getting there will require several hours' hike in the forest.

The laughter had barely died down when Masinop said, "If the sentry did not miss, I will be the first to offer a Mass for the repose of the soul of Lukas."

The men at the table broke again with laughter.

Paulo's mouth hung open in surprise at finding his former teacher has a sense of humor. Like the other children, who studied in the town's primary school, he held Masinop, their very strict head teacher, in awe and fear. The picture of Masinop, going word for word over a sentence written on the blackboard, had remained fixed in his mind. Now, there he is, his former teacher, leaving the quiet, peaceful academic life and taking the path to the violence and uncertainty in the coming revolution.

He swept with his eyes, the rest of the table while his uncle was talking about his observation of the Spanish rule in their town. Seated left of Masinop was Justino Pinalis, the municipal secretary. Seated right of Gayuman, the merchant Leon Ongliko was staring ahead with his shrewd, almond eyes. His trading activities took him as far as in Hong Kong.

Doctor Jose Bihasa was seated at the right side of Ongliko. He was nodding in agreement as his uncle was now speaking about their lives, miserable under their Spanish rulers. Miguel Kabisig was seated at the other end of the table. He was likewise listening to his uncle. He knew Kabisig to have undergone a bit of military training while he was studying in Spain.

He watched them, wondering why they, who enjoyed high social and economic status, are risking everything they have for the danger and the uncertainty in the coming revolution. They did not fit at all, the French rebels, he had read in the French Revolution. They did not seem energetic and daring enough for the difficult and dangerous task ahead of them.

They were dressed like him in ordinary long-sleeved shirts, untucked at the waist. They could very well be discussing, not their dangerous and uncertain goal of throwing the Spaniards out of their country, but commercial matters like the price of rice and hemp or municipal concerns like the lack of water facilities in their hometown.

The town residents, his uncle and the others there being the prime examples, were mostly preoccupied with making a living and pursuing self-advancement. They were known for their drive and aggressiveness. They thrived. Manuel Mulawin was a very good example. A man in his late forties, Mulawin has the self-assured air of someone who had made good in life. He prospered in trade and agriculture. The townsfolk look up to him as their leader.

He also knew that education to them was just as important. The ambition of every family there was to have at least a child, if not all the children, in college in Manila and if they could afford it, even in Europe. The walls in the living rooms of many of the homes there were adorned with diplomas, second only in prominence to the images and the statues of Jesus Christ, Mother Mary and Saint Peter, the town's patron saint. It was their Christian faith, more than anything else, the Spaniards brought with them that made the townsfolk accept, if grudgingly, the Spanish rule in their town. He looked on at the men at the table for the reason for their rebellion. It was in their association with each other, in what they have picked up from reading books like those that filled the bookshelves in Mulawin's library. Copies of Rizal's two novels, their Spanish rulers banned for their exposure of their abuses, could be hidden somewhere in the library. It was due, most of all, they being the best examples, to their independent spirit. It is in their blood. They were descended from the principality that broke away from the kingdom of Namayan, the present-day Manila, and settled there and named it Masakao, many years before the Spaniards came. They kept and nurtured their traditional way of life, their attachment to their town and their families, down to their native surnames.

They did not, unlike those in the other towns in the colony, succumb to the apathy, the cynicism, the feeling of inferiority, the loss of self-confidence and the pessimistic resignation of a totally subjugated people.

They, on the other hand, have a history of resistance to their Spanish rulers, they consider as an unwanted presence in their town. They rose twice in rebellion over some local grievances.

To secure the town from its troublesome residents, their Spanish rulers built there, a stonewalled fort.

Paulo was roused from those thoughts when Mulawin said to his uncle, "I'm so glad, you and Paulo came through safely. We cannot, knowing the Spaniards, be too careful. The checkpoint, the curfew and the Civil Guard patrols should remind us that they are becoming more and more suspicious. The risk that we may be found out grows every day. That is why I confined this meeting to us alone. With only eight of us in attendance, or nine including Paulo, we have nothing to worry about anything leaking out to the Spaniards. We will tell the others at the right time."

Mulawin paused and the others took it as a cue for a smoke. They pulled out cigars from their shirt pockets or helped themselves to a box of cigars on the table. The room, as they smoked, was soon filled with cigar smoke and it now has the smell of stale tobacco.

"The big moment, in any case, is coming," Mulawin continued, I learned in a recent visit to Manila, that some members of the Supreme Council are getting impatient. They think the Katipunan is strong enough to strike at the Spaniards. Bonifacio and another member of the Supreme Council think differently, though, but the time is coming when they will make a unanimous decision. We can only watch from here, how things will develop there and take orders. We must presume, though, that the revolution will break out, anytime soon. The Supreme Council will eventually come to a unanimous decision to start the revolution or the Spaniards will eventually find them out.They will then have no other choice but to fight the Spaniards."

"Are we ready for that?" Masinop asked Mulawin.

"We are not ready from the ideal standpoint," Mulawin replied, "but the revolution will surely come, perhaps sooner than we think."

"We should therefore not just sit here and wait for it to happen," Lukas said. "We must have, before the night is over, a workable plan we will carry out, once the revolution has started."

"I agree," Mulawin said. "We should have the advantage of choosing the time and the place to fight."

"We can," Gayuman said, "join Bonifacio in Manila or fight, right here in our town."

"No, not here in our town," Masinop said. "Our families will be put in danger if we will turn it into a battleground. Let us do the fighting elsewhere."

Lukas said, as he was glancing at Masinop, "We are all concerned here for our families, but it is precisely for them and their future that we must take risks and make sacrifices. We cannot predict its outcome, once the revolution has started. The battles will take place anywhere, but there will surely be a lot of fighting in our town where the Katipunan is active. The matter of doing the fighting, right here in our town, is right and necessary because it will surely take place here. We must fight, right here, for who will liberate our town from the Spaniards, if not we ourselves."

What Lukas said had so profoundly affected the others, voices rose in the room in agreement to what he said.

Gayuman stood up. He leaned across the table and said, as he was shaking hands with Lukas, "You took the words, right out of my mouth."

"I agree with Lukas," Pinalis said. "We cannot join Bonifacio in the fighting that will most certainly take place in Manila. The Spaniards will stop us on our way there. Can we then fight our way through?"

"We cannot allow ourselves," Bihasa said, "to be drawn into a fight, not of our own choosing."

"We are here, let us fight, right here," Gayuman said.

Masinop did not press his opinion when he saw no one had agreed with him although a sour look had remained, fixed on his face.

"Very well, it is settled then," Mulawin said. "We will take our town from the Spaniards, but we must have the arms, for us to do that. Let me show you what we need most."

He stood up and walked toward the desk, near the window. He moved it with Paulo's help, away from the window. Then he pushed aside a rug on the floor, revealing a trapdoor there. He pulled it open and took out there, a long object wrapped in a cloth. He stood up, removed the cloth and held up proudly, a Mauser rifle.

"We will fight the Spaniards with guns like this," Mulawin said as he passed the gun to Pinalis.

"Is it loaded?" he asked Mulawin, who shook his head.

Pinalis pointed the gun to the ceiling and pressed the trigger. He nodded, satisfied with the gun, and passed it on to Masinop who refused to touch it. Lukas took the gun from Pinalis.

"You must get used to handling a gun like this," he said to Masinop.
"How will you fight the Spaniards if you don't even know how to fire a gun?"

"There are many ways of fighting them."

"The best way is to shoot them."

"Teaching English to dumb students is harder than firing a gun like that. I will know everything about it, once I have put my mind to it."

Lukas did not answer back and that put an end to their argument. He passed the gun across the table to Gayuman who, after handling it, passed it on to Ongliko. He passed it on to Bihasa who took a look at it and then gave it to Kabisig who, in his late thirties, was the youngest in their group..

"I have fired a gun like this a few times," he said while handling the gun with skill and confidence.

Then, while the others watched and listened, Kabisig explained the gun's parts and its features. He gave it back to Mulawin when he was finished with his impromptu lecture on the gun. Mulawin then returned it to its hiding place. He moved the desk with Paulo's help, back to its former position near the window.

"We have more of that," Mulawin said when he returned to his seat. He turned to Ongliko and said, "Well, Leon, can we hear from you?"

"I bought with the money we raised," Ongliko said, "five Mausers and five hundred rounds of ammunition."

"That is not enough," Gayuman said. "We should have at least fifty more guns."

"Buying that many guns will require a lot of money," Pinalis said, implying his slim purse.

"Money should be a secondary consideration here," Gayuman said. "Let us see how much money we can raise."

Ongliko cut him short with a wave of his hand.

"It is not that simple," he said. "You don't buy guns as you would buy a box of cigars in a store counter. They are smuggled from Hong Kong. A gunrunner takes great risks in doing that. My friend, a trader in Binondo, from whom I bought the guns, told me he is going out of that kind of business."

"What," Gayuman said to Ongliko, "if we will pay him more?"

"Not even if we will double the price. There is nothing we can do about it. He fears the Spaniards more than he loves to make money."

"Do you have other sources?" Lukas asked Ongliko, who shook his head.

"We have a problem here," Gayuman said. "We cannot mount a revolution with knives, bamboo spears, machetes and a few rifles."

They fell silent, some of them frowning at finding themselves at a dead end in their discussion of the coming revolution in their town.

"Let us take a break," Mulawin then said. "My wife prepared something for us. A full stomach will help us clear our minds."

He stood up, walked toward the door and called for Cipriano to bring in the food.

The conversation among the men stopped altogether as the food was being brought to the table.

Mulawin's hospitality was well-known in the town and he did not disappoint his guests. His wife had prepared fine Spanish food. There was a meat dish mixed with potatoes, green vegetables and sausages. There was a fish dish in sweet-and-sour sauce and a pork dish, heavy with spices and marinated in vinegar and soy sauce. There were pastries of dried cows' milk, rolled in fine white sugar and wrapped in thin white paper. There was beer to wash the food down and brewed coffee to top the meal.

The hour was late, the men were hungry and they ate with zest.

Paulo smiled, his eyes on the food on his plate and the others eating at the table. They object strongly to the oppressive Spanish rule in their town, but not to the fine Spanish food they were eating with zest.

The men were quite cheerful as they went on with their dinner, no one more so than Bihasa. He nodded in appreciation of the beer Cipriano was pouring on his glass. He took a swig and sighed, pleased and satisfied.

"No matter how long I have lived in Hong Kong," he said, "I never enjoyed drinking beer there as much as I do here."

The other men looked at Bihasa with deference. He practiced medicine for more than a year in the British Crown Colony where he not only learned to speak the King's English, but also picked up British traits like pipe smoking and drinking tea in the afternoon. He drank beer in Hong Kong just as he did way back as a young man in the company of Lukas, Mulawin Pinalis, Masinop, Gayuman and Ongliko, all of them, his boyhood friends.

"I don't suppose you are saying that because of your homegrown stomach," Lukas said, smiling, to Bihasa.

"It is not only that," Bihasa replied. "It is just that the pleasure is simply greater in drinking our own beer because of its superior quality."

He set his meal aside, having warmed up to the topic, and said, "It could be due to the malt or yeast, the water we use or it could be due to the way we brew our beer. Whatever it is, our beer tastes better and it courses down your throat more smoothly, more pleasantly. Our beer here and their beer there don't speak, though, of the quality of the British colonial rule in Hong Kong and the Spanish rule over our country. We are worse off in that respect."

"Give an example," Masinop asked Bihasa.

"The British, unlike the Spaniards, run their colony in Hong Kong without being oppressive to the Chinese. They are left alone as long as they pay their taxes and they do not cause the British any trouble. They have relative freedom of movement. The British don't abuse the Chinese as the Spaniards have abused us."

The others nodded in agreement with Bihasa.

"I guess," Gayuman said, "the British, in running Hong Kong, only wanted to make money. They do not impose; they only let their traits rub off on the Chinese."

"We have there, another important distinction between the Spanish and the British colonial rule," Masinop said.

He turned to Bihasa and said, "Let us not forget, the Spaniards came here with an excess of religious zeal, but on empty stomachs. Too much of the former and too little of the latter have brought about this terrible Spanish rule. We will now have to put an end to it."

They laughed, but it was a disagreeable subject and no one pursued it any further. They returned to their dinner.

Cipriano and the maidservant came in later with cups and teaspoons on saucers which they distributed around the table. They left, but came back with a steaming coffee pot and sugar and cream dispensers. They poured the coffee and passed the cream and sugar around. With the coffee served and drunk, their dinner, after a while, was over.

They took whatever they fancied there. Masinop and Pinalis stood up and browsed at Mulawin's bookshelves. The others who remained seated on the table talked quietly or smoked their cigars.

The room was soon enveloped with tobacco smoke. Mulawin looked disagreeably at the smoke, thick around the gas lamps.

Cipriano, at a sign from him, crossed the room and opened the window there.

A sweet scent of flowers then filled the room. It brought with it, the sound from outside of frogs croaking and crickets trilling in the shrubs and trees there, dripping with raindrops.

Cipriano closed the window, once the gas lamps had been cleared of tobacco smoke. The meeting resumed after the table had been cleared.

"We cannot," Mulawin then said, "fight the Spaniards unless we have the arms and what we have may not be enough. What is enough, though, may depend on what we intend to do. How, where and when do we fight the Spaniards? Someone with military training can tell us how we should go about it."

"Tell us," he said to Kabisig, "what you think about it."

Mulawin then clamped a cigar between his teeth, lit it up with a match and settled back on his chair.

Kabisig swept the table with his eyes, narrow and his lips pressed tight which showed him as a highly critical person.

"If you will allow me," he said, "I will get to the point. I heard some fine speeches tonight—the people rising up in arms!

"The image is attractive, but we don't need those beautiful words and that illusion in fighting the Spaniards. What we need is a strategy and a combat force, neither of which we have. That is what I learned in Spain. It is useless, without them, to think about mounting a revolution in our town. If a Prussian drill sergeant will see what we have here and what we intend to do, he will tell us to forget it and just go home."

The others at the table looked away or shook their heads in disagreement to what Kabisig said.

"I'm sorry," he said, "if I offended anyone here by what I said, but it is time we stopped romanticizing the revolution. We must approach it with a cold, clear eye. We need to work out a strategy and raise an armed force. We will not, without them, succeed in our revolution. If you will allow me, I will limit myself to those two very important tasks."

Lukas showed by the frown on his face that his patience with Kabisig had worn thin.

"What I have just heard," he said, "gave me the impression that we are about to engage in some kind of a Napoleonic warfare with flags waving and cannons booming as in the rolling plains in Austerlitz. We will not engage in that kind of fighting."

Kabisig was about to speak, but was stopped by Lukas who had turned the palm of his hand to him.

"Let me finish, first," he said to Kabisig. "I have read about the French Revolution. It did not start out of a preconceived military strategy and a strong armed force which you insist, we must first have. The French people revolted against their king and it rose out of their grievances. They fought, not with a force they had raised beforehand, but with a force they raised when their revolution was already underway.

"It spread, once it started, like a lighted matchstick thrown into a haystack. That is how revolutions are waged. Of course, we have to make preparations, but how? By raising a force of men and women who will wage it? Not all of them need to be trained in warfare. All we need is a small group of trained men who will lead the townsfolk, our real strength, when we mount the revolution in our town."

Everyone in the room, including Kabisig, nodded in agreement to what Lukas said. His eloquence had swayed them to his side in his argument with Kabisig.

"While we are not of the same mind on the need for a military strategy and a sizable armed force," Kabisig said, "I agree with everything else that Lukas said."

"So," Lukas said, "we must now identify our immediate objective."

Mulawin looked at both Lukas and Kabisig. The conflict between them had been resolved. He said as the others nodded in agreement, "Since we have agreed to fight here in Masakao, our obvious goal is the conquest of the town fort."

"I cannot, but agree with you," Kabisig said. "We conquer it and the rest of the apparatus of Spanish power in our town, the civil government and the Church will crumble. Our immediate task then is to find out everything about the town fort, its troop strength and armament. We can, after that, prepare a plan of attack on the town fort."

"I was there yesterday on official business," Pinalis said, "and from what I saw there, the fort must have about forty men."

Lukas asked Pinalis, "How about their arms?"

"I don't know. I did not look around."

"I will say an attack on the fort, based on that information," Kabisig said, "will require a force, two to three times, the number of the soldiers there. We may not have the means to train and equip a force of eighty to a hundred-twenty men, but we can compensate for that deficiency by employing secrecy and surprise. We know them while they do not know us, but that still is not enough. We must know more about the fort. I must check it out, which I will do, tomorrow night."

"Is there no other way of learning more about the town fort?" Ongliko asked Kabisig. "Spying on the fort is dangerous."

"Can you suggest another way?" Kabisig asked Ongliko, who shook his head.

Paulo, who had kept to himself, the entire evening, suddenly stood up. He saw his uncle, staring at him, a puzzled look on his face.

Lukas dropped his jaw in utter surprise when Paulo then said to Kabisig, "You will have to scale the fort wall in spying on the town fort. You will need someone to help you do that. I will go with you."

Chapter Four

The sun was low in the horizon when Paulo went to see his childhood friend, Teresa.

He smiled as he recalled with satisfaction, his uncle's suggestion that he be made a full-fledged member of the Katipunan and he went through the rite. He took before Mulawin, the oath of loyalty to the Katipunan. Mulawin then made with a knife, a small cut on his forearm. He dipped with the tip of a pen, the blood in his forearm and signed with it, his membership paper. He felt, at that moment, bound to the great and noble cause of fighting for the freedom of their country.

The meeting broke up at the crack of dawn, the curfew having been lifted by then.

He and his uncle left at the same time with Doctor Bihasa and Gayuman who also lived on the same side of the town, divided by the river.

"Why," his uncle asked him on their way home, "did you decide to join Kabisig's spying mission?"

"It was a chance for me to do something for our cause."

"I appreciate that, but were you not being rash about it?"

"Perhaps, I was. Do you want me to back out?"

"No. Do what you say you will do, but next time, weigh things carefully before doing something like that. Spying on the fort is dangerous."

He will find that out tonight as he was walking on toward Teresa's house. He saw the town, fresh from the previous night's rain. August was right in the middle of the rainy season in the Philippines, a time welcomed there for the break it gave the country from its hot, tropical climate and for a lot of rainwater, the farmers needed for their rice and other crops.

While the sky was overcast, it was nonetheless a beautiful day. The flowers were in full bloom, the trees were in full leaf. The homes, he was passing by, were made mostly of wood and bamboo and with roofs of palm shingles. A few of them were of stone and wood and with tile roofs.

They were not as well-defined in the dark, the night before when he and his uncle were passing by there in their horse-drawn cab as they were now during daytime when they looked so lovely. Palm and fruit trees and ornamental plants adorned the front yards, the flower boxes below the windowsills decked out with flowering plants.

A gentle breeze wafted its sweet scent to him and he inhaled it deeply and with pleasure. Pleasant too was the sight of the orchards beside and at the back of the homes there and the rice fields spread out farther away.

It was the planting season and the rice fields were waterlogged from the rain falling there for several days now. They will be, a few months hence, carpeted with the rice stalks, full of golden grain. They will then be harvested around November and December.

He walked on, pleased. Masakao was known for its beauty and bounty. It was a jewel of a place located in the eastern side of the Central Plain of Luzon with the river meandering through the town from its headwaters in the mountain range of Sierra Madre.

His heart told him, as he was walking on toward Teresa's home, at how he had lied to himself in ascribing his high spirit to the beautiful day. Neither was it by his acceptance as a full-fledged member of the Katipunan.

It was not any of those, but the expectation of seeing her again that made him so happy and so expectant. He was in love with her. It was a feeling that came slowly, transformed from friendship that went back to that time when they were small children. How he wished, she felt the same way. He must find that out from her before setting out tonight for the town fort.

He was approaching the house when he heard music being played on the piano there. Teresa must be at the keyboard, playing Mendelssohn's beautiful song, *On the Wings of Song.* The music flowed so sweetly to him, it captivated him. He saw in his mind how lovely she must look with the beautiful music she was playing on the piano.

He was so absorbed with the music and the image of her playing it on the piano when he turned abruptly to the sound on the road of a horse's hoofbeat. Julio, Teresa's father, was coming in his horse-drawn rig.

"Good afternoon, sir," he said to Julio.

"A pleasant day to you, too, Paulo. "Why did you not just go in?"

Paulo did not reply, but smiled instead and opened the house gate for Julio. They proceeded toward the backyard.

"I heard you are going to Spain to study law there," Julio said as he got off from the rig and tied the rein to a post there.

"My uncle and I have such a plan, but it will be quite a while before I will leave, not until next year yet."

"Our town benefits when young men like you continue and finish their studies abroad. Your uncle must be proud of you."

What Julio said did not please Paulo, but annoyed him instead. He was not being truthful to Julio. His studies abroad and everything else will be set aside once the revolution has broken out in their town. Julio apparently knew nothing about it.

He glanced at Julio. His face was a dark brown from the many hours he spent working in his orchard, one of the largest in the town, and under the sun in the rice fields with the carabao, his work animal. His arms and his hands were rough and strong from working on the soil. He also raised pigs and chickens in his backyard.

He owned, with his wife Agustina, a small store in the town's commercial area. His daughters Teresa and Esperanza, together with Nieves, their friend and neighbor, helped him and Agustina in running it.

It was all work for Julio in providing for his family.

Julio, who had studied in the town's primary school, has a higher goal for his two daughters. Esperanza has finished with a course in education and she is planning to be a teacher there. Teresa was also studying education in a girl's boarding school in Manila, ran by nuns. She was at home from a short break in her school.

He watched Julio as he was removing a bucket from a post in the house. He filled it with rice bran and fed the horse with it, the other work animal, so dear to Julio, who was also a rig driver. He was now tapping with his palm, the money in his pocket, he earned from a day's work as he also kept beat with the piano music, coming from inside the house.

Paulo said to him, as he was pulling out a sack of rice from the rig's rear compartment, "Let me take care of that, sir."

"Thank you, Paulo, but I can do it."

"Let me do it, sir."

"Very well, you can take it to the rice bin."

Paulo lifted the sack of rice to his shoulders and brought it to the rice bin at the ground floor of the house.

Julio in the meantime had taken out from the poultry house in the backyard, a tin can of chicken feed. The clacking sound he then made with his tongue attracted the chickens and they were soon feeding on the chicken feed, he was throwing into the ground.

He was humming along the piano music when Paulo came back from the ground floor of the house.

"Run along, Paulo and thank you for your help," Julio said to him.

"Very well, sir," Paulo replied.

He walked toward the house and went up on the stairs there. He crossed the balcony, opened the door there and listened, enthralled once again, to Teresa playing still, Mendelssohn's lovely song. She stopped playing it when she noticed him, standing still at the sill of the door.

"There, you are," she said when she turned around and looked at him. "Have you been there long?"

"I've been there long enough in listening to you as you were playing that song so beautifully."

"It is so nice of you to say that."

"It was just as nice listening to you there," he said, his finger pointed to the house gate.

"Why," she said, smiling at the odd figure he cut there, "did you not just come in?"

"I was so entranced by your music and I would have remained still listening to you there if your father had not come."

"Come now, you don't have to overdo it. You know I don't play that well to please a person so highly critical like you."

"But I did enjoy listening to you," he said as he came to her.

He laid his elbow on top of the piano and, his chin resting on his palm, he said as he looked down at her, "You can now see me listening, entranced once again, if you will resume playing Mendelssohn's lovely song."

"I am done with that for the day."

"Play it one more time or you can play another song."

"No, I will not."

"Yes, you will."

They laughed. The pleasure they felt in each other's company showed in this playfulness that came naturally to them even now when they have grown up into a young handsome man and a young beautiful woman.

She stood up suddenly and, wagging her finger at him, she said to him, "I know what you came here for."

"What is it?"

"What else but food, of course! And I have something you will like."

"Thank you, but don't take the trouble. I am not hungry."

"You say that every time you come here."

He watched her, his brow knitted, as she left for the kitchen.

The food she will serve him might divert him from the purpose of seeing her. It will not stop him though from going ahead with it.

He crossed the living room to a small oblong-shaped table by the window overlooking the front yard and the town road. The table will serve his purpose. He sat down on one of the two chairs there, facing each other.

He looked around. It was not a big house. It was bigger though and built better than the nipa huts of some of the town residents. Made mostly of wood, it was roofed with palm shingles.

The house was clean and tidy. Everything there was in its proper place, from the piano, its back against a wall, to the wooden couches, a bookshelf lined with books, the statue of Saint Peter enclosed in a glass cabinet near the door and the grandfather clock in a corner in the living room. The wooden floor and the bamboo beams were clean and shiny. The framed photograph on the wall of Julio, Agustina, Esperanza and Teresa showed them to be by their smile as one happy family. His and his uncle's picture which Teresa and Esperanza had nagged him into giving them, hid by their smile, the sternness in the character of their family.

He was looking on at the statue of Saint Peter when he remembered what Teresa had once told him about his great-great-grandfather Gonzalo. He was a sailor in a Spanish galleon that plied the trade in the Pacific Ocean between Manila and the Mexican port of Acapulco in the last century.

As Teresa had told him about it, the galleon hit the reefs in San Bernardino Strait while it was fighting a Dutch pirate ship. His great-great- grandfather prayed, as the ship began to sink, to Saint Peter for his salvation. He promised that if he survived in the battle, he would have a statue carved in the saint's image. It stood there ever since in the house, a token of gratitude and devotion to Saint Peter. Teresa's ancestor had his salvation.

He, on the other hand, needed more than luck and the intercession of Saint Peter, perhaps of all the saints in heaven, for the cause to which he was now bound of setting their country free of their Spanish rulers. Big things lay ahead, fearful and violent, that will then usher in a new day of freedom for their country.

How he wished he would fare as well as Teresa's ancestor in his first mission tonight in the town fort. How he wished he could tell her about it. He will feel much better then, a knight in shining armor, bidding his fair maiden, a fond farewell. She will perhaps respond in a way he will want her to respond. She might then rush to him and as she is embracing him tightly, she might then tell him how she feared for his safety. She might even beseech him not to do such a dangerous thing!

He watched her as she parted the dining room curtain and moved across the living room, a tray of hot chocolate and pastries in her hands.

He realized he was staring at her and he turned his gaze to the front yard with the palm tree and the ornamental plants there.

She laid the tray on the table and looked down at him who appeared to be in deep thought.

"So, what are you brooding over, this time," she said smiling and expecting no reply from him, for she was used to his short periods of silence.

She said as she then sat down on the other chair, "What you need is something warm and pleasant,"

"This is what I need and want," he said as he suddenly took her hand and touched it to his lips.

He watched her, pleased and satisfied, when she lowered her eyes, her hand limp in her submission to him.

"Father might see us," she said.

"Let him see us."

"You don't have to do that to me."

His face flushed in shame for what he was doing to her, the only woman he cared for.

"I will never do that again," he said as he released her hand when she suddenly touched his face gently.

He felt the same way as she was looking at him with such longing in her eyes, he said to her, "Do you love me as I love you?"

She replied, her eyes now shining brightly, "I do ever since we were small children."

She moved back her hand when Paulo tried to hold it again and sat stiffly on her chair when she heard Julio, humming the Mendelssohn song as he was going up in the stairs toward the living room without having seen nor heard anything unusual there.

Chapter Five

It was raining again when Paulo and Kabisig set out on their spying mission in the town fort. Visibility was poor and by keeping close to the church's adobe and iron grill fence, they managed to slip past the checkpoint by the bridge. It was dark as the two sentries there had sought with their gas lantern, shelter in the roofed bandstand in the town square.

They moved on in the short, narrow road between the church and the municipal hall. It ended at the wide, wooden gate of the town fort. The gate was closed.

There was no sentry standing guard there. The rain had forced him to seek shelter inside the fort.

They must scale the stonewall enclosing the fort if they were to see anything there.

"Help me up," Kabisig said to Paulo who then set his feet firmly on the ground, his hands, he held tightly together.

Kabisig then laid his left foot on Paulo's clasped hands and, his left hand pressed to Paulo's shoulders, he jumped to the top of the wall. Then he pulled Paulo up, beside him on the wet and wide top of the wall.

They looked around. The fort's thick stonewall and the main brick building with its wide windows did not blend with Masakao's scenery of wooden houses, nipa huts, palm and mango trees and rice fields. It was like a fort in Spain moved to Masakao.

The gate led to its right toward the rectangular drill ground. The wall enclosed the fort on four sides, the side where they were watching the fort, the side to their left, separated from the church ground by their common adobe wall, the side facing them with the rice fields behind the fort and the drill ground in front of them. At its right side was the wall along the river.

The main building facing them housed the barracks, the mess hall, the armory, the fort commander's office on the ground floor and his living quarters in the second floor. The building stood between the jail and the stable where, not seen from there, was an iron door to the rice fields at the back of the town fort.

"Let us move on to where we can have a better view of the fort," Kabisig said, his voice kept low.

They crawled toward a spot with a wide view of the fort. They saw from there Lieutenant Zatayde, the fort commander, who was taking his dinner in his quarters, a native orderly serving him. Zatayde's dark profile was shown by the light of an overhanging gas lamp. He has black, wavy hair, his mustache, crowning his upper lip. He has a tall nose and a prominent chin. He was good-looking, but he looked grouchy and disagreeable whenever a smirk formed at the corner of his mouth. He was washing down his dinner with a glass of brandy, tipped to his lips.

They watched the soldiers in their barracks. They were finished with their dinner. Most of them were native auxiliaries from the colony's central region. They spoke a different local dialect and that limited their contact with the town residents. Some of the soldiers, shortly after taking their dinner, were conversing while they were smoking their cigarettes. A window in the barracks showed some of them, lying down on the cots there.

"Have you counted the number of the soldiers there?" Kabisig asked Paulo.

"There are about forty-five soldiers in the barracks or forty-nine if we will include Zatayde, the orderly and the two sentries at the checkpoint by the bridge."

Neither Paulo nor Kabisig saw the guard at the gate who had sought in the jail, shelter from the rain.

"Remarkable," Kabisig said. "We have there, forty-nine soldiers, most of them our own countrymen who have kept a tight hold on our town of several thousand residents."

Paulo frowned as he was looking on at the fort. Their Spanish rulers had them fooled for so long a time. They held power by keeping an illusion of strength through fear. Stories were told countless times about the jail there where the prisoners were kept and tortured. That was the real strength of the town fort—the fear of it, they cultivated in the minds of the townsfolk. The Spaniards had in the forts and detachments they had strung up all over the islands, the chain that kept their country under their terrible rule.

He looked on at the fort. If the Katipunan which is similarly organized in the islands were to attack those forts and detachments, they could have the Spaniards ousted from their country. A smile lit up his face by the pleasant and positive thought.

He turned to Kabisig. His stomach and his elbows on the wet top of the wall, he was likewise watching Zatayde and the soldiers.

"Can we take it?" he asked Kabisig.

"We can, but not through the gate, although a cannon shot can blast it open."

"But we do not have a cannon."

"That is why we will not attack the fort that way."

"So, how should we attack it?"

"We will mount a two-pronged attack where they least expect it, from the river and from the rice fields. We will attack it at night when it is raining, like tonight, when the fort is blind to a surprise attack."

Paulo nodded. Kabisig's plan of attack was simple and easy to carry out. The wall was the fort's main protection and they had scaled it so easily with the cover of the rain and darkness. Without a guard to call out in alarm, they could then rush toward the main building and engage the soldiers in a hand-to-hand combat. In such close fighting with their knives, swords, spears and a few guns, their superiority in number will put them at a great advantage over the well-armed, but much fewer soldiers. He smiled, pleased with Kabisig's plan of attack on the fort.

"If we can take it by surprise, the town fort will be ours," Kabisig said confidently.

"And with the fort now taken, the town will then be ours."

The rain by then, despite the hats on their heads, had soaked them to the bone. Paulo shivered from the cold rain and he blew his warm breath into his cupped hands, he held close to his mouth. It sent him into thinking instead of how soft Teresa's palm was, as it touched his face. He was basking in this pleasant thought and feeling when he turned startled to Kabisig who had nudged his side with his elbow.

"We have seen enough," Kabisig said, "Let us get out of here."

They had not crawled far toward the gate when Kabisig cut his shin on a protruding stone there. He winced from the pain and spun sideways, his weight on his elbow. He swung his shoulders back to regain his balance, but slipped down instead to the wall and into the drill ground.

"Are you all right?" Paulo asked Kabisig who was leaning on the fort wall.

"I cut my shin. Hurry up, pull me up."

Paulo bent down and held Kabisig's hand. He strained his arm until he had pulled him up to the top of the wall.

The soldier on guard duty at the fort gate had seen them. He shouted at them, "Who are you and what are you doing there?"

Paulo and Kabisig looked at each other. They have been found out. They could no longer jump down near the gate, for they will then be trapped between the soldiers in the fort and the sentries in the bandstand.

"Quick, to the river," Kabisig said to Paulo.

They rushed toward the wall along the river with Kabisig hobbling along, his arm on Paulo's shoulders when a gunshot hit Paulo on the left side of his body.

They held on to each other, both of them wounded, and moved on at the top of the wall, from where they then jumped into the river there.

Zatayde rushed to the window when he heard the gunshot. He saw Paulo and Kabisig as they were rushing toward the river.

He rushed there with his soldiers, led by Quatrillo, his deputy sergeant.

The soldier on guard duty came to him.

"I hit one of them," he said to Zatayde, who nodded, pleased.

"Can you see them?" Zatayde asked Quatrillo as he was scanning the river with a gas lantern in his hand.

"No, sir, I don't see them," Quatrillo replied.

"Search the river thoroughly," Zatayde said to Quatrillo. "If you don't find them there in the river, conduct a thorough search in the town, particularly the doctor's house. They might go there."

Zatayde was so angry as he was returning to his quarters.

"I will deal with them even with my bare hands," he said, his teeth clenched.

His anger subsided as he was going up the stairs to his quarters.

He deliberated on the reason for the brazen intrusion into the town fort. It was obviously not to spirit away someone in the jail. It was empty. They could be after the arms there or were on a spying mission.

Whatever was their purpose, his instinct told him, trouble lay ahead. One never knew what those damned *Indios* were up to.

He crossed the sitting room, turned an armchair there toward the window facing the drill ground and sat down there with his boots laid on the windowsill.

"Give me, my brandy," he said to his native orderly.

The orderly left and came back with Zatayde's glass and bottle of brandy.

"Leave the bottle here," he said as he took the glass of brandy from the orderly who then put the bottle of brandy on the floor, beside Zatayde.

He took a swig from his glass of brandy. He felt warm and in better humor, once the liquor had coursed down in his throat. He shut his eyes and smiled grimly at the picture, his mind then formed, in an escape from the boredom of garrison duty in Masakao and before that, in Cuba.

A sword in his hand and a gun in his other hand, he saw himself leading on horseback, a charge against the Indios, slashing here, shooting there and sending them to flight. He now has in the two men's intrusion into the town fort, the chance to show to everyone his true worth as a soldier, to Intramuros' snobbish residents who snubbed him and to Marissa Iglesias, who rejected him. The thought of how they looked down on him pestered like a wound that would not heal.

He looked on at the rain, lashing the fort even harder now. Somewhere out there were the two intruders. What they did in the fort was a sign that something big and serious was going on in the town. What it was, he was not sure yet, but he will take it out from them, once his men had caught them. One of them was shot and could be dead.

Paulo and Kabisig made for the riverbank, once they were far enough from the town fort.

The rain by now had turned into a thunderstorm. Flashes of lightning were cutting across the sky, along with a strong wind sweeping by.

They were shivering from the cold wind and rain as they moved on, both of them wounded, to Doctor Bihasa's house. But for his arm laid on Kabisig's shoulders and Kabisig's arm, around his waist, Paulo might have just then dropped down into the ground. The pain was becoming more than he could bear. His mind at times was as dim as his eyesight failing from the intense pain from the wound on his side.

"We will soon be there," Kabisig said reassuringly to him.

The wooden gate in Doctor Bihasa's house was locked. Kabisig called out repeatedly for the doctor. Teban, his manservant, finally appeared at a window in the house.

"Who are you and what do you want?" he asked them.

"It is me, Miguel Kabisig," he replied. "Paulo and I need the doctor's help."

Teban came out and opened the house gate for them and locked it back. Doctor Bihasa met them at the door. A gas lamp in his hand, he was shocked at the ghastly sight of Paulo and Kabisig. They were soaking wet. Paulo's shirt was spattered with blood while Kabisig was standing on his good foot.

"What happened?" Bihasa asked them.

"We were nearly caught in the town fort," Kabisig replied. "Paulo here was hit by a gunshot while I cut my shin."

"Come inside," Bihasa said to them.

He and Teban helped Paulo and Kabisig step inside the clinic at the ground floor of the house and sit down on the chairs there. Bihasa lifted Paulo's bloody shirt and looked into his wound.

"It looks like a nasty bullet wound," he said. "I must remove the bullet, right away."

He told Teban to get upstairs, the key to the medicine cabinet.

Teban returned to the clinic, his eyes wide with fear.

"There are men coming," he said. "They could be the Civil Guard!"

"Quick, to the stable," Bihasa said. "Hide in the loft there."

Kabisig and Teban helped Paulo move out of the house while Bihasa wiped with a rag, the wet spots on the chairs and on the floor. Then he snuffed out the flame in the gas lamp in his hand and hurried upstairs.

The soldiers were, in a short while, banging at the house gate. They kicked it open when no one who would open it appeared in the house. They rushed toward the house and banged at the door there.

Bihasa was rubbing his eyes when he appeared in a window there.

"What do you want?" he asked the soldiers.

"Did anyone come here tonight?" Quatrillo asked him.

"No one came here."

"Don't lie to us or you will find yourself in big trouble with us."

"I was asleep, all the time."

"Open the door!"

Bihasa went downstairs and opened the door.

"Search the house and the surroundings," Quatrillo ordered his men.

They searched the house and the grounds, but in the dark and with the rain, they did not see much. They returned with blank faces that told Quatrillo, they found no one there. He left with his men.

Bihasa watched and waited until the Civil Guard search party was out of his sight. He proceeded toward the stable. Paulo was so weak by now he had to be helped back to the clinic. They helped him sit down on the examination table there.

Teban stationed himself at the house gate, in case the Civil Guard search party will decide to go back there.

"You will have to bear the pain while I am removing the bullet," Bihasa said to Paulo. "I have run out of anesthesia. We will do without it."

Bihasa left the clinic. He returned there with a bottle of rum.

"Drink as much as you can," he said to Paulo. "It will help numb the pain."

Paulo took several swigs of the rum until he was tipsy.

"Bite into this," Bihasa then said as he was putting a piece of rolled cloth between Paulo's teeth.

Bihasa and Kabisig then laid him down on the examination table.

He watched Bihasa, fear in his eyes, when he turned him on his side. He gritted his teeth and clenched his fists from the excruciating pain when Bihasa then dug his scalpel into his wound. He passed out after that.

He saw, when he regained consciousness, Bihasa and Kabisig looking down at him.

"You are lucky," Bihasa said to Paulo. "The bullet did not lodge in any vital organ or else the gunshot would have killed you."

"Thank you, doctor, for saving my life," Paulo said.

He looked at himself and saw he had been dressed up in a new dry shirt. So was Kabisig's shirt. He was now standing straight, his injured shin having been treated also by Bihasa.

Teban came with food. Paulo and Kabisig wolfed it down.

"Well, doctor," Kabisig said after he and Paulo had finished, eating. "We are very grateful for your help, but we must get going. We cannot stay here. The Civil Guard might come back."

"Where are you going?" Bihasa asked them.

"If you are asking me, I'm going home," Paulo said.

"I will not do that, if I were you," Bihasa said. "Once the search party has returned to the fort, empty-handed, Zatayde himself might lead a thorough search. He might turn the town, upside down, in looking for you."

"But where can we go?" Paulo asked Bihasa.

"We can hide in Gayuman's mine in Alkayag," Kabisig said.

"It is a safe hiding place, but do you know the way there?" Paulo asked Kabisig.

"We must see Gayuman," Kabisig said. "He can take us there."

"But it is too far away," Bihasa said to Paulo and Kabisig, "and you are in no condition to take such a long hike in the mountains, at night and in the driving rain."

"Don't worry about me, doctor," Paulo said. "I'm all right now. I can do it. Just give us some rain gear and please, tell my uncle what happened to us and where he can find us."

"All right, go to Alkayag, if you think you are up to it," Bihasa said to Paulo and Kabisig. "I will see Lukas, first thing in the morning."

Paulo and Kabisig left for Gayuman's house.

They set out, not long after, with Gayuman for his iron ore mine in Alkayag.

"Keep your eyes peeled for the Civil Guard," Gayuman said.

Luckily for them, they did not encounter any Civil Guard search party. The storm passed as they were entering the forest. Gayuman lit up a gas lantern and led the way through the forest. They arrived, hours later in Alkayag, at the hut of Sabedro, Gayuman's Dumagat caretaker of the mine.   The Dumagat tribe village was in the valley below the mine.

Gayuman called out to Sabedro who appeared in a short while at the window in his hut.

"Sorry for waking you up," Gayuman said to him. "These two men with me are hiding from the Spaniards."

"You came to the right place," Sabedro said as he stepped down from his hut.

"Paulo here is wounded," Gayuman said.

He and Sabedro then helped Paulo in stepping up into the hut.

Now rested on a mat in the hut's bamboo floor, Paulo looked around with drowsy eyes at the thatch roof and walls, at the sky and the trees at the bamboo window there.

He watched Kabisig and Gayuman who were now seated on the bamboo stairs, their backs turned to him. They were shadowy figures as they were watching Sabedro who was poking with a stick, the fire he built in a clay stove in the outdoor kitchen, a lean-to roofed with banana leaves placed together into one huge fan.

The smell of coffee soon rose from a clay pot hanging from a bamboo stick, above the fire in the clay stove. Its familiar, inviting smell was in contrast to new thoughts and feelings in Paulo's drowsy mind.

His life in just one day had undergone a drastic change. He is now both a lover and a rebel, the ecstasy of being in love mixing curiously in his heart and mind with the fear of a rebel, being hunted down.   He is bound to a woman's love and to a revolutionary cause, their contrary demands on him, he will have to meet and reconcile. It is a problem about which he has yet to find the answer.

He looked out at the window, at the rain falling again. It must be falling too in Masakao. It must be falling where Teresa now lay asleep.

She will be worried tomorrow morning when she will look for him near the church door and she will not find him there. They had agreed, he will wait for her there and they will then together attend Mass.

He will fail to meet his appointment with her in the church tomorrow morning just as he had failed tonight in his spying mission with Kabisig in the town fort. The thought made him so weary and so disappointed. He will just have to sleep all of that away. He felt like he was now fading into a shadow as he then finally fell asleep.

Chapter Six

The following morning was so unlike the previous Sundays in Masakao when the townsfolk, in worshiping God at the Mass, felt lofty in mind and spirit.

They were gathered in the churchyard, a few minutes before the start of the Mass, their mood anxious and gloomy like the cloudy sky.

They were talking in worried voices about the Civil Guard soldiers banging on doors in search of two men who the night before were caught spying on the town fort.

The town was already under a curfew and this may turn out to be a minor inconvenience compared to the thorough search and the mass arrests, Lieutenant Zatayde might then do in the town.

Julio, his wife Agustina and their daughters Esperanza and Teresa were approaching the church when they heard the talk in the churchyard. They glanced anxiously at each other and walked on toward the church.   Teresa looked around, her face clouded with worry. Paulo was not near the church door where they had agreed yesterday, he will wait for her there before they will attend Mass.

She was very much worried when she sat down on an empty pew, between Agustina and Esperanza, her mind on Paulo who could be connected to the spying incident in the town fort.

That, she feared, could be the reason he did not show up for their appointment there when she suddenly winced from the pain that gnawed at her stomach. She had this old ailment that sometimes struck her when she was terribly upset or worried.

"What is the matter with you?" Agustina said to her.

"It is nothing, Mother," she replied.

She pressed her hand to her stomach to ease the pain and knelt down on the pew so as not to show her looking so worried over what could have happened to Paulo. She looked imploringly at the images of Jesus Christ and Mother Mary at the altar and prayed for their help.

Gradually, as a hand would part a curtain to reveal light, her mind shed that dark, troubled thought. Hope had welled forth in her mind that Paulo is safe from harm. The images at the altar seemed to tell her that. The pain in her stomach then went away.

The church was soon full of people. Among them were Masinop and his family. They were seated, not too far behind the Dumayags. Pinalis and his family were seated across the aisle. Mulawin arrived with his family just as the Mass was about to begin. They sat down in a rear pew.

The congregation stood up and watched Fray Gustavo, the town's parish priest, when he walked in from the rectory to the altar, behind two acolytes. One of them was holding high, a cross, the other, a copy of the Holy Bible.

The priest walked toward the communion table where he began the Mass with the opening prayer. It proceeded solemnly as it always did every Sunday in the town church.

Fray Gustavo passed by Mayor Echeverria and Lieutenant Zatayde as he was proceeding toward the pulpit, at the part of the sermon. They were seated at the front pew, the place of honor. They met him in the rectory before the start of the Mass and told him what happened in the town fort. He agreed to take it up in his sermon.

He paused, out of breath, when he reached the pulpit. He felt at age forty, so old and tired he would pant even at simple physical exertions like going up to the pulpit. He no longer felt as satisfied as he was before in his liaisons with his cook and housekeeper, he had kept since he was appointed the town's parish priest. He was doing what he was not supposed to do as a priest and that added guilt in his mind just as it made his body so tired.

He set aside those thoughts and feelings and felt refreshed by the sight of the congregation, their eyes turned to him for what he would speak about in his sermon. This was the moment when he felt the power as their parish priest. Blood rushed up in his veins, invigorating him. He ruled over their souls and therefore over their minds and bodies, as well. The townsfolk feared God, the Church, the government and him, although, he sometimes felt, not in that order.

He began his sermon. "We see in the life of our Lord Jesus Christ, the best example of unquestioning obedience. While he is God, when he took human flesh as a young boy, he did what he was told to do. The obedience he rendered to his mother and his foster father, Saint Joseph, was his way of showing obedience, not only to his family, but by extension, to the laws of God and the laws of the land. He knew about the suffering and death due him, but what did he say to God the Father who sent him? 'Let thy will be done.'

"This is the message which I will dwell on today. It is our spiritual duty to obey the commandments of God as it is our civic duty to obey the laws of the land. Those who disobey those laws are both sinners and criminals. They are a threat to peace and order. They must be punished according to the gravity of their sin and crime. This will be done to the two men who committed a criminal act last night.

"Some of you may know by now about those two men who were caught spying on the town fort last night. What their purpose was still is not clear, but they had no right, no business to be there. They went there only for some criminal intention.

"They cannot get away with what they did. The town fort is alert to those things. One of them was shot. He fell into the river. His body may still be floating there."

Teresa uttered a cry, she suppressed quickly with her palm pressed to her mouth.

Her mother glanced, annoyed, at her. She said as she pinched the side of her body, "What is the matter with you!"

"Nothing, Mother," she replied, her mind on Paulo.

She was afraid he could be the man who was shot in the town fort. The awful thought made her feel faint. She must leave the church, she needed fresh air, but she could not do that. It will be unseemly of her to leave the church while the priest was delivering his sermon. Her parents will never forgive her for that. She stayed, seated on the pew. She fought her fear. It was unfounded, the result of her imagination having run wild, fed by her love for Paulo. It calmed her down from her anxious mind.

Fray Gustavo said as he neared the end of his sermon, "So, let me say this on behalf of our civil and military authorities. That will not be allowed to pass, just like that. The full weight of our town's authority will bear down on them and the others they have conspired with, for we believe this is much larger than the criminal act by just two men.

"The Church stands with our town authorities in condemning this crime. I stand here to warn those in league with them that they face punishment here and in the afterlife for what they did in disturbing the peace and tranquility in this town."

Mulawin reflected on what happened after the meeting in his house. He was disappointed by the failure of Kabisig and Paulo's spying mission. He was relieved, though, to learn from Doctor Bihasa who came to see him early in the morning that Kabisig and Paulo, though both wounded, were safe. Bihasa also told him he will see Lukas and tell him what happened to Paulo and Kabisig's failed spying mission in the town fort.. He did not see Lukas in the church and he presumed, Lukas must have left for Alkayag to attend to his nephew.

He left with his family at the end of the Mass, depressed by Fray Gustavo's sermon and the failure of their spying mission in the town fort.

Masinop and Pinalis were likewise leaving the church when they saw Mulawin, now crossing the churchyard toward his horse-driven cab on the road.

Their families stayed behind when they approached Mulawin, who was now helping his wife and their two children in stepping up to their cab. Mulawin saw them. They walked away from the cab.

"So," Masinop said, "Miguel and Paulo have failed in their mission." Mulawin then told them that Doctor Bihasa saw him at home and told him everything that happened.

"I will go to Alkayag and see to their needs there," he said to them.

"What do we do now?" Pinalis asked Mulawin. "Are we changing our plans, now that the Spaniards have been alerted?"

"We will discuss that later on," Mulawin replied, his gaze turned to Julio, Agustina, Teresa and Esperanza who were coming on the road.

The dark cloud over the town had passed away during the Mass. Small bands of grayish clouds had replaced it in the sky. The sun peeped through the cloud openings, giving hint of a coming cool and cloudy day.

The Dumayags, like many of the town residents, walked home from the church. Their house was not far from there. Fray Gustavo's sermon weighed on their minds.

Julio then said, "Zatayde will likely use the incident in the town fort as an excuse to make things harder for us," a sentiment Agustina and Esperanza shared with Julio.

Esperanza was so upset, she said, "Fray Gustavo delivered his sermon as if he is not the parish priest, but the town fort commander."

"What else can you expect from him?" Julio said. "He is part and parcel of the Spanish rule in our town."

"It is just too much," Agustina said. "Using the pulpit to threaten people and invoking God, at that. For all I know, the priest may have just made up that story to frighten us and tighten their hold on our town."

Julio met Agustina's outburst with silence. She was only expressing a negative sentiment the townsfolk had toward their parish priest. Fray Gustavo was, with his greed and womanizing, so disliked by the townsfolk. How far different he was from his predecessor, the kindly Fray Augusto. The townsfolk had never forgotten how he died. He drowned in the river in heavy rain when his boat capsized as he was on his way to minister to a dying parishioner, living in a remote riverside village.

"A good priest is up there in heaven," Julio said, his eyes turned to the sky, "while we are stuck here with a bad one."

Teresa, all the while, had kept quiet. She went, once they had arrived home, straight to the bedroom, she shared with Esperanza.

Esperanza joined her there. She was changing into her housedress when she noticed Teresa who was seated on their bed, looking down sadly at the bedroom floor.

She sat down beside Teresa and asked her, "What seems to be bothering you?"

Teresa shook her head.

"Tell me," Esperanza insisted.

"You will tell no one?"

"Yes, I will tell no one. What is it about?"

Esperanza and Teresa never kept anything from each other. They told each other what they would tell no one, not even their parents.

"It is about Paulo," Teresa said.

"What did he do to you?"

"I know what you are thinking of. It is nothing like that, at all."

"What is it then?"

"He is in trouble. I know he is. We agreed to meet in the church this morning. I knew when he did not show up there, that he was the man, shot in the town fort."

"You are only guessing, but why are you so concerned about him? Are you in love with him?"

Teresa did not answer her question. She burst instead into tears and buried her face on Esperanza's shoulders.

Esperanza, in turn, was taken by surprise at this clear sign that Teresa and Paulo were in love with each other.

She brushed Teresa's hair with her palm to comfort her. She was helping her younger sister while setting aside her own feelings toward Paulo, who was in love, not with her, but with Teresa. Nothing of this sort ever came between them and will not, now. She went on brushing Teresa's hair. It had a comforting effect on her.

"I'm sure, Paulo is all right," she said to Teresa. "Perhaps he and his uncle were kept away by something important. I also did not see his uncle in the church."

"I hope you are right," Teresa said as she wiped with her palm, the tears in her eyes.

"Of course, I am right. So he stood you up. That does not mean he is the man shot in the town fort."

"But I could feel it! Paulo was in danger!"

"We will look for him. We will go to his house if you want to be assured that he is not the man who was shot in the town fort."

"Yes, let us do that. I will know then why he did not show up in the church."

"He could be at home and for some reason could not keep your appointment there."

Teresa looked relieved as she then said to Esperanza, "Thank you, my dear sister. You are such a big help to me."

Esperanza in response smiled and tapped Teresa's hand.

"We will leave after breakfast," she said. "So, our parents will not suspect anything, we will tell them we will see our seamstress about some dresses we are having made for us."

The sun was high in the sky when they knocked at the door of Paulo's house. Maring, the elderly housemaid there, opened the door for them.

"Is Paulo home?" Esperanza asked her.

"No, he is not here."

"Do you know where he went?"

"No, I don't. He left yesterday afternoon and has not been back since then."

Esperanza and Teresa looked at each other in alarm. What Maring said to them confirmed what Teresa had feared about Paulo.

Esperanza asked Maring, "How about his uncle? Is he around?"

"He left early this morning with Doctor Bihasa and has not been back, too."

Esperanza thanked Maring and left with Teresa.

Mulawin was seated at the back of his horse-drawn cab, driven by Cipriano, when he saw Teresa and Esperanza who were coming out of the gate in Paulo's house. They seemed so upset and so distracted, they noticed him coming only when the cab was approaching them. He nodded at the thought that they must have been there to see Paulo. There was nothing unusual about them being friends. Just as he had known Paulo since he was a little boy, he had known the two sisters since they were little girls, now both of them having grown up into two young, beautiful women.

He found it unusual, though, for them to be visiting Paulo in his home. The townsfolk frowned on young women visiting young men in their homes. They must have a compelling reason for doing that. His curiosity piqued, he decided to find out more about the two sisters' visit to Paulo's house. He told Cipriano to pull the horse to a stop as they were approaching Esperanza and Teresa.

He said to them, "Can I offer you a ride?"

Esperanza thanked Mulawin, but declined his offer.

He asked them as he was looking at Paulo's house, "Did you come from there?"

"Yes, sir, we were looking for Paulo," Esperanza replied.

"And he is not there."

Esperanza shook her head.

He looked on at Esperanza and Teresa, who seemed to be so depressed. The reason could be the missing Paulo. Since they were at the church, they knew about the shooting incident in the town fort. Since Paulo was neither at the church nor at home, they must have concluded that Paulo was the man who was shot in the town fort. The downcast look in Teresa's face showed him how she must worry about Paulo. They could be more than friends. He must reassure her that Paulo is safe even if he had to lie about it.

He asked them, "How about Paulo's uncle? Is he at home?"

"He is not there, too," Esperanza replied.

"Do you know where they are?" Teresa asked Mulawin.

"I heard Paulo left yesterday for San Nicolas to help in preparing the rice fields there for planting. His uncle must have followed him there."

"Did you see Paulo there yesterday?" Teresa said, a look of relief having appeared in her face.

"No, I did not, but Cipriano, who came back just this morning from San Nicolas, told me he saw Paulo there yesterday."

"But why did he not go home last night?" Teresa said.

"Perhaps he did not leave early enough and was held back by the curfew. I am going to San Nicolas myself. In case I come across Paulo and his uncle, is there anything you want me to tell them?"

Teresa smiled and nodded.

"Tell Paulo. . . ," she said, too excited to say more.

"Tell him to drop by our house," Esperanza said quickly. "We will prepare something nice for him."

"Very well, I will tell him that."

He nodded at Cipriano who had the cab moving away. He hummed a song, very much satisfied, for the good turn he had done for the two sisters.

Cipriano, later on, pulled the rein to the left, at an intersection in the road. It sent the horse running, not toward San Nicolas, but toward Alkayag. Mulawin was going to see Lukas, Bihasa, Paulo and Kabisig.

Chapter Seven

Malacanang Palace on the night of August 21, 1896 was festive and bright with lights all over it.

Its distinguished resident, Governor-General Ramon Blanco, was giving a party for Anton de Luzuriaga, an important man in Madrid, visiting the Philippines. Civil, military and ecclesiastical leaders, merchants and bankers in Manila and the suburbs, government officials and landowners from the provinces—the cream of the Spanish society in the Philippine colony—were in attendance there. Even those in Manila's tiny foreign community were invited. With the governor-general himself as the host, it promised to be a grand night of merriment for them.

It was not only for that why some of those who were invited were so eager to be there. They hoped to learn from the top officials, who were in attendance there, about a native subversive group called the Katipunan whose discovery two days ago had so disturbed them.

The native footman had a busy time attending to the guests arriving in their carriages. He had just finished helping the ladies get off from a carriage when another one drew up in the palace courtyard.

The footman moved quickly toward the carriage and snapped to attention when its door was opened and Colonel Vidal Achutegui stepped out briskly. The footman then reached out to Dona Concha, Colonel

Achutegi's wife, who held on to his gloved hand as she too was stepping out of their carriage.

"It looks like another warm evening," Dona Concha said to Colonel Achutegui.

She turned, startled, toward their son Chemari who, with one jump from the carriage, was in an instant, standing beside her.

"Will you stop behaving as if you are in Lateran with your rowdy classmates and not here in Malacanang?" Dona Concha said, frowning, to Chemari.

He shrugged off, smiling still, his mother reprimanding him. She did not mean it, of course. He is their only child and she doted on him.

He looked himself over in his well-cut coat and brushed back with his palm, his wavy, black hair while his parents were primming themselves. Colonel Achutegui, resplendent in his gala uniform, was brushing with his palm, his sash decked out with medals. Dona Concha in a flowing gown was dabbing her brow with her perfumed handkerchief.

Chemari looked around at the palace as he was waiting for his parents, its grand architecture speaking of the pomp and the power of the office of the governor-general and this was not even the main palace. Blanco ruled the colony from *Palacio del Gobernador* in Intramuros. His predecessors built Malacanang Palace, along the Pasig River, as a country retreat, a haven of peace and quiet, away from the affairs of the state in the colony.

He sighed in admiration of the palace. The men and the women by the tall windows there cast long shadows on the palace grounds. The light from the windows there gave the green grass there, a shade of gold.

Somewhere there was a woman, he hungered to see. He will look for her even if he has to search every room in the palace. His lips and his waxed mustache made sensuous by that thought, he broke into an expectant smile. He looked himself over once more, pulled at the edge of his coat and followed his parents toward the palace's wide staircase.

They halted at the foot of the staircase. Chemari and Colonel Achutegui waited while Dona Concha was dabbing her brow, one more time with her perfumed handkerchief.

"How do I look?" she asked Colonel Achutegui.

"You look fine," he replied, smiling, to Dona Concha.

She held onto Colonel Achutegui's arm as they then ascended the wide staircase.

Governor-General Blanco, at the head of the reception line at the entrance to the main hall, met them with a smile. He was in a dark blue gala uniform with a red sash decked out with medals, his gray hair, mustache and beard adding to his dignified look.

"It is so nice of you to come," Blanco said as he and his wife were shaking hands with Colonel Achutegui and Dona Concha.

"So, you have your dashing young man with you," he said, glancing at Chemari who bowed and smiled, pleased with the compliment. Blanco then introduced the Achuteguis to Luzuriaga and his wife. He told Luzuriaga, as he was shaking hands with Colonel Achutegui, that Colonel Achutegui is the deputy commander of the Civil Guard.

"So, you are the man who quietly runs things here," Luzuriaga said, smiling.

"I try to do my best," Colonel Achutegui replied modestly.

Like Blanco, Colonel Achutegui knew Luzuriaga was there to look around and report in Spain what was going on in the colony.

They were exchanging pleasantries when the Achuteguis saw more guests were coming in the staircase. They nodded at Blanco and Luzuriaga as they then proceeded toward the main hall, bright with the lights from three chandeliers hanging from the ceiling.

It was noisy with talk and laughter while a group of musicians playing a lilting Andalusian song added to the gaiety there.

Chemari looked around for the woman. He frowned, disappointed, when he did not find her there. He turned his gaze to some of the guests clustered at a corner in the main hall, the men standing and the women seated on the couches there. They were listening to a distinguished-looking, middle-aged gentleman who was telling them about the dramatic discovery of the Katipunan.

He listened, out of curiosity and for additional information about the subversive group. His father had talked about it over dinner, the day before. The man apparently did not know much about what happened, for his story was not only inconsistent with what his father had told him, it was also exaggerated.

The man, though, seemed to feel important and knowledgeable in watching the worried look in the faces of his listeners as he then spoke gravely about the imminent, widespread fighting in the colony.

His parents had joined a group of men and women nearby. General Bernardo Echaluce, the military governor of Manila and Colonel Achutegui's superior, was also talking about the Katipunan.

He has heard enough about this subversive group and he whispered to his father that he is going to look for some friends there. Colonel Achutegui nodded and then turned his attention back to Echaluce.

He walked around the hall, full of people having a grand time there. It was, for all their concern about the Katipunan, only a part of the reason, those guests were in attendance there.

They were talking about a host of subjects, the discovery of the Katipunan, being one of them.

A waiter held before Chemari, a tray of wine glasses. He took a wine glass. He liked its bouquet and sweet taste as he took a sip. He then emptied the wineglass with several tips of it to his lips. He complimented the waiter for the excellent wine and returned the wineglass to the tray.

He felt much more cheerful after that. He looked around at the guests who were merry with talk and laughter as they drank their wine and took and ate the finger food in the waiters' trays.

He crossed the hall, avoiding a knot of people there who were conversing and drinking wine, and looked around. The woman he was looking for was not there. He was getting frustrated. He intercepted a waiter, a tray of wine glasses held in his hands, and took a wine glass there.

He made the waiter wait while he emptied his wine glass with several tips of it to his lips. He sighed, having vented his disappointment on the wineglass. He put it back on the waiter's tray and took another wineglass there. He nodded at the waiter who then moved on. He was about to leave the hall when a middle-aged woman came to him.

"I heard you are leaving for Spain soon," the woman said to him.

"Yes, indeed, Dona Cecilia," he replied amiably, "as surely as the sun will rise in the east tomorrow morning."

Dona Cecilia smiled. She lived near the Achuteguis' residence in Cabildo Street in Intramuros.

She touched Chemari's arm and said, "Then you should look up my cousin when you arrive in Madrid. I will give your mother, her address. You will find her family, especially her three daughters, good company."

"She has three daughters? And I suppose, all beautiful?"

Dona Cecilia nodded and smiled.

"Rest, assured, ma'am, the first thing I will do when I arrive in Spain is to look them up," he said as he bowed gracefully and detached himself smoothly from the woman's company.

Near the door to another room, which he had just then entered, was a Spanish military officer conversing in English with two tall young men, apparently Americans from the way they looked and spoke in English.

He listened, his curiosity piqued, while making it appear he was not eavesdropping by looking away and drinking his wine.

"So, Mister McCall, what is the purpose of your visit here?" the Spanish officer asked one of them

"I'm here on assignment from my newspaper, *The San Francisco Sun.*"

"How about you, Mister Shay, what are you after here?"

"I am here to look for the commercial possibilities here for my trading company."

"How long are you staying here?"

"I don't know about Dick here, but I will be around for a week or two."

"I am not staying that long. My ship, bound for Yokohama, will be here this coming Thursday."

Chemari walked away, nodding in approval of the Spanish military officer doing an impromptu interview of the two Americans, never mind if he was doing it, right there in the middle of the governor-general's party.

He knows about the strained relationship between Spain and the United States over the revolution in the Spanish colony in Cuba. Spain accused the United States of meddling in what it considered was an internal Spanish affair while the United States expressed concern over what it saw were Spain's human rights abuses against the Cubans. The two Americans could be in Manila to look around. He was there in Malacanang to have fun, though, not to engage in anything political.

A waiter with a tray of wine glasses was passing by and he gave him his empty wine glass.

The wine he took and the wisps of perfume from the women he had passed by were now beginning to have an intoxicating effect on him. He left the room and entered a deserted hallway.

His ears picked up, as he was walking on, the shuffling of feet to the beat of waltz music from a room or a hall to his left. He was so carried away by the music, he took the hand of a woman he imagined was facing him and he danced with her with complete abandon. He was stopped from dancing by the sight of a beautiful woman in the balcony, at the end of the hallway. He had finally found the woman he had been looking for.

He looked at Marissa Iglesias' beautiful face, etched against the dark background of Pasig River, his eyes feasting on her face, her small nose and thin lips that, with her narrowed eyes, gave him the impression of a woman with an impatient nature. She looked so lovely whatever were her feelings, though, as she was looking on at the river, the woman he has been longing to see in the palace.

He said grandly as he came to her, "What a lucky river that my lovely lady is giving it, all her attention."

She turned and smiled at him.

"So," he said to her, "what are you doing here, all alone in a palace full of people dancing and drinking?

"I am taking a bit of fresh air."

"Or is it because you found no one interesting enough, not until now when I am here with you."

"How highly, you think of yourself!"

He stood back, surprised by her cutting remark. His cheerfulness not having left him, he made light of what she said.

"That was some greeting," he said, smiling still.

She turned her eyes back to the river.

"Why is my lovely one so upset?" he said. "Is it because you missed me so much?"

He saw her frowning and the smile on his face faded away. He felt silly from the pompous way he had addressed her and angry as well as he stood there apparently not wanted by her.

"So, I'm not welcome here," he said as he turned to leave her.

"No, please, don't leave me," she said quickly to him.

He turned back, frowning, and said to her, "What do you really want? You called me conceited, why, I do not know. Then, you made me feel like you did not want me around. Now that I am leaving, why are you asking me to stay here with you?"

She looked humbly at him and he regretted having spoken harshly to her. He looked tenderly at her, keen with a desire to kiss her. He held her shoulders and was about to do that when he saw two men coming from the hallway. He dropped his hands instead, said good evening to them as he then went down quickly with her in the stairs at the side of the balcony.

They passed by the courtyard on their way to the palace garden. All the guests had come in and the footman had left his post there and joined the carriage drivers in another part in the palace's sprawling grounds.

They saw no one in the garden. The scent of flowers there added sweetness to the lovely night, the sky above them, filled with the stars. They were alone. He held her on her shoulders while she leaned her head on his shoulders as they walked on in the garden, close to each other like the young lovers that they were. They halted beside a palm tree there.

She looked sadly at him and said, "Why must we quarrel in the little time we have left together?"

He did not reply to her. He did not want to get into another argument with her. What may have upset her was not so much his flippant remarks nor his lighthearted ways, although they may have annoyed her, but the sad thought that they will soon part. He looked tenderly at her.

"I would not have searched every room in the palace, looking for you," he said, "if I will only end up quarreling with you."

"And I was there, all the time in the balcony, waiting for you. I am sorry, my dear, for having been so nasty to you. I got impatient while I was waiting for you. You are right when you said that nothing and no one interested me. You are the only one who matters to me."

"Despite my conceit?" he said, smiling. "Did you not call me conceited?"

"I called you that, for that is what you are," she said, smiling, too.

He looked at her eyes. She looked back at him expectantly and yielded when he then took her in his arms. She fell in a swoon when he then gave her a long ardent kiss on her lips.

He released her and, smiling mischievously, he said to her, "That is for calling me, conceited."

"I should then call you that more often," she said when she pressed herself suddenly and so tightly to him, he could feel her breast heave as she then wept quietly.

"Please don't cry," he said to her.

He kissed her cheeks, wet with her tears and wiped them with his finger.

"I cannot help it. Only a few more weeks and I will be alone when you will be gone by then."

He sighed and said, "Don't you want me to leave then? But it is for our future. You said that yourself. A law degree in Madrid counts far more than a dozen diplomas here in Manila."

"I know, but how I wish I could go with you to Spain. I miss it. I miss my friends there. I have not been home since we came here."

"This is your home, too."

"No, it is not. Spain is my only home."

He sighed and looked away. He should, by now, be used to the sudden changes in her mood. He felt strongly about it, but decided against pursuing it. He did not want this point of disagreement to come between them. It will just spoil their evening together.

She and her family came to Manila, four years ago, when her father established a trading firm in Binondo. She has never adjusted to the Philippines' hot and humid climate and to life in Manila which she found dull in comparison to life in Madrid, Barcelona and Seville.

He, on the other hand, was born and raised in the Philippines. It is his only home.

"Why don't you ask your parents for permission to visit Spain?" he said to her.

"They will not allow me to leave and interrupt my studies in Colegio de Santa Rosa."

He sighed in disappointment.

"We should go back," he said. "They might be looking for us."

They walked back to the palace and entered a room where young men, some of them Chemari's classmates in Lateran, were dancing with beautiful girls to a waltz played by a pianist and a string ensemble.

A few words, Blanco said in the main hall about the Katipunan was taken as a cue by the other officials and the guests to follow him and Luzuriaga when they proceeded toward the palace library. They could talk freely there, far from the ladies who were getting upset by all the talk about the subversive group.

Everyone there wanted to hear what Fray Mariano Gil, the parish priest in Tondo, will tell them about the Katipunan. He was seated on a couch as he surveyed the other men in the study—the governor-general, his guest Luzuriaga, Manuel Luengo, the civil governor of Manila, other officials, traders and landowners who carried weight in the colony.

"As I have told Manuel," Fray Gil said, glancing at Luengo, "had it not been for a loyal parishioner, I would not have discovered the Katipunan."

"How did you get to know about it?" Isidoro Iglesias, Marissa's father, asked Fray Gil. He was seated in a corner of a couch beside another guest.

His bald head shiny from the light in the chandelier in the ceiling, Fray Gil gave his account on the Katipunan:

"A nun in the orphanage noticed one of the wards, Honoria Patino, crying while she was talking to her brother Teodoro. The poor girl was shocked upon learning that he was a member of a subversive group. By threatening the girl that she will be sent out if they kept anything from her, the nun was able to pry out from Teodoro, the secret about the Katipunan. The nun then told him to come to me and confess his sin.

"Teodoro came to me, the same day, and confessed everything he knew about the Katipunan. My doubts about what he said were settled when I found the lithographic stone used in printing receipts for the Katipunan that he said was hidden in the printing shop of *Diario de Manila* in Palomar. One discovery followed another. We forced open the locker of Policarpio Tarla, another Katipunan member employed in the printing shop and found there, a dagger and subversive documents. We found more incriminating evidence in the house of another Katipunan member.

"All this showed without doubt, the existence of an underground rebel movement poised to strike against us. I reported immediately to our civil and military authorities what I discovered. They have been conducting, since then, a manhunt for the subversives. The rumor about that subversive group, which has been circulating in Manila, is now a fact."

Fray Gil paused in his account. The men showed no sign they had noticed anything wrong with what he did. He broke the seal of the confessional when he reported to the civil and military authorities, everything that Teodoro Patino had confessed to him.

An Andalusian song, sung in the main hall, could be heard faintly in the ensuing silence there. The song's lyrics about the hills and the plains in Spain was a reminder to them that Spain was so far away, they were right now alone in facing this huge problem.

"It looks like Fray Gil has stumbled into something big and serious here," Luzuriaga, who was seated on a couch beside Blanco, said. "If you don't watch out, you might find yourselves facing a revolution. I have seen that happen in Cuba."

"Rest, assured, my friend," Blanco said to Luzuriaga, "that we are doing everything we can to stamp out this threat. We have arrested many of them. We have nipped the rebel movement in the bud."

"And we should spare no effort to get all of them, their leaders especially," Fray Gil said. "I heard that thousands from all over the islands have joined this rebel group."

"Now, now, Fray Gil, don't let your imagination run wild," Luengo said. "This group does not have that many members. It is not that big a threat as you imagined it to be."

"You still cannot see the seriousness of this threat?" Fray Gil said, his eyes blinking in disbelief.

"I am not, whatever you are suggesting, sleeping on my job," Luengo said as he looked sharply at Fray Gil. "We have acted with dispatch and thoroughness in quashing this revolt. What more do you want us to do?"

"You can do more."

"Like what?"

"Like imposing martial law and we should do that right away."

Luengo looked incredulously at Fray Gil.

"There is no need for that, at least, not for now," Blanco said, dismissing the priest's suggestion.

"Imposing martial rule," Luengo said, "will only further alienate the Indios and make the situation worse."

"Are you saying," Fray Gil asked Luengo, "that the measures you have taken are enough to deal with this very serious problem?"

"Yes," Luengo replied. "You can see that by the big number of people we have arrested."

Luzuriaga watched, concerned, the verbal exchange between Fray Gil and Blanco and his subordinate, Luengo. It is a clear sign of a rift between the colony's civil and religious authorities. He learned in the course of his visit there that it is a common knowledge in the Spanish community in Manila that the friars had no love for Blanco and his subordinates like Luengo, whom they felt were too soft to the natives.

The colony's leaders, Luzuriaga noted sadly, were turning at each other instead of working together in fighting their common enemy.

"We have flushed them out of their lairs and now that they are out in the open, they are on the run, like the rats that they are," General Echaluce said. "But we will get all of them."

"Perhaps we should prepare more cells in Fort Santiago for those rebels who are like so much sheep, we are herding in," Colonel Achutegui said.

"Good idea. I think we should do that," Echaluce said. "And now, let us give Fray Gil, our heartfelt congratulations for a job, well done. Had it not been for him, we would not have known about this Indio rebellion, brewing in our midst."

Blanco frowned, annoyed by Echaluce's extravagant remarks. He ended the meeting with the remark that it was time for them to go back to the ladies in the main hall.

The men left the study with Iglesias and Luzuriaga following the others. Luzuriaga was about to speak, but paused and waited instead, until all the others had walked ahead.

"What do you think?" he asked Iglesias.

"I see nothing to cheer about. I don't think the arrests we made have put this subversion to an end. For every subversive, we catch, another one, maybe more, will take his place. The discontent among the Indios is far greater than some of our officials are willing to admit. We are facing a very tough time."

Chapter Eight

Word about the discovery of the Katipunan and the arrest of many of its leaders and members reached Masakao, a few days later. That and the failed spying mission of Paulo and Kabisig had scared some of the conspirators from attending a meeting, Mulawin called in his house. Only Lukas, Doctor Bihasa and Gayuman came. Paulo and Kabisig were advised to stay in Alkayag where they were now conducting military training. Ongliko left the town with his family, so they would be beyond the reach of Zatayde while Pinalis and Masinop begged off from the meeting. They anticipated trouble in Masakao and they took away their families to their relatives in other towns.

"The chaff is being winnowed from the grain," Lukas said to the others.

He could not imagine himself doing what the absent members did although he could not blame them for being so worried about their situation. It was becoming more difficult and dangerous. Aside from the checkpoint at the bridge, more Civil Guard soldiers were now patrolling the town. Many of the houses had been searched. A number of people, Zatayde suspected to be members of the Katipunan, had been arrested and jailed.

"Do you know those who were arrested?" Gayuman asked Lukas.

"I know them." .

"At least the Spaniards know nothing yet about us," Gayuman said.

"But maybe not for long," Lukas said.

"What do we do now?" Bihasa asked Mulawin. "Do we still carry out the attack on the town fort?"

Mulawin glanced gloomily at Bihasa and said, "We might as well forget it."

Lukas frowned, disappointed with Mulawin. His enthusiasm for their cause began to wane once Zatayde had started going after them. Mulawin called for the meeting only after repeated prodding from him. He could not understand what was wrong with them. They were all cowering in fear of Zatayde.

"So, we had those setbacks and we will have more of them," he said. "What do we do then? Should we just run away from the Spaniards?"

He saw Mulawin, his head low in embarrassment. Mulawin maybe their leader, but it is he who is showing them the way to deal with the situation and that is to fight on for their cause.

"While this," he said, "may not be the best time to attack the town fort, we should not rule it out completely. We should attack it, for that is where we can truly hurt the Spaniards. The only thing I doubt in fighting them is our state of readiness, not in our willingness to fight. We now have a small, but respectable fighting unit. Paulo and Miguel told me that the five men we sent there for military training are learning fast."

"What can seven armed men do?" Bihasa said.

"They can do a lot more," Lukas replied irritably, "than a hundred men who do nothing, but run away and hide from our enemy."

"Let us stop that kind of talk," Mulawin said as he reasserted himself. "I will tell you, what we will do. While we have lost the advantage of secrecy and surprise, we still have one thing in our favor— the townsfolk. Once we make the call, they will rise up in arms."

"And then?" Bihasa said.

"We will storm the town fort," Lukas said.

"And make the townsfolk, moving targets?" Bihasa said.

"Whatever we do will involve some risk, some of them at a great risk to our lives, but it is a good move. Like the French Revolution, we will win by sheer numbers."

"But what about the Civil Guard soldiers stationed in San Nicolas and in San Martin?" Gayuman said. "They will surely come to the aid of the town fort."

"That could be a problem," Mulawin said. "Now that we have lost the element of secrecy and surprise in an attack on the town fort, it will be very difficult, if not suicidal, to carry it out now."

Lukas rubbed his fist on his chin and, his eyes turned to Mulawin, he said, "So, what can we do now? We cannot attack the town fort, but neither should we just sit idly. Our problem, I can see it now, is that we have been trying to do everything by ourselves. Before we make any move, why don't we consult first with Bonifacio and the Supreme Council?"

"That seems to be the best thing we can do now," Mulawin said, "assuming that they have not been caught by the Spaniards."

"We can find that out," Lukas said, "if one of us will go to Manila and seek the advice of Bonifacio and the other members of the Supreme Council."

"So, who will go to Manila?" Mulawin said while looking suggestively at Lukas.

"You proposed it, so you should go to Manila," Bihasa said to Lukas.

"Very well," Lukas said, "I will go to Manila."

"Do you want Paulo to go with you?" Mulawin asked Lukas.

"No. It is better and safer, if I will go there alone."

"You are right," Mulawin said. "Miguel and Paulo will in the meantime continue their military training in Alkayag."

"Paulo told me they are running low in some of the supplies, they need there," Lukas said.

"Don't worry about that," Gayuman said. "I will see to it, they will never lack in what they need there."

Lukas nodded approvingly. He has been following up, Paulo's progress with his wound which was nearly healed and his military training. Aside from his occasional secret visits to Masakao, Paulo was now spending all of his time in Alkayag.

He was pleased to see Paulo plunge into learning warfare with energy and enthusiasm, but that did not come as a surprise to him. Having invested with his own blood in the spying mission in the town fort, Paulo now felt completely bound like him, Mulawin and the others, to the revolution. Although not his own son, he felt Paulo was cast in his own mold. He raised him, after all, from his infancy. Paulo's love affair with Teresa, about which he learned from friends and Esperanza, did not diminish Paulo's commitment to their revolutionary cause. His love affair with Teresa was of the heart while his commitment to the revolution sprang from the deepest yearning of his soul to be free of their hated Spanish rulers. If in his youth he came into this same situation, he would have done as Paulo had done it. It brought his mind, back to that time, long ago, when he too had a girl. Maria Celia was an intern in *Colegio de Santa Isabel*. They planned to get married after her graduation. But then, a cholera epidemic swept through Manila and claimed her as one of its victims. He loved her so much that her death closed his heart forever to love for any other woman.

Mulawin asked Lukas, "When are you going to Manila?"

"At the earliest time, tomorrow morning."

Julio took Lukas in his horse-drawn rig to the train station in Malolos. A train then took him to Manila. It arrived there just after noontime. He looked around, the moment he left the train terminal in Tutuban. Calle Azcarraga across the terminal grounds was virtually deserted. A lone horse-drawn rig was running there. The shops at the far side of the wide avenue were closed. What he was seeing there denied what he picked up in the train about the discovery of the Katipunan, that there would be fear and tension, even sporadic fighting, breaking out there.

He noticed with amusement, as he was walking on, that since it was siesta time and with the heat and the humidity, the city residents and the Civil Guard soldiers had avoided any fighting. The residents had escaped to the relative coolness inside their homes and shops while the Civil Guard soldiers may have confined themselves in their barracks in Fort Santiago.

He looked for Bonifacio and the other members of the Supreme Council. No one could tell him where he could find them. He avoided going to their homes. They might be under surveillance by the Spanish authorities.

Mateo Dalandan, a fellow Katipunan member, might know and he proceeded to his hut in Tondo. He passed by the commercial district of Divisoria on his way there. He halted as he was entering Ilaya Street.

It was quiet and deserted except for a stout, middle-aged woman corn vendor in the sidewalk. She was seated on a low, wooden stool, her back against a lean-to of banana leaves that shielded her from the sun. Sweat was trickling down her neck and arms as she was fanning with a cardboard, the hot coals in an iron grill where ears of corn were crackling in the heat.

He was watching the corn vendor, his mind not made up on whether he should buy an ear of corn when two Spanish soldiers came by.

One of them eyed him suspiciously. The soldier was about to approach him when his companion asked him if he wanted to try the roasted corn sold there. The soldier turned his attention to the corn vendor, his mind not made up. The other soldier became impatient and he waved at him for them to move on.

He watched the two soldiers as they were walking toward another street. He then hurried away and walked on through a maze of shops, huts, and alleys. He was now deep inside the working-class district of Tondo. He knew his way there and he walked on until he had reached a catwalk. At the end of it was Mateo Dalandan's hut. It stood on wooden stilts, the ground below, muddy and smelling bad.

A woman peered through a parted curtain in a window there when he knocked at the door of the hut. Salvacion, Mateo's wife, had recognized him and she opened the door and let him in.

She told him, as she was leading him to a wooden bench near the window, that Mateo had gone out to see a neighbor, but will soon be back. Then she asked him, if the Spaniards will come and throw them all in jail.

"Why," he replied, "will they do that?"

"They have been arresting people since the discovery of the Katipunan. They might also come for us."

He cast about for words that could relieve her of her fear of the Spaniards and all that he could say to her was, "Don't worry about that."

What he said was not so reassuring to her, she asked to be excused and she resumed working in the kitchen in the hut. She was cooking their supper in a clay stove in the kitchen.

He looked around while he was waiting for Mateo. The hut was dark and cheerless. It was bare except for a small dining table and two benches. A rolled-up mat stood between an old, wooden trunk and tiers of pillows and blankets. Old, patched-up clothes were hanging from a rope strung up across the hut. On a wall of palm shingles were faded pictures and a calendar.

He twitched his nose at the faint, foul smell swept up by a gust of wind from the soggy, smelly ground through the gaps in the hut's bamboo floor. The hut's depressing sight and the offensive smell of waste matter spoke of the poverty and desperation of Mateo Dalandan's family.

But for their freedom of movement, their condition and in countless other huts like theirs, was hardly any better than the jail, Salvacion was afraid of. Mateo once told him that he did not want his son to grow up poor, wretched and ignorant like him.

A movement in the pillows caught his eyes. A small boy was peering at him. He was Mateo's young son. He waved at the boy who, suddenly overcome with fear of him, ran toward his mother.

He looked outside and saw in the distance, standing on a rise in the ground and dominating the neighborhood, the imposing stone church in Tondo. He frowned as he recalled the horror stories, Mateo and the other Katipunan members had told him about Fray Mariano Gil, the parish priest in Tondo. The priest never allowed a dead person brought inside the church for the last rite unless he was paid first for his religious services. Not everyone could comply immediately with this requirement. It sometimes happened when a coffin would be left in the churchyard, in some cases, for one whole day, until the family and friends of the dead person had raised the money to pay Fray Gil for his religious services. The priest and others like him were, like the civil authorities and the military, responsible for the alienation of the Filipinos from their Spanish rulers.

He had never ceased to be amazed at how, like him, his countrymen had remained steadfast to their Christian faith despite the abuses by some of its ministers. They could distinguish between their Christian faith, which was good and necessary, and a minister like Fray Gil, who was a disgrace to their Christian faith. It gave them hope and comfort in the face of those torments and abuses they endured from a priest like Fray Gil. Now, of all people, it was this priest who had discovered the Katipunan. Fray Gil alerted the civil and military authorities who then went on a manhunt of the leaders and followers of the Katipunan.

He learned all of that in the course of his search for Bonifacio and the other leaders of the Katipunan. He found no one. He could only guess, they have either gone into hiding or have been caught and jailed. He went over again, the question that had nagged him all day—where is Bonifacio? He hoped to get the answer from Mateo who was approaching the hut.

He said to Lukas, the moment he was inside the hut, his voice sharp with fear and anger, "Do you know what the Spaniards have been doing? They have been rounding up people! They have imprisoned hundreds of people in Fort Santiago!"

"Do not panic," Lukas replied, his palm turned toward Mateo, for him calm down.

Mateo sat down on the bench, beside Lukas.

"I have been looking all day for Bonifacio," he said to Mateo. "Do you know where I can find him?"

"He is in Balintawak. He barely escaped capture by the Spaniards. He passed the word for us to follow him there. I have just made arrangements with a friend who will take me there in his rig. You can, if you like, go there with me."

"I will go with you. It is important for me to see Bonifacio."

Salvacion, who was watching them, insisted that they take something before leaving. Lukas was not hungry, although, out of courtesy to her, he took a few bites of the food on the table.

It was time for them to leave. Lukas stepped outside the hut while Mateo was saying good-bye to his wife and his son.

They walked toward the rig, its driver waiting for them, and stepped up into the rig's backseat.

They set out for Balintawak just as the sun was setting in the western horizon, across Manila Bay. The weather had cooled down with the sea breeze now blowing from the bay. The sun, later on, had become a red, brilliant disk sinking slowly into the dark mountain peaks in Bataan.

Lukas looked on, entranced, at the sun. It cast a soft, golden glow on the marshes near the bay and on the bay itself. His eyes remained turned there, his attention divided between Mateo who was talking on about the mass arrests and the beautiful setting sun over Manila Bay.

They had entered the village of Gagalangin when the rig driver made a turn at a fork in the village road. The village was only a short distance from the town of Caloocan. They turned from there, toward the village of Balintawak.

The sun had set by the time they arrived there. With Mateo guiding him, the rig driver negotiated the potholed country road until they reached a house there, near the road.

Lukas and Mateo left the rig. They walked toward the house of Sofronio Navata, a friend of Mateo. He called out a good evening. Sofronio's wife Marcela appeared in the window there.

She told Mateo that they missed Bonifacio by only a few hours. There were so many of them, she added, and her husband had left with them.

"Where did they go?" Mateo asked her.

"They went to Kangkong. It is that way," she replied as she pointed out the way there.

Lukas and Mateo went on foot to Kangkong while the rig driver returned to Tondo.

Night had fallen by then, but a half-moon in the sky lit their way there. They had walked for sometime on the trail, bound on both sides by tall cogon grass, when someone asked them who they were and what they were doing there.

"We are friends," Lukas replied. "We were told to come here."

"Who told you that?"

"Bonifacio."

Lukas and Mateo were, in an instant, surrounded by men armed with knives, swords and bamboo spears. They were the Katipunan sentries. Lukas told their leader, who they were. He was asked for the password. He gave it and he was then told they could proceed to the camp of Bonifacio.

They walked on in the trail until they came to a rise in the ground. They walked up to it and halted at the top, awed by the wonderful sight there of hundreds of men and women gathered in a wide ground surrounded by wooden houses and nipa huts. It was bright with campfires, gas lamps and bamboo torches. They have arrived in the camp of Bonifacio.

Lukas saw Mateo, looking wide-eyed in excitement at the camp and he said to him, "Go ahead, I will join you there, later on."

"I will see you there," Mateo said as he walked down to the camp.

Lukas looked on at the camp. They were not like the frightened men and women cowering in fear in the dark corners of their huts, waiting to be taken out and thrown in jail by the Civil Guard.

He could see instead in the large gathering there, his fellow countrymen poised to strike back at the Spaniards. He could hear from the camp an incessant hum and of voices that echoed the yearning for freedom, he and the others had often expressed in their meetings in Mulawin's house. The uplifting sight there had the effect of removing all the fear and worry that had gripped him the whole day over the fate of the Katipunan.

He was in high spirit when, a few moments later, he walked down toward the camp to look for Bonifacio or a familiar face there. He turned his eyes to a line of men and women moving toward a long table where food was being put by women into the plates held before them.

The sight and the smell of the food there reminded Lukas, how for the few bites of food he took in Mateo's hut.

He was undecided on whether he should join the food line there or look on for Bonifacio when a man there, approached him.

"Am I glad to see you," the man said to Lukas.

"Same here," Lukas replied to Cesar Turiano, also a Katipunan member and a merchant who plied his trade between Manila and Masakao.

"Did you come from Masakao?" Turiano asked Lukas.

"I did. Do you know where I can find Bonifacio? I must see him."

"He is somewhere here. But you must take something first. You look like you have not eaten, the whole day. Bonifacio is not going anywhere tonight. We will look for him, after we have eaten."

Lukas washed his hands in a basin of water there and joined the food line with Turiano. The food served was a simple combination of rice, fried fish and a vegetable dish. He sat down on a bench with Turiano and began to eat with his hands. He ate quietly while Turiano, between mouthfuls of food, told him what happened to the Katipunan in the past two days.

"Had they delayed a little bit," Turiano said, "Bonifacio, Jacinto, Plata and Valenzuela would have been caught by the Spaniards."

Lukas shook his head. What a terrible effect it would have been to the Katipunan if Bonifacio and the other Supreme Council members had been caught by the Spaniards. He knew no one who could take their place.

"Good fortune still shines on us," he said to Turiano.

He stood up with Turiano when they were finished with their meal. They returned the plates and washed their hands.

A man approached Turiano. They were talking when Lukas indicated with his finger pointed outward that he was going to look for Bonifacio.

He walked around in the camp until he finally found Bonifacio. He was facing, beneath a mango tree, a crowd of men and women. A campfire was in front of him.

Bonifacio's profile, small-nosed, his lips thin, his cheekbones so prominent, was tinged a bright bronze by the campfire. He was barefooted, his pants rolled up, just below the knee, a sheathed knife tucked in his belt. There was nothing physically remarkable about Bonifacio except for the fire in his eyes and his commanding presence.

Someone in the crowd asked Bonifacio about his plans for the Katipunan. He did not answer the question, but asked instead for more firewood in the campfire.

He ran through in his mind, as he waited for Bonifacio to answer the question, what he had learned about Bonifacio in the course of his search for him in Manila. Bonifacio has not given a clear and definite answer to a question like that nor did he take any steps nor given any orders to counteract the Spaniards' manhunt of them.

Bonifacio, it seemed to him, was waiting for someone or something, he knew not, who or what.

The longer he waited, the more it became clear to him that Bonifacio was evasive to a question like that. He may not be sure about what step, he should take.

If he were in the place of Bonifacio, he will do only one thing and this was to fight the enemy. Bonifacio had not done that. He may have realized that skill in combat will not just come into play when the occasion to use it had presented itself. It was something that will not just materialize out of thin air.

He knew Bonifacio to be a good leader and organizer. This was evident in the droves of men and women who have joined the Katipunan, but the time for organization had passed. The Katipunan will now face its first test in combat with the Civil Guard..

For all he knew, beyond the field of cogon grass, not far from their camp, Civil Guard soldiers might be looking for them.

A man came with the firewood and put it in the campfire.

Bonifacio saw Lukas, who was standing at the back of the crowd, and he waved at him to come to him. The crowd parted for Lukas as he was walking toward Bonifacio.

"You are a most welcome sight, Lukas," Bonifacio said, his hand laid on Lukas' shoulders. He said, as he turned to the crowd, "My friends, we have here, another comrade. This is Lukas Palanas. He is from Masakao."

The crowd looked on at Lukas.

"How are things in Masakao?" Bonifacio asked Lukas.

"Not good. I was sent here for your orders."

"You will have them in due time. Tell me, how do you size up our situation?"

Lukas, his eyes wide in surprise, looked on at Bomifacio. He did not expect Bonifacio to ask him, a question like that before the crowd. He will not mince his words, though, and he will answer frankly.

"Do you want it given, straight to you?" he said to Bonifacio who nodded in reply. "Very well, it is bad and we have not made it any better by doing nothing, but take the blows and run away."

Bonifacio was so taken aback by what Lukas said, he looked sharply at him, but then his face softened.

"What would you suggest then?" he asked Lukas.

"We must fight back, right away."

He gazed keenly at Bonifacio who seemed to be giving serious thought to what he said to him.

Bonifacio then turned to the crowd and said, "We will set a definite course of action in the meeting of the Supreme Council tonight. Find a place, in the meantime, where you can take a rest. We must conserve our energy for this difficult and dangerous task that lies ahead of us."

The crowd stirred and thinned out until only Lukas and Bonifacio were left there.

Lukas then asked Bonifacio, "Can you tell me now, what you want us to do in Masakao?"

"Do what you suggested a while ago."

"Strike back at the Spaniards?"

"Yes, but do it simultaneously with the rest of us."

Lukas was puzzled by what Bonifacio said to him. He was thinking about it when Bonifacio laid his hand on his shoulders and led him to the house of Apolonio Samson, the headman in Kangkong.

"Have coffee with Jacinto and the others before turning in," Bonifacio said to Lukas.

He left Samson's house, half an hour later. The issue about what the Katipunan should do had remained unsettled. He found a place to sleep beneath a mango tree. He looked around. All activity in the camp had ceased. They were retiring for the night.

The sun, the following day, was already low in the western horizon when Lukas woke up to Mateo shaking him on his shoulders and telling him that they were moving out of there.

He looked around. They were breaking camp. He put his hand over his mouth to stifle a yawn. He had taken a nap, tired by one whole day of discussions, Bonifacio held with the other members of the Supreme Council. Like the night before, they could not agree on what to do, when and where.

"Why," he asked Mateo, "are we moving out?"

"A Civil Guard patrol was seen, not far from here. We are leaving and moving on to Pugad Lawin."

He stood up and looked on, frowning, as men and women removed or stamped out traces of the camp, the remains of last night's campfires, the tables, clay stoves and benches before the Civil Guard patrol will be there. They were running away from the enemy. But then, he nodded in understanding the prudent move made by Bonifacio. An entire regiment of Spanish troops could be following, not far from the Civil Guard patrol.

They made a night-long walk to Pugad Lawin and arrived there at dawn, tired and hungry. They were cheered when they saw food and water set on the tables in the yard of Juan Ramos, the village headman and son of Melchora Aquino, who was one of the first women to join the Katipunan.

An advance party had told the residents in Pugad Lawin about the coming of Bonifacio and his followers. They opened their rice bins, cooked food and drew water for the droves of men and women who had descended on them.

Their camp in Pugad Lawin, as in Kangkong, waited while the Supreme Council then spent the whole morning, discussing how they should respond to the manhunt and the arrest of many of their members.

Bonifacio, Jacinto and Valenzuela were for striking back at the Spaniards. Ladislaw Plata, Bonifacio's brother-in-law, argued that the Katipunan lacked the arms and the men trained in combat to strike back that early at the Spaniards.

Lukas kept to himself. He was seated at the base of a palm tree, tired of the inconclusive discussions by the Supreme Council when he heard there, a lot of cheering and shouting. He stood up and saw Bonifacio, standing on a bench, speaking before a big crowd in front of him.

Bonifacio then raised his arm and shouted, "My brothers and sisters! Do you swear to repudiate the government that oppresses us?"

The crowd shouted back, "Yes, we do!".

"Then bring out your *cedulas* and tear them to pieces! It will symbolize our determination to take up arms!"

"This is it," Lukas said to himself, "the start of the revolution!"

He took out his cedula from his shirt pocket, what tearing it up will mean to him. All adult residents in the colony were required to carry their cedula or identification card with them, at all times. Failure to show it on demand from the authorities meant imprisonment. He will turn into an outlaw if he will do what Bonifacio had told him to do. He tore it to pieces.

The yard, in a short while, was littered with torn cedulas. There was no turning back for them now.

Some men in the crowd shouted, "Long live the Philippines! Long live the Katipunan!"

Lukas was in an instant swept along with the rest of the crowd in shouting the battle cry of the Philippine Revolution.

Chapter Nine

Bonifacio set August 29 as the date for the start of the revolution. Fighting, though, had begun earlier in the town of Makati, near Manila.

They were caught unexpectedly in a fight with a Civil Guard patrol of some forty soldiers that had chanced upon their camp in Pugad Lawin. One Spanish soldier and two Filipino rebels died in the encounter.

Bonifacio had the Civil Guard patrol surrounded and could have overwhelmed it by the sheer force of numbers. He had over a thousand followers in his camp, but the Civil Guard, through some deft maneuver, were able to slip away. Bonifacio, in another apparently prudent move, ordered their immediate withdrawal from Pugad Lawin instead of pursuing the Civil Guard patrol. It could be acting as bait for a bigger Spanish military force, not far from there.

Bonifacio took the offensive, a few days later, when he attacked the gunpowder magazine in San Juan del Monte, an important military facility guarded by Spanish troops. He had nearly succeeded in taking it, but for the timely arrival there of Spanish reinforcements.

Bonifacio, despite that early setback, carried on with the fight with a persistency characteristic of him.

Word about his declaration of Philippine independence spread around rapidly. Various Katipunan chapters, in a spontaneous reaction to it, rose also in revolt. The fighting spread quickly in the districts of

Tondo, Santa Ana, Pandacan, Sampaloc and Mandaluyong in Manila and in the towns nearby of Taguig, Pateros, Marikina and Montalban. Fighting soon broke out much farther in the provinces of Morong, Bulacan, Nueva Ecija, Pampanga, Laguna, Tarlac and Cavite until practically the entire colony was engulfed in the Philippine Revolution.

Masakao, like many of the towns in the colony, was a tinderbox of anger and hatred just a spark could blow it up into a revolution. A terrible incident provided that spark in Masakao.

Lukas returned to Masakao, the day following Bonifacio's declaration of Philippine independence. The town with its empty roads and shuttered homes seemed to him to be in a state of anxious waiting. It was like the calm before a storm.

He was on his way home when he heard someone calling out to him, "Come here quickly, Mang Lukas!"

Agerico, the town artist, Paulo's friend and also a member of the Katipunan, was waving at Lukas from the window in his house. Lukas walked quickly toward the house.

"Zatayde is looking for you," Agerico said to him.

Lukas' face turned grim. So, Zatayde had found him out. He listened as Agerico then told him what happened in Masakao while he was away. Pinalis and Masinop were caught and tortured into revealing, all that they know about the Katipunan. Mulawin, Doctor Bihasa and Gayuman had fled to Alkayag. The Civil Guard had been combing the town for the rebels. Dozens of suspected rebels had been caught and jailed.

"It is not safe for you to go home now," Agerico said to Lukas.

"I know."

"What will you do now?"

"I must flee to Alkayag. I will be safe there."

"I will go there with you."

"We will leave when it is dark."

The fear that gripped the town rebels was the opposite of the confident mood of the town's Spanish authorities. They have taken the initiative and were pressing on, but while Mayor Echeverria and Lieutenant Zatayde shared the same goal of stamping out the rebellion in the town, they differed in the manner of accomplishing it. Their differences broke out in a meeting they held with Fray Gustavo in the mayor's office.

"Have we now put an end to this rebellion?" Fray Gustavo asked Zatayde.

"I cannot say that yet. Their leaders, Manuel Mulawin and Lukas Palanas, have eluded us and we have not found the two spies who are in league with them, but I will get all of them."

"Can you imagine that?" Echeverria said, as he shook his head in utter disbelief, "Mulawin, Palanas, Masinop and Pinalis, leading this rebellion in the town? I know them to be peaceful, respectable people. Pinalis is even working for me. What could have made them, turn against us?"

"Whatever it is, the fact is, they are against us," Zatayde said as he then stood up from his seat. He was leaving the mayor and the priest.

"Wait, before you leave," Echeverria said to Zatayde. "I want you to go easy on those people. The tougher are the measures, we use against them, the more they will rebel."

"So what, if we are tough with them, they are, anyway, already in rebellion. We should not hold back on them. I will put them all in jail and give them the proper treatment there, for that is the best way to end their rebellion. If you will excuse me, I have some work to do."

Zatayde nodded at the mayor and the priest as he left them.

Echeverria and Fray Gustavo sat without speaking, moments after Zatayde had left them. Echeverria reflected on how his authority as the town mayor had been eroded by Zatayde who had been assigned to the town only recently. He could blame no one, but himself for having allowed himself to be relegated into the background by Zatayde, who had taken the initiative in keeping the peace and order in the town. He would not have minded that and would have even commended Zatayde for his zeal except for the brutal methods he was using against the town rebels.

"What do you think?" Fray Gustavo asked Echeverria.

"Lieutenant Zatayde will have to be reined in and fast. The brutal methods he is employing in keeping the peace and order in this town will only alienate further the town residents and bring about a bloody uprising here."

"The strong methods, he is employing are working, though," Fray Gustavo said, who favored them. "Without the curfew and the patrols, the thorough searches, he is conducting, the arrests, he is making, and by your authority at that, we would not have known about this rebellion building up in this town."

"You might as well include the water cure, Zatayde is employing on the prisoners in the town fort jail."

He had seen, disgusted, the water cure, a form of torture, Zatayde introduced there.

The prisoner was laid down on his back to a plank of wood with his arms tied underneath the plank of wood. Water was then forced into the prisoner's mouth until the stomach was swollen. It was then pounded on with a piece of flat wood until the prisoner could no longer endure the pain. The prisoner would then agree to talk, if he was not dead by then.

"We'll have to allow Lieutenant Zatayde, some leeway on that," Fray Gustavo said. "The method he is using shows the strength and firmness needed to keep those Indios under control."

"We can always try to win them back."

A harsh sound came out of Fray Gustavo's throat that sounded to Echeverria was like a cynical laughter.

"But for the fear of God and our arms, they would have strayed from us, a long time ago," Fray Gustavo said to the mayor.

Echeverria gazed, frowning, at the priest. Fray Gustavo was telling him that only the Church and the Civil Guard had kept hold on the town, ignoring the role he played as the town mayor in keeping the townsfolk peaceful and submissive, an amazing feat in the face of their oppressive rule in the town and in the rest of the colony.

"You may have forgotten that it is the civil government and not your provocative Sunday sermons and Zatayde's brutal methods that kept the peace and order in this town," he said to Fray Gustavo.

"That helped, too."

Echeverria was beginning to work himself into a passion, he stood up to calm himself and walked toward a window that looked out at the town square, the churchyard, the river and the outlying waterlogged rice fields. The townsfolk could look forward to another bountiful harvest.

He nodded at Fray Gustavo when he stood up and asked to be excused. He watched the priest who was now walking back to the church. He will be having, within a short time, his afternoon liaison with his cook and housekeeper. He had turned, like a fellow Spaniard, a blind eye to the friar's scandalous behavior. It was a common practice among the Spanish friars in the colony to keep the women working for them as their cooks and housekeepers also as their sexual partners and have children by them as well.

He walked back to his office, his mind on Zatayde. His excesses had so disturbed him he had been wracking his brain for a way to have him relieved from his post of commander of the town fort.

Lieutenant Zatayde at that very moment was patrolling the town with his deputy, Sergeant Quatrillo and two soldiers.

"What do you know about that old man there?" Zatayde asked Quatrillo when he saw Julio raking the dry leaves in his yard into a mound of trash.

"That is Julio Dumayag, sir. He is a storekeeper, a rig driver and a tenant farmer in the friars' agricultural estate in the town."

"Have you come up with anything we can hold against him and his family?"

"We have found nothing yet, sir."

"We will soon find that out. It is just a matter of taking it out from them."

Julio dropped the rake in his hand and came quickly to the house gate when he saw Zatayde and his men were approaching the house.

He bowed his head and said good afternoon to Zatayde, the moment he was at the house gate.

"Are you not giving me the courtesy of letting me in with my men?" Zatayde said brusquely to Julio.

Julio mumbled an apology and opened the house gate quickly.

Zatayde entered the yard with his men and looked around at the house and the orchard there.

"What can I do for you, sir," he asked Zatayde.

"I have a few questions for you. Do you know Masinop and Pinalis?"

"I know the head teacher and the municipal secretary."

"How about Manuel Mulawin, do you know him?"

"I know him, too, sir."

"And Lukas Palanas, do you know him, too?"

"I know him, too, sir."

Zatayde turned his eyes to Teresa who had appeared in the dining room window in the house.

"Is there any anything, we can do for you, sir?" she asked Zatayde, who was left tongue-tied by her beauty.

He was looking on at Teresa when he nodded at something that then came to his mind. He waved at her in a sign that there was nothing she should be concerned about. She left the window.

He turned his attention, back to Julio and said to him, "Come with me, old man."

Julio, though puzzled, followed Zatayde, out into the road.

Zatayde then said to Julio, "Do you know that those people, I mentioned, are all connected with a rebellion brewing in this town?"

Julio nodded. Like everyone in the town, he knew about the arrests Zatayde had made there.

"Now, old man," Zatayde said to Julio, "be good and go to the town fort with my men."

"Why?" Julio asked Zatayde.

"We need you to identify those we have put in jail."

Julio's eyes turned wide with fear about the fort's jail where men were tortured there. He made a feeble attempt to resist, but the two soldiers had grabbed him in his arms.

"Take him to the fort," Zatayde said to Quatrillo. He walked toward the house, once his soldiers were far enough on the road.

Teresa was in the dining room. She was removing at the dining table, the chaff and the stones in a tray of rice when she saw Zatayde leering at her.

She stood up and said, "What do you want? Where is my father?"

"Calm down," he said to her. "My men brought your father to the fort for questioning."

"Why? He has done nothing wrong."

"We will soon, find that out. You can make it easy for your father, though," he said as he approached her.

She stepped back.

"Now, now, just play along."

He tried to grab her, but caught nothing, but air.

She had stepped back until her back was against the wooden wall.

He was breathing hard now when he tried to grab her again.

She was, without room to back into, caught in his embrace.

"I've got you now," he said to her.

He was brushing her cheek when suddenly, he cried out in pain.

She had bitten his finger so hard, her teeth cut, right into the bone. She opened her mouth, releasing his finger and ducked her head when he swung his fist at her face.

She then ran toward the kitchen and picked up there, a kitchen knife.

He was now so frustrated as he was sucking the blood in his injured finger.

"Let me see, how tough you are," he said to her.

He stopped himself as he was moving toward her when she suddenly turned around and faced him, the tip of the kitchen knife in her hand, pointed to her stomach.

She said, her voice, barely a whisper, "You will never take me, alive. Take one more step and I will stab myself."

He looked hard at her, not sure if she was serious or bluffing. He did not expect such a strong resistance from her. Back in Cuba, the native women there, on whom he had forced himself, were just as spirited. They fought, clawed and kicked, but in the end, he overpowered them. This brown beauty will be no exception. Her strong resistance, he had not expected, will only make greater, the pleasure in taking her.

He took a step, but stopped himself abruptly when she then pressed the kitchen knife into her stomach.

He watched, horrified, when blood then appeared at the tip of the knife. She was not bluffing! Never in all his life had he seen anyone do that! He winced at the sight of the blood, now making a line, down in her dress.

He could feel her, as he then looked away from that awful sight, staring at him with so much hatred in her eyes. He left her, subdued by her strong, unexpected resistance and descended the stairs at the back of the house and walked away.

Teresa dragged herself toward the living room, her hand pressed to her stomach to stop the flow of blood. She watched Zatayde who was now out on the road until he was out of her sight.

She was drained of strength, her back against the wall.

"Help me, please, help me," she cried as she then dropped down on the floor.

Her voice, though weak, carried far enough in the quiet afternoon to Nieves, who was tending her garden, beside Teresa's house.

She rushed there and saw Teresa lying wounded on the floor, the bloody knife in her hand. She screamed out in the window for help.

The neighbors soon came to find out what happened there.

Word about what Zatayde tried to do to Teresa spread fast in the neighborhood. Lukas and Agerico were taking a snack in Agerico's house when they heard a woman shouting something, outside on the road. They went to the window and asked the woman, what she was shouting about.

"Our neighbors are rushing toward the Dumayags' house," she said. "Something terrible had happened there."

Lukas rushed with Agerico toward the Dumayags' house and saw a crowd that had gathered there. He asked a woman, what happened there.

"Nieves found Teresa, lying on the floor, a bloody knife in her hand. She has a wound in her stomach, she apparently had inflicted on herself. Nieves, before that, saw the fort commander walk, past her garden. Then she heard Teresa, crying for help.

"Lieutenant Zatayde came here with his soldiers and arrested Julio. He stayed after his soldiers had left with Julio. He must have then come after Teresa, but how she must have fought him."

Lukas and Agerico listened, their lips pressed tight in anger.

"How is she now?" Lukas asked the woman.

"I don't know. She is in her bedroom."

Lukas nodded appreciatively at the woman. He went with Agerico to Teresa's bedroom and knocked at the door there. Nieves opened it. Teresa was in her bed. She was barely awake. She looked pale. A woman, a midwife, seated beside her bed, was attending to her,

"How is she?" he asked Nieves.

"She is all right now. The wound did not run deep. The flow of blood from the stab wound in her stomach has been stopped with the medicinal herbs applied to her by the widwife. She is more in shock than in anything else."

He looked on at Teresa, marveling at her courage. She would rather die than yield to Zatayde.

He asked Nieves about Agustina and Esperanza.

"They are in their store and do not know yet what happened here."

"I will tell them myself."

He told Nieves and the midwife to stay with Teresa.

They left her bedroom, assured that she is quite all right.

The crowd in the living room looked expectantly at Lukas, the moment he and Agerico left the bedroom.

The woman, he talked to a while ago, asked him, "How is she now?"

"She is fine despite what she has been through."

"We should do something about that animal," a young man said.

"What can we do?" an old man said. "He is the fort commander."

"So what, if he is the fort commander," another man said. "We should get rid of that animal."

Lukas' eyes lit up at the crowd, mad at Zatayde for what he tried to do to Teresa.

Here in this crowd, the thought came to his mind, is the dry wood for the fire in the coming revolution in their town.

"I know how you feel," he said to them. "We will not let this pass without doing something about it."

"We will only end up in the fort jail," the old man said, "if we will do anything about it."

"It is Zatayde who will end up, dead or in the jail," Lukas said as he then told the crowd about the revolution that had broken out in Manila.

"The time to strike back at the Spaniards has come," he said to the crowd. "Are you with me when we go after Zatayde?"

"Yes, we are," the crowd replied.

"We will do that soon enough," he said. "But for now, we should let Teresa have some rest. Nieves and the midwife will look after her. Let us all go home and gather whatever weapons we can use, knives, sharpened bamboo poles, machetes, even wooden laundry clubs. Tell the others. We will be back here tomorrow morning with some of our townmates. Gather on the road when you see us there. We will then attack the town fort."

Lukas, Agerico and the neighbors then left the house.

Nieves and the midwife stayed with Teresa until Agustina and Esperanza had arrived home. She would have stayed on there had not Soledad, her mother, called for her. She was about to leave when Esperanza and Agustina tearfully embraced her.

"We cannot thank you enough," Esperanza said to her, "for what you have done for Teresa."

"We are friends and neighbors," Nieves said to them. "We look after each other."

She met Doctor Bihasa when she returned the following morning to see how Teresa was doing. Doctor Bihasa had just then finished treating Teresa of her wound. Agustina and Esperanza were taking their breakfast. They invited her for coffee.

"I will take a look at Teresa first."

"Paulo is with her," Esperanza said.

Like everyone in the neighborhood, Nieves knew Paulo as an old family friend, welcome anytime in the Dumayag household.

She sat down at the dining table and took the cup of coffee, Esperanza gave her. Every effort she made to strike a conversation with them was met with short answers. Agustina looked spent, the lines in her plain, aging face, quite pronounced. The dark bags beneath her eyes showed a sleepless night she spent, worrying and crying for Teresa and Julio. Esperanza looked sad and angry.

Nieves finally stopped asking questions and kept quiet, too. They heard, just then, a lot of shouting on the road, in front of the house.

"What is that all about?" Esperanza asked Nieves.

She stood up and went with Agustina and Nieves to the living room window overlooking the road. They saw a big crowd that had gathered there. More people were coming from both directions in the road.

The crowd, a gathering prohibited by the Spanish authorities, was in an angry mood. They held in their hands, knives, machetes and bamboo spears.

They held them high as they were shouting in reply to Mulawin, Lukas, Doctor Bihasa, Gayuman and Agerico who were working them into hatred toward their Spanish rulers.

Esperanza and Nieves nodded when they saw some of the women there were likewise holding high, wooden laundry clubs in their hands.

"They can use them to bash Zatayde in the head," Nieves said.

"Teresa will love to do that herself," Esperanza said.

They looked on at the crowd, its temper hot like the sun blazing in the cloudless sky.

Teresa thought, how handsome Paulo was, as she was looking at him from her bed. The play of light on his profile, his deep-set eyes, finely chiseled nose and thin lips made him so attractive, what woman could resist him, who was hers.

The time they spent together had eased up her mind of that terrible thing, she went through yesterday.

She told him about it and he said in a low, even voice that betrayed anger, "Never again will Zatayde do what he tried to do to you."

"Don't do anything that might make it worse for me."

"Cast your fears, aside."

She nodded, reassured by what he said. She trusted him completely. Her thoughts were no longer, her thoughts alone, but thoughts, she shared with him. Her life, she felt, is from now on bound to him and that whatever will happen next, she felt as if they were now bound together, with him as her husband and with her as his wife.

He looked out from the window in the bedroom when they heard, loud, angry voices coming from the road.

"What is going on there?" she asked him.

"A big crowd of our townsfolk has gathered in front of the house. It is the start of the revolution in our town."

"I'm afraid of what it might do to us."

"Don't be afraid. We will now get rid of the Spaniards."

He turned to her, who was staring at him. He came to her and mumurred soft, reassuring words to her.

"Why are you leaving me," she said when he said, he had to leave her now as he then moved away from her. She was overtaken with loneliness and tears coursed down her cheeks as she was looking on at the closed bedroom door. He had to leave her. What he is going to do is good and necessary for all of them.

The townsfolk who were gathered on the road fell silent when they saw Zatayde coming with a squad of his men.

Some of them began to move away at the fighting that might then break out there. They stayed there when they saw Mulawin, Lukas, Paulo, Gayuman, Bihasa and Agerico standing still and watching Zatayde who had halted with his men.

"I want you to leave now and go home and I will forget what I'm seeing here," Zatayde said to them, "but I want Mulawin and Palanas to come forward and surrender to me."

No one in the crowd moved away.

"You will be sorry, if you will not leave now," Zatayde said. "I will order my men to shoot you."

He raised his hand for his soldiers to fire at the crowd when suddenly, a volley of gunfire hit Zatayde's men. Three of them were killed or were wounded.

The shooting came from Kabisig and his armed men who were hidden in the bushes and the trees at the side of the road. Mulawin, Lukas and the others had laid a perfect trap for Zatayde and his men.

Zatayde recovered quickly from the shock of finding himself, the attacker, being attacked instead. He turned around and ran away with his men.

He looked so ridiculous, the town fort commander, running away from the townsfolk, it sent them, laughing at him.

"Look at how fast, the coward can run," a young man shouted.

"Don't let Zatayde get away!" Lukas shouted above the laughter. "Go, after him and his men,"

The townsfolk stopped laughing as they wavered between what Lukas had told them to do and their lingering fear of Zatayde. They overcame it when they saw Kabisig and his men, breaking out of the bushes along the road and shooting Zatayde and his men. Another soldier was killed.

Kabisig, his men and the townsfolk then ran after Zatayde and his men. They were far ahead, the fear for their lives having made them running so fast. They reached the fort and had its gate closed as the townsfolk were approaching the road there.

They had been worked up by the chase and they rushed toward the fort. Their knives and their bamboo spears held high, about a score of them had run ahead of the rest of the angry crowd.

They were almost at the fort gate when gunfire suddenly rang out from the top of the fort wall. Four of them were killed, three were wounded. The crowd moved back.

They joined the rest of the townsfolk who had gathered in the churchyard when the church bell in one of the two belfries began to ring. They saw Fray Gustavo, who was in the other belfry. He was waving a large white cloth in trying to attract the attention of the Civil Guard in San Nicolas.

He took fright when he saw, among the noisy, angry crowd in the churchyard, armed men pointing their guns to him. He was stepping back when his left foot slipped on the stone staircase.

The townsfolk were looking on at the belfry when the church caretaker came out of the church and said, "Fray Gustavo is dead."

They stared skeptically at the caretaker. Fray Gustavo was so dominant a figure in the town, they could not believe, he was gone, just like that, not until they saw his body, lying at the foot of the staircase.

"That takes care of the priest," a man said. "Let us now go after the mayor."

The crowd rushed toward the municipal hall. They went upstairs, to the office of Mayor Echeverria who stood trembling before them. A man was about to hit him with a bamboo pole, but Lukas swept it aside.

"Don't harm him," he said," but keep him under guard."

Echeverria was being brought out of the mayor's office when Mulawin arrived there with Gayuman, Paulo, Kabisig and his armed men. They saw, from a window there, the soldiers on top of the fort wall who had kept back the townsfolk from attacking the town fort. The soldiers were completely exposed to them.

Kabisig said to his men, "Shoot them."

They fired, killing three of the soldiers there. The other soldiers jumped down from there and fled inside the fort.

"We can now," Mulawin said, "storm the town fort."

They left the mayor's office. They left there an armed man to watch the top of the fort wall for any soldiers who might dare, go back there.

A large wooden pole was obtained. Five men, along with Paulo and Kabisig, rammed it repeatedly against the fort's wooden gate until it crashed down into the ground.

The townsfolk then surged inside the fort. Some of them were killed or wounded by the soldiers shooting at them from the main building. It did not stop them as they were soon engaged in a close fighting with the better-armed, but outnumbered Civil Guard soldiers.

Paulo rushed toward the fort jail while the fighting was going on in the drill ground and in the main building. He found in a cell there, Julio, Pinalis, Masinop and other men.

"What happened to him?" he asked Pinalis and Masinop when he saw Julio lying on the cell floor, his left arm and leg paralyzed.

"The old man," Pinalis replied, "had a stroke from the torture inflicted on him by Zatayde."

Julio, like Pinalis and Masinop, had welts all over his body.

"I will make that animal, pay for what he did to you," Paulo said to them, his eyes blazing in anger.

He found a crowbar and used it in forcing the cell lock open. The men rushed out of the jail cell when he opened its door.. He carried Julio with Pinalis and Masinop's help out of the jail cell and laid him down at the jail entrance.

"Look, after him," he said to them. "I will go after that animal."

He had barely stepped out into the drill ground when he saw the soldiers being led out of the main building, their hands raised in surrender.

The townsfolk who now filled the drill ground, at the prompting by Doctor Bihasa, Gayuman, Kabisig and Agerico, then shouted joyously at their victory in the town fort.

Paulo's mind was elsewhere, though. He was going after Zatayde. He made his way through the jubilant crowd and rushed toward Zatayde's quarters.

He saw Mulawin and his uncle, who were watching from a window there, Zatayde and Quatrillo who were fleeing on horseback, across the rice fields, to the town of San Martin.

Chapter Ten

Chemari Achutegui halted and looked around as he was leaving the command post in the rain-soaked Fort Santiago. The fort, with its dark stonewall around it, seemed to be standing fast against the enemy, out there in the horizon.

The drill sergeants, at a break in the rain, were shouting orders for the soldiers who had sought, inside the fort, shelter from the rain, to come to formation in the drill ground.

The sergeants' frenzied voices and the soldiers moving toward the drill ground gave Chemari the impression of Fort Santiago reacting swiftly to the revolution, now raging in the colony.

He watched the soldiers as they were now marching in the drill ground and felt a deep affinity with them. Inside his coat pocket were his mission order and appointment papers as a lieutenant in the Spanish Army.

He glanced at the Civil Guard headquarters, wondering how his father was doing. He left for Cavite, a few days ago, with a contingent of troops to help the Spanish Army recover the initiative after that disastrous defeat of General Aguirre's regiment at the hands of Emilio Aguinaldo in the battle in Imus. The rebel victory sent shock waves across the Spanish community in the walled Spanish enclave in Intramuros. If left unchecked, the rebels might soon be attacking Intramuros itself.

How, he asked himself, could the Spanish Army meet this onslaught from Cavite and from the other towns and provinces? It is stretched out so thinly in the colony with its population of more than seven million Indios in an archipelago of more than seven thousand islands. All it had, at the start of the revolution, were 1,500 Spanish troops and 7,000 native auxiliaries.

While several thousand more troops had since then arrived from Spain, they were still not enough to put the Indios under control, thousands of them having joined the revolution. More Spanish troops were needed especially in the battlefields in Cavite, which posed the greatest danger to them. Thousands of Indios from the other provinces had gone there and bolstered the rebel forces there. Bacoor, the nearest town in Cavite, was a mere seven miles away from Manila.

He decided to help face this mortal danger by taking up arms even if it meant setting aside his law studies in Spain. He told his father, after agonizing over it for several days, that he is joining the army.

"If you told me that, a month ago, when things were so different from today, I would have told you to stick to your law course," his father said. "The situation is now completely different with this revolution. You must serve. I will write Personnel, so you will be given your commission immediately."

He shrugged his shoulders in dismissal of those who might call him, a drinking parlor warrior. With the shortcut his father made, regular requirements like a qualifying examination and a period of military training were dispensed with and he was immediately commissioned a ieutenant.

He is not a completely ignorant military officer, though. He learned from his father, some of the rudiments in warfare. A good hunter and marksman, he is familiar with rough places from the hunting trips he had taken in the forest in Morong and in the swamps in Pampanga.

The wagging tongues in Intramuros could say whatever they want to say about him, but he will prove himself in the only place where it really mattered—in the battlefield.

That could be set aside for now, though. He is more concerned with Marissa's likely negative reaction to what he will tell her that he has joined the army. Heaven knows what a dreadful scene she might then make. He has no idea how to tell her that. If he will say it was for his country, she will only laugh at this show of his patriotism. Beating around will not help. It will only make him look so indecisive.

He walked on with his mind so distracted he could only feel he was now passing out of the gate in Fort Santiago. He crossed Aduana Street and walked on toward the square in front of Manila Cathedral. He was now approaching Marissa's house in Beaterio Street, his mind still not clear on how he would tell her that he had joined the army. He might as well simply tell her that and hope she will not react badly.

The homes in Beaterio Street, at a break in the rain, were like the rest of Intramuros, shrouded in a fine mist. It was an occurrence that came rarely with the rains in September.

He welcomed the cool weather after the muggy days at the close of August.

Rain fell again, the moment he reached Marissa's house. He knocked at the door. A maidservant let him in. He brushed away the raindrops on his hair and shoulders before going up to the living room.

It was dark there. The shell-paned window facing the street was closed from the raindrops pattering on the windowpane. It only added to his uneasiness as he waited for Marissa.

She came, her eyes, heavy from an afternoon nap. She greeted him with a smile and looked at him inquiringly.

He forced a smile to keep his composure, for his resolve to tell her straight away that he is now in the army had just then vanished. To make it easy on himself, he did what came easily to him whenever he was alone with her. He looked around and asked her, "Are we alone?"

"Only the maid is here."

"Where are your parents and your brother, Alfonso?"

"They went out to visit my aunt in Santa Ana, but why are you asking me about them?"

"I want to know, how long a time we can be alone.

He then took her in his arms.

She yielded, as she always did, when he kissed her, long and hard. The feel of her body and the sigh she gave him in sheer pleasure from his kiss, sent him lusting for her. He led her to her bedroom, his arm around her waist.

"Why," she asked him, "are you taking me there?"

"I don't want the maid, spying on us in this tender moment, we are together."

She turned her face away when, once they were inside her bedroom, he tried to kiss her again. He was surprised and disappointed that she was making a feeble effort to resist his advances.

But then, he was surprised and pleased when suddenly, she held herself tightly to him. She was giving herself completely to him. They left her bedroom nearly an hour later, happy and fully satisfied with each other.

"Do you like some coffee, dear?" she asked him.

"Yes. I need that to pep me up."

He was slouched on a couch in the living room, fagged out by their intense lovemaking in her bedroom.

"By the way," she said when she was about to go to the kitchen, "you have not told me what brought you here."

"Don't you want me to see you?"

"Of course, I do, but why did you come here?"

He drew a deep breath and sat straight on the couch. It was time he told her the purpose of his visit there.

"I have got something very important to tell you," he said to her. "I have joined the army."

"Why did you do that? It is so stupid."

"When did serving one's country become something stupid?"

"It is, for us! You know we have decided on your law studies in Spain!"

She went to a couch and sat down there. Her arms crossed against her breast, she looked accusingly at him and said, "Why did you do that without telling me first?"

"I am a man enough to make my own decisions."

"You are thinking only of yourself!"

"So are you!"

She looked fiercely at him and said, as she then broke down in tears, "You can now take me for granted after you have taken, all that you can get from me!"

It was getting out of hand. She should not have said that. He loved her even more, now that he had possessed her completely.

He was taken by surprise when she suddenly stopped crying, her eyes turned to the staircase behind him.

Her parents, Isidoro and Consolacion, were looking sternly at them. They heard everything, he and Marissa had said to each other and the suggestion of what they did in her bedroom.

He made an effort to stay calm. He stood up and greeted Marissa's parents, a good afternoon. They did not return his greeting.

Isidoro turned to Marissa and said to her, "Go to your room. I have something important to take up with this young man."

Marissa left quickly for her bedroom. Her mother slammed the door as she was following her, jolting both Chemari and Alfonso who was about to enter his bedroom.

He could hear, despite the closed door in Marissa's bedroom, her mother screaming at her and calling her names. He felt weak in the knees from those dreadful things going on around him and he dropped down on the couch. His nerves were shot. He looked down at the floor and waited anxiously for the blow that will now come from Marissa's father who was looking down at him.

"I heard what you and my daughter did," he said. "Do you take her for a plaything?"

"I don't, sir."

"What you have done to her is clear enough to me."

"I admit what happened, but we did, what we did, because we love each other."

"Then, stand up for what you did."

"What do you want me to do?"

"Marry her. That is the only thing you can do that will satisfy me."

He dropped his head in confusion. What happened that he is now being forced to marry Marissa? His only purpose in seeing her was to tell her that he had joined the army! He loves her and will someday marry her, but not at this time. They are not ready for that. He did not want it, neither did she want it. They have other plans. But then, now that her parents know what they just did in her bedroom, perhaps the right thing to do was to marry her. The thought made him feel noble and righteous.

"I will do that, sir, if that is the right thing to do," he said, his sense of duty overcoming his reservation.

"It is the right thing to do and I want it done, right away."

Isidoro called Consolacion and Marrisa, back to the living room. He told them, when they had sat down on a couch there, that Chemari and his parents will soon be paying them a visit to ask for Marissa's hand in marriage. He also expressed his preference for the Manila Cathedral over San Agustin and Santo Domingo as the church where their wedding will be held.

Chemari saw in the way they looked, acceptance by Marissa and relief for her mother.

He pressed his lips at the thought of how everything had been changed by the lovemaking they did in her bedroom. She will fall into disgrace if it will bear fruit. It could be corrected only by marriage. Only through that will the Iglesias family honor be preserved.

A gust of wind from a window, the maid had opened in the kitchen, swept through the living room. The rain was now falling even harder at the shell-paned window, facing the street.

Chemari came to see his father, later in the week, when the Spanish Army was preparing for a counteroffensive against the rebels in Cavite. He arrived at the friars' estate house, some two miles from Imus, a river town in Cavite, where General Rios, the Spanish Fifth Regiment commander, was holding a conference with his senior officers.

He went up to the main hall in the second floor of the estate house where General Rios and his senior officers were holding a conference, seated around a long table. He nodded at his father when he saw him. He was about to leave and wait downstairs for his father when General Rios took up with his officers, the strategy they will adopt for the coming battle with the rebels. He decided to stay there and watch and listen.

General Rios' regiment was southwest of the main force led by Governor-General Blanco which had just then moved to Bacoor from its base in Paranaque. The two Spanish forces will then attack the rebel positions in Cavite with Rios' regiment moving to retake Imus from the rebels and with Blanco's troops moving west to take Kawit. They will then fan out, south and west, once they have taken those two rebel strongholds, until they have taken most if not the entire province of Cavite.

"We will not," General Rios said, "make the same mistake that put to grief, General Aguirre and his men."

The officers, only a few moments ago, were involved in a spirited discussion of their strategy for the coming battle. They were now silenced by the humiliating defeat of one of the finest regiments in the Spanish Army.

General Aguirre led his regiment, nearly a month ago, in an attack on a rebel force in Imus, led by Emilio Aguinaldo who kept, following the advice of his officers, most of it concealed in thick shrubbery. They allowed General Aguirre's regiment of three thousand soldiers to cross the town bridge before stopping their advance with withering rebel gunfire.

The two forces were exchanging gunfire when Aguinaldo, following once again his officers' advice, ordered the bulk of his forces to cross secretly the river's chest-deep waters and attack the rear of Aguirre's regiment.

The Spaniards were taken completely by surprise. They beat a hasty, disorderly retreat. General Aguirre was killed while many of his troops surrendered or were also killed.

The rebel victory in Imus shifted the focal point of the revolution from Manila to Cavite. It also put Aguinaldo, then an unknown town mayor in Kawit, at the forefront of the revolution.

The conference ended with the disaster in Imus, humbling to them. Their bravado gone, they now viewed the lowly Indios with some respect.

Chemari left the estate house with his father. They walked down in its wide garden, toward a large stone house there, Colonel Achutegui and other senior officers had taken for their quarters.

He said to his father as they were walking on, "I have been assigned to the Third Company of the Tenth Battalion. I wanted to see you before reporting for duty to my company commander, Captain Maestranza."

"Why don't you pass the night here? You can leave tomorrow morning."

"Thank you, Papa, but I must report to my company commander today."

"Is there anything else, you came to see me about?"

"Yes, something very important."

Colonel Achutegui nodded and waited.

"I'm getting married, Papa."

Colonel Achutegui frowned and said to Chemari, "Do you know what you are doing? You have no sooner joined the army when you are getting married? Reconsider what you are planning to do."

"I cannot help it. I have got to do it."

"I will not just stand by and let you to be forced into marriage."

"I am not getting married to just any girl. I love her."

"You do? What do you know about love and marriage?"

"I love her enough to marry her."

"Who is this girl who is so special to you that you are in such a hurry to marry her?"

"It is Marissa Iglesias."

Colonel Achutegui nodded and said, "The pretty girl."

"She is not just pretty. She is the most beautiful woman in Intramuros."

"I have no objection to you, marrying Marissa Iglesias, but why are you in such a hurry to marry her?"

"I have to marry her at the earliest possible time."

Colonel Achutegui sighed and said, "Very well, do what you must do."

"Thank you, Papa," Chemari said.

He hugged his father, who pushed him away.

"You are in the army now. You no longer own your time."

"I know that, but I can get a leave of absence, if you will work it out for me."

"You are pushing things."

"Please, Papa."

"All right, I will talk to Captain Maestranza and explain your situation to him. He might understand it."

"There is one more thing."

"What now?"

"Let us visit Marissa's family with Mama at the earliest possible time and ask for Marissa's hand in marriage."

"You will find that, tough with your mother."

"I know my way with Mama," Chemari said, smiling at how nicely things had turned out between him and his father.

He was in high spirit when he left his father.

He mounted his gray stallion and rode to a village in Dasmarinas, south of General Rios' main force. He arrived there at dusk. He went straight to Captain Maestranza's headquarters, a house along a brook.

He saluted as he introduced himself to his commanding officer, and handed to him his mission order.

"So, you are the son of Colonel Achutegui," Captain Maestranza said. "He was my commanding officer when I was assigned in Vigan. I have never known, a better commander than your father."

"Thank you, sir," he said in appreciation of his commander's high regard of his father.

"You will take charge of the third platoon. You will meet your men tomorrow."

He listened when Maestranza then explained the situation in their sector. The rebels outnumbered their unit of almost two hundred men by a ratio of more than two to one. They faced each other in a rolling expanse of grassland, broken only by a few trees, here and there. The rebels had set up a barricade of rocks, earth, tree trunks and branches. It gave them the cover from where they could spring out for an attack on their position.

"A frontal attack does not look like a good move, sir," he said.

"I know, but that is what our company was ordered to do. We will attack the rebel position, following an artillery barrage by our field guns, but not just yet. We will mount the attack only after we get the necessary reinforcements expected to arrive soon from Spain."

Maestranza paused from his impromptu briefing when he saw Chemari looking so tired from his long ride on horseback from Manila. He called for an orderly who then led Chemari to his quarters—a tent he will share with another junior officer.

He went straight to his tent after dinner in the house. He reflected, as he was lying there, on what he had learned was the army's lack of troops and equipment. He was amazed at how the rebels had failed to see that. If he were in their place, he will mount one attack after another until he will be at the wall in Intramuros.

"But what," he said to himself, "could he expect from those ignorant, barefooted Indios?"

He paused in his thoughts. He was falling into the same arrogance and overconfidence that led to the destruction of one of the finest regiments in the Spanish Army. The rebels did not follow up their victory over General Aguirre's regiment with a general offensive, but instead stayed in their position, preferring to fortify it. They may not have the means to sustain a general offensive or just did not know that the Spanish forces they were facing were then so weak. A good thing they had poor military intelligence.

The drill, marksmanship and other training exercises, he made his troops go through in the next few days had put them in a high state of readiness. He had at the same time acquainted himself sufficiently with them.

His platoon, aside from his master sergeant Bunuelos and a couple of Spanish soldiers, was made up entirely of native auxiliaries. They came from the northwestern region in the colony and were so skillful in warfare. Their familiarity with the terrain and immunity to the heat enabled them to move around briskly and confidently. Bunuelos corrected soon enough their easygoing ways with the hard, disciplinary measures, he imposed on them.

He also knew by then, enough about Bunuelos. He was a veteran in the Spanish Army. A native of Catalonia, he came to the islands, tired of the barracks life in Spain. He wanted adventure and some fighting. He got none of those in the two years he had been in the colony, not until now.

Bunuelos, like the other master sergeants, formed the backbone of the Spanish Army. It made things easier for a green officer like him. He had come to respect his master sergeant's fighting ability and how he whipped up their native troops into a keen fighting force.

He had settled down to army life, some three weeks to the day, he arrived in the village. He is looking forward to the coming battle, confident that the Spanish forces will beat the rebels. The troops from Spain had reinforced considerably the Spanish troops in Cavite. He hoped, if he survived in the battle, to take a leave of absence and marry Marissa.

He woke up, one cloudy morning, to an exchange of artillery fire between the rebels and the Spanish Army that was soon joined by the Spanish naval ships in Manila Bay. Smoke soon mushroomed in the battlefield from the exchange of artillery fire there.

He watched the battle from a high ground with a panoramic view of the battlefield that extended from Imus to the southern shore in Manila Bay.

Blanco's regiment started to move toward Kawit, Aguinaldo's hometown. Moving in a parallel line, a few miles south of Blanco's forces, was General Rios' regiment. It was moving forward for a frontal assault on the rebel stronghold in Imus. The Tenth Battalion, which included Maestranza's company, held the right flank in Rios' regiment.

The battle raged on, the whole day and the next. The rebels, by the third day, gave ground in Imus and Kawit. Their forces facing the Tenth Battalion held their ground, though.

Aguinaldo was, unknown to Blanco and Rios, employing, but on a larger scale this time, the same tactic, he used in Imus against General Aguirre's regiment. While his main body of troops kept the bulk of Blanco and Rios' regiments engaged in the battle, a large force of Aguinaldo's troops was making a sweep from Dasmarinas, farther south, toward Rios' left flank.

Rios saw what Aguinaldo was attempting to do and he reacted quickly. He ordered his reserve troops to meet this rebel threat to his left flank. The Tenth Battalion, including Maestranza's company, was ordered to do the same. To protect what was now his right flank from the rebels facing his company from their barricade, Maestranza ordered three of his platoons, including Chemari's platoon, to maintain their position there.

The rebels attacked their southern force in a flanking movement while their frontal force started to move forward from their barricade, facing Chemari's platoon and the two other platoons.

The exchange of gunfire was so intense as Chemari watched, terrified, scores of rebel troops now advancing toward his platoon. He looked to his right and saw to his dismay, the two other platoons falling back from the enemy attack.

His platoon was left alone and in danger of being swept away by the advancing rebel troops. But if he followed suit and retreated also, the Tenth Battalion and the reserve troops will be cut off from Rios' main force. The Spaniards were facing another military disaster.

The thirty-six men in Chemari's platoon were lying on the ground. They were waiting for his orders that, however, were not coming, not yet, if ever they will come, for Chemari, just then, had broken into sweat in terror of this, his first taste of battle. The firing was getting more and more intense and the shrill shouts of the attackers, the moans of the wounded and the sight of the dead and wounded sprawled on the ground, made Chemari, sick to the pit of his stomach.

He might, any moment now, be hit by bullets whizzing by, or be disemboweled by cannon fire. The urge for him to pull back his platoon was getting stronger. It would be suicidal to stay there with all the firing and the mass of rebels moving toward his position, but then, he was ordered to maintain and defend his position there. He did not know what to do.

He was in such a confused state of mind when Bunuelos came, sliding down on the ground, beside him.

"I can hardly wait for the rebels to be near enough, so I can shoot them with my rifle," Bunuelos said, his gun aimed at the rebels moving closer to them.

Bunuelos' firm and confident attitude had the effect of removing from Chemari, the fear of getting hurt or killed. He was there to fight, not to run away from the enemy. He and his platoon were staying there.

"Keep your heads low," he said to his platoon. "Don't open fire until I tell you."

Their heads kept low on the ground, Chemari's men waited for his order to fire. He watched the advancing rebels, his finger wrapped around the trigger of his gun. They were not near enough. Then he saw them, so close now, he could see their faces, dark with their hats on their heads.

He shouted, once the rebels were near enough to them, "Now, fire, fire, fire!"

A burst of gunfire from his platoon felled some of the rebels. His men then followed it with burst after burst of gunfire. Faced with certain death if they tried to advance any farther, the rebels then fell back to their barricade.

The two other platoons rushed back to their former position when they saw what Chemari and his men had done in breaking the rebel attack.

Chemari's platoon had helped prevent what could have been another disaster for the Spanish Army.

The rebel attack on the Spanish Army's southern flank had petered out. The battle ended in a deadlock.

Chemari took the lull in the fighting as a chance to marry Marissa.   He was, a few days later, within minutes after a grateful Captain Maestranza had granted him a leave of absence, on his gray stallion, on his way home to Intramuros.

Chapter Eleven

Intramuros was gloomy from Blanco's not so successful campaign in Cavite. While the Spanish forces had retaken the towns of Imus and Kawit, the rest of the province remained in rebel hands. That and his failure to keep the fighting from spreading to other provinces had made the situation for the Spaniards as frustrating now as it was desperate then, at the start of the revolution. Blanco's policy of attraction, like his war strategy, was also a failure. Not even a handful of rebel leaders gave themselves up.

Blanco's failures convinced most of the people in Intramuros that the colony could be saved only by a change in its leadersip. The friars, who have been sniping at Blanco, were the most vocal about his removal from office. Madrid responded by sending General Camilo de Polavieja as Blanco's deputy governor-general, prior to his takeover of Blanco's job. Where Blanco was strict, but humane, Polavieja was cold and ruthless.

Polavieja went relentlessly after the rebels in Cavite and in the other provinces, the moment he took over from Blanco. He instituted a policy of terror, sparing no one. It culminated with the execution of Jose Rizal, the foremost Filipino reformist.

Rizal took no part in the revolution and was in fact against it. He sought, not the independence of the Philippines, only its elevation from a colony to a province of Spain, its representation in the Spanish parliament and for a measure of respect and dignity to be accorded to the Filipinos.

That should have put him in a good relationship with the Spanish authorities as a good and loyal subject. But he also had the audacity to write two novels that exposed the Spanish abuses in the Philippines, which he failed to balance with a few good words about the Spanish rule there. He was tried in court and was deemed guilty of treason. Polavieja had Rizal executed by firing squad on December 30, 1896.

While Intramuros was cast in gloom, a corner of it was festive at the wedding in Manila Cathedral of Marissa Iglesias and Chemari Achutegui. Marissa, escorted by her father, walked down the aisle toward the altar, to Richard Wagner's wedding hymn, *Here Comes the Bride,* played in the organ at the choir loft while Chemari stood waiting for her at the foot of the altar. The brave young man in his gala uniform, a medal of valor pinned on his chest, who helped save the day for the Spanish Army in Cavite, was waiting for his bride.

Her hand on her father's arm, Marissa moved gracefully down the aisle. She was never as lovely as she was, this morning of her wedding.

She was in a white, flowing gown, a gold tiara studded with precious stones, crowning her head. The people who filled the cathedral were gazing in admiration of her while she smiled at them, that was quite charming.

She was a beautiful maiden off to marry her man and there was no sign yet that, by then, she was already in that interesting period of early motherhood. But for her mother who helped her and gave her comfort, no one, not even Chemari knew that she had been having this morning sickness, an early sign of pregnancy.

They were in such a blissful state in their honeymoon in Hotel de Oriente in Binondo that they resisted their individual preferences and readily gave in to each other's wishes. Only one thing threatened their newly wedded state—the knowledge that beyond the wall in Intramuros, fighting was raging between the Spanish troops and the rebel forces. Their time together will not last long. Chemari will soon leave for the front.

He brought Marissa, a week later, back to her parents. She will stay with them while their house was being built, near her parents' house, Chemari learned, on reporting for duty in Fort Santiago, that he was given his own command, a company of troops newly arrived from Spain. It will form part of a brigade given the order to wrest back control of the towns at the side of the Sierra Madre mountain range in Bulacan, a province, north of Manila which had fallen into the rebels' hands. He asked for Sergeant Bunuelos to be assigned to his company. It was readily granted.

The brigade slogged through the muddy, waterlogged rice fields in retaking from the rebels, town after town in Bulacan. Chemari, who was by now a seasoned veteran of several military campaigns and a captain, had reached with his troops, the boundary in the town of Masakao.

It was decided in a meeting in the brigade's field headquarters in Santa Maria that Chemari's company of troops will attack the town from his position in San Nicolas, south of Masakao.

Another contingent of Spanish troops from San Martin, northwest of the town, will join him in the attack on Masakao.

Chemari returned to his troops, brimming with confidence. The rebels will be hard-pressed, if not simply overwhelmed by their two-pronged attack. He was not one to underestimate the rebels, though.

He learned from inquiries, he made in San Nicolas, that the rebels in Masakao were tough, that some of them had fought, as far as in Cavite. He will be facing there, a battle-tested rebel force.

He wondered if Paulo Palanas, his friend and former classmate in Lateran, whom he knows is from the town, will be among those he will soon be facing in the battle. The thought made him sad and anxious.

It was early morning, the following day. Chemari was in his temporary quarters in a house in San Nicolas. He was looking at himself in a mirror there, his mind on the coming battle in Masakao. It will be a prize to take. Its flourishing commerce, bountiful lands and a thriving handicraft industry made it one of the richest towns in Central Plain. Taking the town will be the high point of his campaign in the province.

He was interrupted from his thoughts by a knock on the door. He opened it to Sergeant Bunuelos who then saluted as he said their company was ready to go to battle.

"Very well, sergeant, let us get on with it," he said to Bunuelos.

Sergeant Bunuelos said, as they were going down in the stairs, "So, we are off again in another strike for glory."

Bunuelos walked ahead once they were out of the house. He ordered the troops, who were gathered in a wide ground surrounded by huts, to come to formation.

Chemari walked toward the shade of a mango tree there and scanned the landscape with his field glass. The town lay ahead, several hundred yards away. The road to it cut through a few huts and fruit trees, the rice stalks in the rice fields there, rich with golden grain. The church with its two belfries stood serenely in the distance, an island of peace in what will soon be a sea of bitter conflict.

He saw no activity in the town. It showed him, though, an enemy, waiting for him to come. The rebels appeared to hold a strong, defensive position in the orchards, at the approaches to the town.

He looked on, filled with great respect for the Indios for the way they fought him and his troops. Not that he agreed to what the Indios were fighting for. His conviction that the colony should remain under Spain was solid as a rock, but he had learned to respect them for the way they fought. He had seen them fighting even when the sane course of action was to give up and avoid the unnecessary loss of lives. He had seen, how the rebels, their ammunition gone, flung themselves at his troops, armed only with their spears, daggers and machetes.

The Spanish Army was finding it so hard to put down the revolution in the face of such rebel tenacity. The rebels' stiff resistance reminded him all too well of the stiff battle that lay ahead for the control of the town of Masakao

"All right, men," he shouted, "have your guns ready and your eyes peeled for the enemy."

He fell to more musing as he was watching his troops, getting ready for the battle. He has become so good at warfare, he could move around surely, but carefully in the battlefield. That helped him avoid what could have been a disaster for him in the battle in San Manuel.

His troops were pursuing about a hundred fleeing rebels when he saw a forested high ground to his right. His experience in Cavite taught him to favor caution over boldness and he ordered his men to stop the pursuit. His instinct had told him the rebels were leading his troops to a trap. He sent instead a reconnaissance party inside the forest. It ran smack into a large force of rebels waiting to ambush his troops. He lost a few men, but saved his entire company from certain annihilation.

He was, since then, held in even greater awe and respect by his men. He has matured as a soldier. This was brought about, not only by his combat experience, but also by his new outlook on life. It came about with the change in his status from an easygoing bachelor to a responsible husband and future father. He will fight to the hilt, but he will, by being careful, survive in the fighting and be around to see his child, born.

He was interrupted in his thoughts by two soldiers who were moving their field gun forward. They were having a hard time. The ground was soft and muddy from the rain that fell heavily, the night before. A couple of soldiers came and helped them. They gave the field gun a mighty push, but then it struck a rock and one of its wheels broke apart.

"Damn it!" he shouted at them, "can't you do properly, a simple thing like moving that cannon? Have that wheel fixed, right away."

He will have to put off the attack until the field gun has been repaired and is ready to fire.

Paulo watched through his field glass, from the rebel side of the front in Masakao, the Spanish soldiers pulling back their broken artillery.

"The Spaniards have superior firepower, they don't use properly," he said to Agerico as they stood, beside each other in the shade of a mango tree there.

"Let me take a look," Agerico said.

Paulo gave the field glass to Agerico. He said, on looking through it, "What can you expect from them, after what they did to their field gun? If they are that incompetent, we might as well drop our weapons and, in a sporting gesture, fight them with our bare hands."

"Never," Paulo said, smiling, to Agerico, "underestimate your enemy."

He looked around, confident that his troops could keep off the enemy attack despite their disadvantage in firepower. All they have for their arms were the rifles they smuggled from Hong Kong, the guns they took from the town fort and the firearms, they used in Cavite. They have no artillery.

While the Spaniards have the advantage of a larger and better-equipped force and a field gun that, however, needed to be repaired first, he has working to his advantage, the flat terrain and the trench, a defensive measure, Kabisig learned in his research on warfare which they were now applying in Masakao. The Spaniards will have to attack across the rice fields, completely exposed to his troops' gunfire. And he has a surprise for them. His uncle Lukas was leading a contingent of troops hidden in the forest and ready to ambush the Spaniards.

He looked again at the enemy through his field glass, not knowing he was facing across the rice fields, his friend and former classmate in Lateran, Chemari Achutegui.

Across the river, northwest of the town, a larger rebel force was waiting for the Spanish troops that have appeared from San Martin.

Led by Mulawin, Kabisig, Pinalis and Masinop, the rebel troops in that sector have prepared hurriedly for this other Spanish attack. Unknown to them, at the head of this contingent of Spanish troops was an old enemy they chased out of Masakao, Zatayde, who is now a captain.

The town residents, like their troops, have prepared for the coming battle with the Spaniards. While the old people, the children and the women stayed home on the advice of the town leaders, the rest of the townsfolk pitched in for the coming battle. The town's young men bore arms, prepared the defense of the town, or else kept the town's administrative machinery working. The women kept the troops well-provided with food and attended to the sick and the injured.

Doctor Bihasa and Gayuman had converted the town fort into a field hospital and supply center. The townsfolk attended to every task at hand, for it was their hometown they were fighting for.

The townsfolk, particularly the Dumayag family, had no illusion, though, that the peace and quiet, the town had enjoyed since it was taken over by the Katipunan, would last long.

"He will not give up, he will be back," Teresa said to Esperanza, referring to Zatayde.

Their anxiety over Zatayde's possible return to the town was eased up, though, by the sight of the town's young men going through their drill exercises on the road, in front of their house. And there was Paulo at the head of the Katipunan, south of the town. He came to the house whenever he had the time to spare from his military duties. The Dumayags learned from Paulo what was going on in Manila and in the other provinces.

"The Spaniards have retaken most of Cavite and are mounting attacks everywhere," Paulo said to them.

The news about Polavieja's relentless offensive against the Filipinos, added to the presence of Spanish troops at the outskirts of Masakao, brought gloom to Teresa, Esperanza and Agustina. They were in the living room, along with Julio, half of his body remaining paralyzed.

The day passed with Paulo and his troops waiting for the Spaniards to make their move. They saw no activity from them. It was becoming evident to Paulo that the Spaniards were not going to attack yet. It seemed their field gun had not been repaired yet.

Chemari, on the other hand, had sent soldiers to Manila to get a new wheel for the field gun when he was told that the old wheel was beyond repair.

It was getting dark. Paulo knew from his battle experience in Cavite that the Spaniards have no stomach for night fighting. They were going to attack, the following morning yet. He has the time to see Teresa.

"Take over," he said to Agerico who was standing beside him. "I will be gone for just a short while."

"Have fun while you can," Agerico said, a knowing smile on his face.

Paulo was, afterwards, smiling at Teresa who met him in the balcony of her house.

"So, they have not attacked yet," she said as she and Paulo were entering the living room.

"Their field gun broke down," Paulo said. "They will not attack without it."

"Let us not talk about them. It will just spoil our dinner. I will set a place for you," Teresa said as she proceeded toward the dining room.

Paulo helped Julio walk toward the dining room where they had a simple dinner of rice, fish and vegetables. Agustina, Julio and Esperanza, later on, turned in for the night, allowing Paulo and Teresa to be by themselves, seated close to each other in the balcony of the house.

"I don't know what I could have done to prevent the fighting from taking place, right here in our town," he said.

"Stop blaming yourself. You have no control over the course of the revolution. You are doing your part and you are doing it well."

"I have not done much for you, either."

"I want no more than your love," she said in an effort to soothe him out of his depression when she herself was cast in gloom.

They have very little time for each other. She worried so much when he was away and this was not groundless at all. Paulo nearly died when he was shot in the town fort. He was deeply involved in the fighting where he could be hurt or killed. Her fear of what might happen to him so overwhelmed her at times, she would then escape to the bedroom and bury her face on the pillow and cry there silently.

"We will have all the time for ourselves when things have quieted down," she said, her head on his shoulders.

"That is, just it. By then, we will most likely be back to where we were before."

She remained silent, a pained look in her eyes. Paulo had been working too hard for the revolution he had no rest since it began in Masakao.

Paulo proceeded to Cavite, along with Agerico and the town's other young men, after the Katipunan had won in Masakao. He did well there. He led in the attack against the Spaniards holed up in the estate house in Carmona. Built of stone and wood, it was impregnable to their attack with their spears, knives and a few rifles.

He captured and destroyed the estate house with a simple ruse. He had his men, firing continuously at one side of the estate house while he and a squad of his soldiers crept toward the other side of the estate house and set it on fire. Some of the Spaniards there, died in the fire. Those who tried to flee were captured. Aguinaldo commended him for that minor, but brilliant attack. He returned to Masakao, no longer a neophyte rebel who had never fired a gun before, but a veteran officer, now a captain, hardened by the campaign in Cavite. He was second in command to Kabisig who has not been idle, too. He was with General Llanera's forces during their offensive against the Spanish garrisons in Nueva Ecija. They were now fighting, once again, for their hometown.

Paulo had those thoughts while he was seated beside Teresa.

It was time to leave and he said to her, "I have got to go."

"Can you not stay, a little longer?"

"I wish I can, but duty calls."

He hugged her, kissed her long and hard. Then he drew away.

The battle in Masakao began, the following morning with the sound of cannon fire.

Paulo looked on when columns of smoke then rose, northwest of the town. The Spaniards had started their attack on Mulawin and Kabisig's sector. He could do nothing except hope that they could hold on there.

The shelling went on for several minutes with more and more columns of smoke, rising there. The Spaniards were firing indiscriminately at the homes of the town residents there.

"That must be a sadist, leading the Spaniards there," Paulo said to Agerico at this indication of the mad and ruthless enemy, Mulawin, Kabisig and the others were facing there.

Chemari watched in disbelief, the shelling by Zatayde's two field guns of the huts and houses near the rice fields.

"They did not have to do that," he said to Bunuelos who was standing beside him.

He could only watch, frustrated, the battle northwest of the town. The new wheel for the field gun had not arrived yet. He could not mount an attack without softening first with artillery fire, the rebel's defensive position. He could initiate only a probing attack. He ordered a squad of his troops to check the approaches to the town.

He was watching through his field glass, his soldiers moving across the rice fields when suddenly, as they were approaching the orchards there, rebel soldiers sprang out from the ground and fired at them. Four of them were felled by gunfire. The squad had fallen into a trap.

The three remaining soldiers raised their hands in surrender. They were brought inside the orchards.

Chemari shook his head at the loss of a squad of his troops. Now he knew, at least, the rebels were holed up in a trench in the orchards.

A new wheel for the field gun was brought there when it was getting dark, too late for them to mount an attack.

He will have to wait until the following day before he could attack the town. He scanned with his field glass, the other Spanish force, northwest of his position, and saw that it has not gained ground, at all.

"It looks like the other contingent has failed in its attack, northwest of the town," Bunuelos said.

"No doubt because of its incompetent commander," Chemari said.

He spat on the ground in a show of his contempt for Zatayde, the commander of the other Spanish contingent. Zatayde, not only was incompetent, he was bad, very bad. He learned from the barracks talk in Fort Santiago about the bad things, Zatayde did in Cuba. Zatayde also courted Marissa and they met a few times in Marissa's home. Zatayde courted her assiduously and gave up only when Marissa told him to stop coming to her house, for she was in love with someone else. He was that someone else.

Night came, a time of rest for the Spanish troops. It gave them a terrible time instead. The rebels mounted sniper attacks in the entire night. The silence at night was often broken by gunfire and the shouts in anger and frustration of the Spanish troops, shooting back at the unseen enemy.

The Dumagats, the small, dark-skinned tribesmen, led by Sabedro, Gayuman's mine caretaker, hit the Spanish troops, again and again with their poison-tipped arrows.

The only indication of their attack was the cry of pain, as an arrow found its mark in a wounded or dying Spanish soldier. It would have been merciful for those soldiers, had they died instantly. Not only did it prolong their agony, their cries and moans of pain heard throughout the night, demoralized the Spanish troops.

Dawn came and Chemari counted his losses--two squads of his men, dead or wounded. He still has more than enough troops with which to mount an attack. Their field gun, now repaired, he gave the order to attack.

He threw with a platoon of his troops, a feint to his right while his main force of four platoons, following the softening by their field gun fire, moved toward the main rebel position in the middle of the trench in the orchards there.

He was watching, quite satisfied, the rapid advance of his troops when he was shocked to see them, the attacker, being attacked instead.

His platoon on the right flank was retreating before an unexpected rebel attack there.

If that platoon will collapse from the pressure of the rebel attack, his main force of four platoons might be thrown into panic. That would be disastrous. There was only one way to meet this brilliant rebel counterattack.   He set aside all thought about his own safety and he mounted his horse and sent it galloping toward his advancing troops.

Paulo and his men watched, stunned, a Spanish officer speeding on horseback toward the advancing Spanish troops.

"What is that fool trying to do?" he said to Agerico who was also watching the Spanish officer.

He looked out through his field glass and nearly dropped it from shock at finding the Spanish officer on horseback was his friend and classmate in Lateran, Chemari Achutegui!

He nodded in admiration of Chemari's bold, but reckless move to save his troops from the threat on their right flank. He was an inviting target for his men in the trench, their guns now aimed at him.

"Shoot him, once he is near enough," Agerico said to them.

"Do not shoot him," Paulo shouted. "Hold your fire!"

Agerico and their men followed reluctantly, Paulo's order.

Bunuelos, who was leading their attack, saw what Chemari was doing and he ordered two of his four platoons to swerve to the right and meet along with Chemari and the platoon on their right flank, the rebel threat, they now realized, had come from the forest.

Chemari was surprised when the rebels, after only a few shots fired by his troops, began moving back to the forest.

He halted his horse with a pull on the rein and watched the rebels. There was something odd in what they were doing. It dawned on him then that the rebels there were just baiting his troops. They might be, being led to a trap inside the forest.

"Let them go," he shouted at his men. "They are only leading us to a trap!"

His troops immediately stopped their pursuit of the rebels.

He ordered his troops to return to their position, facing the town. He returned to his command post, relieved that he had prevented a rebel ambush from the forest, but he had also lost the momentum for the attack on the town.   His company, for the rest of the day, took no further action against the rebels. Only the field gun, in their half-hearted effort to keep the pressure on the rebels, kept shelling intermittently, the rebel position in the orchards.

The situation was far different in the northwestern side of the town. Unlike the southern approaches to the town, the townsfolk had no time to set up there, a strong, defensive system like a trench or a barricade. They could barely hold their ground when Zatayde mounted his attack. To make it even harder for them, Zatayde attacked without letup. They were forced to abandon their first line of defense in the orchards between the village huts and the rice fields. They were now engaged in close fighting in the town's northernmost village. Zatayde's attack ceased only at dusk.

Paulo, through cunning and the use of threats, was able to pry out from the three captured Spanish soldiers, information that gave him a fair idea about the strength of the enemy. He also learned that Zatayde led the other Spanish contingent.

He was both sad and relieved to learn he was fighting Chemari, a Spaniard, an enemy, but also a good friend.

He shook his head at the strange way, fate sometimes played on men's lives. He expected to see Chemari in Madrid, where they planned to take up their law studies. They were now fighting each other in the battlefield in Masakao instead of debating in a moot court in a university in Madrid. And yet, while he was sad, he also drew some comfort from the fact that he was fighting a friend and a gentleman.

He was worried, though, for Mulawin, Kabisig and the others. They were fighting the mad and ruthless Zatayde. That should explain the senseless shelling of the houses in the northwest part of the town.

He passed on to his uncle, Mulawin, Kabisig and the others, everything he had learned about their enemy.

Paulo, Lukas and the other rebel leaders met that night in the municipal hall to draw up the final defense of their town. They expect the Spaniards to launch another two-pronged attack, the following morning. They were short in ammunition and a number of them had been killed or wounded. The rest were fighting only out of instinct. They were so tired, the moment the shooting from the Spanish positions had ceased, some of them simply dropped down on the ground and closed their eyes and dozed off.

"I hate to say this," Kabisig said, "but we cannot hold the town from a two-pronged attack, the enemy will surely launch tomorrow."

No one disputed it.

"What else can we do then?" Gayuman asked Mulawin.

"Only one thing," Mulawin said. "We must spare the townsfolk from harm and our town from destruction."

"Are you telling us that we should give up the fight?" Doctor Bihasa asked Mulawin.

"What else is there, left for us to do?" Mulawin replied.

"We can fight to the last man. That is the honorable thing to do," Kabisig said.

"But then," Masinop said, "Zatayde might take it out on the townsfolk. They must be spared from that madman."

"It seems there is nothing else that we can we do?" Pinalis said.

"There could be another way," Lukas said. "We must hold the northwestern sector as long as we can. That is where Zatayde will be coming from. We must prevent him from taking control of the town fort, the municipal hall and the church. They are the town's center of power."

"What about the southern sector?" Masinop asked Lukas.

"I will lead a rear guard that will keep Achutegui at bay, long enough for Paulo and the rest of our troops there to withdraw to Alkayag."

"So, you are going to flee," Gayuman said to Lukas.

"Yes, so, we can continue the fight. This is just one battle among the many we will be engaged in."

"But that will still leave the town in the hands of the Spaniards," Masinop said.

"Yes, but under the commander of their southern contingent," Lukas replied.

"Achutegui," Mulawin said.

"Exactly," Lukas said. "The town will be in good hands under Achutegui, but definitely, not under Zatayde. I think that is clear enough."

"What made you say that?" Masinop asked Lukas.

Lukas, instead of answering Masinop's question, glanced at Paulo.

"Chemari Achutegui and I were classmates in Lateran," Paulo said. "He was a dandy then, but I know him to be a gentleman, a good man. We were planning to take up law in Spain when the revolution broke out."

"Well, then," Bihasa said, "that should stop us from worrying about what the Spaniards will do, once they have retaken our town."

"But only if it is Achutegui," Lukas said, "and not Zatayde who will take control of our town."

"I will prevent Zatayde from getting across the river," Mulawin said. "Whoever gets here first will be in control of our town."

"You can count on me," Kabisig said. "I will hold Zatayde back, even if I will die in doing it."

"You can count on me," Masinop said.

"Same here," Pinalis said.

They fell silent. Paulo glanced at Mulawin, Kabisig, Masinop and Pinalis, wondering what made them make this ultimate sacrifice for the sake of their town and the townsfolk. And he had thought of them before as unequal to their arduous and dangerous task. But there they were now, showing simply, without a bit of fanfare and bluster, the kind of stuff they were made of—noble, heroic and self-sacrificing. He is in the best company and he will do no less when his turn will come to do the same thing.

"We have no other choice, but to make this move," Lukas said. "We let Achutegui get control of the town. That way, our town will be spared from Zatayde. At the same time, the rest of our troops will escape to Alkayag. We will continue the fight from there."

"But what," Bihasa said, "if Achutegui will give in to Zatayde?"

"Will Achutegui do that?" Kabisig asked Mulawin.

"Achutegui," Mulawin said, "may not know enough about what Zatayde has done here. He might hand the town to Zatayde."

They fell silent for a moment.

"Someone will have to warn Achutegui about Zatayde, someone he will listen to," Lukas said.

"Are we thinking of the same person?" Mulawin asked Lukas.

"Yes, Mayor Echeverria. We'll ask him to tell Achutegui about the terrible things Zatayde had done here in Masakao, so that Achutegui will not hand to him, the control of the town."

Mayor Echeverria was taken out of his cell in the fort jail and was told about the rebels' plan.

"I will do what you want me to do," he said. "I have been trying to get rid of Zatayde, long before this revolution broke out."

He was not returned to his jail cell and was allowed to stay in the anteroom of the mayor's office under the watchful eyes of a guard.

The meeting was over. They left the municipal hall and bade each other, good luck and good-night.

Paulo pressed his arms across his chest to keep himself warm from the cold night air. He was returning to his sector.

Lukas stayed behind with Mulawin in the mayor's office.

"It was good while it lasted," he said to Mulawin who was seated at the mayor's armchair.

"So it was," Mulawin said about the short period of time, they were in control of their town.

The townsfolk proclaimed Mulawin as their mayor, right after they had defeated Zatayde and his troops in the town fort. It was the first time, since the Spaniards came, that they, the native townsfolk, had regained control of their hometown. It was a heartwarming experience for Mulawin, Lukas and everyone else in the town. It had a fiesta atmosphere then. But it will stay that way only if their revolution will be successful and that was very much in doubt now.

"Well, my friend," Mulawin said to Lukas in a voice that cracked, betraying his effort to maintain his composure. "Here is to the best of luck for all of us. Shall we see each other later on and talk about how we fared?"

"Of course," Lukas replied, a forced smile on his face.

They held each other on their shoulders as they then parted.

The two Spanish forces launched their attack on Masakao, morning of the following day. They started it with the shelling by their field guns of the rebel positions. The battlefield was not yet cleared of field gun smoke when the lead troops in the northwestern sector attacked the rebel position there, only to be cut down by rebel gunfire. The rest of them moved back, the wounded frantically crawling away in the town's warm soil.

Zatayde turned to his troops around him. His breathing, short and labored in anger and frustration, he said to them, "Listen, all of you, I will order another round of the field gun fire. It will be longer and more intense, this time. It will be aimed, not only at the enemy position, but also at the houses behind it. While this is going on, I want everyone, and I mean everyone, to move forward and attack the enemy. I will shoot anyone who hesitates or turns back."

Zatayde's two field guns resumed firing. This time, while the rebels' return fire was just as heavy, Zatayde's troops pressed on. They ran, crawled, paused and dashed again toward the rebels' defensive position.

By the time they got to a rebel position in a hedge, or by a row of trees, the rebels had retreated farther back, among the houses there, some of which were now burning from the field guns' fire. This was reported to Zatayde, who ordered his artillerymen to increase the pounding of the houses with their field gun fire.

The savagery of Zatayde's attack was prompted by what he saw through his field glass of what was happening, south of him. The other Spanish force had made it across the rice fields and seems to have overrun the rebel force there. He could not see much of anything from there, but he presumed, the fighting, south of him, must now be taking place, right inside the town. That meant only one thing—the other Spanish contingent will most likely beat him in capturing the town fort and the municipal hall.

Zatayde's brow was dark at the prospect of losing out in the race for control of the town. It is he, who should conquer the town! All that he wanted to do, for so many days since his humiliating escape from the town fort, was to return in triumph and regain control of the town. Now there is this Achutegui who might beat him to it! There was time yet, if he will move fast enough. To be sure that his troops pressed down on the town rebels, he led the attack himself. He regrouped his troops near a village and ordered his men to push on toward the town's center of power, across the river.

"I want you to be unsparing in your effort and with your gunfire," Zatayde said to his troops before mounting another attack. "Burn down the houses to force down their resistance. I want no prisoners. They will just slow us down! Attack! Attack! Attack!"

Zatayde and his men carried out their attack to the fullest extent. With Sergeant Quatrillo leading them, they swept away the town rebels' resistance. They did not give them any respite. They pressed southward through the rice fields and on the road to the river, where they were met by a blocking force of rebel troops.

It was not a good line of defense, Masinop and Pinalis had set up on the road and in the rice fields there. Except for some huts, bushes and trees there, they were completely exposed to the enemy attack.

South of them, at a distance of a couple of hundred yards, Mulawin was holding another defensive line of rebel troops.

"Take the position by the bridge," he said to Kabisig, "while I will hold the line here."

He knew, while he was watching Kabisig leave with his troops, that it could be the last time, they had seen each other.

The fighting since early morning had gone on with hardly any moment's respite for them. They were nearly faint from fatigue, hunger, lack of sleep and the heat of the sun. They were fighting on, out of their sheer will to keep Zatayde from gaining control of their hometown.

Mulawin had seen his fine home destroyed by Spanish artillery fire, but was thankful for his foresight in having Narcisa and their two children evacuated quickly to his wife's cousin in Nueva Ecija when he learned about the Spanish troops, south and northwest of the town. Many of the townsfolk were not so fortunate. Zatayde's troops fired indiscriminately and men, women and children fleeing from their burning homes were cut down and killed by gunfire.

He shook his head when he saw Pinalis and Masinop's line of defense had collapsed at the initial assault made on it by Zatayde's men. Those who later on raised their hands in surrender were felled by gunfire, Masinop and Pinalis among them.

He looked around at his men, crouched like him on the ground, their guns ready for the Spaniards who were now approaching their defensive position.

His gun in his hand, he shouted, "Fire! Shoot! Shoot!" when the Spaniards came within shooting range.

He saw, just then, from the corner of his eye, a man moving by. He next heard the piercing sound of a rifle shot when something sharp and painful then hit him in his chest. He cried out in pain and spun around on the ground. Darkness then came over him.

Kabisig and his men were on the ground along the river, lying in wait for the Spaniards when someone shouted and pointed at Spanish soldiers moving across the river toward the town fort and the municipal hall.

Achutegui had beaten Zatayde in the race for control of the town.

Kabisig stood up and said to his men, "It looks like our job here is finished. There is no need to hold our position here. Everyone is free to choose between surrendering and escaping, which I will do myself."

He had barely said that when he and his men started taking gunfire from Zatayde and his troops who were now attacking their defensive position.

"There is no time to lose," Kabisig said to his men. "Let us get out of here!"

He jumped into the river. His men followed him and jumped also into the river.

Zatayde himself led his troops in their attack on Kabisig's defensive position. He was among the first to reach the river and was surprised to find the rebels, swimming away there. Then he saw why. Across the river, at the town's main road, in the fort wall and in the municipal hall, other Spanish soldiers were watching him and his troops. He had lost to Achutegui, the race for control of the town. It sent him in a fit of rage and he took it out on Kabisig and his men.

He shouted at his men, "Shoot them! Spare no one!"

Kabisig was among the first to be hit by gunfire. He writhed in pain when a bullet tore through his shoulder bone. He sank and thrashed about when his lungs took in water. Then he remained still as his lifeless body then went down into the river's muddy bottom.

Not one of Kabisig's men had managed to swim away.

Zatayde then ordered his troops to stop shooting. He led them across the bridge and told them to take a rest in the town square.

Chemari's troops had seen, disgusted, what Zatayde and his men had done to the rebels. They kept away from them.

Zatayde went up to the mayor's office in the municipal hall. Mayor Echeverria, Chemari and some of his officers were there. They also saw the town rebels massacred in the river by Zatayde and his troops.

"Well done, Captain, so the town is ours again," Zatayde said to Chemari. "I can only thank you for helping me take over this town."

"I was only doing my duty," Chemari replied coldly to Zatayde.

"I was the commander of the fort here and I will now take over, the control of it and this town as well."

"My mission is to take this town and hold it. I will do nothing less than that. I will give you, neither this fort, nor this town."

Zatayde frowned. He drew himself level to Chemari and shouted, "I said I will take over this fort and this town!"

"Try doing that," Chemari said as he looked straight in the eye at Zatayde.

Zatayde glared at Chemari, who stood firm. Zatayde backed down and left.

"We are rid of him, at least, for the time being," Echeverria said to Chemari. "Thank you for standing up to him."

"I know how to deal with those like him," Chemari said. "They are all bluster. They turn tail, the moment they meet someone who will stand up to them."

"Zatayde will not do anything in this town, for as long as you are here. This is a nice, pleasant town that must be kept away from that madman," Echeverria said, who looked quite well despite his imprisonment in the town fort jail.

"I know," Chemari said. "I have heard a few things about this town from someone who is from here."

"I may know him."

"His name is Paulo Palanas. We were classmates in Lateran. We were going to take up law in Spain when this revolution broke out."

"I met him, his uncle and the other rebel leaders only last night."

Sergeant Quatrillo asked Zatayde, the moment he came out of the municipal hall, "Do we now take control of the town?"

"That damned Achutegui won't give in."

"What do we do now?"

"What else can we do, but go back to San Martin."

"Why don't we finish the job here?"

"What job?"

"I mean, finishing off, the remaining rebels."

"What rebels? Are there any of them left in this town?"

After their offensive and the massacre in the river, Zatayde did not think any significant number of rebels was left in the town.

Quatrillo then told Zatayde what he had overheard from Achutegui's soldiers. A sizeable rebel force had managed to escape to the mountains. Zatayde listened with little interest. He was still mad at Chemari for his refusal to hand to him, the control of the town.

His eyes suddenly lit up as he then said to Quatrillo, "That is just the thing we need to prove who really won here. We will destroy that rebel force while Achutegui is taking it easy here. He may have taken the town, but then, I can say it is I, who wiped out the rebellion in this town."

Chapter Twelve

The Dumagat lookout watched, hidden by the leafy branches of a tall tree there, Zatayde and his troops who were moving in double file in the mountain trail to Alkayag.

It was late in the afternoon, one day after the Spaniards had regained control of Masakao.

The lookout cupped his hands and made a wolf-like call. It was, to an unknowing ear, indistinguishable from the many strange sounds in the forest. A similar call replied from a distance.

Information about Zatayde and his troops was being passed across the forest to the rebel camp in Alkayag.

"The Spaniards are coming," Sabedro said, the moment he entered the hut, Paulo shared with Doctor Bihasa and Gayuman.

Paulo took the news calmly. He expected the Spaniards to come after them. Flushed with their victory in the town, they want to finish off the remaining rebel troops.

He asked Sabedro, "How far are they from here?"

"Two, three hours, half a day, they may never even find our camp," Sabedro replied, smiling.

He and his fellow Dumagat tribesmen and Paulo's men had camouflaged with twigs, rocks, dry grass, leaves and tree branches, the trail where it broke off in a stream, at the side of a mountain there.

"Tell the lookouts to keep us informed about the enemy," Paulo said to Sabedro.

He complied and called out a similar wolf-like call to his lookouts in the forest.

Paulo had the camp alerted as he then drew in a huddle with Bihasa, Gayuman, Sabedro and other men in the camp.

He pointed to the ground with a stick in his hand and said to Sabedro, "Assuming, we are here, point to where the Spaniards are and what lies between us and them. Show to us, where we can best attack them."

Zatayde and his men were, at that moment, conducting a fruitless search for the trail that broke off in a stream. It was getting dark and they still have not found it.

"We will resume the search, tomorrow morning," Zatayde said to his men. "We will make camp in this clearing by the stream."

He looked around at his men, making camp, concerned at the grumbling, he overheard from some of them. He kept it to himself, but he was beginning to realize, he was rash in going after the remaining rebels in their mountain hideout. He was deep inside the forest with no idea of where he was, how to get to the rebel camp or how to go back to the town. The Indio he coerced and bribed as their guide had escaped from them.

The men gathered in small groups as they were preparing their meal. Other soldiers looked around for a place to sleep. The men, as Zatayde ordered, made campfires and formed themselves in a circle with a guard posted every twenty yards, although there was not much they could see in the dark and thick underbrush in the tall trees around, most of their camp.

The sound of rushing water in the stream competed with the strange sounds made by the creatures in the forest. Most of the clearing was surrounded by thick, tangled forest growth. The night deepened and the sounds in the forest became more varied, but they did not alert Zatayde and his troops. They were, unknown to them, being watched by Paulo, his men and the Dumagats who had surrounded the camp, hidden by the thick underbrush of the trees there. They were poised to attack. He was only waiting for the right moment.

He watched Zatayde's soldiers on guard duty, beginning to fall asleep. It was time to attack. Sabedro, who stood beside him, made, at a signal from him, an owl-like call. Anyone familiar with the forest would have noticed this new sound, but the soldiers on guard duty, not knowing any better, remained down on their guard.

The Dumagats then aimed their bows and arrows at the soldiers on guard duty. They released the arrows from their bows, their hissing sound cutting across the varied sounds in the forest. It was followed in an instant by the soft thud and muffled groans when they hit their targets—the guards who then dropped down to the ground, dead or wounded. The Dumagats had done their job on Zatayde's guards.

Paulo, his men and the Dumagats then crept inside the enemy camp. They proceeded silently in killing Zatayde's soldiers with their knives, spears and machetes. Some of them who woke up to the attack were killed as they were reaching for their guns.

Zatayde woke up to Paulo, who was looking down at him. He was reaching for his gun when Paulo swung his machete straight down to his forehead, killing him instantly.

Chemari and Echeverria had, earlier in the day, watched Zatayde and his men leave the town square, doubtful about their expedition to the rebels' mountain camp. They were of one mind about restoring the peace in the town, now that they have regained control over it. It will not serve their purpose with Zatayde and his troops, going after the remaining rebels in their sanctuary in the mountain range of Sierra Madre.

Chemari wanted to reach out to Paulo. He learned, his former classmate led the rebels in escaping to their camp in the mountains. He was confident Paulo will listen to his proposal of peace, if he could get the word to him. He will use Paulo's uncle, Lukas, as his emissary. Lukas was wounded in the leg and was captured, along with Agerico, in his attack on the town.

"We should talk to Lukas Palanas," Chemari said to Echeverria.

Echeverria agreed and Lukas was brought out from his jail cell.

He came in, hobbling on a length of wood, he was using as a crutch. Echeverria motioned Lukas to a chair, in front of his desk, in the mayor's office.

Lukas sat down on the chair, tired by the unaccustomed effort of moving around with the help of a crutch.

Chemari, in a solicitous gesture, asked Lukas about the wound in his leg. Lukas shrugged it off.

"Tell us where the remaining rebels are," Echeverria said to Lukas, the authority he had regained, implied by the commanding tone of his voice.

Lukas replied, his chin thrust out toward Sierra Madre, "I don't have to tell you where they are. Just look, outside the window."

"Your nephew knows me well enough, for you to trust me," Chemari said to Lukas. "I am the new town fort commander. My mission here is to help Mayor Echeverria restore peace in this town. Help us in bringing it about."

"The only kind of peace we will have in this town for as long as you are here is the kind of peace of the dead, the frightened and the downtrodden. Your coming here will not change that."

Chemari looked on at Lukas, frowning in exasperation with him. Had he been another man and not his friend and classmate's uncle, he might have given him a beating. That might put him back to his senses. He could see no reason for the stubbornness of Lukas. It was completely pointless. The rebels' obstinacy had never ceased to amaze him.

He said to Lukas. "We will set you free, if you will promise to talk to Paulo and persuade him to conduct peace talks with us."

"My nephew has a mind of his own."

"You can at least give it a try."

Chemari sat down on a chair and waited for Lukas to reply.

"Very well, I will talk to him," Lukas then said.

Chemari nodded, satisfied. He extended his hand to Lukas.

Lukas hesitated, but then, he said, as he was about to shake hands with Chemari, "I don't usually do this to our enemy, but I will make an exception with you."

"Thank you for giving me the courtesy. We will let you know when you can leave and see Paulo."

Lukas was brought back to his jail cell.

Echeverria asked Chemari why he was letting Lukas go free.

"He is no threat to us," Chemari replied. "He is more useful to us, free than in jail. He will be, as Paulo's uncle, a very useful emissary. Through him, Paulo will get the message that we mean, what we say about restoring the peace and order in this town."

Chemari learned about the fate of Zatayde's expedition, late afternoon, two days later. He was in the fort drill ground when his attention was drawn to a commotion at the fort gate. Zatayde and his troops had returned to the town.

He was surprised to see, not the soldiers marching in, but the remnants of Zatayde's ill-fated expedition to the rebel camp in Alkayag.

Paulo, in a gentlemanly gesture, had allowed the few survivors of Zatayde's expedition to return to the fort with their dead fellow soldiers.

They were seated on carts, pulled by carabaos, their wounds patched up with crude bandages. Lying on the floor of each cart were dead Spanish soldiers, piled on top of each other. A cart brought up the rear where Zatayde's body was laid on the floor.

Chemari, his face in a grimace, looked on when the carts with their loads of dead and wounded soldiers were pulled to a stop in front of him. It was all for nothing. Zatayde's expedition had ended in a disaster.

He checked each cart, said words of comfort to the surviving soldiers seated there, until he came to the cart where Zatayde's body was laid down.

A heavy, bladed weapon had crushed Zatayde's forehead. At the lower end of the wound, blood had flowed down to his cheek and neck, soaking his grimy uniform. Zatayde's face bore no sign of pain, as in a slow, agonizing death. He died instantly. Zatayde's face looked serene as if it spoke of a life he led justly and in peace.

Chemari's jaw tightened at this final deception made by Zatayde's death mask. This is not the real Zatayde, he is looking at. Beneath Zatayde's face was a life lived so bad, it evoked on him, nothing but anger and contempt. Rage welled up in him the longer he looked on at Zatayde. He got what he deserved. He died at the hands of the people he had so abused and tormented, but he also took with him to his death, so many fine Spanish soldiers.

He looked away when he could no longer stand that revolting sight and he gave the order for the treatment of the wounded soldiers and the mass burial of the dead soldiers.

Chemari and Echeverria worked together in the days that followed in bringing peace and normalcy back to Masakao. They set Lukas free, a move questioned in Intramuros. Chemari explained it away with the help of his father and his influential father-in-law as good and necessary to the town. To make the townsfolk put aside their fear of the Civil Guard, Chemari gave them strict orders to behave properly at all times. He also stopped the Spanish practice of torturing the inmates in the fort jail.

He saw another valuable ally in the Church. He and Echeverria briefed the new parish priest, Fray Angelo, about their plan for the town. A priest with missionary zeal, Fray Angelo was so taken by it, that in his sermon at the Mass, the following Sunday, he spoke of peace and justice that will now be the order of the day in Masakao.

The townsfolk took the priest at his word and did nothing in the pursuit of the revolution. They helped the town authorities by doing nothing. Peace reigned in Masakao, a town unusually at peace while in the rest of the colony, the revolution was raging on.

Congratulatory words came from Intramuros. Echeverria and Chemari's efforts were paying off. But unlike, almost everyone else, they were under no illusion that peace reigned in Masakao, only as long as Paulo and his men remained in their mountain camp and did not resume the fight with them. They sought to put an end to it by setting Lukas free, on the condition that he will try to convince Paulo about their offer of peace. They have not heard from Lukas since his release from jail. They have no idea what Paulo's response will be.

Lukas went right away to Alkayag, the moment he was released from jail. The rebel camp was in a plateau hemmed in on two sides by steep mountainsides, their rugged peaks serving as excellent lookouts. The huts there were built around a drill ground where the rebels held training exercises and other camp activities.

The camp's remoteness did not pose much difficulty in keeping the rebel troops there, well-provisioned. Lukas, Mulawin, Bihasa and Gayuman had the foresight to stock up the camp with supplies. Meat was plentiful from the wild game in the forest while Sabedro's fellow Dumagat tribesmen, who lived in the valley below the camp, supplied them with rice, corn and vegetables.

They took the precaution of doing their cooking only at night and in clay stoves encircled by low stonewall to keep the fire from being seen from afar. The smoke from the cooking done in daytime might give away the camp's location in the remote chance of the enemy in the vicinity.

Lukas arrived, early evening in Alkayag while Paulo, Doctor Bihasa, Gayuman, Sabedro and the rest of the camp were taking their austere meal of rice and boiled vegetables, laced with fish sauce.

He said, as they were eating, that Chemari and Echeverria set him free so he could talk Paulo and the others into agreeing to a truce. He also told the others what happened in the town since the Spaniards had retaken it.

The others listened sadly to Lukas who confirmed the sketchy reports they got that Mulawin, Kabisig, Masinop, Pinalis and countless other town rebels had been killed in the battle, northwest of the town and that Zatayde had also destroyed that part of the town.

"We have taken quite a beating," Paulo said. "We are down, but not out. Chemari is in for a long, fruitless campaign against us."

"How well-intentioned, are they?" Bihasa asked Lukas.

"I cannot tell that, but they could mean well," Lukas replied.

"Do they expect us to give up the fight because of their good intentions?" Paulo asked Lukas.

"They are never a reason for us to give up the fight."

"Chemari can be quite naïve," Gayuman said.

"Are the things they are doing, having any effect on the town?" Bihasa asked Lukas.

"Their policy is working with the cooperation of our townmates."

"Too bad they are doing only now, what they should have done, a long time ago," Gayuman said.

"It is good they did not do that earlier," Lukas said.

Paulo and the others threw Lukas, a puzzled look.

"You don't seem to approve of their good intentions for our town," Gayuman said to Lukas.

"I don't approve of them."

"Why?" Bihasa asked Lukas. "Are they not giving us, what we have been asking for, like peace and fair and just treatment by them?"

"So, you too, who is supposed to be so perceptive, has been carried away by their honeyed words."

"Is that not what we want from them?" Sabedro asked Lukas.

"No, that is not what we want from them."

"What then," Bihasa asked Lukas, "do we really want from them?"

"We want no less than our freedom. All those reforms are, without it, meaningless."

"And we can never have our freedom," Bihasa said to Lukas, "as long as we remain under the Spaniards."

"Our country's freedom is contradictory to the Spaniards ruling us."

"Then, for all their good intentions, we must," Gayuman said to Lukas, "continue to oppose Chemari and Echeverria."

"Yes. While I like and respect them for the good persons that they are, they pose a greater obstacle to our revolutionary cause. Their good intentions distract us from our goal of freedom. I find it easier to fight the likes of Zatayde. He was so hateful. Our people needed no prodding and convincing to rise up in arms against him."

"Now that you have explained it, uncle, everything is clear to me," Paulo said to Lukas. "All we will do from now on is to continue the fight until we have won our freedom."

Lukas watched, satisfied, the others nodding in agreement to his views.

He then asked Paulo, "Are we in a position to resume the fight?"

"We are, but in a different way, we will now carry it out."

"What do you mean by that?" Lukas asked Paulo.

"We will not, this time, attack frontally and in massed formations. We will wear them down instead with constant guerrilla attacks."

As they talked on, deep into the night, a perceptible change now came in the way Doctor Bihasa, Gayuman, Sabedro and the other rebels regarded Lukas and Paulo. Paulo's battlefield exploits, topped by his stunning defeat of Zatayde's expedition, had marked him as an exceptional, tactical officer. He now had full rein on military matters while Lukas took charge of policy and strategy.

That arrangement was arrived at by Lukas, Paulo, Bihasa and Gayuman, the remaining leaders of the Katipunan in Masakao, and Sabedro.

A Spanish patrol was ambushed, one night, leaving a soldier dead, another wounded. Another time, a soldier's body was found floating in the river.

While they were mere pinpricks that constituted no real threat to their hold on the town, they happened often enough to upset Chemari and Echeverria. The rebels were waging a fight, in complete disregard of what they were doing for the town and their offer of peace talks.

They spent a great deal of time, discussing ways of meeting the rebels' guerrilla attacks. An attack on their mountain camp was out of the question. This was made very clear by what happened to Zatayde and his troops, but they could not also let the rebels go on sniping at them. Their power and authority will erode, if they will do nothing about it. It will only encourage more rebel attacks.

Chemari ordered more patrols at night when the rebels were most active. He also increased the number of checkpoints and imposed a curfew. He was forced to do some of the things, Zatayde did, which had alienated the townsfolk from the Spaniards.

The rebels were now getting much help from the townsfolk. The Civil Guard patrols reported seeing men sneaking at night into the houses and orchards there. Their investigation turned up nothing.

Chemari and Echeverria had sensed correctly that the rebels were no longer operating solely from their mountain camp, but had descended into the town and, with the townsfolk's help, were now operating there with impunity.

"We are in a bind here," Echeverria said, one day in exasperation, to Chemari. "We can neither move forward, nor backward. We cannot attack the rebels in the mountains, nor hunt them down in the town, for that will harm the townsfolk and alienate them from us."

"Things are not that bad," Chemari replied.

117

He was consoled by the fact that in the rest of the colony, the tide had turned against the rebels.

The offensive, Polavieja mounted before his relief as governor-general in April, the following year, resulted in great Spanish victories over the rebel forces. The rebels, already reeling from the relentless Spanish offensive, were further weakened by the division in their leadership.

This was the unfortunate outcome of the Tejeros Convention, the rebels held in Cavite on March 22, 1897. It was intended to formally establish the Philippine Government and resolve as well the factionalism within their ranks. It was between the Magdalo faction which supported Aguinaldo and the Magdiwang faction which supported Bonifacio.

Bonifacio was chosen as chairman of the convention, a high position with little influence on the delegates. The great majority of them were from Cavite who swore allegiance to Aguinaldo alone. Some provinces had no representation at all.

Aguinaldo, in the convention dominated by his provincemates, was voted President of the Philippine Government over Bonifacio in an election marred by cheating. Ballots were filled before they were distributed to the delegates. There were more ballots than the number of delegates.

Bonifacio settled for the lower position of secretary of the interior, but his qualification for even this lower position was questioned by an Aguinaldo supporter. Bonifacio was so enraged, as much by that insulting treatment, as by the rigged election.

He invoked his authority as chairman of the convention and of the Supreme Council of the Katipunan and he annulled all that had been passed there. Bonifacio also accused Aguinaldo of treason for conducting peace negotiations with the Spaniards. Bonifacio then left the convention hall. He made the fatal mistake of staying in Indang, a town in Cavite, despite the hostility of Aguinaldo, his men and his provincemates.

Aguinaldo disregarded the annulment by Bonifacio of the convention. He took, the following day, in a grab for power, his oath as President of the Philippine Government in a church in Naic, a town in Cavite. Aguinaldo posted guards outside the church to prevent anyone, other than his supporters, from witnessing the oath-taking.

He sent his men, the following month, to arrest Bonifacio on the basis of a letter which alleged that Bonifacio ordered the burning of a village. Aguinaldo used also an unverified report that Bonifacio tried to burn down a church and that, for his food, he stole work animals.

Aguinaldo's men, led by Colonel Agapito Bonzon and Major Ignacio Paua, arrived in Bonifacio's camp in Indang on April 25, 1897. Bonifacio, not knowing their intention, met them cordially.

They attacked Bonifacio and his men, the following day. Bonifacio refused to fight his fellow revolutionaries. Bonzon shot him in the arm while Paua stabbed him in the neck. Bonifacio's brother Ciriaco was killed, his other brother Procopio was beaten up while his wife Gregoria was raped.

Bonifacio was brought to Naic. He and his brother Procopio were charged with sedition and treason. A sham trial was held where the jury was made up entirely of Aguinaldo's men and where even Bonifacio's defense lawyer declared his guilt. Bonifacio was not allowed to confront the state witness on the claim that he was dead, but who later turned out to be alive and with the state prosecutors.

Bonifacio was pronounced guilty of treason and sentenced to death by the sham court. Aguinaldo, in a sadistic move, commuted the sentence, but later on ordered the execution of Bonifacio and his brother Procopio. Bonifacio was so sick by then from his wounds. He was in a stretcher when Aguinaldo's men hacked him to his death on a hill in Maragondon, a town in Cavite, on May 10, 1897.

Aguinaldo took full control of the revolution, now that there was no one who could oppose him in his grab for power.

The terrible events that took place in Cavite showed there were, aside from the heroes, scoundrels in the Philippine Revolution.

Paulo was waging guerrilla warfare in Masakao while all of that was going on in Cavite. Chemari by then had grown so sick and tired of the cat-and-mouse game, his friend and former classmate was playing against him. Had it not been for his Spanish pride, he would have asked to be relieved of his command in Masakao.

Unknown to him, though, his wife Marissa and her influential father had quietly pulled strings in the governor-general's palace for him to be assigned to Intramuros. Marissa had a good reason for wanting Chemari to be with her. Her time to give birth to their child was coming near.

Chemari got his orders to return to Intramuros. He was leaving the town without much regret. Foremost in his mind now was to be around at the birth of his child. Echeverria, though, was sorry to see him leave. They liked each other. They had a fine teamwork.

Captain Laguerte, Chemari's replacement, arrived in Masakao, a few days later. The whole town now knew that Captain Achutegui was being replaced by another officer.

Spanish troops, in a ceremonial parade, then came marching from the town fort, to the road between the church and the town square.

The townsfolk, who came to like Chemari, watched from the roadside and the churchyard, the Spanish troops passing in review before the town's civil and military officials and the parish priest who were standing in a makeshift platform, built for that purpose in the town square.

Captains Achutegui and Laguerte looked imposing in their gala uniforms while Mayor Echeverria and Fray Angelo stood next to them, the mayor in a formal coat and the priest in his cassock. It was the first time such a gathering had taken place in Masakao since the revolution began.   Paulo held Chemari in such a high regard that he ordered his men to cease every guerrilla activity so that nothing will mar the farewell parade being held for Chemari.

He felt, as he was looking at the crowd, Paulo himself could be there, watching him, unrecognizable along with the men there with their straw hats, slanted over their eyes. He watched the parade with an ironic smile on his face. Here he was, being honored with a parade, for having accomplished virtually nothing of what he had set out to do for the town. He was putting up a brave front; that was all.

His chin thrust out to his troops, passing in review, he did not show what he was feeling then as he stood there and watched them. They were fine soldiers who served him well. They fought well and it was just too bad they had to engage in a kind of warfare in which they were ill-suited. His former classmate was right in waging guerrilla warfare against him.

He looked on at the crowd and got again a vague feeling that Paulo was there, watching him.

How they had changed from the time they were students in Lateran. They were then two young men, their eyes turned to their future as lawyers.

They were both new in Lateran when, one time, they nearly came to blows over something, he could not remember anymore. Friendship, from that inauspicious start, grew between them. That was another time, though, another world, the carefree life of two young students. Life was good then.

A brass band was playing a marching song as it was passing by, at the end of the parade. It was time to leave. Chemari turned around and walked with the other town officials toward the town fort for a last meal with his troops.

Chemari was, within an hour, headed home to Intramuros.

Chapter Thirteen

Paulo sensed something important when he saw a stranger standing near the door to the hut, he shared with his uncle, Doctor Bihasa and Gayuman.

He walked past the stranger and looked over the shoulders of his uncle who was seated before a table, reading a note in his hand. Facing him there were Gayuman and Doctor Bihasa.

"Well, what does it say?" Gayuman asked Lukas.

"Aguinaldo is calling for a meeting in his headquarters in Biak-na-Bato. We have been ordered to attend it."

Lukas wrote a reply, which he then gave to the stranger, Aguinaldo's courier. The courier saluted and left.

"When will Aguinaldo hold the meeting?" Bihasa asked Lukas.

"It will be held on Thursday, three days from today."

They have been waiting for such a meeting. It was a chance for them to ask Aguinaldo for help and guidance. They were short in ammunition and could not carry out as many guerrilla attacks as they wanted to, against the Spanish troops in Masakao.

Captain Laguerte, unlike Chemari, was pursuing them relentlessly, but having learned from the lesson of the disastrous Zatayde expedition, he never ventured, deep inside the forest. He made it a point to pull his forces, back to the town before nightfall when it would be Paulo's turn to take the initiative with his guerrilla attacks. The fighting thus swayed, back and forth, in the foothills, in the rice fields, in Civil Guard checkpoints and against their patrols. The townsfolk heard in this exchange of gunfire between the two forces, clear evidence that the revolution was very much alive in Masakao.

Most of the rebel forces, on the other hand, particularly those directly under Aguinaldo, had by then retreated to the mountains and other remote areas in the colony. But while the Spaniards now controlled most of the towns, the end of the revolution was not yet in sight. The rebels fought on from their mountain camps and their sanctuaries in remote villages.

Lukas, Paulo and the other field commanders learned, three days later, the reason Aguinaldo called for the meeting in Biak-na-Bato. It was to frame up a constitution for the country. It will also formalize the break with Spain, which Bonifacio made, months before, with his declaration in Pugad Lawin of the Philippine independence.

The meeting was held in a wood-and-bamboo house in Biak-na-Bato. It was a remote mountain village in Bulacan. Aguinaldo set it up as his new headquarters after he fled from Cavite, following his battlefield losses there.

Paulo, as a lower-ranked officer, stood behind his uncle Lukas who was seated with other senior commanders around a table in the house.

Aguinaldo was seated at the head of the table. A commander asked him about the kind of constitution, he has in mind.

"What we should have for the present," Aguinaldo replied, "is an authoritarian form of government."

It was another term for a dictatorship.

No one posed any objection, for Aguinaldo had impressed on the men there, the need for this form of government. It could wage the revolution speedily and in a unified manner and not be hampered by time-consuming debates and power-sharing practiced in a republican form of government. The discussion was then simply on the powers of the commander-in-chief—Aguinaldo himself. They agreed that the successful prosecution of the revolution required that they be final and absolute.

Aguinaldo, in the break that followed, talked to the officers individually. He came to Paulo.

"Well, major," Aguinaldo said to Paulo, "I am glad to see you again."

"So am I, sir, and thank you for addressing me as a major," Paulo replied with familiarity that caught the attention of the other officers.

"I have just promoted you to major," Aguinaldo replied. "I heard you are doing many times in Masakao, what you did in Carmona."

Paulo smiled. Aguinaldo has not forgotten that minor engagement in Carmona, from among the many battles waged in the colony for so many days now. He captured the estate house there with a simple ruse, an achievement that impressed Aguinaldo.

"The Spaniards will never have it easy in Masakao, sir," Paulo replied.

"That is the spirit. Carry on with the good work," Aguinaldo said as he turned to another officer, standing next to Paulo.

Lukas and Paulo and the other field commanders left the meeting, their spirit raised by Aguinaldo's determination to carry on with the fight. They were so encouraged and with fresh supplies, they intensified in the following days their attack on the Spanish patrols and checkpoints in Masakao. The time had come to attack the town fort itself.

Paulo outlined his plan of attack with his finger pointed to a crudely drawn map spread out on the table in their hut.

Lukas, Gayuman, Doctor Bihasa and Sabedro stood around the table and watched and listened.

He said, "We will attack the town fort when and where, they least expect it, that is, on a moonless night and from the river. We will divert their attention, before we start the attack, with a feint at their outpost, south of the town."

The others nodded in agreement with Paulo's plan of attack on the town fort.

"It is a good plan, easy to carry out," Lukas said, "and with the very important element of secrecy and surprise. When will you carry it out?"

Paulo was about to reply to his uncle's question when a soldier at the hut entrance said a courier from Aguinaldo's headquarters was waiting, outside the hut. The courier was let in. He handed a note to Lukas.

Lukas frowned as he was reading the note.

"What does it say?" Gayuman asked Lukas.

He did not reply, but passed the note instead to Gayuman.

He read it and shouted as he threw it to the floor, "Why, in the name of all the the saints in heaven, did he do that?"

"Do what?" Paulo asked Gayuman as Doctor Bihasa was picking up the note from the floor.

He frowned too as he was reading it and passed it on to Paulo who shouted after reading it, "Has Aguinaldo lost his mind?"

"We fought for nothing," Gayuman said, "We have been sold out."

The note said that Aguinaldo had entered into a peace pact with the Spaniards. He is going into exile in Hong Kong in exchange for amnesty and indemnity. The note ordered them to lay down their arms and that Aguinaldo will call bandits those who will not follow his order and continue the fight. He also ordered Paulo to join him as an aide in Hong Kong.

The courier looked on nervously at the men's angry reaction to the note. To Lukas, however, the anger expressed by Paulo and Gayuman now had the opposite effect of calming him down. Aguinaldo must have a good reason for giving up the fight. He wrote a reply to Aguinaldo. They will lay down their arms while Paulo will join Aguinaldo in Hong Kong. He gave the note to the courier who saluted and left.

"We are all angry at what Aguinaldo did," Lukas then said, "but he must have a good reason for what he did."

"Which is," Gayuman said to Lukas.

"I don't know," Lukas replied irritably. "But what would you rather do? Go on fighting? We will not last a month if we will continue to fight by ourselves and at the same time be called bandits."

Bihasa asked Lukas, "Did you see any sign that Aguinaldo is giving up the fight when you saw him last week?"

"I saw nothing to indicate that. But that is academic now. We must follow his order. We must lay down our arms. As for you, Paulo, you are going to Hong Kong with Aguinaldo."

"I am not going there," Paulo said sullenly.

"An order is an order," Lukas said, his finger pointed to Paulo. "Don't ever forget that. For you and for all of us, it is duty above everything else. As for you, Paulo, you are going to Hong Kong with Aguinaldo."

Paulo sulked while Bihasa, Gayuman and Sabedro left their hut.

Lukas watched them as they were walking away. He could not blame them for objecting to the truce. He himself is against it. But then, Aguinaldo may have agreed to the truce because he may have realized that they had lost in the fight. He should have seen the sign when Aguinaldo fled to the mountain village in Biak-na-Bato.

He realized now that Aguinaldo's stunning victory in the battle in Imus was just a fluke. Aguinaldo never won a single battle after that, but one defeat after another.

Aguinaldo was now acting more like an outlaw than as the head of the revolution. In entering into a truce with the Spaniards, Aguinaldo was trying to salvage with an amnesty and indemnity, something out of their lost cause.

He shook is head sadly. They have failed in their revolution. They remained under Spanish rule. The sacrifices they made were all in vain.

He looked away in anger at how he was also a victim of the misplaced optimism at the Biak-na-Bato meeting. He did not realize it then that Aguinaldo held it in a desperate move to make up politically for his reverses in the battlefield. The field commanders came to Biak-na-Bato demoralized. They have suffered terrible losses, they were in retreat, they were barely fighting on, but as the meeting went on their demoralized state underwent a remarkable change from the brave and confident words of Aguinaldo who had taken heart at the presence and unquestioning obedience of his field commanders.

What he found most galling was the secretive way, Aguinaldo made a deal with the Spaniards. He did not consult with his field commanders, whose opinion about this course of action, he should have sought and respected. Aguinaldo acted instead like a dictator, not a true revolutionary leader like Bonifacio.

Lukas thought bitterly, all of that is now over.

He said to Paulo, now that they were alone in the hut, "I am sorry, if I have been hard on you."

"It is all right, uncle, I understand. We must set aside our thoughts and feelings for the cause. As you said, it is duty above everything else."

Lukas stepped out of the hut with Paulo and told him to assemble the troops in the drill ground.

He was facing afterwards the assembled troops with Paulo, Bihasa, Gayuman and Sabedro. He has the sad, thankless task of telling them that they were giving up the fight. To prepare them for the blow, he commended them first for their bravery, loyalty and sacrifice.

He continued: "A courier came here a while ago with a message that Aguinaldo has entered into a peace pact with the Spaniards. It put an end to our revolution. Aguinaldo, in exchange for amnesty and indemnity, has agreed to go into exile in Hong Kong. Joining him there will be your commander, my nephew, Paulo.

"We must, as ordered by Aguinaldo, lay down our arms. We are returning to our families, to our homes in Masakao safely and without fear of reprisal by the Spaniards. As we leave our camp, let me say the privilege is mine for having fought with you for our country's freedom."

The troops took the blow with silence. There were no mutterings or loud voices raised in angry protest to Aguinaldo's order. Lukas was gratified at how calmly their troops had accepted the order for them to lay down their arms. Paulo and Kabisig had drilled loyalty and obedience into their minds.

There was heaviness in his heart, though, at the thought that they were giving up the fight with the freedom, they fought for at such a terrible cost, had remained beyond their reach. He could say no more. Paulo took over and gave the order for their troops to pass in review.

Lukas felt his spirit lifted at the sight of their soldiers marching by. They are not a mob going back to the town, a dangerous one with anger in their minds and arms in their hands. They are giving up the fight in perfect form, like the true revolutionary soldiers that they are.

They dispersed afterwards and returned to their quarters to prepare for their return to Masakao, the following day. Lukas had ordered an advance party of his troops to leave for the town and inform the town fort and the townsfolk that they were coming home.

Lukas, Paulo, Gayuman and Doctor Bihasa returned to their hut. Lukas was putting his things in a bag when something came to his mind.

"I'm not sure," he said, "if the truce will last. It may fail."

"What are you getting at?" Gayuman asked Lukas.

"We must not abandon our camp completely. Sabedro and his fellow Dumagats will keep it ready. We will leave our best arms here, for we may have to fight again in case the truce will fail."

The rebels left Alkayag, midmorning of the following day. It took them, most of the day to reach Masakao. They moved silently in the town while the townsfolk who lined the road watched them just as silently. They moved on, their heads held high, for they were not coming home in humiliating defeat.

Some of the soldiers in the column waved back in acknowledgement of the greetings by their friends and relatives who were standing on the roadside or were watching them from the windows in their homes. They were their sons, brothers, husbands and fathers, friends and loved ones who fought the good fight and who were now coming home.

Mayor Echeverria and Captain Laguerte watched Lukas, who was at the head of the column when it entered the town fort, marched toward the drill ground, halted and faced them.

Lukas then stepped forward and faced Mayor Echeverria and Captain Laguerte, after which he removed his sheathed sword and laid it down on the ground. He did the same with his sidearm.

The rest of them then filed past the Spaniards and laid down their arms, their guns, swords, machetes and bamboo spears. The pile of weapons rose higher and higher. The rebel troops then filed back in formation.

Mayor Echeverria then spoke about the terms of the Pact of Biak-na-Bato. He assured them of Spain's benevolence, that there will be no vindictiveness and that now that peace had been restored, it was time to rebuild the town and bind and heal the wounds caused by the revolution.

"You are free to return to your homes and start anew," Mayor Echeverria said in conclusion.

Captain Laguerte spoke in the same vein. Lukas then turned toward his troops and gave the order dismissing them.

The townsfolk were kept outside the fort. They watched their troops when they came out of the fort. Teresa, Esperanza and Nieves stood behind the townsfolk there.

They smiled and waved at Paulo when they saw him coming out of the fort with Lukas, Gayuman and Doctor Bihasa.

"Go ahead, make them happy," Lukas said to Paulo.

Paulo was in low spirit since they left Alkayag. It was lifted up when he saw Teresa. He came to her, but was stopped from taking her in his arms by the townsfolk who will disapprove of such a public show of their affection for each other.

Here, he is, close to her, her lover who seldom saw her and there she is, eased of the constant fear of death that might take him away from her, so close to each other and he could not even hold her hand. That, he decided, he could at least dare do. He held her hand, but released it when he noticed some of those in the crowd were looking at them.

He turned instead to Esperanza and said to her, "How is my future sister-in-law?"

Esperanza looked at Paulo and said with feigned disapproval, "What made you think, I approve of you as my future brother-in-law?"

She poked suddenly and playfully Paulo on his ribs and the four of them laughed. It was just like the old times when they were young children.

Paulo turned to Nieves and said to her, "How is my dear friend."

"Still, your dear friend," Nieves replied to Teresa and Esperanza's laughter.

They joined the crowd moving away from the town fort.

"So, you came straight from Alkayag," Esperanza said to Paulo.

"Yes. We started out this morning."

"Have you eaten anything since then?" Teresa asked Paulo.

"We ate something around noon. It was not much, though."

"You must be very hungry by now," Nieves said to Paulo.

"I can, right now, eat a horse if I can find one."

Teresa, Esperanza and Nieves laughed.

"We have only our faithful horse," Teresa said.

"Give Father the choice between giving up his arm and his horse and he will readily give up his arm to giving up his horse," Esperanza said to their laughter.

"But we have chicken, fried and marinated, pork, noodles, soup. What else did we prepare?" Teresa asked Esperanza and Nieves.

"A lot more food, you will like," Esperanza said to Paulo.

"I can hardly wait to get to your house," Paulo said.

He asked as they were walking home, "How is your father?"

"He can now walk around in the house and in the yard," Teresa replied, "and do light things, like feeding the chickens."

"His favorite exercise," Esperanza said as she then made a clacking sound with her tongue in imitating the manner by which Julio called out to the chickens on their feeding time.

Julio and Agustina, after the customary exchange of greetings, led Paulo to the dining table for their evening meal.

The food, the women had prepared, was as Paulo had expected, something he could not resist filling himself with. After the austere meals in their mountain camp, the food on the table was a veritable feast to him.

He ate with gusto while the others at the table plied him with questions about the revolution and the peace pact.

They were finished with their supper as the church bells were ringing the Angelus. They prayed after which they cleared the table and washed the dishes.

That task done, Paulo, Teresa, Esperanza and Nieves repaired to the balcony and there talked as they did when they were small children.

It was getting dark. Esperanza lit up the candle inside a Christmas Star, hanging in the living room window, facing the road. She then proceeded to the bedroom, she shared with Teresa.

"I'm going, too," Nieves said as she left for her house nearby.

It was early evening in December. Teresa was seated on the rocking chair, facing Paulo. Her sandaled feet pressed to the floor sent her rocking chair in a rhythmic to-and-fro movement. She was happy and satisfied with Paulo now back to her, safe and sound. He was seated on the balcony's wooden sill, his back against its wooden post. He was facing the night sky with its garlands of light in the distant stars.

Out there in the town road, young men were walking by and talking in cheerful voices. The glow in the lit ends of their cigarettes trailed now and then in the dark road, the men smoking them indistinct figures on the road. The shadow of a cypress tree was lying across the front yard, its tip pointed to the road.

The town was never as lovely as it was at this time of the year when the windows in the homes there were bright with the Christmas Stars. They were patterned after the Star of Bethlehem, which guided the Three Wise Men on their journey to pay homage to Jesus Christ at his Nativity. They were signs of the coming Christmas. The townsfolk eagerly waited for that day, they spent in the celebration of the birth of Jesus Christ and his message of love, peace, hope and the salvation of mankind.

The thought came pleasantly to Teresa that it meant for her and Paulo, a wonderful life awaiting them.

She felt as she looked on at Paulo that it was time for them to talk about it.

"What are you going to do," she asked him, "now that the revolution is over? Are you now going to pursue your law studies?"

She stopped rocking her chair and waited.

He looked on at the night sky, full of the stars. Then he said, "It is not over yet."

"It is not over yet? Aguinaldo has given up. You have laid down your arms. What revolution are you still talking about?"

"Uncle is not convinced, it is over and I agree with him."

"Your uncle maybe right, but I am speaking about us."

"I cannot make any plans for us, not yet."

"Why can we not make plans for us?"

"I have been ordered to join Aguinaldo in Hong Kong."

Teresa looked hard at Paulo and said, "What did you tell him?"

Paulo did not reply. He looked away instead.

"You are going to Hong Kong!"

"I have no choice. An order is an order."

"What about us?"

"There will be time enough for us."

She looked hard at Paulo, their life together dashed by him, leaving her and going into exile with Aguinaldo in Hong Kong. She realized now, how insignificant a part, she played in his life.

She looked bitterly at Paulo, her breast heaving from rage welling up inside her. She would have broken out into brutal language about how he had taken her for granted, how he had only used her, but the sight of him, so remote and so despondent, tempered her anger.

She sought to understand what had come between them. It was their separation. He had been away from her, too long. His mind, his entire being had been so focused on the revolution, he set everything else aside, including her. He could not face the fact that they have lost in their revolution, that it was time for them to set it aside and start a new kind of life for the two of them.

Paulo was talking on, more to himself than to her about continuing the revolution. His voice droned on, upsetting her even more.

"Have it your way then," she said. "So be it, if your revolution is more important to you, but leave me from now on, out of your life!"

She stood up and turned to leave. Paulo stood up also and held her arm.

"Wait, don't go," he said pleadingly to her, "let us talk about it."

She wrenched her arm away from him and said, close to his face, "It is pointless to talk to you! You have no love left for me, for this town, or for anything else except for your silly revolution!"

He looked on, shocked, as she then stamped out angrily from the balcony. He made a move but stopped himself from following her to the living room. He waited instead in the balcony, hoping she will come back there. When, after a while of waiting, she did not come back, he stepped down in the staircase and left the house sadly.

Part Two

Chapter Fourteen

Chemari mounted slowly the stone staircase in Fort Santiago as dawn was breaking out in Manila. It was his habit to walk around a bit, refreshed by the fresh morning air before going home, his eyelids heavy from a night as the fort's duty officer.

He perked up once he was on top of the wall, at the sight of the city cast in the thinning dark haze of the night. The sky above was still grayish-black, but orange streaks of the coming day had broken through the clouds in the eastern horizon. The mountain peaks in Morong were taking definite shapes with the daylight rising behind them.

The churches in Tondo, Binondo, Quiapo and Santa Cruz across the river stood solemnly watching over Manila. Their massive frames were, in the dark, not yet as clearly defined in the daytime landscape there of those churches with their belfries and the tile-roofed homes and buildings there.

The Chinese quarter in Binondo, across the Pasig River, had as usual roused itself early. The shopkeepers there were opening their stores and putting out goods in the storefronts.

Chinese peddlers were coming out from an alley, hats on their heads and bamboo poles on their shoulders. Hanging on each end of the bamboo poles were round bamboo baskets containing food and other products they will peddle in the city streets.

Intramuros, on the side of the fort, was still in slumber, its medieval churches overlooking the tile-roofed homes there, their windows kept wide open for the cool breeze from Manila Bay that warm May night in 1898.

Chemari walked around as he was taking in the cool morning breeze. He halted at a corner parapet and looked down at the rhythmic ebb and flow of the bay waters on the sandy shore, near the base of the wall in Fort Santiago. Manila Bay, west of him, was still cast in darkness.

He was in one place in Manila, whose view all around, even in the dark, was a happy combination of what nature had done there and what man had made there. He was glad to be a part of it all, in this city of his birth.

He fell to more musing. He is a lucky man. He has a beautiful wife and a wonderful son. While the Achuteguis were a highly respected family, it helped a lot that he was married to Marissa. Her family was one of the richest and most influential families in Intramuros.

He will leave the army in a few weeks after serving it with distinction. He smiled as he recalled how Marissa's face lit up when he finally agreed, after so much nagging from her, to leave for Spain with her and their child and take up there, his law studies.

The possibilities after that were many and wonderful maybe even the governorship of a province nearby. Its grand style of living will please him, as it should satisfy her.

His brow was suddenly creased with worry over what could threaten his excellent prospects. War had broken out between Spain and the United States over Cuba. The Philippines was a Spanish colony and it could be drawn into the war.

But as he had thought over for so many times, Cuba was an ocean away from the Philippines. The war could not get that far, there in the Philippines where America had no interest. All indications pointed to the war being confined in Cuba and he could put that war behind him once he is in Spain with Marissa and their child.

The soldier on guard duty interrupted Chemari in his thoughts.

He said to Chemari, his finger pointed to the mouth of Manila Bay, "Will you take a look, sir, at those ships coming in the bay?"

Chemari took a look at the dark western horizon. It showed him nothing and he said to the guard, "I don't see any ships, you are talking about."

"They are right there, sir."

He kept on looking until he saw the ships. They looked like warships.

"I can see them now," he said to the guard.

The warships seemed headed toward Manila.

"Are they our ships, sir?"

He looked doubtfully at the strange warships. He knew their warships had arrived the day before in their naval base in Sangley Point in Cavite, some nine miles south of them.

He was shaken when he realized those could be American warships, a squadron of them!

The warships then turned south in battle formation.

He was looking on when the shore battery in Sangley Point opened fire at the American warships.

The shock waves it generated jarred Chemari and the soldier as they were watching, their mouths hanging open in astonishment, the start of the naval battle in Manila Bay between the Spanish and the American warships.

"Ring the alarm bell!" he shouted at the soldier as he then ran

Several soldiers had gone there ahead of him. They were standing by the shore battery.

"What are you waiting for?" he shouted at them. "Load those guns and turn them toward those American warships!"

He looked on while the soldiers were loading the guns with shells and setting them in firing position.

"Now, start firing!" he shouted at the soldiers.

He looked out at the bay, his hands on the cold parapet.

He pursed his lips in disappointment when he saw the shells were exploding harmlessly in the water, too short of the American warships.   He shook his head sadly. There was nothing, Fort Santiago could do to help their warships in Sangley Point.

The United States, at the outbreak of the Spanish-American War on April 21, 1898, considered the defeat of the Spanish naval force in Manila Bay as very important in winning the war against Spain.

America's Asiatic Squadron, under the command of Commodore George Dewey, was then stationed in Hong Kong.

He was ordered to proceed to Manila Bay and destroy the Spanish Pacific Squadron stationed there.

Dewey had six warships in his squadron, his flagship, the battleship *Olympia,* the cruisers *Baltimore, Raleigh* and *Boston* and the gunboats *Concord* and *Petrel.*

The Spanish Pacific Squadron, led by Rear Admiral Patricio Montojo, had seven warships: his flagship, the battleship *Reyna Cristina,* the cruisers *Castilla, Don Juan de Austria, Don Antonio de Ulloa, Isla de Luzon, Isla de Cuba,* and the gunboat *Marquez del Duero.*

The Spanish warships were way below the American warships in size, armament, speed and mobility. They were manned by poorly trained crews. Their warships were so poorly maintained, some of their engines were not even working.

The Spanish squadron was based in Subic. It moved to Cavite on April 30, 1898 when it learned that the American Asiatic Squadron had left Hong Kong and may now be headed toward Manila.

Dewey's squadron of warships approached the mouth of Manila Bay, past midnight of the same day. A Spanish shore battery there fired a few rounds. They fell short of the American warships.

Dawn was breaking when the American warships veered toward the Spanish naval base in Sangley Point. Its shore battery then fired at the American warships. The shells fell short of the American warships, which were still out of range of the shore battery.

Dewey said to the captain of his flagship, the *Olympia,* once the American warships were near enough to Sangley Point, "You may fire when you are ready, Gridley."

The American warships then swung to their right and fired their port guns at the Spanish warships there. Then they swung around again and fired as they were turning left, at a closer range, their starboard guns toward the Spanish warships.

The Spanish warships and their shore battery fired back at the American warships. The shells they fired either fell short or missed their targets. It was turning out to be an uneven fight between the American and the Spanish warships with the Spanish warships getting a severe beating.

The battle was going on when suddenly, at around eight o'clock, Dewey received an urgent message. His warships had only fifteen rounds of ammunition left per gun.

He ordered the immediate withdrawal of his warships from the battle. The order he gave left the American warships' crews stunned, confused and disappointed. He then said, to keep their morale, that he gave the order for their warships' withdrawal from the battle so they could take their breakfast.

He learned in a conference he later on held at the *Olympia* with his ship captains that the message about the fifteen rounds of ammunition left per gun in their warships was so garbled, what it actually meant was that only fifteen rounds of ammunition per gun in their warships *had so far been used.* The ship captains also reported at the conference that explosions were heard and fires were seen in the *Reyna Cristina* and the *Castilla.*

The Americans resumed action, some two hours later. The *Don Antonio de Ulloa* was fired at and sunk. The crew of the Spanish transport *Mindanao* abandoned it when it was fired at by the *Concord.*

The Spanish warships were by now offering very little resistance.

Montojo saw his squadron was now in such a hopeless situation, he ordered his warships to simply ram the American warships. His flagship, the battleship *Reyna Cristina,* then charged toward the American warships. It turned back at the intense firing by the American warships. It was so badly damaged when it returned to the naval base, Montojo ordered it to be sunk. The *Castilla* was also so badly damaged, it was likewise sunk. The cruiser *Marquez del Duero* lost an engine and had only one gun left with which to fire back at the American warships. The captain of the *Don Antonio Ullao* was killed while most of its crew was wounded when it was hit by a shell below the waterline. The cruiser *Isla de Luzon's* guns were all destroyed.

Montojo then ordered his remaining warships to be sunk.

The *Olympia, Baltimore* and *Boston* then turned their guns toward the shore battery in the Spanish naval base in Sangley Point and put it out of action. The gunboat *Petrel* then fired its guns at the government offices there. A white flag was then raised there and the firing ceased.

The naval battle in Manila Bay was over, its outcome in an American victory, clear from the very start.

Dewey won the battle in Manila Bay with one cruiser damaged, nine crewmen injured and an officer who died from a heart attack.

The losses on the Spanish side were severe. Two cruisers were scuttled, one battleship, four cruisers and one transport ship were sunk. 77 crewmen were killed, 271 were wounded.

A detachment of marines then landed in Sangley Point. The Americans now have a foothold from which they could carry out a land war against the Spaniards in the Philippines.

Dewey ordered later on two of his warships to move northward, near Manila. They sent warning signals to Fort Santiago, not to fire its shore battery there or it will likewise be blown to bits. American warships had Intramuros and the rest of Manila, now blockaded in Manila Bay.

Chapter Fifteen

The Spaniards in Intramuros were made painfully aware of the American blockade every time they looked in the direction of Manila Bay. Their stonewalled enclave in Intramuros and for that matter, the entire colony itself, had now become like a big prison to them.

They could still leave the Philippines by way of the overland routes to the ports in Legazpi and Sual. No Spaniard in his right mind would take, though, those perilous trips through the dangerous Philippine countryside where the Filipino rebels were active again.

They had nowhere to go. They were virtually imprisoned in Intramuros by the American warships in Manila Bay. It depressed Chemari while it upset Marissa. She complained about it, at all hours of the day and night.

"We should be in Spain by now if you had only rid yourself earlier of your grand notions about this damned colony," Marissa said to Chemari, one evening in their living room.

Chemari remained silent. He will not be drawn into another pointless argument with her that led nowhere. He blocked his view of her by burying his nose on the pages of a newspaper, he was reading. She kept on talking. It made him so upset, he stood up and without saying a word to her, he left their house for a more pleasant time in a bar in Solana Street.

He entered the bar and sat down on a stool in the bar counter, across the bartender, a middle-aged man with a droopy mustache. He caught the tail end of the conversation between the bartender and the customer seated beside him, who was bent over his glass of wine.

The bartender was shaking his head in reaction to the customer's comment that things had turned from good to bad in Intramuros ever since the American warships had blockaded it in Manila Bay.

Chemari ordered beer. The bartender complied by pouring into a glass, a bottle of beer. He drank, upon getting it, half of it with one tip of the glass to his lips. He was one more customer who came to the bar to drown in his glass of beer, the American warships in Manila Bay.

He saw in the mirror behind the bartender, four men at a corner table. They were having a heated argument. He listened to them.

"For all we know, another fleet has been assembled in Spain and is now on its way to Manila," one of the men said.

"Do you expect me to believe that?" another man said. "We are finished!"

"What do you want us to do then? Give up, just like that?"

"What else can we do? Fight and die for nothing? The Americans have us, by our throats."

Chemari frowned at the dreary talk at the corner table there and drank his beer. He needed no one to remind him that their situation in Intramuros was grim and desperate. While the stonewall around it gave them a sense of security, he was under no illusion that it could keep away an American army that was now most likely being assembled in the United States. It will then land its troops in the former Spanish naval base in Sangley Point in Cavite. That was the assessment in Fort Santiago.

He shared the opinion there that, in the ground war that will follow, the Spanish forces in Intramuros, despite an abundant manpower supplied by its population swollen by refugees from the provinces, will be as mismatched to the American army, as their navy was to the

American navy. Just as worrisome, the rebels who remained hard to control despite the peace pact were active again.

He emptied his glass of beer with one swig of it and ordered another beer. He finished it, again with one swig of it and ordered another beer.

"You must have a good reason for the way you are drinking, as if it is water and not beer that you are drinking," the other customer at the bar counter said to Chemari.

"I have my reason," he said with a sour face.

"Which is?"

"Tell me yours first."

The man drank his wine and sighed.

"I was, only last month," the man said, "one of the richest men in Batangas. I had a wide tract of land, planted to coffee, rice and coconut. Cattle roamed it. I lost all of that when the Indio rebels returned to the province. I fled here with my family. I am now living on the generosity of my wife's family, here in Intramuros."

One more refugee, Chemari thought contemptuously of the man, seated beside him. His bloated stomach, his coat could not hide, and his bloated cheeks showed the man's fondness for food and wine. The man lived on the fat of the land worked for him by his Indio tenants.

The man, for all that had happened to him in Batangas, did not seem to be down and out. He could not take his tract of land with him, but he must have taken with him, his money and his jewelry. He knows about the hoards of money, gold, silver and jewelry kept there in Intramuros by those landowners and government officials who had sought refuge there.

He looked around at the bar, at the man in the counter and the men in the corner table. The abuses they and all the rest of them did to the Indios brought about the revolution. They will rise up in arms again. That was the assessment in Fort Santiago. Aside from the American warships stationed in Manila Bay, they will soon face an American army and the rebel Indios. They faced nothing, but defeat and destruction.

Blood surged up to his head in anger at everyone and everything there. He was tempted to say to the man, seated beside him, that he got what he deserved, but then, one fight with his wife was enough for one night.

He was there to get drunk and then go home and sleep in peace. He finished his beer, paid for his drinks and left the bar.

The dark homes along the narrow cobblestone streets in Intramuros brooded over him as he was walking home on his unsteady feet. He met no one. He stepped aside at the sound of the hoofbeat of an approaching horse-drawn cab and watched it as it ran on in the cobblestone street.

He resumed walking and heard from the homes, he was passing by, men conversing, children engaged in a game and a woman singing an Andalusian song to a piano accompaniment. The residents in Intramuros were keeping their domestic life as normal as possible. It was as if there were no American warships blockading them in Manila Bay. The beer, he drank had made him keen of feeling and he observed with a heavy heart, how the wonderful life he led there in Intramuros will soon come to an end.

Chapter Sixteen

Spencer Pratt, the American consul in Hong Kong, had expected even before the naval battle in Manila Bay that the Philippines, a Spanish colony, will soon be drawn into the war between Spain and the United States. He promised American aid to Aguinaldo if he will resume the revolution. That will put the Spaniards in a very difficult situation of fighting at the same time, the American soldiers and the Filipino rebels.

Aguinaldo took the offer without hesitation. He had good reasons for resuming the revolution. The Spaniards did not keep their promise of total amnesty and full indemnity. Some of the rebels were arrested while not all of the promised indemnity was given to him. He agreed, on the other hand, to the peace pact only for the breathing spell it gave him from the fighting that had been going against him. He will resume the revolution, once he had the arms to do it.

The arms Aguinaldo could buy with the indemnity will not be enough, though. Now, with the American aid offer, he will have all the arms he needed to resume the revolution and, after that, gain the independence of the Philippines. Aguinaldo, though, was in deep diplomatic waters there and he did not even know how to swim.

His ignorance of international law was shown by what he wrote: "The United States would at least recognize the independence of the Philippines under the protection of the United States Navy, that there was no need for entering into a formal written agreement because the word of the Admiral (George Dewey) and of the United States Consul (Spencer Pratt) would be fulfilled to the letter. . . "

Aguinaldo took Dewey and Pratt's offer of American arms aid as equivalent to America's formal, written recognition of an independent

Philippines. Both Dewey and Pratt denied having the authority to do that, for only the United States Congress had the authority to do that.

The Filipinos rose up in arms again upon Aguinaldo's return to the Philippines in an American warship on May 19, 1898. Aguinaldo declared, a month later, on June 12, 1898, in his hometown in Kawit, Cavite, the independence of the Philippines. Many of the provinces had by then fallen into the Filipino hands.

Paulo returned to the Philippines with Aguinaldo. He was so tied up with staff work for Aguinaldo, it was only after several weeks had passed when he sought and obtained Aguinaldo's permission to lead a contingent of Filipino troops that will liberate Masakao from the Spaniards.

He proceeded to his hometown, expecting a stiff fight there with the Spaniards. He was met instead by some townsfolk who told him that the town was now theirs. Mayor Echeverria and Captain Laguerte had fled to Manila, a few days earlier. He was even more pleased to learn that the townsfolk had proclaimed his uncle as their new town mayor.

"Your uncle went straight to work. He did not even bother to celebrate," the townsfolk said to him.

Paulo left his troops in the town fort and proceeded to the municipal hall. He paused at the door to the mayor's office and looked around at the men and women who filled the room before turning his eyes to the novel sight of his uncle, seated at the mayor's desk.

A discussion going on there ceased as he was approaching his uncle who stood up when he saw him coming. He took his uncle's outstretched arm and touched the back of his uncle's hand to his forehead in a sign of respect for an elder. Lukas was smiling as he then held Paulo on his shoulders.

He said while looking closely at Paulo, "Am I so glad to see you again. You look fine."

His fine military bearing showed in the way he stood straight in his gray uniform and boots, an officer's cap on his head and a holstered sidearm on his belt.

"You look fine too, uncle," Paulo said.

"Work makes me feel and look good."

He turned to the men and women in the room and said to them, "I suppose, you all know my nephew here."

They all knew Paulo as the brave young man who led the town's rebel troops, who went in exile with Aguinaldo in Hong Kong and who was now a rising commander in Aguinaldo's staff.

A man seated near Lukas' desk offered his chair to Paulo. He thanked the man, but waved his offer aside. The man persisted. Paulo complied and sat down on the chair.

"Don't let me interrupt your meeting," he said to Lukas.

They were discussing the agricultural estates in Masakao, abandoned by their owners, a friar order and the Ilustrado landlords. They fled to Manila at the outbreak of the revolution. They returned there during the truce and left again, following the naval battle in Manila Bay.

The agricultural estates were either leased to, or were worked on by the town residents. They were descendants of the original Indio owners of those lands, taken away from them by their Spanish rulers.

A middle-aged man, standing near Lukas' desk, delivered an impassioned speech about the abuses, he endured from his Ilustrado landlord and how, like his forebears before him, he tilled that same piece of land and got only a pittance for all the work he did there. Now that the Spaniards had left and the town was theirs, the man said, the land he tilled should be his by simple occupation. The others in the room voiced their agreement. It was a delicate matter, put in the hands of Lukas.

"We are in the same situation here," he said. "You all know, I am a lessee myself. I have been tilling that land for years, a part of it, I sublet to other tenants, but I cannot just claim it as my own land."

"I don't know about you, mayor, but I will now occupy, my piece of land," a young man said to Lukas.

"You are already occupying, a part of it. But that did not make you its rightful owner, not yet anyway. No tenant in this town can just claim any of those lands for himself or herself. Ownership of those lands remains in the hands of the friars and the absentee landlords. I suggest that you continue tilling those lands until we have worked out something that is lawful, fair and just to both of you, the friars and the landlords."

Paulo saw something different in the way his uncle conducted the meeting. It confirmed the commendatory words he heard from the townsfolk, he met on his way to the municipal hall. His uncle had not changed at all despite the political power, he was now wielding in the town.

He nodded in admiration of his uncle at the precise, passionate and eloquent manner by which his uncle advanced his views, so that he won over even those who in the beginning were opposed to him. There was nothing in his uncle of the ignorance, confusion, corruption and arrogance, he had seen in the other revolutionary leaders who have taken from the Spaniards, the control of those towns.

He had been sent, as a member of Aguinaldo's staff, on various errands to those towns. He was so disappointed to find those new town mayors, so ill-suited to their jobs. They were pompous, arrogant and ignorant who used their political power only for their own advantage.

His uncle was refreshingly different. He was conducting himself, honorably and effectively as the mayor of Masakao. That did not come as a surprise to him, though.

He knows his uncle as a man of character, integrity, honesty and commitment to public service, a man who looked at public office as one of stewardship and not as a means for self-advantage. There was also his uncle's faith in God. His uncle was a religious man who held the view that political power came from the people and therefore from God: "*Vox populi, vox Dei*—"The voice of the people is the voice of God"—as his uncle had often said with the few Latin words he knew.

The meeting ended and the men and the women left Lukas' office.

Paulo said, now that they were solely by themselves, "You handle your job, uncle, as if you were born to be our town mayor."

Lukas shrugged off Paulo's admiring comment as he sat down, so relaxed on the armchair, now that he was alone with Paulo. It was not with the air of vanity and authority, but with fondness and familiarity that he responded to Paulo's admiring comment.

"I try to do my best; that is all," he said to Paulo.

"Our townsfolk are fortunate to have you, for our mayor."

"That is so nice to hear, but I see things differently from where I am now seated."

"How different, is it?"

Lukas stood up and walked toward a window there. He said, as he was looking at the river and the rice fields there, "I was not lacking in the best of intentions when I took this job which, by the way, should have been Manuel Mulawin's job, had he not died in fighting Zatayde. I have learned in the short time, I have occupied this position, how precious little I can do in bringing about the changes we need in our town. Our town's ways are set. We have what God has given us. We are part of a feudal system evolved through the centuries that cannot easily be changed and not by a mere town mayor.

"You have seen one very serious problem—land tenancy. Some of our townsfolk want to take over those lands owned by the friars and the absentee landlords by simple physical occupation. You heard me say that I am all for that, but that it cannot be done merely through that. We have laws to follow. We have here a complex situation that needs wise and effective policy, fair and patient administration and the resources for the transfer of ownership of those lands to their tenants. Before we can even do that, we have to prepare and educate first the tenants on the responsibility of land ownership.

"I see the town differently from where I now stand and no longer with the zeal and naivete when we were fighting the Spaniards. The risk and the danger set aside, it was far simpler to remove the Spaniards through the revolution than to run this town and our country, the way they should be run. For our country to be like the more advanced countries, we must remove our bad traits and habits and be true to ourselves. That is basic."

"How should we do that?"

"We must, first of all, do that by getting rid of those two maladies that afflict us. Where our crab mentality makes us pull each other down instead of pulling each other up, our colonial mentality makes us bow down to and imitate our Spanish rulers."

"Is it that important to remove them?"

"It is, for they afflict too much and too many of our people. Their ambition is to be like the Spaniards. They consider, as marks of distinction, of high social status, anything Spanish they acquire, practice and imitate, from the Spanish surnames they acquire, to the slang Spanish they speak, down to the Spanish social graces, they practice when those are, in fact, nothing more than examples of their imitation of our Spanish rulers. They do not know or do not care that they are imitating those people who oppressed us for hundreds of years."

"The glamour in a Spanish surname is that strong among our people. But, if they feel good about that, why then should we not grant them that?"

"Because, like the fly perched on a carabao, which thinks it is big and strong like the carabao, it swells their heads into thinking what they are not. It gives them this grand, but false opinion of themselves and the imaginary sense of being superior to those who have kept what are native to us."

"But are we not expected to imitate our Spanish rulers?"

"Not, if we will look at our neighbors. Did the Malays and the Indians change their native names to English names and imitate the British? Did the Indonesians change their native names to Dutch names and imitate the Dutch? Did the Vietnamese, Cambodians and Laotians change their native names to French names and imitate the French? Not one of them did that.

"You know why? They have the self-respect to imitate their foreign rulers. They take pride in their history, culture and way of life to imitate their foreign rulers. They have those things, which unfortunately we did not have. That is one reason, we imitate the Spaniards. If the Americans will take over from the Spaniards, they will do the same thing, they did with the Spaniards."

"We will then have to just accept it."

"No. We were in an underdeveloped, divided state before the Spaniards ruled us. It will be hard to do, but it can be done again. We can develop what we were before they came. We had in the *Barangay,* a system of government, the regional languages we can develop into one national language, a social, economic structure. We can do that again in the spirit that we are one nation with the same natural endowments, other nations have."

"I can see from that, a strong dislike that you have for the Spaniards."

"I am not that biased, Paulo. You know that. I am objective and fair-minded enough to admit that there are some good things the Spaniards have brought and done to us, like their fine cuisine and their beautiful language. Like you and our townsfolk, aside from our own regional dialects, I also write, read and speak in Spanish because it is a necessary means of communication with the rest of the world. We also owe it to the Spaniards for uniting our many tribes and principalities into one nation and, the most important of all, for the Christian faith they brought to us."

"Speaking about that, should we not also discard our Spanish baptismal names and adopt only native baptismal names?"

"We don't have to go that far. We have baptismal names in Spanish, not so much in imitation of our Spanish rulers, but more in keeping with our Christian faith. The name chosen at a child's baptism could be in Spanish, English, French, Indian, Italian, or in any other language. This is in keeping with the universality of our Christian faith."

Paulo nodded when Lukas then said, "It is time for us to chart our own destiny and live up to our true identity as a nation. But then, even if we should gain our freedom, we cannot amount to much as a people, not until we rise from our deficiencies, we make up for with our boastful nature, not until we rid ourselves of our bad traits and habits, not until we stop imitating other people and be true to ourselves."

"I cannot, but agree with that, uncle. So, how do we go about it?"

"We must, first of all, settle this question of national identity. Once we become an independent country, we should call it, for what it is, not as a country named by our Spanish colonizers after their king, Philip the Second."

"Is that not a radical idea?"

"It is, and that is what we need—that which is radical. Our revolution itself is an example of a radical idea that grew into a radical movement. So should it be with the way our country is named. The Philippines as the name of our country, our Spanish rulers imposed on us, is acceptable only as long as we are a Spanish colony. It becomes an anomaly, once we become an independent country."

"What, by then, should we call our country?"

"We should have a name fit for it. We can name it *Silangan* as a country in the Far East. We can also name it *Kalayaan,* which means freedom. Most appropriate of all, as the only Christian nation, as the missionary outpost of the Christian faith in this part of the world, we should call our country, *Kristiana* or Christland. I cannot think of a better way we can express our faith in Jesus Christ than by naming our country after him."

"I agree with you, uncle. So, when do we start on that?"

"Right away, but our leaders are so engrossed with and are so sharply divided on the issue of the changes needed in our country. We can see the division on this issue quite sharply in two contrasting persons—Jose Rizal and Andres Bonifacio."

Lukas paused, a faraway look on his face. He seemed to be organizing his thoughts. Then he said, "Both of them were after change in our country. Where they differed is in the kind of change, we want and need and how it should be brought about and by whom. Their way of thinking about it was influenced by the kind of persons they were, their backgrounds and the social, cultural environment in which they lived.

"Our countrymen look up to Jose Rizal as the foremost Filipino, and I agree with that, looking at Rizal as a person. He was a highly cultured man with a brilliant mind who came from a well-off family. A doctor admired for his charm and intelligence, he mingled in the social, intellectual circles in Europe. He wrote poetry, novels and essays. He spoke several languages. Rizal was a man who could stand up to anyone in the world.

"Many of our countrymen, on the other hand, look down on Andres Bonifacio, he being a poor, simple company messenger and warehouseman with limited formal education. He made up for it with the books he read, like the lives of the American presidents, the Spanish translation of Victor Hugo's *Les Miserables* and Rizal's two novels, *Noli Me Tangere* and *El Filibusterismo.* He had never been abroad. He mingled mostly with poor, unsophisticated people like him who often walked around, barefooted.

"They must be judged, not so much for their personal attributes, but for what they wanted to do and did for our country."

"There, I cannot but agree, is how we should look at them."

"Rizal wanted change brought about from above, through reforms made by our colonial rulers. Bonifacio wanted change brought about from below, through the revolution by our people. Unlike Bonifacio who fought for our country's freedom, Rizal did not want an independent Philippines. What he wanted was for us to be a province of Spain with representation in the Spanish parliament and for us to be accorded the same status and respect as the Spaniards.

"Rizal is a good example of a person afflicted with colonial mentality. He wanted us to be what we are not while Bonifacio was the foremost example of what we should be, by being true to ourselves. What Rizal advanced, that is for us to remain under Spain and be treated like the Spaniards, is the exact opposite of the freedom for our country and from all the bad Spanish influences, Bonifacio fought for and died for." "But Rizal loved our country, did he not? He even died a martyr for our country. He wrote before his execution, *Mi Ultimo Adios,* that beautiful farewell poem to our country, I never tire of declaiming by myself."

"No one doubts that Rizal loved our country. But he loved our country, not as an independent state, but as a vassal state of Spain. Rizal died a martyr, both for Spain and our country. Rizal is the foremost example of a brown Spaniard."

"Is that possible?"

"For Rizal to die, both for Spain and our country, seems to be contradictory. It is not. Rizal simply tried to reconcile the two. He had the interests of Spain and our country in writing those two novels that exposed Spanish abuses in our country. The Spaniards saw that as treason to the way they ruled our country and for which they executed Rizal by firing squad. The Spaniards were blinded by their arrogance and ignorance to see Rizal's purpose in exposing their abuses through his novels."

"What was Rizal's purpose in writing them?"

"He wanted Spain to change the way it treated us, for us to be treated justly. Rizal tried to bring to Spain's attention, the truth essential to an effective foreign rule."

"Which is?"

"The best way to keep the loyalty of foreign subjects is by treating them well. Rizal wanted Spain to keep us, by treating us well."

Paulo shook his head in regret. He said, "What a powerful combination it would have been, had Rizal and Bonifacio worked together. Did Bonifacio try to win Rizal over to the revolution?"

"Yes. Rizal was exiled in Dapitan by the Spaniards when Bonifacio sent there, Doctor Pio Valenzuela, a member of the Katipunan Supreme Council, with an offer for him to escape from Dapitan and lead the revolution, we were planning then. Rizal rejected it. He recommended instead, Antonio Luna, the finest military man in our ranks, for the fighting inherent in a revolution."

"Why did Rizal reject the offer, Bonifacio made for him to lead the revolution?"

Lukas replied with a sour smile, "Rizal called it premature."

"It looks to me, like a flimsy excuse."

"It is. Rizal ignored the fact that we have endured, far too long, for more than three hundred years, the oppressive Spanish rule over us.

"Bonifacio made one more try. Rizal was aboard a ship docked in Manila, on his way to Cuba to serve as a doctor there in exchange for his release from exile in Dapitan. Bonifacio, Emilio Jacinto and Guillermo Masangkay went to the pier, disguised as Filipino sailors, to take Rizal out of the ship. Jacinto was able to talk to Rizal who rejected their rescue offer. Rizal was later arrested, jailed, brought to trial, where he was deemed guilty of treason and executed by the Spaniards.

"Had Rizal agreed to Bonifacio's rescue offer, he would still be alive today and leading the fight for our country's freedom."

"But why was Rizal so against the revolution?"

"The mere idea of a revolution may have horrified Rizal, not only for the violence, destruction and death it will bring about, it will also put to an end, the kind of life he loved and enjoyed so much under Spain. Rizal enjoyed the best time in his life in Spain and in the rest of Europe."

Paulo nodded, impressed by his uncle's insight, radical ideas and far-ranging vision and he said, "It is just too bad for Rizal, Bonifacio and our country that they never worked and fought together."

Lukas shook his head and said, "Those are problems and concerns, a mere town mayor like me cannot address, let alone, solve. I don't have what ultimately is the most important factor—the power to direct the course of events here and in the rest of our country."

"Who holds that?"

"You are in Aguinaldo's staff, you should know that. Anything Aguinaldo does in Cavite will affect us here in Masakao."

"What are you trying to tell me, uncle?"

"The fate of our town depends ultimately on what will happen to the rest of our country. We cannot even say our country is now ours. The Spaniards are still around even if they are now confined in Intramuros while the Americans are preparing to take over our country."

"But are they not helping us, fight the Spaniards? They even provided us with the arms to fight the Spaniards."

As a member of Aguinaldo's staff, Paulo followed Aguinaldo's thinking that the Americans were benefactors helping them rid the Philippines of the Spaniards.

"They are helping us," Lukas said, "only because it is convenient for them to do so and a fine thing they are doing of letting us do the fighting for them."

"What made you say the Americans are planning to take over our country?"

"I said that because that is what they will do."

Paulo pressed his lips in reflection of his uncle's analysis. If it is correct, after disposing of one enemy, they will have to fight another enemy, this one posing as a friend and benefactor. His uncle could be right, though. He saw a sign of a very serious rift with the Americans when Commodore Dewey, after expressing privately American support of the Philippine Revolution, stayed away when Aguinaldo proclaimed the Philippine independence in Kawit. It was an unspoken sign the Americans did not support an independent Philippines. Dewey's blockade of Manila was a very important sign that the Americans have designs on the Philippines.

"What is Aguinaldo doing now?" Lukas asked Paulo in changing the subject of their conversation.

"Nothing much since we started chasing the Spaniards, out of the countryside. We have no sooner come to a town when Spanish opposition would melt away."

"That is what also happened, here in Masakao."

"How did you take over the control of our town?"

Lukas smiled and said, "When I learned that Aguinaldo is back, I knew it meant only one thing—the resumption of the revolution. It was not hard to do that here. Our townsfolk did not have to be persuaded to take up arms again. I gathered as many men as I could. We went to Alkayag and took the arms, we kept there. Mayor Echeverria and Captain Laguerte fled when they learned, we were coming. The town was ours. Can you imagine that, the town's brass band met us! I was not surprised the Spaniards gave up our town so easily. They are so demoralized now."

"It makes it easier for us to take Intramuros. Our troops are now surrounding it."

"Taking Intramuros is vital to our cause. We conquer and occupy it and we remove the symbol of Spanish rule over us. It is vital for the Spaniards to keep it as it is vital for us to get it. Considering its importance to the Spaniards and to us, why does not Aguinaldo attack it now?"

"The wall around Intramuros may have discouraged Aguinaldo from attacking it. It cannot be scaled as what Miguel and I did at the wall in the town fort. It is more than double the height and the width of the town fort wall. It can be breached by cannon fire, but we have no artillery."

"That is what the British did when they successfully breached the wall in Intramuros. But what we lack in resources, we can make up for with the use of our imagination. We can use ladders in scaling that wall. That seems to have escaped the attention of Aguinaldo and his staff,"

"What really kept Aguinaldo from attacking Intramuros was Dewey's advice for him to wait for the American troops with whom we can then attack Intramuros."

"I simply cannot understand how Aguinaldo can be so dumb and ignorant! Our troops can take Intramuros without American help. Moreover, in a joint action with us, the Americans will not take a secondary, but the leading role. We will unfortunately end up there in Intramuros as mere spectators, not as its conquerors."

"Aguinaldo has already agreed on a joint action with the Americans. Is he too trusting of the Americans?"

"He is not only too trusting of the Americans he is also too submissive to them. He should not have made that agreement with Dewey. That is a very bad judgment, like that he made in the case of Bonifacio. His execution, on Aguinaldo's order, led to division in our ranks and to the loss of the living symbol in our revolution.

"I fear what is coming. After fighting the Spaniards, we will next find ourselves, fighting the Americans. This time, though, we will not be fighting a colonial power in decline, but a young, vigorous country moving its arms across the sea. America is now doing that in Cuba and will next do that, here in our country."

Paulo shook his head at the possibility, his uncle mentioned of another conflict. He had embraced Aguinaldo's thinking that the Americans were simply helping them in getting rid of the Spaniards.

"But enough of this dreary talk about war and politics," Lukas said as he led Paulo out of the mayor's office.

He said, as they were descending the stairs, "Will you have dinner with me, at home?"

"I have to see someone," Paulo replied, "but I will be home, later tonight."

He left Lukas at the foot of the stairs where men were waiting to talk to him.

Paulo was low spirit when he came to see Teresa. He would be glad to see her again, but he was not sure, how she would greet him. They quarreled, the last time they saw each other.

He was approaching her house when he saw her, alone in the yard.

She was seated on a low wooden stool, trimming a potted plant of its dead branches and leaves. He opened the gate and went in.

Whatever worries he had about her frigid welcome were removed by the smile in her face when she saw him, coming. She rushed to him and held herself, tight to him.

He said, as he was brushing her hair, "Am I forgiven?"

"No, you are not," she replied, holding on more tightly to him. "I will never forgive you for leaving me without even saying good-bye."

He smiled and was about to kiss her, but held himself in check when he saw a woman, the neighborhood gossiper, had halted on the road and was watching them.

He will not let the woman see them in an embrace and be the talk in their neighborhood. He released Teresa from his embrace and made it appear as if they were engaged in a conversation. He asked her about Esperanza and their parents.

"Father and mother are at home," she replied, "Esperanza is in our store with Nieves."

The neighborhood gossiper left, but then another woman was coming on the road. The best thing to do, he decided then, was to go away from there. He took Teresa's hand and led her inside the orchard where they soon gave in to what they felt deeply to each other.

They returned after a while to the yard, happy and satisfied with each other.

He watched her as she resumed working on her potted plant.

"Now that you are back here," she said to him, "are you going to help your uncle, run our town?"

"I wish I can do that."

"Why can you not do that?"

"I came here with a contingent of troops to liberate our town. It is now ours, so I don't have to stay here. I am needed elsewhere."

"So, you are needed elsewhere, but not here."

"It is not only that."

"It is, and you came here only to use me in enjoying yourself."

"You know that is not true."

He watched her, his jaw dropped from shock, when she then swept away the potted plant and returned, frowning, to the house, leaving him, scratching his head in bewilderment.

Chapter Seventeen

Captain Bill Shay and Dick McCall were on the deck of a troopship as they were watching, wide-eyed in amazement, the squat, frail-looking nipa huts holding fast against a storm lashing the rice fields around the new American naval base in Sangley Point in Cavite.

They watched, even more amazed, two barefooted men walking on in the rice fields, seemingly unconcerned about the storm lashing them.

The deckhands were also ignoring the storm as they continued to take down to the naval base, supplies and war materiel from their troopship.

Dick said, "I never saw a storm like that in San Francisco."

"Neither have I in Iowa."

Their troopship was among the first American ships to dock in Sangley Point, following the American victory in the naval battle with the Spanish fleet in Manila Bay.

"Do you expect a stiff fight with the Spaniards in a land war with them?" Dick asked Bill.

"No. Their army will be as mismatched to our army, as their navy was to our navy."

The storm passed. The soldiers, rifles in their hands and duffel bags on their shoulders, started moving out of the troopship.

"Are you not going down?" Bill asked Dick.

"I will stay here for a while."

Bill picked up his duffel bag and walked down on the ship's gangplank.

A band there then played up, *The Star-Spangled Banner..*

Dick's head swelled with pride. This land, he is certain, will soon be the farthest frontier of the United States of America.

A sufficient number of American troops had arrived in Cavite by the first week in August, 1898 for the United States to start a ground war against Spain.

The first aim of the American ground forces was the conquest of Intramuros, the political heart of the Spanish colony and to accomplish that without the unnecessary loss of life and damage to property. It was a mission they kept from Aguinaldo.

They could not attack it, though, for by then, except for the west side in Manila Bay and the north side in Pasig River, Aguinaldo had it completely surrounded by his troops.

The Americans, if they were to attack Intramuros, needed a corridor through the Filipino lines. To get it, General Francis Greene, the commander of the American frontline troops, worked on General Mariano Noriel, who commanded the Filipino line from Singalong to Malate, at the shoreline of Manila. Noriel faced Fort San Antonio Abad, the advance post of Intramuros. Greene told Noriel, he will need artillery, which Noriel did not have, if he were to take Fort San Antonio Abad and after that, Intramuros itself. Greene then told Noriel, he will give him five artillery batteries sitting idly in Cavite, if Noriel will allow the Americans to occupy the left flank of his line at the shoreline in Manila.

Noriel replied, he had to consult first with Aguinaldo. Aguinaldo wanted a written request. The Americans will not do that, for that will then mean, they were recognizing the Filipinos as their ally and that was not in their minds.

Greene promised to submit to Aguinaldo, a formal written request as soon as the Filipinos have given the Americans, the corridor they needed for their attack on Intramuros. Aguinaldo incredibly agreed to that.

Greene, not surprisingly, did not make the written request, once his troops had occupied Noriel's left flank at the shoreline in Manila.

The Americans now have the corridor through which they could attack Fort San Antonio Abad and, after that, Intramuros itself.

The Spaniards in Intramuros knew they were in a hopeless situation. They were hemmed in on all sides—in the east by the Filipino troops, in the south by Filipino and American troops, in the north by the Pasig River and in the west by the American warships in Manila Bay.

Commodore Dewey and General Wesley Merritt, the commander of the American ground forces, asked Fermin Jaudenes, the new Spanish governor-general, to surrender Intramuros.

The only sane course of action was for the Spaniards to surrender to the Americans. Jaudenes would not do that, though, out of their Spanish pride.

That, to Jaudenes, was also preferable to fighting, much less to surrendering to the Filipinos who were full of vengeance toward the Spaniards.

Jaudenes, in response to Dewey and Merritt, sent secretly an emissary to them with the message that the Spaniards will surrender

Intramuros only after they had put up, a semblance of a fight with the Americans. It will then show to the world, the Spaniards did not give up Intramuros without a fight. It will then preserve Spanish honor even if it will be done in a superficial manner. The Americans agreed to Jaudenes' proposal.

Jaudenes, a few hours before the sham battle, inspected together with General Achutegui, who was newly promoted to that rank, the Spanish defensive position in Intramuros.

Chemari accompanied them in their inspection of his troops and field guns in his sector at the Rampart of San Gabriel.

They faced, across a wide open ground, the Filipino rebel troops massed in the former Chinese quarter in Parian. Jaudenes nodded, satisfied with their troops' state of readiness there.

He next went with Chemari and General Achutegui to Chemari's command post in the main building of the College of Saint John of Lateran.

It stood along Muralla Street, at the back of the Rampart of San Gabriel. It has a broad view, not only of Parian, but also of the districts of Binondo, Santa Cruz and Quiapo, at the north side of Pasig River.

Jaudenes watched, concerned, the Filipino rebel troops in Parian.

"Young man," he said to Chemari, "under your command is the most important sector in our defense of Intramuros. You must prevent the Indios from getting over the wall. They must be kept out, at all cost."

"I have prepared for that, sir, even for a long siege."

"There will be no siege. The battle will be very short."

Chemari glanced at his father for an explanation, but General Achutegui deferred to his superior and he kept quiet.

Jaudenes then said to Chemari, "Keep our strategy to your self. I don't want to demoralize our troops and sow panic among our people. We will not stand for a long siege. It will only prolong the agony and cause our people unnecessary hardship. Our strategy is to keep the Indio rebels away while we will allow the American troops, entry into Intramuros. We will formally surrender to the Americans, once their troops are here in Intramuros."

Chemari looked in disbelief at Jaudenes. They were going to just fake a fight, not engage in a real battle with the Americans!

General Achutegui pressed his finger to his lips in a sign for Chemari to keep quiet, but something inside him had snapped.

"So," he said, "we will just fake a fight with the Americans."

"Look at it, anyway, you want to," Jaudenes said sharply to Chemari, "but that is the only thing, we can now do and it is not for you to question your superior's orders. Just follow them!"

"I will, sir, as I always do," Chemari replied sarcastically.

Jaudenes left with General Achutegui, upset by Chemari's disrespectful remarks.

Chemari regretted immediately what he said to Jaudenes. But for his father's presence there and his fine military record, the governor-general could have given him a tongue-lashing or worse, Jaudenes could have him relieved of his command, right then and there. But he could not accept this sham battle that his superiors had planned to stage with the Americans. The rest of the Spanish Army may fake a fight, but he will fight a real battle. He will see to it the Indio rebels will never get over his sector of the wall.

He looked out from the window at Pasig River. Malacanang Palace was at a bend in the river, not far from there. It was not too long ago when he and Marissa danced the night away in the palace. He then went home, drunk and happy. He sighed. That was a good time, now gone, just as everything else in Intramuros will soon be gone.

An increase in the rebel troops' activity in Parian interrupted him in his thoughts. They seemed poised to attack. He swept with his field glass, the Filipino troops there, not knowing that someone known to him was among those leading them. He was fighting, once again, his friend and former classmate, Paulo Palanas. He returned to the Rampart of San Gabriel to supervise the artillery shelling, once the rebels had started to attack Intramuros.

General Merritt gave the order to attack Intramuros, the same day he received Jaudenes' message about the sham battle. It began with Dewey's warships in Manila Bay and Greene's field guns, laying an artillery and naval gun barrage at Fort San Antonio Abad and Intramuros. The booming sounds and the smoke that rose in the sky from the explosions on the ground were frightening to see. A sharp observer would have noticed, though, that the artillery and naval gun shells were exploding outside, not inside Intramuros.

Dick McCall watched with the leading American infantry company, their artillery shelling at Fort San Antonio Abad. The Spaniards responded with their own artillery barrage. Clumps of earth shot up into the air from an artillery shell that exploded on the ground, a mere fifty yards or so from where he was standing.

He dived into the ground, but stood up, embarrassed, when he saw a soldier nearby, standing pat to the explosion near them. The soldier showed his contempt for the Spanish artillery by spitting on the grass.

Dick was impressed. He took out his pen and notebook from his shirt pocket and began to write.

"Are you a newspaper guy?" the soldier asked Dick.

"Yes, I am."

"Perfect. You can report to your readers how Sergeant Robert Whittaker of Mayfield, Ohio led the charge on Fort San Antonio Abad and Intramuros."

Dick went on writing. What the soldier told him will make for a dramatic human-interest side story to the article he is writing about the Americans' attack on Intramuros.

He watched, the moment the shelling had ceased, the American troops now moving toward Fort San Antonio Abad. It fell in just a short while of fighting. The Americans then began to move toward Intramuros.

Paulo watched the Americans, who now seemed poised to attack Intramuros. He arrived in Parian only the other day and took command of a battalion of troops there. He was facing, across the wide open ground in Parian, the wall of Intramuros and behind it, his alma mater, the College of Saint John of Lateran. The few residents in Parian had anticipated the coming battle there and they quickly evacuated it.

He knew the Spaniards hated night fighting and he was planning to attack tonight yet that sector in Intramuros. He changed his mind when he saw the Americans, south of him, had started to move toward Intramuros.

"We must not let them beat us to Intramuros," he said to his subordinate officers.

"But are we not," a lieutenant said, "planning to attack tonight, under the cover of darkness?"

"It will be suicidal for us to attack now," a captain said, "when we have to cross that wide open ground and ford the moat there as well before we can even get to the wall there."

"We will have to take that risk," Paulo said. "The Americans have started to move toward Intramuros. We must do the same. If we delay, there will be nothing left for us to get there."

He shouted for his troops to start their attack. The lead soldiers then rushed toward the Rampart of San Gabriel. They have not gone far when they were stopped by heavy artillery fire. To go on with the attack will risk the lives of so many of his troops, he reluctantly ordered them to pull back. He must find another way of attacking that sector in Intramuros.

A plan came to his mind. He was in a short while discussing it with the commander of the battalion at his right flank which held the ground along Pasig River. He will create a diversion with another attack on the Rampart of San Gabriel while, north of his troops, the other battalion will attack the Spaniards, holed up at the Gate of Isabel II, near Pasig River.

He was returning to his command post when the Spaniards resumed firing their field guns. An explosion on the ground sent a stone ricocheting and grazing his left temple. A soldier stopped the flow of blood with a bandage wound around his forehead. The treatment over, he glanced at the other battalion and was upset to see that it had started the attack, too early. It allowed the Spaniards to concentrate their artillery fire on that battalion which then prevented it from advancing toward the Gate of Isabel II.

He looked on, puzzled by the heavy concentration of enemy artillery fire in his sector. There was something odd about it. He scanned with his field glass, the district of Ermita, south of Intramuros and was dismayed to see the American troops there, now advancing rapidly in a front, some three hundred paces wide, toward Puerta Real and the Rampart of San Andres at the south wall of Intramuros. He saw there, no Spanish resistance, at all.

A sour smile broke out of his face as he then realized the Spaniards were using in Intramuros, the same tactic, he and his uncle had used against Chemari and Zatayde in Masakao. The Spaniards were keeping them at bay while allowing the Americans to enter Intramuros.

He saw, after a while, the American flag raised at the guard tower in the Rampart of San Andres. The Americans were now, right inside Intramuros.

Dick McCall paused to catch his breath after all the running he had done in catching up with the American troops as they were advancing from Malate to Intramuros. He was right with them, now that they were spreading out in the narrow streets in Intramuros.

Why, he asked himself, was there no sign of damage in Intramuros after all the artillery shelling there? It remained intact.

His attention was next turned to a Spanish general as he was handing his sword to an American colonel in a ceremonial surrender of Intramuros. The American colonel accepted the sword and returned the salute by the Spanish general. Then, following the general's command, the Spanish troops behind him, laid down their arms. They were then escorted by American soldiers for confinement in Fort Santiago.

The surrender by the Spanish troops came as a big surprise to Dick. He had expected a fierce fight there between the American and the Spanish troops. His heart that had beaten fast in his excitement had slowed down, now that he realized there had been no fighting that took place there.

He followed the colonel and his contingent, moving on in Muralla Street. A detachment of Spanish troops was waiting on the ground between the main building of Lateran and the Rampart of San Gabriel for another ceremonial surrender there.

He was near enough to see the Spanish commander, his troops behind him, facing stiffly the American colonel.

The Spanish commander, he noticed, was very young like him. He showed in his face, anguish almost like physical pain, at the ceremonial act of surrender to the Americans.

Chemari Achutegui, the Spanish commander, went through with it, bitter at the thought of how the Spanish Army had faked its last battle in the colony. That he and his troops fought well and had kept out of the wall, the Filipino rebels, gave him very little satisfaction.

It pained him to think that the Americans might see him as one of those who fought the sham battle.

He watched, one of them, apparently a journalist, who was writing something on a note pad. He will be reporting to the world, how they faked the battle with the Americans. He became even more anguished.

A captain, at the colonel's command, stepped forward. Chemari gave his sword to the captain and then, escorted by the Americans, he moved on with his troops for confinement in Fort Santiago.

Dick saw, as he was walking on, some Spanish residents watching in a street corner there, the American troops passing by. The glum look in their faces and the shuttered windows in the homes there showed the Spaniards trying to shut out the presence there of the American soldiers. There was no doubt about it, though, that they, the Americans, now owned Intramuros.

Spain and the United States, in an ironic twist of fate, not known to the combatants, had agreed in the treaty in Paris on a cease-fire, the day before the sham battle in Intramuros. The news never got to Manila on time.

Commodore Dewey had, a few days earlier, ordered the submarine cable linking Manila to Hong Kong, to be cut.

The Philippines was then isolated from the rest of the world. Only when the submarine cable was connected again did those in Intramuros learn about the cease-fire agreement.

The Americans, in accordance with the cease-fire agreement, should pull out their forces from Intramuros and return to their pre-battle position near Fort San Antonio Abad in Malate.

The Americans went instead by the convenient principle that possession is nine-tenth of the law and they stayed in Intramuros.

They allowed the Spanish residents to leave Intramuros and most of them, followed that. They besieged the shipping companies for passage in the ships that will dock in Manila on their way to Spain and the rest of Europe.

Marissa and her father, Isidoro, booked their family and the Achuteguis as well for passage in a British steamship headed for Spain and the rest of Europe when they learned that Chemari, General Achutegui and all the Spanish soldiers will soon be released from Fort Santiago

Their ship was expected within a week in the port in Pasig River. With their money and their connections, they got posh berths on the port side of the ship. Marissa also sold their house to a British realty company.

"We are leaving; we are going to Spain," Marissa said to Chemari, the moment he arrived home.

He looked at her and said nothing. He did not argue against it, for there was nothing else that he could do.

She took the initiative to everything in the next few days prior to their departure for Spain while Chemari simply watched or mumbled his assent or grumbled his objection to whatever Marissa was saying or doing there.

He stayed for hours, seated in an armchair, near the window in the living room, staring at the street below and the house across the street or in burying his nose on a book or a magazine. He would rise from the armchair only at mealtime, when he had to go to the bathroom or when it was time for him to go to bed.

She asked Chemari, one time she was sorting out some clothes scattered on the floor, "Which of these should we take with us to Spain?"

"You can decide on that as you have decided on everything else in this house."

She glanced sadly at Chemari and put the clothes in a wicker basket. Then she called their maid and pulled down with her, the curtains in the room and replaced them with new, clean ones. They were putting everything in order in the house. The American journalist who rented their house from the British realty company will be glad to see it, clean and tidy.

They were set to leave, a few days later. Chemari looked on from his armchair when Marissa called to the living room, their maid and their manservant who also served as their carriage driver.

"You have been good to us," she said to them. "Thank you for your great service to us."

The maid broke down in tears while the manservant looked down sadly at the floor.

"I want to see, no more of that," Marissa said to them.

She then took out from her handbag, two leather purses containing silver coins and gave one, to each of them.

"They are," she said to them, "tokens of our appreciation for your great service to us. You may also be interested to know about the American journalist who leased our house from the British realty company. His name is Dick McCall. He might need your services, so stay around. He will come in a day or two."

They were, a few minutes later, inside their carriage bound for the port in Pasig River. Chemari and Marissa were seated, side by side, while their child was seated on the maid's lap. Chemari kept his eyes to the street and the houses they were passing by, the last time he was seeing Intramuros.

He kept to himself and not a word passed between him and Marissa.

The only sound in the passenger compartment was of the horse's hoofbeat and of the carriage wheels running on the cobblestone street. It joined a stream of carriages making their way through the crowd that filled the port. They got off where the British steamship was docked.

The sky was cloudy and it was cool in the port. Marissa followed Chemari who led their way through the crowd, their child in his arms. The servants followed with their luggage. The crowd in the port was noisy.

"Don't forget to write," a woman passenger said from the deck of the ship. "And look after my house. I may be back, next year."

The crowd cheered the woman for her optimism.

Chemari and Marissa went up on the gangplank with their child while their servants gave their luggage to the waiting porters. The ship's purser checked their names and took their tickets.

They waved in good-bye at their servants and proceeded with a steward to their cabin with the porters, carrying their luggage, following behind them. Their cabin was right beside the cabin of Marissa's parents and her brother Alfonso who, they saw through the open door, were putting their things inside the cabin closet.

Isidoro Iglesias joined them later on in their cabin.

He said to them, ""Do you like it? We are on the port or the better side of the ship. It will not face the warm morning sun, on its way to Spain."

It was cool inside the cabin. Chemari, after putting their clothes inside the cabin closet, had nothing else to do there and with Marissa and their child settled there, he left them to check on his parents.

General Achutegui and Dona Concha were in their cabin, putting inside the cabin closet, their clothes laid on the bed when Chemari came in. He stayed there only for a short while. Then he went to the upper deck.

The ship blew its horn. It was about to leave the port. Marissa, her child in her arms, her parents and her brother and Chemari's parents joined Chemari in the upper deck for one last look at Manila.

He looked around sadly, his elbows on the deck railing, at Binondo and Escolta, the Puente de Espana Bridge, the belfries in the Manila Cathedral, Santo Domingo Church and San Agustin Church, the Lateran, the Palacio del Gobernador, Fort Santiago and the homes in Intramuros. He will never see them again. He had lost a dear part in his life.

The ship moved out slowly toward Manila Bay.

The ship's passengers and the crowd at the port waved in good-bye at each other. Some of them cupped their hands and shouted in good-bye at the crowd. Some of the women passengers took out their handkerchiefs and wiped with them, the tears in their eyes.

The ship moved on, away from Pasig River, toward Manila Bay.

It was late afternoon, the sun now down in the western horizon, in the mountain peaks in Bataan. As the ship plowed on, the port, the churches, the wall in Intramuros, the homes there, everything about Manila was receding in the distance until it was just an outline in the eastern horizon.

Chemari stayed in the deck while everybody else, including his family, returned to their cabins.

Marissa came back, his jacket in her hand.

"You might catch cold," she said as she draped it on his shoulders.

He nodded in appreciation of her caring gesture, but kept his eyes to the bay.

"I can hardly wait for us to be in Spain," she said to him. "You will love it. It is a beautiful country. A great future is waiting for us there."

He said nothing, his eyes fixed to the bay.

"It is getting cold here," she said as she then touched his arm. "Let us go back to our cabin."

"Go ahead. I will follow, later on."

She walked away.

He shook his head at how far apart, they were from each other.

He was sad and lonely now that he was all alone there. The ship was taking him to Spain. It made no difference to him if he is being taken instead to France, Italy or in some other European country. His life had lost its goal and purpose regardless of what Marissa had said to him about the great life waiting for them in Spain.

Mayor Echeverria was, unknown to him, in the lower deck. He saw Chemari as he was going up to the upper deck.

"So, you are, like the rest of us, also going to Spain," he said to Chemari. "It is gone, just like that. You know, things might have turned out differently for us and we might not be leaving today had we done things differently in this colony.

"Had we been just and humane to the Indios, had we given them the simple reforms they asked for instead of jailing, torturing and killing many of them, as what we did to Rizal and the three reformist priests, this revolution may not have happened, at all. Instead of fighting us, they might have then fought the Americans, side by side with us. We might have then defeated the Americans."

Chemari said nothing. Echeverria took it as a hint that he wanted to be left alone. He walked away, but then he turned back.

"Come now, enough of that brooding," he said to Chemari. "Let us have some cheering up. They must have a bar in this ship. We'll have a few drinks there."

Chemari stood up. They left the deck as the ship was moving on in Manila Bay, now dark and gloomy, early in the night.

Chapter Eighteen

Filipino and American troops watched each other in the next few weeks. The Americans now occupied, aside from Intramuros and Fort San Antonio Abad, other areas in Manila, the Filipinos had abandoned as indefensible. Most of the city remained in their hands.

America's intentions were becoming clear with the arrival there of more American troops. They were now disembarking, not only in their naval base in Sangely Point, but also right there at the port in Pasig River.

The war with Spain in the Philippines was over and there was no need for more American troops there unless the Americans were anticipating another war, this time against the Filipinos. Faced with this possibility, the Filipinos built up their forces with whatever resources they had.

Prominent Americans like the politician William Jennings Bryan, the industrialist Andrew Carnegie and the writer Mark Twain were against the annexation by the United States of the Philippines.

Their objection was put to rest when President William McKinley issued on December 21, 1898 a proclamation of "benevolent assimilation, substituting the mild sway of justice and right for arbitrary rule for the greatest good of the governed. As a result of the victories of American arms, the future control, disposition and government of the Philippine Islands are ceded to the United States. It will be the duty of the commander of the forces of occupation to announce and proclaim in the most public manner that we come, not as invaders or conquerors, but as friends to protect the natives in their homes, in their employments, and in their personal and religious rights."

President McKinley also expressed America's intentions toward the Philippines:

"1. We cannot give them back to Spain—that would be cowardly and dishonorable;

"2. We could not turn them over to France or Germany—our commercial rivals in the Orient—that would be discreditable.

"3. We could not leave them to themselves—they were unfit for self-government, and they would soon have anarchy and misrule over there worse than Spain's was.

"4. There was nothing left for us to do but to take them all and to educate the Filipinos, and uplift and civilize and Christianize them, and by God's grace do the very best for them, as our fellowmen for whom Christ also died."

McKinley was one hundred percent correct in the first two points, and partly correct in the third and fourth points.

The Filipinos had by then shown their capacity for self-rule with the Philippine Republic they established on January 23, 1899. The Philippines, on the fourth point raised by McKinley, was like a Catholic convent in more than three centuries it was under the Spanish rule.

McKinley's intentions toward the Philippines were put in concrete and specific terms by Secretary of War Elihu Root. In his instructions to William Howard Taft, the head of the Second Philippine Commission before he was elected President of the United States, Root defined America's colonial policy toward the Philippines:

"In all forms of government and administrative provisions which they are authorized to prescribe, the Commission should bear in mind that the government which they are establishing is designed not for our satisfaction or for the expression of our theoretical views, but for the happiness, peace and prosperity of the people of the Philippine Islands, and the measures adopted should be made to conform to their customs, their habits, and even their prejudices to the fullest extent possible consistent with the establishment of the indispensable requisites of a just and effective government."

With Secretary Root's instructions as the basis of its colonial policy, American administration of the Philippine Islands was so magnanimous and so unlike the oppressive and exploitative rule by Spain.

President McKinley also had the map of the Philippines superimposed on the map of the United States. It will stay there, he said, as long as he is the President of the United States.

The Philippines actually remained an American colony far longer than that, in fact, for nearly half a century.

Now that most of the country was in their hands, Aguinaldo, on the advice of his political strategist, Apolinario Mabini, presented the world with a de facto Philippine Republic. He called for a constitutional convention in Malolos, the capital of the province of Bulacan, where delegates representing the provinces worked on the Philippine Constitution and proclaimed the Philippine Republic with Aguinaldo as the President.

Paulo visited his uncle, the day before Aguinaldo's inauguration as President of the Philippine Republic on January 23, 1899.

The harvest was over and with the planting season still half a year away, the rice fields were left baking in the sun.

He came on horseback and took the road between the rice fields.

It was a warm day, but he was pleased and satisfied to see the townsfolk undeterred by the heat and the humidity from working in the open.

He saw in the front yards, in clusters of huts and houses, most of them newly built from the destruction wrought there by Zatayde, men and women engaged in various tasks.

They were tending their vegetable plots and their poultry, mending fences or at work on some handicraft. He saw children playing in the yards in their homes there while the older ones were fishing in the river. The town was preoccupied with work and play.

He went to the municipal hall where he was told his uncle was in the town's primary school. He left his horse in their house and walked toward the school.

Lukas was with some men and women in the school grounds. He was helping out in making palm shingles, used for the roofs and the walls of nipa huts and wooden houses. Finished palm shingles laid in a row on the ground were drying in the sun.

"How are you, uncle?" Paulo said as he was approaching Lukas.

The men and the women looked on approvingly as he then took his uncle's outstretched arm and in a sign of respect for an elder, touched the back of his uncle's hand to his forehead. Lukas then led Paulo to a bamboo bench in the shade of a mango tree there.

Paulo watched for a while, the workers who were grouped in a circle, making palm shingles. They were seated on low wooden stools or on the grass.

The men were stripping the palm fronds with their knives while the women were folding the strips of palm fronds over bamboo sticks and stitching them together with bamboo needles into individual palm shingles. It was routine, even dull work, they were doing with zest.

"I see you are busy at work, as usual," he said to his uncle.

"As you might expect, one is hardly finished with a task when another one is waiting to be done."

Lukas looked on at Paulo. He was in a gray military uniform with boots on his feet and an officer's cap on his head.

"You look fine in that outfit," he said to Paulo.

Paulo smiled, pleased. His eyes lingered on the newly sewn insignia of a colonel on the shoulder board in his uniform.

He was back in Aguinaldo's staff. He has been doing errand work for Aguinaldo and the other leaders who had gathered in Malolos for the constitutional convention and the inaugural rites. The town was some fifteen miles southwest of Masakao.

"I have never seen our townmates enjoying so much, what they are doing here," he said to Lukas.

"They are just small tasks, just small tasks."

"But I have never seen them work with so much zest and on a hot day like this. The rest of the town, I passed by a while ago, has never been so busy at work. I can only guess who brought all of that about," he said, smiling suggestively at Lukas.

"All I did was to tell them that with the Spaniards now gone, what they gain from their work is now entirely theirs. Can you think of a better incentive than that? That has made them work, as they never did before."

"And they did that on your leadership and encouragement."

"I'm only doing my job, like what our friends here are doing theirs. They maybe small tasks, but they are the building blocks of our nation we were not allowed to develop by Spanish intervention and forced rule, not until the idea of freedom that lay dormant for centuries was stirred awake by Rizal's propaganda movement and fought for in the revolution, led by Bonifacio. Is there anything related to all of that which you came to see me about?"

"I bring you, great news. Aguinaldo will be inaugurated tomorrow in Malolos as the president of our republic."

The men and the women, listening all the while to them, glanced at each other at this vague, but apparently important subject.

An old man laid aside, a palm frond in his hand, and said, "Our own republic? What does it mean for us?"

Paulo knitted his brow at the old man's question he felt he should answer as simply as he could.

"It means we are now on our own," he said. "We now have a basic body of laws and a government that will put into effect the freedom we fought for in our revolution."

The man seemed not to understand what Paulo said to him. He was about to speak, but Paulo had turned to Lukas and said, "You must come, uncle, to represent our town."

"Of course, I will come. I have been waiting for an occasion like this when I can wear my embroidered shirt that has long been gathering mold and dust in my clothes chest."

Paulo and the others laughed. Lukas was, beneath the serious expression in his face, a warm, friendly person with a lively sense of humor.

"This is a long time in coming," Lukas then said, smiling. "This is something, really something! We now have our own republic!"

The old man, mystified by what Lukas said, fixed his eyes on Lukas and asked him, "What do we need a republic for?"

"My nephew has answered that question, has he not? Anyway," Lukas said patiently to the old man, "We need a government representative of the people, for us to be a democratic independent nation. It is also our way of saying we are no longer under Spain or anyone else. We're now free."

"Does it mean the Americans, like the Spaniards, will now leave?" the old man asked Lukas.

"I certainly hope so."

"What, if they don't leave?" the old man asked Lukas.

"It could mean war with the Americans."

The men and the women looked, wide-eyed from shock, at Lukas.

"Let us hope it does not lead to that and it may not," Paulo said to them, "but for now, the important thing is the inauguration."

"We will be there," Lukas said. "We will leave very early tomorrow so we won't miss any of the festivities in Malolos."

"Very well, uncle. I have got to go," Paulo said as he stood up. "There is someone, I have got to see."

"You will have dinner at home, won't you?" Lukas said to Paulo. "Doctor Bihasa and Gayuman are coming over."

"I will be there," Paulo replied.

He felt like a returning town hero from the friendly greetings and admiring glances of the townsfolk, he met on the road, on his way to Teresa's house. They provided a pleasant distraction from the thought of Teresa's likely chilly reception when they will meet again. Things once again went badly between them, the last time he saw her. The image remained fixed in his mind of her, furiously sweeping away a potted plant in her angry reaction to what he said to her that he could not stay in Masakao.

He entered the yard in Teresa's house and saw, not her, but Esperanza. She was at the edge of the orchard, pulling away the ripe fruits in a guava tree there.

"Look, who is here? Do I know you, sir?" she said to him when she saw him coming.

He smiled in reply to her as he took the basket from her and helped her with her task.

"That is it," she said, once the basket was full of the guava fruit. "We have more than enough guavas to last us for a while."

They heard, as they were going up to the house, Julio, Agustina and Teresa talking about their old well which was drying up.

Esperanza took the basket from Paulo when they reached the balcony. She thanked him for his help as she proceeded to the dining room. Paulo entered the living room and said good afternoon to Julio, Agustina and Teresa. She did not, unlike her parents, return his greeting. She stood up instead and followed Esperanza to the dining room.

Paulo sighed sadly for having been snubbed by Teresa. He sat down on the large couch Agustina had offered him and asked, as a matter of courtesy, about Julio's health. Julio then spoke about the progress, he was making in overcoming his illness, what medicines he was taking and the light exercises he was doing in bringing the dead muscles in his feet, back to life.

Julio suddenly stopped talking, his attention, like Paulo and Agustina, turned to the dining room where Esperanza and Teresa were having an argument.

"What are you doing here?" Esperanza said to Teresa. "Why don't you attend to Paulo?"

"Let our parents do that."

"A fine way to treat him, the few times he comes to see you."

"I am only doing this, for the way he is treating me."

"So, how is he treating you?"

"Like a toy. He comes to see me only when he has nothing else to do."

"What do you want him to do then? Do you want him to just sit by your side at all hours of the day?"

"Yes."

"What you need then is a pet dog, not a man. Don't you see how he tries to see you every chance he has? And now that he is here, what did you do? You snubbed him! You walked away! You were rude and childish!"

Paulo caught Julio and Agustina, looking at each other. Now they know for certain that there was something going on between him and Teresa.   He saw no disapproval in their eyes. They may have seen as inevitable for one of their daughters to fall in love with him. He was that close to both Teresa and Esperanza. He was considered, a part of their family, so why not as their son-in-law? He smiled, pleased with the thought. He next heard the clatter of plates in the dining room and that pleased him even more. Esperanza and Teresa must be preparing an afternoon snack for him

.   "Now, go back there and bring this to Paulo," Esperanza said to Teresa. "Be nice to him. What are you waiting for? Go there now!"

He watched Teresa, pleased and amused, as she was coming out of the dining room, a tray of snacks in her hands.

What, he said to himself, a scolding by an older sister could do!

She laid the tray on the coffee table and sat down on the big couch, beside Paulo.

Had they been alone, the least he would have done then would be to hold her hand or maybe even hug her.

She picked up the cup of coffee and gave it to Paulo. He nodded and thanked her, but mindful of the conversation, he was having with Julio and Agustina, he drank his coffee with his eyes turned to them.

"We have a new government," he said to them, "now that work on our constitution is finished. Aguinaldo will be inaugurated tomorrow in Malolos as the president of our republic."

"Can you imagine that," Agustina exclaimed, "our own republic!"

"How I wish," Julio said, "I could go to Malolos and see that great event myself."

"You are not well enough to do that, Father," Teresa said, "but Paulo will witness it for us. So will, his uncle. Am I right?"

"If that is what you want me and my uncle to do, then that is exactly what we will do," he replied to Julio and Agustina's laughter.

Esperanza came in from the dining room and sat down on an arm of the big couch. She led, seated in this uninhibited, casual manner, the talk about Masakao, their orchard and other subjects with Teresa and Paulo spicing them up with humorous asides.

It was just like the old times when Julio and Agustina were then and now, the indulgent parents and Paulo, Teresa and Esperanza were like small children, uninhibited in their behavior.

It was getting dark when Paulo took his leave. The family asked him to stay for dinner, but he begged off from their invitation and said his uncle was expecting him home for dinner with Doctor Bihasa and Gayuman.

Teresa showed him out in the balcony where she threw herself in a tight embrace with him. He in turn gave her a long and passionate kiss on her lips. They parted this time, happy and satisfied with each other.

Lukas and Paulo arrived, morning of the following day in Malolos, overflowing with people.

They left their horse-drawn cab in the yard of the house where Paulo was billeted and walked toward the main street, cordoned off from vehicular traffic for the parade that will pass there.

Lukas smiled, happy and amazed, at how the town had turned out for the festivities. Swaying in the breeze were multicolored buntings, strung up above the street. Draped on the windowsills in the homes along the street were new Philippine flags with their field of red, white and blue colors and a yellow sun with nine rays representing the city of Manila and Bulacan, Laguna, Cavite, Batangas, Pampanga, Tarlac, Bataan and Nueva Ecija, the first city and provinces to rise up in the revolution against Spain. Providing a melodic counterpoint to the excited voices of the crowd that filled the street was marching music played by a brass band, passing by in the street.

They made their way through the festive crowd and entered a big tile-roofed house along the parade route. The house was full of people. Lazaro Garces, the homeowner, met them at the top of the stairs.

"I'm so glad, you came," Garces said smiling and shaking hands with Paulo and doing the same when he was introduced to Lukas.

"Did you come, all the way from Masakao?" Garces asked them.

"Yes, we did," Paulo replied.

"You must be hungry by now."

"We had a full breakfast."

"Take something, just the same, the parade will not start yet," Garces said as he then led them to the dining room.

Garces had a dining table full of food as expected of a rich town merchant like him. They ate there with Garces keeping them company.

"We have been very busy since the start of the constitutional convention," Garces said to Lukas, referring to his role of seeing, along with the other town leaders, to the needs of the delegates to the constitutional convention, members of Aguinaldo's Cabinet, the military and Aguinaldo himself. They had taken quarters in Malolos for a number of days now. Paulo had, as a member of Aguinaldo's staff, met with Garces and the other town leaders, befriending them in the process.

"I can imagine all the work you have been doing here, but it is worth the effort," Lukas said. "I have never seen such a happy, grand and meaningful event in my life."

"I agree," Garces said. "This is one event of a lifetime."

He talked on while they ate until they were finished with their meal. Garces then led them to the wide window in the living room overlooking the town's main street. The people there gave them and Garces room, for they appeared to be Garces' special guests from the personal attention, he was lavishing on them.

They were an admirable sight as they stood at the window. Paulo looked splendid in his uniform, a ceremonial sword on his side, and an officer's cap on his head. He was looking with his deep-set eyes at the festive crowd in the street below.

Lukas looked similarly distinguished in his embroidered shirt, his dignified bearing, accented by the lofty gaze he was taking with his keen, perceptive eyes of the festive crowd below them in the street.

Chairs were obtained for them. They sat down there and watched the crowd in the street.

"Five brass bands came from Bulacan alone," Garces said proudly. "We spared no effort in making this affair, something to remember."

Lukas felt a deep sense of satisfaction as he was watching the festivities, below them in the street. The people in the street were there, out of curiosity or a sense of pride. The role, he and Paulo had played in their revolution maybe small, but it helped in making this celebration possible. They had done well, but it was likely the high point of everything they had done and fought for. The rest could be downhill. Everything that will follow from their republic's inauguration was dark and uncertain. Miles away, south of them, the Americans were poised to strike against them.

One of them was in the crowd, looking around, but also making himself an object of curiosity.

Dick McCall stood out in the crowd, taller by a head, his brown hair in contrast to the people in the street with their black or white hair.

"What is that white man across the street doing there?" Garces asked Paulo.

"He is not an American soldier. They are not allowed to go beyond their lines. He is, more likely, a newspaperman. They are allowed to move around here."

"You mean to snoop around."

"Not really. Aguinaldo gave the order, on Mabini's advice, to allow them to go anywhere. That way, through their newspaper reports, the Americans and the rest of the world will know what is going on here."

"He can report to his readers and convince them that the Philippine Republic now exists."

"That is exactly the purpose."

Lukas listened, his chin rested on his palm, to the conversation between Paulo and Garces. He doubted if the newspaper reports on the festivities there could be of any help to their cause. They were proclaiming the Philippine Republic with the American army in control of Intramuros and parts of Manila, the American navy in control of Manila Bay and with the Philippines having been ceded by Spain to the United States. War between the new Philippine Republic and the United States was imminent. He kept those thoughts to himself so that he will not spoil the others' enjoyment of watching the festive crowd in the street below them.

They watched Dick who was now proceeding toward Barasoain Church, site of the inauguration ceremonies, until he was out of their sight.

The crowd's attention was then turned to the sound of marching music. The parade marshals urged the crowd with the pushing motion of their hands to move back, to give room for the parade participants due any moment now. The crowd moved back.

They cheered, moments later, and clapped their hands when a brass band playing marching music came by at the head of the parade. Right behind it was the honor guard with the blazing colors of the Philippine flag and the various military flags and banners. They came marching down in perfect step with the marching music.

Paulo stood up and saluted as the honor guard was passing by in the street. Then he sat down, a proud expression on his face as he then watched the troops by the hundreds, his fellow soldiers marching by to the beat of the marching music played by the brass band.

The members of Aguinaldo's Cabinet then came by, led by Apolinario Mabini, Aguinaldo's confidant, the Prime Minister of the Philippine Republic who was called, "The Brains of the Revolution."

Mabini was seated on a wheelchair as it was being pushed forward by an aide. A lawyer, he compensated for the loss of the use of his legs from an attack of polio with the use of his mind that was active, sharp and brilliant. Mabini guided Aguinaldo through the complexities of government and foreign affairs, subjects that were way above the head of Aguinaldo.

Lukas watched the Ilustrados, passing by in the street, frowning in profound dislike of that privileged class of people who were descended from Spanish officials and adventurers. They got along with the friar orders, royal grants to the huge tracts of land, including those in Masakao, that were taken away from the native Indio inhabitants by their Spanish rulers.

He looked on at the Ilustrados, his eyes narrowed in anger. They snubbed the revolution, considering it beneath them to join it because it was a plebeian uprising. They joined it when it was gaining ground, but then abandoned it when the Spaniards gained the upper hand. They brokered the truce and thus put themselves in a good light with both Aguinaldo and the Spaniards.

He was so upset at how they wormed their way to the vital position of delegates to the constitutional convention which drew up the constitution when Aguinaldo declared his intention of establishing the Philippine Republic.

He said, the tone of his voice, sharp with sarcasm, "They certainly know how to turn to where the wind is blowing."

"Who are you referring to?" Garces asked Lukas.

"I'm referring to those opportunists walking down there in the street."

"You don't like them?"

"I don't."

"Aguinaldo likes them, though or else, he would not have picked them as the delegates to the constitutional convention."

"Aguinaldo likes them and looks up to them because they have what he wants—wealth, a tall nose, a Spanish surname and a fair complexion."

"It is to their advantage that they team up with Aguinaldo," Paulo said.

"It will not last long," Lukas said. "They will abandon Aguinaldo when they see it is to their advantage for them to do that."

He remained frowning, his enjoyment of the parade spoiled by the presence there of the Ilustrados.

He turned his gaze to Aguinaldo, who was coming at the tail end of the parade.

Aguinaldo was seated, all by himself, in a grand open carriage pulled by a team of four magnificent white horses.

Lukas smiled sarcastically as he was looking on at Aguinaldo. He knew that when the Philippines was under Spain, only the governor-general, as the head of the civil government and the military, and the archbishop of Manila, as the head of the Catholic Church, went around in carriages pulled by teams of four white horses. So did Aguinaldo now, as the head of the Philippine Republic.

Aguinaldo acknowledged with a nod, a smile and a wave of his white-gloved hand, the cheers from the crowd in the street and by those watching from the windows in their homes at the side of the street.

Some men suddenly broke off from the crowd and blocked the carriage.

The parade marshals pushed them back until enough room had been made for Aguinaldo's carriage to move on.

Aguinaldo kept all the while on smiling and waving his white-gloved hand at that show of enthusiasm by the crowd.

Lukas, though, was frowning at the sight of Aguinaldo who was in tails and top hat. Here is their president, an Indio dressed like the Spanish nobility and he said, "He is yet to be inaugurated as our president and he is already aping our unlamented Spanish rulers in his mode of dressing."

"What would you rather have him wear then?" Garces asked Lukas.

"Something like this embroidered shirt, I'm wearing."

He looked on admiringly at his shirt that was not tucked at his waist and brushed with his palm the fine, delicate texture of his shirt.

They were not allowed, when the Philippines was under Spain, to tuck in their shirts. Lukas, in wearing his shirt, not tucked at the waist, was now making into a sign of honor what before was a sign of their servility to their Spanish masters.

"Aguinaldo," he said, "could have worn also, a gala military uniform to show the revolutionary character of our republic."

A man, another guest of Garces, was at the window, listening to the talk there. He said to Lukas, "You don't seem to approve of Aguinaldo. Why are you then attending his inauguration as our president?"

"I came here," Lukas replied, "to honor the office of the president of our republic, not the man occupying that office. If Bonifacio is alive today, as the founder of the Katipunan and the Father of the Philippine Revolution, he should be the one being inaugurated as our president, not Aguinaldo."

Lukas' real feelings toward Aguinaldo, long dormant in his heart and mind, had finally come out in the open. He could never forgive Aguinaldo for what he and his men did to Bonifacio, his brothers and his wife.

He looked on, frowning, at Aguinaldo who was now passing by in his carriage, below him in the street, as he moved on toward Barasoain Church.

What followed afterwards was one whole day of merrymaking, far greater than the town fiesta in Malolos. The center of activities by nightfall had shifted to the state banquet for the new president and other dignitaries. The rest of the town was merry with festivities. There was feasting in many homes, marching music in the streets and dancing in the town square.

Lukas and Paulo returned to Masakao, the following day.

Chapter Nineteen

The Filipinos and the Americans were, in less than two weeks, at war with each other.

What precipitated it was a minor shooting incident when an American sentry shot dead a Filipino soldier in a bridge in San Juan, a suburb in Manila. The American soldier claimed the Filipino soldier had strayed into their line of battle.

It was the excuse, flimsy as it was, used by the new American commander, General Elwell Otis, to go to war against the Filipinos.

The Americans were, within a few minutes of that minor shooting incident in San Juan, laying an artillery barrage at the Filipino troops' positions in Manila and in the suburbs.

Aguinaldo tried to stop the fighting. He sent an emissary to Otis for talks. Otis replied, "Fighting having begun, must go on to the grim end."

The United States Senate, which had the final say on the matter, was influenced by the falsely presented event of the United States now at war with the Philippines. It then voted, by one more vote than the required majority, for the annexation of the Philippines.

General Antonio Luna had just then been appointed as the field commander of the Filipino army. The most brilliant Filipino general, Luna will conduct the war against the Americans differently from the way Aguinaldo conducted the revolution against Spain.

Where Aguinaldo fought the Spaniards instinctively and with a good measure of guess work and plain luck, Luna will fight the Americans, out of his knowledge of and experience in military strategy and tactics.   Where clan, town and provincial loyalty dominated the way Aguinaldo conducted the revolution against Spain, Luna, in the war against America, will instill discipline and duty to their country.

Paulo, a week earlier, was given the command of a battalion of troops. They were, at the outbreak of the war, in the yard of an abandoned mansion in Quiapo District in Manila. He held a staff meeting there.

"We will hold our defensive position here, from Pasig River to Calle Azcarraga," he said, his finger pointed to a map on a table.

His battalion, that same day, was attacked by the Americans from San Miguel. He held on to its position for several days when another large American force came from Sampaloc and attacked his left flank. That put his battalion in danger of being cut off from the rest of the Filipino forces.

Luna then ordered Paulo's battalion to fall back and form another defensive position in Santa Cruz. He abandoned it, a few days later, when superior Americans forces threatened to overwhelm his battalion.

He retreated farther west, toward Gagalangin.

"We have the whole country to fall back into," he said to his troops.

Rain fell continuously in the following days, impeding the Americans' offensive. Many of their field guns were stuck in the mud.

General Arthur MacArthur, Jr., the American field commander in the northern front, thought it unwise to press forward during such a bad weather and he ordered his troops to stand down.

MacArthur's order gave the Filipinos, the chance to regroup their forces and mount an attack on the Americans..

Luna took up with his senior officers, his plan of attack while rain was sweeping by in the tile roof and the shuttered windows in Luna's temporary headquarters in the rectory of the Catholic Church in Caloocan.

It was, Paulo thought as he listened, simple and brilliant.

"This is the best time," Luna said, "to attack the Americans when they least expect it with this very bad weather.

"We will strike at the heart of Manila. Our strategy calls for a two-pronged attack. Generals Mariano Llanera and Pantaleon Garcia will attack Maypajo. East of them, Generals Maximo Hizon and Servillano Aquino will attack La Loma. The two armies will push southward and complete their attack in the plaza in front of Santa Cruz Church. They will then push on toward Pasig River. We will, by then, be in control of the northern half of Manila."

Paulo left the rectory after the meeting to check on his troops. He pulled them out of Gagalangin, two days earlier. They were now bivouacked in the church nave, full of soldiers. He was making his way to his troops there when he overheard a soldier worrying about his family in Tondo.

"I heard you say, you are from Tondo," he said to the soldier.

"Yes, sir, I live there in Tondo," the soldier replied.

"What is your name?"

"Mateo Dalandan, sir."

"I want you to be assigned to my battalion. I'm Colonel Palanas. I am not so familiar with that area. A guide will be of great help to me."

His eyes turned wide in surprise, Mateo said to Paulo, "Are you related to Lukas Palanas, sir?"

"He is my uncle."

"We were together when Bonifacio declared the Philippine independence in Pugad Lawin."

"Small world," Paulo said, nodding and smiling at Mateo who then said, "I will be glad to join your unit, sir."

Mateo was, within a few minutes, assigned to Paulo's battalion.

The Filipinos launched their surprise attack, just before sunrise on February 22, 1899. The right or western flank of General Llanera's army was led by Paulo's battalion. Its point platoon crept toward the Americans' advance post and disposed of it without alarming the rest of the American troops there.

Then, at the precise time of the attack, Paulo's battalion and the rest of Llanera's army fired at the Americans' position across a front, a few hundred feet wide.

The Americans were taken completely by surprise. They fired back with small arms as they retreated while the Filipinos went after them. Their field guns, the Americans' one huge advantage over the Filipinos, were of no use in the fighting at close quarters.

Llanera's army had reached Canal de la Reina by early afternoon, at a point where it flowed in a westerly course toward Manila

Bay. His army pressed on until it reached the wide Calle Azcarraga, which ran from east to west, along almost the entire length of northern Manila.

The Americans dug in at the street's southern side. They halted from there, the Filipino troops' offensive.

Things did not go well for the troops of Generals Hizon and Aquino at the eastern side of their two-pronged attack. The Americans held on to their position in La Loma. The Filipinos could have overwhelmed the American troops there had they pressed on with their attack, but Hizon and Aquino's Pampango troops were so tired by then.

Luna then ordered the fresh Kawit troops from Cavite of Captain Pedro Janolino to relieve the tired Pampango troops and press on with their attack against the Americans.

Janolino refused to follow Luna's order. He said he took orders from Aguinaldo alone. Janolino's insubordination cost the Filipinos dearly. Without those fresh Kawit troops, Hizon and Aquino's offensive faltered in La Loma. The other claw in the Filipinos' two-pronged attack was missing when the troops of Llanera and Garcia reached Calle Azcarraga.

The Filipinos' sudden massive attack took General Otis completely by surprise. He was in his headquarters in Fort Santiago, listening all morning to distressing field reports when General Arthur MacArthur. arrived there.

"I need more troops to stop the enemy attack," MacArthur said to Otis.

"Intramuros will be left defenseless, if I will give you the troops here."

"We will be in far worse shape if we will allow the Filipinos to take the northern side of Manila. We should counterattack at the earliest possible time, using all our available troops. I will lead it myself."

"How will you carry it out?"

"We will first hold our defensive line, along the entire length of Calle Azcarraga. The street is wide and we can stop the Filipinos from crossing it, if we have enough troops to hold it, particularly its southern side. We will then, once our reinforcements have arrived there, mount a massive counterattack, all along the wide avenue and at the La Loma salient."

Otis nodded and said, "Get the troops you need, but leave one regiment to secure Intramuros."

MacArthur went over with Otis' chief of personnel, Colonel Smith, the units he could muster for his counterattack. Among those drawn up was Captain Bill Shay's Iowa Volunteers.

He was at the head of his troops within a few minutes, moving through the narrow streets in Intramuros.

He halted his troops in Beaterio Street. They waited while he was knocking at the door of a house there.

Dick McCall, from the second floor of his house, asked Captain Shay, "What is up, Bill?"

"Do you want some big news?"

"What is it about?"

"The Filipinos are attacking us in the northern side of Manila."

"I know. I have just cabled my story about that."

"We are going there to push them back. Would you like to tag along and watch some interesting fighting there?"

"Give me a minute."

Dick gathered his things and pulled out from a closet in the room, a bag containing his clothes and other things, he kept handy for any emergency. He then dashed out of the house.

They were soon moving toward the Puente de Espana Bridge, which spanned the Pasig River.

They arrived in Calle Azcarraga to an exchange of gunfire between the Filipino and the American troops there.

The increased amount of gunfire coming from the American side in Calle Azcarraga showed Paulo that American reinforcements had arrived there. It wll not be long now when they will counterattack.

A series of explosions then rocked the area, west of his position. American warships in Manila Bay have started their own offensive.

He was relieved to find the explosions, falling short of his defensive position, the farthest point of which was in Ilaya Street. The Americans' naval shelling was hitting instead, the huts and shops in Tondo, near the shore in Manila Bay.

He turned to Mateo, his guide, who had rushed to him.

"They are shelling Asuncion Street," Mateo said, his eyes wild with fear and worry. "My house is not far from there! Could I check on my family there, sir?"

"But you cannot go there. The whole place is about to be destroyed by the Americans' naval gunfire."

"Please, sir, let me go there."

Paulo had barely nodded in assent when Mateo was already running toward Asuncion Street. He disappeared in an alley bound by huts, burning, a short while later.

Paulo watched and waited. When Mateo did not come back, he turned with a heavy heart, his attention, back to the American troops who were now firing with great intensity from the southern side of Calle Azcarraga.

He saw from the Americans' intensive firing that they will soon be charging across the wide avenue. His battalion is in a dangerous, untenable position, but to break off now would be risking a disorderly retreat by his battalion and possibly its annihilation.

He conferred hurriedly with his subordinate officers. They agreed on a way out for their battalion.

The Americans started their counterattack, a few minutes later, not knowing that Paulo's battalion had abandoned its position there and had retreated, north to Moriones. A company of his troops covered his battalion's withdrawal from Calle Azcarraga.

He could hear in Moriones, the exchange of gunfire as his rear guard fought the American troops, now charging across Calle Azcarraga.

He pulled his troops out of Moriones when his position there later on became untenable, too. He took another defensive position at the northern bank of Canal de la Reina. The only way across the canal was by a small bridge and it was well-covered by his troops. They held on to their position there despite the furious attack by the American troops from the other side of the canal. The Americans mounted another furious attack, the following morning. Paulo and his troops held them back, once again.

Captain Bill Shay watched with grudging respect, the Filipinos' tenacious defense there.

"They certainly are a stubborn lot," Bill said to Dick who was busy taking down notes.

"What will you do now?" he asked Bill.

"We'll destroy that outfit, if it will take all our field guns to do that."

Bill then told his communications officer, "Get the coordinates of the canal's northern bank. Then send a message to headquarters to obliterate it with all our available field guns. If our foot soldiers cannot dislodge them there, our field guns can."

Paulo's battalion, at the start of the Americans' artillery barrage, had withdrawn from its position at the northern side of the canal. A company of his troops once again covered his withdrawal, northward to Gagalangin.

General Luna gave the order for a delaying action and orderly retreat in the face of the American troops, now pressing on, all across the front.

Paulo's battalion then retreated farther north to Caloocan, along with the rest of General Llanera's army. They bivouacked in the town square, in front of the church. Hundreds more troops from General Garcia's army had also retreated to Caloocan before the day was over.

Caloocan was an important, strategic point. Roads from there, fanned out, east to Balintawak, west to Malabon and Navotas, and north to the towns in Bulacan. Equally important to both the Filipino and American forces was the Manila Railroad, which passed through the town. It had its marshaling yard and repair shops there.

The battle in Caloocan started the following day, bloodier than the battle in Calle Azcarraga. The result was the same. Filipino troops disengaged from the massive pounding by American artillery. They retreated northward, along the railroad tracks, set up a defensive line in Malinta, then in Meycauayan and in the outskirts of Malolos, a prize catch for the Americans, since it was the capital of the Philippine Republic.

General MacArthur preceded his attack on Malolos on March 31, 1899, with a bombardment that laid waste to large areas in the town. American troops then rushed toward the town. They found the Filipino troops' resistance there, light, mostly sniper fire from the shuttered houses there. They moved toward Barasoain Church and saw, not a soul there.

Aguinaldo's government and army had retreated, a few days earlier, farther north to San Fernando, Pampanga.

The Filipino forces were to all appearances taking a severe beating from the American forces. It was actually a part of a grand strategy, Luna had conceived. He was fighting a delaying action in battle after battle; in one defensive line after another while he was preparing, much farther north, his stronghold in the mountain range of Central Cordillera.

He will conduct there, no longer a conventional, but a guerrilla type of warfare. American artillery and cavalry, which had wrought havoc on the Filipino forces in a conventional warfare in the lowlands, will be practically useless in the rugged, mountainous forest-covered terrain of Central Cordillera. The Americans will also be fighting there, the Igorots, a common term for the highland tribes of the Ifugaos, Ibalois, Bontocs and Kalingas. They fight battles silently and effectively with their machetes and poison-tipped arrows as often in the daytime as at night.

Luna's ultimate goal was to wear down the Americans to the point that they will settle for talks to end the war and eventually leave the Philippines. It will then be finally, a free country.

Luna had, by then, overshadowed everyone else, Aguinaldo in particular. As the commander of the Filipino forces, he was doing the fighting while Aguinaldo, as the president, was relegated into the background. The conduct and the outcome of the war depended, not on Aguinaldo, but on Luna. There was also, from Aguinaldo's point of view, the possibility that Luna, in the war against the Americans, might do to him, what he did to Bonifacio in the revolution against Spain.

This situation, intolerable to Aguinaldo, did not last long.

Aguinaldo moved his government from San Fernando, Pampanga to Cabanatuan, the capital town of Nueva Ecija. He sent on June 2, 1899, a telegram to Luna, calling for a meeting with him in Cabanatuan. Luna was then in Bayambang, Pangasinan, preparing the Filipinos for an expected American landing there. He proceeded to Cabanatuan and arrived in Aguinaldo's headquarters on June 5, only to learn that Aguinaldo had left for Tarlac without informing him about the cancellation of their meeting.

Aguinaldo had laid a trap for Luna.

Luna was met instead by Captain Pedro Janolino and his men. He was the same Captain Janolino who refused to follow Luna's order to attack in the battle in La Loma salient, for which Luna lost in the battle, the only offensive the Filipinos were able to mount against the Americans. Instead of being punished for his insubordination to Luna, Janolino was made the commander of the Presidential Guard by his townmate, Emilio Aguinaldo.

A heated exchange of words ensued between Janolino and his superior, Luna. Janolino then struck Luna in the head with his sword. His men followed suit, by shooting Luna who had staggered out into the street where he died with thirty bullet wounds in his body.

General Pantaleon Garcia later on said, he was ordered by Aguinaldo to carry out the assassination of Luna. He said he was so sick at that time to carry out Aguinaldo's order.

Aguinaldo denied, he had anything to do with the murder of Luna.

The Filipinos lost, with the death of Luna, the only general fighting the Americans effectively. The Filipino forces, soon afterwards, fell in disarray with the field commanders fighting the Americans virtually on their own initiative and resources.

Luna was killed in the Philippine-American War, not by American arms, just as Bonifacio was killed in the Philippine Revolution, not by Spanish arms. They both died in the hands of Aguinaldo and his men. Behind their death, loomed the shadow of Aguinaldo.

There were Filipino heroes and scoundrels both in the Philippine Revolution and in the Philippine-American War.

Chapter Twenty

General Henry Lawton led an equally awesome force moving northward, parallel to General MacArthur's army. His army was sweeping through the towns in Bulacan, on the eastern side of the Central Plain of Luzon.

Lawton got only as far as in the town of Quingwa in Bulacan where he was killed by a sniper's gunfire. He was the highest ranking officer in the American army, killed in the war.

Captain Bill Shay was at the head of his company in another town in Bulacan. He was surveying the grand vista of the rice fields laid bare before him.

He was in the heart of the Central Plain of Luzon. It was summertime and the rice fields there were left to the weeds, golden-hued in the sunlight.

The place reminded him of the cornfields in Iowa.

His attachment to the soil, long dormant in his heart, came back to life and instilled joy in him. He looked on with his blue eyes at the grand view before him, a soft easterly breeze stirring his blond hair lightly. It was the first time, he found some delight in this tropical country laid bare before him. The heat no longer bothered him as much as it did before and he derived a certain comfort in the coolness of the night.

It was made even more pleasant and satisfying to him by his successful military campaign. The rest had been easy after the intense battles in Calle Azcarraga, in Canal de la Reina and in Caloocan.

Dick McCall was with him, a great part of the time. He asked Dick, "We are going to take the towns, northeast of here. Do you want to tag along?"

"I don't mind making you famous with my news reports."

Captain Shay's company was made the vanguard of Colonel Andrew Morgan's battalion because of the speed by which it led its offensive in the towns at the foothills of the mountain range of Sierra Madre.

Captain Shay was also promoted to a major.

It took his company only five days to sweep through three towns in Bulacan until it reached and conquered the town of San Nicolas.

The town of Masakao, a short distance away, lay open to Major Shay and his troops.

It was early morning in San Nicolas and Major Shay's company was bivouacked in the common yard of a cluster of huts, abandoned by their owners. Between them and Masakao were the town's rice fields.

Colonel Andrew Morgan, the battalion commander, was farther back in the town of San Miguel.

Major Shay ordered a squad of his troops to investigate the town. The squad moved carefully in the rice fields. They were approaching the orchards at the edge of the town when gunfire suddenly broke the silence there. The entire squad was killed except for one soldier who managed to run back before he was also felled by gunfire.

Major Shay watched, shocked, the annihilation of his squad of soldiers.

"This town," he said to himself, "will not be an easy target."

Unlike the other towns, he had conquered so easily, Masakao seemed to be defended by battle-hardened troops. A camouflaged trench also girdled the town. Removing them there will not be easy.

It was Major Shay's first setback, although a minor one, since the Americans' northward offensive began in Central Plain. He now viewed, after having been thwarted, the enemy with some respect.

He would not have given the order that sent a squad of his soldiers to their death, had he known about their camouflaged trench there. He had become smug, careless and overconfident after the battle in Caloocan because everything since then had gone his way. He was in this state of mind, a frown on his face, as he was looking at the enemy position when Dick McCall came to him.

Dick had also seen the disaster and he said to Bill, "It looks like a tough nut to crack."

Bill waved away, Dick's comment and said, "Watch me make my move. You have not seen yet what I can and will do."

"See what?"

"Just watch. I will make them pay for what they did to my men," he said. He then ordered his field guns moved to firing position.

Lukas watched the Americans who were positioned in a cluster of huts and trees at the edge of the rice fields. They will not attack yet, not while they were still smarting from the death of their squad of soldiers.

He won in the intial skirmish because he had the element of surprise, but this is only the beginning. How he wished Paulo were with him, but he was elsewhere in far bigger battles than this one.

He was in a tree-shaded rise on the ground, hidden from the Americans' view by expert camouflage of bamboo and bushes that covered the trench. It formed the town's only line of defense. The town beyond the trench lay open to the Americans. He had made all the necessary preparation. He and his townmates, veterans in the revolution against Spain, were now fighting another enemy.

The Americans, as he knew them very well, will in the end break through and conquer the town and not only the town, but sooner or later, the entire country itself. He could see no way they could win against the Americans with their vastly superior arms who were helped at the same time by the traitors among them in another betrayal by the Ilustrados. They made a deal with the Americans and were now fighting their own countrymen.

He cast those thoughts aside as distractions from the task he faced of defending the town against the Americans. His brow was knitted with worry when he looked across the rice fields. The Americans have lined up their field guns, facing the town. He had only the trench to protect him and his troops, once the Americans have started firing those field guns.

He had, though, a big surprise in store for the Americans. He will use the same tactic, he and Paulo used against the Spaniards. He will withdraw with his main force to Alkayag, leaving behind, a small number of his troops to cover his withdrawal, once the Americans were going to break through their defensive line. They will then learn, as the Spaniards did before, that taking the town would be far easier than defeating its defenders. He rebuilt their camp in Alkayag with the help of Gayuman, Doctor Bihasa, Sabedro and his fellow Dumagat tribesmen. They will, from there, continue to fight even after the town had fallen into the hands of the Americans.

Major Shay, for his attack in Masakao, did something never done before in the town. The ground in the approaches to the town was pockmarked a few minutes later by the pounding by the Americans' ten field guns. The Spaniards never had that much firepower.

He watched, satisfied, when the artillery shells exploded on the trench. His troops then began to advance even before the smoke had cleared from the artillery firing. They were shocked when they were met again by deadly enemy gunfire. More American soldiers fell dead or wounded in the warm soil of Masakao.

The town's defenders had anticipated a massive artillery attack on the trench. The trench they then dug was deep and narrow. They crouched at the bottom of the trench during the shelling, so that, other than a direct downward hit, the shells exploded harmlessly on the ground. They moved up, once the shelling had ceased, and fired with deadly accuracy at the advancing Americans.

He watched, frowning, his troops who had fallen back. He ordered another, more intensive artillery barrage. They then overran the trench, which they found out was defended by only a few Filipino soldiers.

He realized, by then, that most of the Filipino troops who fought from the trench had withdrawn while the shelling was going on. He ordered the town searched for the enemy troops while he proceeded to the town fort and the municipal hall, abandoned by the Filipino troops.

Colonel Morgan conferred with his officers, the moment he arrived in Masakao with the rest of the battalion. The word by then had gone around that most of the Filipino troops, who defended the town, had fled while the shelling by their field guns was going on.

"Why," a captain suggested, "don't we round up the men here and interrogate them?"

"We will leave the civilians alone," Colonel Morgan replied. "We don't want to make more enemies than we already have."

Major Shay said as he pointed at Sierra Madre, "There is no other place, the enemy troops could have fled to except in that mountain range."

"Should we," a captain asked, "go after them in that mountain range?"

"Yes," Major Shay replied, "if that is where they fled."

"We will do, just that," Colonel Morgan said. He turned to a cavalry officer and said, "Mount up your charges, Richards, and go after them. You, Morrison and Campbell, follow Richards."

"Well, Bill," he said to Major Shay, "your company has done enough fighting, not only today, but in the entire campaign. You and your men need some rest. You will stay here and maintain our hold on this town."

Major Shay then proceeded to his troops who were taking a rest in an orchard of mango and other fruit trees.

He said to them, "You can take it easy. We are staying here."

Major Richards' cavalrymen caught up with Lukas' rear guard in the foothills in Sierra Madre. The rear guard, in the ensuing firefight, was wiped out, but Lukas' main force had managed to escape to the forest. The American cavalrymen galloped after them, only to be met by a hail of gunfire. Four American soldiers were hit and thrown off from their mounts.

"Get back, get back!" Major Richards shouted at his men.

They retreated to a level ground and dismounted from their horses. They charged again at Lukas' troops, who were now moving, deep inside the forest. What followed was another wild firefight at close quarters between the two forces.

The arrival of Morrison and Campbell's troops, who had likewise dismounted from their horses, gave the Americans an overwhelming superiority in number of troops and firepower. They soon had the Filipinos fleeing deeper inside the forest. Another firefight broke out near a stream, among its boulders and in the vegetation along its banks.

Lukas was sweeping aside with his hands, the thick undergrowth around him when he tripped on a root protruding from the ground. He pitched forward, dropped his gun and fell into a ravine. A soldier near him grabbed his hand and was pulling him up when a gunshot rang out. The soldier was hit in the arm and he lost his grip on Lukas' hand.

"Go! Don't worry about me," he said to the soldier.

His eyes darted to the Filipino soldier who had stood up and the American soldier who fired again, but missed the Filipino soldier who then fled. He watched the American soldier who was now looking around. He was gripped with fear when he saw the soldier, now moving in his direction. He dived into the tall cogon grass, in a corner of the ravine.

He landed unfortunately near an anthill where ants were soon all over him and biting him. He gritted his teeth from the pain of the ant bites, but dared not move a muscle so as not to give his presence away. He was relieved when he heard someone, apparently an American officer, shouting, "All right men, that is enough work for today. We are going back to the town."

He stayed in his hiding place and listened. The forest was now quiet except for the crickets trilling in the trees. The Americans had left.

He moved out of his hiding place, now that he was out of danger, and brushed away the ants, biting him. It was time for him to leave, too. He was staggered by the sight of an American soldier who, on seeing him, fired at him. The bullet tore through the base of his neck, barely missing his throat, but sending blood spurting out from his neck. The force of the bullet sent him falling back into the ravine.

The American soldier walked over to the edge of the ravine and looked down at Lukas. He was sprawled on the ground and he appeared to be dead. The soldier then walked away and joined the other Americans who were leaving the forest.

Lukas regained his consciousness, the following day to a throbbing pain in his neck. His arms and legs were also aching from the ant bites. A shaft of sunlight, when he turned around, hit his eyes, nearly blinding him.

He sat up and looked around. Sunlight was piercing through the gaps in the leafy branches of the trees that towered over him.

He sat still, his breathing, short and labored.

"Thank God," he said to himself, "I'm still alive."

He felt cold, right after he had said that, from his own blood, he now saw had soaked him all over his body. Unless he got help soon, he will die from loss of blood.

But where, he asked himself, could he get help? It was available in Alkayag, but getting there will mean, a hike of several hours on the rugged mountain trail. He did not have the strength to do that.

If he will go back to the town, which was much nearer and where the terrain was easier to negotiate, he risked capture by the Americans. It was not as bad as the prospect of dying there.

He raised himself up with a tree branch, he used for a crutch. He managed, despite the difficulty, to climb out of the ravine. He took drafts of air before trudging back to the town.

He often took a rest to catch his breath, and it took him so long a time before he reached the outskirts of the town.

The slow and difficult walk, he took in the forest and in the foothills, his wound and the blazing sun had so weakened him, he felt he could not make the remaining distance to the town.

He detoured instead to a mango tree in the middle of the rice fields. While it was only a short distance away, he was so tired when he got within its shade, all he could do now was to press his back against the tree trunk and slide down into the ground.

He began to chill and he wrapped his arms around his knees to keep himself warm. All the effort he took, had left him so tired, out of breath and barely conscious.

A whip of wind roused him from his flickering consciousness and he opened his eyes to a wonderful view of Masakao.

There it is, peaceful and beautiful, as always, basking in the sunlight splashed on the church, the thatch-roofed huts and the tile-roofed homes, the fruit trees, the bamboo groves and the rice fields there.

He is now leaving it for his just reward. He has done his part and has given the best that he could. Paulo and the others will now carry on, the fight for their country's freedom.

He pressed his hand to his faintly beating heart and turned his eyes to the cross on top of the church dome, cast in brilliant sunlight.

The cross seemed to draw him to it, sapping him of his remaining strength. It will soon be over for him and he prayed. The hope and comfort, it gave him was as warm and bright as the cross in the church dome. His breathing, now short and labored, he then shut his eyes for the last time.

A teenage boy crossing the rice fields, seated astride a carabao, found Lukas, dead in the shade of the mango tree. He was curled up on the ground, like a baby in a womb.

The boy rode back to the town and reported what he saw there. The townsfolk started coming for the wake,. by the time Lukas' body had been washed, dressed in new clothes and laid on a cot in the living room of his house, The whole town by sunset knew about his death.

Julio was seated on his rocking chair while Agustina was doing embroidery work in the living room when Nieves came with the news about the death of Lukas. They could, for a moment, only stare, shocked, at Nieves who then proceeded to Esperanza and Teresa's bedroom.

Agustina wept quietly while Julio looked down sadly at the floor. They stayed home when the Americans came and occupied the town yesterday. They had no idea what kind of people they were. They could be bad like Zatayde and now they learned about the death of Lukas.

The town, more than ever, needed him who was wise and strong and who could stand up to the town's new conquerors.

"Should we attend the wake for Lukas?" Agustina asked Julio.

"I don't see why we should not. The least we can do is to pay him, our last respects. He was a dear friend. He was our family, too."

"How about the Americans who could be bad like Zatayde," Agustina said, her eyes turned anxiously toward the town fort.

"Why will they stop us from holding a wake for our dead mayor?"

"We'll go there after I have cooked some food for the wake."

Agustina stood up and went to the kitchen to prepare the food while Julio turned to the sound of weeping in his daughters' bedroom.

Teresa, Esperanza and Nieves came out, after a while, from the bedroom, their eyes red from weeping. They sat down on the big couch.

"Paulo must be told about his uncle's death," Teresa said to Julio.

"He could be anywhere."

"I will look for him, if no one will."

"Don't do such a foolish thing. You cannot go anywhere with this war going on. We will ask around. There must be someone in the town who knows where to find Paulo."

Lukas' house and yard were, by nightfall, full of people. They were standing or were seated on stools and benches in the yard, bright with gas lanterns hanging in the trees there. They were keeping to themselves or were conversing in low voices.

The sound of the rosary being prayed, the smell of frying pork, chicken and fish inside the house and the crowd in the yard showed the townsfolk, holding a wake for Lukas.

The lights and the presence of many people in Lukas' house and yard, in sharp contrast to the darkness and silence in the rest of the town, caught the attention of a squad of American soldiers patrolling the town.

Some of them stayed outside on the road and watched the crowd in the yard while the rest of the patrol, led by a sergeant, returned to the town fort and reported what they saw to Major Bill Shay. He was, refreshed by a bath and fortified by a good dinner and a few drinks, taking it easy in his quarters in the town fort, along with Dick and the other officers.

He listened to the sergeant, his brow furrowed. He asked him a few questions and dismissed him.

His company was assigned as the town's occupation force while the rest of the battalion pushed on to the other towns at the base of the mountain range of Sierra Madre. He had taken the precaution of setting up a checkpoint and conducting patrols in the town. He was confident, though, that the rebels did not pose any serious threat to him. They had been severely defeated and their remaining troops had fled to the outlying mountains. He was disturbed, though, by the sergeant's report. It could be a political meeting and he could not allow that.

He said to Dick, "Do you want to tag along and see what this is all about?"

"I won't mind, doing that. A little walk will be great after the heavy meal, we just took."

They proceeded to the house of Lukas with a squad of soldiers.

"Mighty fine night for a walk," Dick said as they were walking on toward the house of Lukas.

Bill nodded. He was likewise taken by the clear night sky and the sweet scent of flowers in the gardens of the houses they were passing by on the town road. He liked what he saw there. He saw nothing of the hostility, he had expected from the townsfolk, only resignation in their stoic faces. They were used to foreign rule.

He saw there a nice combination of people and nature, a beautiful town with rice fields in the plain, rolling hills and mountains, a river meandering through it, the modest-looking homes there suggesting a simple kind of life led there by the townsfolk.

It was a country life similar in some respects to his hometown in Iowa.

But much, as he was attracted to the town, he had no illusion about him and his troops, not being welcome there. He was there to occupy the town and keep the peace, nothing more and nothing less.

"We will know soon enough, what those natives are up to," he said to Dick. "I'll have to break it up, if it is a political meeting."

The house, when seen from a distance, with the lights and with a lot of people there, gave the impression of something festive going on there.

They saw, when they came near the house, gathered in the yard, men and women on their feet or were seated on the stools and benches there. Some of them were engaged in quiet conversation while the others seemed to be by themselves, talking to no one and looking downcast at the ground. There seemed to be nothing political in the gathering there. Neither was there anything festive there—no music, no dancing and no merrymaking.

Bill and Dick walked toward the house, to the curious stares and worried looks of the people in the yard.

A dignified-looking gentleman met them at the gate.

"Good evening. Is there anything, we can do for you?" he said to them in flawless English.

Bill and Dick glanced at each other, surprised to hear someone in the town, speaking in English with a British accent.

"Yes," Bill replied. "What is going on there?"

"We are holding a wake for someone who died."

"And who are you?"

"I'm Doctor Bihasa. Like everyone here, I am a friend of the deceased."

"And who is the deceased?"

"He is our mayor, Lukas Palanas, a dear friend of everyone here."

The gathering was, whatever was its purpose, seemed to Bill, an act of defiance to his authority.

"I suppose, you are well aware that we have taken over this town."

"That has not escaped our attention."

Bill said, his eyes narrowed in annoyance with Doctor Bihasa, "You are not supposed to leave your homes by nightfall."

"We are not aware of such an order."

Bill and Dick glanced at each other. Bill did not issue such an order. He took it for granted that the townsfolk, afraid of the Americans, had stayed inside their homes, once it got dark.

"We want to take a look, inside the house," Bill said in a tone of voice, now resonant with his authority.

Doctor Bihasa nodded. The soldiers stayed in the yard except for two of them who escorted Bill and Dick when they went up into the house with Doctor Bihasa.

Bill saw, the moment they entered the living room, men and women, some of them seated on chairs while the others were on their knees. They stopped abruptly from praying the rosary.

Their fingers on their beads, some of them gazed curiously while the others gazed apprehensively at Bill, Dick and the two soldiers.

Bill felt, he had intruded into their prayer and he said to them, "I'm sorry for the interruption. Please, go on with your prayer."

He turned his eyes to the dead man, laid on a cot. The scratches and bruises in the man's face and the wound in his neck showed him that he was engaged in the battle yesterday. A rosary, clasped in his hands, the dead man looked peaceful from the light cast on him by the candles, placed on the stands at each corner of the cot.

A bookshelf lined with books and a wall adorned with pictures and diplomas showed Bill that the dead man was an educated man. He noticed, as he looked again at the dead man, pain was likewise on his face from the wounds he suffered in fighting them.

He reproached himself for making an opinion about the dead man, and he looked elsewhere at the people attending the wake, his eyes settling down on three young beautiful women, seated beside each other.

They were so near him, he could, if he bent down a little, even touch them. They were so beautiful, so different from the women he had seen before in the islands, women whose dark complexions, flat noses and thick lips, their eyes staring blankly were a letdown to him who had expected women in the southern seas to be beautiful and sensuous. But there they were now, the most beautiful women he had seen, since he came to the colony.

He was so drawn by their beauty he could not help glancing at them again. They seemed to have a quality of reserve and demureness that made them even lovelier and more desirable, qualities he had never seen in any women, he knew before. They had a light brown complexion, soft facial features and thin, lovely lips. Two of them with similar features looked like they were sisters. The older-looking one, who was looking away, showed by the amused smile in her face, that she knew, he was staring at her.

He was embarrassed for having been caught, staring at her, and he turned his gaze toward a window there. He could not help it, though, and he took, from the corner of his eye, another look at the woman who had caught him, staring at her.

Dick, he saw, was looking on, amused, at him. He had also noticed him, staring at the three young, beautiful women when suddenly the younger-looking of the two sisters, looked up at him. He saw, by the frown in her face, how she detested him.

He looked elsewhere, so disconcerted by her stern gaze, as he then left the living room with Dick, Doctor Bihasa and their escort.

He halted when he was about to pass out of the house gate with Dick and glanced at Doctor Bihasa, who had accompanied them there. The doctor could be useful to him.

"I want that observed as a wake for the dead, nothing else, nothing political, or I will have to order, all of you to go back home," he said to Doctor Bihasa. "I will assign four soldiers to keep watch at the wake and the burial. I want you to come to the fort tomorrow. You can tell us a lot about this town. You can work for us, as our doctor, liaison and interpreter."

He was out on the road with Dick when, on a sudden impulse, he looked back at the house and caught two of the women, one of them the older-looking sister, looking at them. They averted their eyes instantly. They seemed approachable and appeared to be mildly curious about him and Dick. It was something to look forward to.

"So, what do you think?" Dick asked him.

"What do I think, of what?"

"Those three young, beautiful women, we saw in the house."

"They certainly will make garrison duty in this town, a pleasure."

He walked back to the fort with Dick, now feeling differently about the town. A while ago, on their way to the wake, he viewed his assignment there, simply as a military duty. He now felt, not only a liking for the town, but also a longing to be welcome there, all because he had seen there, those three young, beautiful women.

So did Dick. He could tell that from the way Dick had also looked with great interest at the three young, beautiful women. He was, even then, clear about it, that as he looked on at the older one of the two sisters, what he felt then was something called, love at first sight.

It was quiet in the mayor's office. Bill was writing a progress report, Dick, a news story. Three days had passed since they investigated the wake for Lukas. They turned their eyes to the town church when they heard its bells tolled.

"What is that, all about?" Bill asked Dick.

Dick, instead of answering Bill's question, stood up and went to the window overlooking the town church.

"A funeral procession, probably for the town mayor, is at the churchyard," Dick said.

Bill joined Dick at the window. They looked on as Lukas' coffin was taken out of a cart and brought inside the church.

Some of the women there were, in a sign of mourning, dressed in black.

They watched with great interest, Teresa, Esperanza and Nieves, who were walking beside each other.

They learned about their names from the inquiries they made about the town from Doctor Bihasa who had agreed to work for Bill.

"Are you thinking, what I am thinking about?" Bill asked Dick.

"Yes. How we can be friends with them."

They smiled.

They returned to work when the funeral procession had entered the church. Their minds, though, were elsewhere.

"Do you have to leave tomorrow?" Bill asked Dick.

"I have got to file my stories and cover other fronts."

"Is there something about me in your news and feature stories?"

"I have written enough about you," Dick said in a faked rebuke.

Bill had become a celebrity in his hometown in Iowa from the news and feature articles, Dick had written about him. They also put Bill in good stead with the army headquarters in Fort Santiago and he was retained as the town administrator and fort commander in Masakao.

"Continue doing that when you get back to Manila," Bill said to Dick.

"So you will be kept here."

"It is also in your interest, for me to be kept here."

It was late in the afternoon when Lukas's mortal remains were brought to the town cemetery for his burial beside the graves of his brother Marko and his sister-in-law Leticia.

Father Madaluan, the new Filipino parish priest in Masakao, was saying a prayer for the dead as his coffin was being lowered by rope into the ground.

Many of the women there then broke into piercing cries of mourning that carried far in the quiet afternoon across the rice fields in Masakao and to the foothills in Sierra Madre.

Paulo, with an escort of soldiers, was there, secretly watching the burial beneath a mango tree there. The soldiers, not wanting to intrude at this moment of his bereavement, kept themselves at a distance from him.

His eyes were blurry with tears when he bent down, his chin on his clasped hands, as he prayed for the repose of the soul of his uncle.

He felt, right after he had prayed, as if he was then being tossed around by a succession of thoughts and feelings.

His uncle was gone for his just reward in heaven. The sadness, he felt when he learned in Tarlac about the death of his uncle, was now heavier with the feeling of regret and deep loss. His uncle died when there was so much of life ahead of him and there was so much need for him.

The responsibilities, his uncle carried and carried so well, for their town and their country, were now placed on his shoulders. The deep sadness that had overtaken him was eased up by the ennobling thought that he must carry on where his uncle had left off.

His mind then turned to the memory of his life with his uncle. His uncle then seemed to him was very much alive. He wept when sadness, so strong this time, overtook him once again.

He stood up when he saw everyone in the cemetery had left. He walked toward his uncle, his father and his mother's graves and prayed for them.

He went afterwards, back to his horse and mounted it. The soldiers with him also mounted their horses.

One of them asked him, "Are we going back to Tarlac, sir?"

"Yes, but we are coming back."

Chapter Twenty-one

With Lukas dead and Paulo elsewhere, with Doctor Bihasa now working for the Americans and with Gayuman, ill, the town's troops were left leaderless. Those who managed to escape to Alkayag returned quietly to the town. Peace reigned once again in Masakao.

The townsfolk accepted willingly the Americans' occupation of their town when they found them to be friendly. They saw this in Major Bill Shay who was so different from the cruel and sadistic Captain Zatayde. It had the effect of removing the townsfolk's initial fear and distrust of the Americans. Bill had the town completely under his control when Dick came back, two weeks later, after covering the war in other fronts.

His work in the town fort and the municipal hall done for the day, Bill went riding around the town on horseback with Dick.

The afternoon heat had kept the townsfolk inside their homes and they were all alone, the silence there broken now and then by their horses' hoofbeat on the gravel road.

Dick was talking about the war and how the Filipino soldiers, the Americans now called insurgents, were taking a beating from them.

"The amazing thing, though," Dick said, "is that they keep on fighting when, from the military point of view, all is lost to them. What do you think about it?"

Bill would ordinarily expound his views on the fighting, but he remained quiet. His mind was elsewhere. Dick knew what was on Bill's mind and he asked him about the three young, beautiful women.

"I saw them one time when I was passing by their store," Bill replied in a dull tone of voice.

"Did you talk to them?"

Bill shook his head.

Dick sighed in disappointment and said, "You could have gone to their store and on the pretext of buying something there, talked to them. It is at least a friendly gesture."

"You don't expect me to do that, do you?" Bill replied in a harsh tone of voice that took Dick by surprise.

He was pressing too hard. He realized this when he saw the annoyed and frustrated look in Bill's face. His friend is in a difficult situation. Bill could not go beyond the bounds of his own authority. The townsfolk could interpret a friendly gesture for courtship and it would be demeaning and poor politics for Bill, the town administrator and fort commander, to be seen going after a local girl, Esperanza in particular. Bill had indicated, he had his eyes on her. But most of all, he could not stand the humiliation of being rejected should it turn out that Esperanza is not interested about him.

They rode on with no particular destination in their minds, but then they found themselves on the road toward the Dumayags' corner store in the town's commercial area.

They were approaching the store when they saw it, already closed. Good fortune was on them, for they saw, far ahead at the other road, Esperanza, Teresa and Nieves walking on their way home.

Dick turned his horse toward the women.

Bill hesitated but then he sent his horse abreast of Dick's horse.

"What," he asked Dick, "are you doing?"

"Do I have to explain it to you?"

They followed the women, but kept themselves, far behind them. They halted and looked on when the women passed through a house gate and entered the house there.

Julio was in the yard, raking into a mound, the tree leaves there when Dick and Bill came to the house gate.

"Good afternoon, sir," Dick said in Spanish to Julio. "That is a lush, beautiful orchard, you have there."

A pleased look was on Julio's face as he replied, also in Spanish, "Thank you for the nice thing you said about my orchard."

"I cannot help but take a look at your orchard whenever I'm passing by here. I tried my hand at gardening without much success. It must take someone good at it to make those plants and trees grow like they do in your orchard."

"Making things grow is not that hard."

"I wish I could say that about myself."

"All you need is a lot of patience. Let me show you around."

Julio opened the gate and motioned Dick and Bill to come inside the yard.

"Nothing will please us more," Dick said, smiling.

They dismounted from their horses and entered the yard.

"By the way, my name is Dick McCall," Dick said as he extended his hand to Julio.

Julio gave his name as he was shaking hands with Dick.

"And I am Major Bill Shay," Bill said to Julio.

Julio also shook hands with Bill.

They tied their horses' reins to a post there, looked around and listened to Julio as he explained, his finger pointed to a mango tree there, how with proper care, it bore sweet, luscious fruit.

"You will have a taste of it," he said to Dick and Bill, "when we harvest the fruits during summer."

"Thank you," Dick replied, smiling. "We will look forward to that. It sure is nice to have a taste of that fruit. We don't have that in America."

It took them a while to look around in the large orchard.

Julio plucked two ripe fruits from a branch in a guava tree there. He said, as he gave them to Dick and Bill, "I don't know, if you have them in America."

He watched, pleased, when Bill and Dick, as they were eating the fruit, smiled and nodded at its delicious taste.

"We don't have these too in America," Dick said. "What is it called?"

"It is called guava."

"It will be nice if we can have a guava and a mango tree in our garden and vineyard in San Francisco."

"You can dry the seeds and plant them there."

Dick, like Bill, had feigned interest in the beginning, but had since then admired Julio's lush orchard.

"It must," he said to Julio, "take a lot of your time in taking care of them."

"My wife and my two daughters help me in taking care of them."

"It would be nice if we can meet them."

He glanced at Bill, who nodded and smiled.

"You should meet them; they are all at home," Julio said as he then led Dick and Bill to the house.

They saw no one in the living room.

"I will call my wife, she must be in the dining room," Julio said as he motioned Dick and Bill to the large wooden couch there.

Bill and Dick looked around as they sat down on the wooden couch. The living room was neat and cozy with the feminine touch evident in the indoor plants, the curtains in the windows and the crocheted table runner on the coffee table. One of the photographs on a wall, they noticed, was that of the dead mayor and a young man beside him. There was a bookshelf and the statue of a saint inside a glass cabinet. A piano set against a wall spoke of the home, rich with music. A grandfather clock stood in a corner.

"Nice place," Bill said, "like the rest of the town."

Dick nodded and smiled. Bill had indicated by his comment, a growing attachment to the town. They both have this wanderlust, he as a journalist who wanted to see the world and write about it and Bill as a civil engineer who went from one job site to another in America before he joined the army. Could it be, he asked himself, that he and Bill have found there, the place where they could settle down? He smiled, pleased with the thought.

A woman in the dining room was talking to Julio in their local dialect. While Bill and Dick could not understand, a word that she was saying, the sharp tone in her voice told them that she was scolding Julio.

He appeared, after parting tbe curtain to the dining room, with a woman. A sheepish look was on his face as he introduced her as his wife Agustina. She smiled shyly at Bill and Dick who had stood up and greeted her. She turned her gaze to the bedroom door, opened by Esperanza. Teresa and Nieves were beside her.

They glanced curiously at Bill and Dick, who nodded and smiled at them.

Julio introduced the three women to Bill and Dick and said to them, in Spanish, "I was in the yard when Major Shay and Mr. McCall came by and told me how much they liked our orchard. I showed them around. I thought you should meet them."

Dick caught Esperanza and Nieves, looking at each other. So, they knew all along that he and Bill were following them home. They could have guessed then that their interest in the orchard was only a pretext to meet them. Esperanza and Nieves smiled. Dick knew then that he and Bill were welcome there. Teresa, though, was frowning, her eyes averted from him and Bill. She seemed displeased by their presence there. She asked to be excused and went with Agustina to the dining room.

Bill and Dick sat down on the large wooden couch while Esperanza and Nieves sat down on the two small couches by the side of the large couch. Julio remained standing. They picked up from where they left off in their conversation in the yard.

"We can apply in America, some of the things that you do here," Dick said to Julio.

"You are far more advanced there."

"But we don't have those plants and trees that you have here. I have never seen such fruit trees. Your orchard is a virtual paradise. You have everything here. I wish I can have and do the same thing in my little garden and vineyard, at the back of our house in San Francisco."

"It is not, that hard. An orchard needs just a few things. Good seed is one, but most of all, you must have plenty of water."

"And where does your water come from?"

"We have a well in our backyard."

"Does it provide enough water for your needs? How about your drinking water? Where do you get it?"

"We collect rainwater or else we boil the water we draw out from our well."

Dick turned to Bill and said in English, "What they need here is a safe, reliable source of water."

"A water system," Bill replied, "based on a dam built upstream in the river can provide the homes here with potable water and the rice fields with irrigation water. It will take a lot of money and effort, but it can be done."

"Did I hear you right, Major Shay, that you can build a water system in our town? If you can do that, you will have the people in our town, praising you to heaven," Esperanza said in English which took Bill and Dick by surprise.

"We need that badly in our town," Nieves said, also in English.

Julio saw Dick and Bill, looking at each other, their eyebrows raised in surprise at Esperanza and Nieves speaking in English. He told Dick that they, along with Teresa, learned English in the town's primary school.

Agustina came back with a tray of two cups of coffee. She set it down on the coffee table and motioned to Bill and Dick to take them.

Bill and Dick were picking them up when Julio, at a nod from Agustina, asked to be excused. He left the living room with Agustina.

Bill and Dick drank their coffee.

"This is fine coffee," Bill said.

"It is our famous Batangas coffee," Esperanza said.

Dick took another sip and nodded.

"This coffee is as fine as the music you must make there on the piano," he said boldly and suggestively.

"You should hear Esperanza play on the piano," Nieves said. She turned to Esperanza and said to her, "Why don't you play something."

Esperanza sighed as she stood up and went to the piano. She waved at Nieves to join her there.

"Let us try the *Barcarolle,*" she said to Nieves.

Bill and Dick finished their coffee quickly and sat back on the couch and waited eagerly. They listened, entranced, Dick especially, the moment Nieves began to sing the beautiful song. It seemed to him that her voice was like that of a nightingale warbling music on a summer day.

Their eyes met in the middle of the song and locked to each other. Dick was pleased and flattered. She was singing the song to him. After a few bars, though, Esperanza shifted to another key. Nieves got distracted and she missed a note. She blushed in embarrassment, but went on with the song.

Dick nodded and smiled at her in a sign, not to mind it, his enjoyment of her singing, remaining undiminished. He listened, entranced like Bill who, he saw was looking seemingly entranced at Esperanza.

He seemed to be captivated by her beauty, by her piano playing, or by both of them. He seemed so absorbed with Esperanza's beauty and her music that he was startled when, at the end of the song, the grandfather clock chimed the time.

The music ended to Bill and Dick's applause.

"I never heard that song sung and played on the piano so beautifully," Dick said, smiling.

"Thank you very much," Bill said, smiling as well. "How I wish we could stay longer and listen to you make more beautiful music."

Bill glanced at Dick. It was time for them to return to the fort for the flag-lowering ceremony.

"Duty calls," Bill said as he and Dick stood up from the couch, "but I can tell you, we never had such a grand time. Thank you very much."

"You make such beautiful music, we will never get tired of listening to you," Dick said.

Julio, Agustina and Teresa appeared from the dining room.

"You will hear them play on the piano and sing anytime you come here. You are most welcome here," Julio said as together with Nieves, Esperanza, Teresa and Agustina, he walked Dick and Bill to the balcony.

"Thank you very much for the grand time, you gave us," Bill said.   "We look forward to having more of it," Dick said.

They nodded and smiled at their hosts as they descended the stairs and walked toward their horses. They went back to the town fort, smiling at the grand, wonderful time they had at the Dumayag household.

Chapter Twenty-two

The townsfolk were startled one evening by gunshots, which they have not heard for a long time. They listened anxiously to the exchange of gunfire, the shouts of command and voices, raised in pain or in anger. The townsfolk learned the following morning that an American patrol had been ambushed and an American soldier was killed.

Paulo was back in the town with vengeance.

More American soldiers fell dead or wounded in the days that followed to the insurgents' nighttime sniper attacks. This dire development in Masakao soon reached the American headquarters in Fort Santiago.

Dick returned there one day after covering a fruitless search for Aguinaldo who had by then disappeared like a common outlaw in the mountain range in Central Cordillera.

The Filipinos by then were severely defeated in conventional warfare and they turned to guerrilla warfare.

Dick was leaving Fort Santiago when he overheard two soldiers talking about the fighting in a town in Central Plain. He paid no attention to this minor engagement, one in the scores of battles going on that very moment, all over the islands. He halted when he heard the name of the town mentioned.

"What," he asked them, "did you say is the name of that town?"

"It is called 'Mash a cow."

"What happened there?"

"The insurgents have been waylaying our patrols and checkpoints there. Two of our soldiers there have been killed."

Dick left Fort Santiago. He will go to Masakao.

He saw no marked change in the town. The townsfolk were doing their usual tasks in the gardens and orchards there. It was as if nothing serious and troubling was happening there.

His view of things changed when he saw Bill in a meeting with his subordinate officers in the town fort.

Bill pointed to an empty chair when he saw Dick. Then he returned to the question under discussion, the threat posed by the Filipino insurgents.

It sometimes got sidetracked when some of Bill's officers expressed their anger and frustration with negative views on the colony, in general and the insurgents, in particular.

Dick was pleased and satisfied to see Bill was no longer the same Major Bill Shay who used to ride on that kind of talk about the Filipinos. He even rebuked his subordinate officers by putting in a good word about the town and its residents.

Their discussion became emotional and Bill led it back to its original track, the move they must take in counteracting the insurgents' nighttime guerrilla attacks.

He said to Dick, "You can give us your two cents' worth of opinion on what we should do about the insurgents. They have killed two of our troopers, one of them, only three nights ago."

"Do you have any idea where they might be operating from?"

"They have a camp, deep in the mountains, which they have kept from the time of the Spaniards. It is a remote mountain village called Alkayag."

"I heard that name before."

"Yes, on the first day we took this town when we chased the insurgents to the foothills and the edge of the forest. They were then retreating to their mountain lair in Alkayag. We should have finished them off, then and there."

"Why did you not do that?"

"We were not supposed to fight the enemy in a terrain like that, not good for our health. But now, it seems, we have to attack Alkayag, after all, and destroy it."

"We don't have much choice," a lieutenant said. "The insurgents will continue to harass us, as long as they have that camp."

"I know," Bill said. "We'll have to destroy that rebel sanctuary, once and for all. It will be a tough job, though. The insurgents, from what I have gathered, are led by this young, able commander."

He turned to Dick and said, "You might be interested to know him. His name is Paulo Palanas. He is the nephew of the town mayor whose wake and funeral procession, we saw a few weeks ago."

The Americans, in the following days, made preparation for their attack on Alkayag. Bill asked for and was given additional troops. Native scouts working for the Americans were sent to him. They were highly experienced in jungle warfare.

Bill's utmost concern was an engagement at night in the forest. He learned about the disaster that overtook Zatayde and his troops when they attempted to attack Alkayag.

He was going to avoid getting his troops, caught inside the forest at night. Also on his orders, the native scouts gave his troops, a crash course in jungle warfare.

The townsfolk saw in the big number of American troops arriving in the town that an American offensive against the Filipino troops in Alkayag was about to take place. Word about it reached Paulo.

"So, they are going to attack us," he said to his men. "Let them, come. We are ready for them."

He was poking with a stick, the embers of a campfire around which he, Sabedro and other soldiers were gathered.

The men around Paulo had served him and his uncle since the start of the revolution. He was facing a formidable enemy in the person of this Major Bill Shay who was not a madman like Captain Zatayde.

He swept with his eyes, his men gathered around the campfire. They will, as always, give a good account of themselves. He watched with casual interest, Sabedro, who had stoked back to life, the campfire's dying embers. He smiled at a big surprise he had in store for the Americans.

The Americans, two days later, moved out at daybreak toward Alkayag. As Bill had anticipated it, within an hour, he and his men were inside the forest, the insurgents, hidden by the trees and their dense undergrowth, were attacking them with guns, bows and arrows.

He was ready for them. His troops, following their native scouts' advice, met with concentrated gunfire any movement and any sound, no matter how slight, in the undergrowth and in the trees around them. The tactic paid off with some insurgents killed, wounded or captured. He pushed on with his men despite the insurgents' intermittent attacks.

The weather favored them. The rainy season was over and the ground was dry and easy to walk on. They had hiked up to what, by

Bill's estimate, was the last mountain peak before reaching Alkayag when they encountered the heaviest insurgent attack. They fought the insurgents that left them with several men, dead or wounded. They eventually prevailed with their bigger number and firepower. The attack ceased; the insurgents withdrew as silently as they came.

He pressed on until late afternoon when he saw smoke rising from the trees, east of them. There was no mistaking it—the insurgents were burning down their camp. He could not quite understand why the insurgents were giving it up, just like that, after having fought them tooth-and-nail inside the forest.

He reached the camp with his troops. It was fairly large with several dozen huts, some of them reduced to ashes while the others continued to burn. It covered a wide ground cleared mostly of trees and shrubs. A brook was running through in a corner in the camp.

His soldiers were asking each other, what they had accomplished, after all the fighting they went through in the forest. They came upon the camp, abandoned and destroyed by the insurgents.

Bill looked on, so disappointed at the destroyed rebel camp.

A captain asked him for his orders. He told the captain to set up a defensive position around the camp. They were staying there for the night.

Dick came and dropped down on the ground beside Bill.

"So, the fish got away," he said.

"A clever fish," Bill replied, a sour expression on his face. "He left nothing, but ashes."

"I can see why they fled, but must they burn down their camp, as well?"

"They did that to prevent us from using it."

"They may have set up another camp, where we do not know."

Bill stared at Dick and then turned his gaze to the camp. Dick could be right. The insurgents may have built another camp or maybe a number of small camps inside the forest. They will be much harder to find and destroy. He pursed his lips at how the enemy had outwitted him.

The Americans set up camp. They put up a barricade of tree branches and shrubs around the camp. It will be their defensive perimeter from the attacks, the insurgents are expected to launch tonight. They also set up piles of dry wood and twigs at intervals of twenty feet and forty feet in front of their barricade. They will keep the piles of wood burning the whole night to give them visibility of the camp and its surroundings.

Bill, as a final defensive measure, divided his troops into two groups, each group of almost a hundred soldiers doing sentry duty for a period of two hours each. They had then a lot of firepower, ready at any given time for the insurgents' attacks.

The soldiers on guard duty kept watch behind their barricade while the rest of the troops took a rest in the middle of the camp.

Bill was lying down on the ground, a few feet away from Dick who went to sleep immediately after their evening meal. Dick was so tired from their trek and skirmishes with the insurgents in the forest.

He was kept awake, though, by his responsibility as the commander of the troops and by the sporadic sniper attacks. They ceased after a while and he turned his gaze to the night sky. It was so peaceful, up there, his thoughts turned to Esperanza. She was so lovely and desirable as she played the beautiful song on the piano. A volley of gunfire interrupted him in his thoughts. He turned around, his elbows on the grass.

The insurgents were attacking. It was not as intensive as their last attack inside the forest. The bonfires had kept the camp and its surroundings, so well-lighted they prevented the insurgents from attacking beyond their forest cover.

Bill looked on at the forest, his mind working. The insurgents were attacking on orders from their leader. They will only be like a mob without him. The key was their leader.

The shooting ceased and Bill looked again at the night sky. The stars shining brilliantly now seemed to him to be trapped in the dark void of the universe.

A thought flashed in his mind and he formed from it, a plan so simple and so obvious, he asked himself why he had not thought of it before. Their leader, like those stars above him, maybe brilliant, but like them, when trapped, he would be just as confined and helpless as those brilliant stars. To get him will be far easier and less costly than this expedition he took to the enemy camp. The more, he thought about his plan, the more he was convinced that it will work. He finally fell asleep.

It was still dark, although sunlight had peeked out in the eastern horizon, when Bill woke up to Dick, who was shaking him on his shoulders. They took a light breakfast, broke camp and returned to Masakao. It was late in the afternoon when they arrived in the town.

Bill, Dick and his subordinate officers were in Bill's quarters, a few hours later, washing down their dinner with beer and rum.

"I hope that was the first and the last of our excursion to the mountains," Dick said to the other officers' laughter.

"Consider yourself fortunate for the exercise, you just had," Bill said, smiling and pointing at Dick's stomach. "You need that. With all the good food you are eating in this colony, your bay window is now quite noticeable."

Dick replied, smiling, as well, "I have ways of removing this bay window, but certainly not by hiking to those mountains."

"It was not a wasted effort, though," Bill said as he drank his beer. "We now know the enemy camp's location, how to get there and how to fight in the forest. Their mountain hideout is no longer of any use to them."

"There will be no letup in their sniper attacks," a captain said.

"No doubt about that," Bill said, seemingly unconcerned, which struck Dick as unusual.

He knew Bill well enough and that he did not disregard the insurgents' sniper attacks. Bill could be planning something.

Paulo resumed his sniper attacks, a few days after the Americans attacked his camp in Alkayag. He was emboldened, as the week wore on and more American soldiers fell dead or wounded to his troops' sniper attacks, to operate more frequently in the town from the two small camps he had set up in clearings inside the forest and much nearer to the town.

He concluded from their weak response to his nighttime attacks that the Americans, like the Spaniards, had no stomach for night fighting. He could very well take a stroll in the town roads at night. He could even pay Teresa, a visit, anytime he wanted to. The more he thought about it, the more he felt, a keen desire to see her.

He came to see her, one evening with an escort of three men. She was waiting for him in the dark balcony. A courier saw her earlier in the day and told her about his visit there tonight. He came alone in the balcony. His escorts stayed in the orchard to give them privacy.

She dropped into his arms, the moment he came to her. They then talked quietly, mostly about the war, for it bore so much on their lives.

"How is it going?" she asked him.

"We have the Americans frustrated here in Masakao, but I cannot say the same thing about the rest of the country. It is going badly for us. We can only hope to wear them down with our guerrilla attacks. That is all that we can do now."

"Do you see the end of the war soon?"

"I cannot tell that yet."

"Do you want the war to end soon?"

"I'll keep on fighting, as long as I can. But how about you, do you want the war to end soon?"

"Yes, so that we can get on with our lives."

"Should we, even under the Americans?"

"Yes, we should even under them. I care only for our future. We cannot have that with this war separating us."

He pulled her close to him. His warm breath, brushed her cheek as he then kissed her. She held on to him tightly. They remained locked in an embrace until he gently drew away. It was time for him to leave her.

She looked at him apprehensively and said, "You should not come here again. It is too dangerous."

"What are you afraid of? The Americans, right now, must be sound asleep in the town fort. You have nothing to worry about."

"Please be careful," she said as he was stepping down in the stairs.

She then hurried inside the house, locked the door and went to her bedroom.

Esperanza was in bed when she walked in and sat down on the bed. A radiant smile on her face, she seemed to be in a trance as she was looking out at the night sky, framed by the bedroom window.

Esperanza smiled. She said as she was watching Teresa, "That is what ardent kisses can do."

She tilted her head back and said to Esperanza, "You are only envious."

Esperanza made a face, so teasing Teresa playfully hit her with a pillow. They laughed, so sheer in delight they were made completely unaware of a commotion in the orchard.

Bill's native scouts had jumped on Paulo and his men and struck them down with wooden clubs and bamboo poles. He was knocked down to the ground with blows to his head, back and arms. He was only dimly aware of his arms then being tied behind his back and of being dragged out of the orchard and into a horse-drawn rig that then sped toward the town fort. Bill's native scouts, after days of discreet surveillance, had finally caught Paulo.

He was taken to the jail's interrogation room dimly lit by a gas lamp on a table in the middle of the room. He was made to sit down on a stool, surrounded by the native scouts who captured him.

They were flush with pride and excitement over what they had accomplished. One of them boasted that it was the punch he threw at Paulo's face that sent him down on the ground that enabled them to tie him up. The others mocked Paulo and called him names.

He sat straight and his head held high, he ignored the native scouts. His defiant posture had so provoked one of them that he punched

Paulo on his face just as Bill, Dick and a couple of guards were entering the interrogation room.

"Stop that!" Bill shouted at the native scouts.

They snapped to attention. Bill shook his head when he saw what they had done to Paulo. He had black eyes, his nose and lips were a bloody mess, his cheeks were swollen, his arms were bruised and there was a lump on his head.

He told a guard to untie Paulo. Then he turned to the native scouts who told him how they captured Paulo. He said nothing to the native scouts and dismissed them.

They left, looking so disappointed, for Bill did not commend them for capturing Paulo.

He turned to Paulo instead and said to him, "You may consider yourself as our unwilling guest here. You will undergo tactical interrogation tomorrow. It is all a part of our routine. Be assured, you will be treated as a gentleman and a military officer and not the way, your own countrymen had so violently treated you."

Paulo gazed sullenly at the floor and said nothing. His wrists rubbed raw by the rope and the pain in various parts of his body showed him otherwise. He will get the water cure. Zatayde applied that form of torture on Masinop, Pinalis, Julio and the other prisoners in the fort jail. The Americans will likely do that to him, too.

"Get the doctor. Tell him, we have a patient here," Bill said to a guard.

Doctor Bihasa came in a short while with his medical bag.

"Will you take a look at the prisoner?" Bill said to Doctor Bihasa.

Their eyes met as Doctor Bihasa was taking a look at Paulo's wounds.

"Don't get any wrong ideas about me," Doctor Bihasa said to Paulo in their local dialect. "I agreed to work for them so I would know what they are doing or are planning to do in our town."

Paulo nodded, satisfied with Bihasa's explanation.

"Are they going to give me the water cure?" he asked Bihasa, a look of concern on his face.

"I never saw nor heard them do that."

Paulo nodded in relief. He sat stoically, bearing the pain as Doctor Bihasa then treated his wounds.

"Take care now," Bihasa said to Paulo at the end of the medical treatment.

He picked up his medical bag, nodded at Bill and Dick and left.

Bill ordered the guards to take Paulo to his cell. Then he left the interrogation room and returned with Dick to his quarters in the town fort.

"How did you capture the insurgent leader?" Dick asked Bill as they were going up in the stairs to Bill's quarters. "How did you even know, he will be visiting someone in the Dumayags' home?"

"It was just a hunch."

"It is more than that."

"Do you remember the picture of Paulo Palanas and his uncle, the mayor, in the Dumayags' house? Their picture gave away their special relationship with the Dumayag family, especially Paulo. I sensed who among them has a special feeling for him, from the way she treated us."

"You are referring to Teresa."

Bill nodded and said, "She dislikes us or may even hate us because we were fighting her lover and for killing their mayor, her lover's uncle. Once I have established that, I needed only to be patient and capture Paulo with the native scouts when he would see her."

"That is a fine analytical work, you have done," Dick said as they sat down on a couch in the sitting room of Bill's quarters.

"I have also done myself a favor."

"And what is that?"

"Now I am quite certain, Esperanza is not the object of Paulo Palanas' affection."

"What if she is the insurgent leader's girl?"

"I don't want to even think about that."

"Would you then turn your attention to Teresa? You will have to admit, she is the most beautiful among them."

"No doubt, she is so beautiful, but then, I have got to admit that, neither you nor I, stands the chance of getting the insurgent leader's girl and I don't like losing—in love or in war. In any case, I have already made my choice. I like her sister, not her. How about you, who are you after, among those three beautiful women?"

"We are not competing for the same girl. I like Nieves. Not only is she pretty and friendly, she has a beautiful voice and I think she likes me."

"And liking is just an embrace away from loving."

"You said it exactly right."

Bill stood up and took out from a cabinet, a bottle of brandy and two glasses. He filled them with the liquor and, as he sat down on another couch, he gave Dick, one of the two glasses.

"Let us have a toast," he said, "to the capture of Paulo Palanas and the end of the insurgency in this town."

They raised their glasses and tipped them to their lips. They sighed in pleasure as the liquor coursed down their throats.

Dick said, after he had taken a good measure of his liquor, "It is ironic how this man who is the most serious threat to the peace in this town could also be its best hope in the future."

"You seem to have taken a liking to the prisoner."

"Why should I not feel that way? You have got to hand it to him for fighting on, despite the odds against him. Only a committed person will do that. He is the kind of person you would rather have for a friend than for an enemy. When you fight him, you are also fighting the whole town. The townsfolk look up to him. They will take his capture badly."

"It is my duty to capture him. He is an enemy or have you forgotten that?"

"He is an enemy today who could be a good friend, a very good friend tomorrow."

"I hope so, too. Good treatment might change him from an enemy to a good friend, a very good friend."

"Doing that will hardly make any difference from the way some of our forces are treating the enemy. We might end up like the Spaniards who came and left, hated and unwanted."

"We are different from them. We don't abuse and exploit other people. We have good intentions for this colony. We are here to bring to them, the many benefits of our rule. We will do that once we finish off this insurgency. You know that, too."

"The good intentions you are talking about just don't match with what some of our forces are doing to the natives. You know that, too. You know how the concentration of some of the towns had caused terrible hardships to the people there."

"War regrettably makes some of us do what they will never do in time of peace, but once we have finished this insurgency, you will see what our country will do for those people."

"That may be so, but that is a long way off yet. In the meantime, we have this problem with the prisoner. Never mind Teresa, we just cannot get to her, but what I am concerned about is how Nieves and Esperanza will take Paulo Palanas' capture and imprisonment."

Dick and Bill were not getting anywhere with them. They were friendly, that was all. They could even lose that friendship with Paulo's capture and imprisonment.

"He will be out of the jail in no time at all," Bill then said, "if he will stop fighting us and take the oath of allegiance to our country. I will give him, if he will refuse to do that, privileges that will make his imprisonment, not so disagreeable to him and the three ladies."

Dick, two days later, went around the town on horseback. He was alone. Bill, who usually went riding with him, could not pull himself away from work.

Nieves was, just as he had hoped, tending her garden when he came by. He greeted her a good morning and asked her, how she was doing with her gardening. She nodded and went on with her gardening.

He shook his head at her cold reception. She was not happy with the capture of Paulo Palanas.

He steered her to a more agreeable subject with a comment in their local dialect, he picked up from the townsfolk, on how the flowers in her garden were blooming so beautifully. He smiled, amused, at how she then busied herself all the more with her gardening. She was trying to ignore the compliment he made of speaking to her in her local dialect.

"I have a fingertip-size garden and vineyard at the back of our house in San Francisco," he then said to her, "but they don't grow as well and as beautifully as the flowering plants, there in your garden."

She busied herself all the more with her gardening.

He looked away, disappointed. He was not making any headway with her. He then said, his eyes turned to the Dumayags' house, beside her garden, "You and your friends there could see someone badly in need of your company."

She stopped abruptly from her gardening, her eyes, large in utter surprise, now turned to him.

"Major Shay," he continued, "is not only allowing you, Esperanza and Teresa to visit Paulo Palanas and bring him food every day. He will be set free once he accepts the American rule and takes the oath of allegiance to the United States."

He saw her, now smiling. He had made up with her. He tipped his hat to her, said good day to her and had his horse moving away from there.

Nieves looked on at Dick, who was so magnificent on horseback. She should not have been so cold to him. It was necessary, though, to show to him that she did not approve of them in capturing Paulo. But he is not a bad sort, at all. He said they could even bring food to Paulo everyday. He will even be released from jail, just by taking the oath of allegiance to the United States. She was now, more than ever, convinced about Dick as a good, friendly man.

Her footsteps were light and quick as she then crossed her garden and went up to Teresa and Esperanza's house. They were in the living room, doing embroidery work. She told them, they could see Paulo and bring him food.

"We can see him and bring him food?" Teresa and Esperanza said.

"Not only that," Nieves said, smiling. "He can be out of the jail in no time at all. All he has to do is take the oath of allegiance to the United States."

"Paulo could be out of there, by doing just that?" Teresa and Esperanza said.

Nieves nodded and smiled even more broadly.

Teresa suddenly stood up and went to the bedroom. She had changed into another dress, a shawl over her shoulders, when she returned to the living room.

"I am going to see Paulo," she said to Nieves and Esperanza.

"Are you not bringing him something?" Esperanza said to Teresa who was already at the door to the balcony.

She halted and said, "Like what?"

"Like *Adobo*, his favorite food," Esperanza said. "Paulo will like that after the terrible food, I can imagine, they are feeding him there."

Teresa remained at the door, undecided on what to do.

"Very well, go ahead," Esperanza said with a sigh. "Nieves and I will follow with the food."

"The Adobo will be fine and easy to cook," Nieves said.

Teresa smiled and went down quickly in the stairs.

The jail's receiving room was cold and damp, the heat from the morning sun, not having penetrated it yet. Teresa was seated on a bench before a table there. She was facing the door that led to the cells where Paulo will be coming from.

She pulled at her shawl tightly around her arms to keep the cold away. How hard it must be for anyone to be confined there. She knew about the terrible things done to the prisoners there. Her own father had a stroke from the terrible treatment by Zatayde and his jailers.

She trembled at the thought of Paulo who might also be suffering from the same kind of treatment from the Americans. But the American soldiers had been behaving well, she suspected on orders of Major Shay, who may not be so unlikeable. Her face softened at the thought of Major Shay's nice, friendly gesture of allowing her to visit Paulo and bring him food. He was even willing to set Paulo free.

A guard ushered in Paulo and left. He looked sullen as he sat down on the table across Teresa who was looking at him, her mouth hanging open and her eyes wide from shock. His cheeks and lips were swollen; he had dark crescents beneath both of his eyes; a bandage was wound around his head and in both of his arms. Paulo's wounds showed her, he had been treated so badly in the jail.

She touched his face tenderly, her eyes blurry with tears and said to him, "What have they done to you?"

"This," he replied, "is the work of the scouts, our own countrymen who waylaid me and my men in your orchard."

She said as she was wiping with her palm, the tears in her eyes, "How about the Americans? How are they treating you?"

"I have nothing to complain about that."

"I came as soon as I learned that I could see you. Esperanza and Nieves are coming with the Adobo, your favorite food."

He smiled at the mention of the food, but then, his face had lapsed again into a tired, weary look.

She sighed. Not even her presence could lift him from depression, but she came bearing good news. It will lift his spirit and she said, "You can be out of this jail, anytime you want to."

"What!" he said, his eyes wide in astonishment.

"Mister McCall told Nieves a while ago that Major Shay will set you free once you have taken the oath of allegiance to the United States. Is that not wonderful?"

"I will never do that."

"Why? What is so hard about saying a few words?"

"They are not just words."

She was about to speak again, but he cut her short with a curt wave of his hand. He did not want them to talk about it.

Days passed. Bill, in an effort to soften Paulo's resistance, gave him as many privileges as he could. Teresa, Esperanza and Nieves were allowed to visit him every day and bring him food, which Bill heartily approved of, for they also set aside portions of the food for him and Dick, whenever he was in town. The townsfolk were allowed to visit Paulo, once a month. He was also allowed to receive books which, with time in his hands, he read avidly. He tried writing poetry, but was devoid of feeling that he could express with the written word. He wrote instead political essays, which Teresa smuggled out of the jail.

Bill and Dick watched how those privileges worked in bringing down Paulo's resistance. He remained steadfast. They were at first disappointed, but were later satisfied and were even pleased when they realized how Paulo's resistance was working in their favor. Teresa, Esperanza and Nieves brought him food everyday and set aside portions for them. Out of this frequent contact, a deep kind of friendship had developed between them and the women, not possible under other circumstances. It was, as Bill and Dick were hoping, a step toward a more meaningful relationship with Esperanza, in the case of Bill and with Nieves, in the case of Dick.

This situation did not last long, though. Bill was ordered, a few weeks later, to bring Paulo to Manila. He will, from there, be sent into exile in the island penal colony of Corona.

Doctor Bihasa and Gayuman gathered the townsfolk at the fort entrance, the morning Paulo was to be taken out of the jail and brought to Manila. They were seeing him off, their leader they admired for his battlefield exploits and his unyielding resistance to the Americans.

Julio and Agustina stayed the shortest of those allowed to see Paulo in the jail's receiving room. They said words to comfort him and then took turns in hugging him as if he was their own son. They approved of his future marriage to Teresa, which now seemed to be so remote. They stepped outside after saying good-bye to him.

Esperanza said, as she was embracing Paulo, to keep himself in good health. Nieves, at a loss of what to say, repeated what Esperanza said.

Teresa watched them quietly, for she was too distressed to say anything. Paulo was going to a dark, forbidding island, far from her, a prospect he seemed to face bravely as he stood, facing calmly, Esperanza and Nieves. He was the same unflinching Paulo who bore stoically whatever ill wind was upon him.

Seeing him like that, thus gave Teresa momentary hope. They will both endure as they had in their previous partings. But those were far different partings from this one. He could then see her anytime, he wanted to. Those were only temporary partings, unlike this one. He was going to a forbidding island. No one, her troubled mind had imagined, had ever left it alive.

Esperanza and Nieves had left the room. Now alone with him, Teresa could no longer hold back her tears. She embraced Paulo tightly, the last time she will hold him for a long time, maybe even for the last time!

She trembled at that thought and clung even more tightly to Paulo. This did not have to happen, he did not have to leave her, but she could not ask him to change his mind about taking the oath of allegiance. It was pointless to even mention that.

Chapter Twenty-three

Paulo was taking a nap, dressed only in his shorts because of the heat in the ship's hold, when the ship blew its horn, announcing its arrival in Corona. He dressed up quickly, went up to the deck and looked out at the island. It was beautiful. Sea waves were lapping gently at its white sand beach, the leaves of the palm trees there, swaying gently with the wind.

He would have been charmed by its beauty, had he arrived there for some other reason. It only added to his loneliness. He was looking at the island with the eyes of an exile, a beautiful island far from those dear to him. He was there for his refusal to take the oath.

The ship dropped its anchor. Some of the island's residents appeared on the beach and watched what the ship was bringing in.

Paulo went down in the accommodation ladder at the side of the ship and boarded a rowboat the ship's crew had lowered into the water.

He wedged himself between sacks and boxes of supplies for the prison camp. The boatswain and a crewmember then paddled the boat toward the island. It was, in just a short while, alongside the island's tiny concrete pier. The boatswain went up first to the pier.

Paulo followed the boatswain. His bundle of clothes tucked under his arm, he stepped up into the pier. His leather sandals scraped its surface of stone and coral as he walked on with the boatswain. A sergeant met them.

"So, we have another prisoner here," the sergeant said to the boatswain. "Do you know the way to the camp?"

"I have been here before," the boatswain replied. "I will bring this prisoner to Captain Croyce myself. You attend to the supplies."

Paulo and the boatswain proceeded toward the interior of the island. They arrived in the camp which Paulo saw was identical in some respects to his camp in Alkayag. It was on a flat ground about triple the size of his camp in Alkayag and fenced with barbed wire. Rows of bamboo huts stood facing across an open space, the camp commander's office and quarters, a wooden building roofed with palm shingles.

A guard let them pass through the gate.

Captain Walter Croyce, the prison camp commander, watched from a window in his office, Paulo and the boatswain as they were crossing the prison camp.

He returned the boatswain's salute, the moment he and Paulo had entered his office.

"We have another prisoner here, sir," the boatswain said as he was giving Captain Croyce, Paulo's file in a sealed envelope.

The boatswain saluted again, turned around and left.

Paulo sat down as he was directed by Captain Croyce to a chair in front of his desk.

Captain Croyce then returned to his desk.

He has a husky build, his bearded, tanned face with its rough features spoke of a life he had spent mostly outdoors. He was in his early thirties. He towered over Paulo, at his height of more than six feet, by nearly a head. He sat down, opened the envelope and read the file on Paulo.

He raised his eyes to Paulo to confirm what the file said about him. His youthfulness, haggard looks and slim build did not fit with what the file said about him as a fanatical insurgent leader.

He certainly does not look like it, Captain Croyce said to himself as he was looking on at Paulo. But he does not expect any difficulties with him. He was just another lost and defeated insurgent leader. This new arrival was one more inmate in the prison camp of three dozen recalcitrant insurgent officers out of a prison population of two hundred twenty-three inmates, the great majority of whom were ordinary convicts.

"It says here, you speak English well," Captain Croyce said to Paulo. "Where did you learn it?"

"I learned the basics in school. The rest I taught myself."

"What school did you go to? Was it, elementary or high school?"

"I was in college. I was going to take up law when the revolution broke out."

"It also says here, you are a colonel."

"That is correct."

"Say, 'sir,' when you are addressing me."

"You are a captain, I am a colonel. I will not say, 'sir,' to you."

"Damn you, boy. I don't care, if you are a general. You are just a prisoner here."

Paulo stared ahead, a defiant look in his face, but he remained silent.

Captain Croyce was fuming still as he returned to Paulo's file. He was jolted by what he read there. The military headquarters in Fort Santiago wrote that Paulo is a brilliant insurgent leader and that he, Captain Croyce, should go easy on him, make every effort to win him over and to encourage him to take the oath of allegiance to the United States. It said further that with the prisoner's educational attainment and fine qualities of leadership, he could later be useful in the American administration of the colony.

Captain Croyce sighed. An order is an order.

He said to Paulo, "You will be confined in an area separated from the rest of the prison camp by a chain-link fence. The main prison camp is for ordinary convicts. They are not let out. You are a political prisoner and you are allowed to move around at a fixed time of the day. But don't even think about escaping from this island. The only way out of here is by the sea. There are a few fishing boats in this island, but they are kept under guard at all times. This island has a native population of about three hundred people. You are free to socialize with them at the time when you are let out, but don't engage in anything political or subversive."

Captain Croyce opened a drawer in his desk, pulled out a sheet of paper there and gave it to Paulo.

"Those," he said to Paulo, "are the camp regulations. You will conduct yourself accordingly. You will also be provided with supplies for your personal use.

"The length of your stay here depends on no one, but yourself. You are a political prisoner brought here because of your refusal to accept American rule of this colony. You can choose to take the oath of allegiance to the United States and be returned to Manila in the same ship that brought you here or you can choose to rot here. Which one is it?"

"I would rather rot here than take the oath."

"All the political prisoners say that when they arrive here. Like them, you will soon eat your words."

Captain Croyce dismissed Paulo with a curt wave of his hand. A soldier then accompanied him to the supply hut.

"Politics," Captain Croyce said to himself as he was watching Paulo who was crossing the prison camp to the supply hut.

He was given a mat, a pillow, a blanket, a toothbrush and a tube of toothpaste, a towel and a bar of soap. The soldier with him then showed him, his quarters, a bamboo hut he was to share with five other prisoners. The hut was empty. Its occupants were at work in the shops and in the fields.

"This is your first day here, so you are excused from work, but tomorrow, like all the others, you will work in the fields and in the shops," the soldier said and left.

He removed his sandals and laid down his things on the bamboo floor. He looked around. There were men's things and clothes laid neatly in a row along a wall of palm shingles. They gave him a sense of order and purpose in the hut that looked so dreary.

This will be the home, or more correctly, the prison quarters of a man like him, a man with no future, a man whose only ardor left was for a lost cause and a lost love.

He had enough of those gloomy thoughts and he turned to the practical matter of learning about the camp regulations. He picked up the sheet of paper Captain Croyce gave him and read it. It was a monotonous litany of what he could and could not do in the prison camp.

A cool breeze passing through the gaps in the bamboo floor made him drowsy and he soon dozed off. He woke up moments later when he heard men talking as they were entering the hut. He blinked his eyes and rubbed them as they adjusted to the sight of five men who were looking down at him. He stood up and faced them.

The hut, he noticed, was now cramped with six of them standing there.

"So, you are the new arrival," one of them, apparently their leader, said to him.

Paulo nodded and said, "I hope I have not taken anyone's sleeping space here."

"No, you have not," the man said. "That space is yours. It was vacated, two weeks ago."

"Why, what happened?" he asked the man.

"The fellow who used to sleep there ended up where all of us may end up, too—in the camp cemetery," the man replied, baring uneven teeth as he broke into a cynical laughter.

"Where did you fight the Americans?" another man asked him.

"I last fought them in Masakao."

"Where is that?" the man asked him.

"Is that a part of the Philippines?" another man asked him.

"It must be an island, somewhere in the Pacific Ocean," another man said as they laughed at him.

Paulo's eyes were narrowed in anger at the men. They were patronizing him. They were making fun of him. They were looking at him dubiously at his youthfulness and slim build. He wondered who they were. If they were with the top leadership, he would have met and known them.

"And where are you from?" he asked them.

"We are from the Visayas," the man with the uneven teeth replied about the central region in the colony.

"Have you been to Manila?" he asked the man..

"We never had the chance to go there."

"So, you have never met Aguinaldo."

"Have you met him?"

"I am a colonel in Aguinaldo's staff in Hong Kong, in Cavite and in Malolos. I was twice in command of a battalion of troops."

The men looked, stunned, at Paulo. He is their superior officer.

"I'm sorry, sir, if we have been rude to you," the man with the uneven teeth said.

He nodded in acceptance of the man's apology. His authority over them was implied by the way the men, in their embarrassment, now averted their eyes from him. Thankfully for them, lunchtime was then announced by the clanging of the iron triangle in the prison mess hall. He nodded, giving the men permission to move out of the hut.

He took his time in going there, where he brought up the rear of the prisoners lined up at the food counter. He took a plate from a tower of plates there and held it before a kitchen helper standing at the other side of the counter. The kitchen helper then scooped with a dipper, rice from a large pot there and put it down on Paulo's plate. He did the same procedure with a small fried fish and a vegetable dish.

Paulo found no delight in eating the food that was tasteless, but for the salt in the fried fish. It was not like the delicious food brought to him every day in the town fort jail by Teresa, Esperanza and Nieves. He would not have touched the food, at all, but he was so hungry, he ate and finished it quickly. He had only bread, butter and coffee since the ship left Manila.

The political prisoners went back to work. They were allowed a free time of two hours before supper. They left for the village individually, in pairs, or in small groups. Most of them stayed in the camp grounds and engaged there in small talk.

Paulo kept to himself. He walked around the camp, but tired of it, after a while. He was so depressed. He was like that since he left Masakao. The best thing to do then was to sleep it away. He went back to the hut and went to sleep. He woke up, moments later, to the sound of footsteps on the bamboo floor. The other men had come in. They moved on a tiptoe so as not to disturb him. Then he heard mats being rolled out on the floor. Silence followed, broken later by the men breathing deeply as they slept. It was the end of another day in what was an unchanging pattern of life in the prison camp.

He was falling asleep when the crickets in the trees around the camp began to trill. The sounds they made brought his mind back to the last night he was with Teresa in Masakao. The crickets that night also trilled there. How he wished, he could be with her once again and hold her in his arms. He missed her so much.

Paulo adjusted quickly in the next few days to life in the prison camp. He was up and about at the clanging of the iron triangle, early in the morning when it was still dark. He was, like the other prisoners, allowed a few minutes to wash up in the bathhouse. He was, after a simple breakfast of fried rice, fish and coffee, off to work in the fields and in the shops. Lunch was at noon at the mess hall and, after an hour of rest, it was more work in the fields and in the shops.

The prisoners raised their own vegetable crops. He was gratified by work. Not only did he love to make things grow, work also kept him occupied and away from depressing, idle thoughts.

A few days had passed when he decided to make use of his free time by going to the beach. He chose a hollow in the sand, in the shade of a palm tree to take in the quiet, beautiful scenery. The sea breeze, as he expected, was invigorating. The rhythmic advance and retreat of the sea waves on the beach, a fishing boat out in the dark, blue sea, the palm leaves swaying with the cool sea breeze and the flight of birds in the cloudless sky were all very touching to him.

He sat there for a while, his elbows on his knees and basked in the silence and beauty of the beach and the sea. It would have been a good time and place to write a letter to Teresa if he had a pen and paper.

Captain Croyce, he noticed, was watching him in his first few days in the prison camp, what was on the camp commandant's mind, he could only guess. He was satisfied, later on, when Captain Croyce treated him with indifference. It will stay that way simply by following the prison camp regulations.

He took in the sea breeze and the scenery for a few more minutes, glad of the time, he had spent well there. Then he stood up, brushed away, the sand from the seat of his pants and walked toward the village.

The village road, he found out, was more of a wide trail than a road, the trees at its sides cleared of their underbrush. The houses there stood in small clearings, set back a few yards from the road. But for the houses there and the trees cleared of underbrush, the village appeared to him as just like the forest in Alkayag.

It was midafternoon and the shrubs, the houses and the trees there were now dotted with sunlight. Children playing tag on the road, paused from their game and looked on as he was passing by them.

He was walking on when he saw a store and huts around a wide ground, in what looked to him was the center of the village. A young woman tending it watched him as he was coming to the store. He said good afternoon to her.

She nodded and smiled at his friendly greeting and looked on from behind the glass counter as he then bent down for a look at the fruits and the pastries in the lower shelves.

A young man just then walked in and asked the woman about a tool he was looking for. The woman replied, he should first look for it in the toolshed before asking her about it. The man was about to leave when he saw Paulo.

"Is that you, Paulo?" the young man asked him.

He stood up, his mouth hanging open in surprise, and said to the young man, "Agerico, of all people! What are you doing here?"

"I should ask you, the same question," Agerico replied, smiling.

They laughed and slapped each other's arm while the woman looked on curiously at them.

"You have not changed, at all," Agerico said to Paulo. "Well, you look thin, just a little bit. But what brought you here? No, you don't have to tell me. You are an inmate in the prison camp."

"What other reason, do I have for being here?"

"I was brought here for the same reason."

"How come you are running a store here and not confined like me in the prison camp?"

"It is a long story."

Agerico wrapped his arm around the woman's waist and said to Paulo, "I would not have stayed in this island, if not for Consorcia here, my dear, lovely wife."

He said to her, "You have finally met Paulo."

"Rico has told me a lot about you," she said to Paulo.

"Good things, I hope."

"Rico always said good things about you. Hardly a week passes by without him telling me something about you, your uncle, your townsfolk and your hometown. I hope to visit it someday."

"Please do."

"Wait, wait," Rico said to Paulo, "let us not just stand here."

He led Paulo toward the door at the side of the store while Consorcia left for the kitchen at the back of the store to prepare something for Paulo.

He halted as he stood beside Agerico at the sill of the door and looked around at the living room, opened by Agerico. It was cluttered with boxes of merchandise piled on top of each other.

"I know, you don't have to tell me," Agerico said as they were crossing the room toward a large wooden couch there. "It is not like our homes in Masakao. It is making money above everything else here."

He said, as they sat down on the couch, "Consorcia comes from a family of merchants. This is their house."

"Where are her parents?"

"They are both dead, her mother, a couple of months ago, her father, two years ago. She has a brother; he lives in Cebu. She inherited this property."

"You told me what made you stay here, not what brought you here."

"It was for the same reason that brought you here, although it was the Spaniards, not the Americans, who exiled me in this island."

"How did it happen?"

Agerico stretched his legs on the floor and the back of his head on his clasped hands, he looked up at the ceiling as he collected his thoughts. He said as he was turning to Paulo, "Do you remember the battle we waged against Achutegui and Zatayde? Your uncle and I were captured while we were covering your withdrawal to Alkayag. Achutegui freed your uncle so he could convince you to give up the fight. Of course, nothing came out of it. I was transferred from the fort jail in Masakao to Fort Santiago. I was brought here, a few days later, with other prisoners. I have been here since then."

"You could have returned to Masakao."

"I have thought of doing that, but then I married Consorcia. I have been occupied ever since with raising a family and making a living here."

"So, you have children."

"That is the sad part. We are still childless. Consorcia and I may not be trying hard enough to have one."

Consorcia came in just then, her face flush in embarrassment. She heard what Agerico said. She glanced sharply at Agerico as she was putting on the coffee table, a tray of coffee and rice cake. She left the room, frowning.

Agerico pointed to the tray. Paulo complied. He drank the coffee and finished eating the rice cake with several bites of it. It was the most delicious food he had eaten since he arrived in the penal island.

He asked Paulo, "A lot must have happened in Masakao since I was brought to this island. How did the Americans get you?"

The question rekindled painful thoughts, but Paulo felt he had bottled them up, long enough. Agerico listened as he then spoke at great length about the truce, the resumption of the revolution, the war with the Americans, what he did in Masakao, Malolos, Manila and the events that had transpired since then. He also talked about the death of his uncle.

"I loved your uncle as much as you did," Agerico said. "I was in the fort jail when I learned that Mulawin, Kabisig, Masinop and Pinalis were dead. It seems everyone is dead."

"Not everyone. Ongliko fled to Hong Kong and never returned to Masakao. Gayuman and Doctor Bihasa are still in town although Gayuman has been quite ill lately."

"They died for our freedom that remains beyond our reach."

They fell silent, their faces gloomy.

"You will join us for dinner, won't you?" Consorcia said to Paulo when she returned to the living room.

"Thank you, but I'm still full with the rice cake," Paulo said as he then stood up. "I have got to go. I should be back in the camp, by now."

Agerico stood up also and said, "Come back tomorrow. Come here everyday and have dinner with us."

"I am not allowed to take dinner, outside the prison camp."

"I'll see what I can do about that."

"Can you?"

"You will find that out, soon enough."

Paulo nodded and walked hurriedly toward the prison camp.

He was back in Agerico and Consorcia's house and store in the afternoon break, the following day. Like the day before, Agerico asked him more questions about the town and the war. He spoke with great warmth and enthusiasm about Masakao, but was depressed when he talked about the war.

"It is going badly for us," he said to Agerico.

"You mean, we will lose the war."

"I am not ready to accept that. We can still bring the Americans to a stalemate if we can wear them down with constant guerrilla attacks until we reach the point when they will settle for talks to end the war."

"That means the end is not yet in sight."

"It is far from it."

"So there will be more struggle and hardship, more pain and death."

"It looks that way. Among those spared from all that horror are those who were involuntarily kept away from the war, like you. Are you a prisoner here with conjugal and live-out privileges?"

"No. After the Spaniards left and the Americans took over this prison camp, I took the oath of allegiance, as I, by then a civilian, was asked to do. I saw no point in continuing the fight with the Americans."

Paulo had a mind to reproach Agerico for allowing himself to be so taken by the Americans, but he decided not to talk about it. Their contrary views about the Americans did not have to come between them.

"Why did you not go back to Masakao?" he asked Agerico. "You and Consorcia could set up a store there."

"I have thought about that, but we have already settled down here and I have been doing here, what I have always wanted to do, that is, to paint without much distraction. Let me show you something."

Agerico led Paulo to an adjoining room, an artist's studio. There were paintings hanging on the walls there and canvases laid in rows against a wall. An easel stood in a corner.

Paulo looked at the paintings, his eyes bright in admiration of them and Agerico.

There were paintings of Masakao and its people. There were battle scenes like the one they fought against Chemari Achutegui, south of the town. It was a panorama of the townsfolk on the trench who were shooting at the Spaniards who, led by Chemari mounted on a gray stallion, were charging toward them.

Another painting showed people gathered around Mulawin and his uncle as they were urging them to rise up in revolt, moments before their confrontation with Zatayde. Another one, on the fighting for the town fort, showed the townsfolk ramming down the fort gate with a large wooden pole. Fray Gustavo was shown waving a large white cloth in the church belfry.

Paulo looked on gravely at the paintings. Agerico had done them in dark somber and harsh colors with the subjects shown to be in pain, anguish or in anger. It was not Agerico's style of painting and it did not conform with his cheerful outlook on life.

He found the paintings disturbing and he turned to the other side of the studio. He nodded in approval of the more pleasant subjects of the paintings there—the town scenes.

Agerico was in his element there. He painted them in his signature sweet and light colors.

There was a painting of boys, straw hats on their heads, fishing in the river with the bamboo poles in their hands.

There were paintings that marked the seasons, of farmers planting or harvesting their rice crops, of the countryside, of a nipa hut in a quiet summer afternoon and of the men engaged in a cockfight, their favorite pastime.

He turned to the portraits of Mulawin, a cigar clamped between his teeth and of his uncle who was shown to be in deep thought. His eyes lingered at a portrait of Teresa, who was shown looking out from a window, her beauty, haunting and inviting and there he was in a portrait of a passionate young man.

He looked at the other paintings of various scenes in the island, portraits of Consorcia and Agerico's self-portrait done in Agerico's sweet light colors.

"Well, what you have shown in those paintings! They can fill a gallery," he said. "They are so lifelike, so beautiful!"

Agerico, he noted in admiration of his friend, had with brush and paint recreated on the canvas the varied spectacle of people living, loving and waging war.

"You have seen one more reason why I stayed in this island," Agerico said to Paulo.

"It is an eminently good reason. You are doing your life's work as an artist. I'm amazed at how you have painted our townsfolk, myself included, and those scenes from memory and rendered them in a way that they appear on the canvas as if they are in flesh and blood. They are, my friend, great artistic creations."

"I like to recreate on the canvas, persons, places and events dear and memorable to me."

They talked for the better part of the afternoon in great detail about the paintings. Not only did Paulo see in those paintings, great artistic creations, they brought him back to Masakao, making him nostalgic about their hometown.

Blank canvases and other painting materials in a corner of the room caught Paulo's eyes.

"You seem to be well-provided with supplies," he said to Agerico.

"You will be surprised to know that everything, I need to paint, came all the way from America, compliments of your camp commandant."

"Captain Croyce?"

Agerico smiled. "Yes, the one and only Captain Croyce."

"How did you and the camp commandant become friends?"

"It came about accidentally. I was on the beach one day, drawing a seascape with charcoal on a piece of paper, one of the few pieces I had then. Captain Croyce came by. He had been assigned to the island, just a few days then. 'Remarkable,' he said, from behind me. I turned around and saw him, looking at my drawing. He asked me a few questions and left. I was summoned to his office, the following day. I went there, worried that I might have done something wrong. My worries turned out to be groundless.

"Instead of an interrogation, I was worried about I had a pleasant time with Captain Croyce. He talked about his wife and his two children, he left in Indiana. He showed me their pictures. He asked me, 'Can you paint them, for me?' I replied I would be glad to do that, but I have no painting supplies. He told me to write down everything I needed to paint.

"I had, within two months, enough paint, brushes, canvases, even an easel to paint as much as I wanted to. If I ran out of anything, all I had to do was tell him. And I did paint his wife and their two children. The paintings now grace his home in Indiana. His wife wrote to him that everyone who saw them liked them and admired them. They included his portrait, which I did in his office and other paintings about the island. I had Captain Croyce eating since then from the palm of my hand."

"So, that is what you meant when you said, you will see what you can do about me, taking dinner here."

"That and other things," Agerico said, smiling.

Paulo, through Agerico's intercession, was given relative freedom and privileges like eating out in the house of Agerico and Consorcia. He was happy to see Captain Croyce become so well-disposed to him he was now treated, less as a prisoner and more as a well-liked acquaintance. Captain Croyce would ask him, every time they ran across each other, how he was getting along or he would ask him, a thing or two about the colony.

The other prisoners soon deferred to him when they learned about his rank, the position he occupied in Aguinaldo's staff and his combat experience. But he had no desire to be so close and intimate with anyone of them. Agerico and Consorcia were enough company for him.

Life in the island was, for the most part, pleasant for him. He would, in those times when he was feeling sad and lonely, stroll down the beach, the sea breeze and the sea's constant rhythmic advance and retreat on the beach eventually calming down his sad and troubled mind.

One privilege, he treasured, was the mail he could send out and receive. Teresa was, between him and her, the more avid letter-writer. She wrote a lot about what was going on in Masakao. He, on the other hand, had very little to write about in the penal island. The only persons he cared to write about were Agerico and Consorcia and there was not much that he could write about them except that they were very happy and satisfied with the life they were leading in Corona.

He was amused to learn from Teresa's letters that Dick McCall was courting Nieves while Major Bill Shay was courting Esperanza.

"Neither of them made the mistake of wooing me or else I will laugh at him and out of our town," Teresa wrote one time. "My heart will accept no love, but yours."

He nodded, proud and pleased, but he could imagine, the tough time the two Americans were having in courting Nieves and Esperanza.

As Teresa also wrote, "They must draw a lot of water and cut a lot of firewood before they could even get a nod of approval or a word of encouragement from Esperanza and Nieves."

He smiled, amused by the reference Teresa made to the manner of courtship in Masakao although, he thought proudly, he did not go through that humbling experience in courting her.

The town suitors had to prove their sincerity and industry as prospective husbands. They cut firewood, drew water and made themselves virtually servants of the women they were courting. Major Shay and Dick McCall may not cut firewood or draw water, as the town's suitors do, but to be kept waiting and hoping—that was humbling enough for the two Americans. How Teresa must enjoy watching them go through that.

She also wrote that the townsfolk had grudgingly accepted the American rule of their town because it was the practical thing to do. Without him, their leader, they had lost the will to fight. The townsfolk had turned instead to peaceful pursuits like agriculture, home industry and something novel there, a school set up by Dick McCall and Major Shay at the ground floor of the municipal building. They followed the fad among the American soldiers of starting such schools in the towns they now occupied. They taught English, reading, writing and arithmetic, American literature and history. It supplemented the town's primary school, now managed by Masinop's associates and new teachers like Esperanza.

The school, as Teresa reported, was set up for the children, but adults eager to learn English and other subjects attended its special classes. Esperanza and Nieves know their English, they having been Masinop's star pupils, but they attended the school to make themselves more proficient with the English language. She kept away, though, from the school. Her indifference did not stop the two Americans from dropping by their house on the pretext of following up with homework, their classroom instruction to Esperanza and Nieves. They in turn taught them, their local dialect.

A neat arrangement, Paulo thought, smiling in amusement. It was, for the two Americans, a good substitute to drawing water and cutting firewood.

He had no doubt, though, that the two Americans will eventually win the love of Esperanza and Nieves. Once this happened, that will be the end for both of them. How Esperanza and Nieves will then run their lives! He could see them doing that now from what Teresa wrote. Dick McCall and Major Shay, who were Protestants, were very friendly to Father Madaluan, the town's new Filipino parish priest. Something might come out of that.

Then came, what he expected would happen. Teresa reported in a subsequent letter that Nieves seemed to be falling in love with Dick McCall and Esperanza with Major Bill Shay.

He smiled. There was nothing, love could not bridge, not war, not race and not religion. Love conquered all. It was in the air. Peaceful pursuits like getting married, raising a family and making a living will take over from the pursuit of the war.

Major Shay, as Teresa also wrote, was staying in the Philippines. He will, once he had returned to civilian life, start a construction company. Among the things, he planned to build will be the town's waterworks and irrigation system and the road to Gayuman's mine in Alkayag. As for Dick McCall, he was putting up a newsmagazine in Manila.

All of those that Teresa reported to him had made him, for the first time, favorably disposed toward the two Americans.

It was inevitable that Teresa will mention his return to Masakao.

She wrote, "The town needs you for the great changes about to take place here. Gayuman is ill while Doctor Bihasa's sole interest now is in his medical practice. Major Shay's assignment as the town administrator is coming to an end. The Americans will soon set up a civil administration, all over the islands and I heard we will be given as much local government as possible. You should be our town mayor. The townsfolk are waiting for your return home from exile, there in Corona."

He liked her suggestion of him as the mayor of Masakao. It played on his ego. In the end, though, he rejected it, for it meant, giving up the fight. Not even the prospect of being the town mayor could make him do that. Teresa scolded him when he wrote back that he will not go back to Masakao and be its mayor, for it meant going down on his knees before the Americans.

"You are so hardheaded," she wrote. "You never listen to reason."

"That is not true, at all," he said to himself, in reply to her.

He agreed with her, though, that their town needed a leader. That put him in a dilemma. He spent countless hours debating on whether he was right in preferring exile in Corona to freedom in Masakao at the price of bending his knees before the Americans.

His uncle will tell him, if he is alive, on how to deal with it and that is for him to remain firm to his duty. He was doing just that and he had remained in exile in the penal island.

His uncle will then say, it is the price, he must pay for keeping his duty. He could do the next thing, though, and that is to use the enemy as what his uncle once taught him.

He came home, one time, from school with a black eye and a bruised lip from a fistfight with a bigger boy.

"Never," his uncle then said, "get into a fight with someone bigger than you; use him instead."

The phrase stuck in his mind. He will use the enemy when the occasion presented itself, not in his confined condition in Corona, but later on, in Masakao.

If, as Teresa wrote, the Americans will turn over to them, the local civil administration of the islands, there was then the chance for him to run Masakao, the way his uncle, ran it so well. He will do it simply by doing what his uncle had done for the town and by applying the American principles of democracy and free enterprise in his hometown. He will then in a way be getting back at the Americans. He will be using their own tools in running a local government. It was a nice thought that he knew, though, belonged yet to the future.

He considered Teresa's letters too personal for him to show them to Agerico. He told him instead, the gist of her letters.

He was, one time, watching Agerico as he was putting the finishing touches on a still-life painting when he mentioned Teresa, who was upset over his refusal to take the oath of allegiance so he could return to Masakao and be the town mayor.

"Teresa is right," Agerico said. "You are so stubborn for your own good. You are missing this great opportunity to be the mayor of Masakao."

He frowned. No one could see his point.

"I am not," he said, "an opportunist panting after the position of town mayor. If I will go back there, it will not be on my knees, like what you did before the Americans."

And he stormed out of Agerico's house.

It was bound to happen.

Paulo stopped going to Agerico's house. They had worn out each other's company and they had different interests and political views. To Agerico, his wife, his art and their business mattered more to him than anything else. Masakao belonged to his past while Masakao to Paulo will always be home to him. He wanted to go back there and be with Teresa, but not on the condition of taking the oath of allegiance to the United States.

They avoided each other until Agerico went to the prison camp at Captain Croyce's request. Fort Santiago had inquired about the progress, he had made in persuading Paulo to take the oath. He knew Paulo, by then, as a very stubborn man. He could not do it alone. He needed help. He turned to Agerico. He knew by then that Paulo and Agerico were very good friends who hailed from the same town.

Agerico listened quietly as Captain Croyce spoke about what Agerico could do in making Paulo take the oath.

"I will see, what I can do," he said.

"Thank you," Captain Croyce said. "I am grateful for your help. I also have something for you."

He pointed at two boxes of painting supplies in a corner of his office and said, "I will have Paulo help you, take them home."

Agerico nodded, pleased, and thanked Captain Croyce for the gift.

Paulo came a short while later, his shirt soaked with sweat. He was supervising the digging of a well, a hard task done in the heat of the sun. He walked straight to Captain Croyce's desk.

"You sent for me, Captain?" he said to Captain Croyce.

"Yes. I want you to help Agerico, carry those painting supplies."

Paulo nodded in compliance with Captain Croyce's order.

He left with Agerico, each of them carrying a box of painting supplies. They crossed the camp grounds in silence. Where Paulo was indifferent, Agerico was conciliatory.

Agerico said, as they were passing out of the camp gate, "Let us take these boxes home first, and then we will go to the beach. I would like to paint a seascape from what you once told me is your favorite spot there. Can you show me where it is located?"

"I'll be glad to show it to you."

They put the boxes in the studio and took the items, Agerico needed to paint. Paulo carried the easel and a blank canvas while Agerico carried a bottle of water, a box of painting supplies and a gunnysack, he picked up, outside the door. They stopped by the store and Agerico told Consorcia to prepare something special for their dinner.

"I will be glad to do that," she said.

"I always enjoy, your fine cooking," Paulo said to her.

She watched them, smiling, as they were walking toward the beach. They were friends again.

Paulo led Agerico to the shade of a palm tree with a great view of the calm blue sea meeting the bright blue sky in the horizon.

He set up the easel on the sand and put on it, the blank canvas while Agerico swept with his eyes, the beautiful scenery. He was ready to paint. He mixed with the brush, the paint on the palette and began to paint.

"Do your thing while I do mine," Paulo said to Agerico.

He sat down on the sand with his back against a tree trunk and watched the scenery. Lulled by the waves gently rolling onward and then receding from the sand, he yawned, stretched out his arms and dozed off.

He woke up with the sun now low in the horizon. He rubbed his eyes, stood up and walked toward Agerico who was finished painting and was now washing the brush and the palette with the bottle of water, before putting them back in the paint box.

The painting was an interpretation of the scenery. Unlike the bright blue sky above them, the sky Agerico painted on the canvas was dark with streaks of lightning breaking through the storm clouds. Unlike the calm blue sea before them, the sea on the canvas was rough with turbulent waves.

"It shows," Paulo said, "far more than what I see there."

"I painted, not what I see of the sea and the sky, but of what I feel and think about them."

"What are you trying to show there?"

"Unlike here in Corona, Masakao is still in the midst of a storm of continuing warfare."

Paulo looked away, discouraging Agerico from any further talk about the painting. He would rather not be told by Agerico that Masakao needed him in moving away, the storm of continuing warfare there.

"Let us take a walk," Agerico said, "while we are waiting for the paint to dry."

He picked up the gunnysack and walked on the beach.

Paulo looked on when Agerico halted and picked up a clump of seaweed in the sand.

"I learned about this from Consorcia," he said as he was rinsing the seaweed in seawater before putting it inside the gunnysack.

"What will you do with it?"

"We will, later on, eat it with Consorcia."

"Raw?"

"Of course not," Agerico said, smiling, as he was picking up more seaweed and rinsing them in seawater. "I will wash them thoroughly when we get home and then dip them in boiling water. Mixed with salt, vinegar, pepper, sliced onion and tomatoes and garnished with shrimp fry sauce, they will make an excellent salad. When eaten with rice and fried fish, they are a veritable feast in this island paradise."

"It is your island paradise, not mine."

"We make our own heaven or hell. You can leave your hell here and have a taste of heaven, if you will go home to Teresa."

"Now, you are talking like the devil's disciple."

"I am only saying what a stubborn nitwit you are."

"What?" Paulo shouted as he swung his hand toward Agerico's face.

Agerico moved his head back to avoid the blow. Paulo held him instead on his shoulders.

"Damn you!" he shouted at Agerico. "Can't you see how I have long wanted to go home to Masakao? I would have left this damned island, if only I could!"

He released Agerico from his grip on his shoulders and looked away.

The shock, Agerico felt, subsided at the sight of Paulo now looking, so sad and dejected.

"What, then," he asked Paulo, "is keeping you from taking the oath, so you can leave this island?"

"It is duty! I am not just being proud and obstinate in refusing to take the oath! It is duty to our country that has kept me from taking it! I am not like you, now a civilian. I remain even in prison, an officer in our army. I will be committing treason if I will take the oath of allegiance to America, for we are still at war with it! I just cannot do it!"

Paulo walked away. Agerico picked up the gunnysack and walked after Paulo. He dropped his hand on Paulo's shoulders when he caught up with him. He said to him, "Now that I know that, I'll never mention it again."

A ship arrived in Corona, a few days later. Its boatswain delivered an important message for Captain Croyce. He read it and he immediately gave the order for the political prisoners to assemble in front of his office.   They came from the shops and the fields and watched Captain Croyce who was at the window in his office.

"I have here, a very important message from Manila," Captain Croyce said, a piece of paper held high in his hand. "It will affect your stay here. Aguinaldo has been captured."

The prisoners took the news in stunned silence.

Captain Croyce continued: "He has taken the oath of allegiance to the United States. You are also called upon to take the oath. Those who will take it will be brought to Cebu and Manila on the same ship that brought this message here. Now, those who will take the oath, raise your hands."

Captain Croyce nodded. All the prisoners raised their hands.

"We will have the oath-taking done, right now. Raise your right hands and repeat after me," he said as he then recited slowly, the oath of allegiance to the United States.

Paulo, later on, went to see Agerico and Consorcia.

They were in their store. They watched him as he was coming on the road.

"We have been expecting you," Agerico said to Paulo.

"So, you have heard about it."

"This is a small island. News like that spreads   fast here."

Paulo smiled and said to them, "I can now go home."

Paulo looked on at the sea, his mind keen in anticipation of his return home as the ship was passing by Corregidor Island at the mouth of Manila Bay. Manila was just a blur in the horizon, but as the ship plowed onward, the churches in Tondo and Binondo, the wall in Intramuros, the church and the tile-roofed homes in Ermita and Malate were now more clearly defined in the bright afternoon sun.

He watched amazed as the ship was moving toward the port in Pasig River at the great amount of activity going on there. He never saw the river before choked with so many watercraft, steamships, barges, tugboats and fishing boats moving in the river or were docked in the port. Buildings near and far were in various stages of construction. At the southern side of the river in Parian, a construction gang was widening the road to the main entrance in Intramuros and to Saint John of Lateran. The school itself, like Fort Santiago and the other Spanish buildings in Intramuros, stood somnolent to the onslaught of building activity, going on there.

He was seeing for the first time in all that activity, the new American rulers turn from the fury of the war to the frenzy of peaceful construction. The Americans were making their own mark in Manila.

He wondered if a similar activity was taking place in the countryside, in towns like Masakao. The thought about his hometown made so keen, the anticipation he felt on his return there.

The ship moved sideways to its berth in the port, full of people. Passengers were boarding another ship while in their ship, passengers were disembarking, the crowd in the port welcoming them or bidding them good-bye. Dockhands were bringing up cargoes into the other ship while the deckhands in their ship were lowering cargoes into the port.

Someone he knows might be in the crowd and he smiled and waved his hand when he saw, standing beside a carriage, Teresa, Nieves and Esperanza and beside them, Major Bill Shay and Dick McCall.

He picked up his cloth bag, Agerico's gift of paintings inside aluminum tubes tied together and boxes of pastries, sweetmeat and dried fish, Consorcia had prepared for him.

He walked down on the gangplank and made his way through the crowd to meet Teresa, who was rushing to him.

He dropped on the pavement, the things he was carrying, the moment he came upon her, who had thrown herself in a tight embrace with him as she then wept with tears of joy.

Esperanza said suddenly to them, "Enough of that! It is my turn!"

They had hardly released each other when Esperanza was already hugging him. Nieves, not a moment too soon, was tapping Esperanza on her shoulders and saying, "It is my turn." Esperanza drew away as Nieves then gave him, a big hug.

He smiled, very much pleased. The three of them were outdoing each other in welcoming him.

"How did you know, I'm coming home?" he asked them when he had somewhat recovered from all the hugging, the women had done to him.

"Their connections," Esperanza said as she glanced at Major Shay and Dick McCall who were now standing beside her. "They were kept informed about the ship coming from Corona and its passengers. We knew that with the capture of Aguinaldo and the oath of allegiance he took, you will soon come home. We are here to meet you and take you home."

"The whole town is waiting to welcome you," Teresa said.

He smiled, at a loss of what to say. He turned to Major Shay and Dick McCall.

"We are so glad to see you again," they said as they shook hands with him.

The three women smiled at the friendly greetings between Paulo, Major Bill Shay and Dick McCall.

"You can now call Major Shay, simply Bill, since he is no longer in the army," Esperanza said.

They proceeded toward the carriage with Bill and Dick helping Paulo in carrying his things. They passed them on to the carriage driver. Then they helped the women in stepping up into the carriage's passenger compartment with Paulo seated between Teresa and Esperanza while Nieves was seated between Bill and Dick.

Bill looked around and, finding everyone there, now settled comfortably, he leaned out of the carriage window and told the carriage driver to get them moving. The driver then, with a flick with the rein, sent the horses moving the carriage out of the port and into the narrow streets in Intramuros.

The Tutuban train terminal was undergoing repair and improvement. The carriage will then take them to the Caloocan train station where they will take the train to Malolos and then proceed to Masakao.

"Bill and Dick are doing a lot of things, now that the war is almost over," Esperanza said, breaking the momentary silence inside the carriage. "Bill is now a builder. He will build a shopping arcade across the river and he will soon build the town's waterworks and the road to Alkayag."

"It is time for peaceful pursuits," Bill said.

"Like the newsmagazine, Dick is putting up here," Nieves said.

"So much waits to be done," Paulo said, "here in Manila, in Masakao and in the rest of the country."

"Like the great things waiting for you on your return home to Masakao," Teresa said.

"And what are those?" he asked Teresa.

"You will see them soon enough," Teresa said eagerly. "But you will be glad to know, the whole town is waiting for your return home, complete with a brass band and lots of food.

"The festivities will start tomorrow morning with a Mass in the church in thanksgiving to God. It will be followed by the feast in the churchyard and in the town square."

"Tell us about the food for the welcome feast for Paulo," Dick said to Nieves.

"We have," Nieves said, "roasted or cooked in other ways, pigs, dozens of chickens, pails of fish and a lot more that will be laid out there."

"Are they that many?" Bill said.

"That many and more," Esperanza said to Bill. "You will have to hand it to Mother and Father, to Nieves' folks, to Gayuman, Doctor Bihasa and the townsfolk to go all out for Paulo, on his return home. But I am not even sure if all of that will be enough. The whole town will be there and you should see how our townsfolk eat."

"I don't know, if I deserve all of that," Paulo said.

"You do. Everyone there is glad for your return home," Teresa said.

"That includes us," Dick and Bill said.

The effort they took in healing the wounds of war, their friendliness, the things they will do for the country, their affinity for the town and their love for Esperanza and Nieves had removed whatever remaining reservation, Paulo had toward Bill and Dick. They, after all, now shared a common fate. They were caught by the women and there was no way, they could ever leave them.

Paulo and Teresa were looking out from the carriage window at a beautiful view of Manila Bay and the marshes by the bay when Teresa suddenly held his hand tightly and looked sternly at him.

She was, by what she was doing to him, letting him know that she will never let him, leave her again.

He looked tenderly at her.

They were now smiling as they looked on, entranced, at the sun now setting in the mountain peaks in Bataan, across Manila Bay.

It cast a soft, golden glow on the marshes by the bay and on the bay itself as they moved on, homeward to Masakao.

Chapter Twenty-four

It was morning of the day, following the feast, the town of Masakao held on Paulo's return there. It took the whole day and into the night when the town, for the third time in its history, had a native resident for its mayor.

The first to be thus proclaimed was Manuel Mulawin, following the defeat of Zatayde in the battle for the town fort. Paulo's uncle Lukas was the second town mayor during the short-lived, but heady days of the First Philippine Republic.

The Americans, who were in control of the town and virtually the entire country, posed no objection to Masakao having another town mayor, not by election, but simply by acclamation by the townsfolk.

It was after all their intention, even while the war was still going on, to give the Filipinos as much authority as possible in running the colony's local governments.

Dick and Nieves were in the balcony of her house. He and Bill were going back to Manila, following the festivities, the town held for Paulo.

"Can you not stay, a little longer?" she said to Dick.

"How I wish, I can do that. You know how I love every moment, I am with you, but I have a job to do."

"What a sweet tongue, you have, my dear," Nieves said, smiling. "Very well, off you go."

They embraced and kissed each other, after which, Dick went down the stairs and out into the road.

Bill, who had done earlier, a similar gesture to Esperanza, was waiting for Dick in Julio's horse-drawn rig. He will take them to Malolos. They will then proceed from there to Manila.

Dick, once they were in Manila, will drop off Bill in the compound beside the mouth of Pasig River of his newly established construction company, the Pacific & Gulf Construction Company.

He will then proceed to the editorial office in Plaza Cervantes of his newly established newsmagazine, *The Philippines Newsmagazine.*

"The war has not made any great changes here," Dick said as they were looking around, seated in a horse-drawn cab, "but changes will be made here, now that the war is just about over."

"It is not over yet, far from it," Bill said at the fighting still going on in some towns and provinces in the colony.

The Filipinos had by then shifted from the conventional to the guerrilla type of warfare, the Philippine-American War being like a fight between a tiger and a dog.

The Filipinos resorted to this form of warfare to give them at least a fighting chance against the Americans with their vastly superior arms. Some American military men called the Filipinos savages, for waging that kind of warfare against them.

Dick saw, in a letter kept in a file at the U.S. military headquarters in Fort Santiago, what could influence the turn of events in the Philippines and the subsequent United States policy toward the Philippines.

He turned out to be correct in his assessment of the letter. It later on had a profound effect on the conduct of the American troops in the Philippines and, more important, in the development of American policy toward the Philippines.

The letter, written by Apolinario Mabini, the chief political strategist of Aguinaldo and known as the "Brains of the Philippine Revolution," was addressed to General J.F. Bell, a top-ranking officer in the United States Army.

Dick, as he read the letter, was impressed as much by Mabini's wisdom and the fortitude of the Filipino people as on what had prompted them to employ guerrilla tactics against the American troops and on how the Americans should treat the Filipinos. He asked for and received the permission to reprint the letter in *The Philippines Newsmagazine:*

August 31, 1900
Manila, P.I.

General J.F. Bell

My dear and distinguished General:

The reading of your personal letter of the 28th instant has made me very happy. After having considered closely the points treated in it, I cannot but acknowledge the loftiness of your intentions and the nobility of your sentiments. I shall try to match your kind attention and courtesy and give you, with the greatest clearness and frankness, my private opinion on the subject under consideration, with so much more pleasure, as I am no less anxious to find a solution of the same.

You bewail that the Filipino people do not know how to appreciate the efforts and sacrifices of the Americans. May I take the liberty to tell you that until now all the efforts and sacrifices of the Americans tend only to show their devastating strength, and this fact the Filipino people understand.

When the American authorities turn back their eyes to reason and justice, making less use of force, I can assure you that the Filipino people shall at once know how to appreciate the change of procedure.

You yourself corroborate my estimate of the situation when in your letter you set up this principle: "The only justifiable condition of war, whatever circumstances, is the possibility of success."

Were this principle true and were it constantly put into practice, the solution of all international and civil questions would have to be sought in force, and men would have to blot out with a stroke of the pen the eternal principles of morality and justice written with the blood of many generations, and bring back mankind to its primitive state.

You could not invoke the words "humanity" and "civilization" without demolishing your principle. If in real life the strong nations so easily make use of force to impose their claims on the weak ones, it is because even now civilization and humanitarian sentiments that are so often invoked are, for some, more apparent than real.

In accordance with your principle, it has to be admitted that the war which the Americans are waging in the Philippines is just and humanitarian, because the Filipinos are weak, which trend of reasoning not even the most ignorant Filipino will believe to be true. I am the first to deplore deeply the guerrilla and ambush system of warfare which the Filipinos have been forced to adopt, because I have always considered the fight that offers equal risks to both combatants more noble and more worthy of men.

But the laws of war that authorize the strong nations the use of their powerful weapons of combat in their fight with a weak people who lack said weapons, are the very laws that persuade the people to make use of the guerrilla and ambush system, especially when it comes to defending their homes and their freedom against an invasion. In this extreme case, those very laws implacably order the weak people to defend their threatened honor and natural rights under pain of being called uncivilized and incapable of understanding the responsibilities of a proper government.

I agree with you in this: force as the only factor used in the solution of all kinds of questions among rational beings is not only criminal in itself, but it is also the cause of all the miseries and ruin that have afflicted humanity and the peoples of all ages. For the reasons that I have stated in the previous paragraphs, the Americans and not the Filipinos should be reminded of this lesson from history.

The Filipinos know only too well that by force, they can expect nothing from the United States. They fight to show the United States that they possess sufficient culture to know their rights even when there is a pretense to hide them by means of clever sophisms. The Filipinos hope that the fight will remind the Americans of the struggle borne by their ancestors against the Englishmen for the emancipation of the colonies which are now the Free States of North America. The Americans were then in the same place which the Filipinos are today.

If at that time the justice of the American cause found defenders in France, the Filipinos hope to have on their part the very Americans when the latter will realize that the fight is not motivated by hatred of race, but by the same principles sealed with the blood of their own ancestors.

The Filipinos know also that the art of governing, like all other practical knowledge, is acquired through experience and that, in order to be good citizens and be able to conduct rightly a republican form of government, it is necessary that they know how to appreciate honor and defend justice. This does not destroy the natural disposition of people to learn the art by themselves as the American people learned it without the help of any other men.

If the Filipinos, giving up the faculties that by nature belong to them, would let the Americans govern the Islands by themselves as the latter claim to do, the Filipinos would never learn the art of governing, and they would give the Americans a cause to say that the Filipinos are by nature incapable to govern. The Filipinos cannot believe in the promised help because the conditions required for the granting of said help make the realization of the promise impossible.

I hope the Americans will understand the present state of culture of the Filipino people shall not put up with subjugation by force as a permanent condition. The Filipinos may be vanquished now and again, but as long as they are denied every kind of right, there will not be lasting peace.

The Spaniards are able to rule the Islands without great trouble for three centuries because the Filipinos were then sunk in the most complete ignorance and they lived without consciousness of national solidarity.

Today it is different. Today, the Filipinos share in the life of other nations and they have tasted, even if only for a short time and in an incomplete manner, the joys of independent life.

I can understand that it is impossible, nay, even pernicious, that the Americans should abandon the Islands to the mercy of other ambitious world powers. The Filipinos know likewise that the union between the two peoples is the only thing that can undo and avert the dangers of the future. Mutual convenience demands the prompt cessation of hostilities, because as the war drags on, it will necessarily engender hatred and make it impossible for the Americans and the Filipinos to lead a common life together.

In the Revolution of 1896, the Filipinos were only asking Spain the concession of certain privileges which the Spaniards enjoyed, but the Spanish government refused to grant them their request. Had those requests been granted, the Revolution would not only have been stopped, but the Filipinos would have found common cause with Spain in the war against the United States.

The Filipinos are ready for an understanding as long as said understanding would not demand an unconditional submission to the claims of the Americans, but the acceptance of a formula in the advantages and disadvantages of which both sides would equally share. The Filipinos would not have faith in the promises of the American authorities while the latter pin them down to the cruel alternative of dishonor or death.

In the meantime that American sovereignty is not content with limiting the prerogative inherent to the Filipino people, and would go so far as to claim the complete annulment of the same, such sovereignty shall be hated by the Filipinos who will see in it the origin of their humiliation.

If the war does not prevent the organization of municipalities, much less can it prevent the creation of a constitutional project that will lay the cornerstone of the political future of the Philippines. When the Congress of the United States shall become convinced that the completion of said project will paralyze the fighting, it will make it into law.

Any reference to the just claims of the Filipinos, far from weakening among them the prestige of the Americans, would make it more firm to serve as a base on which the solidarity of interests, which is the best guaranty of union and peace, would stand.

For my part, I shall do everything that I can to facilitate such understanding. The one branded as uncompromising will give a clear and practical proof of the greatest adaptability, because he knows that he who lives in this world has to undergo the inconveniences in it.

Hence, I shall not advocate absolute independence, knowing that I cannot obtain it now. Neither would I talk about independence with protectorate nor of autonomy, because both are purely theoretical. Protectorate is a limitation the nature and importance of which depends upon the mutual agreement, tacit or expressed, between the protector and the protected. Autonomy, on the other hand, involves in itself the idea of independence more or less restricted. To discuss these formulas, therefore, is to waste time on abstract questions.

I shall go direct to the point as is commonly said, following the example of the Americans who are a very practical people. I shall limit myself to point out the bases on which, in my opinion, the political edifice of the Philippines should stand, to wit:

1st. The enjoyment by the Filipinos of the same individual rights, natural as well as political, the citizens of cultured and free nations enjoy;

2nd. Complete equality between the Americans and the Filipinos within the territory of the Philippine Islands; and

3rd. The organization of government which would offer the best guarantees for the realization of the first two conditions.

I should like to see a project of the Constitution that would fix the rules which shall serve as basis for the solution of the questions that may arise from the three capital points which I have specified; and should I find it acceptable to the majority of the Filipinos, I would not have any inconvenience in advising my countrymen the acceptance of the same. My uncompromising attitude has no other purpose but the assurance of a real peace; hence, I cannot accept conditions which, in my opinion, will not lessen the unrest of the minds.

Please forgive me if I have written long and if, involuntarily, I have expressed myself with more frankness than courtesy. I wanted to have these poor lines reflect faithfully the sentiments of the majority of Filipinos, and I hope I have achieved it. Many maybe, cannot or will not like to express their real thoughts on these questions; but it does not matter. Everything that I have said beats to the core of the hearts of all Filipinos.

I have the greatest pleasure to be your most humble servant.

A.P. Mabini

Mabini was a powerful and highly influential figure in the Philippine Revolution and in the Philippine-American War. His letter to General Bell contained his thoughts on the Filipino people and their aspiration for freedom and what should be the American policy toward the Philippines.

Such is the power of the written word the reaction by the United States government to what Mabini wrote was implied in the policy it then adopted toward the Philippines.

It was the guiding principle in almost half a century of its rule in the Philippine Islands, a kind of rule that was exceptionally just, enlightened and benevolent.

The capture of Aguinaldo on March 23, 1901 in Palanan, Isabela, and the call he made for the Filipino troops to give up the fight and take the oath of allegiance to the United States did not end the Philippine-American War.

It only showed Aguinaldo as so isolated by now from the rest of the Filipino forces. The fighting continued with the Filipinos, now relying more and more on guerrilla tactics.

The most glaring example, which so profoundly affected the Americans' conduct in the war, was the so-called Balangiga Massacre.

Balangiga was a coastal town in the island province of Samar. A major source of revenue for the townsfolk and the rest of the province was the Manila hemp, used in shipping and in the industries.

Brigadier General Robert P. Hughes, who commanded the Department of the Visayas, the central region in the Philippines which included Samar, waged a campaign in the summer of 1901 to deprive the inhabitants of Samar, but most of all, General Vicente Lukban, the commander of the Filipino forces in Samar, a big source of revenue from the Manila hemp. He did this by closing the port in Balangiga to shipping, along with the other coastal towns of Basey and Guiuan. That might then force General Vicente Lukban, the commander of the Filipino troops in Samar, to give up the fight against the Americans.

It had the opposite effect of encouraging the Filipinos in Samar to strike back at the Americans at the first opportunity.

The troops of C Company of the 9th U.S. Infantry Regiment arrived in Balangiga on August 11, 1901 with the order to close the port there and prevent supplies from reaching the Filipino troops in the island's interior.

The relationship between the town residents and the troops of C Company, under their commander, Captain Thomas Connell, was in the beginning, so friendly. They even engaged in drinking sessions with the town's male residents of the local palm wine called *Tuba*. The American soldiers also introduced baseball there. It became so popular, not only in the town, but years later, in the rest of the Philippines.

What brought about the change in their friendly relations was something trivial and unfortunate.

Captain Connell was told, the U.S. Army inspector general will soon visit the town. He engaged the services of some of the men in the town to clean it up and make the town clean and presentable to the inspector general.

The workers, as a precautionary measure, were kept overnight in two tents. Their single-bladed machetes, called *Bolo,* which they used in their clean-up work, were taken away from them along with their supply of rice. This enraged the townsfolk and they decided to get even with the Americans. The town leaders, led by Balangiga Mayor Pedro Abayan, and the staff of General Lukban then planned an attack on the American troops stationed in Balangiga.

They organized a town fiesta that would coincide with the visit there of the inspector general. Captain Connell approved their plan since it will also make festive, the visit there of the inspector general. The townsfolk gave the American soldiers a lot of the local palm wine so they will be drunk the following day when they will carry out the attack.

The women and the children were moved out of the town secretly, a few hours before the attack. It was still dark, early in the morning, when a group of men dressed as women came to the town church, carrying small coffins.

The American sentry there checked the first coffin. He was told the dead child laid there had died of cholera. The rest of the party carried other coffins with their weapons concealed there. They were allowed to move on toward the church which was near the Americans' camp.

They carried out their attack on the American troops who were then taking their breakfast in their mess hall. They fought back with kitchen utensils, steak knives and with their bare hands.

36 soldiers of Company C's complement of 74 officers and men were killed. All the officers, led by Captain Connell, were killed.

28 of the townsfolk were killed. They captured the American soldiers' weapons and their ammunition.

The American soldiers who survived the attack escaped to Basey and the town of Tanauan in the nearby island province of Leyte.

Captain Edwin Buckmiller, the commander of G Company, based in Basey, learned about the rebel attack in Balangiga. He sailed there immediately with his troops. They found the town deserted. They burned it down and buried the American soldiers who died in the rebel attack there.

The attack on the American troops in Balangiga and the death there of so many of them, dispelled the general belief among the Americans in the Philippines that they had put to an end, the Filipinos' resistance to their rule there.

The rumor even went around that the Filipinos might soon launch a guerrilla attack in Manila itself. The American men there then started carrying sidearms. Governor-General William Howard Taft was so worried about the safety of his wife Helen, he had her moved to the British Crown Colony in Hong Kong.

The Americans in the United States were shocked by the report about the massacre of American soldiers in Balangiga.

President Theodore Roosevelt then ordered Major General Adna Chafee, the military governor in the Philippines, to take the measures to pacify Samar. General Chafee passed the President's order to Brigadier General Jacob Smith. General Smith was so enraged by the massacre of the American troops in Balangiga, he gave the following order to Major Littleton Waller, the commander of a battalion of marines in Samar:

"I want no prisoner. I wish to kill and burn; the more you kill and burn, the better it will please me…The interior of Samar must be made a howling wilderness."   -- Gen. Jacob H. Smith

General Smith also ordered Major Waller to kill everyone in Samar who could bear arms. When Major Waller asked him about the age limit of those who could bear arms and be killed, General Smith answered: anyone older than ten years. It was an age when a boy or a girl could barely carry a rifle much less shoot people with it.

To starve the Filipino guerrillas in Samar to submission, food and trade to the island province were cut off. Waller and his troops carried out, at the same time, a campaign of shooting people, destroying homes and killing draft animals to force the province's inhabitants to stop supporting General Lukban and his troops. It was hoped, this would then force them to support the Americans out of their fear of starvation and General Smith's campaign of terror where 2,000 Filipinos were killed with 200 homes burned down.

The American newspapermen covering the war were so outraged by General Smith's order to Major Waller, they mocked him with names like "The Monster," "Howling Jake," "Hell Roaring Jake Smith," and "Howling Wilderness Smith."

The American people were similarly outraged by the brutality committed in Samar by General Smith and Major Waller.

Secretary of War Elihu Root then sent, in response to the public outcry, the order relieving General Smith and Major Waller of their command. They were both ordered to face a court-martial.

As Secretary Root then said, "The President desires to know and in the most circumstantial manner all facts, nothing being concealed, and no man being for any reason favored or shielded. For the very reason that the President intends to back up the Army in the heartiest fashion in every lawful and legitimate method of doing its work, he also intends to see that the most rigorous care is exercised to detect and prevent any cruelty or brutality, and that men who are guilty thereof are punished."

Major Waller in the court-martial was not found guilty. General Smith was found guilty and was forced to retire from military service.

The Balangiga Massacre had a profound effect on the American soldiers' conduct in the war. This was to fight the Filipinos and at the same win their goodwill.

It then became a common practice for the American soldiers to teach young Filipinos in the schools they established in the towns they now occupied, at the same time that they were fighting their elders.

That practice and the American soldiers' friendliness had a profound effect on the Philippine-American War. It soon came to an end with the Americans, now on friendly terms with the Filipinos.

Part Three

Chapter Twenty-five

Universal primary and secondary education was one of the principal goals of the new American rulers. Large numbers of American schoolteachers are now going to the Philippines. The largest group of six hundred American schoolteachers arrived in Manila on August 21, 1901, on board the U.S. transport *Thomas*. They and those who came earlier or later were soon called the *Thomasites.*

Public schools for primary and secondary education were built in the towns and in the provincial capitals. Opportunity for college education was later increased with the establishment of the University of the Philippines. The brightest students, called the *Pensionados,* were sent on scholarships in colleges and universities in the United States. They later on provided the Filipino leadership in government, business and education.

Where the Spanish language was denied to the Filipinos during the Spanish colonial rule, English was taugh everywhere under the Americans so that it became virtually the Philippine national language.

With the protection of Philippine products in the American market and the introduction of American business know-how, trade and agriculture flourished. The Filipinos, after more than three centuries of ignorance, poverty and oppression under the Spanish rule were, right at the beginning of the Americans' benevolent rule, on the road to education, peace, progress and prosperity.

A couple is a good example of those American schoolteachers.

Samuel Tyler looked away, an embarrassed smile on his face when Dorothy Dickinson caught him staring at her again.

"Time for a smoke," he said to divert her attention as he then took out from his coat pocket, his pipe, a match and his tobacco pouch.

He sighed and shook his head when he saw the pipe bowl, clogged with tobacco residue. He took out a pocketknife from his coat pocket and began to scrape it away.

It was Sunday afternoon, the second day they were off from teaching in San Isidro's public school. Dorothy and Samuel were taking pleasure in each other's company, seated across each other at the small oval table by the window in Don Camilo Monte Araztea's house.

It was tiresome watching Samuel engaged in this tedious task of cleaning his pipe. Dorothy turned her gaze outside, to the town's main road and saw the boy coming.

While he was yet at some distance from the house, she could see how he had grown up since a year ago when he appeared at the door of her classroom, a sorry-looking boy with a black eye and a bruised lip, his wooden clogs caked with mud. A sullen look was on his face as Mr. Welk, the school principal, was holding him on his shoulders.

"Here is one more student for you, Miss Dickinson," Mr. Welk said to her. "His name is Leandro Sumaka. As you can see, he has been in a fistfight."

He looked down at the boy and said to him, "You get into another fight and you are out of this school."

She told the boy, after Mr. Welk had left, to step forward. She asked him what happened, why he got into a fight.

"They made fun of my family name, ma'am," the boy replied.

"Why, what did they call you?"

The class erupted with laughter when he said the word. Her stern gaze silenced them promptly. She looked again at the boy, sorry for him, who was so out of place in that roomful of boys and girls in their spotless u niforms.

"You may take a seat at the back row," she said to the boy.

She looked out through the classroom's shell-paned window as she was waiting for him to take his seat.

It was raining again. How cold and wet it was out there in the school grounds and in the outlying rice fields and how warm and cozy it was inside her classroom. It was the first day of school in her second year of teaching in San Isidro's public school.

The scent of flowers from outside the window wafted sweetly inside the classroom and it was with keen pleasure that she then lectured in her class in English and American literature.

She was just as pleased now when she said to Samuel, "Leandro Sumaka is coming."

"So, that is him," Samuel said as he looked out over his shoulders at the boy on the road.

"That is him, all right, the boy who got into a fight over his surname. Won't you do the same thing, if someone made fun of your surname?"

"I certainly will."

She smiled, pleased with Samuel's forthright answer. She was now, even more impressed with this Philadelphian who is so handsome, his tall nose and his thin lips so well-formed, his furrowed brow wide and his brown hair combed to the oval shape of his head.

He could be a good match to her, a beauty herself. She could see how smitten he was with her whenever his eyes were fastened to her face, her brown eyes and her auburn hair. Everything about her seemed to charm him, even the heart-shaped pendant of a necklace hanging in front of her long-sleeved dress buttoned up to her neck.

She caught him staring at her again and he turned his gaze, back to the boy.

"So his classmates called him, not Leandro Sumaka, but, Leandro Sumuka instead, which means to vomit in their local dialect."

"I'm sorry for him."

"I'm also sorry for that boy, a butt of jokes with a surname like that. Sumaka means to farm in their local dialect. It is a fine surname that unfortunately rhymes with something gross in their local dialect. He can change it to a grand Spanish surname and be like the others in this town."

"He will never do that."

"Good for him, he is not like the rest of them," he said as he resumed cleaning his pipe.

He tamped the tobacco residue on the windowsill and blew it away.

"That will make a good fertilizer," he said, smiling, as he was looking down at the plants and the grass in the front yard where the tobacco residue had landed.

Dorothy smiled too when she looked again at the boy who had halted and was now looking at a house along the road.

It was more than a month since he came to her as she was going to her classroom. He had moved up to the next grade and she seldom saw him now. He was quitting school and he asked her, if she could help him, find a job in Manila.

She would have declined such a request, had another student made it. It will set a bad precedent with her students, but this is Leandro Sumaka, her favorite student, asking for her help. She liked him for his drive and intelligence and for the fact that he was so poor and in need of help.

He had very high grades, but without the connections, the money and the social standing, he could not go on to college, nor could he obtain a scholarship in the United States. The Insular Government was creating in the colony, a pool of thoroughly Americanized young people called the *Pensionados* who will be its future leaders.

She was not surprised that, with further education beyond his reach, he came to her about getting a job. The problem was, she knew no one well enough who could give him a job.

There was Bill Shay, who owned a construction company in Manila, but she had met him only once and briefly, at that. Samuel was in far more familiar terms with Bill. They became good friends in the course of Bill's visit to San Isidro to inspect the annex to the school building he built there and the new town market.

She told Samuel about Leandro. He agreed to help him. Samuel wrote Bill Shay about Leandro. Bill wrote back about a job opening for a messenger and janitor in his company. Samuel told her about it. She in turn told Leandro to visit her today, so he could talk to Samuel about the job. He also wrote a letter of introduction for Leandro. The envelope was on the table.

She smiled as she was even more pleased with Samuel for the good thing he had done for Leandro. He has been courting her from the very first day they met on the ship that took them from San Francisco to Manila on this mission to educate the young minds of this new American colony, The Philippine Islands.

This was the grand adventure she sought, way back in Burlington, her lovely hometown in Vermont where she finished a college degree in education precisely for a foreign mission like this.

She and Samuel arrived in the Philippines, two years after the largest batch of six hundred American schoolteachers arrived there on board the U.S. transport *Thomas* in 1901. It was just a few years after the U.S. Army had won in a tough and bloody fight with the Filipino insurgents, following an easy American victory over the colony's Spanish rulers.

Samuel had finished cleaning his pipe and she looked on when he put there, fresh pipe tobacco. He clamped the stem between his teeth and lit it up with the match. He sucked in the smoke, removed the pipe and blew the smoke, out of his mouth.

"I will not be surprised if the boy, when he sees you smoking, will pick up that habit," she said to Samuel.

"Good for him, if he will also do that. It will set him apart even more from the townsfolk."

"You don't seem to like them."

"I don't for the way they treat that boy. They make fun of his native surname because they have grand Spanish surnames that, however, do not match with their meanness and their sour looks."

"What a sharp tongue, you have!"

"I speak of what I see and what I see are those people so pathetic in trying to be what they are not and could never be."

"You really don't like them."

"I like them and I feel sorry for them. They have been so badly treated by their Spanish rulers, but this does not mean, I approve of their bad traits and habits."

She smiled at Samuel for his sharp mind and tongue. He saw more than what was simply a source of amusement to her.

She looked away, discouraging Samuel from talking further about the townsfolk in San Isidro. She looked instead at the dining room where Agustina, the cook and housekeeper, is preparing their afternoon snack. She may have heard Samuel and felt alluded to with her distinguished-sounding full name of Agustina Mariana Santos de los Divinos and she does not want her feelings hurt. Agustina had picked up enough English, the same way she knew a smattering of Spanish that helped her do her job in the house.

She did not see Agustina. She could be too far back in the house to hear what Samuel had said about them.

They were by themselves with Agustina in Don Camilo Monte Araztea's house. She lodged there, one of the town's biggest houses, with Misses Winslow, Hayworth and Robinson, her fellow teachers in San Isidro's public school.

They left a few hours ago at the invitation to the town fiesta in San Rafael. Their happy and excited voices when they left in Don Camilo's carriage echoed yet faintly in her ears. She was also invited, but she declined the invitation.

She had been avoiding those town affairs after the last town fiesta she attended where the townsfolk, much to her annoyance, had ogled at her. She was not relieved of her displeasure even by Samuel's joking explanation that the townsfolk did that and even had to do that because they saw her as a beautiful foreign white goddess who had condescended to mix with them.

It did not please her also to be served with an array of food, for which, she knew very well, the townsfolk had saved and scrimped on lots of things. But, more important, she stayed behind for Samuel and Leandro's visit there this afternoon.

Samuel was blowing smoke from his pipe when Dorothy, in an afterthought, said, "What is wrong with them, copying their former rulers?"

"It does not speak well of them."

"Why?"

"It shows how hung up they are to their Spanish colonial legacy."

"Is that not to be expected of them?"

"With them, yes; with the others, no. Look at their neighbors. They were colonized by the French, the British and the Dutch, but they did not imitate their colonial rulers as the Filipinos did with their Spanish rulers. They, unlike the Filipinos, have the self-respect and the national pride that kept them from imitating their colonial rulers."

Dorothy nodded. Samuel had said the same thing discussed in the briefings she attended prior to her departure for the Philippines, one of which had remained in her memory:

"The Filipinos are a collection of tribes and principalities largely independent of each other that fell under the colonial rule of Spain for more than three hundred years. Spain formed them into a nation and brought to them the Christian faith. The Spaniards left their mark in the only impressive structures in the colony: their stone churches, their town halls, their stone-and-wood homes with tile roofs, their walled enclave in Intramuros and the palace of their governor-general.

"The flimsy nipa hut, the most common type of native dwelling, has remained the same through the centuries. It symbolized their lack of progress and innovation. They copied from the Spaniards as they will now copy from the Americans for lack of the ability and the inclination to develop and improve things of their own."

"At least," she said to Samuel, "they are over and done with Spain. Would it have been good for them if, after defeating Spain in the battle in Manila Bay, we left them alone? I heard that from, not a few people here and in the United States who made that observation."

"That would have been unfortunate for them. This colony would have then ceased to exist as it was formed by Spain."

"Why? Are you not willing to grant that, had they succeeded in their revolution against Spain, they could have developed into a nation with a strong, stable government?"

"It is possible, but highly unlikely. A civil war was more likely to follow that would have dismembered this colony. They were still fighting the Spaniards and us, later on, when their top leaders were already murdering each other. Factionalism was a big factor in their defeat, both in their revolution and in the war against us.

"The fact is, they were never left alone. If the Spaniards did not come, this archipelago may have become an Indonesian province or a Chinese or a Japanese colony.

"War broke out between Spain and our country, following their revolution. There was no way Spain, its empire on its last legs, could keep it. The German fleet was not too far when Dewey was fighting the Spanish fleet in Manila Bay. British, French and Dutch warships were roaming its seas. The European colonial powers were casting covetous eyes on it while we in America were then debating on what to do with it. It was up for grabs. The European colonial powers would have divided it among themselves, had we left after we defeated the Spanish naval fleet in Manila Bay."

Samuel's impromptu lecture on Philippine history did not take Dorothy by surprise. It added to her good impression of this social science teacher who was seated across her at the table, his face now and then veiled by the tobacco smoke, he was blowing, out of his mouth.

"I see you have done your homework," she said.

"I boned up on this place, way back in Philadelphia when I was accepted as a social science teacher here."

"So will they, copy from us, now that they are under us."

"And there are a lot of good things they can copy from us."

"One thing they would want us to address is this land tenancy problem. It is quite pronounced here in San Isidro."

Don Camilo Monte Araztea owned, along with a friar order and a few families, all of them of Spanish descent, virtually all the lands in San Isidro and in the towns nearby. They were previously owned by and taken away from the town's native inhabitants by their Spanish colonial rulers.

Dorothy was not keen about lodging in Don Camilo's house. It identified her with the town lord. But she did not choose to live in this house. It was arranged for her, long before she and the other American schoolteachers arrived in the colony.

To ingratiate himself with their new American rulers, Don Camilo offered his house for rent, for a nominal fee, and moved out with his wife to their married son Enrique's house in Santa Ignacia. Their daughters Marrieta and Carmina were married and living in Spain.

Don Camilo's house came, complete with a staff of a housekeeper who worked also as the cook, a carriage driver who also worked as the gardener and handyman and a woman who came, three times a week to do their laundry. It was one of the few houses in San Isidro with facilities like plumbing, suitable to Dorothy and her fellow American schoolteachers.   That should have satisfied her to board in Don Camilo's house. It did not. She did not approve of the way Don Camilo treated the town as if it was his personal domain and the townsfolk as if they were his serfs. She did not consider it right for one man or a few families to own so much while the rest of the townsfolk were living in perpetual poverty and bondage to the town's landlords.

The town was like the rest of the colony, which was divided into land grants by the Spanish colonial authorities and given or sold to the friar orders and the Spanish and mestizo families like the Monte Arazteas.

She was born and raised in New England where it was considered a farmer's right to own the land he tilled. But she came to this colony to teach English and American literature and, much, as she was inclined to, she was not in a position to help change its unjust system of land tenancy.

Agustina was coming from the dining room and Dorothy glanced, satisfied with her plumpness.

The first time, she saw her when she was newly arrived in San Isidro, Agustina, like many of the native women in the town, was thin and sickly. She and the other teachers, out of pity for her and the other servants, gave them complete access to the food in the house. Their health improved and all of them had gained weight.

"The food is ready, ma'am," Agustina said about the snack of coffee and rice cakes, she had prepared for Dorothy and Samuel in the dining room.

"Thank you, but we will first have a few minutes with that boy. Will you, please, let him in?" Dorothy said to Agustina as she was looking at Leandro who was waiting to be let in at the gate to the house.

Agustina likewise looked out from the window. Then she left it, her footsteps light in the clean and shiny wooden floor.

Dorothy watched Leandro as he was passing through the gate, Agustina had opened for him. Unlike the time in her class when he was in short pants, he was now dressed in long pants and a long-sleeved shirt with his feet now wearing leather sandals.

He had grown taller by an inch or two and had also gained weight. Otherwise, he looked the same: a face, brown-hued from long exposure to the sun, his cheeks a bit hollow and his hair brownish-black and wavy. Unlike the pug-nosed and thick-lipped townsfolk, he had a sharp nose and full lips.

"Good afternoon, ma'am, good afternoon, sir," he said to Dorothy and Samuel from the flagstone path to the house.

They returned his greeting. Dorothy then told Leandro to come up to the house.

He was in a short while at the door to living room. To avoid his sandals from leaving dust and dirt on the clean and shiny floor, he removed them from his feet and pushed them aside with his right foot.

He paused when he was about to step inside the living room, awed by the living room's luxurious furnishings. His eyes darted from the chandelier to the tall mirror set against a wall, the mahogany coffee table with a Persian rug underneath, the large vases, the cabinet of glass menagerie, the leather couches and heavy tasseled drapes so out of place in the tropical climate, the Monte Araztea family picture of Don Camilo, his wife Dona Isabella and their children, on top of the piano.

Don Camilo's life-size portrait in gilt frame, hanging in a wall, caught his eye. The Spanish mestizo town lord was gazing imperiously at his domain—the rice fields seen through the window that stretched far into the horizon.

Dorothy wondered, as she was watching Leandro, if this was the first time he had set foot there. He was looking around at the living room, his eyes wide and his mouth hanging open in awe of what he was seeing there.

A sheepish smile was on his face as he was approaching her and Samuel. He bowed as he greeted them, a good afternoon. He waited to be addressed with his shoulders slightly stooped and his hands clasped to his stomach.

He seemed anxious. To put him at ease, she introduced him rather casually to Samuel who said to him, "Miss Dickinson told me that you are quitting school. Don't you want to go to college?"

"My folks cannot afford it, sir. It is time, I started earning a living. It is time, I got a job."

"And you cannot find it here in San Isidro."

"Land, our only source of livelihood here, was taken away from us by Don Camilo, the friars and the other landlords."

Dorothy and Samuel nodded. They understood perfectly Leandro's feelings toward them. They both knew the serious land tenancy problem in San Isidro.

She heard from Samuel, a while ago when they were by themselves, only harsh words about the townsfolk in San Isidro. He was now so kind to Leandro, but frank to her then because he must feel, he could speak his mind freely to her who admired him for his sharp tongue, mind and eyes. They were so sharp he could even see what was in her heart and mind.

"Do you know Mister Bill Shay?" Samuel asked Leandro.

"No, sir, I don't know him, although I have heard about him."

"He owns the construction company that built the school buildings here in San Isidro and in the towns nearby. I told him in a letter that you are looking for a job. He replied, he has a job opening for a messenger and janitor. Do you want to give it a try?"

"I certainly want to, sir."

"Very well," Samuel said. He picked up the envelope and gave it to Leandro. "That is your letter of introduction to Mister Shay. I mentioned Miss Dickinson to add a good word about you. See the personnel manager and give him the letter as per Mister Shay's instruction. Don't keep them waiting. Go there as soon as possible. The company address is written on the envelope. It is in Parola near the mouth of Pasig River in Manila."

"I will go there, sir, right away, tomorrow morning."

Then he bowed in a stiff and solemn manner and said, "I cannot thank you enough, ma'am, sir, for your help and kindness. I will always be grateful to you. I will never forget this."

"It is no big thing," Samuel said, waving away in dismissal, Leandro's profuse expression of gratitude.

Dorothy smiled, impressed even more with Samuel.

"Good luck on your job, young man," Samuel said to Leandro. "Is there anything else, we can do for you?"

"That is all, sir," Leandro replied, smiling.

"So, there is no need to detain you any further. You may go now," Samuel said as he tamped on the windowsill, the tobacco ash in his pipe, blew it away and returned his pipe, the match, his pocketknife and his tobacco pouch to his coat pocket.

Leandro had turned to leave, but Dorothy stopped him with her hand raised.

"Wait," she said to him, "before you leave, I almost forgot, I have something for you."

She stood up, her ankle-length dress rustling against a leg of the table as she proceeded to her bedroom. She returned in a short while, a copy of *The Adventures of Tom Sawyer* in her hand.

"It is a souvenir of the time, you were in my class," she said as she gave Leandro the book.

He said as he was putting Samuel's letter inside the book, "I'll never forget this, ma'am, sir. I will always be grateful to you."

He bowed once again and left them.

She was watching Leandro as he was passing out of the house gate opened for him by Agustina when Samuel suddenly held her hand.

She let it remain there, for it came to her then that he was doing that as the reward for the good thing, he had done for the boy.

She realized how wrong she was when the feel of his hand sent radiating into her heart, the love he was showing her by holding her hand. It was almost like being locked in an embrace with him.

Agustina was coming in the living room, reminding them about their afternoon snack in the dining room.

"The coffee will get cold," she said to Samuel.

They stood up and were following Agustina to the dining room when Samuel held her hand again. She smiled as her hand remained, held by his hand.

Chapter Twenty-six

Leandro left Don Camilo's house, smiling at the thought of the job waiting for him in Manila. He will be a janitor and messenger, a lowly job, but, he nodded, a job is a job. It will be just the first of the many steps he will take in making a mark in the world. From nobody, he will be somebody. He could hardly wait to be in Manila. He will leave at the earliest possible time. By tomorrow then, he will be gone from San Isidro.

The smile on his face faded away as he looked on sadly at the church ahead and to his left, at the orchards, the bamboo groves, the rice fields, golden-hued under the summer sun, and farther away, the hamlet of Bangar. He was leaving them on his first journey into the world, way beyond his hometown.

He smiled and shook his head. He was yet to leave his hometown and he was already missing it, although not all of it when he glanced at the large stone and tile-roofed homes at the right side of the road. They no longer held him in awe as they did a while ago when he passed by there on his way to see Miss Dickinson and Mr. Tyler.

He will prove himself a better person than the Ilustrados, those Spanish mestizo landlords living in those big houses. He will make good on his own merit without hurting or depriving anyone as they had done to him and the poor townsfolk in San Isidro. They live like Don Camilo in comfort and luxury from the bounty of the land which they took away from and were now tilled for them by native peasants like him. They feasted everyday on sumptuous meals washed down with wine while a peasant boy like him ate nothing, most of the time, but gruel in their dining table.

No one else was on the road. The landowners and their families have been kept by the warm afternoon sun inside their cool and grand, comfortable homes set back from the road by front yards lush with fruit trees and flowering plants and fenced with stone masonry or iron grill.

It was a grand place so different from the humble nipa huts in the hamlet of Bangar where he lived, a wooded area a mile or so away from where he was. The hamlet there was lush too with fruit, palm and forest trees and bamboo groves, the lone road there, cutting across the rice fields.

He walked on, his mind on the hard life, he led there. He has been working his entire young life. He was at age six, doing household work, from cleaning the hut, to gardening, to feeding the sow, the chickens, the carabao, their work animal, to drawing water from the well. He was at age ten, toiling in the rice fields with his uncle Julian, his aunt Tarcila and his cousin Candido.

They were, at the crack of dawn, out in the rice fields. They worked except for a short lunch break until sundown. They nursed the tender rice shoots during planting time, often on their knees, their hands often cut, until they had grown up into rice stalks, bent with golden grain by harvest time.

He halted when he came to a large stone house along the road, just as he halted there a while ago on his way to see Miss Dickinson and Mr. Tyler, hoping to catch at the window there, a glimpse of Angela Rosablanca.

A girl with long tresses and dimples in her cheeks, she was the girl of his dreams whom he had embraced in countless dreams. But all that he had managed to do in a year they were classmates in Miss Dickinson's class was to smile at her and mumble a greeting and, once her back was turned to him, to look longingly at her.

He was inhibited from making friendly overtures to her by shyness and the fear of getting rebuffed, for he was a poor peasant boy while she was a pretty rich, aristocratic, Spanish mestiza girl.

As luck would have it, there she was, seated by the window, talking to an older woman. Their eyes met and he froze, confused. Is she friendly or cold and indifferent? He was not sure. He could walk on as if he did not see her, but then, if he dared to talk to her, she might then ask him to drop by for a chat with her. But what could he say to her?

He was confused, the longer he stayed there, when he remembered having heard somewhere that when in doubt, one must be bold.   "Good afternoon, ma'am," he said. "Good afternoon, Angela."

She barely nodded. She turned her eyes to the older woman and resumed talking to her. She ignored him. He thought quickly. He must say something that will catch her attention and impress her as well.

"I am," he said to her, "leaving tomorrow for Manila. I've got a job waiting for me there."

What he said had no effect on her, for she went on talking to the older woman. It was as if he was not there on the road, talking to her. It was as if, he did not even exist!

Then, quite abruptly, she and the older woman left the window. His brow burned in anger and humiliation. She snubbed him, a poor peasant boy not good enough for a pretty rich girl like her. She will regret the way she treated him, once he had made it big in Manila!

He walked away, kicking in anger a pebble on the road as he tried to banish her from his mind. There are other girls in the world and he now has one more important concern in his life: his job.

The church to which he now turned his eyes stood ahead in the road, solemn and majestic, its dome silvery in the sunlight, its lone belfry pointed to the sky.

He passed through an open side gate and walked in through a side door. The church was deserted, but for the old church caretaker who was sweeping the stone floor clean with a broom in his hands.

It was so unlike earlier in the morning when it was full of people attending Mass, where he served as an acolyte. He listened then, slightly bored, for he had heard, once too often, what Father Saludo, the parish priest, said in his sermon about the wages of sin. It did not bother him a bit, for he led a good life, free of sin.

He knelt down on a pew his eyes he directed to the figure of Jesus Christ nailed to the cross and prayed for everything to go well for him in Manila. He prayed for his family and his friends, for Miss Dickinson and Mr. Tyler, for Angela Rosablanca as well, never mind if she snubbed him.

The time he spent there had a salutary effect on him he was in high spirit again when he left the church.

He was crossing the town's main road when he frowned, his eyes turned to the town hall across the town square. It looked gloomy and forbidding despite the sunlight washing over it. It was a bad, very bad place during the revolution when the Filipino rebels captured by the Spaniards were jailed and tortured there.

He nodded satisfied at how the American soldiers in the war that followed the revolution, had changed it into something like a school. What were then heard there were no longer the cries of pain of the rebels being tortured there during the revolution, but of the children singing nursery rhymes and reciting simple English words and phrases.

The American soldiers had converted the ground floor into classrooms where they taught the children, reading, writing and arithmetic.

Those informal classes, they held there and in other towns they had conquered and occupied, helped change the Filipinos' attitude toward the Americans from fear and hostility to acceptance and friendliness. His uncle Julian kept him away, though, from those classes.

"They are only using the children like you to get to their elders like me," his uncle once said to him.

He was disappointed, but he understood his uncle's negative attitude toward the Americans. His uncle did not like them. He was a noncombatant who treated the sick and the wounded during the revolution and in the war that followed. He was captured and was set free only after he reluctantly agreed to swear allegiance to the United States.

He was walking on, in the town's main road, when he heard a horse running behind him. He looked back and saw a horse-drawn rig raising dust and fast approaching him. He ran and turned right to the road in the town's commercial area and watched the rig running on, in the town's main road. He sighed in relief. He had avoided, catching the dust on his clothes, he will wear again on his trip tomorrow to Manila.

The new town market at the end of the road was closed for the day. He and his aunt Tarcila sold there yesterday, a basket of tomatoes. They sold there a week ago, a dozen eggs. The money they earned helped them with their family expenses.

The rice mill was also closed, but the shops, stores and the livery stable were still open. He was going to see there, Rustico, a friend and neighbor in Bangar, about taking him and his folks, tomorrow morning in his horse-drawn rig to the train station in Santa Ignacia for his trip to Manila.

He was on his way to see Rustico when something came to his mind as he was passing by Angsiang's general store. He saw Angsiang working near the store entrance as he was entering his store. A yardstick in his hands, Angsiang was measuring a bolt of cloth on a table there.

They nodded at each other. He was well-known there. He walked on, his thoughts on the Chinese merchant. Angsiang and Liaolu, the other Chinese merchant, monopolized the retail trade in the town.

A dress in a rack of ready-made dresses looked to him like a nice parting gift for his aunt Tarcila. He took it out, but returned it promptly to the rack when he saw its price tag. He could not afford it. The other dresses had the same price. He will instead give his aunt, a parting gift that will please her as much and will cost him nothing as well.

Azucena, Angsiang's wife, was standing behind a glass counter of sweets and pastries. He came to her, the reason he went there to the store. It was not to shop there, but to see her, this one last time before leaving the town tomorrow.

He was, at a very young age, infatuated with her from the very first time he saw her, five years ago. She was then a poor pretty girl, newly hired by Angsiang in his store.

He felt sorry for her at how she had changed since then. Her eyes, bright and eager then, now looked tired from lack of sleep. Her breast, small and firm then, was now large and hanging down loosely in her dress. She was worn out by childbearing. Not a year passed since she was married to Angsiang that she was not pregnant. She now has four children.

One of them, a boy, was nagging her over something. She told the boy to stop bothering her, for she was busy attending to him, who had bent down for a close look at the sweets and pastries in the lower shelves of the glass counter, his mind not made up on what to buy there.

He was, in fact, thinking of her. She could have married anyone of the young men who courted her, not Angsiang who was not only old and ugly, but was an alien town merchant.

The talk went around in the town that Angsiang, with what he did to Azucena, had put her in a situation where she could quit her job in his store and sue him for seducing her and remain poor or she could marry Angsiang to a life of plenty. Liaolu, the town's other Chinese merchant, was known to have done the same thing to his employee, Consuelo.

He had stayed long enough at the pastry counter and he pointed at a chocolate bar and said to her, "I will take that one."

"You really have a sweet tooth, Leandro," she said to him. "You never fail to buy something sweet every time you come here."

He smiled and paid for the chocolate bar. He ate it as he was leaving the store, pleased by its sweet taste and for having seen Azucena for one last time before leaving the town.

He came to Rustico who said, as he was closing up the livery stable, "You can ride home with me."

"Thank you, but I am not going home yet. Can you take me tomorrow morning to the train station in Santa Ignacia? The train will be there, around eight o'clock."

"Why? Where are you going?"

"I'm going to Manila. I have a job waiting for me there."

"Why, you lucky boy, I will give up my left arm for a job there. Very well, I will pick you up at around seven o'clock."

"Thank you. I will see you tomorrow."

He walked back to the town's main road and smiled as he was approaching the town's public school.

It took his uncle Julian almost a year before he was allowed to study there. It was long after the construction of the school building was finished and the American schoolteachers had started teaching there.

His uncle had also refused to let him study in the classes held earlier in the town hall by the American soldiers.

His uncle relented only when Candido said, in exasperation with his father, "Do you want Leandro to grow up an ignorant, uneducated fool like us?"

He was, a few weeks later, enrolled in the town's public school at the start of a new school year.

He had, despite that incident on his first day in the school, a wonderful time there.

He entered the school grounds, spurred by that thought and looked around. At the back of the school building was the mango tree in whose shadow he got into a fistfight.

He was seated on a bench there, waiting for the bell to ring at the start of the classes when two boys came, mocking him with their insulting song:

> *"Oh, Leandro Sumuka!*
> *Oh, why did you vomit again?*
> *Oh, why on your teeny-weeny tail!"*

The two bullies had not finished with their insulting song when he swung his fists at them, never mind if he was outnumbered and they were both bigger than him.

A good thing, Mr. Welk came by just then and stopped the fight or he would have ended up with more than a black eye and a bruised lip. But he got to kick one of them on the shin and punch the other on the nose. Word about the fistfight spread throughout the school. No one, from then on, dared to make fun of his surname and provoke him into a fight.

He entered the school building, his mind full of memories, and walked down the corridor. Last Friday, his last day in school, the corridor, during the few minutes' break between classes, was swarming with students noisy with talk and laughter. It was now quiet and deserted.

He turned toward a door and was glad, on turning the doorknob, to find it unlocked. He opened it and stood still at the sill of the door and looked around at Miss Dickinson's classroom, just as he did, a year ago.

He could see even now, Miss Dickinson silencing with her stern gaze, the other students in the class who were laughing at his surname. He repaid her kindness by studying hard. He never came to her class, unprepared. He was always ahead of his classmates. His eyes would light up each time Miss Dickinson announced to the class that he had topped a test.

He had gone far from his first day in the school when he stood at the door of Miss Dickinson's classroom, a lonely, angry boy with a black eye and a bruised lip. He closed the door and walked out of the school.

He was going to the cemetery, the last stop in the last look he was taking of the town before leaving tomorrow for Manila.

A short walk from the school, the cemetery reflected by the dead buried there, the social, economic disparity between the town's rich landlords and their poor tenants.

He entered the cemetery and walked on through the section where the dead landlords were buried. The graves there were set in concrete and at an elevation from the ground. Each grave had a stone cross. A grave there had an angel in stone blowing a trumpet triumphantly.

The graves of the poor dead tenants were simply mounds of earth overgrown with weeds.

He stood for a while at the foot of his mother's grave, a mound of earth at the head of which was a wooden cross, leaning on its side. Written on a piece of wood below the cross were his mother's name and her dates of birth and death: Milagros Kamao-Sumaka, April 7, 1870— March 1, 1890.

His mother died a few days after he was born. He never knew when or where his father Leonardo died. He learned about the little that he knew about them from his father's brother, his uncle Julian, His mother was taken ill from a broken heart when his father left her. His father joined the Katipunan, the rebel group which mounted the revolution against Spain. His father may have died in one of the many battles fought by the rebel group.

While he never knew his parents, he had long decided, as his uncle Julian had described them, to be brave and resolute like his father and kind and caring like his mother.

The thought about his dead parents, heavy on his mind, he turned to distract himself, to the task of cleaning up his mother's grave.

He laid the book on the grass. Then he removed his shirt and put it, beside the book.

He set the cross upright after which he pulled out the weeds there and tamped the grave flat with his hands. Deep down there were his mother's mortal remains and up there in the sky, the soul of his mother must be looking down at him.

His task there done, he put on his shirt and picked up his book.

He prayed, as he then stood at the foot of his mother's grave, for his mother and his father. He prayed for himself as well for him to do well in Manila.

He left the cemetery, sad at the thought that it could be the last time he had visited his mother's grave.

Beads of perspiration had gathered in his brow as he was then walking on the road to the hamlet of Bangar. It cut through the rice fields, bright with sunlight.

He halted and picked up his sandals. He must save on the leather. He resumed walking, the callused soles of his feet allowing him to walk barefooted, but comfortably on the hamlet's rough gravel road.

Chapter Twenty-seven

He arrived in the hamlet at siesta time. It was quiet there, but for the crickets trilling in the trees and the shrubs there. It was deserted, but for his uncle Julian and a young girl nearby who was playing hopscotch by herself on the hamlet's sandy ground.

The nipa huts there stood in two rows. They faced each other, across the hamlet's common front yard.

Julian was seated on a low wooden stool, in front of their nipa hut. A wiry middle-aged man with a coarse, sunburned face, he was brushing with his palm, the feathers in his gamecock.

He set it down on the ground and removed a cigarette dangling in his mouth when he saw Leandro coming. He knew about Leandro's meeting with Miss Dorothy Dickinson and Mr. Samuel Tyler

"How did it turn out?" he asked Leandro

"I got it, uncle. I have got a job!"

"Good."

"I have Mister Tyler's letter that will introduce me to Mister Shay. He built our school building, its annex and the new town market. Mister Shay has a job for me in his construction company in Manila."

"You are lucky you have those American teachers who helped you in getting get a job there. Do you have everything ready?"

"I will just have to put my things in my bag."

"When are you planning to leave?"

"Mister Tyler told me to be in Manila at the earliest possible time. I will then leave tomorrow morning."

His uncle nodded.

"I saw Rustico at the livery stable about the rig we will need for the ride to the train station in Santa Ignacia. He will pick us up at seven o'clock, tomorrow morning."

"Good."

Julian then turned his attention, back to his gamecock. He lifted it with one hand and inspected its head, shaved of its comb and wattles. He nodded satisfied and blew cigarette smoke at his gamecock's head.

Like the town's cockfighting enthusiasts, Julian held the notion that the cigarette smoke and the hot peppers he fed his gamecock will make it stout of heart, a feathered gladiator ready for a cockfight in the cockpit in Santa Ignacia, the next Sunday..

He watched his uncle, neither surprised nor resentful, that he was now showing more interest in his gamecock than in his departure tomorrow for Manila. His uncle, like his aunt Tarcila, was not keen about him, leaving them in Bangar. While they did not object to him in making a try for a better life in Manila, they also wanted him around to help them with the farming and other tasks there. He sighed. Whatever were their feelings about his departure do not matter now. He was set to leave.

He dropped his sandals on the bamboo floor and pushed them aside with his right foot as he was entering their bare and flimsy nipa hut. It was as familiar as it was so depressing to him.

A small cabinet with several drawers stood in a corner of the hut. On top of it was an alarm clock and a few books, his uncle read avidly, which made up for his lack of formal education. A bamboo bed stood near the hut's wall of palm shingles. Underneath the bed was a clothes chest. A wooden bench stood by the window overlooking the front yard.

A pile of pillows, mosquito nets and bedsheets stood in another corner of the hut. Beside it were two rolled-up mats leaning on the wall of palm shingles. The walls were bare, but for a small framed mirror and a calendar with a picture of the Holy Family.

Their nipa hut standing on their plot of land, the carabao, their work animal, the chickens, the sow and its piglets, the vegetable plot, the bamboo grove and the fruit trees in the backyard were all that his aunt and his uncle owned in the world.

He was a while ago in Don Camilo's large stone house with its luxurious furnishings. Their hut showed the sharp contrast between their landlord's life of ease, luxury and plenty and their life of toil, poverty and misery.

He glanced at his aunt Tarcila, who was at the dining table, mending a dress. She was dark and thin, her back turned to the sunlight coming through the window in the kitchen behind her. The bamboo stairs to her right led to the backyard. To her left were the enclosed bathing area and the bamboo footbridge to the elevated outhouse. Steam was rising from a clay pot above the fire in the clay stove in the kitchen.

"Is that," he asked his aunt, "our supper, you are cooking?"

"No. I am boiling our drinking water."

He nodded, glad and satisfied. He had finally prevailed upon his aunt to take up that hygienic measure, he learned in school. She had previously refused to do that, arguing that she had, all her adult life, been drinking water taken from the well in the backyard and never got sick from it and that boiling their drinking water was just an extra chore and a waste of firewood. His aunt changed her mind when he told her what he picked up in school about a cholera epidemic brought about by contaminated water that swept through a convent in Manila recently.

"I have got the job in Manila," he said as he was approaching her. "I am leaving tomorrow morning."

She said nothing and went on working on the dress.

He shrugged his shoulder in dismissal of his aunt, ignoring what he said. He busied himself instead in getting his things ready for his trip to Manila tomorrow.

He put inside his canvas bag, his clothes and his purse with his savings of a few bills and coins. Then he took out from the cabinet, a piece of paper. He wrote there his uncle Berting's address at 128 Maria Clara Street, Palomar. That will be his home address in Manila. His uncle Berting and his uncle Julian were second-degree cousins. They wrote to each other about his plan to look for a job in Manila. While he had memorized the address, he took the precaution of writing it down on that piece of paper, in case he will forget it, once he is in Manila.

He put the piece of paper inside the book, Miss Dickinson gave him. He smiled at her parting gift to him. He turned the pages and stopped at what was written on the flyleaf. It was a dedication from her teacher. Dated March 15, 1905, it read:

To Leandro Sumaka,

A young man whose thirst for knowledge is equaled only by his zest for a life lived fully and well.

Dorothy Dickinson

His teacher had thought so well of him, not only did she help him get a job she also gave him this wonderful parting gift.

He was singing a song as he was putting the book inside his canvas bag, which he then put in a corner in the hut.

He was changing into his work clothes, rolling up his pants to just below the knee when he heard his aunt, coughing. There was something he could do for her.

He said to her "I will see if I can catch some fish in the pond."

The fish he will catch there will be his parting gift to her.

Chapter Twenty-eight

Leandro stood still in the pond's earth embankment, his round bamboo fish-trap, he held ready in his hand. He was watching a fish moving around and making ripples on the surface of the pond. He stepped down into the pond and crept toward the fish once it had stopped moving around.

He was only a few feet away and was poised to plunge his round bamboo fish trap on the fish when it sensed his presence there. It swam away and disappeared in the murky water. He stooped down and searched for the fish, but failed to find it. It may have embedded itself in the muddy bottom of the pond or in any of the nooks and crannies there. He left the pond, so disappointed.

He walked back, frowning, to the solitary tree in the embankment, sat down in its shade and laid the fish trap beside his wicker basket where he kept his catch. He will catch that fish yet. It will show up again. All he needed was a little patience.

He thrust his elbows on his knees and looked around at the pond. It was round-shaped, the tree and the grass, the only vegetation in the embankment there. The sky was a clear light blue with a soft breeze slightly touching his hair.

It was a perfect summer day in the pond. It was his own domain, the master of every living thing in the water, including the elusive fish.

He fell to more musing, his eyes raised to the rice fields which stretched far into the horizon, to the distant peaks of Central Cordillera in the north and to the town, not far from the pond. The fertile soil in the rice fields there yielded an abundance of grain, of which only a small part went to tenants like his folks. Their share of the harvest was cut down even further after Don Camilo had deducted a certain amount for the seed and what they owed him.

There were, for all the backbreaking work they were doing in the rice fields, those times when their share of the harvest was so little, it could not tide them over for the rest of the year. To survive until the next harvest season, they borrowed money at a usurious rate from Don Camilo and this only added to what they owed their landlord. It had been like that for as long as he could remember.

A fish appeared moving around in the surface of the pond. He watched it, wondering if it was the same fish, he was after. He could not determine also whether it was a mudfish or a catfish. It was farther away and the water was murky. It looked like a big fish, though, perhaps a foot long, maybe even longer. He waited for the fish to stop moving around.

Such a catch, that fish and the three others, two mudfish and a catfish now secure inside his wicker basket, will please his aunt Tarcila.

Boiled with cabbage and potato, fried or broiled in hot coals, they will make a fine supper. His aunt could also preserve in salt and rice, some of his catch.

The fish had stopped moving around. It was time to strike. He stood up, picked up his fish trap and returned to the pond.

He swung his fish trap once he was near enough to the fish and brought it down on the fish and into the muddy bottom of the pond.

The fish swam wildly inside the fish trap in its vain effort to escape. He then shot his hand through the fish trap's round opening at the top, felt for the fish and clamped his hand around it. It was scaly, a mudfish. He had caught a female fish by the feel of his hand on its full belly.

He took it out of the fish trap and smiled at the fish, twisting in his hand. It was a big one, about a foot long.

He walked back to the shade of the tree and put the fish inside his wicker basket. He now had quite a catch and it was getting late, but why should he stop fishing when the going is good? Fishing is his pastime and it helped in putting food in their dining table.

His aunt, besides that, will like to have as many fish as she could preserve in salt and rice.

He was rewarded, as he was looking at the pond, by the sight of another fish moving around. It was much farther away, at the far side of the pond.

He picked up his fish trap and, his eyes kept to the fish, he walked back to the embankment. He was about to step down into the pond when he heard his name called He looked back and saw his cousin Candido coming, astride his carabao.

"Have you caught any fish yet?" he shouted.

He did not reply to Candido. Had he said just a word, the sound of his voice might scare the fish. It might then move away. He raised his hand instead, four of his fingers pointed up to show the number of fish, he had caught so far.

He looked back at the fish, his brow knitted with worry. It might have swum away and disappeared in the pond. He nodded. It moved just a little from where he last saw it. It was time for him to get the fish. He stepped down into the pond and moved slowly, carefully toward the fish. He brought his fish trap down on the fish, once he was near enough to it. He took it out of the fish trap and was delighted to find it just slightly smaller than the other fish, he had caught earlier.

He walked back smiling to the embankment. He has something to show to his cousin.

He raised high, the fish in his hand and shouted at Candido, "Look at this big mudfish, I just caught!"

Candido was not to be outdone and he showed to Leandro, his catch in his wicker basket, tied to the carabao's broad neck. He had simply taken out the fish from the bamboo fish cage he had laid across the creek, at some distance from the pond.

Both the pond and the creek were in the section in the rice fields, they tilled for Don Camilo. They agreed, the pond to be his fishing preserve, the creek, Candido's fishing preserve.

He walked back to the shade of the tree and put the big mudfish inside the wicker basket. He watched and listened when Candido, after getting off from his carabao, began to sing their favorite song:

The sun shines bright in the old Kentucky home,
This summer, the darkies are gay;
The corn-top's ripe and the meadow's in the bloom
While the birds make music all the day.

He kept beat with the song by tamping his feet to the ground as he then sang along with Candido, the song's refrain:

Weep no more, my lady, O weep no more to-day.
We will sing one song for the old Kentucky home,
For the old Kentucky home far away.

It occurred to him then that he will be, by tomorrow, far away from home. Where he is going will not be as far as Kentucky, wherever Kentucky is, but Manila will be far enough from San Isidro.

"So, you have caught five fish; not bad," Candido said as he was approaching Leandro.

"They are more than enough for one good meal."

"Do as much fishing there as you can," Candido said as he was looking at the pond. "It looks like it is drying up fast. The water level there, the other week, was almost a waist-high."

"I know," he replied as he was likewise looking at the pond.

The fish there will then hibernate in the pond's nooks and crannies or deep in the mud, turned into clay during summer. They will come out at the onset of the rainy season when the pond will be filled again with water.

"Let me see your catch," Candido said as he was looking down at the fish in the wicker basket. "They are big! What will you do with them?"

"It is up to your mother, but I guess, she will cook the three small ones and preserve in salt and rice, the two big ones. Why don't you and Maria have supper with us?"

"But, of course, we will," Candido said, smiling and rubbing his hands in keen anticipation of a good meal. "Tell Mother to make soup with the mudfish and put there, a lot of vegetables."

Candido then walked back to his carabao. He said as he mounted it, "The fish I caught are small compared to the fish you caught."

"I was just lucky."

"You are always lucky."

The carabao moved forward when Candido flicked its side with the rope in his hand. He left the pond, singing once again, their favorite Kentucky song.

He was watching Candido until he was no longer in his sight when he decided to take one more look for fish in the pond. The fish trap in his hand, he walked slowly around the pond, halting now and then as he was looking at the water for any sign of fish there. He did not find any. It was time for him to go home, too.

His left cheek warmed by the sun, he crossed the rice fields and took the path that then merged with the hamlet's lone gravel road. He blinked his eyes from the shafts of sunlight piercing through the gaps in the leafy branches of the trees on that side of the road.

He saw, on his arrival in the hamlet, the common front yard now lively and noisy with children playing games there while on the ground between two huts, a small crowd of men was watching two cockfighting enthusiasts making a practice cockfight with their gamecocks.

Genoveva, the hamlet gossiper, was at the foot of the stairs in her hut. She was busy pounding rice on a large wooden mortar with a wooden pestle in her hand.

She said as he was passing by her hut, "I heard you are leaving for a job in Manila."

"Yes, ma'am, I am leaving for a job there."

"I hope, you will make good there."

"Thank you, ma'am, I do hope so."

He crossed the hamlet's common front yard, his thoughts on her. Everyone in the hamlet will know by nightfall that he is leaving for Manila, for a job there. It showed, though, how much they know or are close to each other. They are all related to each other, either by blood ties or by their common bondage to Don Camilo.

He entered their hut and went straight to his aunt.

"Here it is, auntie, my parting gift to you," he said as he showed to her, the fish inside the wicker basket.

"What a nice parting gift," she said as she was looking at the fish. "Those two mudfish are big. Thank you, my son."

She called him by his nickname, Andro, and seldom called him, her son. He was touched and, like a helpful son, he took from the bathing area, a large iron basin, they used in doing their laundry. He put it down on the dining table and looked on, proud and happy, when his aunt then dropped the fish into the iron basin.

"Let me see," she said to herself. "I'll preserve the two big mudfish in salt and rice, the rest I will make into soup with cabbage and tomatoes."

"That is what Candido wants you to cook. He and Maria will join us for supper."

The fish must first be clubbed dead, cleaned and their entrails removed before her aunt could do anything with them.

He took from the bathing area, the implement perfect for the purpose—the wooden club they used in doing their laundry.

"Let me do it," she said as she took the wooden club from him. "Go, now, you need to wash up."

The water level in the clay jars in the kitchen and in the bathing area was low and he filled them with water, he drew out from the well in the backyard.

He came back to his aunt later on, now fresh from a bath there.

"Can I be of some help, auntie?" he said when he saw her, now cleaning the fish.

"No. You better have your things ready for your trip tomorrow."

"I have already done that."

He could not just stand there and watch his aunt, working. He went down in the bamboo stairs at the back of the hut.

His uncle, after watching the practice cockfight in the hamlet's common front yard, was now cutting firewood in their backyard.

His uncle asked him, "Did you catch any fish?"

"I did, uncle. I caught two catfish and three mudfish, two of them rather big."

His uncle resumed working. He also went to work.

He watered the vegetable plot and removed the dead branches there. The sow in the pigpen was lying on its side while its litter of piglets was suckling at its teats. He left it alone. He also left the carabao alone when he saw it, feeding on a mound of hay.

He glanced at his uncle's gamecock inside its locked bamboo cage. His uncle will not let anyone, but himself, to handle or feed it. The chickens were everywhere in the backyard. They were scratching for food on the ground. They were soon all around him, feeding on the broken grain he was throwing into the ground.

"I don't see the brown mother hen," he said to his uncle.

"Adiong took it for a party, Don Camilo is holding this week."

"The hen should be deducted from what we owe him."

His uncle, in response, merely shrugged his shoulders. It was such a gesture of helplessness and resignation that filled him with pity for his uncle and hatred for their landlord. His uncle, like the other tenants, followed every wish and whim of their landlord.

Tarcila appeared in the kitchen window and asked Julian for firewood. He gathered an armful and brought it up to the hut.

Leandro was finished feeding the chickens. He sat down on the bamboo stairs, frowning at the kind of arithmetic Don Camilo did that they were never out of debt to him. They paid him with part of their share of the harvest and whatever they had there, like the mother hen, Don Camilo's manservant Adiong took, and by doing servant's work in Don Camilo's house before he rented it to the American schoolteachers. His uncle did handyman work for Don Camilo while his aunt helped wash the dishes at the parties Don Camilo held in his house. His mother, so he was told, when she was still alive, did laundry work for Don Camilo and his family.

They will always be in debt to Don Camilo, he thought bitterly of their feared and hated landlord. He held Don Camilo with such loathing, he could not stand the sight of him and he avoided Don Camilo every time he dropped by their hamlet.

Don Camilo always came on horseback, imposing and fearsome in his safari suit and helmet, his tall shiny boots in stirrups and a gun inside the holster in his belt. He was so short-tempered, he would shout, "Damn you!" at anyone who incurred his displeasure. He was a violent man who once lashed a tenant with the whip in his hand.

He looked around as a way of removing all thought about their feared and hated landlord. He was at the time of the day when done with his tasks there, he had nothing else to do, but to wait for his aunt Tarcila to call him to supper.

It was dusk. The bamboo grove and the fruit and palm trees now blending in the gathering darkness, along with the crickets trilling in the trees, made this, their plot of land, a place so dear to him.

He has a special feeling for this spot on earth. It nurtured him and his folks. The grain they planted and harvested in the rice fields, their pigs and chickens, the vegetables in the garden and the fish, he caught in the pond, all of those sustained them whatever was the time, lean or plentiful, that was upon them. The beauty of the place somehow made up for the impoverished, desperate lives they led there.

The sound of footsteps coming from inside the hut interrupted him in his thoughts. He leaned sideways to give his uncle room as he was going down the stairs.

Julian took out a small wooden box from the cabinet in the ground floor of the hut. He returned to the backyard and sat down on a bamboo bench, a few feet away from Leandro.

He took out from the wooden box a strip of thin white paper on which he sprinkled shredded tobacco. Then he rolled the paper into the shape of a tube. He had made his own cigarette which he then lit up with a match.

Not a word passed between them. Leandro watched the now increasingly dark surroundings while his uncle went on smoking.

His uncle, after a while, said, "I will say this before you leave tomorrow. If things don't work out for you in Manila, don't hesitate to come back here. We will be glad to have you, back. After all, we are your family."

"I wish I did not have to leave, but I have no future here."

"You are like your father. He could not accept the way things were here. He sought change with the revolution. He met there death instead."

"My father was a rebel."

"We are a family of rebels."

He nodded. His uncle looked meek, but now that he was talking about the rebellious streak in their family, his uncle had then assumed a proud and defiant expression in his face. His uncle at that moment was not a meek tenant farmer, but a fierce tribal fighter. This rebellious spirit ran through generations in their family. His uncle's voice was animated as he then spoke about their forebear, Grandfather Pedro.

"He was the foremost fighter in our family," Julian said. "He fought in a local rebellion the Spaniards were able to stamp out only after so many years of fighting."

"You told me once that for his involvement in that rebellion, he was exiled in Guam, where he died."

"He preferred to be exiled in that island in the Pacific Ocean, never to return here rather than bow down to the Spaniards. He refused, unlike our townsfolk, to adopt a Spanish surname, as most of them did. It was nothing more to him than a doglike subservience to our Spanish masters. He will be amused to see how those who took those Spanish surnames have made into a symbol of high status what actually was an example of Filipino slaves aping their Spanish masters."

"But why did he not drop his baptismal name, as well?"

"He kept his baptismal name in keeping with our Christian faith. It is one good thing the Spaniards have brought to us."

"At least we are now through with them."

"But we now have the Americans."

"You are against them, too."

"I just want us, to be left alone."

"Will the Americans do that?"

"It is not likely to happen."

"We will then have to accept, they will be around for sometime."

"They will indeed be around, I cannot tell, for how long."

"What can you say about that, uncle?"

"I must admit, they are not like the Spaniards. They have not taken for themselves, those lands the Spaniards stole from us. But I am waiting for the day when those lands will be returned to us. I will be pleased if the Americans will also investigate the abuses of Don Camilo and the other landlords. But that will never happen. We have seen them, getting instead into the good grace of the Americans. We may just have to continue to bear the indignity and the injustice of tilling those lands our forebears owned, but were forcibly taken away from them by our Spanish rulers. Candido and others like him have considered taking them back, by force."

"Will they succeed, if they will do that?"

Julian was so absorbed with the question he noticed his cigarette only when it was beginning to burn his fingers. He flicked it away.

The backyard was by now cast in darkness except for a light on the ground. It came from the kerosene lamp on the worktable there.

"Resorting to force," Julian then said, "as Candido and the others want to do, can be justified only by its success and that is so doubtful. They cannot remove by force, Don Camilo and the other landlords. They should work instead on what I heard are the Americans' sense of justice and fair play. They must be encouraged to take over those lands. They could then apportion those lands to us, the tenants, with us paying for them on installment over a period of time.

"I'm waiting for that day. I heard the Americans are here, not to exploit and abuse us, as the Spaniards have done to us, but to bring to us the many benefits of their rule. They must initiate land reform. It is one good thing that they can do for us."

He gazed at his uncle, impressed by the soundness of his reasoning and by the change in his attitude toward the Americans. He himself liked, respected and admired the Amercans for the help and kindness of Miss Dickinson and Mister Tyler who got for him, a job in Pacific & Gulf.

He sighed. All those concerns will be far behind him by tomorrow. He will be in Manila by then, a good future waiting for him there. It will be so unlike that of his uncle, whose life in Bangar held no good prospects for him.

Tarcila appeared again in the kitchen window.

"Come up here, supper is ready," she said to them. "You will have gas pain from all the talking you are doing there on your empty stomachs."

They went up to the hut.

Julian took the kerosene lamp in the kitchen and put it on a hook connected to a bamboo beam in the dining area. It provided enough light on the dining table. The rest of the hut remained partly in darkness.

Candido and his wife Maria have not arrived yet.

"I will tell them, supper is ready," Leandro said.

He was walking toward the hut's front stairs when they arrived with Miguel, their baby in Maria's arms. They live in their hut across the hamlet's common front yard.

"A perfect timing," Candido said, smiling.

He often said that every time they came over for lunch or supper. They often did this for a varied meal and to keep Candido's parents, company ever since his two sisters, Luisa and Paz, had married and started their own families, far from them.

Candido had a baby's blanket over his arm while his other hand was holding a plate of fried fish, the same ones, he caught in the creek.

He said, as he was putting the plate of fried fish on the dining table, "Come and get them while they are still hot from our kitchen."

Julian and Tarcila nodded approvingly of the fried fish as Candido was putting the baby's blanket on the bamboo floor.

He stood up and drummed playfully Miguel's stomach with his fingers as he was about to take him from Maria.

"Stop that! You will upset his stomach," she said as she turned their baby away from Candido.

Leandro said, as he was watching them, "I have a better idea."

He took Miguel from Maria and danced with him around the hut.

"Stop that, Andro," Candido said to Leandro. "That is not the way to dance, not with two left feet. You are only making my baby dizzy with that kind of dancing, you are doing."

Leandro went on dancing with the baby.

"Do you want him to throw up on your face with that kind of dancing, you are doing?" Candido said to Leandro who promptly gave the baby to Candido.

"What made you do that?" Candido asked Leandro.

Leandro simply shrugged his shoulders. He went smiling to the kitchen and washed his hands there, after which he sat down at the dining table beside his aunt Tarcila.

Candido laid Miguel on the blanket and then joined Maria in washing their hands in the kitchen. They sat down beside each other, facing Leandro and Tarcila. Julian, as the head of the household, was seated at the head of the table.

They prayed and then they proceeded with their dinner. They ate with their hands. Candido carried the talk at the table. The others ate and listened when he told them how he settled a fight between two housewives in their hamlet. Both women, though much older than

Candido, deferred to him. He has a way with people, a jovial, backslapping fellow, a natural leader. He was eight years older than Leandro. Candido, at twenty-two years in age, was considered, the future headman in their hamlet.

The talk turned to the food on the table. Maria complimented Tarcila for the delicious soup. Candido brought laughter to the table with the comment that his mother had cooked so much soup it could fill the pond with water and keep it from drying up.

The laughter at the table had barely died down when Candido turned to Leandro and said, "I heard, you are leaving tomorrow for a job, waiting for you in Manila. You did not tell me that in the pond, this afternoon."

"I forgot to tell you about it."

He wanted Candido to learn about it, not from him, but from somebody else. He did not want to see his cousin, reacting badly if he himself had told him about it. Both of them wanted to try their luck in Manila. They had talked about it, a wonderful place full of people, big buildings, theaters, stores, gaslight in the streets, ships in the river and in the bay and homes with plumbing and running water.

"How did you get a job in Manila when you are living here in Bangar?" Candido asked Leandro.

"Miss Dickinson, my teacher, and Mister Tyler, who is also a teacher, helped me in getting a job in Pacific and Gulf Construction Company. It built our school building, its annex and the new market here."

He looked on at Candido. He seemed to be, both glad and resentful, he has a job waiting for him in Manila while he was stuck in Bangar. Trying his luck in Manila was, for Candido, out of the question. The only way he could provide for his family was by staying in Bangar and working as a tenant of Don Camilo.

He was pleasantly surprised when Candido suddenly stood up and, leaning across the table and holding him on his shoulders, he said to him, "Good for you, Andro, good for you! I know you will make good there. And don't you forget us when you have made it big in Manila."

The others laughed while Leandro smiled in relief.

"Do you have everything ready?" Candido then asked Leandro, who nodded in reply.

"We will see Leandro off at the train station in Santa Ignacia," Julian said.

Maria asked Leandro, "How about our ride to the train station?".

"Rustico will take us there in his rig, tomorrow morning."

"Do you know the time the train will be in Santa Ignacia?" Julian asked Leandro.

"It will be there at around eight o'clock."

He knew the train schedule from the many times he had been to the train station and watched people boarding the train bound for Manila. He will soon be doing that, too.

"We will miss you," Maria said to Leandro.

The mood at the dining table suddenly turned gloomy.

He looked sadly at the others at the table. Tonight might be the last time he was sharing a meal with them.

Miguel woke up, crying. Maria, after washing her hands in the kitchen, picked him up and began breastfeeding him. The others were finished eating and Leandro cleared the table and washed the dishes while Julian went downstairs. Candido waited for Maria while Tarcila sat quietly at the dining table.

He was finished with his task in the kitchen at the same time that Maria was finished breasfeeding Miguel. He walked with them across the hut and watched them as they crossed the hamlet's common front yard and entered their hut.

It was early evening, a time for song and good cheer in the hamlet. A group of young men, Rustico among them, was having a drinking session around a table in front of a hut. It was strictly a male affair although some women were watching them from the windows in their huts.

The host filled a tin cup from a pitcher of palm wine and drank a good measure of it. He nodded and said the wine had aged well. The others complimented him for his skill in winemaking.

The tin cup was passed around and everyone there had a fill of the wine. They accompanied, the drinking they were doing with what they heard about the unusual event of someone in their hamlet going to Manila for a job there. They all wanted to live and work in the Big City.

The young men were at some distance from where Leandro was watching them. He could guess, though, that their eyes often turned to him, they were talking about him although they could hardly see him, it being dark in the window in the hut.

He is waiting for Candido to come out of his hut. Candido liked to be with people. He watched him when he came out of there and joined the young men. The tin cup of wine was passed to Candido. He took a good measure of it and said something he could not quite catch due to the distance and the noise at the table. It seemed to be funny, though, from the laughter that followed what Candido said.

While the young men were having a good cheer with their home-brewed palm wine, Julian and the hamlet's other elderly men were holding their own session, seated on benches in the front yard, a few feet away from where Leandro was watching them. He listened when they talked about something going on between a landlord and the wife of the municipal secretary in Santa Ignacia.

He began to lose interest when the talk turned to the land tenancy problem. He and his uncle had talked enough about it. He yawned. It was time for him to retire for the night.

He stood up and made his bed, a mat he spread out on the bamboo floor on which he laid a pillow and a blanket, above which he hung up a mosquito net. He watched with drowsy eyes as he was now lying down on the mat, the dark starry sky framed up by the window. He then heard a guitar strummed up from a distance. A man then began to sing a sad love song. Its lyrics of a lover leaving his loved one filled him with love and sadness.

He was likewise leaving this town that he loved. He was leaving those whom he loved, his family and his friends, a teacher with brown eyes and auburn hair and a girl with long tresses and dimples on her cheeks. He was leaving them, filled with the song about a lover, leaving his loved one.

Chapter Twenty-nine

Leandro had a special breakfast of coffee, fried rice, fried fish and eggs and sliced tomatoes, ready at the dining table and his lunch of bread, a bottle of water and two hardboiled eggs inside his canvas bag while his uncle and his aunt were still asleep in their bamboo bed.

He was dressed up by the time they woke up. His aunt called him to breakfast as Candido and Maria were entering the hut with Miguel in Maria's arms.

"Join us," Julian said to them from the dining table.

"Thank you, Father," Candido said, "but we have just taken our breakfast."

The food looked inviting, though, and Candido said, "I won't mind, taking a bite."

He sat down at the dining table and asked Maria to join him there. Maria shook her head and looked on as they went on eating. The food was good. They seldom have that kind of breakfast, but mindful of the time, they ate hurriedly.

Leandro, after they had finished eating, cleared the table and washed the dishes with Candido helping him. Then he said to his uncle and his aunt who were dressing up, that he is going to see Rustico about their ride to the train station.

He had stepped down to the foot of the stairs, his bag in his hand when he saw Rustico coming in his horse-drawn rig. He was early. He pulled the horse to a stop, the moment the rig was beside Leandro.

"Hop in," he said to Leandro, "and give me your bag."

He gave his bag to Rustico, who put it beside him in the driver's seat.

"What are you waiting for? Why don't you climb in," Rustico said when Leandro made no move to step up into his rig.

"I'm waiting for the others," he replied.

"I thought you are going alone to the train station."

"My folks are going to see me off. They will be down shortly."

"In that case, you can just drop me off at the livery stable. Candido can drive the horse."

"Are you not going to see me off at the train station?"

"There is not enough room for all of us and I cannot bear the agony of watching you, leave our town."

Leandro smiled and shook his head in reaction to what Rustico said. His eyes lit up when he saw their neighbors, looking at him from the windows in their huts.

"Take care now and good luck," Genoveva said.

"Don't forget to send us money," another woman said.

The neighborhood was soon noisy with the neighbors giving him advice and wishing him well.

He smiled and waved at them. They were looking up to him, a peasant boy like the other boys in their hamlet who will make it big in Manila. His departure for a job there was a big, unusual event there. It was the first time in his life to be the center of attention, his head swelled with pride.

Three teenage boys, Leandro's friends, were coming. Like him, they too had dreamt of someday going to work in Manila. Now, there he was, on his way to realize their common dream. They hugged him and tapped him on his shoulders and back in effusive farewell gestures.

Rustico was watching them from his rig.

One of the boys said, "Hey, Rustico, are you sure that nag of yours can still make it to the train station? If it cannot, it might be better for Leandro to just walk to the train station."

They roared with laughter. Rustico did not reply, but smiled in good humor for his horse with its droopy head and thin legs looked like it had long passed its prime.

Julian, Tarcila, Candido and Maria with Miguel in her arms had come down from their hut. They exchanged greetings with their neighbors. Candido took Miguel from Maria as Leandro was helping her and his aunt in stepping up into the rig. They took the backseat while Candido and Julian took the front seat. There was no room left for Leandro.

"Why don't you just walk beside the rig?" a boy said to Leandro, to the others' laughter.

"Better still," another boy suggested, "Why don't you race that nag to the train station?"

Rustico ignored them and said to Leandro, "Take my seat."

"But where," he said, "will you sit down?"

"That is no problem," Rustico replied as he sat down on the floor of the rig.

"Could I drive the horse?"

"Go ahead."

Leandro stepped up into the rig and sat down on the driver's seat. Everyone there was waiting for him, to get them going. He waved in good-bye at his friends and their neighbors. Then he whipped up the horse with the rein, sending it moving away from the hamlet.

They dropped off Rustico at the livery stable and proceeded to the train station.

The horse was so slow, no amount of prodding, Leandro made with the rein, could make it run faster. They might miss the train.

After what seemed like a long time to him, the train station finally came into view. Now that he was freed from worry, he relaxed his hold on the rein, his eyes turned to the train station.

It stood out in a landscape of rice fields, the weeds carpeting them rendered golden hued by the summer sun.

He was looking at it when something risky but thrilling that took place there, crossed his mind. It was the battle between Filipino and American troops during the Philippine-American War. Candido spoke about it:

"It was a short, but savage fight. Our troops fought from the train station. They were no match to the Americans with the firepower of their artillery. The battle lasted only half an hour or so. Our troops then retreated farther north, along the railroad tracks. I was scared when the Americans started moving toward the train station. I was hidden by the tall cogon grass, a mere hundred yards or so away from them. A good thing they did not see me."

Candido's report, instead of scaring him, made him determined to see also how the battle went there, a risky thing to do. The Americans by then had occupied San Isidro and the towns nearby. Many of them, young and excitable, they might shoot him if they will see him.

Candido did not stop him from going there, but told him to be careful. He kept his plan from his uncle and his aunt.

He went there the following day in the fastest route, in the railroad tracks. The trains were not running. He met no one along the way.

The effect of the battle was immediately known to him from its collapsed tile roof, pockmarked brick walls and shattered awnings, doors and glass windows.

His face was grim when he entered the train station at more signs of the fighting that took place there in the rubble, the empty shells and cartridges, tattered clothing and blood on the floor.

He was pleased to learn, a few weeks later, that the Americans had fixed the train station and had the trains running again. He was encouraged to go there again and watch the people, going to Manila.

They arrived at the train station which looked like it was newly built. The collapsed tile roof and the shattered glass windows, the door and awnings had long been replaced, the bullet holes in the brick wall cemented over and given a fresh coat of paint, the blood on the floor washed away, a long time ago.

His uncle took Miguel from Maria as he was helping her and his aunt in getting off from the rig.

They entered the train station while Candido brought the rig to the parking area.

They watched and waited when he joined the line to the ticket teller's window. He was next in line to the ticket teller when he felt Candido, tapping him on his shoulders.

"Let me take care of your train fare, cousin," Candido said. "It is my parting gift to you."

"Thank you," he replied, "but I will buy it myself."

"No, I will do it," Candido said as he moved toward the ticket teller's window.

He shrugged his shoulders. It was useless to argue with Candido, once his mind was made up.

He thanked Candido again as he was giving him his ticket.

"Nothing to it," Candido replied, smiling. "It is only money which I just gave away."

Tarcila was watching them and she said to him, "Don't be like your cousin. Be careful with your money."

"I will auntie," he replied, amused at his aunt's warning, not to be like Candido who had an easygoing attitude toward money. She had a point there, though. If he is not careful, he could get lost in Manila with no money in his pocket. He felt for his purse. It was safe inside his pocket.

Candido then led them through a noisy crowd in the train station, the noisiest among them, the food vendors selling their products.

He caught bits of conversation as he was walking on, behind his uncle. An old woman was telling a young man beside her to visit his cousins in Manila. Two women were bidding each other, good-bye. Most of the crowd though was just standing there, their eyes often turned northward where the train will be coming from.

They sat down on a bench, its back against the wall with him seated beside a man, eating peanuts. Candido, Maria, his aunt and his uncle occupied the rest of the bench. The man was making a mess with the empty peanut shells scattered around his feet.

He ignored the man and looked around at the train station.

It was a familiar sight to him from the many times he had visited it. An onlooker then, he was now also a train passenger. He was taking his first train ride to Manila itself when the provincial folks were going there. They were, like him, lured there by the jobs, the attractions and amenities of life in the city.

He glanced at his uncle and his aunt, sorry for them, they were not going with him to Manila. They were too old to move out of Bangar. So too with Candido who could provide for his family only by working as Don Camilo's tenant while Maria will always be, by the side of Candido.

Smoke appeared in a short while in the horizon. It was coming from the train, an iron caterpillar painted orange. It bellowed a deep hollow sound as it was approaching the train station. The sound of its iron wheels resounded in the iron rails in the train station.

The passengers and the vendors surged toward the train cars, the moment the train had stopped beside the platform in the train station.

"It is time, Andro," Candido said to him.

They stood up from the bench. He smiled at Maria and playfully squeezed Miguel's nose. Then he hugged his aunt who said to him, "Take care now and always be a good boy."

He was surprised when he hugged his uncle to hear from him, a strange wheezing sound as if he had trouble breathing.

His arm on his shoulders, Candido said to him, "Remember what I told you, cousin, do not forget us when you have made it big in Manila."

"I will not and wish me good luck."

They looked on sadly as he then walked toward the train. It has a number of train cars and he took the one, nearest to him. He smiled and waved at them once he was inside the train car.

The train then moved away.

He saw a seat ahead had a vacant space. He took it and put his bag in the overhead baggage compartment. The stout man seated beside him was snoring as he slept with his straw hat over his face.

He will not let this snoring seatmate spoil his first train ride and he ignored the man and looked out through the train window. The man obstructed part of the view. He saw nonetheless, a few miles away, across the rice fields, San Isidro recognizable with its church with a lone belfry.

He sat back on his seat, once the train had passed the town, his heart pained with sadness. He may have seen San Isidro for the last time. He had seen his folks a while ago, perhaps also for the last time. He had no way of knowing that. He had a feeling, though, that his life in San Isidro was over.

The train conductor came and checked the passengers' tickets, distracting him from his sad thoughts. His turn came and he gave the conductor his ticket. The conductor examined it, punched a hole on it with the puncher in his hand and returned the ticket to him.

The train made a stop in the next town. It looked just like San Isidro with its church, also with a lone belfry, and its landscape of trees, nipa huts, stone houses and rice fields. The sight made him feel like he was going back to San Isidro. He smiled as he shook his head. He was gone for less than an hour and he was already missing his hometown.

The train ran on. The sameness of the view in Central Plain and the train's rhythmic, slightly swaying movement had such a dull effect on him, he dozed off like the stout man seated beside him.

He watched on waking up with no particular interest, the crowd in the station where the train had made its next stop. He went back to sleep, once the train had started to move again. He slept, like the man seated beside him, through the next stops the train made.

A young girl tugging at his shirt sleeve woke him up. She was holding in front of him a rice cake, wrapped in banana leaf. Hanging from her arm was a basket of rice cakes.

"You will like this rice cake, sir," the girl said. "It is delicious. It will make a good lunch and it is very cheap—only two centavos."

He was annoyed, the young girl had disturbed him while he was sleeping, he said to her, "Go away. I have my own lunch."

The girl looked down sadly at the train floor.

She was walking away when something about her made him look back at her. She was so thin and so small she must be only seven or eight years old. Her dress was so patched up a slight tug might tear it apart.

She was a very young girl, earning a living selling rice cakes, competing with older and bigger vendors who swarmed the train aisles, each time the train made a stop in a train station. He was suddenly filled with pity for the young girl.

"Come back, here," he said to her. "I will buy your rice cake."

The girl returned smiling and gave him a rice cake. He paid for it and put it on his side. He stood up to get his lunch in his bag in the baggage compartment when the stout man stirred in his seat.

He watched from the corner of his eye, the stout man who had raised his hat, revealing a pig-like face with his thick lips and round, bloated cheeks.

The man asked the girl for a rice cake. She left, as the man was removing the banana leaf wrapper of the rice cake, he bought. He ate like a pig, finishing the rice cake with two big bites and concluding his meal with a loud burp. The man then pulled his hat over his face and went back to sleep.

The man looked so disagreeable he turned his gaze to the other side of the aisle, to the more pleasant sight of the other passengers taking their lunch from the food on their laps.

He took out from his bag, his lunch of bread and two hardboiled eggs. He was so hungry he finished it and the rice cake with a few bites of them and then washed them down with the bottle of water he also carried in his bag.

The lunch he took had made him so drowsy and he slept through the next stops, the train made.

He woke up later on as the passengers across the aisle were talking with loud voices.

He looked out through the window. The long shadows cast on the ground by the trees at some distance from the railroad tracks showed him that it was now late in the afternoon.

The train later on passed by the fishponds in Bulacan, their surface of water, bright in reflection of the late afternoon sunlight.

It began, not long after, to slow down. He watched, curious and excited, houses, people walking on the sidewalk and horse-drawn rigs running in the street, near the railroad tracks.

The train had arrived in Manila. It entered, soon after, the terminal building in Tutuban.

He stood up from his seat and pulled out his bag from the baggage compartment. He was about to leave when he noticed the man, seated beside him, was still sleeping. He slept practically all throughout the trip. The train might later leave the terminal with the man still on board, sleeping there. He might then find himself, on waking up, back to where he came from.

He looked on at the man, undecided on whether or not, he should wake him up. Some people, when roused from sleep, could be so nasty. The man might snarl at him when he was only being helpful. Let the train conductor wake him up, he said to himself, and he left the train.

The terminal lobby was full of people. Ten train stations like the one in Santa Ignacia will easily fit there. And what a bustle! Some of the people there were the passengers, who just got off from his train. Other passengers, their bags and luggage in their hands, were hurrying toward an outgoing train. People were lined up at the ticket tellers' windows. Some of them were lounging on the benches, reading, talking or simply looking around, their boxes and bags at their feet. Others were milling around. There were children playing in the lobby's tile floor while other children, seated on benches beside their parents, were talking to each other or were, like him, looking around at this very busy place, full of people. He heard in all that activity, the din of human voices and the rhythmic wheezing sound of a train engine.

He had seen enough of the train terminal lobby and he walked on toward its wide entrance, his eyes wide in awe of what he was seeing there.

A wide avenue near the grounds of the terminal building was busy with vehicular traffic. Horse-drawn cabs and rigs and steam-driven trucks were running in opposite directions in the avenue. People on the sidewalk were waiting for their ride in the horse-driven cabs and rigs running there. On the far side of the avenue were two-story wood-and-stone buildings with wide sloping tile roofs. The upper floor with tall shell-paned windows looked, just like the landlords' homes in San Isidro. The buildings' ground floor with their open arches and glass display windows showed them to be built for business.

Shoppers were inspecting or were haggling with the salesgirls there the merchandise spread out on the tables there or were displayed in the glass cabinets in the stores and shops there.

Angsiang and Liaolu will drool with envy at that big crowd of shoppers they seldom had in San Isidro.

He never imagined Manila to be such a busy place with so many people and what he is seeing there is probably, just a small section in the city.

The view was marvelous, but it had also distracted him from his immediate task of finding his uncle Berting's house. He could not just wander around and end up, lost and confused, in this very busy place. He needed direction. A police officer could help him, but he saw no one around. He hesitated about asking strangers for direction. Someone working in the train terminal could help him.

He took out from the book in his bag, the piece of paper with his uncle Berting's address, written there. He showed it to a ticket teller and asked him where he could find the address written there.

"It is not far from here," the ticket teller said to him. "It is in the street at the left side of the train terminal. You will not miss it. Just walk over to it."

He left the train terminal and, following the ticket teller's direction, he proceeded to Maria Clara Street in Palomar, where his uncle Berting resided.

He took note, as he was walking on, of the street numbers posted in the houses there. He had passed by a house numbered 115 and an alley next to it when he was puzzled at the next house, now numbered 145.

Where, he asked himself, his brow knitted in bewilderment, were the houses numbered from 116 to 144? His uncle Berting's house was numbered 128. His uncle Berting's house could be somewhere there, inside the alley.

He looked on at the alley that was narrow and dark. The huts that lined both sides of the alley were so close to each other, their roofs nearly touched each other, nearly blocking out the sunlight.

He noticed, as he then entered the alley, that the huts there were like those in Bangar. They were made of wood or bamboo and walled with wood or palm shingles. There were no flowering plants there except for the few potted plants hanging from the windowsills in some of the huts there.

The stench in the alley made him squirm in disgust and he had thought before that the homes in Manila had modern toilet facilities.

They were far better off in Bangar where every home there, even those of the poorest families, had its own outhouse.

He was, by now, deep inside the alley, in a low section where flanks of wood had been laid, a foot or so, above the soggy, smelly ground. He walked on until he came to a fork in the alley. He took the branch that led to a higher ground and walked on to an open ground, surrounded by huts and a small store.

Seated there, across each other on the bamboo benches, were five tough-looking young men, thugs who were idling the day away.

"Who do we have here, if not a provincial boy," one of the thugs said to the others' laughter when they saw him wearing leather sandals, not leather shoes or rubber sneakers.

He felt, he was in danger there and he walked back to the alley.

"Hey, you," one of the thugs shouted at him. "Who are you? What brought you here?"

He walked on, pretending, he heard nothing.

"He is ignoring you, Bruno," one of the thugs said.

"We will see about that," the thug called Bruno said as he and the other thugs then rushed toward him and surrounded him.

. "So, you want to play tough," Bruno said as he gripped his shirt front.

"Punch him in the face, Bruno," the thug, beside Bruno, said.

"Who are you and why did you come here?" Bruno asked him, who was struck dumb with fear.

"Don't we have a deaf-and-dumb fool here," Bruno said to the other thugs' laughter.

"Punch him in the face, I said, if he doesn't speak up," the thug beside Bruno said again.

Bruno, on the prompting by the other thug, swung his arm to punch his face when suddenly, a tall and muscular, but older man appeared from the alley.

"Enough of that, Bruno," the man said.

Bruno broke into a sheepish grin and released his shirt from his grip.

"I was just getting acquainted with this provincial boy," Bruno said to the man.

"Very well," the man said to Bruno. "You may leave him alone, now that you are acquainted with each other."

Bruno returned to the store with the other thugs.

"Thank you, sir, for your help," he said to the man.

"Nothing to it," the man said. "They are not bad; they just are not used to seeing strangers here."

"They seem to look up to you, sir."

"They do. I am the headman here. What brought you here?"

He told the man, he was looking for his uncle's Berting's house.

"Go back to the alley," the man said. "When you reach the fork there, take the one on wooden flanks. Walk on until you find a house with a green door. That is Berting's hut."

He thanked the man and walked back to the alley until he had reached the hut with a green door. He knocked at the door. An old woman looked out from the window near the door.

"What do you want?" she asked him.

"Good afternoon, ma'am," he replied. "I'm looking for uncle Berting. I'm his nephew, Leandro. Uncle Julian wrote about me."

"So, you are Leandro. I'm your aunt Agueda. We have been expecting you."

She left the window and opened the door.

"Come in, come in," she said to him.

He entered the hut, pushed his sandals aside with his foot and put down his bag on the floor. Then he turned to his aunt, took her hand and touched it to his forehead.

A man, just then, came in from the back of the hut. It was his uncle Berting.

"You must be Leandro," Berting said.

"Yes, uncle," he said as he also took his uncle's hand and touched it to his forehead.

"Are you not too young to make a try here in Manila? The last time I saw you, you were only this tall," Agueda said, her hand raised to her shoulders.

"Come now," Berting said to Agueda, "that was six, seven or eight years ago. You can see how he has grown up since then."

He has only a vague recollection of his uncle Berting and aunt Agueda. They did not look as his uncle Julian had described them. They were about the same age and thin like his uncle Julian and aunt Tarcila.

His uncle Berting, as his uncle Julian had told him, was employed in a tailoring shop while his aunt Agueda was a plain housewife. All their three children were married and living elsewhere in Manila.

"You look tired and hungry from your long trip," Agueda said to Leandro. "Have a seat. Make yourself comfortable while I prepare something for you."

He sat down on a bench there, glad at the thought of food. He was hungry. The lunch he took in the train was so little.

Agueda went to the kitchen while Berting sat down on the other bench there.

"I gathered from Julian's letter that you came here to Manila for the same purpose we left San Isidro," Berting said to Leandro.

"I have no future there, uncle."

"It is also not easy to make a living here. You will need a lot of luck and patience to get a job here."

"But I already have a job, waiting for me."

"You do, where?"

"At the Pacific and Gulf Construction Company."

"You got a job there!" Berting said, his mouth hanging open in astonishment. "Why, you, lucky boy! I will give up my left arm to work there!"

He blinked his eyes, wondering why his uncle was so enthusiastic about his job in Pacific & Gulf. It was just a job to him, but it made him look so special in his uncle's eyes.

"Why," he asked his uncle, "will you give up your left arm just to work in Pacific and Gulf?"

"Why? It is a top American company! The best among the best! You are assured of a good future once you become a part of that company. It is one of the good things that ever happened here. It is building just about every road, bridge, wharf and school here. Imagine yourself, a part of all of that!"

"I have seen something of that, uncle. It built our school buildings in San Isidro and in the other towns nearby, but I never imagined the extent of construction work it is doing."

"It is all over the islands. But, tell me, how did you get a job there when you were living, far away in San Isidro?"

He told his uncle about the help he got from Dorothy Dickinson and Samuel Tyler.

"Good for you, you have those American teachers who helped you get a job there. It takes Americans for us to get through to other Americans. If you will apply on your own, you will never get, past the company gate. I tried it myself, but failed to get a job there. You are very lucky you got a job there. When will you start working there?"

"I'll go there, right away, uncle, tomorrow morning."

"Very well, if that is what you want to do, although I would rather that you spend your first few days here, sightseeing. You must see what Manila is like before you start working."

"I can do that anytime, uncle."

"But we still have time for me to show you around and most important of all, I will take you to the Pacific and Gulf compound so you will know your way there tomorrow. We will leave after you have taken your snack."

Berting looked pleased with himself for the help he was giving Leandro, he hummed a song, he accompanied by drumming his fingers on the space in the bench between his thighs. He stopped humming when he saw Leandro's bare feet and his sandals, near the door.

"You cannot work in Pacific and Gulf, wearing those sandals," he said. "You must buy a pair of rubber sneakers or leather shoes."

Agueda called from the kitchen, "I need water for the coffee."

"I will get it," Berting said.

"Can I be of some help?" he said to his uncle.

"Take it easy there," Berting said as he stood up and proceeded toward the kitchen.

He looked around as he was waiting for his snack. The hut with its few furnishings was bare like their hut in Bangar. Its dark wall of palm shingles made it seem even more dismal and decrepit. Life in Manila for his uncle Berting and his aunt Agueda was hardly any better than the life he led in Bangar.

He sighed, wondering if, in living in this place mired in filth and poverty and infested by hostile, violent people, he might also suffer the same fate of his uncle Berting and his aunt Agueda. In that case, it would be much better if he never left San Isidro, at all. But he has this job in Pacific & Gulf. That made all the difference. As his uncle Berting had told him, a job there assured him of a good future. Tomorrow then will be a big day for him when he will go to Pacific & Gulf.

Chapter Thirty

Bill Shay woke up to the ringing of the alarm clock in the night table, beside his bed. He shut it off and looked around at the bedroom, bright with sunlight. It was seven-ten of a Tuesday morning.

He swept the bed sheet aside. He stifled a yawn, his hand over his mouth as he sat down on the side of the bed. He glanced at the other side of the bed where Esperanza had slept. The shape of her head on the pillow showed her having slept facing him. He smiled, pleased and satisfied. She had risen ahead of him and she must be in the kitchen, preparing their breakfast. While they have a cook, she preferred to do this housewife's chore herself.

The thought of a good breakfast prodded him out of the bedroom. His face that greeted him in the bathroom mirror was full and youthful, unlike the time he was in the army when he looked so thin. The bright expression his eyes gave his face showed him, a life he led that was so happy and so fulfilled. He looked downward at himself. The few pounds, he had gained were not so noticeable yet except in the midriff.

He had tarried long enough before the mirror and he removed his pajamas and went quickly to the shower stall. He was in the closet, a few minutes later, refreshed by the shower he took, his overnight beard and mustache shaved and his blond hair combed as well.

He said to himself, as he was dressing up in a white shirt, a blue tie and a white drill suit, at how nice he looked, a handsome young man on the go. He looked so different from his army days when he was in uniform, day in, day out now that had the choice of what to wear.

It was also during the war while he was fighting the Filipino insurgents that he saw the many possibilities offered by this colony to an army engineer like him. It was a raw, frontier country badly in need of infrastructure. He decided then and there that he will build there badly needed roads, bridges, wharves, dams, buildings, school buildings and a lot more.

Dick McCall who covered the war for his newspaper, *The San Francisco Sun,* had the same thought. Dick saw a lack in the colony of mass publications. He resigned from *The San Francisco Sun* and put out his newsmagazine—*The Philippines Newsmagazine.*

He established, around that time, the Pacific & Gulf Construction Company. He named it after the colony's location in the world's largest body of water—the Pacific Ocean---and the Gulf of Mexico where, as a teenager from Iowa, he saw the sea for the first time in his life and dreamed of someday crossing it to distant lands.

He and Dick were of the same mind about making a mark in life, more challenging in the Philippines because of its raw economic state than in the highly advanced industrial economy of the United States

All of those were quite true, but his wife's picture in the night table told him there was one more compelling reason why he stayed in the colony. It was love. He fell in love with Esperanza as Dick did with Nieves, the first time they laid their eyes on them. It was just a day after he had conquered their hometown of Masakao, following a tough battle there with the local insurgents.

They were later married, a handsome foursome, at the town church. The town had never seen a twin wedding like theirs of two Americans marrying two local women. They knew him quite well, though, for he was then the town administrator and fort commander. Dick was just as well-known there as a friendly young American, like him.

The whole town came out for their two weddings, he to Esperanza and Dick to Nieves and for the wedding feast that followed, not in the homes of Esperanza and Nieves. Like the homecoming feast for Paulo, the insurgent leader who later became their very close friend, it was held in the church grounds and in the town plaza.

He and Esperanza made their home, built by his workers, in this corner in the suburban town of Caloocan, north of Manila. Dick and Nieves had their home, built nearby.

He shook his head at the thought of Dick and Nieves who had remained childless. They did not have enough of the genes, according to the doctor who examined them, for them to have a child.

Although they were childless, he could say that they, like him and Esperanza, are very happy in their married life.

Those were Bill's thoughts as he was looking at himself before the mirror in the bedroom closet. It was confirmed by the smile on his face as he then left their bedroom.

It looked like another warm day. He saw this from the sunlight washing the screened windows, giving the wooden floor in the living room, a deep shine. Their home was a ranch type. Its rattan furniture and large screened windows overlooking the lawn, along with the trees and the plants there and in the neighbors' orchards, gave it the look and feel of country life.

He was born and raised in the cornfields in Iowa and he liked Caloocan for its countryside setting. It was also near enough to Manila, making it convenient for him to commute to work.

The living room was quiet, but for the ticking of the grandfather clock in the corridor leading to the rest of the house.

He smiled as he shook his head. How different it was then, when early morning would find the house, full of people, complete strangers, seeking jobs. Right after he and Esperanza had settled down there, word about his construction company spread around in the neighborhood.

A neighbor came uninvited, one morning, looking for a job. He did not have the heart to turn the man away. He seemed like a good bet and then and there, he took him in. Word about it spread around in their neighborhood. The house was soon full every morning of people seeking jobs until Esperanza put a stop to those impromptu job applications.

She did not want their home turned into an employment agency and she said to the jobseekers in a polite but firm way to apply instead in the company office in Parola. Word about that also got around and the number of people coming uninvited dwindled until no one seeking a job came anymore to the house.

He walked toward his son Michael's bedroom and peered inside at Michael who was still asleep. He will grow up like him with a blond hair and a tall nose and like Esperanza, with a cheerful expression on his face.

He closed the door and went to the kitchen where, a turner in her hand, Esperanza was frying eggs, sunny side up, while Teofila, their cook and Michael's nanny, was putting fried rice on a plate.

The shapeless housedress Esperanza was wearing did not show her nice figure that went so nicely with her beautiful face. Her profile showed those keen eyes and all the rest of her that attracted him to her, the first time he saw her a few years ago.

The fried eggs, she was putting on a plate reminded him about food, another thing that so attracted him to her. She is a very good cook.

He laid his arm on her shoulders and said with a peck on her cheek, "How beautiful you look, as always, this morning."

"Thank you, my dear handsome husband," she said as she smiled, "you don't have to flatter your way to a good breakfast. It is there, waiting for you."

He left her smiling too and sat down at the head of the dining table. He looked pleased at the food laid out there, a combination of Filipino and American breakfast of ham and fried eggs, fried milkfish on a bed of lettuce and sliced tomatoes, bread and fried rice, rich with sausage, fried scrambled eggs and green onion shoots.

Teofila filled a cup with coffee and gave it to him. He took a sip as he was waiting for Esperanza to join him at the breakfast table.

She sat down to his right and prayed, after which he passed on to her, the plate of fried rice. They proceeded with their breakfast. He took a portion of everything on the table. Like her, his attention in the next few minutes was on the food they were eating with zest.

"A good thing, I am not in the army anymore," he said to her. "I would have been demoted from major to private with all this good, tasty food you are making me so stout."

"I would rather see you stout than thin that you were, the first time I saw you."

His eyes lit up in remembrance of his army days. His appetite was often dulled by the bland taste of the food often served in his quarters in the town fort that he sometimes skipped lunch or dinner. He regained his appetite only when Esperanza started cooking food for him. She had, by then, become quite fond of him, which was quite a feat on his part, for they first met under inauspicious circumstances.

It was at the wake of Lukas Palanas, the mayor of Masakao, just a day after he and his troops had taken the town from the Filipino insurgents. Dick was with him. Esperanza was seated beside her sister Teresa and their friend Nieves. She was curious while Teresa was hostile.

They saw him then as an enemy who killed the uncle of Teresa's lover, Paulo Palanas. Love won and he and Esperanza and Dick and Nieves were later married. Paulo and Teresa were likewise married. He and Paulo, now the mayor of Masakao, have since then become very good friends.

"How," he asked Esperanza, "are they doing in Masakao?"

"Teresa is six months pregnant with their second child."

"Paulo must have a lot of time in his hands that he could have another child so soon. Anyway, a man does find the time for that kind of pleasurable activity."

"So do you, my dear handsome husband," Esperanza said, smiling, but then she said, "Paulo cannot do much in Masakao with his two main projects there, still hanging in the air. He pins his hope for the town's progress on the water system and irrigation dam and the road to Alkayag that you promised to build there."

"My men and I are ready but there is nothing we can do but wait for the Insular Government to give us the go-signal to start work there. It is, after all, providing the funds for those two projects."

"They mean so much to Masakao, the rest of the province and the Central Plain," Esperanza said as she was eating a spoonful of egg and fried rice.

He did the same. They ate as they talked.

"I know but, you must understand," he said, "government finances are stretched to the limit with so many programs and construction projects going on at the same time. It must set priorities."

"Like the breakwater and the new port, you said, you will soon build in Manila?"

"You may include the electric streetcar system, the school buildings, the hospitals, the roads, the commercial buildings, the vacation resort city in Central Cordillera, the ports in every large coastal town, the roads and bridges, and so much more."

"All of those, all at once?"

"Not, all at once, but they will all be done, all in good time, all in good time."

He saw in Esperanza's smile, happiness and satisfaction at what his company and the Insular Government were doing there when suddenly she shook her head and said sadly, "That is a terrible thing that happened in San Francisco," about the great earthquake and fire that killed a lot of people and destroyed large areas in the city on April 18, 1906.

"Dick was about to go there when he learned his folks and his home there were both safe. The city though is fast recovering from that disaster."

"Will Dick put you again on the cover," she said in changing the subject again, "like what he did in the last anniversary of his magazine?"

"I don't know. Anyway, it is far off yet," he said in reference to the party, Dick McCall will hold on the fifth anniversary of his newsmagazine.

"I would not know what to wear there, certainly not the native dress, I wore, the last time around. I felt so out of place then."

"You turn heads, my dear lovely wife, whatever you are wearing."

"Thank you, my dear. You never run out of nice things to tell me."

"There are so many of them, I will never run out of them."

They were both smiling when they left the dining table.

He went to the bathroom, one more time, and then picked up in the library, his briefcase crammed with reports, studies and documents, his workload, the night before at home.

Esperanza was waiting for him at the main door of the house when he came to her. He kissed her on the cheek and was about to step out of the house when Michael appeared in the living room. He was rubbing his eyes and dragging his stuffed toy bear on the floor.

"There you are," he said to his son who then dropped his toy bear and rushed to him.

He dropped his briefcase too as he took Michael in his arms.

"What do you want, Daddy, to bring you home?" he asked him.

"A toy bear."

"But you already have a toy bear."

"Give Daddy, a big hug," Esperanza said to Michael. "Hurry up. We don't want Daddy to be late for work."

"Yes, Mommy," Michael said as he gave Bill, a big hug.

Esperanza then took Michael from Bill and looked on as he picked up his briefcase and walked toward the carport where Tibo, the gardener and Teofila's husband, was waiting for him.

He stepped inside his car—an Oldsmobile curved-dash runabout. Tibo then cranked up the engine, at the same time that he was pulling out the throttle lever. It roared to life and settled down to a steady hum when he pushed back the throttle lever. He was set to go.

He waved, smiling at Esperanza and Michael, and drove out into the street.

A plaything of the rich in the United States was now, for him, a convenient and necessary means of transportation. A man in a hurry, going to work should not take too long for him, like it used to when he was riding in a horse-drawn cab. He was, aside from his construction business, also taking part in ushering in the motorized age in the colony.

The car engine purred smoothly as he drove on in Mabini Street, the town's main street, south toward Manila. Pacific & Gulf had only recently paved it with asphalt. His company had also paved many of Manila's old dirt roads and cobblestone streets with that paving material that made driving there, much faster and smoother.

He drove on, amused, at the people on the sidewalk who were looking at his car. It was a novelty to them and there were only a few of them, running down there.

It was his regular route to work. He crossed in Maypajo, in Caloocan, the bridge spanning the narrow channel, the boundary between Caloocan and Manila. Except for the change in the name from Mabini Street to Juan Luna Street, there was no marked difference between what he had passed by in Caloocan and what he was seeing now in Tondo, the old section in Manila. The more durable homes of wood and stone had replaced both in Manila and in Caloocan, many of the flimsy nipa huts that used to line those streets.

"Progress, progress," he said in satisfaction with himself. He is playing a great part in changing the face of Manila and the rest of the islands in bringing progress there. He felt good about this land, his second home. He has the important role of helping in making the Philippine Islands, an example of American administration and enterprise.

He slowed down, a short while later, and looked around as he was crossing Azcarraga Avenue. He fought there, his first big battle with the Filipino insurgents, a few years ago.

He drove on, his mind dwelling on how he had, since then, changed from a soldier fighting them, to a builder bringing so much progress to them. He was quite satisfied with himself as he then turned right on reaching Muelle de la Industria.

The street ran parallel to Pasig River. It was busy with maritime traffic. A tugboat was pulling a barge upstream. Ships were docked in the city port on the south side of the river. A barge laden with products was lying alongside the concrete riverbank on the north side of the river, near Muelle de la Industria.

The church bells in Manila Cathedral, across the river, were ringing the time—nine o'clock—as his car was approaching the compound of Pacific & Gulf in Parola.

He owned his time as the president of Pacific & Gulf Construction Company. He has the privilege of coming in much later than his workers who must clock in at eight o'clock in the morning or earlier.   The security guard opened the gate quickly when he saw him coming. He saluted as his car was entering the company compound. It was a slight military-like gesture, he required from his security guards.

There was no one, other than the security guard, in the company compound. Everyone in Pacific & Gulf was already at work.

He glanced, on getting out of his car in its parking slot marked "President," at the other cars parked there: Tom Guernsey's, Packard, Philip Beldry's Studebaker, Mark Clavier's Buick and John Stroheim's Oldsmobile, which differed from his Olds, only in color. His Olds was in flowing black and yellow while John's Olds was a red tinged with orange. His executives were already at work.

He nodded as he was looking at their cars, at the good team that he has there. Guernsey was the vice president of the fabrication division, which made the materials, from asphalt, creosote and concrete to wood and steel, they used in their construction work. Beldry was the vice president for operations, which handled all the field projects, from roads to bridges, ports, wharves and breakwaters, to buildings of whatever type, schools, offices, warehouses and so much more. Stroheim was the vice president for the administrative division under which were the accounting, cashier and payroll, personnel, medical, security, communications, property and maintenance. Clavier was the personnel manager.

He went up in the staircase instead of taking the elevator in the administrative building as part of his daily workout. He looked around as he was entering the anteroom to his office.

It was quiet, but for the chatter of the typewriter keys, hitting the bond paper in the typewriter rollers.

"Good morning, people," he said to Nancy Jamieson and the three other members of his executive staff.

They looked up from their desks and returned his greeting. Nancy Jamieson, his efficient, though plain-looking, executive secretary, was typing on the Underwood typewriter, an office machine new in the Philippines. The three others, a woman and two men, were at work, bent over their desks. One of them was likewise typing on another Underwood typewriter.

He glanced at Nancy as he was approaching his office. She was, following the fashion of the day, wearing a long-sleeved dress buttoned up to her neck, like the prim and proper schoolteacher that she was before she joined Pacific & Gulf. She stopped typing and followed him as he was entering his office.

She asked him, the moment they were inside there, "Would you like a cup of coffee to start your working day?"

"Thank you, but not, right now."

He took out the folders from his briefcase. He put some of them on his desk, the rest he gave to Nancy.

He usually started work by giving to her for typing, filing, or passing on to the concerned division, the work he had done at home.

He sat down on his swivel chair and looked up at Nancy who was standing in front of his desk.

"You look like you had a great time in Tagaytay," he said about the resort town, Pacific & Gulf had built in the highlands in Batangas.

"You can say that again. How I love its cool climate. It is so unlike this warm, humid weather, we are having here today."

She said, as she then looked up at the ceiling fan, "That reminds me, you need that."

She crossed the room and turned on the switch of the ceiling fan. Cool air was in an instant swirling inside the room.

He smiled and nodded in appreciation of her thoughtfulness.

"I can understand how you feel about the warm weather here in Manila after you have enjoyed the cool climate in Tagaytay."

"Baguio is much cooler than Tagaytay."

"I know. It is on a much higher elevation at four thousand, eight hundred ten feet. As Dick had so beautifully described it in *The Philippines Newsmagazine,* it will be, when are finished working there, like New England without the snow."

"That is a very beautiful way, Dick described Baguio."

They were talking about the tiny Ibaloi village, deep in the mountains in Central Cordillera the Insular Government was developing into a vacation resort city, the future summer capital of the Philippine Islands. It will be an ideal escape with its cool, bracing climate from the heat and the humidity in the lowlands, especially during summer.

Pacific & Gulf was picked as the lead company, among a large group of companies, in the construction of the various facilities in making Baguio, a modern vacation resort city.

It has already built, or is in the process of building, or will soon build there, vacation homes like the Mansion House for the governor-general, parks, the city hall, retreat houses, a market, schools, a cathedral, a university, roads and bridges, a telephone, power and water system, a country club, a military camp, a hospital, commercial buildings and a lot more.

Many of the rich people in Manila and in the provinces were now buying lots there for business and their vacation homes, following the go-signal given by the Insular Government.

"I will soon be spending, my vacation there," Nancy said as she was leaving the room, the folders in the crook of her arm.

Now that he was alone, Bill turned his swivel chair toward the window for a brief, idle viewing of the company compound and Manila Bay before going to work. It was cut short by a knock on the door.

"Come in," he said.

Mark Clavier appeared at the door and walked toward Bill's desk.

"What is up, Mark?" he said pleasantly to his personnel manager.

Mark was in his usual outfit of white pants and long-sleeved white shirt, topped at the neck with a dark blue bow tie.

"I have got this boy, Leandro Sumaka, applying for the job of messenger and janitor. He showed me this letter."

Bill read Samuel Tyler's letter and put it down on his desk.

He asked Mark, "Has he been through the usual tests?"

"Yes," Mark replied, referring to the company's standard procedure in hiring a job applicant—the forms filled out, the aptitude test taken and the interview with the applicant.

"How did he make out?"

"He passed it."

"So, we now have the man for the job."

"Yes. Would you like to see him?"

"Bring him in."

He made the final decision on every successful applicant for a regular position in the company. In meeting them, even briefly, he knew at least by the face, his regular workforce now numbering several hundred employees.

Mark stepped out of the office, but was back in a short while with the person in question who, Bill was surprised to see, was no more than a teenage boy.

He looked on at Leandro, who was standing in front of his desk. He was looking at him from beneath his brow, his shoulders slightly stooped and his hands clasped in front of him. He had seen in the boy's fellow countrymen that kind of submissive posture whenever they were facing Americans of high rank.

He motioned Leandro to a chair in front of his desk to put him at ease.

Leandro nodded and sat down on the chair.

"So, you are the young man, Mister Tyler has written me about," he said. "You have done well in the test and in the interview. Congratulations and welcome to Pacific and Gulf."

"Thank you, sir."

"When can you start working?"

"I will, right away, sir."

Bill raised his eyebrows, very much surprised at this teenage boy's enthusiasm for his job. It was not everyday that he met someone like him. Other successful applicants usually took it easy for a day or two before starting on their jobs. He took an immediate liking of Leandro.

"Good for you," he said to Leandro. "Mister Clavier will now fill you in, on your duties."

Leandro rose from the chair and bowed before Bill in gratitude for his job. He then left the room with Mark Clavier.

Bill watched them leave, satisfied with himself. Taking in a new worker was a part, though tiny, but still a part of what his company was doing for this, his second home, the Philippine Islands.

He turned his swivel chair around for a brief, idle viewing of the company compound and Manila Bay, satisfied with the many wonderful things his company was doing in this American colony.

Chapter Thirty-one

Leandro was smiling as he was leaving Bill Shay's office. He is now officially an employee of Pacific & Gulf Construction Company. It was replaced by a worried look as he was walking on in the anteroom with Mark Clavier. Cleaning the offices and the grounds will be easy enough, but doing errand work could be, a bit daunting. He has yet to familiarize himself with Manila and its suburbs. What, if he were asked to deliver something in Malacanang Palace or in the suburbs of Ermita or Malate? He has only a vague idea of where they are located.

He did not see much of Manila from the tour, his uncle Berting gave him yesterday. They started out on foot and went first to a shoe store where he bought a pair of rubber sneakers. Then they took a horse-drawn cab, so he could see more places in the city. They went first to

Pacific & Gulf's compound in Parola. He took a careful note of the way there.

Night had fallen by then.

The streetlights were of little help. They did not provide enough light by which he could have a sense of direction there. No matter. The important thing is that he knows the way to Pacific & Gulf. The company compound, to him, is the most important place in Manila, never mind if he knows nothing yet about the rest of the city. He will, in due time, know his way around there.

As he understood it from Mark Clavier, the work of a messenger meant doing errands, not only for Bill Shay, but also for Mark Clavier himself, the other company executives and maybe even for the four employees working in Bill Shay's anteroom.

One of them was Nancy Jamieson, who was going over some files in her desk. Another girl was doing filing work in a steel filing cabinet while the two male employees were doing typing work on the typewriters on their desks.

He watched them, marveling at how the typewriters made writing neat, faster and easier. The chatter of the typewriters was a wonderful new sound to his ears.

A big black box with what looked like was a round-shaped mouthpiece in the blonde woman's desk began to ring. It stopped ringing when she picked up a similar mouthpiece that was attached to the side of the black box.

She pressed it to her ear and began to talk to the mouthpiece in the black box.

He looked on, amazed. It was the first time, he had seen a telephone. He did not notice it before on his way to Bill Shay's office. His mind was then on his meeting with the company president.

He walked on, marveling at those office machines, when he suddenly felt a strong gust of wind sweeping by his head and shoulders. He looked up and saw the source in a ceiling fan swirling air in the anteroom.

Mark Clavier had walked ahead to the elevator at the end of the anteroom and pushed the elevator button on the wall. He watched Leandro, smiling in amusement as he was waiting for the elevator door to open.

Leandro's cheeks flushed in embarrassment. He has been gaping, like an ignorant provincial boy, at those wonderful office machines, but then, back in Bangar, he did not even know that they existed!

He walked fast toward the elevator, but paused as he was about to enter it. He had quite a scare, the first time he took it in going up with

Mark Clavier to Bill Shay's office. It was like being entombed in a steel box, but he must not keep the personnel manager waiting and he stepped quickly, inside the elevator.

He held his breath while his hand was gripping the handrail, the moment the elevator began to drop down to the ground floor. He sighed in relief when it came to a stop. The door opened and he stepped out into the lobby. His feet on solid ground again, he now walked confidently with Mark Clavier. They turned from the lobby to a corridor there.

"You might be wondering about the very large area, you have to keep clean and tidy," Mark said to Leandro. "You will not be doing that alone. You will coordinate with a janitorial service on the work in the company compound and in the other buildings. You will meet their supervisor, later this week, but this building is your sole responsibility."

They walked on in the corridor and then entered a cubicle there.

"This is your work station," Mark said to Leandro.

It was dime-size with a small desk, a stool and a closet at the back. Mark opened it, revealing there, mops, brooms and other cleaning equipment.

"Those are your work tools," Mark said to Leandro.

He barely glanced at them, his attention drawn to a small bell nailed to the wall, near the closet. Written on a board below the bell were the names of the company executives with an electric bulb beside each name. What, he wondered, were they for?

Mark saw him staring at the board and the bell. He said to him, "It rings whenever anyone in the list of names below the bell needs a messenger service. If, for instance, it is from me, you will see the electric bulb beside my name, lit up. You can turn off, both the light bulb and the ringing of the bell in the switch below the board."

"Is that my priority job, sir?" he asked Mark as he was looking on, in admiration of that example of American ingenuity and gadgetry.

"It is. Drop whatever you are doing and attend to it first. You can get in the cashier's office, near my room, the money you may need in doing errand work for me."

He then asked Leandro, "Do you have any other question?"

"I have none, sir."   .

"Now, if you will come with me," Mark said as they were leaving his cubicle. "I will now fill you in, on other matters. Carlos Yturalde, one of my assistants, will afterwards show you around the company compound."

They went back to Mark's glass-paneled room where Mark had earlier interviewed Leandro. The security guard directed him there on his arrival at the company gate, earlier in the morning.

Mark sat down on his swivel chair and pulled out from a drawer in his desk, a copy of the company handbook.

He gave it to Leandro who remained standing and told him to read it in its entirety in his spare time. Mark also told Leandro about his pay of thirty pesos a month. He never felt, so rich in his life.

Mark then said to him, "You will have your time card, ready in the time card shelf, near the gate at quitting time at five o'clock in the afternoon. You will punch it on the time clock when you report for work at eight o'clock in the morning or earlier, but never later than that time; before and after you take your lunch break of one hour at noon and when you stop working at five o'clock in the afternoon. Do you have any questions?"

"I have none, sir."

"That is it then," Mark said to Leandro.

He waved at a young man at work on his desk, for him to come to his office.

"This is Leandro Sumaka, a new hire," Mark said to the young man as he was entering the room. "He will do messenger and janitorial work. Show him around."

Mark then turned to Leandro and said, his finger pointed to the fair-complexioned young man, "That is Carlos Yturalde; he will tour you around, the company compound."

Leandro looked around, astonished at the huge size of the company compound, as he was stepping out of the administrative building with Carlos. The whole of Bangar, including his beloved pond, will easily fit there and with plenty of room to spare. It has, by his rough estimate, a land area of thirty to forty acres.

It was square-shaped. A concrete wall defined its northern and eastern boundaries. The compound housed several buildings and a huge warehouse. Piles of construction materials were arranged neatly and ready for transport at the marshaling yard, near Pasig River. The riverbank formed the company compound's southern boundary.

Workers were loading in a boat docked there, materials for the company's various construction projects. A fishing boat was moving out toward Manila Bay. Its shoreline formed the company compound's western boundary.

He listened as Carlos then told him about the various company facilities that he will show him.

They entered a big building.

"This is the fabrication division," Carlos said to Leandro.

They walked around the building, noisy with men talking, calling out instructions or working on the machines, cutting, sawing, pounding, grinding and riveting construction materials of various shapes and sizes.

Carlos often had to raise his voice in explaining to Leandro, the work being done there.

He could only nod back. He could not hear well with all that noise in the seemingly organized chaos of workers welding iron bars, pounding metal sheets, sawing wood, fabricating and assembling various construction materials.

He left the building later on with Carlos, relieved that he was not assigned there. All that noise might break his eardrums, in no time at all.

Carlos next led Leandro to the marshaling yard. They looked on as the workers there picked up and carried on their shoulders wooden crates which they then brought to a boat docked in the wide, concrete riverbank.

"Where are they taking them?" he asked Carlos as they were following a couple of workers to the concrete riverbank.

"I cannot tell, where in particular," Carlos replied, "but they are all going to the company's many construction projects in the islands."

He looked around as he stood there beside Carlos at a panoramic view of Manila, Pasig River and Manila Bay. The churches and the commercial buildings in Binondo and Escolta on their side of the river stood there grandly, early in the morning. A boat on the river, its flag flapping with the wind, was moving out toward Manila Bay.

He could see there in Intramuros, across the river, Fort Santiago, the churches, schools, buildings, homes with their sloping tile roofs, of what he had only imagined before, from what he had read about it in a history book in San Isidro's public school, was the heart in Manila of the past Spanish rule in the Philippines.

It soon became obvious to him that the difference between Manila and San Isidro was in the amount and variety of human activity and its imprint on the land.

The church, the homes, grand or humble, the trees, the shrubbery, and the rice fields formed the landscape in San Isidro while Manila was made up mostly of buildings, homes, streets and other man-made structures. Where nature is dominant in San Isidro, man ruled in Manila.

He nodded. The more men like Mr. Shay are doing there, the more economic opportunities they are bringing about, the greater is the progress in Manila. But like the ripple effect, the fish made in his pond in Bangar, those activities had very little or no effect at all in San Isidro. All that were being done in Manila were bringing about opportunities for a better life, not found in San Isidro. The only worthwhile economic activities there were in the landlords' agricultural estates and they have remained the same since they were under the Spanish rule.

It seemed to him, as he threw a sideward glance at Carlos, that the nice panoramic view there had the same salutary effect on him, for he then said, "I feel good every time I take a look at Manila from this vantage point. You can see from here, something of its past grandeur, as in Intramuros, something of its vigorous present, as in those roads and buildings being built, and something of its future that is full of hope and promise.

"You can also see in Pasig River, that which has remained unchanged through the ages. It flows on and on into the bay. This is the city of my affection."

"So, you are here from Manila."

"Yes, although we came originally from Toledo in Spain, my family has lived in San Miguel, not far from Malacanang Palace, for the past seventy years or so."

Carlos pointed at a tile-roofed, beige-colored building at the northeastern corner of Intramuros, the view of its lower floors hidden by the Customs House..

"I studied there, in Lateran," he said. "I could have gone on to a scholarship in the United States, but I missed the qualifying tests by just a few points. I went instead to a Jesuit college there, where I finished my Bachelor of Arts degree. You can see its building there, across the river."

He looked on, in the direction Carlos was pointing at, a sullen expression, now on his face. The building was inside Intramuros and its glorious Spanish past, which has no relevance to his own life in Bangar. Carlos had made him feel inferior by talking about himself. Who is he, but a poor, ignorant provincial boy with little education in comparison to this well-educated, wealthy Spanish mestizo? Carlos would not have taken the trouble of showing him around the company compound, had he not been ordered to do so by Mr. Clavier.

They are, in that respect, almost on equal terms. They are both employees of Pacific & Gulf. Not quite, though. Carlos as a personnel assistant is definitely superior to his job of janitor and messenger, perhaps the two lowest positions in the company. But he is only starting there. The lower is his position now the sweeter will be his achievement in the future when he, being that confident, will be occupying better and higher positions in Pacific & Gulf.

He has an edge over just about everyone there. A very good worker used to hard work, hard work having been his life in Bangar he will work harder than ever in Pacific & Gulf. The harder, he worked there, the greater will be the reward for him.

"Are you not glad to work here in Pacific and Gulf?" Carlos said which took him by surprise.

He looked away, wondering why Carlos had so abruptly turned to another topic. It came to him in an instant. Carlos was not so conceited as to talk endlessly about himself. Carlos was not showing off, but had only mentioned where he lived and where he studied from the prompting by the wonderful view of Intramuros and from the question, he himself asked him, if he is from Manila. His resentment toward Carlos died down.

"My future," he replied to Carlos, "is tied to my job here."

"And it is a very good future. You will have a very busy time here with so many things, we are doing here."

"I can see that."

"Take that thing there, for example," Carlos said as he pointed out a line of rocks protruding in Manila Bay, a few hundred yards away from the shore.

"What is it?" he asked Carlos.

"That is the first of two breakwaters, we are putting up there. The other one will be located farther south."

"What are they for?"

"I thought that should be obvious to you. They will keep the water inside the breakwaters, calm and safe enough for ships to dock even in bad weather in the finger piers we will build there, starting from the shoreline in Intramuros."

"And where do the rocks come from?"

Carlos pointed at the western horizon in Manila Bay and said, at the dark outline there, "That is the mountain range in Bataan."

"What about it?"

"The rocks for the breakwaters are quarried there. So are the rocks we will use in reclaiming the foreshore of Intramuros where we will build the finger piers. We will have, when we are finished working there, a new port and the best harbor in the Orient and one of the best in the world."

"And Pacific and Gulf is doing the work there."

"So we are."

"So, all those ships we now see in Pasig River will be docking instead in those finger piers, once we are finished building them."

"So, take a look now at those ships. Once they are gone, so will be the romance of Pasig River."

"I did not know you have a romantic bent."

"I can hardly wait to say that to a girl, for it might then send her heart, fluttering with pleasure."

They continued their tour of the company compound. A tall smokestack stood, some distance from the riverbank. It looked like a giant cigar set upright, its top discharging smoke into the sky.

"What is it?" he asked Carlos.

"It is a smokestack. Is that not obvious to you? All that it does is clear out into the sky, the smoke emitted by the boiler in the adjacent building."

Carlos caught him as he was staring at a row of giant iron cylinders of various lengths.

"We treat wood there with creosote," Carlos said, his finger pointed at the iron cylinders.

"And what is a creosote, what is it for?"

"We apply creosote, which is a chemical preservative that comes from coal and wood tar, to make the wood pilings, power line poles, fence posts, railroad ties and sawn lumber we use in construction, resistant to the elements, to termites and other bugs, to salt and dry rot. Wood treated with creosote usually lasts for fifty or more years."

He nodded. Carlos had been showing him the company's varied operations and facilities that have nothing to do with his job as a janitor and messenger.

He asked Carlos, "Why are you showing me all of those when all I will be doing here is run errands and keep this place, clean and tidy?"

"Consider yourself a special case. We don't do this to every new employee. Mister Clavier must have seen something about you that he asked me to tour you around. You are being shown, the company's varied operations and facilities on the reasoning that you may, in the future, be assigned to any of those departments. You don't expect to stay here, a janitor and messenger forever, do you?"

"No, I don't," he replied with a firm shake of his head.

"So, now you know why I am showing you around."

He smiled in appreciation of those bits of information, Carlos had put into his head. They could be useful to him, sometime in the future.

They walked back to the administrative building.

"What I have shown you, should give you a good idea of what we are doing here," Carlos said. "You will learn more about the company as you go along. You can be proud to be a part of Pacific and Gulf. It is known for quality work. We have a good team here."

"I have seen a little of that."

"We have, in just a short time, made Pacific and Gulf, dominant in construction. We have never seen anything like it when we were under Spain. Time stopped for us then."

"Nothing changed in my hometown, too. Only when the Americans came, did we have a public school in San Isidro. It is a town, north of the Central Plain."

"So, I have here with me, a provincial boy."

He glanced sharply at Carlos, but then he realized quickly enough that Carlos was not patronizing him. He may have been simply surprised to learn that he came from the countryside. He gave it no further thought.

He continued walking with Carlos in the company compound.

"If the Americans came here earlier," Carlos said, "say, fifty years earlier, around the time they forced Japan to open itself to world trade, like Japan, we would have been much better off, by now."

He looked on at Carlos, his jaw dropped in utter surprise. He did not expect Carlos, a Spanish mestizo, to be so admiring of the Americans. He deemed it prudent, though, not to pursue the subject.

He said instead, "We can make up for that lost time by working hard, very hard."

"You will do well here with that kind of positive work attitude."

He smiled, pleased by what Carlos said about him. There is, to him, nothing unusual about working hard in Pacific & Gulf, for that was how he worked, back in Bangar.

Carlos said, as they were walking toward the administrative building at the end of their tour there, "That is it! Don't hesitate to ask me anything, if you need help."

"You can show me, where you take your lunch."

Carlos smiled and said, "I'm sorry, I forgot to show you the cafeteria, the most important facility here."

He was also smiling as Carlos showed him the cafeteria, located at the ground floor of the administrative building.

"The workers, when they get tired of the food served here, take their meals at the food stalls, outside the company gate," Carlos said. "Is there anything else, you want to know?"

He shook his head and said. "Nothing else, thank you for showing me the company facilities. See you later."

Carlos, in a friendly gesture, tapped Leandro on his shoulders as he then walked away.

He looked on at Carlos, happy for his job and a newly found friend.

Chapter Thirty-two

Bill Shay arrived in Pacific & Gulf much earlier, the following day, so he could see the unloading of a big shipment of construction equipment and materials from the United States.

He was pleased to see Leandro already at work, cleaning the anteroom in his office. It was only seven-quarter in the morning and most of the employees were yet to come in.

He entered his office and found it spotless. The boy is a good worker.

He sent Leandro, later in the morning, to deliver some documents to the Ayuntamiento, the Insular Government building in Intramuros, and to the electric streetcar station in Paco.

Pacific & Gulf was the principal contractor in building the streetcar stations and laying out the rail tracks of a modern and efficient mass transportation system in Manila.

The electric streetcars will replace in most of Manila, the steam-driven cabs and the horse-drawn cabs and rigs running in the city streets.

It was, Leandro found out, easy enough to go to the Ayuntamiento. All that he did was hire a cab in the street corner, outside the company gate, which then took him across Pasig River on the Puente de Espana Bridge to Intramuros and dropped, right at the front steps of the Ayuntamiento.

He paid the driver and stepped out of the cab, his eyes wide in awe of the Ayuntamiento. He heard it called the Marble Palace and he could see why. It was a jewel of a building with its pillars, walls and floor made mostly of marble.

He looked around. Near the Ayuntamiento were the Plaza de Roma, the Manila Cathedral and Fort Santiago.

That small area in Intramuros, as he had read about it in a history book, represented the three cornerstones of the Spanish colonial rule in the Philippines: the civil government, the Catholic Church and the military. He is now standing there, awed by their beauty, history and the power they held. The Americans' Insular Government ruled the colony from the Ayuntamiento, Fort Santiago and Malacanang Palace, just as the Spaniards did before them, but with the Church, then included.

He realized, he must have looked odd, standing awestruck there on the pavement that people passing by were glancing curiously at him. They were Americans in white drill suits, walking purposely out of or toward the building. He was loitering around when he should be attending to what he came there for.

He did the same in their manner of walking and he walked purposely toward the lobby. He was directed at the information desk to the concerned department where he delivered some of the documents, he carried. That was one quick work, he had done there.

The majestic building prompted him to wander around its lavish corridors adorned with porcelain vases and woodcarvings. The people he saw there were Americans, dressed mostly in white suits with a couple or a group, here and there, engaged in quiet conversation or were walking purposely toward the offices, lining the corridor.

The serious look in their faces and their dignified bearing showed him they were the people involved in the serious business of running the Insular Government. He could tell, as well, the heavy responsibilities they carried in the important titles and positions posted at the doors of the offices lining the corridor.

A glance he took at a wall clock there showed him the time—eleven-fifty. He had been there too long and he hurried out of the Ayuntamiento. He flagged down a horse-driven cab, which then took him to the train station in Paco.

It was deserted, but for a man seated on a bench, eating peanuts and the security guard, standing on his post there. He approached the security guard.

"Excuse me, sir," he said to the security guard. "Can you tell me where I can find the station manager? I have important papers for him. I am from the Pacific and Gulf."

"The station manager had just left for lunch," the security guard replied. "You can give them to me. I will take them to the manager's office."

Leandro nodded appreciatively at the security guard and he gave him the documents and a receipt, which the security guard then signed. It was the proof that they were properly delivered and received.

His mission there accomplished, he looked around, like what he did in the Ayuntamiento, before leaving the train station. It was bigger than the train station in Santa Ignacia, but much smaller than the train terminal in Tutuban. Except for the concrete columns at the entrance, it looked no different from the train station in Santa Ignacia.

There was not much to see there and he stepped out of the train station. He saw from the sun in the sky that it was already noontime.

The ground in the train station and the street outside were deserted. It might take a while before a cab or a rig will come by and he decided to walk back to the office by retracing the route the cab took to the train station. He could also flag down a cab or a rig, should he see one, on his way back to Pacific & Gulf.

The shadow, the sun cast on the trees in the train station, could be useful as a guide. He could then see the westward direction, he must take in going back to Parola, but it was noontime and with the sun directly above him, the shadow it cast was straight down to the ground and not at a slant in the shadows of the trees that could then give him a sense of direction.

He halted as he was leaving the train station and looked around. There were two streets ending in the street alongside the train station. He has no idea where they led to, nor could he recall which of those two streets the cab driver took from the Ayuntamiento.

It was then, solely by instinct, that he took the street at the right side of the train station. He came later on to an intersection. He halted, undecided on what direction, he should take. He turned right again. He met a couple of women as he was walking on. He asked them for direction to Parola. One of them said, she had never heard of such a place in Manila.

He walked on, disappointed and with growing fear that he might be lost. He was tempted to backtrack to the train station, but he was now in such a confused state of mind, he was doubtful if he could even find his way back to the train station. He was relying solely on his instinct and he walked on, in the same direction.

He had walked for sometime when he came upon a small stone bridge. He was pleased, on looking down at the creek below the bridge, to find it so clear, he could see minnows moving in the water and sand and pebbles at the bottom of the creek.

It occurred to him then that the creek might lead to another body of water, perhaps to Pasig River itself. He changed course and walked along the creek, the pace by which he was walking, now fast in his excitement. He saw, after sometime, the creek flowing into Pasig River. He finally found the way back to Pacific & Gulf.

It was now, just a simple matter of walking along the river on its westward course toward Manila Bay.

He slowed down, sometimes even halting, now that he knew he was going in the right direction, as he looked at the grand homes there of the rich and the powerful residents in the city. He was just as pleased to see there, various kinds of watercraft, from a tugboat pulling a barge to an outrigger. He had explored by accident, a place in Manila he would never know had he not decided to walk back to the office.

He walked on until he saw, pleased and satisfied, across a wide open ground, Intramuros and to its right, the Puente de Espana Bridge.

He ran into Mark Clavier, the moment he arrived in Parola.

"How come," Mark asked him, "you are back only now? Did you lose your way here?"

Perspiration, the size of grain, glinted in Leandro's brow, a broad smile on his face.

"No, sir," he replied, "I did not lose my way here, but I could not find a cab or a rig in Paco station so I decided to walk back here."

"Did you do that?" Mark said, his voice, raised in astonishment. "Paco is quite far! That is some walking, that you did."

"I'm used to that, sir," he said, who looked tired and hungry.

"Have you taken your lunch?"

"No, sir, I've not taken it yet."

"Then, run along now and take your lunch before you faint from hunger."

Mark looked on as Leandro then proceeded toward the cafeteria.

Leandro, later that day, did something that impressed Bill Shay and Mark Clavier. He was mopping the floor in the ladies' room when he saw a purse, someone had left there. He gave it promptly to Mark Clavier who then told Bill Shay about it.

Bill nodded, pleased. Leandro, not only is a good, hardworking employee, he is also honest.

Bill Shay arrived in the office on Friday, the last day of their week of work, expecting to find Leandro already at work there. He was not around. He was late in coming to work. He may have been held up by traffic or something. He gave it no further thought and went to work. He met Mark in the lobby as he was leaving at the end of the day.

"The boy did not come today," Mark said.

"Did he, at least call?"

"No, he did not. He just did not show up."

Bill frowned sorely disappointed with Leandro. He was not, as he pretended to be, a good, responsible employee.

"Tell him," he said to Mark, "he is fired, should he come in next week."

Bill and Mark did not know it then, Leandro failed to report for work because of something terrible that happened to him, the day before.

He was on his way home when the same thugs who ganged up on him, the previous Monday, caught him in the alley.

"Who do we have here, if not the same deaf-and-dumb provincial boy again," Bruno said to his gang who had surrounded Leandro. "If you know what is good for you, you will give us, liquor money."

He was only too willing to give Bruno and his gang, liquor money. He wanted no trouble with them. The problem is, he did not have, even a penny in his pocket. He was so concerned about losing his money that he had with him to work, just enough for his lunch and his transportation fare.

He could try to talk his way out of there, or he could run away. He was a fast runner, but the thugs had him surrounded.

Bruno became impatient.

"Don't keep us waiting!" he shouted as he then hit Leandro on the back of his head.

It sent him into a blind fury and he threw a punch at Bruno's face that sent him crashing backward against the wall of a hut there.

He turned to run away, but dropped instead to his knees when one of the thugs stabbed him on the left side of his body.

"Finish him!" Bruno said to the thug who stabbed Leandro.

A man suddenly appeared in the window of the hut.

"What is going on there!" he shouted.

Bruno and his gang ran away, leaving Leandro bleeding in the alley. He managed to stagger back to the street. Fortunately for him, a rig driver saw him and brought him to San Lazaro Hospital.

The knife had penetrated, deep in his body, and there was also the danger of infection. He remained unconscious, between life and death, for three days, after the doctors had treated his wound, but he was a young, strong boy, he came around on the third day, the fever having gone down by then. He saw, when he opened his eyes, his uncle Berting and aunt Agueda, looking anxiously at him.

"How do you feel?" Berting asked him.

"Hungry and all right now."

"We will have you eating to your heart's content, but you will do it gradually," Agueda said at a bag of food on a table, she and Berting had brought for Leandro.

"How did you find me here?" he asked them.

"It took some doing," Berting replied. "We were worried when you did not return home last Thursday. I went to Pacific and Gulf last Friday. I was told you did not report for work that day. I went to the police, but they had no report about you. I found you here, yesterday."

"So, the police never knew what happened to me."

"You had no identification card for the hospital people to report to the police."

"I had nothing, not even a penny in my pocket."

"Tell us what happened."

He was not inclined to talk about it, but they were entitled to know about it and he told them what happened to him in the alley.

"A good thing, you got away from those bad people," Agueda said.

"Do you know who they are," Berting asked him, "so the police can arrest them?"

"It happened so fast and it was already dark. I did not have a good look at them," his voice breaking at the lie, he said.

He would rather that they will not know who attacked him. Bruno and his gang will get back at him if they are reported to the police. He might then end up with something far worse than a stab wound on the left side of his body.

"Let Leandro rest for now," Agueda said. "He needs to eat, too."

They propped him up on the bed with several pillows placed on his back. Agueda then began feeding him.

Berting, the following Monday, took the morning off from work and reported to Mark Clavier what happened to Leandro. Mark left Berting in his office when he went to see Bill Shay.

He felt bad when Mark told him what happened to Leandro.

He shook his head at how he had so unfairly judged the teenage boy. He fired him, an innocent victim of a gang of thugs while he was fighting for his life in a hospital.

"Where did it happen?" he asked Mark.

"It happened in an alley near his home."

"It happened, right there? He is risking his life every time he leaves and returns home. He should move out of there."

"Is there anything in your mind?"

"Yes. Let us find a place where he can stay for the time being, one that is safe for him."

Bill Shay was beginning to have a personal interest in Leandro's welfare.

"There is a bunk in the warehouse loft."

"Good. That will do for the boy until he can get his own place. You can tell him that when he reports for work."

"I will tell his uncle. He is waiting in my office."

Leandro returned to work, three weeks later, when he was fully healed of his wound. He took up residence in the warehouse loft. He was only too glad to move out of his uncle Berting and aunt Agueda's home. They were just as relieved to see him, leave them, for his life was in danger there. As he eventually told them, he was stabbed in the alley by the neighborhood thugs—Bruno and his gang.

His temporary stay in the warehouse loft brought about a change in his work routine.

He was watching the other workers, punching out their time cards at the end of the first day on his return to work. They were all going home except him. He is staying behind, for home to him now is right there where he is standing, in the company co mpound.

He punched out his time card at the thought of dinner. He walked out toward the food stalls, outside the company gate. One was still open.

A young girl waited on him as he was looking at the food trays in the glass counter there. He ordered rice topped with fried pork and steamed vegetables. As he began to eat, the food stall proprietor, a middle-aged man, joined the girl and asked him, "You are a new hire here, are you not? What is your name?"

He gave his name and said he is indeed, new in Pacific & Gulf.

"Good for you, you were taken in there," the man said.

He ate while the man kept him company. He gave his name of Mang Emong. He said he and his wife, Aling Pacing, who was attending to another patron there, were from the town of Arayat in the province of Pampanga. They moved to Manila when their daughter Crisanta was still a small girl. He was a tailor by trade, but both he and his wife were good cooks. They put up their food stall there within a few days when Pacific & Gulf started operations there.

He saw, as he was eating, the girl now putting the leftovers inside a carton box. They were just waiting for him and the other patron to finish their supper before closing their food stall. He finished his meal quickly, thanked Mang Emong, Aling Pacing and Crisanta for the delicious food, paid for his meal and left.

It was too early to bed and he went back to the administrative building to check if there was anything that he could do there.

Bill Shay was going out of his office when he saw him, cleaning the desks in the anteroom.

"So, you're still at work," Bill said to him on his way to the elevator.

"Yes, sir," he replied as he continued cleaning the desks.

He was finished working there in a few minutes and he left the building. He was on his way to the riverbank for an idle viewing of the city when he saw in the marshaling yard, lumber left scattered on the ground by workers apparently in a hurry to go home. He set about in arranging them in a neat pile when a security guard on night duty saw him working.

"What are you doing there?" the security guard said to him. "Why are you still here? Everyone has gone home."

"I am not going anywhere. I am staying here, at the warehouse loft. I am putting in a neat pile, these pieces of lumber left, scattered here."

The security guard frowned and said, "That does not mean, you can do whatever you want to do, like working beyond normal working hours. I want you to stop, what you are doing there."

He ignored the security guard and went on working.

"Did you not hear what I said!" the security guard shouted at him.

"I heard you," he replied, sore at the rude way he was being treated by the security guard.

He dropped the piece of lumber in his hands and said to the security guard, "Is there any company regulation that prohibits me from working beyond normal working hours? I have read the company handbook. There is nothing there that says, I cannot do what I am doing. If you feel so strongly against what I am doing, you can report me to your supervisor and I will do the same and report you to Mister Shay and Mister Clavier."

He watched, satisfied, how mentioning the names of Mr. Shay and Mr. Clavier had so jolted the security guard, he then said, "You don't have to do that. I'm only doing my job."

"Your job is to secure the company premises. You have no business, no authority to tell me what I can and cannot do. So, stop meddling with what I am doing."

The security guard walked away, humbled.

He watched the security guard, frowning at how his duty of securing the company premises had gone to his head. He knows, it is a trait that is common among them, of getting swellheaded by power or authority, no matter how slight it was. The abuses they suffered under their past Spanish masters had made them also an abusive, power-hungry people.

He resumed working. He picked up the piece of lumber he dropped on the ground and put it in its proper place in the pile of lumber.

The following days showed him doing extra work for the company. He liked to spend his free time that way, occupied with work, before retiring for the night. He stayed away from the security guards on night duty when he overheard them, backbiting, the other workers.

He could read in his spare time, the book Miss Dickinson gave him, but he was so tired after each hard day's work and reading in his bunk with its poor light was a strain on his eyes. He went straight to sleep instead. The book, though, was a precious gift from Miss Dickinson. He kept it inside his locker. He will read it, sometime in the future.

It was all work for him, a habit he developed at an early age in Bangar. He worked there for the food he ate, for he did not eat enough, if he did not work, hard enough. He carried over this work habit in Pacific & Gulf. No task was too menial or insignificant, whether it was in picking up a crumpled piece of paper, dropped on the ground or in sweeping with a mop, a wet spot in a restroom.

Bill Shay was on his way to his office when he saw Mark Clavier.

Mark said to Bill, "Have you heard about the talk, going on about our new hire, Leandro Sumaka?"

"What is it about?"

"The boy is doing other things and is working, late into the night."

"So he does," Bill said, not surprised about it.

He had seen Leandro from his office, working way past quitting time in the creosote-injecting iron cylinders, at other times in loading construction materials in the boat, docked in the riverbank.

"He seems to enjoy the extra work," he said to Mark. "Let him continue what he is doing."

"Some of the workers seem to resent, what he is doing."

"Why should they?"

"I am not sure why, but from what I have gathered, they are saying the boy, a newcomer, is trying to make a good, but false impression of himself in working at night and that he is actually stealing company property under the cover of darkness."

"That is malicious talk! How did the boy react to that?"

"He seems to ignore or maybe he is not aware of that kind of talk going on behind his back."

Bill frowned in anger at this kind of talk going on among some of his workers. He was even more infuriated, knowing that he could not put a stop to it.

He could not penalize, much less fire the guilty parties on the basis of an unsubstantiated report that they were backbiting the boy. But he could not tolerate it.

"I want you to put a stop to that kind of talk," he said to Mark.

He slapped the wooden railing in anger as he was going up in the staircase to his office.

What a despicable, hypocritical lot! They were so submissive and respectful to him and their other American superiors, but how mean they are to each other!

His executive staff, he watched satisfied, was deep at work on their desks while Leandro was busy, mopping the floor. The boy deserved something a lot better for the kind of work he is doing for the company, not the shabby treatment, he is getting from some of his fellow workers. He decided to do something about it.

Chapter Thirty-three

"How is Leandro doing?" Dorothy asked Bill as they were walking toward the lobby of Columbus Club with Esperanza and Samuel. They arrived at the same time in the club's driveway. They were going to attend the fifth anniversary celebration of Dick McCall's newsmagazine, *The Philippines Newsmagazine.*

Dorothy and Samuel have not heard from Leandro since he left San Isidro, several months ago.

"The boy is doing great," Bill replied.

"I am not surprised to hear that," Samuel said to Bill. "From what I have gathered from Dorothy here, he is a diligent, hardworking boy."

Dorothy caught Esperanza looking inquiringly at Bill and Samuel and she said to her that Leandro was a former student of hers, Samuel had recommended for a job in Pacific & Gulf.

"He must be a fine worker for Bill to say that about him," Esperanza said.

"He is a very good worker," Bill said as he was looking around at the elegant appointments—the chandeliers, the paintings on the walls and the marble floor—in the lobby of Columbus Club.

Neoclassic in design, it was a fine example of quality work of Pacific & Gulf. It was, within a year after its inauguration, a hub of the social life in Manila.

Bill walked ahead toward a table near the door to the banquet hall where the celebration was being held. He gave his name and those of Esperanza, Dorothy and Samuel to Dick's staff members, all of them Filipinos, who were seated at the other side of the table. They checked Bill and the others' names with their list of guests. Everything was in order and they then pinned on them, their guest tags with their names and assigned tables written there.

A doorman opened for them, the door to the anteroom of the banquet hall. It was full of guests, the rich, the prominent and the powerful men and women in the colony. The men were in suits while many of the women there were wearing gowns, some of them wearing on their heads, tiaras full of precious stones.

The party in celebration of the fifth anniversary of *The Philippines Newsmagazine,* was notable for the presence there of both the Americans and the Filipinos. Some of the guests were from Manila's foreign community.

They were making good use of the time left before the start of dinner by engaging in conversation, sipping wine and trying out the finger food, the waiters in white coats, were serving them. Dinner will be served upon the arrival of the special guest of honor, Governor-General William Howard Taft and his wife Helen.

Bill and Samuel took from a waiter bearing wine glasses, wine for Esperanza, Dorothy and themselves. They looked around for Dick while they were taking sips from their glasses of wine.

Dick, not seen by them, was at a corner of the anteroom with Nieves. They were talking to Paulo Palanas and Teresa.

"How is the baby?" Dick asked Teresa as he was looking down at her round midriff.

"It is getting bigger and more active with each passing day," Teresa replied while she was rubbing gently, her round midriff.

"Must be a boy," Nieves said.

"How is Masakao?" Dick asked Paulo. "Nieves and I have not been there for quite a while."

"Not much is going on there," Paulo replied.

"Not much?" Teresa said. "What about the new cottage industries that you introduced there? And the new market, Bill's company had just finished building there?"

Dick and Nieves smiled.

"My husband is too modest for his own good," Teresa said.

"Paulo is an unusual kind of town leader. He does not crow over his achievements," Nieves said.

"He and Dick are alike; both of them are modest and unassuming," Teresa said to Nieves, "but then, unlike Paulo here, Dick is not a politician and does not have to keep himself in the public eye."

"I put people in the public eye," Dick said, smiling. "But tell me," he said to Paulo, "how are your two major projects, getting along?"

"Bill," Paulo replied, "is waiting for the Insular Government's go-signal for the construction of the dam and the road to Alkayag."

"You will have, both of them in due time," Dick said.

He waved back when he saw Bill, waving at him.

"Good, Dick has seen us," Bill said to Esperanza, Dorothy and Samuel. They moved in a single file through the other guests toward Dick who was also approaching them with Nieves, Paulo and Teresa.

Bill had just then found himself facing someone who, while smiling and extending his hand, said to him, "Am I so glad to see you, Mister Shay!"

"So am I, Mister Quezon," Bill replied.

They shook hands. Another man joined them.

"I am pleased to see you again, Mister Shay," he said.

"Same here, Mister Osmena," Bill replied as he was shaking hands with him, too.

He introduced to them, Esperanza, Dorothy and Samuel who were looking on, from behind him.

"A great party," Osmena said.

"All of Dick's affairs are great," Bill said.

"You mean his social affairs and not that kind of an affair," Quezon said as he winked mischievously at Bill.

The other guests within hearing smiled at what Quezon had alluded to. So did Bill at the two gentlemen, both of them, young, rising politicians. Quezon was from the province of Tayabas while Osmena was from Cebu. They had sought Bill's help for funding by the Insular Government of their pet projects in their respective provinces.

"I hope you won't mind," Quezon said to Bill, "if I will ask you, right in the middle of this grand party and so does, I suppose, my friend here, if you have taken up with the governor-general my Atimonan port project and his school building program."

"I have not had the chance," Bill replied, "to talk to the governor-general about your projects, but I have taken them up with his staff."

"What did they say?" Osmena asked Bill.

"They said there are no funds this year for those projects. I'm sorry."

Both Quezon and Osmena shook their heads in disappointment.

"You can take them up directly with the governor-general," Bill suggested. "I am sure he will listen to you."

"I think we should do that," Quezon said.

Bill then asked to be excused and he left Quezon and Osmena. He made his way toward Dick with Esperanza, Dorothy and Samuel.

"So nice of you to come," Dick said as he shook hands with them.

More handshaking followed when Dorothy and Samuel were introduced to Nieves, Paulo and Teresa.

Dick knew Dorothy and Samuel very well. He had featured them in *The Philippines Newsmagazine* as two fine, young American schoolteachers, providing the young people in the colony, the education they need for a good future in life.

"I saw you detained by Quezon and Osmena," Dick said to Bill. "What are they after now?"

"The usual, their pet projects."

"Quezon's aggressiveness and Osmena's quiet persistence are hard to resist," Dick said.

"And both of them have the good looks to go with those fine qualities of theirs," Esperanza said.

"Exactly," Dick said, smiling.

Someone from his staff came rushing to him and told him that Taft has arrived with his wife Helen. He asked to be excused and left with Nieves to welcome them.

They returned to the anteroom, a few moments later, with Taft and his wife Helen. The guests gave them room as they proceeded to the banquet hall. The guests then proceeded to their assigned tables.

The members of the presidential party, led by Taft and Dick, took their seats at the presidential table with Taft seated beside Dick and his wife Helen seated beside Nieves. While there were other high-ranking guests there, Dick picked Bill and Esperanza, Paulo and Teresa as some of the guests to be seated there because they were his close friends.

The orchestra then struck up *The Star-Spangled Banner* and everyone in the hall stood up until it had finished playing America's national anthem.

Dinner was then served by waiters, bearing silver trays of food, to the strains of the lovely song, *Beautiful Dreamer.*

It was a sumptuous affair with French and American dishes served, along with French wine, Spanish brandy and Southern whisky. Entertainment was provided by the orchestra, a group of Filipino boys and girls who performed a number of Filipino folk dances and a pretty Filipino singer who sang popular songs of the day.

Bill stood up toward the end of the dinner and said, "Ladies and gentlemen, let us offer a toast to the man who founded *The Philippines Newsmagazine,* Dick McCall."

The guests stood up and raised their wine glasses to Dick.

"Thank you, my dear friends, honorable guests, ladies and gentlemen," he said. "Tonight is a special day for us in *The Philippines*

Newsmagazine. We have gone through the first five years of our newsmagazine and we have done even then and will always do the service to our country and the people of these islands as our great objective."

The guests applauded. He continued: "We shall carry on, as we have done from the very beginning, happy and grateful for the support we have received and shall continue to receive from all quarters, from the farmers in the countryside to the highest government officials overseeing and working for the progress and prosperity of these islands, led no less by the governor-general himself.

"Ladies and gentlemen, I am privileged to present to you, our most distinguished guest, the honorable Governor-General William Howard Taft."

Taft, in his speech, spoke of the efforts of the Insular Government in bringing to the Philippines, the many benefits from America's benevolent rule. He concluded his speech with a tribute to Dick and *The Philippines Newsmagazine* as the Insular Government's valuable helper in its pursuit of peace, progress and prosperity for the people of the Philippine Islands. Taft's speech was met with cheers and a rousing applause.

The orchestra then played *The Blue Danube Waltz.*

Many of the guests, drawn by its melodic, swaying beat, stood up and moved toward the dance floor.

"Shall we dance, dear?" Samuel asked Dorothy.

"If you want to," Dorothy replied.

They stood up and followed other couples to the dance floor. They held each other's hand as they danced gracefully. The other dancing couples threw them, admiring glances, prompting them to go on dancing in perfect rhythm with the waltz's swaying beat.

It was just as well that they were dancing to the lovely music so that no one, but Samuel had noticed a shadow that had then crossed Dorothy's face. She was now dancing with less spirit, almost mechanically, her eyes turned to something far away.

The waltz had not ended when they left the dance floor. They went to the balcony and sat down on a marble bench there screened from the banquet hall by tall ferns and potted plants.

Dorothy looked sad and Samuel said to her, "Are you thinking about it again?"

"I cannot help it. I cannot blind myself to the fact that you are going away, that you are leaving me."

"But I will be gone for just a short while; a year or two, at most."

"I cannot bear, not seeing you that long."

"How I wish we could have it our way and you could be with me."

They both knew, this was out of the question. She had to stay behind and continue teaching in San Isidro while he will be studying anthropology in the United States.

The dark expanse of the grass in Luneta Park, across the street from Columbus Club, seemed likewise cast in gloom as Dorothy reflected sadly on how a simple trip, Samuel took to Central Cordillera had changed the course of their lives.

What Samuel saw there made him decide to take up anthropology so he could conduct a thorough research in Central Cordillera. He will henceforth devote so much of his time and effort in the study of the mountain tribes there—the Ifugaos, the Bontocs, the Ibalois and the Kalingas—and the magnificent rice terraces they built in Banaue, Hapao, Batad, Kiangan and Mayoyao.

He will study anthropology in the United States to equip himself for that task. He enrolled by cable in his old school and was readily accepted as an alumnus with an outstanding academic record.

Dorothy, in trying to fathom what underlay Samuel's decision, remembered his interest in the ethnic communities. He had been to the Southwest to look into the Indian tribes there.

She was not against Samuel pursuing anthropology, but she was against what it would do to their relationship.

In conducting his study of those mountain tribes, Samuel will be spending a great deal of time and effort in Central Cordillera, far from her in San Isidro. She threatened to break off their engagement. Why should they get married if they could not live together as husband and wife?

Fortunately for them, Samuel learned about an Episcopalian missionary named Brendan who was establishing a boarding school for American boys in Baguio, the Ibaloi village, deep in the mountains in Central Cordillera, being developed into a modern vacation resort city by the Insular Government and private business and industry.

Samuel applied for teaching positions for both of them in the boarding school and were both readily accepted. He will, like her, after his study in the United States, also teach in Brendan School and pursue at the same time, his research and study of those mountain tribes while based in Baguio, right at the heart of Central Cordillera. They could then get married and live together as husband and wife.

Dorothy will start teaching in Brendan School, once the construction of the school buildings, the faculty housing and other facilities was finished while Samuel was studying anthropology. All of those somehow eased up the sadness Dorothy felt at Samuel's impending departure for the United States.

It was a lovely evening. She could see it now in the dark, cloudless sky with its pinpricks of light from the stars and the marvelous view before her. The weather was cool, following the first rains in May.

After the noise and the music in the banquet hall, the silence and the cool air in the balcony were refreshing, both to mind and spirit. The dark grass-carpeted stretch of Luneta Park was no longer cast in gloom. The wall in Intramuros stood out against the night sky, the lights in Binondo outlining the churches and other buildings in Intramuros.

She was alone with Samuel, lovers making the most in this precious moment they were so close to each other. She held her breath when Samuel turned to her and took her in his arms. She clung to him tightly and she will cling tightly to him forever, if only she could.

Dick said to Dorothy and Samuel when he saw them, back in the banquet hall, "You make a lovely couple. When are you getting married?"

Dorothy and Samuel smiled at Dick, but said nothing. There will be the time for that.

Chapter Thirty-four

Mark Clavier gave a hint that it was time for Leandro to look for his own place, two months to the day, after he took up residence in the warehouse loft. He was so happy and content in lodging there, he had forgotten, it was only a temporary arrangement, Bill Shay had made for him, out of his concern for his safety. But where could he find a place to live? He turned to Carlos for help. He invited him to a snack at the cafeteria and told him about his problem.

"That is not a problem, at all," Carlos said. "There are many apartments and boarding houses in Manila."

"But I don't know where to look."

"Ask yourself first, before looking for it, what you want and need and what you can afford. Since you will be living alone, renting a house is out of the question. You may consider an apartment, but that may still be too big for you. A simple bed space may not also be enough for you, since you will need some privacy. Let us settle then on a room. It is just right for you. You can share the kitchen and the bathroom with the other tenants. How does that suit you?"

"It is fine with me."

"Let us go over the places where you can rent a room. San Nicolas is nearby, but it is mostly residential. Binondo is too expensive. Santa Cruz is okay and so are Quiapo and Sampaloc. Pandacan is too far. You can try San Miguel."

He looked skeptically at Carlos. A poor country boy like him will be out of place there, where Malacanang Palace was located.

"Only rich folks like you live there," he said. "I will not fit there."

"Who says, you cannot live there? I, for one, will be glad if you will live near our house there."

He nodded, won over by what Carlos said. Living near his house is a good idea.

He asked Carlos, "Are there any rooms, for rent there?"

"There just might be. I will look around. I will tell you when I have found one."

Carlos told Leandro, two days later, that he found a room, just right for him.

"It is not far from our house. Don Anastacio, the owner of the house, has fallen on hard times. He subdivided, to increase his income, the ground floor of his house into several rooms and put them up for rent."

"How much is the rent?"

"It is four pesos a month and one month security deposit, paid in advance or initially, a total of eight pesos."

Leandro nodded. He could easily afford the rent.

"We will meet in my place on Sunday and take a look at the room," Carlos said. He then gave Leandro the address and the direction to his house in San Miguel.

Leandro went to see Carlos that Sunday, after attending Mass.

His impression of San Miguel as a fine residential place was confirmed before his eyes when he went walking in the shade of the acacia trees that lined Real Street, where Carlos resided. The homes there conveyed wealth and gracious living. They were built, like the homes of the landlords in San Isidro, of stone, brick and wood and with tile roofs. The windows in the lower floor were barred with sloping iron grills.

He was passing by a house there when he heard a lovely melody being played on a piano there. He was so taken by the music, the first time he heard it, that he halted and listened in sheer pleasure until whoever was on the keyboard had finished playing Beethoven's lovely song, the *Fur Elise.*

He waited for more piano music, but the house now remained silent. He resumed walking, humming the song along, until he had reached Carlos' house. He pressed the gate bell button on the wooden gate. He looked at the house and its surroundings while he was waiting for someone who will come and let him in.

It was an old, two-story stone house with a tile roof and a balcony, facing Real Street. Leading up to the house was a roofed stone staircase. A garden decked out with flowering plants and fruit trees set it back from the street. The right side of the house was a garden, full of plants, fruit and palm trees. A driveway at the left side of the house led to the garage.

A maid soon came and opened the house gate for him. He was going up in the stone staircase when he paused at the sight of a beautiful girl tending a potted plant in the garden, at the right side of the house. He looked on at her, wondering who she was, when she looked up at him.

"You must be Leandro," she said to him. "Carlos told me about you. I'm Regina, his sister. He is waiting for you."

He nodded and smiled at her. He went up in the staircase, his mind fixed to her. So, Carlos has a beautiful sister. What a bright smile and sunny disposition, she has. She seemed self-assured, not shy, like most girls of her age. He was so lost in thought about her that, on entering the living room, he nearly collided with Carlos, who then held him back on his shoulders.

"I'm sorry," he said. "I was looking down, I did not see you."

"It's all right. Did you have any trouble in finding your way here?"

"No."

"Would you like to take something before we take a look at the room?"

"No, thank you. I just had a full breakfast."

"Let us get going then."

They were about to pass out of the house gate when Carlos saw Leandro, looking back at Regina.

"That is my sister, Regina," Carlos said.

"I know."

"Have you met her?"

"I did, briefly, as I was going up to your house."

"So, there is no need to introduce you to each other."

"See you later," Carlos then said to Regina as he and Leandro were passing out of the house gate.

"Regina," he said to Leandro as they were walking on in Calle Real, "is at home for the weekend. She is a student boarder in Ascension College. It is a school in Malate, ran by the Sisters of Saint Mary."

Leandro was stunned by what Carlos said. Ascension College was the school, he heard Angela Rosablanca say as the school where she will study after her graduation in San Isidro's public school.

He resumed walking with Carlos, his thoughts on Angela. She must be, by now, enrolled in that school. It occurred to him then that he has not thought of her since he left San Isidro. He was so preoccupied with work, he has completely forgotten her. Could it mean, he asked himself, that he is now through with her?

He shrugged his shoulders. "So be it," he said to himself.

"Here we are," Carlos said when they reached the house.

He pressed the house gate bell button and looked, together with Leandro, at the house.

It seemed, like its sagging wooden gate, to have been through better days. The paint was peeling off in the tile roof, dark brown with age.

Don Anastacio came out and opened the gate. Carlos introduced Leandro as his friend, looking for a room there.

"What I have got is the best in the house," Don Anastacio said in a bit of sales talk.

He led Carlos and Leandro inside the house. The room was at the end of a corridor. It was small and square-shaped, measuring about twelve feet across the wooden floor. It has a single bed, a cabinet, a chair beside a desk that faced a window barred by a sloping iron grill.

Leandro moved toward the window, pleased to find that it looked out into a tiny garden. It was a bare simple room, but far better than where he slept before in the bamboo floor in his uncle Julian and his uncle Berting's nipa huts.

"I have three other tenants here; all good people," Don Anastacio said. "I might as well tell you that we have house rules here. Pets are not allowed here. Visitors are welcome, but are not allowed to spend the night here. Drinking inside the room is allowed, but drinking parties are also not allowed here. I have kept this, a peaceful, quiet house in this peaceful, quiet neighborhood by keeping those simple house rules."

"Could we?" Leandro asked Don Anastacio, "Take a look at the rest of the house?"

He showed them the bathroom and the kitchen, which they saw were small, but clean.

Leandro nodded at Carlos. Everything about the room and the rest of the house is satisfactory to him.

"Talk it over," Don Anastacio said. "I will be back in a few minutes."

He said, when Don Anastacio returned there, that he is taking the room. He gave Don Anastacio the security deposit and the first month's rent while Don Anastacio gave him the keys to the gate, the room and the door in the ground floor of the house.

"I know, you will like it here. Enjoy your stay here," Don Anastacio said, smiling, as he then left them.

"I will get my things in Parola," Leandro said to Carlos.

"And I am going home, but I will be back after about an hour. Will you be back by then?"

"Make it an hour and a half."

Leandro was back in his room, more than an hour later. He was putting his few belongings inside the cabinet when Carlos came in, lugging a folding chair.

"I noticed, there is only one chair in your room. I brought this, so I will have a chair to sit on when I visit you here," Carlos said, the chair he then put beside the desk.

Leandro in the meantime had taken out a book from his suitcase and put it down on the desk.

Carlos glanced at it and said, *"The Adventures of Tom Sawyer,* a wonderful book for children. So, you have not outgrown that."

"It is," Leandro said, smiling, "a gift from Miss Dickinson, my teacher in San Isidro."

"Your teacher must have liked you so much, she gave you that book."

"She has done much more than that. It was through her and another American teacher's recommendation that I got the job in Pacific and Gulf."

Carlos nodded and smiled. "It takes Americans for us to get through to other Americans."

"You are not the first person to tell me that. I am lucky to have made friends with good people, like those two American teachers."

"Good fortune, like the sun outside, shines on you."

Carlos looked outside at the garden bright with sunlight. The shadow cast on the ground by a solitary tree there showed that it was noontime. He took out his pocket watch and checked the time.

"It is twelve-ten, time for lunch," he said to Leandro. "You will have it with us. Everyone in my family will be there."

Leandro weighed in his mind whether or not he should accept Carlos' lunch invitation. While it is a chance for him to be acquainted with Regina and the rest of Carlos's family, the very idea of taking lunch with them, intimidated him. They belonged to Manila's best society while he is a poor peasant boy, not even sure about his table manners.

He ate with his hands, back in Bangar and in his uncle Berting's nipa hut in Palomar. He could not do that with the Yturaldes. While he had familiarized himself with the use of the fork and spoon from the meals he had been taking at the cafeteria and the food stalls, that may not be enough. He might make one mistake after another and end up making a fool of himself.

"Thank you, for your lunch invitation," he said to Carlos, "but not today, perhaps some other time."

Carlos was not to be put off, though.

"Come now," he said. "You don't want to disappoint my mother and my sister, do you? I have already told them, I am taking you with me to lunch with them. They have prepared a fine lunch for us."

That, Leandro decided, left him with no other choice but to accept Carlos' lunch invitation. He could say no to Carlos and he will not feel offended. His mother and his sister, on the other hand, might not only be disappointed, but even be offended if he will not take lunch with them.

"All right," he said to Carlos, "lead the way."

They arrived in Carlos' house to his family waiting for them in the living room. Carlos introduced Leandro to them and then led him, right away, to the dining room. It was, like the living room, opulent in furnishings and had likewise a big chandelier hanging over the long hardwood dining table.

Leandro sat down beside Carlos who took the corner chair, left of his father, Don Alfonso who sat down at the head of the table. Don Alfonso was distinguished-looking with his gray hair, his white drill coat and blue tie. Carlos faced Regina across the table with Menardo, the oldest son, seated beside her. Seated to Menardo's right was his wife Alicia who faced their young daughter Amanda across the table, at the left side of Leandro. Carlos' mother, Dona Magdalena, was facing Don Alfonso. She was flanked by their two younger sons, Ricardo and Sebastian.

The dining room, Leandro observed, has a friendly, casual atmosphere and this put him at ease. Alicia and Dona Magdalena were comparing notes on a musical they saw in a theater, the night before, their conversation spiced up with laughter at the antics of some of the actors. Don Alfonso and Menardo were discussing their family business. Ricardo and Sebastian were making funny faces at each other while they were waiting for the start of lunch. Regina, best of all, was throwing him friendly, curious glances. He felt like he was being treated like someone familiar and welcome to them.

He looked on, pleased, when the maidservant brought in from the kitchen, a meat dish and put it at one end in a row of dishes laid on the sideboard. Nailed to the wall there was an impressionist still life painting of fruits and vegetables.

They were having sumptuous Spanish food for lunch—*Arroz ala Valenciana, Pescado con Agrio Dulce, Morcon, Camaron Rebosado* and *Torta de Cangrejo.*

Now, Leandro noted, pleased with himself, he will be feasting on the same kind of mouth-watering Spanish food, he knows Don Camilo and the other Ilustrado landlords in San Isidro also ate at their dining tables.

He bowed with his eyes closed and joined the others in saying grace. His mouth hung open in bewilderment when, at the end of the prayer, he opened his eyes and saw the utensils arrayed before him on the dining table.

A large plate with a bowl on top of it and a napkin folded in the shape of a fan, laid on top of the bowl, were right below him. At the right side of the plate were a teaspoon, a regular spoon, another spoon with a round end and a knife. Laid left of the plate were two forks. A fork and a spoon will do. So, he asked himself, what were the other utensils for? And what was he supposed to do with the napkin?

He looked on at the utensils, his eyes blinking in his confusion on what he should do with them. He will soon be found out to be lacking in proper table manners, but he had been through in other tight situations before and he did what he saw the others were doing at the dining table.

He glanced at Carlos and likewise picked up the napkin and spread it on his lap. He took the cue from Don Alfonso who was using the spoon with a round end in eating the soup, the maidservant had ladled into the bowl. He did the same with Regina on the Morcon. He cut it first into bite size with the knife and ate one small piece at a time instead of swallowing it whole. He followed this with the rice which he took with the regular spoon. He glanced at the other utensils. The other fork must be for the cake, the maidservant had put on the sideboard. The teaspoon, he guessed, will be for stirring the coffee with sugar, both of which should come later on, at the end of their lunch. He thus conducted himself like a perfect gentleman at ease in dining with the wealthy, sophisticated Yturalde family.

Don Alfonso and Menardo ate, at the same time that they were discussing the ranch and the coffee plantation in Batangas, their main family business.

"How do you size up the coming coffee crop?" Don Alfonso asked Menardo.

"It looks like we will have a good harvest this year," Menardo replied. "The weather has been good to the coffee beans. Even better, the price quoted in the market is higher today than last year."

The pleased look that then appeared in Don Alfonso's face and the chorus of approval that rose at the table over Menardo's glowing report showed Leandro that the Yturaldes were a closely knit family.

He learned a few things about their family business from Carlos. Their coffee plantation was spread out, alongside their cattle ranch, in the highlands in Batangas. Menardo managed both. While he now had his own home in Ermita, he spent almost half of his time in the other Yturalde house in Batangas in overseeing the work there. Don Alfonso was a lawyer of the upper crust in Manila. He was also a minority partner in a trading company, based in Rosario Street.

Leandro wondered why Carlos was working as a mere personnel assistant in Pacific & Gulf when he could be a boss in their family business. Carlos must want to make a mark in the world, just on his own.

Leandro concentrated on his food, satisfied to listen to the talk at the table. Don Alfonso, midway in their lunch, turned to him and asked him, "So, young man, what do you do in Pacific and Gulf?"

He did not expect to be asked about his job and he hesitated before giving an answer. They will look down on him once they will learn he is a janitor and messenger in Pacific & Gulf, but what could he do except to tell them the truth?

He was about to speak when Carlos said to his father, "Leandro is our all-around person there. He may be a new hire, but the talk going around there is about the big things in store for him in the company."

Leandro could barely suppress a smile at this bit of exaggeration, Carlos had said about him. He made him look important to his family, especially to Regina, who was looking at him admiringly.

The image of her, smiling at him, lingered in his mind when he left the Yturaldes, nearly an hour later.

He had pulled it off. He had done well in passing himself as a young, sophisticated gentleman. He walked back to his room, savoring still the great time he had with Carlos and his family. That, he said to himself, was the best lunch, he had ever taken.

It also marked a change in his social life. He was a loner before that. It was all work for him in Pacific & Gulf. He spent by his lonesome self, his two days' off from work on Saturday and Sunday.

It was simple routine like his janitorial work in Pacific & Gulf. He would watch a show at the Teatro Libertad or in some other theater in Manila. He would attend Mass on Sunday in any of the churches in Intramuros, Binondo, Santa Cruz and Quiapo.

He would take his lunch and dinner in any of the Chinese and Filipino restaurants in Binondo and Santa Cruz, window-shop in Rosario and Escolta Streets, take a stroll in Luneta Park and watch the lovely sunset in Manila Bay before calling it a day.

He was happy with that kind of life, he was leading, but felt, something was lacking. What it was, he found in the company of Carlos and Regina. Proximity allowed him to spend now, most of his weekends with them in their home or in watching shows, attending Mass, window-shopping, taking a stroll in Luneta Park and in watching the glorious sunset in Manila Bay.

Time thus passed pleasantly and uneventfully for Leandro until, a few months later, he received both on the same day two important news, one of them good, the other one bad.

He had just returned to his cubicle when he heard the bell ringing and saw the light bulb beside Mark Clavier's name, lit up. He went to Mark's office right away.

"How would you like to do field work?" Mark asked Leandro. "A position of general assistant is open in Operations. It goes with a higher pay, much higher pay."

Leandro's eyes shot wide in delight. That will be doing work, right at the heart of the company's field operations.

"I will be glad to take it, sir," he replied.

"Very well, see Mister Beldry about it."

He left Mark Clavier's office brimming with happiness. He must share it with someone. He approached Carlos who was watching him from his desk.

"Did you take the job?" Carlos asked him.

"I did. So you know about it."

"That is what we are here for."

"Why did you not take it yourself?"

"Why should I? Even if I want it, which I don't, my family will not let me take it, for it will mean, I will be working, far away from them. The thing is, I was not even considered for that job. I heard Mister Shay, the Big Boss himself, picked you for the job."

"Is that so?"

"The Big Boss seems to like you."

"He likes all of us."

"I'm not sure about that. You should be glad you are among those who have found favor with the Big Boss. Well, enjoy your new job. It will take you places."

"That is fine with me. I live alone. No one will miss me after I have left for my new job."

"Are you sure about that?"

"What do you mean by that?"

Carlos did not reply. He resumed working, a knowing smile on his face.

"See you later," Leandro said as he then walked away.

He was approaching the Operations building when he suddenly halted. Carlos was referring to Regina as the person who will miss him.

He had forgotten her in his excitement over his new job. It meant being far away from her. That made him suddenly sad and lonely. They have become fond of each other, but he has no choice. He could not pass up this chance for advancement in the company. He will no longer be a lowly janitor and errand boy, but someone who will be doing important work for the company's field operations.

He proceeded to Philip Beldry's office. He has done a few errands for him. He knows him quite well by now. The frequent visits he made to Operations had made him familiar with it, although the bulk of its work was in the job sites. He will be respectful as always, but no longer deferential as he was, the first time he came to Pacific & Gulf. He was no longer an outsider coming in, but an insider on his way up in the company ladder. That he was being taken in at Operations on orders of Mister Shay, the Big Boss himself, added to his confidence when the secretary ushered him into Philip Beldry's office.

"Your first assignment will be in Zamboanga where we are building a wharf, aside from other construction projects there," Beldry said to Leandro. "You will be an all-around person in addition to specific tasks you will be assigned to by Joseph Kirkpatrick, the field manager there. You will take the boat leaving on Wednesday. You have only two days to settle your affairs here, so get moving now."

Leandro left Philip's office, impressed by the way he conducted their meeting, quick and to the point, it took only a minute.

He was walking back to his cubicle when his thoughts returned to Regina. He will be leaving without seeing her. He must see Carlos about it.

He said, the moment, he met Carlos, "I wish I can see Regina before I will leave on Wednesday, but the nuns in her school don't allow visitors on weekdays."

"I will tell her you have been assigned to Zamboanga and that you have to leave, right away. I will help you, get your things ready."

They left work together. They took an early supper in a restaurant in Quiapo before proceeding to Leandro's room. It did not take them long to pack up Leandro's belongings in a new leather suitcase with the Tom Sawyer book, tucked inside.

He had added a few things to what he carried, the first time he came to Manila. He was not a spendthrift; he deposited in a bank most of his pay. He also returned the chair, Carlos gave him.

He saw Don Anastacio after Carlos had left and told him, he is leaving his room. He checked his mailbox on his way back to his room and found there, a letter from Candido. It contained bad news.

Candido wrote, "Father is terminally ill with tuberculosis. He hardly eats now. He is very weak. He spits blood every time he coughs. I am afraid for Mother, too. She may have caught the disease from Father. Do visit us, if you can. It will mean so much to Father. Don Camilo is back in San Isidro in a wheelchair. He had a stroke. He can no longer walk, much less, ride a horse."

He took it to mean from Candido's letter that with Don Camilo, back in his house in San Isidro, Miss Dickinson and the other American teachers were no longer boarding there. Their posts in the town's public school must have been taken over by the Filipino trainee teachers. Miss Dickinson may have returned to the United States.

The letter, held in his hand, he looked out sadly at the tiny garden in the house. What, he asked himself, was happening to the people, he cared for? His uncle was dying, his aunt was also sick while his teacher was gone.

He wrote back to Candido, regretting that he could not visit them in Bangar for he is leaving for Zamboanga in two days. He also enclosed money for his uncle, his aunt and Candido's son Miguel.

Chapter Thirty-five

"Is it from Leandro?" Maria asked Candido when she saw a letter in Candido's hand.

She was tending the fire in the clay stove in their kitchen for a gruel she was cooking for Julian and Tarcila who were now too ill to cook their food.

"It is from Leandro," he replied. He opened the envelope and said, "He sent us money."

"That is so nice of him."

He pulled out a letter there and read it aloud.

"It is too bad, he cannot visit us."

"He was leaving for Zamboanga. At least, the money he sent us will be of great help to Father and Mother."

They turned to someone, calling for Candido from the front yard. He went to the front window in their hut.

"Don Camilo wants to see you," Adiong, Don Camilo's manservant and carriage driver, said to Candido.

He nodded. Their landlord seldom called for his tenants unless it was for something urgent and important.

"Don't keep Don Camilo waiting," Maria said. "Go there now. I will bring the food to Mother and Father."

He left the letter and the envelope with Maria and went right away with Adiong to Don Camilo's house.

"I heard about your father," Don Camilo said to Candido, the moment he was seated in the living room in Don Camilo's house.

"My father is too far gone in his illness. The doctor said it is only a matter of weeks, maybe days."

Don Camilo drew a deep breath, his face clouded with worry. It was bad enough, he had a stroke. He must also avoid catching that dreadful disease that will soon send Julian to his grave.

"I asked you to come here," he said to Candido, "if in the event that your father dies and that, as you told me just now, may happen soon, I want to know if you are willing and able to take over the land, he is tilling for me."

Candido nodded.

"I want a categorical answer."

"Yes, sir, I am willing to take over from my father, the land he is tilling for you when the need arises."

"Do you know what it means?"

"No, sir, I don't."

"It means that, aside from tilling that land, for which you will receive your share of the harvest, you will assume what your father owes me."

Candido stared hard at the floor and said, "If that is what it means, I am sorry, sir, I cannot take over the land, my father is tilling for you."

Don Camilo frowned. He did not expect to be rebuffed and in so direct manner by this tenant. He tried another tactic and said, "You are your father's son. You owe your father, your life itself. This is your chance to repay your father for that."

"Not to the extent, sir, of me, assuming what my father owes you."

Don Camilo bristled. The reply Candido made was such an affront to him, he would have lashed Candido with his whip, if only he had it in his hand.

He kept his temper. A threat to his livelihood might force Candido to change his mind.

"If you will not assume that responsibility,' he said to Candido, "I see no reason why I should keep you as my tenant."

Candido kept his eyes to the floor and said nothing.

"I want this matter settled while your father is still alive. I heard your cousin Leandro has a good job in Manila. You can ask him to help you pay, what your father owes me."

"I cannot ask him to do that. Why don't you ask him, yourself?"

Candido's refusal and disrespect were so glaring it sent Don Camilo in a fit of anger.

He stood up and, his hands pressed to the wheelchair's armrest to support himself, he shouted at Candido, "Why, you impertinent dog! You refused me, first, my offer! Now you are telling me to plead to your cousin to pay me, what your father owes me! Get out of here! I will have you whipped, if I will see you again in this town!"

Candido stood up and left Don Camilo.

Adiong, Agustina and Dona Isabella were in the kitchen when they heard Don Camilo, shouting. They rushed to the living room and found him slumped on his wheelchair.

"Quick, get the medicine!" Dona Isabella shouted at Agustina and Adiong.

She bent over Don Camilo and massaged his chest. Agustina looked on, paralyzed by fear, while Adiong watched, confused, Candido who was going down the staircase and Don Camilo who was slumped on his wheelchair. The sight of Dona Isabella frantically massaging Don Camilo's chest sent him running toward their bedroom. He came back with the medicine and put a tablespoon of it in Don Camilo's mouth. His breathing, after a while, returned to normal.

"Take me to the window," he said to Adiong.

Adiong pushed the wheelchair there while Dona Isabella kept on massaging Don Camilo's chest. He looked up at her and said to her, "I'm all right now. Go back to whatever you were doing in the kitchen."

Dona Isabella returned to the kitchen while Don Camilo was looking out from the window, an old problem with the Sumakas, dredged out of his mind.

The Spanish colonial authorities expropriated the Sumakas and the other natives in San Isidro of their farmlands for some vague public use. Don Cipriano, Don Camilo's great-great-grandfather, obtained a big part of it as a land grant with a huge bribe, he gave the governor-general.

To appease the Sumakas and the other natives who protested the expropriation of their farmlands, Don Cipriano allowed them to keep their small plots of land in their hamlet in Bangar. He had the ownership papers drawn up and handed with flourish to the poor, ignorant natives.

Don Cipriano kept them as his tenants, since they had no other means of livelihood. That gesture did not satisfy the Sumakas and the other tenants. They have been, since then, demanding for the return of their farmlands taken away from them, through deceit and coercion, by the Spanish colonial authorities.

Don Camilo sighed, his eyes turned to his farmlands that extended, far into the horizon. He did not want any trouble with the Sumakas, not that he feared them, for he feared no one, but because the doctor had warned him to avoid any kind of trouble. It is bad for his heart and it will send his blood pressure, soaring.

But now, trouble lay ahead. He knows Candido is an agitator. Much as he wanted to, he could not have him evicted from Bangar and all because of his great-great-grandfather's misplaced magnanimity. He could have Candido dealt with summarily, had they been still under Spain. He could also have him evicted from Bangar or thrown in jail on some trumped-up charge or even secretly dispatched as what he did to Candido's uncle, Leonardo. But now that they are under the Americans, there is this blasted rule of law that he had to follow, like everybody else. He could not deal with Candido, the same way he did with his uncle.

He sighed. Had he kept his temper, he could have avoided that row with Candido. He could, had Candido remained as his tenant, continue to exercise some control over him, but he could not keep his temper as he could not keep his sexual appetite under control. What happened sixteen years ago was then dredged out of his mind.

He was on horseback, one morning and was passing by the church, when he saw there, a wedding party at the churchyard. He knew the man, a tenant of his, but not the bride who was from another town. He was so taken by the bride's beauty and fine, slim body, he resolved to possess her.

The man's wife did the laundry in his house in payment for what his family owed him. The opportunity came one day when his family was invited to a friend's baptismal party in Santa Ignacia. He stayed behind, claiming he had a headache. He sent Agustina on an errand, after Dona Isabella and their children had left, so he could be alone with the woman.

He wasted no time. He attacked her, but she resisted so fiercely and had fled after she had bitten his finger to the bone. He had a tale ready when Dona Isabella and the children returned home.

He told them, he sent the woman away for ruining his clothes. As for the wound in his finger, he said it was caught in the door, which he slammed shut in anger at the woman.

He was, later that day, inspecting with Nicasio, his farm overseer, a piece of land, he owned in a remote part of the town, when the woman's husband came to him and made threats, a fatal mistake on the part of the man. He will never let anyone make threats on him and get away with it. He whipped out his gun and shot the man, dead.

They buried the body secretly, assured with the warning he made of his overseer's silence. They covered up the man's disappearance with a tale they spread around the town that the man had joined an underground movement in Manila, plotting against Spain.

He learned from Nicasio, a few days later, that something terrible had happened to the man's wife. The sudden, mysterious disappearance of her husband and what she had been through were too much for her to bear. She lost her mind that very day. Her tongue from then on was silent except in those few times when she would suddenly break out into fits of laughter and weeping. The woman had lost her mind.

The woman was Milagros and the man was Leonardo, Leandro's parents. Milagros died, a few moments after she gave birth to Leandro.

Their death haunted Don Camilo ever since. He was, as a salve to his conscience, almost benign in his treatment of the Sumakas, not until now, in that row he had with Candido. An agitator, he meant trouble, big trouble. The only way to deal with him, short of murder, which he could no longer do, was to run him out of town.

He found the answer to the question of how he will do it when he saw his son Enrique who was coming in his carriage with his wife Conchita and their young children, Joaquin and Margarita. But for the mustache above his upper lip, Enrique looked just like him. Enrique will be the solution to his problem.

Joaquin and Margarita were all over Don Camilo, laughing and hugging him, the moment they arrived in the living room with their parents. Dona Isabella returned to the living room. The two grandchildren then rushed to her and happily threw their arms around her.

Enrique and his family's visit was always a happy occasion for Don Camilo and Dona Isabella. They will be happier if their two daughters, Marietta and Carmina, were with them, but they were now married and living in Spain.

"You arrived, just as we were preparing lunch," Dona Isabella said to Conchita.

"I will help you," Conchita said.

They left for the dining room with the two children. Enrique sat down on a couch, near his father.

"So, how are things in Santa Ignacia?" Don Camilo asked Enrique. He has not been there since he returned to San Isidro.

"It is the same as when you used to live there," Enrique said. "Like here in San Isidro, there is very little, going on there."

"That is what you think. We are in for a big change with the local elections coming."

The election of local officials was a basic step the Insular Government was taking toward making the Philippines an autonomous and eventually an independent country. It was the first time in the world that a colonial power was doing this voluntarily to its colony. It meant, as a first step, the control of the local government passed on to the Filipinos. Its importance was not lost to Don Camilo.

"I know that," Enrique said. "Should we get involved in it?"

"Of course, we should."

"Why?"

"We can better protect our farmlands, if we control the local government."

"Who are we supporting in the election, here and in Santa Ignacia?"

"We will leave Santa Ignacia alone. It is in good hands. Juan, the son of my friend, Don Nicanor, is running for mayor there. It is San Isidro, I am worried about."

"You have not found any suitable candidate yet?"

"I now have—you."

"Me? I don't even live here."

"You will, starting today."

"But why should I run for the town mayor?"

"So we can control the local government. Who can better do that, than someone in our family?"

Enrique nodded and Don Camilo smiled, pleased and satisfied.

"It is settled then," he said. "You will be the mayor of San Isidro."

He looked out at the rice fields. They will be best protected with Enrique as the town mayor.

He saw a man walking on the road to Bangar. It was Candido on his way home to the hamlet. Don Camilo's eyes narrowed in anger. He will have that impertinent dog chased out of San Isidro, once his son is the town mayor.

Candido was walking home toward Bangar, so distracted by the row he had with Don Camilo, the callused soles of his feet hardly felt the rough surface of the gravel road. His feelings alternated between anger, jubilation and worry. He was angry, Don Camilo had removed him from the land, he was tilling as Don Camilo's tenant, making him a farmer with no land to farm. He was jubilant at his newly found freedom. Don Camilo no longer has any hold on him. But how will he now provide for his family? He knew no trade. He had no skills. Farming was the only thing he knew.

He searched in his mind on how he could now earn a living. He could ask Leandro for his help in getting him a job in Pacific & Gulf, an idea that he dropped right away. Leandro was a mere janitor and messenger there. His recommendation will carry no weight. He could ask the friars who owned an agricultural estate in the town or the other landlords to take him as their tenant. It was an idea, he also dropped. The friars and the other landlords will never, out of their shared interests with Don Camilo, take him as their tenant.

He halted, suddenly seized with panic. He knew no other way, he could earn a living. He looked around, feeling helpless and desperate, when something he saw there, came to his mind. The land around him could be the answer to his problem. The land tenancy problem had caused bitter resentment in every tenant in San Isidro. They were always talking about it. He was the most aggressive and the most articulate among them. They look up to him to lead them in the fight for the return of those lands to them. He will do that by running for the town mayor!

He could then use the power and the resources of the mayor's office against Don Camilo, the friar order and the other landlords. The timing was perfect. They will hold within a few months and for the first time in San Isidro, the election for the town mayor and other local officials. It will not be like during the Spanish time when the provincial governors, with the approval of the governor-general, appointed the local officials. Now that they were under the Americans, anyone could run for public office, like the town mayor.

Mayor Candido Sumaka. His name and the title sounded so nice to him. He was so elated by that thought, he now felt like he was walking on a cloud with his bare, callused feet hardly touching the gravel road.

"How was your meeting with Don Camilo?" Maria asked Candido when he arrived in their hut.

"I'm no longer working for him. He fired me when I refused to assume what Father owes him."

"What! It cannot be true!"

"It is true. I am no longer his tenant," he said, a sour smile on his face.

"You seem to be even happy about it!"

"I am."

"Why should you be when you have just lost our only source of livelihood?"

"I have found another way. Instead of a tenant farmer, I will be the town mayor."

"What!" she shouted, so shocked by what Candido said, she dropped on the dining table, the plate in her hands. It did not fortunately break.

She sat down, shaken, on a bench there.

"Have you lost your mind?" she said as she stared, wide-eyed, at Candido. "You!, running for mayor when we don't even know where we will get our next meal?"

"I know, it sounds crazy, but that is what I am going to do."

"It is crazy! You have got no chance of winning! You will just be laughed out of our town!"

"I have as much right as anyone in our town to run for mayor."

"You may be right about that, but what do you know about running our town?"

"I can learn. I can do as well, even better, than those Spanish mestizo morons who have been running our town. Things are so different now. We have in this election, the first time we will hold it in our town, a chance for a poor man like me to lead and I can lead. I am a born leader! Don't you see how the folks here look up to me to lead them? And that is what I am going to do, by running for the town mayor!"

She nodded and said, "I guess you have got something there, although it still sounds incredible to me. I will have to get used to the idea of you, our town mayor."

"I will, right now, help you with it," he said as he pulled her up from the bench, took her in his arms and kissed her.

He said, now that things were settled between them, "I will tell Father about my plan to run for mayor."

"He will be glad to hear that."

The letter envelope in his hand, Candido went to his parents' hut. He was filled with pity for his father as he was approaching him.

"Don't come, near me," Julian, who was lying on his bamboo bed, said in a weak, raspy voice. "I don't want you to catch this dreadful disease."

He ignored his father's warning and sat down on the bed, near his mother who was seated on a bench at the foot of the bed.

Julian's body, ravaged by tuberculosis, was all skin and bones. His face had a mournful look from sadness and resignation. He was a dying man. He asked Candido, "How was your meeting with Don Camilo?"

"It turned out to be, both good and bad."

"Give me the bad part, first."

"Don Camilo fired me for refusing to assume, what you owe him. I am no longer his tenant. I am free."

"Free, but hungry," Tarcila said. "How will you now, provide for your family?"

"I will get to that, for that is the good part. I have decided to run for the mayor of our town."

Julian gazed uncomprehending at Candido, but then his eyes lit up and he nodded and smiled.

"I like that," he said, his voice now so cheerful. "You can, as the mayor, do a lot for our town and for yourself."

"I can even make a living from that."

"But, can you win?" Tarcila asked Candido.

"I am confident about that, although it may depend on who will be my opponent."

"So, who is your opponent?" she asked Candido.

"I don't know yet, but I will run regardless of who will be my opponent."

"If only Leandro were here, he will be of great help to your campaign for mayor," Julian said to Candido.

"I know. He might send us more money, once he learns I'm running for our town mayor."

"Did he send you money?"

"Yes, Mother. It is in this letter, which I got a while ago in the post office. He said it is for your medical expenses. A small part of it is for Miguel."

He took out most of the money from the envelope and gave it to his father.

The money in his hand, tears clouded Julian's eyes.

"I will be happier," he then said, "if Andro is here and he himself will give me this money."

"Who knows, he may just appear here, one of these days," Candido said.

He did not have the heart to tell his father that Leandro was in faraway Zamboanga and that he may soon die without seeing Leandro, for one last time.

Chapter Thirty-six

Leandro, that very moment was seated on a deck chair in a ship bound for Zamboanga. He was writing on a pad of paper, a letter to Regina.   He had so far written the following:

"Dear Regina,

"I am sorry for leaving you without saying good-bye."

It was a good beginning, but he could not proceed. His pen in his hand, he was poised for quite a while now to continue writing, but was at a loss on what he should write to her.

He looked out, long and hard, at the sea for a word or a phrase that could help him continue writing. His mind remained blank. It was useless to go on. He returned the pen and the pad of paper to his suitcase beside the deck chair and looked out sadly at the sea.

He shook his head in regret at the thought of the nuns in Ascension College who might have allowed him to see Regina, had he gone there and explained himself to them. What he could have done then. He could express himself better, facing her than writing her a letter. What he could not convey with the written word, he could by simply speaking to her.

The more, he thought about that missed opportunity to see her before leaving for Zamboanga, the more he felt bad about it. Brooding over it will not help and he turned to the next thing he could do. He took out the Tom Sawyer book from his suitcase and began to read it. He had been catching up on his reading since the ship left Manila.

Excited voices coming from the ship's bow suddenly broke the silence in the deck. The ship was approaching Zamboanga.

He returned the book to his suitcase and walked toward the ship's bow where he saw, after more than a week at sea, the town of Zamboanga.

He watched, his eyes bright with delight, the town's coastline fringed with palm trees and the blue sea marked by small boats, the wind bellying them forward on their smart, colorful sails.

Zamboanga, as he had imagined how it looked like from what he had read about it in a history book, appeared to him as a town where land and sea meet, a town the lives of whose people are tied to both the land and the sea.

It was once, as he had also read about it, the southern outpost when the Philippines was a Spanish colony. The Spaniards, with the military power they projected from there, controlled Mindanao and the islands of Basilan, Sulu and Tawi-Tawi.

He could see quite clearly, now that the ship was getting closer to the town, the old Spanish fort with its dark stonewall, the town hall with its sloping tile roof, the old church and other buildings in what must be the town center. They were partly hidden by an abundance of palm and other fruit trees. They were the remains of the past Spanish rule in the town.

The American flag, flying in the town fort, showed the Americans were now in charge there and for that matter, in the entire Philippine Islands.

His eyes lingered at a strange-looking village at the eastern side of the town. The homes there seemed to rest on bamboo stilts, several feet above the water. A tower stood at the entrance to the village. Beside it was a building with a strange-looking, onion-shaped dome. He had seen a similar picture in a book in his geography class in San Isidro. He was now seeing for the first time, a real Muslim village.

The coastline, he next watched, was picturesque with the beach there fringed by tall palm trees, their leaves swaying with the wind and carts and horse-drawn rigs moving on the seaside road there.

The new wharf being built by Pacific & Gulf stood directly ahead, not far from the dilapidated wooden wharf no longer in use, the Spaniards built decades earlier.

The ship blew its horn, a signal that it was about to dock at the wharf, half of which was still under construction. He walked toward the port side of the ship that was now moving sideward toward the finished side of the wharf.

The deckhands, right after the ship had docked there, threw down long thick ropes to the waiting dockhands who then tied them around the wharf's iron cleats. Other dockhands were at the same time moving a gangplank toward the side of the ship.

He left the ship and looked around. The first thing he must do there is to report to Joseph Kirkpatrick, the regional manager and superintendent of the wharf project. He asked a dockhand for direction to the field office of Pacific & Gulf.

"It is, right there," the dockhand said at a huddle of one-story wooden buildings near the entrance to the wharf.

He saw, when he entered the field office, Filipinos at work on their desks. Kirkpatrick, the only American there, was looking out at the sea from a window behind his desk.

He introduced himself as he was approaching Kirkpatrick.

"So, you are Leandro Sumaka," Kirkpatrick said. "I have been expecting you. How was your trip?"

"I had a fine trip, sir."

Kirkpatrick then said he will work under Marquez, the warehouse custodian, and that he will also help out in the construction of the wharf.

"As you must have seen from the ship," Kirkpatrick continued, "so much remains to be done at the wharf. Only one-half of it is finished. Your ship just the same had to dock there. It is not safe to dock at the wharf, the Spaniards built, long ago. Do you have any questions?"

"I have none, sir."

Kirkpatrick then called out to Saniel, a stout, middle-aged man, who was removing some files in a steel filing cabinet, to come to his desk.

"This is Leandro Sumaka," Kirkpatrick said to Saniel. "He is assigned here from our Manila office. Take him to the barracks and to Marquez. Then show him the work we are doing at the wharf."

Leandro left, proud and happy, with Saniel. He is no longer known as a provincial boy from the town of San Isidro, but as someone from the main office in Manila.

Saniel took Leandro first to the company barracks, near the field office.

"You can take any of the unoccupied bunks," Saniel said as they were walking in an aisle between two rows of double-deckers.

Leandro took a bed there. Then he removed and put in a locker there, the contents of his suitcase, which he then put underneath the bed.

They moved on to the warehouse and passed by workers stacking up the construction materials and supplies that have just been taken from the ship.

Saniel introduced Leandro to Marquez, the warehouse custodian.

"So," Marquez said to Leandro, "you are the young man from our Manila office. Mister Kirkpatrick has told me about you."

Leandro smiled, the second time, he was known as from Manila.

"The boss told me to show the wharf to this young man," Saniel said to Marquez.

"Very well, you will start working here tomorrow," Marquez said to Leandro. "Take it easy now and enjoy the sights in this beautiful town."

"It is, sir," Leandro said, "even if I have seen only a small part of it from the ship."

He proceeded to the wharf with Saniel. The dockhands there were loading into waiting carts, the rest of the cargo the ship's crane had brought down into the wharf from the ship's hold. The crane, after it was loaded with cargo from a stack of cargoes in the wharf, was then swung upward into the ship's hold. Passengers bound for other ports were watching from the ship's deck, the port dockhands and the ship deckhands at work.

Leandro was beside himself with excitement as he was walking on with Saniel in the finished part of the wharf. He will now be doing construction work in Zamboanga, no longer the kind of work he did before in Parola of doing errands and keeping the administrative building and the ground there, clean and tidy.

They walked on toward the edge of the finished part of the wharf. A row of dark, creosote-treated poles stood there, about ten feet above the sea level.

Saniel explained the work being done there. Leandro listened to Saniel, at the same that he was watching the workers engaged in various tasks there. Some of them were hammering wooden beams on the wooden poles. Other workers were applying additional coat of creosote on the wooden planks, placed above the wooden beams.

Lording over the work there was the operator of a steam-driven pile hammer, pounding a long pole, deep down into the sea floor.

The sea waves crashing against the wooden poles next claimed his attention. He was looking down, fascinated by their rhythmic advance and retreat at the wooden poles, when he suddenly felt dizzy, at the same time that he was feeling a tingling sensation in the soles of his feet.

He had an attack of vertigo. He shook off the feeling so casually, Saniel noticed nothing to alarm him. He thought it prudent, though, to step back from the edge of the wharf. Another dizzy spell might send him falling down into the sea.

A worker was coming in a carabao-drawn cart, loaded with planks of wood.

He was, the following day, doing the same kind of work in providing the construction crew there with the materials they needed in working on the wharf. He was also doing odd jobs in the wharf, whenever he was not too busy in the warehouse.

His complexion, after just a few days there, which had become a shade lighter in Manila, had become darkly hued again from long exposure to the sun in Zamboanga.

He attended the Mass, held in the town church, the Sunday of his arrival in Zamboanga. It was his day off from work and rather than spend his free time in idleness in the company compound, he decided to walk around in the town and see what it was like.

He was pleasantly surprised to find it, though bigger and livelier, similar to San Isidro in some respects. Its church was as old and as big as the church in San Isidro, but its town hall was much bigger and it had more Spanish-type homes that stood grandly along the town's tree-shaded streets.

It took him a while before he noticed something distinctive about the town. It was the sight and the smell of flowers. Zamboanga was a town of flowers. It had such an abundance of flowering plants in the sidewalks and in the gardens of the homes there. He had never seen anything like the orchids in Zamboanga, never in San Isidro, a few times in Manila.

Zamboanga, as he had seen it from the ship, was much bigger than San Isidro. He was therefore not surprised to find the market which he next visited, much bigger and livelier than the market in San Isidro.

He was drawn, in particular, to the fish section, where vendors were selling fish, caught fresh from the sea by fishhook or by fishing net. They were laid out in the stall counters or were thrashing about in large iron basins. He watched, fascinated, varieties of fish like the tuna and the swordfish and strange-looking sea creatures like the manta rays, the octopus, the squids and the turtles.

He saw, as he was walking around in the town market and in the streets, that Zamboanga had a more diverse mix of people than San Isidro.

A few of them looked like the Spanish mestizos in his hometown. The Chinese were standing behind the counters in their stores. A few American soldiers were taking in the sea breeze.

While most of the men there were dressed like him, some of them were garbed in colorful jackets. The women were wearing even more colorful clothing with intricate designs, their necks, wrists and ankles adorned with beads and trinkets.

Many of the men were wearing headdresses, most of which were nothing more than white cloth wound around the top of their heads.

They were short, rendered dark brown by the sun and the sea, their teeth blackened by betel nut, they were chewing with gusto. While they had similar facial features and were brown-skinned like him, they were different in the local dialect they spoke, in their mode of dressing and in other ways he could not yet define. They were the Muslims, he had read about in a school book in San Isidro.

The ship had docked in the wharf, a few days ago, when he saw in the village, in the eastern side of the town, the tower standing near a building with its unusual onion-shaped dome. It was not too far from the town and he decided to walk to the village for a close look there.

A man in a white headdress appeared at a window in the tower as he was approaching it. He halted and watched the man as he then cupped his hands close to his mouth and made what sounded to him was like a call to prayer.

He watched, fascinated, when, a man walking in the village road suddenly halted, knelt down and bowed his head, close to the ground. The man then uttered something that sounded to him was like a prayer in monotone, at the same that he was tapping his chest and forehead repeatedly.

He felt, while he was looking at the man on the ground and listening to the man in the tower, as if he had set foot in another country.

The following week was a busy time for Leandro with various tasks at the warehouse or at the wharf and in doing whatever Kirkpatrick had assigned him to do there.

He got along with everyone, particularly with Saniel, who was a local hire. Saniel invited him one day to his home.

"It is my wife's birthday, this coming Sunday," Saniel said to him. "I'm inviting you to a little celebration, we are having at home."

He agreed readily to Saniel's invitation. He had no social life there and he welcomed this chance to meet people.

He proceeded that Sunday, after attending Mass in the town church, to Saniel's house, not far from the church. He met there Saniel's family and friends and had a great time with them and his fellow workers in Pacific & Gulf who were also invited to the party.

The birthday party for Saniel's wife also yielded for him a pleasant surprise. He learned from Saniel that he was an avid fishing enthusiast and that he was only too glad to teach him, a thing or two about sailing and deep-sea fishing.

He loved fishing. It was his pastime and it helped in putting food on their dining table in Bangar.

He learned, in no time at all, through Saniel's expert instruction, how to ride a boat with the use of a sail or a paddle and how to catch fish, like the yellowfin tuna and the swordfish.

He went, from then on, deep-sea fishing on his days off from work with Saniel or by himself. Saniel allowed him to use his fishing boat.

Fishing in the sea in Zamboanga was, he found out, much more thrilling, challenging and rewarding than fishing in his tiny pond in Bangar. The fish in Zamboanga were much bigger and more varied. The swordfish gave a stiff fight before he could land them in the boat. A few of them broke his fishing line and got away.

He was, one time, fishing by himself and all that he had caught after hours of it was a foot-long mackerel, a midget of a fish compared to what he had caught there before.

"That is it, it is not my day," he said to himself.

He still has bait left, though. It will be such a waste to throw it away and he decided to keep on fishing. He put fresh bait into the fishhook, a fish bigger than his palm, and cast it into the sea. The line became tight in just a short while.

He could tell by the feel of his fingers on the line that he had caught a big fish. It swam away when he tried to pull it in. He fought with the fish for what seemed to him was like a long time that hurt his hands and made his arm and back, stiff and aching.

The fish suddenly shot out of the sea. He watched it, delighted, before it dropped back into the sea. He had caught a giant yellowfin tuna. It was, by his estimate, if set upright on its tail, taller than him.

It gave up the fight after a long time of struggle with him.

It was so big and heavy, when when he hauled it into the boat, it nearly tilted that side of the boat into the sea

He had an even bigger scare, once he had the fish in the boat. It was so heavy it lowered the boat so much, leaving it with a clearance of only a few inches above the water.

The sea was, fortunately for him, so calm that day, the wind barely disturbing the sea. Had it been just a bit rough, a wave just a foot high might have then swamped the boat with water and sank it.

He paddled the boat toward the sandy shore. His fellow workers gaped at the fish when he brought it to the company kitchen with the help of a teenage boy.

Word about his huge catch spread fast in the wharf and in the company compound. It was seldom that a fish that big was caught in Zamboanga. He became there an instant celebrity.

He gave Kirkpatrick, Saniel, Marquez and the teenage boy, big parts of the fish. Celestino, the company cook, made several dishes out of it. The biggest part of it was cut into small pieces and broiled in hot coals in an impromptu feast the company workers held that night on the beach where for the first time in his life, he was induced to drink locally distilled firewater.

He was in Zamboanga by just a few weeks when he learned in a letter from Candido about the death of his uncle Julian. Candido wrote that his father died happy knowing he was running for mayor of San Isidro and that his opponent was Don Camilo's son, Enrique. As Candido wrote, "Father said to me, a few days before he died, 'Beat him, for my sake.' "

The letter in his hand, he reflected sadly on his uncle's unrewarded life of endless toil. His uncle fell ill when he could not take it anymore. He should have seen the sign long before, the day he left San Isidro. He was hugging his uncle before boarding the train when he felt his uncle's chest heaving as if he was trying to catch his breath. He had thought then that his uncle's heart was heavy with sadness over his departure for Manila.

He now knows that it was the disease brought about by poor nourishment and endless toil and not his departure for Manila that accounted for his uncle's labored breathing. He failed to see it as a sign that his uncle was wasting away from tuberculosis.

He sighed. They will all go on their appointed time. This was a lesson, his uncle had taught him about life.

He went back to his bunk and put Candido's letter inside his locker. It was the last connection between him and his uncle. His uncle's generation was passing away. It was now the turn of his generation. It should do better. His elders did no better nor worse than those who came before them in what mattered most to them: the land tenancy problem which had remained unresolved. But now something will be done about it in San Isidro should Candido win in the coming election. His uncle died happy knowing that his son might succeed where his generation had failed. His uncle must have been also happy that he, who was like his own son, was moving up in Pacific & Gulf with his new job of general assistant.

He smiled. So, Candido's opponent will be none other than Don Camilo's son, Enrique. The mighty Monte Arazteas must now be trying to win the support of the townsfolk, they had so abused and exploited.

How he wished, he is back in San Isidro so he could help Candido and see for himself how he will beat Enrique. He wrote back expressing grief over his uncle's death and confidence in Candido's poll victory. He also enclosed money for Candido's campaign for mayor of San Isidro.

Chapter Thirty-seven

Dick McCall read, his chin rested on his palm, what he had written on the newsprint, he had rolled out from his typewriter. The article was about the election for mayor in San Isidro. He stopped writing it when he could not find the right word to go on and finish a sentence in the article. Forcing himself will not do.

What he needed was a slight diversion and he turned his gaze through the glass panel in his office to the editorial room of *The Philippines Newsmagazine.* His two young editorial assistants were at work. One was typing a feature article while the other one was proofreading a galley proof. His layout artist was drawing the editorial cartoon for their special issue on the election of local officials in the colony.

The slight diversion helped him in finding the word he was looking for. He rolled the newsprint back into the typewriter and completed the sentence. He continued typing until he had finished writing the article.

He was using San Isidro as an example of how well or poorly the Filipinos had learned and applied basic democracy in the local elections.   He read the article:

"The townsfolk in San Isidro, a town in Central Plain, had for the first time in their town's history, a say on who will govern them for a period of four years. Enrique Monte Araztea promised better roads, additional classrooms in the town's public school, a bigger market. Candido Sumaka campaigned on a platform of social and economic change with land reform as its centerpiece. The election was clean, honest and peaceful. Candido Sumaka lost to Enrique Monte Araztea.

"The result in the election in San Isidro was decided on the basis of a unique Filipino social disease called colonial mentality. It afflicted the townsfolk, like the rest of the colony. It influenced their choice of town mayor. Enrique Monte Araztea is the only son in a wealthy Spanish mestizo family of landowners. Educated in Spain, he belongs to the best society in the colony. His opponent, Candido Sumaka, is a poor native peasant until lately a tenant of the Monte Arazteas. His highest educational attainment is an informal study of the three R's—reading, writing and arithmetic.

"Candido Sumaka could have won the election had he enjoyed the support of the peasants. They make up the overwhelming majority of the voters in the town. A peasant himself, Sumaka could best represent the interests of this lowly, exploited class of people. His fellow peasants did not see it that way, though.

"He is one of them and like them, he is poor and uneducated, not someone they could look up to. They want in their mayor, the qualities they idealize and aspire for in life: wealth, power, education, social distinction, a foreign or Spanish name, a tall nose and a fair complexion. Enrique Monte Araztea had all those qualities, so they voted for him and not for Candido Sumaka.

"The Filipinos, in this local election, were given the right and the power to choose their local leaders, a right denied them in more than three centuries they were under Spain.

"This is only a small part of the many great changes being brought about in the Philippine Islands by the United States. It ranges from the establishment of a democratic, republican form of government to free universal elementary and secondary education, to public works, health and sanitation and a booming free enterprise economy.

"The economy is one area where the natives, who make up the overwhelming majority of the population, continue to play a very limited role. Local commerce is in the hands of the Chinese merchants while British and American trading firms control international trade. Banking and finance are in the hands of the Americans, the Catholic Church and the Spanish and Chinese mestizo families. The friar orders and the landowners control agriculture. American entrepreneurs are dominant in construction and industry, the two most promising sectors in the colony's economy.

"And where does the native Filipino fit there? He shares only by his sweat and brawn. He is a factory and construction worker, domestic help, clerk, janitor or messenger in the city and a tenant farmer in the countryside. He was and is and will likely remain as the colony's servant class.

"One area where the Filipino peasants, by their great numbers, could be dominant is in politics and local government. But they must first overcome this colonial mentality where someone with a fair complexion and a Spanish or foreign-sounding name is automatically favored over one who has none of those qualities. They must support each other. Had they done that in San Isidro, the winner would have been the native peasant candidate, the poor, brown-hued Candido Sumaka, and not the wealthy landowning Spanish mestizo candidate, Enrique Monte Araztea."

It seemed to Dick that three paragraphs of what he wrote, did not fit with the theme of the article. He weighed in his mind on whether he should retain them or cut them out for future use in another article. They could also be taken as an expansion, an elaboration of the theme of the article. He decided to keep them. He called the copy boy and gave him the manuscript for typesetting in the printing room.

While everything that Dick McCall wrote about the election in San Isidro was correct, he failed to see two other factors that bore on its outcome. These were fraud and bribery. He failed to see them, for they were kept hidden from the prying eyes of visiting American journalists like him. He never knew, much less see, bribe money passed on to the voters. Neither did he see, cheating in the counting of the votes.

This was the work of Don Camilo's manipulative mind. He was insuring his son's victory in the election by bribing the voters to vote for Enrique and the poll clerks into counting the ballots in favor of Enrique.

As he said to Enrique, "If your great-great grandfather could bribe his way into getting so much of the lands in this town, so can we, in our drive to make you the mayor of this town."

Enrique's campaigners knocked on doors, concluding each visit with an envelope with money and carbon and plain paper inside thrust into the hands of the head of the household.

The bribed voter, on the day of the election, slipped the carbon and plain paper underneath the ballot, making an exact copy of what was written there, proof of a vote for Enrique. The carbon and plain paper were then returned discreetly to Enrique's campaigners waiting outside the polling place.

Those who accepted the bribe money did so from need, from a cynical regard for the electoral process and for getting something, even just a peso, out of the election. Unlike most of the townsfolk, Candido's relatives and neighbors in Bangar and in a few other hamlets flatly rejected Don Camilo's bribe offer, out of their hatred of the Monte Arazteas.

Candido was furious, but could do nothing about the fraud and the bribery. He was supported by poor people like him. He could not match Enrique, peso for peso. And even if he had the money, he would not use it to cheat and bribe voters. He had decided long before that if he will win, it will be because the townsfolk wanted him as their mayor and not because he bribed, coerced and cheated his way to the mayor's office.

While Candido practically shouted himself hoarse about his goals for the town, Don Camilo made money, talk for Enrique. "A peso for a vote for Enrique" was the catch-phrase passed around the town in whispers during the campaign. It spoke quietly, but effectively in Enrique's poll victory over Candido.

Don Camilo took one more measure in insuring Enrique's poll victory. He had the poll workers also bribed, so that they counted most of the votes in favor of Enrique. To avoid the suspicion that the election was rigged, Don Camilo ordered the bribed poll workers to allow Candido, a few votes, here and there.

The townsfolk knew about those poll irregularities, but faced with the threat of reprisal from the Monte Arazteas, they kept what they knew to themselves. Those poll irregularities were not noticed by the authorities in Manila. They did not have the manpower to monitor the election in every town, much less in every precinct where the poll irregularities were committed. The local officials and the teachers who managed the election succumbed, like the townsfolk, to coercion and corruption.

Dick McCall was, however, so impressed by what he saw was a clean, peaceful, honest and orderly election in San Isidro, he wrote in his newsmagazine, "This is one example of the Filipinos' capacity for self-rule." It was a comment, he regretted later on.

The election also spurred the independence movement in the colony. It was henceforth an important issue in every election there.

Dick's view on the role played by race, social standing, wealth and the voters' colonial mentality was evident, both in the local and national politics.

The newly established Philippine Assembly, the Philippine counterpart of the United States Congress, was dominated by two young politicians who were classmates in college.

Manuel Quezon was a Spanish mestizo from the province of Tayabas, whose mother was the daughter of a Spanish friar. Sergio Osmena, who was of Chinese descent, was from the province of Cebu.

Candido wrote to Leandro that he lost in the election, not because the townsfolk favored Enrique over him, but because they were bribed or coerced to vote for Enrique. He also mentioned cheating in the polls where the poll workers counted most of the ballots in favor of Enrique. The local poll officials ignored his protests about those poll irregularities.

The first time they held an election in San Isidro, Leandro noted sourly, it was marred by fraud, coercion and vote-buying. Nothing had changed there. The landlords, led by the Monte Arazteas, remained entrenched in San Isidro. The situation of the tenant farmers was desperate as ever. His cousin was worse off. Not only did he lose the piece of land he was tilling for the Monte Arazteas, he also lost in his bid for mayor of San Isidro.

Fortunately for Candido, an American businessman visiting the town was so impressed by the way he ran his campaign, he offered him a job in case he will lose in the election. The American was with a group of American businessmen who had put up a sugar mill in Santa Ignacia.

Candido accepted the job of timekeeper.

"It may not be in the same class as the town mayor, but the job means my family will not go hungry," Candido wrote. Leandro smiled. His cousin lost in the election, but not his sense of humor.

Candido reported for work in the sugar mill in Santa Ignacia, the very day, Enrique took his oath as the town mayor. He thus avoided the humiliation of being around in Enrique's assumption into office and the feast that followed in Don Camilo's house.

Don Camilo was not happy as he expected to be. He was seated on his wheelchair, a grave look on his face. He had failed to anticipate one outcome of the election. Candido lost in the election, but his candidacy had made him too much of a public figure to be hounded and persecuted.

How he wished he could do away with him, the way he did with Leonardo, Candido's uncle, but that was before, when they were under Spain. Things were now so different under the Americans.

His mind dwelling on those dark thoughts, Don Camilo cut an odd figure, an ailing old man imprisoned in his wheelchair, frowning while everybody else in the Monte Araztea house and its wide grounds was having a grand time at Enrique's poll victory.

Chapter Thirty-eight

Kirkpatrick wired Manila, while the construction of the wharf in Zamboanga was going on, to send a geodetic engineer who will check out the feeder wharves in the islands of Basilan, Jolo and Tawi-Tawi.

James Lehigh arrived there, more than a week later.

Leandro was by now so good at sailing, Kirkpatrick assigned him to man the boat for Lehigh's survey work in those islands.

They first went to Isabela, the largest town in Basilan, the island nearest to Zamboanga.

They scanned its coastline as they were approaching the town. Its tiny feeder wharf, the Spaniards built long ago, looked so broken down it might not be safe for them to dock there. Lehigh told Leandro to steer the boat toward the beach where soldiers were coming to meet them.

They jumped into the water and pushed the boat into the beach. One of the soldiers identified himself as Captain Campbell, the station commander in Basilan. Lehigh introduced himself and Leandro. He told Captain Campbell, the purpose of their visit there. Captain Campbell said he had been informed beforehand about the inspection that will be made on the feeder wharf.

He asked Lehigh, "Would you like to take a rest first in my camp or go straight to work?"

Lehigh replied he would like to take a look, right away, at the feeder wharf.

Captain Campbell said on their way there that he and his men had tried to fix it. Lehigh nodded, but said nothing. He halted when he and the others were about to step into the feeder wharf. He shook his head as he was looking closely at its wooden planks and railings. No amount of repair work could fix it. It had been, so eaten away by the elements that merely stepping on it posed a risk to life and limb. It must be demolished and replaced by another wharf. It could be built, right there or in another location.

"We will survey the area," Lehigh said to Captain Campbell.

"All right, if that is what needs to be done," Captain Campbell said.

He watched Lehigh and Leandro who went back to their boat.

Leandro, following Lehigh's direction, steered the boat, back and forth, while Lehigh took notes with the measurements he made with a line and other equipment of the current and depth of the water in the area at both sides of the wharf. He also measured the shore with an engineer's chain.

Lehigh decided, following his visual survey and the measurements he made, that a cove some two hundred feet away from the feeder wharf and where the water was calm, will be a good location for a new feeder wharf.

Kirkpatrick then sent men and construction materials for the new feeder wharf in Basilan. They finished its construction in one week instead of the expected two weeks.

Lehigh and Leandro then visited, on Leandro's suggestion, the island's interior. Captain Campbell assigned two soldiers to escort them. They found the island's inhabitants called Yakans, friendly. Unlike the seafaring Badjaos and Samals in Zamboanga, the Yakans were farmers. Leandro left the island, more aware of Zamboanga's varied culture.

They next went, farther south to Jolo, the principal island in the chain of islands in Sulu Sea. They reported on their arrival in the capital town of Jolo to Captain Hayes, the station commander there, and went straight to work. They inspected the feeder wharf there and found it in good condition. It needed only minor repair work. Then they surveyed the town's coastline.

They worked, watched closely by the American soldiers, for Jolo was not yet a completely pacified place. Captain Hayes warned Lehigh and Leandro that Jolo was infested with Muslim suicide killers called *Huramentados* who attacked people without warning or provocation.

"So, am I supposed to cringe in fear of them?" Lehigh replied to Captain Hayes' warning.

Leandro smiled, amused. Lehigh was not concerned, much less worried, about the Huramentados there. He learned, in the course of their work, a few things about the tall and muscular Lehigh.

He was a former soldier who fought the Apaches in Texas and New Mexico. Lehigh feared no man, not the Indians in the American Southwest and not the short Filipinos in the Philippines. He considered them falling short in many ways, his condescension, he often expressed with a popular song of the day often on his lips, and to which Leandro listened in annoyed silence, about the monkeys in Zamboanga having no tails.

Where Lehigh was condescending to the Filipinos, he was friendly to Leandro. It was a kind of friendliness, though, that Leandro knew, he deserved. Lehigh treated him with respect for the efficient way, he worked with him. He noticed, pleased and amused, how Lehigh watched him, impressed with the expert way he sailed their boat in the open sea. Lehigh's racial prejudice aside, they made a good team.

He saw also that Lehigh was not interested in the island's inhabitants, but in what he could do there. He was interested, in particular, in what the soldiers, watching over them, had told them about Panakol, a fishing village at the other side in the island of Jolo. It might be a suitable location for another feeder wharf in the island.

Lehigh decided to survey the fishing village. He told Captain Hayes, after they had finished their work in the capital town of Jolo, about his plan to survey Panakol. He asked for a security escort. Captain Hayes turned him down.

"I cannot allow you to go there. It is a dangerous place," Captain Hayes said to Lehigh. "It is infested with the Huramentados."

"I fought the Apaches in Texas and in New Mexico. They are much tougher than those Huramentados."

"That may be so, but that does not make those Huramentados, less dangerous than they are."

Lehigh was exasperated and he said, "Look, captain, I will not let those crazies stop me from doing my job."

"I don't want you to be harmed by those Huramentados while you are under my jurisdiction."

"Will they harm me for doing something good for them?"

"They will."

His face grave with worry, Leandro watched Lehigh and Captain Hayes locked in argument.

"This is not getting us anywhere," Lehigh finally said. "Leandro and I are going there with or without your security escort."

Leandro gasped at how rash, Lehigh was. It will be suicidal for them to go to Panakol, unarmed and without a security escort.

The argument with Lehigh had worn out Captain Hayes and he said, "I will provide you with a security escort, if you are really bent on going there. It is faster, if you wll go overland and be careful."

"Thank you, Captain," Lehigh said. "Rest, assured, we will be careful."

Leandro sighed in relief.

They set out for Panakol with four soldier escorts in two horse-drawn rigs, driven by native orderlies. They arrived on market day in the fishing village. An open space there was converted into a market. Ringed by stalls and lean-tos, it was noisy with shoppers milling around, inspecting or haggling with the vendors, the seafood, poultry, fruits, rice, pearl and coral products, clothing and other products being sold there.

They were passing by a side in the market when Lehigh told the driver to stop, right there.

"Why did we stop here?" Leandro asked Lehigh.

Lehigh replied, his eyes fixed to a lean-to there, "I have found what I have been looking for, a nice present for my wife when I return to Manila."

He alighted from the rig. Leandro and two of their soldier escorts followed him. The two other soldiers stayed in the other rig and watched them.

Lehigh went to the lean-to where pearl and black coral earrings, bracelets and necklaces were spread out on a mat. He picked up a necklace with three pearl pendants and looked at it admiringly.

"It is a beauty," he said. "My wife will love it."

"Let me haggle with the vendor," Leandro said. "I have picked up a little of their local dialect."

Lehigh and the two soldiers watched Leandro as he then went into a lively haggling with the woman vendor.

She was considering his final offer when she suddenly turned her eyes, wide in alarm, to what she saw behind Leandro, Lehigh and the two soldiers.

They turned to where the vendor was looking at. The crowd there had parted for four men, wielding wavy-bladed swords called *Kris*. They were the Huramentados, Captain Hayes had warned them about.

They yelled and ran toward Lehigh, the two soldiers and Leandro, who had turned rigid from fear and shock.

One of the two soldiers fired a warning shot above the heads of the Huramentados. It did not stop them. The other soldier fired at and hit in the arm, the Huramentado running ahead of the other three Huramentados. It did not stop him as he rushed toward them, directly toward Leandro.

The Huramentado was about to strike Leandro in the head when the soldier felled him with a shot at his chest. The three other Huramentados withdrew quickly and disappeared in the crowd.

They stirred up the crowd which had now turned menacing. They began to move toward Leandro, Lehigh and the two soldiers.

The two other soldiers in the rig stopped the crowd with warning shots, they fired above their heads.

"Don't show fear," Lehigh said to Leandro as they walked back to the rig.

They left the market with the soldiers, ready to fire at the crowd.

Leandro sigh in relief at their narrow escape from death, once they were far enough from the village.

Lehigh noticed, he was still holding the pearl necklace.

"I don't think, I should keep this," he said and he threw it away.

They arrived in the military station in Jolo at dusk. Lehigh and Leandro sailed back to Zamboanga, the following day. They told Kirkpatrick, the moment they arrived there, about the incident in Panakol.

"You cannot stay here," Kirkpatrick said to them. "If I know those people, they will try to get even with you. You are taking, James, the first ship leaving for Manila. As for you, Leandro, you are going to Davao. That is far enough from them."

"I hate to leave Zamboanga. I like working here," Leandro said.

"It is not safe for you to stay here," Kirkpatrick said.

"I can't understand why they attacked us, and why me in particular."

"They saw you as an enemy."

"Why did they see me as an enemy when I look like them?"

"You may look like them, but you were with the American soldiers, they consider as their enemies. That made you their enemy as well."

The word spread around about Leandro and Lehigh's hair-raising encounter with the Huramentados in Jolo, Lehigh's return to Manila and Leandro's assignment to Davao. Saniel organized a farewell party for Lehigh and Leandro who left Zamboanga, the following day.

Chapter Thirty-nine

Leandro and the ship's purser watched from the deck, the town of Davao shrouded with mist and rain as the ship was approaching the wharf there. It was, like the wharf in Zamboanga, also under construction..

Davao seemed dreamlike to Leandro, what with all that mist and rain all over the town and with the plain and the forest there blurry as well with mist and rain. It looked like an impressionist landscape painting, he had seen in an art book in the library in San Isidro's public.school.

"What is it like?" he asked the purser with whom he became acquainted during the ship's three-day voyage from Zamboanga.

"It is a pioneering town. It is just starting out. You will see that later on in its muddy, unpaved roads, the homes and the buildings there that look as if they were built only last week."

So, it will not be like Zamboanga, Leandro thought of the old town with a storied past.

The purser then said, "While you will not, right now, see much of that place with all that mist and rain, everything there is big, in the plain and in the mountains, in the sea abundant with fish, and in the trees in the forest, so big and so straight they shoot up into the sky. The soil there is so rich, thrust a stick into the ground and you will see within a week, branches, leaves and even fruits and flowers appearing there."

"Is it really like that?" Leandro said to the purser's exaggerated description of the town.

"You will soon find that out."

"You seem to like this town."

"I do. I grew up there."

The ship then docked at the wharf. The dockhands there placed immediately a gangplank to the side of the ship. Leandro said good-bye to the purser and walked down on the gangplank, his suitcase in his hand and a field hat and rain gear shielding him from the rain.

His impression of the town as dreamlike and its gushy description by the purser were out of his mind, the moment he had stepped down into the wharf's solid planks of wood. His immediate concern was in finding the field office of Pacific & Gulf. He asked a dockhand about it.   "It is, right there," the dockhand replied at a huddle of one-story wooden buildings near the entrance to the wharf.

He reported to Teddy Williams, the Davao area superintendent, in his office and handed to him, a note from Kirkpatrick.

"So, you had a close brush with the Huramentados in Jolo," Williams said after he had read the note.

"It was a close call, sir. A good thing the soldiers with me were quick on the trigger. They felled one who was about to strike me in the head with his sword."

"You must live a charmed life. Well, while we may not have that kind of excitement here, we do just as much work here, if not more. We are constructing, aside from the wharf, a school building, government offices and a road that will go deep into the interior. It will open up vast areas for agriculture. We have just finished building a new market."

Williams then said to Leandro, "You will do the same kind of work you did in Zamboanga as supply assistant of Rogaciano, the warehouse custodian.

"You will also do the marketing for Reynes. He runs the mess hall and the commissary."

Leandro asked himself, how he will do the marketing when he did not even know where the town market was located.

"The man handling the marketing there has been assigned to Cebu only last week, so they are short there in personnel," Williams said. "As for the market, this is a small town and it is easy to find. Since you are new here and do not know yet, your way around here, don't hesitate to ask for help."

He then told a clerk there to take Leandro to the barracks and to Rogaciano and Reynes.

They first went to the barracks where Leandro took the lower bunk in the middle of two rows of double-deckers. Then he removed and put in a locker there, the contents of his suitcase, which he then put underneath the bed.

He asked the clerk to take him next to the section of the wharf under construction. Leandro was introduced to the workers there. He was not surprised to find the wharf there of the same size and design as the wharf in Zamboanga.

A master plan and design had been drawn up in the main office in Manila for the wharves it was constructing in important port towns in the Philippines. It meant big savings for the company in time and money.

The clerk then brought Leandro to Rogaciano who showed him around the warehouse. They went afterwards to the mess hall which had several rows of tables and benches. The workers took their meals there.

They next went to the kitchen where Leandro was introduced to Reynes, who was preparing their supper with a girl helper beside him.

"You came at the right time," Reynes said to Leandro. "We have a labor shortage here."

He introduced Sophia, the girl working with him. She was mixing with a dipper in a large cast-iron pot, pork and vegetables into a fat-rich delicious stew.

"That is Marina over there in our commissary," Reynes said, his chin thrust out toward the girl, at the other side of the mess hall. She was wiping with a piece of cloth, the glass counter in front of her.

They are pretty, Leandro noticed. Marina and Sophia were wearing colorful dresses that, along with the beads and trinkets adorning them, showed him they must be from the local ethnic community.

Reynes saw him looking intently at the large-sized kitchen equipment.

"Everything here in the kitchen is large-sized," Reynes said. "We are feeding here, some sixty workers."

He was sauteing in a large pan, diced pork, garlic, onions and vegetables. The mixture in a short while had browned enough. He then poured the pan's contents into a large pot of boiling water, turning it into a delicious soup.

Reynes was whistling a tune as he then took out a bowl from a cabinet and put a spoon there. Then he poured with a dipper, the soup into the bowl and gave it to Leandro.

"Try it for its taste," he said to Leandro.

He took several scoops with the spoon and nodded approvingly.

"It is delicious," he said. "Adding pepper and fish sauce might make it even tastier."

Reynes nodded. He scooped with the dipper, soup from the pot and blew on it. Then he slurped the soup, once it had cooled enough.

"You are right," he said. "It needs a little more pepper and fish sauce."

He dropped a dash of pepper and several spoonfuls of fish sauce into the pot and stirred it with a basting spoon.

Leandro in the meantime had finished with his soup. He thanked Reynes and washed the bowl and the spoon in the kitchen sink. Then he wiped the utensils dry with a towel and returned them to the cabinet.

He looked again at the pretty girl in the commissary and said to Reynes, "Mister Williams told me that I will be doing the marketing. Perhaps Marina can give me, a few pointers on how to go about it."

"Go ahead," Reynes said.

Leandro walked toward Marina and introduced himself. Up close, she looked much prettier. She had large, bright eyes and an olive skin; her lips were shaped like a sea wave, her nose was narrow and straight, her deep-black hair, flowing down to her shoulders.

She cleared her throat. Only then did he realize, he had been staring at her. He said quickly to her that he had just arrived from Zamboanga and that he was assigned there in the mess hall and in the warehouse, that he will do the marketing and that he will appreciate it very much if she could fill him in on the work they were doing there.

She smiled at his detailed overture and she was soon also talking about herself and her work in the commissary and the mess hall, and that she and Sophia were cousins, that they were Manobos who had converted to Christianity, that they live in a village near the town and that most of the items in the kitchen and the commissary were purchased in the town market and in the general store of Yupang, a Chinese merchant.

He told her then that, being new in the town, he did not know yet, his way around there. He asked her if she could help him with the marketing. She replied, she would be glad to be of help to him.

They set out to do the marketing, the following morning in a hired carabao-drawn cart, driven by a hired teenage boy. Leandro's pocket was full of money, he received earlier from the company cashier. Marina had with her, a list of the items, she and Reynes needed for the kitchen and the commissary.

They first went to Yupang's store. He and Marina knew each other and they greeted each other casually. The Chinese storeowner, portly and animated, nodded and looked slyly at Leandro when she introduced him as the new purchasing agent of Pacific & Gulf.

She gave Yupang, the list of the items, she needed: several cartons of cigarettes, boxes of cigars, matches, gallons of cooking oil in tin cans, dried fish, sacks of rice and beans, coffee, sugar, salt, chocolate bars, toothpaste and toothbrushes, bath and laundry soap.

Yupang and his native helper then took out those items from their respective shelves, boxes and barrels and put them in sacks and boxes.

Leandro and Marina checked each item in the list and loaded them into the cart with the help of their driver and Yupang's helper. Leandro then helped Marina climb aboard the cart.

He went back to the store to pay Yupang for what they bought there.

Yupang was waiting for him at the cashier's counter. He counted the money, Leandro gave him, put most of it in the cashier's box and, his hands lowered out of Leandro's sight, he put some bills inside an envelope. Then he gave Leandro a receipt for what he and Marina had bought there.

He was about to leave the store when he saw Yupang pointing his thumb toward the store's back room in a sign for him to go there with Yupang. He put the envelope in Leandro's hand, once they were inside the back room, and said to him, "That is for you."

"What is it?" Leandro asked Yupang as he was opening the envelope. His eyes turned wide in surprise at finding money there.

"It is a token of my appreciation for bringing me so much business," Yupang said. "You will get something in return every time you buy something here for your company."

Leandro blinked his eyes in confusion. It was the first time in his life to experience something like that. He bought things in Angsiang and Liaolu's stores in San Isidro, but they never gave him money in return for buying things in their stores. There was something strange, maybe even wrong about what Yupang did. He could not accept the money.

"Thank you, but I cannot accept it," he said as he returned the envelope to Yupang.

"No, take it, take it," Yupang said, as he put the envelope, back in Leandro's hand. "Call it whatever you want to, a rebate or a token of my appreciation, but it is not a kickback. Do not think that, in accepting it, you are shortchanging your company, you are not. Whether you accept it or not, the price is the same of whatever you buy in my store. So, take it."

Leandro blinked his eyes in confusion at the Chinese merchant's elaborate, but twisted reasoning. It gave him, though, the excuse for accepting the money. He put the envelope in the back pocket of his pants.

"It is strictly between us," Yupang said. "Nobody, but you and me, will know about it."

They were walking back to the store when Yupang suddenly laid his arm on Leandro's shoulders.

"You are young and you have a lot to learn," he said to Leandro, "and I have just given you, one free lesson on the ways of the world."

Leandro left the store and sat down beside Marina in the cart. A knowing smile was in Yupang's face as he was waving in good-bye at Leandro and Marina. She waved back at Yupang while Leandro kept his eyes to the road ahead.

The cart driver, with a flick of the rein, sent the carabao moving toward the town market. He kept watch at the goods in the cart as Leandro and Marina then proceeded toward the town market.

It was a large structure, open on all sides. It stood on tall and large iron posts. It was roofed with corrugated, galvanized iron sheets. It smelled partly of cement, which showed its construction was finished only recently.

The ground outside the market was still wet with puddles of water remaining there from the rain that fell yesterday, until late last night. The sky though was now bright with sunshine.

"You can imagine what our market was like, before we built that," Marina said.

"What was it like then?"

She said, her finger pointed to the sky, "It has that for the roof." Then she said, her finger pointed downward, "And it has this solid earth for the floor."

He laughed, glad to find Marina has a lively sense of humor.

They entered the market, followed by a teenage boy she hired for his pushcart where they will put whatever they will buy there.

The market was noisy and full of shoppers. They went from one stall to another where, after much haggling with the vendors, she bought pork, fish, chicken, eggs and vegetables.

He looked on and paid for them. The vendors had no receipts and she made them sign or mark on a piece of paper, each item she bought from them.

They were finished with the marketing in just a short while. She did, on their way back to the company compound, all the talking about the money she had saved for the company with all the haggling that she did with the market vendors.

He, on the other hand, remained quiet. His mind was still on the envelope of money inside the back pocket in his pants.

They put the goods in the kitchen and in the commissary with the help of Reynes, Sophia and the cart driver.

He paid the cart driver for his services. He thanked Marina for her help who then said to him, "Let me know anytime you need help. I am at your service."

There was money left and he returned it to the cashier, along with the list of their purchases and the receipt from Yupang.

His marketing task done, he reported for work in the warehouse, busy with men storing or removing the construction materials stored there.

He kept himself occupied with work, the rest of the morning, what took place in the backroom in Yupang's store, out of his mind in what was the first moral crisis in his life.

He stopped working at lunch break, Reynes announced by clanging with a short length of iron, the iron triangle at the entrance to the mess hall. He joined a line of workers moving along the food counter where Sophia and Marina were putting food on their trays.

Reynes was standing beside them. He was checking on his notebook, the meals taken there by the workers. They were deducted from the workers' pay, given every fifteenth day and end of the month. Reynes also took care of replenishing the food in the food counter.

Leandro exchanged a few friendly words with Sophia and Marina as he was lined up at the food counter. The large amount of food they put on his tray, took him by surprise. He nodded and smiled at them. Then he proceeded to a table in the mess hall, noisy with talk and laughter. He took his lunch quietly and finished it in just a short while.

There was time yet for a nap before he must go back to work. He went to a tool shed, facing the sea, where it was cool and quiet. He shut his eyes once he was seated on a wooden box there, his back against the tool shed's wooden wall. Nagging thoughts kept him awake.

He could not, until now, make up his mind on whether he should keep the money or return it to Yupang. If it was a token of his appreciation, as Yupang put it, and not a kickback, as he saw it, how come he did not feel good about accepting it? But then, he could do a lot with all that money that will now be coming his way and he did not have to feel guilty about accepting it. He was not shortchanging the company.

Yupang had assured him that he will pay the same amount for the purchases, he made in his store, with or without his token of appreciation. Why, he asked himself, should he then feel guilty about taking the money?

He smiled at Yupang's shrewdness. Yupang had made him, by giving him a rebate, a captive customer in his store. He cannot do business with the other town merchants, so as not to offend Yupang or else word about the rebate or kickback, as he saw it, might then reach the ears of his superiors and that might put his job in jeopardy. He will just have to keep quiet about it or return the money to Yupang.

He sighed. Yupang must be doing that to his important customers. It must be a business practice employed not only by Yupang, but also by the other Chinese merchants who keep them by giving them kickbacks or tokens of their appreciation. This culture of corruption with their important customers must be prevalent among them.

They controlled the retail business in the colony. They wield, with so much money in their hands, tremendous economic power and exerted great political influence, as well. That could be the reason even the high and the mighty Monte Arazteas and the other landlords in San Isidro treat Liaolu and Angsiang with great respect.

A serious look was on his face as he remembered Azucena. Like the poor folks in Bangar, she led a life where she worried where her next meal would be coming from. It was the question of food and money that had prompted her to favor Angsiang over the young men who courted her. That was how it also went with Liaolu, who won Consuelo for his wife over the young men who also courted her.

He nodded at the thought that it must be a common practice among the Chinese merchants to go after the women, working for them. They were men who left China in need of female company. Their money and the expectation of a life of comfort and plenty were more than enough to overcome the women's resistance to the prospect of marrying them.

He shook his head. Marriage out of economic need was, to him, unacceptable. People, to him, should marry out of love and nothing else.

As for Yupang's rebate or bribe money, he is returning it. He has no need for it. He is leading a good, uncorrupted life with his salary in Pacific & Gulf that is much more than enough for his personal needs.

The calm blue sea before him was so restful and he dozed off, satisfied with his insight and the decision he made of returning the money to Yupang. He woke up, a few minutes later, to the clang of the iron triangle. It was time for him to go back to work.

The song, *Home on the Range,* was in Leandro's lips as he was driving his borrowed horse-drawn cab on the road, built by Pacific & Gulf. It cut across the vast cogon-covered plain of Mandala. The plain at the left side of the road extended, far into the horizon. It ended to his right at a range of hills, thick with forest trees. Ahead of him, for many miles, was the dark-blue outline of a mountain range.

He is going to his "kingdom," as he called his homestead, a ten-acre plot of land beside the Kafalen family's homestead in a corner in the plain.

The Insular Government had opened it for development at the completion of the road. It was due to be inaugurated, later in the month, along with the wharf, a school building and the municipal building.

The shadow, the tall cogon grass cast along the road showed him, it was now late in the morning. He hurried up. He lashed the horse with the whip, sending it running fast.

A horse, fit for the racetrack, it was now running to a headwind that swept his hair back. He came, not long after, upon a gaunt tree near the road. It marked the corner boundary of their homesteads.

The horse slowed down when he pulled the rein. He saw then to his right, near a hut and a tree with its branches spread wide, Marina, Sophia and their folks moving about or attending to some task. They were already at work in their homestead.

He slapped his knee in annoyance with himself for having arrived there, so late. He attended the previous night, a drinking party in the house of his boss, Rogaciano. He woke up late and missed the first Mass in the town church, today being a Sunday.

The rig had entered the boundary between their two homesteads when he saw Marina, waving at him. He waved back and then pulled the horse to a stop, beside the Kafalen family's horse-drawn cart. A sheepish smile on his face, he apologized to Datuk Kafalen, Marina's father, for coming late.

"There is no need to apologize," Datuk said. "We just got here ourselves."

"I can see, you have gone straight to work," he said as he was watching them engaged in various tasks.

Sophia was chopping vegetables on a wooden board in a bamboo table in the shade of the tree. She was preparing lunch with Uday, Marina's mother, who was building a fire in a clay stove in the open-air kitchen.   Marina, not far from them, was turning the ground with a hoe in her hands. Datuk had put her to work in preparing some vegetable plots there. Her brother Marcelino was clearing a section of their homestead of cogon grass while Magno, Sophia's brother, was drawing water from a brook nearby.

They were working, this time for themselves, in those two parcels of land grown wild with cogon grass in the vast fertile plain of Mandala.

It was on Datuk's suggestion that he applied with him for their homesteads. Having a land of his own, who never owned, even a square inch of land, appealed immensely to him. It cost him nothing and it made him a proud landowner that put him somewhat in the same class as Don Camilo and the other Spanish mestizo landords in San Isidro.

Datuk knew Mandala, like the palm of his hand. Their homesteads were flat like a tabletop on the left side, a rolling terrain at the other side, which then ascended toward a range of low-lying hills. A brook was running at the boundary of their homesteads.

Working in their homesteads in his two days off from work had made him close to the Kafalen family. He was now, a year since he was assigned in Davao, spending his two days, off from work, less by fishing at sea, like he used to do in Zamboanga, and more in Marina and Sophia's company in their village and in their homesteads.

He went immediately to work with Datuk, Magno and Marcelino in clearing their homesteads of cogon grass. It was a hard work of pulling out the thick grass to their roots, so they will not grow back. They stopped working only when Uday, Sophia and Marina called them to lunch. They went back to work after taking a simple lunch of rice, fish and vegetables. The sun, later in the day, was now low in the horizon when Uday came to Datuk and said to him, "Our work animal, the chickens and the pigs have yet to be fed."

It was time for them to return home. Datuk called the others. They went to the hut where, with Leandro's help, they gathered their things and loaded them in their cart. They climbed aboard the cart except Marina, who kept on working in her vegetable plot.

"Come on, Marina, you are keeping everyone, waiting," Marcelino said to her.

"Go ahead, I am not finished here," she replied.

She turned to Leandro, who was standing beside the cart, and said to him, "You will take me home, won't you, Leandro?"

"Of course, I will. But why don't you go with them. You can do that, some other time."

"I don't like to leave unfinished, whatever I have set out to do," she said as she kept on hoeing the ground.

Leandro smiled and shook his head. Magno and Marcelino laughed while Sophia looked away, frowning.

"She has a mind of her own," Datuk said to Leandro.

"Don't be home late," Uday said to Marina.

"I won't," she replied.

"Will you join us for dinner?" Datuk asked Leandro.

"Yes, of course," he replied. "That reminds me, I'll see if I can catch some fish for our dinner."

"Good idea," Marcelino said.

He watched them leave. Then he took from the cab, his box of fishing equipment.

He caught in the brook, the week before, two big catfish.

They had a fine dinner with them in the Kafalen home. He might be just as lucky today.

The box in his hand, he approached Marina.

"Did you see any earthworms here that I can use as a bait?" he asked her as he was looking around at the ground.

"I saw one, a while ago."

He looked down for an earthworm in a hollow in the ground still wet from an early morning rain. He found one and took it out.

"Wish me luck," he said to Marina as he went to the brook.

He cast, in just a short while, after making the necessary preparation, his fishing line into the water. He then waited for a fish to take the bait, his back on the grass-covered ground that sloped down to the brook with the back of his head, rested on his clasped hands.

He sat up when he saw Marina coming.

She asked him, "Have you caught any fish?"

He said, "Nothing yet."

"How come?" she said, "I thought you are an expert in catching fish."

He smiled. She liked to tease him. They had grown close to each other in a year he had been in her company, at work or with her folks.

"The fish there must be taking a nap," she said as she sat down on the grass, beside Leandro.

She picked up a pebble and threw it near the fishing line.

"That should wake it up," she said, "and make it take the bait."

"Stop that," he said. "You are scaring the fish away."

"It will come back, once it sees the earthworm there. Let me do it," she said as she took the fishing line from him and twirled it in her fingers.

"Stop that," he said as he took back the fishing line from her.

He was about to tell her to leave him alone when he saw her, now looking at him from beneath her brow, like she was up to something.

He looked at her, puzzled by that expression in her face and was startled when suddenly, she held his hand. The feel of her hand gave him a strange new feeling for her that also left him confused. No woman had ever done that to him. He could try removing her hand gently, but that might then offend her. He could let her hold his hand, but what then?

He saw her, now looking at him with such intense longing, he finally understood what all of that meant. She wanted him to take her.

He laid her then, down on the grass.

She was now breathing hard, her eyes turned to the sky, as she waited for him to come to her.

Bill Shay and Philip Beldry arrived in Davao, a week later, for the inauguration of the company projects there. Dick McCall, who was writing   some articles about Mindanao and the outlying islands, was with them.

He was undecided about the title in one of them, whether it will be "The Land of Promise," or "America's Farthest Frontier."

Bill helped Dick settle it with the suggestion that Dick could use both titles in two articles in *The Philippines Newsmagazine,* for they both describe what the Americans were doing in the Philippines.

They went straight to the stage, near the wharf entrance, set up for the inauguration ceremony, right after the ship had docked at the finished wharf. A big crowd there was waiting for them.

Bill was seated in the front row of the stage with Dick and Philip. He looked around while he was waiting for the start of the inauguration ceremony. He saw Leandro in the crowd with Marina and her family. He waved at him to come over.

He was, in an instant, walking fast toward the stage.

Bill said, as he then stood in front of him, "Well, my boy, I have been hearing a lot of good things about you."

"Thank you, sir," he replied, smiling proudly.

Everyone there, his fellow workers, most of all Marina and her family, will now know, he is quite close to the two top bosses in Pacific & Gulf. The editor of *The Philippines Newsmagazine* might also write something about him.

"What do you think, if we will have this young man assigned to Masakao?" Philip said to Bill.

Bill nodded. "He is just the man, Joseph needs there."

He turned to Leandro and said, "Now that most of our work here is finished, Mister Beldry and I are assigning you to another project. We are building a dam and a mining road in a town called Masakao. You will assist in the procurement of supplies and equipment there, like what you did here and in Zamboanga. You will be working under your old boss, Joseph Kirkpatrick."

"Thank you, Mister Shay," he said, "thank you, Mister Beldry, for this new assignment."

The inauguration ceremony was about to start and he left the stage and rejoined Marina and her family. He showed nothing of the relief he felt, now that he has a very good reason for leaving Davao, for leaving Marina.

She told him, her face grave with worry, a few days after they made love in the homestead, that she missed her period.

He had, since then, a terrible time.

He kept it to himself, but he felt obliged to marry her for the sake of their child. The obstinate woman that she is, she will then insist that they should live in their homestead in Davao. He would then spend the rest of his life there, no better than the life he left in Bangar.

She told him, two days later, that her period had only been delayed. That freed him from his self-imposed obligation of marrying her. But the risk of getting trapped into marrying her will remain for as long as he is residing there. He must leave Davao. His assignment to Masakao gave him the perfect excuse for doing that.

He had, three days later, a sad, tearful good-bye at the wharf with Marina. He was leaving in the same ship with Bill Shay, Philip Beldry and Dick McCall. She did not object to him in leaving her, for he was leaving her, for leaving Davao, on orders from the Big Boss himself.

He was about to step up into the gangplank when he said to her, to soften the blow of his departure that he is coming back.

He entered the ship quickly after he had said that, his brow burning in shame for having lied to her. He is not coming back.

Chapter Forty

Leandro left Davao, a warehouse assistant and purchasing agent. He arrived in Manila, nearly two weeks later, a warehouse custodian and purchasing agent. The voyage gave him the opportunity to brief Bill Shay and Philip Beldry on his work in Zamboanga and Davao.

He made such a good impression on them, Bill gave him the bigger responsibility of setting up the warehouse and supply system for the two projects in Masakao.

There was also a bonus from Dick McCall who told him, he will write an article about him as a young man who has done a lot of good work for Pacific & Gulf in Mindanao.

Bill allowed him, since he had no place to stay while he was in Manila, to take once again for his temporary quarters, the bunk in the warehouse loft until his departure for Masakao.

He went to see Carlos on his arrival in Parola.

He said when he saw Leandro coming to his desk, "Well, look who is here, if it is not Gulliver back from his travels."

He stood up from his chair and tapped Leandro in the arm while Leandro smiled, delighted at finding himself, now nearly as tall as Carlos. He had gained a couple of inches more since he left Manila, three years ago. As for Carlos, he saw no change in his friend. He was the same cheerful, friendly fellow.

"You have not changed," he said to Carlos.

"I cannot say that about you. You look awful with that beard and mustache in your face."

"Never mind, how I look," he said, slapping the air in dismissal of Carlos' tart remark. "I misplaced my razor, so I did not shave, the entire time I was in the ship. Anyway, how are your folks? How is Regina?"

"They are all fine. I am going to see her tomorrow at the fair they are holding in their school. You can come with me, if you like."

"I will be glad to be there," he said, smiling broadly.

Leandro was smiling, not only broadly, but expectantly as well, the following day, on his arrival with Carlos in Ascension College.

Its campus had been converted into a fairground. It was full of people walking around, talking and laughing, watching the various exhibits in the booths there, or waiting for their turn at the amusement rides in the Carousel and the Ferris Wheel.

They were a novelty in Manila and Leandro watched, fascinated, as the Ferris Wheel with its twenty or so seats was moving vertically in a circle in a steel tower. He could already see himself, seated there with Regina. They will have as much fun, riding on the wooden horses, moving up and down on their posts in the Carousel's circular platform.

His eyes, bright of the fun, he will have in those rides with Regina, he entered with Carlos the lobby of the school's main building, eager to see her.

"There is someone I've got to see first," Carlos said. "We can see Regina later on."

"Very well, if that is what you want us to do," he replied in a disappointed tone of voice.

He would rather that they will see Regina, right away. Now that he is not going to see her yet, he took his time by walking around leisurely and halting to read the school notices, posted in the bulletin board there.

Carlos, in the meantime, had walked ahead. He halted at the door in a classroom there. A couple of schoolgirls were showing to a group of visitors, the exhibits on display there.

One of them came to Carlos and said to him, "I thought you were never coming."

"Fret, no more, my dear," he said to the girl. "Here I am, in your graceful presence."

He glanced at Leandro who had joined him at the classroom door.

"Do you know each other?" he asked him and the girl when he saw them staring, wide-eyed, at each other.

"We were classmates in the public school in San Isidro," Leandro said to Carlos, his eyes fixed to Angela Rosablanca.

"Well, what a coincidence," Carlos said, smiling. "So, you two studied in the same school while Leandro and I are working in the same company."

"It was just a mere coincidence," Angela said coldly.

"But we are here," Carlos said, "not out of coincidence. What can you offer us that will make our visit here, worth our time and yours?"

"What," she asked Carlos, "did you come here for?"

"I came here to see you."

"Is that the only reason that you are here?"

"Now that you have asked about it, why don't we see Regina? We can then take a snack in your school cafeteria."

"So, that is what you came here for."

"Not really, but I'm hungry. I skipped breakfast at home because I was in such a hurry to see you."

"What a sweet, lying tongue. Very well, let us see Regina. Then we'll go to the cafeteria."

Angela's classmate nodded when she pointed at the corridor in a sign that she was leaving her.

They went to Regina's classroom with Leandro walking behind Carlos and Angela.

Angela, he noticed, has not changed, at all. She is still the same haughty Spanish mestiza, now snubbing him again. She is not succeeding, though, if her intention is to hurt him. He is no longer, the poor, naive peasant boy in Bangar who used to moon over her. He is now a sophisticated young man, wise with the ways of the world.

"Look, who are here," Regina said when she saw Carlos and Angela at the door in her classroom.

She was with some classmates, attending to the visitors who were taking a look at their clothing and handicraft exhibits there. She asked to be excused and she walked toward Carlos and Angela. She was startled when she saw Leandro there.

He said to her, "How are you, Regina?"

She barely nodded in response to his greeting.

"You know what?" Carlos said to Regina. "Leandro and Angela are not only townmates; they studied in the same school there."

"It is a small world," Regina said coldly.

She turned to Angela and said to her, "Did you have a lot of visitors to your exhibit?"

"We had a few. All the trouble and the effort we made in preparing our exhibit may not be worth it."

"It is still early," Carlos said, "and people are only starting to come." He then said at the exhibits there, "Are those, what the nuns are teaching you here, how to sew clothes and make shopping bags?"

Regina laughed, Angela so hard at Carlos making fun of them. Ascension College was an exclusive girls' school known for the liberal arts, not for the domestic arts.

Leandro felt, on being left out in their conversation, that he was not welcome there. He might as well, stay away from them.

He asked to be excused and was about to leave when Carlos said, "I must go, too—call of nature."

Carlos left for the men's room while Leandro went to the fairground. He walked around there, lonely and depressed in the company of strangers, he returned to Regina's classroom. He was about to enter her classroom when he heard, from his side in the classroom's wooden wall, Regina and Angela talking about him. He halted and listened.

"So, Leandro had his eyes on you," Regina said. "What did you do about it?"

"I did nothing. I simply ignored him."

"Why?"

"I did not want to have anything to do with him."

"Why?"

"Why? He was so poor—that is why. The first time he showed up in our classroom, his feet were in muddy, wooden clogs, not shoes. He had a black eye and a bruised lip from a fight with a couple of boys who called him Leandro Sumuka!"

Regina and Angela broke into peals of laughter while Leandro turned rigid in anger. They were making fun of him and his surname!

"I cannot," Angela said, "imagine myself, becoming Missis Sumaka, a peasant boy's wife, a butt of jokes with a surname like that. He will never amount to anything unless he changes it into something elegant and distinctive."

"Like Carlos Yturalde?" Regina said as they laughed again. "But he now has a job and a very good one, too. Is that not something good, you can say about him?"

"That is not enough for me. Will you take to him, if you were in my place?"

"No, I will not."

"Did he have his eyes on you, too?"

"Yes."

"What did you do about it?"

"I was friendly to him, but only because he and my brother are very good friends. He is a nice fellow, but that is not enough for me to take to him. I have not seen him for so many years."

He was about to walk away, hurt and angry at what Regina and Angela had said about him, but then he saw Carlos, coming. He will not walk out on his friend.

They seemed startled and worried when he appeared in the classroom door with Carlos and that he might have overheard what they had said about him.

He pretended, he heard nothing when he said to Carlos, "Are we going to just stand here, the whole day?"

He felt even better when he saw Regina and Angela looking so relieved.

"Thank you, for reminding me about that," Carlos replied. "Let us go to the cafeteria."

They left the classroom with Leandro walking behind Carlos, Angela and Regina who were walking beside each other.

The school cafeteria was full of people, but a couple was just then leaving a table there. Regina and Angela took it while Carlos and Leandro went to the food counter and placed their order of soda and sandwiches. They distributed them at the table and sat down, Carlos beside Angela while Regina and Leandro sat down, separated by a corner in the table.

He worked in his mind, as he began to eat his sandwich, how he would start a conversation with Regina. It may take some doing. She was sore, not once did he write to her in the three years, he was away. But they were good friends before and they could be good friends again. He could tell her about his work and experience in Zamboanga and Davao. She might even show concern at his close brush with death in Panakol. That might then change her view of him.

He cleared his throat with a sip of his soda. He was about to speak when Regina suddenly turned her eyes to a young, well-dressed Spanish mestizo walking toward her. He pulled a chair from a table nearby and put it down at the corner of the table, between Regina and Leandro.

"What took you so long?" Regina said to the young man.

"What a nagger," the young man replied as he sat down on the chair.

Leandro watched Regina and the young man at the way they were looking at and talking to each other. They seemed to be on very close terms.

"I would like you to meet Ruy Villa del Conde," Carlos said to Leandro who nodded and smiled at the young man.

"I'm Leandro Sumaka. I am glad to meet you," he said to Ruy, who glanced at him before turning his attention, back to Regina.

"You have not answered my question," she said to Ruy.

"What took you so long?" Angela also asked Ruy.

"I overslept."

"So, you went out, last night," Regina said to Ruy.

"And I know where he went—to those horrid cabarets," Angela said.

"What do you expect me to do?" Ruy said to Regina and Angela.

"You could have stayed home," Regina said to Ruy.

"What do you take me for—a domestic servant? I saw a musical in Zorilla. I had dinner afterwards and played billiards at Tommy's. That is all that I did last night."

"How was the musical?" Carlos asked Ruy.

"It was the same old tearjerker."

Leandro looked coldly at the others, sore at having been snubbed by that mestizo, Ruy Villa del Conde, and at being left out in their conversation. He was out of place there, but could not summon the will to leave them.

He saw, as he was eating his sandwich and drinking his soda, from the way Carlos and Angela were now looking at and talking to each other, that they were on very intimate terms. He would not mind Carlos, having Angela for his girlfriend. He has no claims on her. She was never his girl. He was even glad that where he failed, Carlos had succeeded with Angela. As for Angela, she snubbed him before and he did not care, she snubbed him again. It was a different matter with Regina, though. It pained him to realize now that he had only deluded himself into thinking, she had a warm feeling of affection for him. He must face it. They do not belong to each other, never did and never will. He is of poor peasant origin while she is an aristocratic girl from a wealthy Spanish mestizo family who kept him in her company only because he is her brother's friend and fellow worker in Pacific & Gulf. As for the spoiled boy, Ruy Villa del Conde, he is like the Monte Arazteas and is just as rude and detestable.

The sandwich he was eating did not taste fresh and good, but he continued eating it, so that the others at the table will not notice him, watching them and listening to them.

He nearly choked on his sandwich when he saw, from the corner of his eye, Ruy and Regina, now holding hands.

He took a sip of his soda to clear a lump that had then blocked his throat, his brow burning with envy and anger. He asked to be excused when he could not stand that sight anymore and he left their table.

His brow burning still in anger and envy, he passed out of the school gate so distracted, he took no notice of the people he met and passed by on the sidewalk.

Neither did he notice the horse-drawn rigs and cabs running in the street. He walked on with no particular destination in his mind.

He was crossing the rail tracks in the middle of a street, so lost in thought he did not notice an electric streetcar coming. Its warning bell alerted him, just on time and he crossed the rail tracks quickly.

He was shaken, but was glad to see an electric streetcar now running there. Thanks to Pacific & Gulf, which laid those rail tracks and built the train stations, Manila now has in the electric streetcar, a modern, mass transportation system.

What he saw in the electric streetcar filled him with resolution. He will, from now on, set aside all personal cares and concerns and attend solely to his job.

He will cut all ties with Regina and Angela, the same way he did with Marina. His job is the only thing that mattered to him now. Great things, after all, are in store for him in Pacific & Gulf.

He walked on, his eyes now bright with wonder at the many changes that have taken place in that section in Manila, he last saw, three years ago.

But for the old church in Malate and a few old Spanish-type homes there, he would not have recognized that section in Manila

It was, three years ago, mostly shrubs and rice fields. It had, since then, been developed into a modern, American-style suburb. Its asphalt-paved, tree-lined streets carried in the street corners, names of American states like Dakota, Colorado, Georgia, Tennessee, Indiana and Pennsylvania. The streets were lined with new screened bungalows, painted mostly white and green.

He saw, in one of the homes there, a blonde American woman cradling in her arms, a blonde American baby.

He smiled and thrust his chin out proudly at the thought that Pacific & Gulf built those homes and paved those streets.

He had passed through several blocks and was now deep in the heart of Ermita when he halted at the sight there of great buildings, just about finished in their construction. They were in a style, he had never seen before, with their tall, massive columns at the front entrance.

A worker nearby was shoveling dirt into a wheelbarrow.

"Excuse me, sir," he said to the worker. "Can you tell me, what those buildings are?"

"You are looking at the University of the Philippines."

"It would be nice, if I can study there."

"I am too old for that, but I heard the children of those who helped build it will be given priority when it opens, a few months, if not weeks, from now. My children are looking forward to that."

"Good for you," he said to the man as he then turned his eyes to several new buildings in a compound, across the street.

He asked the man, "What are those buildings there?"

"That," the man replied, "is the compound of the Philippine General Hospital. Construction of those buildings was finished just a few months ago. You must be new, here in Manila."

He ignored what the man said and walked on, filled with regret. While money to him is not a problem, he could not study there, in the University of the Philippines or in any other school, not with him being assigned from one construction project to another. He will never be a well-educated man with the initials of a college degree, after his name. It was enough, though, that he has this great job in Pacific & Gulf.

He walked on, crossed the Pasig River on the Puente de Espana Bridge and turned west, toward Manila Bay. His stomach was making its familiar gurgling sound for food when he arrived at the food stalls, outside the company gate in Parola.

The sight and the smell of the food displayed at the glass counters in the food stalls there whetted his appetite. He proceeded to a food stall and sat down on the bench there. The girl there waited as he was considering what to order of the food displayed in the glass counter there.

"What will you have, sir?" she asked him.

He looked up at the girl and was pleasantly surprised to see, how she had grown up since he last saw her, three years ago, into a pretty young woman.

"Don't you remember me?" he said to her. "I used to eat here."

The woman peered at him.

"Why, it is Leandro," she said, smiling. "I have not seen you around for a long time. Where have you been, all this time?"

"I was away on assignment in Zamboanga and Davao. I got back only yesterday."

"I'm so glad to see you again. You now have the pleasure of eating again the delicious food that we serve here."

"That is why I am here."

He looked again at the food counter, his mind, not made up on what to order there. They all looked delicious.

He asked her, "What would you suggest for my lunch?"

"Try either or both the pork omelet and the fried noodles. I cooked them myself."

"Very well, I will have both of them for lunch."

He looked on as she scooped into a plate, the food he ordered, and nodded. She was attractive in her own way, a native girl, light brown in complexion with a small nose, brow and lips, her hair swept back into a bun. She was friendly, simple and sincere and was so unlike Regina with her faked friendliness and Angela with her cold haughtiness.

He took a bite of the food and nodded at its delicious taste. Even better, serving it was this pretty, young woman whose name, he now remembered, is Crisanta Mercaida.

Chapter Forty-one

Leandro proceeded later on to the motor pool to check for a company truck that might be going to Masakao. One was leaving within a few minutes. He hurried up to his locker in the warehouse, took out his suitcase there and hitched a ride in the truck. It was midafternoon when it arrived in Masakao.

He went straight to the company's temporary field office, a room at the ground floor of the municipal hall and reported to Joseph Kirkpatrick, his old boss in Zamboanga, who was also assigned there.

"I'm glad to see you again," Kirkpatrick said to him.

"So, am I, sir," he replied.

He put his suitcase down on the floor and sat down across Kirkpatrick's desk.

"Have you been briefed about our projects here?" Kirkpatrick asked him.

"Yes, sir, I've been briefed about it."

"Good, but it bears repeating that we will soon build a dam here in Masakao and a mining road to the remote mountain village in Alkayag. It is known, even during the Spanish time, to have extensive iron deposits.

"The dam will increase by so much the agricultural yield, not only here in Masakao, but also in other towns in Central Plain. Mining operation will start in Alkayag, once the construction of the mining road is finished. It will be a source of material, vital to industry. So, you can see the tremendous economic benefits those two projects will bring about, not only to this and the other towns, but to the entire colony itself."

He heard that refrain about the company projects, a few times before. He was glad to hear it again from Kirkpatrick. It made him feel good to be working in the company, doing so much good to his country.

"This town is special to Mister Shay," Kirkpatrick continued. "His wife Esperanza comes from here. Her sister Teresa is married to the town mayor, Paulo Palanas, who is a good friend of Mister Shay. The Big Boss, in pushing through those two projects, had to pull a lot of strings in the Insular Government."

Leandro nodded, flattered by what it meant to him. The Big Boss handpicked him for those projects that were important to him and his wife. Not only did Mr. Shay have confidence in him, he is also fond of him, as Carlos once said to him.

"That," he said, "should prod us into doing a very good job here."

"You will do well here, if you will do the same kind of work that you did in Zamboanga and Davao. But there is a big difference for you now. You will be in charge of the warehouse and the purchase of construction materials once we start work on those two projects. You will not be doing much purchasing here, though. Most of our supplies will be coming from Manila."

"In the meantime that I am not doing that kind of work, at least not while I am waiting for the start of the work on the dam and the road, what do you want me to do?"

Kirkpatrick looked around at the room.

"As you can see," he said, "I'm rather cramped here, but this is only my temporary office. We are putting up our own offices, barracks, a mess hall and a warehouse."

"Are they those wooden structures, I saw were being built in the open space at the back of the bandstand in the town square?"

"They are. The workers there need close supervision and you are the man who will do that. Let us take a look."

They left the office, crossed the road to the town square on their way to the company compound at the back of the bandstand.

He confirmed with his own eyes, the moment they arrived there, what Kirkpatrick said about the workers there who need close supervision. Some of them were not doing any work. They were seated on a stack of lumber on the ground, smoking and conversing idly. They stood up and went through the motion of working when they saw him and Kirkpatrick coming.

He walked around in the compound with Kirkpatrick and looked into the work being done there. Some of the men were mixing cement; others were cementing the floor of the buildings while others were doing carpentry work. They were working in such a disinterested manner, he saw Kirkpatrick, frowning.

"Are they locally hired, sir?" he asked Kirkpatrick.

"They are. They were recommended by the local politicians here."

He nodded at what Kirkpatrick had implied was the reason for the men's disinterested manner of working. They have the notion that with their political backing, Kirkpatrick could not be strict with them.

He knew Kirkpatrick well enough to be soft-spoken, but firm and resolute. He waited expectantly when Kirkpatrick asked a worker nearby, for the foreman. The frown in Kirkpatrick's face showed him, he will give the foreman, a scolding.

The foreman, thin and gray-haired, came. Kirkpatrick said to him, "I don't think I have impressed on you, strongly enough, that work here should be finished by the end of the month."

"We need more men, sir," the foreman said.

"You have enough workers. You are not working as hard as you can and should. That is the problem. I am giving you, a fair warning. If you do not finish the work here, by the end of the month, none of you will be hired when we start the construction of the dam and the road and when the mine in Alkayag will be operational."

The foreman looked shaken; he bowed his head humbly.

Kirkpatrick then turned to Leandro and said to the foreman, "This is Leandro Sumaka. He will run things here when I am not around. Do as he tells you."

He looked hard at the foreman. Compared to him, who was eyeing him skeptically, he was just a teenage boy, younger than the workers there. If only the foreman knew what he had been through!

Kirkpatrick saw the foreman looking away, a sarcastic smile on his face and he said to him, "Leandro here is a veteran worker of Pacific and Gulf. He has worked in far bigger and more difficult projects in Zamboanga and Davao. He has even faced Muslim suicide killers in Jolo. He may be young, but he has more know-how and experience than you or anyone of the workers here."

The foreman glanced, surprised, at Leandro..

"You may now go back to work," Kirkpatrick said to the foreman.

They were leaving the company compound when he said to Kirkpatrick, "Thank you, sir, for what you said about me."

"You are welcome. As you must have noticed, they are all slackers. You must whip them up into working hard."

They returned to the town hall and went up to the office of Mayor Palanas.

Leandro was surprised, the moment he and Kirkpatrick had entered the mayor's office, to find him so young. He could be of the same age as Candido.

"What can I do for you?" Mayor Palanas said to them.

"Leandro here needs a place to stay while we are building our barracks," Kirkpatrick replied.

"You can also stay in my house," Mayor Palanas said to Leandro. "You can share the other bedroom downstairs with Jones. Do you know where I live?"

"I don't, mayor."

"I will have one of my men, take you there."

Leandro and Kirkpatrick thanked Mayor Palanas and left.

Leandro went to the company compound, the following day, supervising the work there.

Kirkpatrick came, later in the day, and told Leandro to accompany him to the river at the foothill side of the town, for the dam site being surveyed by Ralph Jones, a civil and geodetic engineer.

They took a horse-drawn cab and arrived, after a while, in the area. They got off from the cab and walked up to an elevation in the ground. It sloped down on the other side by about fifty feet to the riverbank.

The river, from that point, was by Leandro's estimate, about two hundred paces wide. It was summertime. Not as much water was coming from its headwaters in Sierra Madre and the water level there was low.

Jones was standing on the riverbank, his surveyor's level, beside him. He was giving instructions to the workers who, while fording the river, were putting down there, a surveyor's chain.

Leandro nodded. He had done that too in Basilan and Jolo.

He looked on. Jones, from where he was standing, was measuring the distance to the riverbank across the river, its depth and its current, the elevation in the hill on the other side of the river and the elevation on the ground where he and Kirkpatrick were watching Jones.

"How are you doing there?" Kirkpatrick asked Jones.

Jones looked up at Kirkpatrick and replied, "We are doing fine."

"How does it look as the dam site?"

"It looks promising, but we can be more definite about it after we have made our measurements and checked the bedrock."

"How long will it take you to do that?"

"Two to five days. The river here, during summer, is not as deep as during the rainy months. That will make it easier for us to determine the depth of the bedrock."

The bedrock, as Leandro knew it, will be the critical part of the dam project. They are not going to build the dam on sand and mud as it will collapse in no time at all. It had to be built on solid rock.

He listened while Kirkpatrick and Jones were discussing the dam site. It will bring about great positive changes to many people. Once it was finished, the farmers in Masakao and in other towns will no longer depend on rain alone to water their crops. They could have, by then, multiple cropping. The increase in their incomes will redound to the benefit of Masakao and much of the rest of Central Plain.

The dam, aside from that, will provide Masakao and other towns nearby with a steady supply of safe drinking water. They no longer have to depend for that on the wells they dug on the ground or on rainwater.

He was standing at a vantage point and he turned his gaze to a panoramic view of Masakao. Its old stone church was like the church in San Isidro except for its two belfries. The church in San Isidro had only one belfry. Many of the homes there were, like his hometown, made of wood and bamboo and roofed with palm shingles. Some of the homes there were built of stone and roofed with tile similar to the homes of the landlords in San Isidro.

The sudden realization that he was making a comparison between Masakao and San Isidro caused him to start. It was a sign of homesickness, but why should he miss his hometown when he is not even keen about visiting it, now that his uncle Julian and his aunt Tarcila were both dead and Miss Dickinson was no longer teaching there? San Isidro did not even look like Masakao.

Being so close to Sierra Madre, much of it is rolling terrain, unlike San Isidro which is flat like a tabletop. Masakao is a river town, the foothills near the river, lush with forest growth.

It will look different, weeks from now, when the construction of the dam will be in full swing. Perhaps work will begin right there where he is standing. It will be up to Jones. He will determine the best location for the dam.

"When do you expect to finish, surveying the other possible sites for the dam?" Kirkpatrick asked Jones.

"One week, two weeks, it is hard to tell."

"Very well, keep it up," Kirkpatrick said.

He waved in good-bye at Jones as he and Leandro were leaving the elevation in the ground.

"We must finish the work in the company compound, by the end of the month. That is less than three weeks from today," Kirkpatrick said as he and Leandro were returning to the town.

"We can finish the job, if we will lean hard on the men."

"Do whatever it will take to finish the job on time. The Big Boss wants the construction of the dam and the road started at the earliest possible time. He himself will come to start their construction."

They parted at the town's main road with Kirkpatrick proceeding to his office in the municipal hall and Leandro, walking toward the company compound.

He resumed work where he left off in supervising and helping out in the construction of the various facilities in the company compound. He was under pressure to finish everything there, by the end of the month and he was everywhere, inspecting, asking questions, giving orders and taking part in the work there.

The workers grudgingly accepted his authority even though he was younger than all of them. But he has the full backing of Kirkpatrick and the alternative to indolence and insubordination was dismissal.

He made veiled threats about it, at the same time that he was not lacking in commending a job well done.

It was late afternoon, at the end of the work in the company compound. Leandro was on his way to Mayor Palanas' house, tired but satisfied with the work he and the men had done there.

He halted when he came near the mayor's house and looked at it. It took his eyes, like the first time he went there yesterday, not because there was anything distinctive about it. It was a very ordinary house, hardly different from the other houses in the neighborhood and that was what he found striking about it.

It was so modest for a town mayor. It was made of wood and roofed with palm shingles. It has two floors and, like most of the houses there, only the upper floor must have been previously used and occupied.

Like their hut in Bangar, the ground floor was probably open on all sides, its floor similarly of packed earth before improvements were made there.

He noticed, as he was entering the ground floor, that it was newly walled with wooden boards, its floor of packed earth, newly cemented. Mayor Palanas' house was small and modest, but his achievements were big and exceptional, in contrast to Enrique Monte Araztea who lived in a very big house, but whose achievements were so small. But what could he expect from Enrique? He ran for mayor only to keep his family in power.

That was the gist of the few letters he received from Candido when he was in Zamboanga and Davao. Candido wrote that his mother, his aunt Tarcila, had passed away and that the trainee Filipino schoolteachers had replaced the American schoolteachers in San Isidro.

He went to the bedroom, he shared with Jones. He came out, a minute later, with a towel and fresh clothes in his hands for a bath in the bathroom there. He had barely stepped out of the bathroom, a short while later, when Kirkpatrick and Jones arrived there from work. He waited until they had also taken a bath. They went upstairs afterwards for their dinner there.

Mayor Palanas met them in the living room with his wife Teresa, who arrived, a few hours earlier from a few days' visit to her sister Esperanza, Bill Shay's wife.

Kirkpatrick and Jones addressed Mayor Palanas, sometimes simply as Paulo, now that he was at home with his wife and without the protocol of public office.

"You must be hungry from all the work you have been doing, the whole day," Teresa said to them.

"We'll be amply rewarded with what you have prepared for us," Paulo replied as he was leading them to the dining room.

They were soon having a simple, but ample dinner of fried fish on a bed of tomatoes and pork spareribs, supplemented by soup and salad.

Kirkpatrick asked about their two children, Lukas, whom Paulo had named after his late uncle, and Demetrio. Teresa replied they have taken their supper, ahead of them.

The men repaired to the living room after dinner where, over rice wine, they talked shop, mostly about the work being done in the river and in the company compound.

Leandro spoke only when he was asked a question. Otherwise, he just watched and listened there. They were his superiors, conversing with the town mayor. It would be rude and presumptuous of him to be too familiar with them.

The talk turned to the Philippine-American War, nearly a decade ago where Paulo Palanas and Bill Shay fought each other in Masakao.

"You see, we had to find out first in the fighting, if Bill and I deserved to be friends," Paulo said as the others smiled.

"Who won?" Jones asked.

"Do you have to ask that?" Kirkpatrick said to Jones.

Jones then said, "The Big Boss must have crowed after the battle, '*veni, vidi, vici*—I came, I saw, I conquered.' "

"So he did," Kirkpatrick said.

"Not exactly," Paulo said. "Bill came and saw, all right, but in the end, it was he who was conquered, not by me, but by a lady in our town, Esperanza, my wife's sister."

Kirkpatrick said, "A woman's charm is mightier than a man's spear and sword."

"You can say that again," Teresa said as she was coming from the dining room.

They stood up from their seats. She had a tiring trip from Manila with her two children and, in coming to the living room, she was giving a hint that she wished to retire for the night with her husband.

They thanked Paulo and Teresa for the nice dinner and went to their rooms downstairs. Leandro could hear, a short while later, Jones in the other bed in the room, now sleeping soundly.

Chapter Forty-two

Mayor Paulo Palanas was beside himself with excitement as he was standing on the wooden stage in the town square. It was a special day for him and the townsfolk. Construction of the dam, the survey of Alkayag and the trail there will soon begin. The two projects were the fulfillment of the promise of progress and prosperity, he made to the townsfolk gathered with him in the town square. He established two public agencies that will oversee them, once they were operational. A group of local residents set up a company that will handle the marketing of the iron ore to be mined there.

The town's brass band playing the overture in Rossini's *The Barber of Seville* made the occasion as festive as the bunting flapping in the wind, made it so colorful.

He glanced at his son Lukas who was playing with his wooden toy truck in a corner of the stage and turned his gaze to the town square.

"Any sign of them?" he asked Teresa, who was standing beside him.

She did not answer the question, but glanced, frowning, instead at Paulo. He was slapping his thigh repeatedly, as if he was swatting an insect that had crawled inside his pants. He developed only recently this mannerism of slapping a part of his body, his thigh, this instance, whenever he was so excited and he was, this morning. Some of those in the crowd facing the stage were looking on in amusement at what he is doing.

"Will you please stop, what you are doing," Teresa said in a low voice, close to Paulo's ear. "The people around have noticed it. Relax, please! Bill and his party will be here, any moment now."

Paulo glanced sheepishly at Teresa and hid his hand, inside a pocket in his pants. He smiled as he waited for the arrival of Bill Shay's party.

How different it was now from a few years ago when he and Bill fought each other during the Philippine-American War. How things have since then changed between him and Bill. From enemies, they have become very good friends. If his uncle Lukas, who died in defending the town from Bill's attack, were alive today, he will also be very happy.

His face suddenly was clouded by the sad memory of his uncle and the other town leaders who fought and died for their country's freedom in the revolution against Spain and in the war against America. Not one of them was still around to celebrate this happy event in the town. His uncle, Bihasa, Gayuman, Mulawin, Kabisig, Pinalis and Masinop were all dead.

He was roused from the sadness that had overtaken him by a young man running toward the stage and shouting, "They are coming! The Americans are coming!"

Bill Shay, the man, everyone in the town square was waiting for, had just then entered the town's main road, at the head of a motorcade. He has been to Masakao many times before and for many months during the war, he was the town administrator and fort commander. His visit today is special to Paulo, Teresa, Esperanza, the townsfolk and himself.

He is leading a party that included Esperanza, their son Michael, William Fowley of the Insular Government, Dick McCall and Nieves, and Philip Beldry for the ceremony that will start the work on the dam and the trail to Alkayag. His workers, Kirkpatrick, Jones and Leandro, have everything, ready for them. Construction of the field office, the warehouse and the mess hall was completed only a few days before, thanks to their and the local workers' untiring effort.

Work on the sleeping quarters was finished even earlier. Kirkpatrick, Jones and Leandro had moved there to give room to the members of Bill's party in Paulo and Teresa's home. Dick, though, will stay with Nieves in her home near the Dumayags' house.

Jones had finished with his survey of the dam site even earlier. He had determined that the best location for it will be in the same spot where Kirkpatrick and Leandro had paid him a visit, three weeks earlier.

The rumbling noise, the truck engines were making, faint at first, was now so loud as the motorcade was approaching the town square.

Bill Shay was at the wheel of the lead car. A wide smile on his face, he was waving happily at the crowd, lining the road. They were smiling, clapping and waving their hands and cheering him.

Esperanza moved forward from the backseat of the car and said to Bill, "What a wonderful welcome, dear. How they love you!"

Bill smiled with pride and pleasure.

"How is that for your second conquest of the town?" Philip Beldry said. He was seated beside Bill in the front seat of the car.

Bill smiled. The first time he came to the town, he was met with gunfire and then with silence, the townsfolk having stayed inside their homes, their shuttered windows signs that he was not welcome there. That was then. Here he was again with the townsfolk now welcoming him with open arms, for he was back to wage war, this time not against them, but against poverty, their old enemy. Where before he came with the weapons of war, he now came with the tools of industry, the noise made by the truck engines, music to his ears.

Michael stood up from the backseat between Esperanza and his nanny, Teofila, and shouted a Tagalog greeting, *"Mabuhay! Mabuhay!"*

William Fowley was behind Bill's car. He acknowledged the crowd's cheers with a smile and a wave of his hand. So did Dick McCall and Nieves from their car behind Fowley's car. Following behind Dick's car were the company trucks and their trailers loaded with earthmoving machines and construction equipment. The supply trucks brought up the rear in the motorcade.

The crowd lining the road followed the motorcade. The cars halted at the side of the church's iron grill fence while the trucks moved on toward the company compound at the back of the bandstand.

Paulo and Teresa stepped down from the stage and welcomed Bill and his party as they were leaving their cars. They were exchanging pleasantries when they turned to Esperanza who asked, her voice raised in alarm, "Where is Michael?"

The boy had escaped from Teofila and had wandered away, forgotten in the flurry of greetings and handshaking between Paulo, Teresa, the guests of honor and the town's other officials.

"He is there with Lukas," Teresa said as she pointed at Michael and Lukas.

The two cousins were not so far from them, but they were partly hidden by the crowd. They were showing off to each other, the toys in their hands.

"Come here, you two," Esperanza, upset but relieved, said to them.

The boys obeyed her. Esperanza and Teresa then took them by their hands and followed the others to the stage. The two cousins sat beside each other in the front row, beside their mothers. The band struck up the *The Star-Spangled Banner* and everyone in the stage stood up.

Paulo remained standing while the others in the stage had sat down at the end of the anthem-playing. He welcomed the guests and thanked Bill and Fowley for the dam and the road.

He described in glowing terms what those two projects will bring about in Masakao. He also thanked Dick for the publicity he had given the town in his newsmagazine.

Fowley then spoke at great length about the Insular Government's efforts in bringing prosperity to the town and the rest of the colony.

Michael and Lukas had, in the meantime, become restless from Fowley's long speech which they did not understand, much less cared about. They slid down from their chairs and began playing with their toys on the stage floor. Esperanza and Teresa's faces flushed in embarrassment. Their children were drawing the crowd's attention, away from Fowley, who had paused from his speech and was also watching the two boys.

Esperanza signaled to Teofila, who was with the crowd, to get the two boys. Teofila stepped up quickly to the stage and, ignoring their protests, took the two boys away from the stage.

Bill, unlike Esperanza and Teresa, merely smiled at the interruption, his son and his nephew had made in the ceremony. They were just boys who liked to play and it served Fowley right for being so long in his speech. He saw from the bored expression in the townsfolk's faces that they too had no patience for long speeches.

He spoke, as the last speaker, briefly and from his heart. He said Masakao is a second home to him for the great friends, he made there and for the love of his life, he met there. The crowd gave him a hearty applause.   Paulo and Teresa smiled, pleased, while Esperanza gave him, a tender, loving look.

The band played a marching music, the signal for the start of the tour of the warehouse, the field office, the mess hall and the barracks.

Led by Bill and Paulo, they left the stage with the townsfolk following behind them.

They walked on, six or seven abreast, with Bill and Esperanza, Paulo and Teresa, Dick and Nieves and Fowley forming the first line. Behind them were Philip, Kirkpatrick, Jones, two town officials and

Julio, who had just then joined them. Agustina stayed behind in their house to babysit with Teofila, Michael, Lukas and Demetrio. Other local officials formed the next few lines, followed by the company workers and the townsfolk.

Leandro had gone ahead to the warehouse where he waited at a corner of its tall and wide open door to tour the guests around.

"So, this is your new business address," Bill said to Leandro as he and the others were entering the warehouse.

Leandro smiled proudly at the brief attention, he got from the Big Boss.

Bill looked around, satisfied with the work done in the big and clean warehouse. It was walled with wooden boards and paved with cement, its roof made of corrugated, galvanized iron sheets.

The shelves there were now empty. Once the guests had left, the equipment and the supplies will be unloaded and brought there from the supply trucks parked outside in the company compound.

Everyone was looking around at the warehouse when Teresa whispered something to Esperanza.

She turned to Bill and said to him, "What do you think, dear? Won't this warehouse later on make for a nice social hall for the town?"

Bill rubbed his chin while he was thinking about Esperanza's suggestion.

"They can have it," he said, "all in good time, all in good time."

They left the warehouse with Esperanza and Teresa, smiling, pleased and satisfied. They walked on toward the yard between the field office and the barracks.

Esperanza asked Bill, "How about those facilities? Don't tell me, you will tear them down at the completion of those projects' construction. Paulo can do a lot with them, too."

"Come now, my dear beautiful wife," Bill said, smiling, to Esperanza. "You talk as if you are an employee of Paulo."

Teresa, Dick and Nieves broke into peals of laughter.

"How I wish," Paulo said to Esperanza, "you are working for me. You can do a lot with your connections, but I cannot afford you."

"I will at least get paid if I will work for you," Esperanza said to Paulo. "My husband here does not pay me for what I am doing for him."

"I make you happy, my dear, lovely wife, is that not enough?" Bill said, smiling still, to Esperanza.

"Of course, my dear handsome husband," Esperanza said. "I am the happiest wife in the world."

"Aside from me," Teresa said, smiling.

"And me," Nieves said, smiling, too.

Paulo and Dick nodded, pleased with Teresa and Nieves.

Bill, at the end of their tour of the company compound, said to Esperanza, "All right, my dear beautiful wife, I will donate to the town, everything we built and will build here, if that will make you happy."

"It will make me, Paulo and the others, very happy," Esperanza said, smiling. "You have a generous heart, my dear handsome husband."

Paulo and Dick glanced at each other. The frank way Bill and Esperanza showed their love for each other was a standing joke with them.

Bill left the compound with the others, satisfied as well with what had been done there. He was looking forward to seeing more of that kind of work at the dam site, where they were now going.

There, in an elevation in the ground with a commanding view of Masakao, in a simple start-up ceremony, as those around them cheered and clapped their hands, Bill, Paulo, Fowley, Dick, Philip and the other town officials scooped from the ground, clumps of earth with the shovels in their hands and tossed them into the riverbank below. The earthmoving machines then slid down in the slope and into the riverbank. Construction of the dam will now begin.

Bill watched, satisfied, the start of the work at the dam site and busy as well when he met people later on in the municipal hall and in the company's field office.

He woke up, the following day, in high spirit although with a slight hangover from the wine he drank at the celebration in the town square last night at the start of the dam's construction. He had done enough merrymaking, though. Today will be just another working day for him, the trek to Alkayag the most important of what he will do.

He stood up from the bed and went to the bathroom. He was, a few minutes later, watching Esperanza and Teresa with the help of Maring, their elderly housemaid, and some housewives in the neighborhood, as they were preparing their breakfast in the kitchen and in the dining room.

"There you are, my dear," Esperanza said to Bill. "Breakfast is almost ready."

"Have coffee first with Paulo, Philip and Mister Fowley," Teresa said to Bill. "They are in the living room."

"Where is Michael?" Bill asked Esperanza. He has not seen his son since yesterday morning.

"He and his cousins are with our parents."

"I hope they are not giving the old folks, any trouble."

"No, they are not; they are good kids. As for our parents, they like nothing better than to have their grandchildren around."

Bill nodded, assured about his son's whereabouts. He joined Paulo, Philip and Fowley in the living room for coffee.

Dick and Nieves arrived just then from Nieves' house. She proceeded to the kitchen to help prepare their breakfast while Dick joined the others for coffee.

"So," Paulo said to Dick, when he was about to drink his coffee, "you will be going again with Bill to Alkayag."

"I went there before," Dick replied, "to write what Bill will do there then, which was to destroy it. I am going there again to write what you, Bill and the others will do there now, which is to build something there for the benefit of this town and the rest of the colony."

Dick had alluded to the attack, Bill made with his troops against Paulo and his men in their camp in Alkayag during the war. Bill was going back there, this time to build a road that will connect it to the town. Mining the iron deposits in Alkayag will begin, once the construction of the road is finished.

Kirkpatrick, Jones and Leandro arrived in the house, just as Esperanza had announced that breakfast is ready. They proceeded to the dining room.

The town officials joining the trek to Alkayag arrived in the house, a few minutes later. Teresa invited them to breakfast.

"Thank you," one of them said, "But we have taken our breakfast."

The living room, where they waited was quiet and they could hear there, the talk in the dining room about the dancing and the merrymaking, the previous night in the town square.

It showed how the townsfolk had so liked the Americans for what they had done for them in the past, and are doing now and will continue to do the many good things for their town.

How the Americans took it was reflected by the gaiety at the dining table.

"For an old war horse, like you, Bill, you certainly remain nimble on your feet," Philip said. "How you danced, the night away with Esperanza."

"Some dancing that my husband did," Esperanza said. "No one could outlast him on the dance floor."

"With one exception—me," Dick said.

"I will grant you that, although you could not even keep pace with me when we went to Alkayag," Bill said to Dick, to the laughter of the others at the dining table.

Paulo's friend Sabedro, the mine's Dumagat foreman, and another Dumagat, arrived in the house, just as the men had finished their breakfast. They thanked, but refused Teresa's invitation for them to have breakfast there as, they said, they took something on their way to the town.

The men left in horse-drawn rigs and cabs that took them to the edge of the forest, outside of the town. They went on foot, the rest of the way to Alkayag. Paulo had the foresight of having Sabedro and his fellow Dumagat tribesmen clear the trail, a few days earlier.

It was early March, the start of summer. The time was just right to go to Alkayag when the current in the mountain streams was not swift and difficult to cross as they were during the rainy season when they could be drenched as well with rain.

They made their way, led by Paulo and Sabedro, in the forest. Paulo remained familiar with the trail. He visited Alkayag, a few times, since he returned to the town. Bill, Dick and Fowley walked behind Paulo and Sabedro. The rest of the party followed them. The other Dumagat brought up the rear and looked after anyone who might lag behind or lose his way.

Leandro walked beside Jones, who was stopping now and then to put markers, check his compass and write something on his notebook. Leandro stayed with him for any help, he could extend to Jones' initial survey of the trail. Once they were done, with the Dumagat guiding them, they walked briskly and had soon enough caught up with them.

They reached Alkayag at noontime. The old rebel camp was in a plateau about the size of a baseball field. The Dumagats had planted a great part of it to rice, corn and root crops. It also had fruit and palm trees and banana plants. Other than its topography, nothing there was familiar to Bill and Dick. Whatever Paulo and his men had built there, they themselves had burned down or had been reclaimed by nature.

"What do you think?" Bill asked Philip as they were looking around at the former rebel camp.

"It will make for an ideal mining campsite," Philip replied.

"The Dumagats have made good use of it," Kirkpatrick said.

"Where is the mother lode?" Bill asked Paulo.

"It is right there," Paulo replied as he pointed at the side of the mountain peak that sloped down to the camp.

The party went around, inspecting the area and the base of the mountain peak while Jones, with Leandro's help, made measurements with a surveyor's level and chain. Then they went up to the location of the iron deposits.

Jones removed there with a pick, clumps of iron ore and passed them around. They looked at them that were mostly gray and purple in color. A geologist from the Bureau of Mines had visited the area and took there ore samples, confirming the extensive iron ore deposits there.

Bill asked Dick, who was looking around, "Well, what do you think?"

"I'm looking at you and Paulo," Dick replied, "and at Masakao and Alkayag from several angles—you and Paulo, from foes to friends, Masakao and Alkayag, from fields of strife, to fields of peace and progress. You and Paulo, together with Fowley as the representative of the Insular Government, will make a nice cover in *The Philippines Newsmagazine.*"

They saw, just then, smoke rising from a corner in the plateau.

"Is that," Fowley asked Paulo, "a forest fire?"

"No," Paulo said, smiling. "That is the smoke from our lunch being prepared by the Dumagats."

"What are we waiting for?" Dick then said. "Let us go there now. I am hungry and so are all of you. "

They walked down to where the smoke was coming from and saw in a thatch-roofed shed and in the open-air kitchen there, some Dumagat men and women who were preparing their lunch.

A Dumagat girl was barbecuing venison in hot coals.

A Dumagat man, a bolo in his hand, was cutting away on a bamboo table, the husk of a coconut until he got to its shell. He then punctured it with the tip of his bolo. He held the coconut above a large clay vessel until all of its water had flowed down into the clay vessel. It will make for a cool, refreshing drink.

They watched and waited as the Dumagats were now putting the food on a bamboo table in the middle of the shed. They were dishes the Dumagats had learned to cook when it was a rebel camp.

They then took their lunch of the food laid out in banana leaves on the bamboo table. They ate with their hands or with the forks and spoons, the Dumagats had learned to use when it was a rebel camp.

Paulo, at the end of their lunch, interpreted for Bill who thanked the Dumagats for the delicious food, Paulo had secretly paid for in advance.

Leandro was seated on a sawed-off tree trunk, taking it easy after their hearty meal, when Bill asked him, "So, how do you like your job here in Masakao?"

"It is not like Zamboanga and Davao, sir," Leandro replied. "But I like it here. It is like being back in my hometown."

Bill, since his arrival in Masakao, had seen very little of Leandro. His time was crowded with people to meet and things to do and see.

Leandro was about to speak about his impressions of Masakao, but Bill had turned his attention to Jones, who was standing nearby.

"What do you think of the trail?" he asked Jones "Will it do for a mining road?"

"Those, worked on by the Dumagats, will do," Jones replied.

"Wonderful! The Dumagats have done a good job with it," Bill said, nodding in approval of Sabedro and the other Dumagats who had just then taken their turn at the dining table.

"You can tell your Dumagat friends," Bill said to Paulo, "I am impressed by their building skills. You can also tell them, they will have the priority in the jobs for the construction of the dam and the road and later on, in the operation of the mine."

"I will be very glad to do that," Paulo said, smiling.

Bill and the others watched Paulo as he then spoke to the Dumagats in their local dialect. They nodded, pleased and satisfied, when the Dumagats then broke into excited talk.

Paulo led them as they then approached Bill and the others.

"I have just been appointed as spokesman of Sabedro and his fellow Dumagats," Paulo said to Bill and the others who nodded and smiled. "They asked me to tell you how grateful they are for your kindness. You have their assurances they will work hard, very hard."

"I am looking forward to that day when we shall be working together on the road, the dam and the mine," Bill said to the Dumagats.

Paulo translated again for the Dumagats. They smiled and nodded at Bill as they then returned to their lunch.

"Their capacity for hard work will go well with the technical and management prowess of Pacific and Gulf," Philip said to Bill.

"We will soon see how hard they work especially on the trail, a terrain familiar to them," Kirkpatrick said.

"There are areas, though, where it would be better to build a road than to widen the trail," Jones said.

"We will do whatever will have to be done to make this place accessible to motorized transport," Bill said. "We will do it, at the least possible cost, finish it at the earliest possible time with the work done of such a quality that it will last, long after all of us here are gone."

Leandro nodded. Bill Shay said the same thing at the inauguration of the wharf, the road, the school and the municipal building in Davao. It was the Pacific & Gulf's operational guideline.

The Dumagats were finished with their lunch and Sabedro and the other Dumagat guide were standing by, waiting for orders. It was time for them to go back to the town.

Bill looked around at the mountain peaks and inhaled deeply, the cool bracing mountain air there.

"Nothing," he said, "like clearing up your lungs with clean mountain air before going back to the town."

They returned to Masakao with Sabedro, once again leading the way and the other Dumagat, bringing up the rear. They were now mostly going downward and more familiar with the terrain, so that their return to Masakao was easier and faster. It was midafternoon when they arrived in the town.

While Bill spent part of the following day in enjoying the festivities there, for it was like the town fiesta, he was there mainly to work. He went to the dam site, one more time, watched the work being done there and discussed the dam's technical details with Fowley, Philip, Kirkpatrick and Jones. He also spent time in discussions with Paulo, Dick and Fowley on the Insular Government's economic development program for the colony, especially in the countryside. The land tenancy problem was one subject they did not take up with Paulo.

"I'm glad Paulo did not bring it up," Dick said to Bill as they were approaching their cars at the end of their visit to Masakao,

"So am I," Bill said.

They came to Masakao solely for the purpose of starting the construction of the dam and the road to Alkayag.

Paulo wanted the agricultural lands there, owned by the friars and the Ilustrado landlords, to be bought by the Insular Government and given to the tenants. They in turn will pay for them on installment. Both Dick and Bill knew the powerful landlords and the friars will resist that move.

Dick then said to Bill, "Our government cannot solve the tenancy problem because it cannot cover all of those lands. A big part of them are friar lands. They are protected under the Treaty of Paris, between Spain and the United States. The Catholic Church took the initiative in solving the land tenancy problem when it sold for $7 million, 170,000 hectares of the friar lands. That move needs to be sustained. Because they won't be hampered by the Treaty of Paris, the Filipinos, once the Philippines becomes an independent country, can solve this problem, but only if they have the strong will and the financial resources to do that."

Bill and Dick did not want to be caught between the tenants who wanted those lands returned to them and the Spanish mestizo landlords who wanted to keep them.

They returned to Manila while Jones with Leandro, Sabedro and other Dumagats' help, now surveyed in earnest, the mining road to Alkayag. Work in both the dam and the road was done typically of the projects of Pacific & Gulf—methodically and efficiently. Work on the tunnel that will divert the water, prior to building the dam, was started within a few weeks. Jones' survey of the road was finished by then. Earth-moving equipment then began building the road to Alkayag.

The projects meant jobs, not only for Masakao's townsfolk, but also for the residents in other towns and the Dumagat tribesmen in Alkayag. Paulo's reputation as a political leader spread far and wide.

He was soon known all over the colony with Dick, having put him, Bill and Fowley on the cover of *The Philippines Newsmagazine* as model partners, two Americans and a Filipino, in bringing so much progress and prosperity to the Philippine Islands.

Chapter Forty-three

Since Masakao was only a few hours' ride to Manila by car or by truck, it was near enough for Leandro, as the two projects' warehouse custodian and purchasing agent, to make his purchases there. That took him quite often to Manila.

Unlike in Davao, where he dealt mostly with Yupang, he bought the supplies for their two projects in Masakao, mostly from the Chinese storeowners in Manila. No one offered him a rebate as Yupang did in Davao. He was certain this was a business practice, common among the Chinese storeowners. Balemal, the company's chief purchasing officer, was most likely getting the rebates. He was, to those Chinese merchants, just a subordinate of Balemal doing errand work for him and should not be let in, on their secret trade practice. He did not care for that, though. What mattered to him was his job in Pacific & Gulf.

He took his meals in Crisanta and her parents' food stall whenever he was in Parola. The food there was delicious. Even better, serving it was Crisanta herself. He was hardly aware of it, but he was increasingly being drawn to her.

He was kept, one time, by work at the warehouse from taking his dinner early enough. He saw, when he went to the Mercaidas' food stall, Crisanta wiping clean the empty food counter while Mang Emong and Aling Pacing were putting in a carton box, fresh leftover beef and vegetables. They were closing up their food stall.

"I'm sorry for coming late," he said to Crisanta.

"I'm sorry, too," she said. "I wish we can offer you something, but we are cleaned out here."

Leandro glanced at the other food stalls. They were either closed or were also closing.

"I cannot bear the thought of you, passing the night on an empty stomach," Crisanta said to Leandro. "We are about to leave. If you like, you can have dinner with us, at home."

"Thank you," he said. "That will save me a long walk to the restaurants that may still be open in Carvajal Street."

He caught Aling Pacing, frowning at Crisanta. She forgot to ask first for her parents' permission in her eagerness to invite him to dinner in their home. It was not considered proper for a nice girl like her to extend such an invitation to a mere acquaintance like him.

Mang Emong was more permissive, though. He said to Leandro, "We will be glad to have you join us for dinner at home."

Aling Pacing looked away, frowning, but said nothing.

Leandro looked down at the ground. He was in a quandary. He would have preferred it, if Mang Emong was of the same mind as Aling Pacing. He would then thank, but refuse Crisanta's dinner invitation and walk away with no hurt feelings. He could take his dinner elsewhere. But there he was, invited to dinner by Crisanta and Mang Emong over Aling Pacing's silent objection. He was pleasantly surprised when Aling Pacing said, "Very well, you can have dinner with us."

"Thank you, ma'am," he said. "I really don't want to go to bed, hungry."

The joke he made eased up what was then a tense situation for him.

He carried the carton box of food and waited with Crisanta and Aling Pacing while Mang Emong was closing up their food stall. They walked toward the street corner where a horse-drawn rig was parked.

Mang Emong asked the rig driver, who was taking a nap in the driver's seat, if he was taking any fare. He asked Mang Emong where they were going. Mang Emong gave the address. The rig driver mentioned the fare. Mang Emong nodded in agreement to it. Then he helped Crisanta and Aling Pacing in stepping up into the rig. They took the backseat while Mang Emong and Leandro took the seat behind the rig driver with the carton box of food in Leandro's lap.

It was not a long ride to Nicodemus Street in Tondo where Crisanta and her parents resided. The rig entered the narrow street which ended at the shore of Manila Bay. It was late afternoon and the sun was now low in the horizon. Young girls playing hopscotch in the street stepped aside as the rig was passing by.

The rig driver, at Mang Emong's direction, pulled the horse to a stop in front of a small wooden house with a porch, the home of the Mercaida family.

Leandro got off from the rig with Mang Emong. He offered to pay the rig driver. Mang Emong waved it aside and paid the driver while he was helping Aling Pacing in getting off from the rig. He then held Crisanta's hand as she was also getting off from the rig and felt sorry for her, whose hand was made rough by the work she did in their food stall.

He followed them to the house. It was typical of the homes in the working-class district of Tondo. Like his uncle Berting's hut in Palomar, it was raised a foot above the wet ground. Unlike his uncle Berting's hut, it was walled with wood, its roof made also of palm shingles.

He gave the carton box of food to Mang Emong as he was about to enter the house. The wooden floor, he noticed at the door, was clean and shiny. He would not want his rubber sneakers to soil it and he bent down to remove them from his feet.

"You don't have to do that. Come in, come in," Crisanta said to him as she was opening the window overlooking the street. "Make yourself comfortable while we are preparing our dinner."

He stepped inside the house, sat down on a large wooden couch there and looked around at the house.

It was bigger than the hut in Bangar and shaped differently. A door at the right side of the dining area probably led to Crisanta's bedroom. Her parents probably slept on the bamboo bed, set against the wall at the other side of the dining area in the middle of which was the dining table. Behind it was the kitchen and beside it was another door probably to the bathroom, Crisanta had just then opened and closed.

He watched Aling Pacing who was slicing into thin strips, the chunk of beef she had taken out of the carton box. Then she mixed the meat with soy sauce and citrus juice.

Mang Emong, a few feet behind her, was building a fire in the clay stove in the kitchen. Then he put on top of the stove, a frying pan and dropped there several spoonfuls of lard. He put in the frying pan, when it was hot enough, slices of onion and the marinated beef. The house was soon rich with the mouth-watering smell of frying beef and onion.

Crisanta came out of the bathroom and joined Aling Pacing at the dining table who said to her, "I can manage this. Attend to your guest."

"Very well, Mother," she said.

She said, as she sat down on a small couch near Leandro, "I'm glad you have been assigned to Masakao. It is not far like Davao and Zamboanga. You can now come to Manila as often as you need to."

"And that is often enough—every two weeks or so."

"How long will you be in Manila, this time?"

"I will be here until Sunday. I am going back to Masakao on Monday yet."

"You have no work then. What will you do on your day off?"

"I have not thought about it yet," he said, but then his eyes lit up. She might agree if he will invite her to spend Sunday with him. They could first attend Mass and afterwards have lunch in a restaurant in Carvajal Street. They could afterwards take a stroll in Luneta Park and cap the day by watching the beautiful sunset in Manila Bay.

"How would you like to attend Mass with me?" he said to her. "We can go to Manila Cathedral or Binondo Church."

"So, you are a Catholic."

"Yes, I am a Catholic. You are also a Catholic, are you not?"

"Not anymore. We have converted to Methodists."

He pursed his lips in disappointment. Taking her to Mass was not only out of the question, so would be any farther association with her and her parents. He will be committing venial sin, as he was taught by Father Saludo in San Isidro, every time he kept company with a Protestant like her. If he did that, often enough, the venial sins will add up to a mortal sin and just one mortal sin will be enough to send him to the fires in hell.

It was a big issue for him. The presence of the American Protestant ministers in the Philippines meant they were, after more than three hundred years, no longer solely under the pastoral care of the Catholic priests, many of them, Spanish friars. Now, here they are, the American Protestant ministers undertaking their own evangelizing work in the Philippines. One result of their work was the departure of Crisanta and her parents from the Catholic Church.

His mind was made up. He will stay away from Crisanta, but he is at least staying for dinner. It will be rude of him if he will tell them that he could not, a Catholic, share a meal with them because they are Protestants.

Crisanta's mind was on other things.

"How long," she asked him, "will it take you to finish the dam and the road in Masakao?"

"It may take a year, maybe two years. I can only make a guess. I am not an engineer. Why did you ask me about that?"

"I want to know, how long you will be going, back and forth, between Manila and Masakao."

"I cannot tell you that, but it is far better than working for a long time in faraway places like Davao and Zamboanga."

She nodded, smiling. She turned her gaze to Aling Pacing who was calling them to dinner.

The simple meal, Aling Pacing and Mang Emong had prepared of fried rice and fried beef and onion was delicious, like the food they served in their food stall.

That did not come as a surprise to him. Crisanta and her folks came from Pampanga, a province noted for its fine cuisine.

They finished their dinner in just a short while. He stayed for a while, out of courtesy to them, and talked about his work in Masakao. He left after thanking them for the nice dinner.

He felt, on stepping out into the street, Crisanta looking at him from the window in the porch. He did not look back at her. What for when he is never going there again? She will be, from now on, nothing more to him than a nice woman who served good food in their food stall. He is a Catholic while she is a Protestant. They are incompatible.

It was early evening and it was cool with a soft breeze now blowing from the bay. He took a horse-drawn cab for his return to Parola.

The cab's slight swaying movement from the horse running in the street, as he was seated at the cab's backseat, induced him to reflect on his relationship with women. Something somehow had to spoil it. With Crisanta, it was religion—he was a Catholic while she was a Protestant. With Regina and Angela, it was racial, social and economic—he is a poor native peasant boy while they are rich, socially prominent Spanish mestizas. With Marina, it was cultural—he is from the mainstream Philippine society while she is from an ethnic minority. Add to that the sex they had that nearly forced him into marrying her. It could have turned his life, upside down.

He sighed. He is young and he might have better luck with other women. But he must, for now, set them aside and concentrate on his job. It is the only thing that mattered to him now.

All the thought about the women who had touched his life had been vanished from his mind, by the time he arrived in Parola. He was focused solely on his job, by the time he was back in Masakao.

He avoided any socializing in the town despite the pretty girls he had seen there. He followed without fail his daily routine of waking up, early in the morning, taking his breakfast at the company mess hall, then off to work in the warehouse or as often at the job sites where he brought supplies and equipment and helped in building the dam and the road to Alkayag.

He was back to work after a lunch break of one hour, then off to their barracks, retiring early evening after supper at the mess hall. He made an arrangement to have the supplies and equipment brought to Masakao. That way, he did not have to go to Manila and thus avoided seeing Crisanta.

He was about to enter the town church, one Sunday morning, when someone at the church entrance gave him a palm leaf. He remembered then, as he was accepting it, that it was Palm Sunday, the start of the Holy Week. He entered the church to a sea of palm leaves, some of them held high by those waiting for the start of the Mass.

Work on the dam and the road to Alkayag slowed down and stopped altogether on Holy Thursday. This was in keeping with the observance of the Holy Week.

This forced idleness induced him to spend the day, by taking a nap in the company barracks. He woke up, late in the afternoon, when he heard voices reading in singsong manner, a passage in the Holy Bible.

He left his cot and dressed up. He took his dinner at the mess hall and then went out to the town square, a short walk from the company compound. It was full of people, seated on the concrete benches there or were huddled in small groups, engaged in conversation. The road between the town square and the church was full of people walking by singly, in pairs, or in groups.

He entered the bandstand, improvised as a chapel for the Bible reading. Two couples seated beside each other were reading in singsong manner, a passage in the Holy Bible, placed on a table in front of them.

About a dozen old people were seated behind the Bible readers. They were waiting for their turn to read passages from the Holy Bible. It will go on continuously into the night and up to the following morning on Good Friday.

As he also knew it, the next religious rite will then be held in the town church. This will be the discourse, starting at noon, by the parish priest on The Seven Last Words, as they were called, that Jesus Christ uttered at his crucifixion.

All those rites will culminate, early morning of Easter Sunday, at the celebration in the resurrection of Jesus Christ.

He knew all those rites, way back in his boyhood as an acolyte in the church in San Isidro. All those religious observances and celebration were general all over the Philippines with its predominantly Catholic population.

He left the bandstand after a while and joined the crowd, taking a walk in the town road. He walked toward no particular destination, his interest drawn to young people like him. They were enjoying themselves. It was as if they were taking a stroll in Luneta Park in Manila.

The smile in their faces and their cheerful talk showed him that it was not so much in the observance of Holy Thursday that they were out there in the town road as in the enjoyment of each other's company.

It was the only day in the entire year when it was socially acceptable for young, single women to walk around in the town road in the company of young men. The young men, for their part, took it as a golden opportunity to press their suit with the young women in their company. For those young men and women, taking a stroll in the town road on Holy Thursday was a perfect time for courtship. He smiled at the thought that he could do that too to a girl, if he had a girl.

A tent improvised as a chapel for the Bible reading was set up, some distance from the town square. He stepped inside. He was watching and listening to a hymn being sung in accompaniment with the Bible reading when he overheard a young couple near him who were having an argument. He listened to them.

"Let us take a seat there and wait for our turn to read the Holy Bible," the girl said in a low voice to the young man, standing beside her.

"Only old people do that," the young man replied.

"Who said so?"

"But I don't know the tune."

"Just sing along, it is that easy."

The young man hesitated. The girl frowned and said, "Very well, I will do it alone."

The girl left the young man and walked toward the empty chairs there. The young man followed her and sat down beside her.

Their argument and the smile they now gave each other showed Leandro that they were a young man and woman in love with each other.

He watched them, filled with envy. The young man had his girl beside him while he, standing alone at the back, had no girl he could call his own. He sighed in regret. If only Crisanta had remained a Catholic, he would be by her side now, watching the same rite in a church in Manila. They could then, later in the evening, do the *Visita Iglesia*, a religious practice they picked up from the Spaniards of paying seven churches a visit in remembrance of the last hours their savior, Jesus Christ, spent before he was crucified for their redemption from sin.

It was already dark when he walked back to the company compound. The road and the town square were now even more crowded as more people were encouraged to go out in the open by the cool night air. He walked on, feeling lonely in the crowd, he being a stranger in the town, the people he knew and cared for, far from him.

He retired early to voices reading in singsong manner, a passage in the Holy Bible. Out there in the town square and on the road, young men like him had the time of their lives wooing and winning the love of the young women in their company. The thought made him so lonely and depressed. Thankfully for him, he finally fell asleep.

Time passed. Leandro had long been attached to nature from his life rooted to the land and the sea. He could tell by the feel of the wind on his face, the changes in the season, warm and humid during summer, damp in the rainy months and cool in the late months of the year. So was the sun, harsh and glaring during summer, screened by dark, heavy clouds in the rainy months and softer, its rays tempered, later in the year.

All of those showed him, without having to look at the preparations being made in the town, that Christmas was coming. He could feel an air of anticipation in Masakao getting keener as Christmas Day drew near when the spirit of the season became more and more pervasive.

Grand or humble, every home in the town was by now decorated with the Christmas Stars in the windows, the candles inside lit up at night. The homes there now had Christmas trees in the living rooms, an evidence of the growing American cultural influence in the colony.

It was just as pronounced in the hymns that now filled the air in the church, in the town school and in the homes there. The Americans brought with them, beautiful hymns like *Silent Night, Holy Night* and *O Come All Ye Faithful,* now sung along with that enduring legacy from the Spanish time, the lively hymn of *Nacio, Nacio Pastores.*

He has no family or friends with whom he could share in the festivities. He is a loner, a workaholic devoted solely to his job. He has not heard from Carlos. Regina, Angela and Marina were all forgotten. He has not written to Candido and has not received any letters from him. As for Crisanta, he avoided her food stall, the few times he went to Parola.

All work stopped, the day before Christmas Day, to allow the workers to be home with their families. Kirkpatrick and Jones had left for Manila where they will spend Christmas with their families. The only worker in the company compound, aside from the security guard at the gate, was the locally hired cook who also left after providing Leandro with his evening meal.

He was all alone in the barracks with nowhere to go to. There was Mayor Paulo Palanas and his wife Teresa, but it would be presumptuous of him to go knocking at the door of the home of the town mayor and the sister-in-law of the Big Boss.

It was Christmas Eve. The company compound was cast in darkness except for the light in the security guard's outpost at the gate and the solitary light in Leandro's corner in the barracks.

He was debating with himself whether or not he will attend the Midnight Mass to be held within half an hour in the town church, across the town square. But he was lethargic from having done nothing the whole day, he might as well skip it and attend instead, the morning Mass on Christmas Day.

He was about to turn off the gas lamp near his cot when he was startled by the sudden appearance there of Bill Shay.

"What are you doing here, all alone?" Bill asked him.

"I'm keeping an eye, sir, on the company property."

Bill regarded him keenly.

"Well, now," he said, "while I like your zeal and dedication to your job, are you not overdoing it, a bit? It is Christmas Eve! Why are you not, at home with your folks?"

"This is my home, sir," he replied. "I have got no family with whom I can spend Christmas."

He was wondering at the same time what the Big Boss was doing there in the company compound on Christmas Eve.

"In that case," Bill said, as he gave him a kindly look, "I am inviting you to spend the *Noche Buena* with us, after the Midnight Mass. We will hold it in the home of Esperanza's parents. Paulo and Teresa will be there, so will be, Dick and Nieves. The whole family will be there. Celebrating Christmas Eve with us is better than staying here, all alone, is it not? I saw the light in your quarters as I was taking a look around here."

"Thank you, sir," he said, smiling. "I'm so glad and honored to accept your invitation. I did not know, you are a Catholic, sir."

"I am not, although I have taken the initial steps in converting to a Catholic. Mind you, I did this only to please my wife as what I have been doing from the time we were married in the town church here."

"I did not know the Catholic Church allows that, sir."

"Not ordinarily; we got a special dispensation for that."

"I am so glad to hear that, sir," he said, more for himself than for the Big Boss, for it occurred to him then that, if a non-Catholic like the Big Boss could marry a Catholic like Esperanza, so could he, a Catholic, at the very least, make friends with a Methodist like Crisanta.

Philip Beldry, a few days later, sent for Leandro. He knew why. Bill Shay had told him at the Noche Buena that he was going to be assigned to a much bigger company project in Baguio.

"You have done well in Masakao," Philip said to Leandro when he came to see him in his office in Parola. "You are now in for bigger things. Mister Shay has told you about your assignment in Baguio."

"Thank you, sir," he replied, "for that assignment in Baguio."

"Do you know what Baguio is like and what we are doing there?"

"I have heard about it, sir. It seems, we are building something big in a tribal village there, deep in the mountains in Central Cordillera."

"We are building there, a modern vacation resort city. We are the lead company in a consortium of companies doing work there. We have several projects there, from road and bridge building, to the construction of parks, schools, a cathedral, a power, telephone and waterworks system, a country club complete with a golf course, vacation homes, housing for the workers, office and commercial buildings, a hospital, a military camp and academy. We are widening and paving the roads to the copper mines and the mountain tribes, up in the north and a lot more."

He nodded, very much impressed by what Philip Beldry said. He never imagined the extent of Pacific & Gulf's work there. No such massive undertaking had ever been attempted before in the Philippines.

He left Philip Beldry's office, so lost in thought of the magnitude of the work being done by Pacific & Gulf in Baguio that, on stepping out of the building, he nearly collided again with Carlos.

"Well, look, who is here," Carlos said to him. "Are you not a sight for my sore eyes?"

"So am I."

"Enjoy your short stay, here in Manila."

"So, you know about my assignment in Baguio."

"Of course, I do know that."

They walked on, in the company compound.

"How are you getting along?" he asked Carlos.

"I'm not sure how to answer that question, now that I am getting married," Carlos said, a sour smile on his face.

"You are, to whom?"

"To Angela, of course."

"Congratulations! You make a happy couple, but are you not in a hurry to get married? She is not through with her studies, is she? Or is she quitting school?"

"No."

"Can you not wait until she graduates?"

"I wish we can, but we cannot."

"Why not?"

"She had this 'accident,'" Carlos said as he then made a curved motion with his hand in front of his stomach.

Leandro shook his head. Carlos and Angela were going to have a child and they did not want it born out of wedlock.

"When," he asked Carlos, "are you two getting married?"

"This coming Sunday."

Carlos halted and said to Leandro, "How come you don't know that? You are in the guest list. Angela is supposed to send you an invitation."

He kept silent. He never got any invitation from Angela. She had purposely left him out of their wedding, but he is going to attend it, not for her, but for Carlos. He let the matter pass.

"This calls for a celebration," he said to Carlos.

"And we will start it with a lunch at the cafeteria."

"Better still, if we will have it at a food stall. I must see someone there."

Carlos said, as they were approaching the company gate, "You might as well know that Regina and Ruy are also getting married."

Leandro halted, startled by the news of Regina, getting married to Ruy. He pursed his lips, concerned for her. She is making a big mistake in marrying that spoiled boy. Whatever they did was none of his business, though, and he walked on with Carlos.

He passed out of the gate with Carlos and led him to Crisanta's food stall. She was alone.

"Look, who is here," she said, smiling as he and Carlos were approaching her food stall.

"How are you?" he said to her.

"I am fine," she said, smiling still. "I have not seen you around. Where were you, all this time?"

"I was in Masakao, busy working as usual."

She glanced at Carlos.

"Do you know this fellow?" he said to her, his finger pointed to Carlos. "He is Carlos Yturalde. He was my guide when I was new in Pacific and Gulf."

Carlos nodded and smiled at Crisanta.

"Crisanta and her folks serve the most delicious food here, the cafeteria included," he said to Carlos.

"Is that so?"

"I see you pass by, often enough," Crisanta said to Carlos, "but not once have you tried the food we serve here."

"About time, you did," Leandro said, rebuking Carlos.

"I now have the chance to try it."

They sat down on the bench there, their eyes turned to the food counter in front of them.

Crisanta asked them, "What can I offer you, gentlemen?"

Leandro replied, "Can you give us something special?"

She said, smiling, "For you, it is always something special."

Carlos' eyes darted to Leandro and Crisanta, an amused smile on his face.

"It is not for me," Leandro said to her, "but for this fellow here, beside me. We are celebrating with the food you will serve us, his forthcoming marriage."

"Congratulations! For that, you will indeed have something special."

"Consider yourself as invited, too," Carlos said to Crisanta.

"Me?" she said, her mouth hanging open in astonishment.

"Yes, you," Carlos said. "I consider the friend of my friend here also as my friend."

"Thank you. I am honored, but I don't even know the girl you will marry."

"You will get to know her, soon enough."

"Allow me to escort you to their wedding."

Crisanta smiled and nodded in agreement to Carlos' invitation to his wedding. She put in two plates, something special for the lunch of Carlos and Leandro.

Crisanta's parents saw nothing improper about her attending with Leandro, Carlos and Angela's wedding and they did not pose any objection.

The wedding was held in San Agustin Church. The reception that followed was held in Columbus Club. The cream of Manila's high society was there. So were the landlords in San Isidro, including the Monte Arazteas.

Leandro was seated at a table, beside Crisanta. The look on his face showed him to be proud, happy and satisfied. He was cutting an impressive figure of himself. To Angela and Regina, he has with him, a girl, attractive in her own way. To Don Camilo and his family, he was no longer the poor, peasant boy in San Isidro, but a young man on his way up in the largest construction company in the islands.

Streams of waiters in white coats served in every table, various dishes and French wine and Spanish brandy. Glasses were raised and clinked to each other for the happiness and prosperity of Carlos and Angela Yturalde. The orchestra then struck up a lovely waltz.

Carlos and Angela left the head table and were soon on the dance floor, dancing to the waltz's three-quarter beat.

Leandro and Crisanta did not know how to dance, but they were nonetheless enjoying themselves in watching Carlos and Angela and other couples, dancing the waltz. He was happy and satisfied enough in holding Crisanta's hand. The others at the table did not notice it, for their hands were locked underneath the table, hidden from their view by the tablecloth.

She resisted at first when he tried to hold her hand and she tried to pull it away, but then he held it so firmly, her hand eventually went limp in her submission to him.

Leandro took his lunch in Crisanta's food stall, the day following Carlos and Angela's wedding. He was leaving in the afternoon for Masakao to wind up his work there. He will be back in Parola on Saturday.

He said to her, the moment her parents' attention was turned to Aling Nelia, the owner of the food stall, next to theirs, he would like to take her out on Sunday. They will take their lunch in a restaurant in Binondo and then spend the rest of the day in Luneta Park and watch there, the lovely sunset in Manila Bay.

"I would love to do that, but I cannot," she said to Leandro. "It will not look nice if I will go out with you. My parents will not let me."

"You can ask a cousin or a friend to go out with us."

"I will ask my cousin Armando. He cannot resist a free lunch."

Leandro listened as Crisanta then said to Aling Pacing, "Leandro and I are going out on Sunday."

"A decent girl does not just go out with a man."

"You allowed me to attend the wedding of Leandro's friend."

"That is different,"

"I will have Armando to chaperone us."

"All right," Mang Emong said, ending their argument. "You can go out with Leandro, but be back before sundown and only if Armando is with you."

Leandro came knocking, the following Sunday morning, at the door in Crisanta's home.

"You look so lovely in that very nice dress," he said to her when she opened the door.

She was wearing a blouse with sleeves that reached down to her elbows and a skirt that reached down to her feet.

She led him inside the house. Mang Emong and Aling Pacing were at the dining table. He greeted them, a good morning. A stout boy wearing rubber sneakers was seated on the couch. Crisanta told Leandro, the boy was her cousin Armando, their chaperone.

"We are going now," she said to her parents.

They looked on approvingly as Crisanta was leaving the house with Leandro and Armando.

He held her hand when she stepped up to a horse-drawn rig, waiting for them in the street. The rig driver then took them to a restaurant in Carvajal Street. He ordered a sumptuous lunch. The food he ordered came within a few minutes. He glanced, amused, at Armando, whose eyes were big and bright, as he was looking at the food on the table. The boy ate with gusto while he and Crisanta ate sparingly. Their attention was not so much on the food as on each other.

They window-shopped after lunch in Escolta, one of Manila's two principal shopping streets. They were passing by a jewelry store there when they saw, displayed there, a gold necklace with a pearl pendant.

"It sure is a fine jewelry," he said to her.

"Any girl will love to wear it."

"Let us go inside."

He asked a saleslady there to bring to them, the gold necklace.

"It will look nice on you," he said as he was then holding the gold necklace.

"At that price," she said, her eyes on the price tag, "it should look nice on any girl."

"Never mind the price. Just try it on."

He nodded at the saleslady who then put the necklace around Crisanta's neck. She smiled as she looked at herself before a mirror there.

"Do you like it?" he asked her.

"Of course, I like it. Any girl wearing this necklace will like it."

He took out his wallet and paid for the necklace.

She asked him, "Are you really buying this for me?"

"I am."

"Why?"

"It is my belated Christmas gift to you."

"Thank you, but I have got nothing to give you in return."

"You can pay me back by cooking for me, something delicious."

They were both smiling when they left the jewelry store with him pleased with the necklace now around her neck. Not only did it look nice on her, it will remind her of him, every time she is wearing it.

They proceeded to Luneta Park to watch, later in the afternoon, the beautiful sunset in Manila Bay.

Chapter Forty-four

Leandro looked to his right as the truck was passing out of the gate of Pacific & Gulf. He saw Crisanta and her parents serving several patrons in their food stall.

He sighed as the truck moved on, in Muelle de la Industria. He is leaving for yet another place, this time to Baguio, a place he heard was like no other place in the Philippines.

It might be a long time before he will see Crisanta again. His mind on her, he glanced indifferently at a boat moving in Pasig River toward the bay. Dockhands in the riverbank were busy loading crates and bales of goods into a boat, docked there.

The truck turned left toward Rosario Street. Leandro looked on with little interest at the people on the sidewalk and at the stores and shops lining the street. It gave him a fleeting impression of Manila he is leaving for yet another time.

He is looking forward to his assignment in Baguio, a beautiful place, he heard, that is so unlike the rest of the Philippines. It also reminded him about the itinerant nature of his job.

It had regretably resulted in his short-lived relationship with people, especially with women. But he is young and adventurous and he has yet to see a lot of other wonderful places and meet other wonderful people in his lifetime of many journeys.

And yet, he got, after witnessing Carlos and Angela's wedding, the feeling that it may be time for him to settle down, too. He has, in Crisanta, the woman with whom he would love to spend the rest of his life.

He was not inclined to talk about this personal matter with Esteban whom he first met only this morning as they were entering his truck. He looked around instead as they were passing by Binondo Church.

"Sit back and relax. It will be a long trip to Baguio," Esteban said, breaking the silence inside the driver's cabin.

"Have you been there before?"

"I have, countless times. I shuttle between Manila and Baguio, where I live.

He glanced at Esteban and said, "It must be nice to live there, a tribal village up high in the mountains, our company is converting into a modern vacation resort city. I have heard it described as "like New England without the snow.""

"That is a very nice way to describe Baguio although I have no idea what New England looks like."

"I have a good idea about it, from what I learned about it in school. How long will it take us to get there?"

"It varies. It may take five, six, seven hours. It depends on the traffic and the condition in Kennon Road. It is the mountain road to Baguio. We have to stop at certain one-way sections of the road and wait for our turn to move on. Landslides sometimes block some sections of the road. That is to be expected. It is a newly built road and it is still undergoing a lot of improvement."

They fell silent. The truck ran on, the steady hum of the engine, the only sound inside the driver's cabin.

Leandro crossed his arms and gazed idly at the street ahead. He saw no remarkable change in the scenery there of homes, old and new, that lined it, not even, after they had crossed the bridge spanning the channel, the boundary between Manila and the suburban town of Caloocan.

Esteban, not long after, glanced at Leandro and said, "Do you know that Mister Shay, the Big Boss, lives here in Caloocan?"

"Is that so?"

"Would you like to see his house? It is only a block away from Mabini Street, the town's main street."

"Sure, I would like to."

Esteban drove on. He turned right after a while from Mabini Street. Then he turned left toward another street. He had the truck, now moving at a crawl. It stopped at the iron grill gate of a house in the street.

"That is where the Big Boss lives," Esteban said as he pointed at a ranch-type house painted white with screened windows and a galvanized iron sheet roof, painted green. Its lawn with palm and fruit trees set it back from the street.

Leandro looked on at the house, surprised and disappointed to find the home of Bill Shay so modest for the president of Pacific & Gulf, the largest construction company in the Philippines.

Bill Shay's home looked just like the American bungalows, he had seen in Malate and Ermita. He expected it to be like Malacanang Palace or at least like the homes of the landlords in San Isidro. As one of the richest men in the colony, the Big Boss could even afford a home as grand and opulent as the official residence of the American governor-general in the Philippines.

He was looking on at the house when his disappointment turned into an admiration of the Big Boss. His home is so modest, for it reflected the kind of person that he is, the opposite of Don Camilo. Where Don Camilo is brusque, arrogant and ostentatious, Bill Shay is kind, friendly and unpretentious. Where Don Camilo is feared and hated by his tenants, Bill Shay is loved and respected by his workers. Where Don Camilo stole their land, Bill Shay is building on their land, schools, homes, roads, bridges, ports, hospitals and a lot more.

"What do you think about it?" Esteban said as he drove away.

"It looks nice," he said, "although it looks no different from the American bungalows, I have seen in Manila. It may have been built from one of several architectural designs by Pacific and Gulf."

They were about to turn right on Mabini Street when he saw what looked like was a vacant lot at the end of the street.

"Can we take a look there?" he said as he pointed at the vacant lot.

Esteban threw him a puzzled look. He drove the truck, just the same, right in front of the vacant lot which Leandro saw was a very big lot bound with a chain-link fence. He saw a lagoon at the back of the vacant lot, its waters blue in reflection of the sky. A narrow strip of land separated it from Manila Bay. Farther away in the horizon was the dark outline of the mountain range in Bataan.

He will, he said to himself, own that big lot. He will build there his home with a fantastic view of the lagoon and Manila Bay and he will be living near the home of the Big Boss. It is also near enough to Manila and it has the rustic quality of the countryside, like the hamlet in Bangar.

He thanked Esteban for accommodating him who then drove the truck, back to Mabini Street, past the homes and shops lining it, the town church, the town hall and the town square luxuriant with plants and trees.

"I will live in this nice town," he said to himself, "near the Big Boss' house."

The rest of Caloocan was, from there, except for the train repair shops and marshaling yard, mostly shrubbery and huts, solitary or huddled together and homes, built of stone and wood, more shops and stores.

The truck then sped, past a marshland. The land near the road had been converted into fishponds in square patterns. The surface of the water there was bright in reflection of the morning sun, looking at it, hurt Leandro's eyes. He looked down instead at the truck floor and dozed off.

When, after sometime, he woke up and looked around, rice fields were all that he could now see at both sides of the road. They have passed the fishponds in Bulacan. They were now in Central Plain. The harvest season was over. The rice fields there lay idle in the sun until the start of the planting season when the rain will start falling there again.

He looked out at the horizon. Somewhere there, far to the northwest, is San Isidro. It seemed like ages ago since he left his hometown, but that was only four years ago. He had changed so much, since then, from a naïve peasant boy to a seasoned worker and traveler, wise with the ways of the world.

The sameness of the landscape made him drowsy again and he said to Esteban, "Wake me up when we'll stop for lunch."

Esteban did just that when they arrived, hours later, in the roadside village of Carmen, a popular stopover for travelers. They had a leisurely lunch in a roadside restaurant there. They boarded their truck, after Esteban had a smoke, and were soon on the road again.

Leandro saw, nearly an hour later, that they were now leaving the Central Plain with the mountain peaks of Central Cordillera, looming ahead. The truck engine began to labor when it started its ascent. Where the asphalt road, back in the plain, ran flat and oftentimes straight, it was now ascending and winding beside a mountainside.

He was seeing on the road, but on a much larger scale, the same marvelous engineering employed in building the road to Alkayag. The road, he noticed, was most of the way, built alongside a stream. The other side of the stream was a mountainside covered mostly with grass.

They passed by a waterfall at the mountainside, so slim and bright, it looked to him was like a white bridal veil.

The view to his left of the mountainside was marvelous, but not of the road itself which he noticed was now strewn with soil and stones.

"We may be coming to a landslide," Esteban said.

He slowed down the truck until, at a turn on the road, he stopped it behind another truck at the end of a line of ten or so trucks and cars. A landslide had indeed taken place on the road. It blocked the road's right lane and it could handle only one-way traffic.

He passed the time by watching the trucks and the cars that came from Baguio. A construction worker overseeing the traffic, after a while, waved with a red flag in his hand, for them to move on.

Esteban drove the truck slowly, past the workers who were removing by hand or with shovels, the rocks, stones and soil blocking a part of the road. He followed, frowning, the truck ahead of them. It was so slow it had been left far behind by the trucks and cars ahead of them.

He turned the truck, after a few more minutes of patient driving, toward a one-story building in an open ground. They have arrived in Camp One. It was a field office and marshaling yard of Pacific & Gulf which handled part of the construction and maintenance of Kennon Road.

"We will remove some of the supplies here," Esteban said as he parked the truck there. He then proceeded to the field office there.

Leandro left the truck too and walked around to limber up his legs which felt stiff for so long a time, he was seated inside the truck.

Esteban returned afterwards with a couple of workers who removed some of the construction supplies and equipment from the truck.

Their task there done, they boarded their truck and drove back to Kennon Road. Esteban sometimes drove the truck to the shoulder of the road and waited for his turn to drive on at sections in the road, not wide enough to accommodate two-way traffic.

He followed the same procedure and allowed a car coming from Baguio to cross first, a one-lane steel bridge.

Leandro felt as they were going higher on the road, the air there was now much cooler.

Esteban was saying something, but all that he could hear from him was a monotonous trilling in his ears, as if they were full of crickets.

"Will you say that again?" he said to Esteban who laughed and then shouted, "Can you hear me now?"

"I can hardly hear you."

"Swallow hard, several times," Esteban said which he showed by opening and closing his mouth. "Your hearing will then go back to normal."

He did what Esteban told him to do. He then heard something snap inside his ears and he could hear well again. He could even hear now, the hum of the truck engine and the crunching sound, the truck tires were sometimes making on the asphalt road.

"What," he asked Esteban, "made me so hard of hearing?"

"I'm not sure, what brought it about. It may have something to do with our ascent, something like air pressure on the ears. Anyway, you can hear well again—that is the important thing."

"How far are we now from Baguio?"

"We should be arriving there in just a short while."

The truck continued its ascent. Leandro looked down from the cabin window at sections of the road, they drove through a while ago that were now far below them.

He was looking at the view there when he felt suddenly dizzy, at the same time that he was feeling a tingling sensation in the soles of his feet. He had another attack of vertigo, just like that which he had in Zamboanga. He looked on at the road ahead, the dizzy spell he felt, having passed away, his attention now drawn to the trees near the road.

He had never seen before, trees like them. Thin and straight, they had gnarled barks, dark brown in color. They had, instead of leaves, what looked to him were like long brown and green needles.

Esteban saw him looking wide-eyed at the trees and he said, "They are pine trees. They grow only in high places like Baguio."

Leandro then turned his head out of the cabin window and said, as he was inhaling deeply, the cool, fresh mountain air, "They smell fine, too."

Esteban afterwards drove the truck off the road and stopped at an open ground there.

"There it is—Baguio," he said to Leandro.

He looked out through the windshield. All he could see were mountain peaks and the sky. The truck's hood and the ground a few feet ahead had obstructed the view below of Baguio.

"Let us go outside," Esteban said, "where we can have a good look at Baguio."

They moved out of the truck. Leandro was about to shut the door when cold wind swept by him. He returned quickly to the truck and took out his jacket from his suitcase there. He had the foresight to bring with him a thick jacket by what he was told about Baguio's cold climate.

He moved out of the truck, now comfortably warm in his jacket, and savored with a deep breath, the scent of the pine trees and the cold wind sweeping by.

He joined Esteban near the edge of the ground and saw a section of Baguio spread out, below them. It was mostly rolling terrain with winding roads lined by buildings and tall pine trees.

He saw in a hill there, buildings of uniform size and shape of what looked like a military camp, he learned later on, was Camp John Hay. He saw below the camp a market, no doubt from the crowd there and buildings, finished or under construction that lined a street, he learned later on, was Session Road, Baguio's main street. He saw near the market, a park with a grass-carpeted open space, bound by pine trees, a kiosk and in the middle, a long and wide rectangular man-made lake.

It was, he learned later on, the Burnham Park, named after Daniel Burnham, the American architect who designed Baguio from a tiny Ibaloi village into a modern American-style vacation resort city. There were buildings, some of them, near the marketplace. Some were finished, some were under construction. Right down below them was a football field.

He nodded, thrilled by what he was seeing there. Everything built in Baguio was in harmony with nature. The result was this beautiful vacation resort city. The magnificent view of what was natural and man-made, the bracing wind, the scent of the pine trees and flowers were so invigorating, he exclaimed, "What a lovely, wonderful place!"

"You can say that again and again," Esteban said. "I often make a stop here after the long trip from Manila and just look around. It makes me feel good to be back, here in Baguio."

Leandro nodded. It is like no other place he had been to. It is like being in another country. The thought came to him then that it must look like New England from what Miss Dickinson once told her class in San Isidro about her hometown in Vermont, a typical state in New England.

It was now, late in the afternoon. Thick fog had descended on them and everything else around them.

Leandro felt, as the fog then enveloped him with a cold, grayish haze, like he was up high in the clouds.

"Let's go," Esteban said, "we cannot see anything, anymore in this thick fog."

They walked back to the truck. Esteban was, in a short while, driving it slowly, its fog lights and low-beam headlights piercing through the grayish haze of the thick fog enveloping the road.

They had dinner in a restaurant in Session Road before proceeding to the company compound. Esteban had been shuttling between Baguio and Manila and he knew the company mess hall will be closed by then. They went to the field office and saw there, the night supervisor.

He knew Leandro and Esteban were coming from a telegraph message sent there, ahead of them.

"You will report tomorrow to Mister Fitzsimmons," the night supervisor said to Leandro. "He is the big boss here. I will show you, your quarters while Esteban is unloading the supplies in the warehouse."

"Why don't I help Esteban first?" Leandro suggested.

"Very well, we will all do it together," the night supervisor said.

Esteban drove the truck to the warehouse. They put there the construction supplies, they removed from the truck. Esteban then left the truck in the motor pool and proceeded to his home in Aurora Hill. The night supervisor, on the other hand, took Leandro to the company barracks.

"Have you taken your dinner?" the night supervisor asked him. "The mess hall is closed. There is nothing to eat here, tonight."

"It's all right. I have taken my dinner with Esteban."

They said good night to each other. Leandro then set about in retiring for the night. He put inside the locker, everything he took out from his suitcase except for his sweater and his nightclothes. Then he removed his shoes and pushed his suitcase underneath the bed.

He shivered from the cold night air as he was removing his street clothes. He changed quickly into his nightclothes with a thick sweater he wore over it and a thick blanket covering him, up to his chin.

He could still feel the cold night air. He took it with humor, though. What he needed to get used to the cold climate in Baguio is a skin as thick as the hide of a carabao. He smiled at that thought as he then fell asleep.

He was at eight o'clock, the following morning, in Anthony Fitzsimmons' office.

A bow tie, adorning his neck, Fitzsimmons was wearing a smoking jacket over his white shirt. He had thin, brown hair. A handlebar moustache crowned his upper lip. He looked more British than American.

"Well, Sumaka," Fitzsimmons said to him, "I have heard a few things about you. You have got quite a record, but I will make this clear. I am interested only in how well you will do your job here. We are engaged here in the biggest construction job ever undertaken in the Philippines. Pacific and Gulf is the lead contractor and you are a part of it."

"I will do my best, sir."

"Good. We all have to work together in this gigantic operation. We are engaged with other firms in building, out of this mountain tribal village, a modern vacation resort city, complete with the amenities of civilized life. We are building, here a model American resort city that with its cold climate is so unlike this hot, tropical colony. This is a massive, complex operation led by our company and I am on top in all of it."

"I am glad to be a part of all of that, sir. What am I supposed to do here?"

"You will assist De la Pena, our warehouse custodian and purchasing agent. You will see to it that every project, we are handling will never go short in supplies and equipment. Do you have any questions?"

"No questions, sir. Can I go now to the warehouse? There is so much to do here and I would like to start working, right away."

He glanced, amused, at Fitzsimmons whose eyebrows were raised in complete surprise to what he said. Fitzsimmons may outrank him, as a general outranked a corporal, but he knew, he could do just as well in the volume and quality of the work there. He did it before in Manila, in Davao, in Zamboanga and in Masakao and will do it again, here in Baguio.

"Itneg, the man you saw, outside my office, will introduce you to De la Pena," Fitzsimmons said as he dismissed Leandro.

He learned soon enough that working in Baguio was no different from the other company projects, he had been assigned to. They were doing, much, much more, but the method of doing things was the same. It was always, according to the company's operational guideline. Baguio, though, with its cold climate, was so different from the warm, tropical climate in the rest of the Philippines.

He liked Baguio for its cold climate. It made him so energetic that he remained eager to continue working at the end of his working day.

The warehouse department soon became very efficient with Leandro doing yeoman work there. He attended personally to the provision of supplies in the construction sites, so that in just a short time, he knew what they needed, when and where. By then, he knew all about Pacific & Gulf's projects in Baguio, planned, completed, or under construction, by itself or in partnership with other construction companies.

The list is long: The widening and maintenance of Kennon Road, called before the Benguet Road and its steel bridges, whose construction was started by the U.S. Army Corps of Engineers under Colonel Lyman Walter Vere Kennon, the construction of Wright Park and Burnham Park, the Mansion House, the vacation home of the governor-general, the City Hall, the Baguio Cathedral, the Dominican and the Jesuits' retreat houses, vacation homes for government officials in Cabinet Hill, housing in Aurora Hill for the company workers and city residents, the roads and the city streets, the lampposts and the streetlights, the water, telephone, telegraph and electricity systems, the Saint Louis University, private and public schools, the buildings in Baguio market, commercial buildings in Session Road, the Halsema Road to Bontoc, deep in Central Cordillera, Camp John Hay and the Philippine Military Academy, the Baguio General Hospital, the Baguio Country Club, the road to the copper mines.

He learned how to drive a company car so he could attend quickly and personally to whatever he needed to provide in the many construction projects there of Pacific & Gulf.

He would return to his quarters at the end of his working day, tired but satisfied from having done another day of good work. He would take his supper after taking a rest of a few minutes, after which he would retire early so he could rise early the following morning for more work except on Saturday and Sunday, his two days, off from work.

As in Manila, he spent Sunday by first attending Mass at the chapel of the Belgian missionaries, a block away from where they were building the Baguio Cathedral.

He would then, most often, proceed to Burnham Park, the one place, he loved best in Baguio. He was so taken by its natural beauty and what were built there, so that he spent a great deal of his time, biking, skating, horseback riding, or boating in the park's man-made lake, all of which, except for the boating, he learned to do in Baguio.

He preferred at other times to just sit down on a bench in Burnham Park or in Wright Park filled with the scent of the pine trees there and feel in his face, the cold, bracing mountain air in Baguio.

He had been in Baguio for just a few weeks when, one Saturday morning, while he was taking a walk in Session Road, he saw there a big number of American families riding in their cars or eating in the restaurants there. He also saw more American families enjoying themselves in Burnham Park. He saw the same thing happen, a week later and in the following week. He asked Esteban about it when, sometime later, they saw each other again in the company motor pool.

"They miss the cold climate in America," Esteban said. "They want to enjoy it, even for just a few days, here in Baguio."

Leandro nodded. That should also explain the big number of cars, he saw, coming in Kennon Road from Manila on Friday afternoon and just as many cars, going back on Sunday morning, from Baguio to Manila, after a three-day vacation in Baguio by those Americans.

Seeing those droves of Americans in Baguio made Leandro lonely for company. He is once again by his lonesome self, no Carlos, no Crisanta to keep him company. He went occasionally to the public market for the thrill at the sight and sound of commerce and to rub elbows with the shoppers, many of them Ibaloi women, although he saw occasionally American women shopping there. He would, at other times, just walk around in Burnham Park, in the city streets, particularly in Session Road, Baguio's equivalent of the Escolta and Rosario Streets in Manila.

He saw Nancy Jamieson, one morning, leaving a restaurant in Session Road with a big bag, probably of snacks, that she must have bought there. She crossed a street and walked on toward Burnham Park.

He walked fast, so he could say hello to her.

She must be, he thought, one more of the Pacific & Gulf executives and employees who have been going to Baguio to enjoy, even for just a few days, the fruits of their company's extensive construction work there.

He was about to approach her, as she was now standing at a street near Burnham Park, when a car stopped beside her. Its right rear door was opened and she entered the car.

He was surprised to see, as he was approaching the car, Bill Shay at the wheel of the car. Esperanza was seated beside him. Their son Michael was at the backseat with his nanny, Teofila.

Bill was about to drive the car away when he saw Leandro coming.

"Well, if it is not, Leandro," he said to Esperanza.

Leandro greeted them as he was approaching their car.

"How are you doing, here in Baguio?" Bill asked him.

"I'm doing fine, sir,"

"Good. We were just leaving after a few days of leisure here."

He nodded and said, "Have a safe return, sir, mom, to Manila."

He watched the car as it sped away. So, the Big Boss, just like the other Pacific & Gulf executives and their employees, had just spent with his family and Nancy Jamieson, a few pleasant days of a bit of America in the cold, beautiful resort city of Baguio.

It became, later on, a status symbol for Filipinos as well to spend, even for just a few days in Baguio, a city so like America and so unlike the rest of the Philippines. Droves of them, by then, were going there especially during the Holy Week for their spiritual renewal in Baguio Cathedral and in the Dominican and Jesuit retreat houses there. It was also a fun-filled time in Burnham Park that was like a summer carnival with the horseback riding, skating, biking, boating and the amusement rides in the Carousel and the Ferris Wheel,

Leandro had been working in Baguio for several months when, one Sunday morning, while he was walking around in Baguio Market, he saw to his complete surprise, Dorothy Dickinson. He thought all along that she had returned to the United States.

She was bent over a low table, inspecting the vegetables spread out there while the Ibaloi vendor waited on her. She picked up a bunch of lettuce, asked for the price and put it in her shopping bag.

He approached her as she was paying for the vegetable.

"Good morning, Miss Dickinson," he said to her.

Dorothy turned to him, her eyes wide in complete surprise.

"Why, if it is not, Leandro," she said. "It is so nice to see you again. What are you doing, here in Baguio?"

"I have been assigned here, ma'am. Pacific and Gulf has a lot of construction projects here. I have been here for so many months now."

"I'm so glad to hear that. Would you like to come with me? You can tell me and Mister Tyler, how you have been doing here."

"Did you say, Mister Tyler, ma'am?" he said, a puzzled look in his face.

"I'm no longer Miss Dickinson. I have been married to Mister Tyler for two years now."

"That is great, ma'am! Congratulations, ma'am! Mister Tyler is a lucky man, Miss Dickinson . . . I mean, Missis Tyler."

"You will see him soon enough. He is at home."

"So, you are now living, here in Baguio."

"Yes. Both Mister Tyler and me are teaching in Brendan School at the same time that he is pursuing his anthropological study of the mountain tribes here."

They proceeded to her car, parked in the market's parking lot.

Her fragrance and the scent of the flowers and pine trees wafted sweetly inside the car as she drove on in Baguio's winding roads with Leandro seated in sheer pleasure, beside his lovely teacher.

The car, after a while, passed through the gate in Brendan School, the large windows in the main building there, reflecting the morning sun.

She drove on through the campus and slowed down to a crawl as it was approaching a cottage there. It was partly shaded yet from the morning sun by the pine and other trees there and set back from the campus road by a lawn of verdant green grass.

Samuel Tyler was bent over a flower box, below the cottage picture window. He cut away with a pair of garden scissors, the dead branches of a flowering plant there. The task done, he gazed admiringly at the flower box.

It was summertime in Baguio and the flowers in the flower box, the roses, the hyacinths, the gardenias and the carnations were all in full bloom.

He laid aside the scissors on the windowsill and picked up his smoking pipe there. He was rewarding himself with a smoke in his pipe for the work he was doing there.

The pipe's stem, clamped between his teeth, he was about to light it with a match when he turned to the sound of the car coming in the cottage driveway.

He watched Dorothy and Leandro as they were stepping out of the car.

"Who," he asked Dorothy, "is that young man with you?"

"Don't you remember Leandro Sumaka?" she replied, gently rebuking Samuel for being so forgetful. "You recommended him for a job in Pacific and Gulf."

"But, of course, your student in San Isidro," he said, nodding in sudden recognition of Leandro.

"I'm so glad to see you again, young man," he said as he shook hands with Leandro.

"So am I, sir."

"Come inside, dear. I will make coffee," she said to Samuel.

"I will join you there as soon as I'm through here."

Leandro walked quickly toward the cottage. He opened the screened and the main doors for her and followed her, inside the cottage.

"Make your self comfortable while I am making coffee," she said to Leandro.

He sat down on a rattan couch in the living room while she proceeded to the kichen. She laid her shopping bag on the worktable there, where her housemaid was preparing their lunch.

"Is Alfred still asleep?" she asked her as she was filling a kettle with water from the faucet in the kitchen sink.

"Yes, ma'am," she replied. "He woke up, after you left. He went back to sleep when I gave him, his bottle of milk."

"So, the Tylers have a child now," Leandro said to himself. Everyone close to him has gone through a transition in life. His teacher, Miss Dickinson, is now married to Mister. Tyler. So is Carlos to Angela. Regina must be married by now to that detestable Ruy Villa del Conde.

He felt suddenly lonely for Crisanta. He is truly in love with her. He sighed, not sure if she is also in love with him. It was depressing. He looked around at the cottage to banish the thought from his mind.

He has never been inside an American home and he marveled at the elegant, but functional simplicity of the Tylers' cottage. There was nothing showy or unnecessary there. It was carpeted to help keep the cold out. It was furnished with a large rattan couch, in front of which was a coffee table, also in rattan. Facing the small rattan couch where he was seated was another small ratttan couch. A rolltop desk stood in a corner, beside a tall bookshelf full of books, magazines and manuscripts. A grandfather clock was a few feet away from the fireplace.

He turned his gaze to Dorothy who was coming from the kitchen with a tray of three steaming cups of coffee which she put down on the coffee table.

Samuel came in at the same time with a bunch of flowers.

"Those are nice flowers," she said to him.

"I know it is not your birthday, but I want you to feel like it is your birthday with this as my gift to you."

"Thank you, my dear. You make me feel so special," she said, smiling as they then embraced and kissed each other.

Leandro looked away, embarrassed by their spontaneous show of affection for each other. He had never seen anything like that before.

Samuel saw him looking away and he released Dorothy from his embrace. He was smiling as he then gave her the flowers.

"I have a nice vase for these flowers," she said as she went back to the kitchen with the flowers.

Samuel sat down on the couch, facing Leandro. He took one of the cups of coffee on the coffee table and said to Leandro, 'Take one, before it gets cold."

Leandro took a cup of coffee and began drinking it.

"So, young man," Samuel said to Leandro, "how have you been doing, all this time?"

"I'm doing fine, sir. I must thank you and Missis Tyler, once again, for your help in getting me, a job in Pacific and Gulf. Baguio is my latest assignment. I have worked before in Zamboanga, where we built a wharf and feeder wharves; in Davao, where we built another wharf, a school, a municipal building, the town market and the road that cuts across the wide plain in Mandala. We are building a dam and a mining road in Masakao. It is a town at the foot of the Sierra Madre."

"That is a lot of work you have done in Pacific and Gulf."

Dorothy returned to the living room with the flowers, now in a nice porcelain vase. She put it on a table near the window. Then she sat down on the large couch and took the remaining cup of coffee in the coffee table.

"I understand, Pacific and Gulf is doing a lot of work, here in Baguio," Samuel said to Leandro.

"Yes, indeed, sir, ma'am. Pacific and Gulf is the lead company in a group of construction companies building a lot of infrastructure here."

"It is amazing," Samuel said, "how Baguio has been transformed from a small Ibaloi tribal village during the Spanish time to a modern vacation resort city, complete with the amenities of modern life."

Leandro nodded and said proudly, "We are building, or have built, or are planning to build the city's power, water and communication facilities, roads, bridges, a military academy, the Burnham Park and the Wright Park, Camp John Hay, a country club complete with a clubhouse and a golf course, the Baguio General Hospital, the City Hall, the

Baguio Cathedral and Saint Louis University, the religious orders' retreat houses, school buildings, vacation homes for government officials, housing for workers and government employees in Aurora Hill, the Mansion House, the governor-general's vacation home in Baguio.

"We have just finished building and paving the roads to Bontoc and the copper mines, a few miles, east of Baguio. There are a lot more that we are building here."

"It is good, you built the road to Bontoc," Samuel said. "It makes it easier for people to see those fantastic rice terraces in Central Cordillera, particularly those in Banaue."

"Have you been to Banaue?" Dorothy asked Leandro.

"No, ma'am, I have not been there although I have heard about the rice terraces there.. What are they like?"

"They are like a series of grand stairways to the sky," she said, smiling

"You can see how your teacher is charmed by that man-made wonder," Samuel said. "She has been there."

"Don't miss the chance to visit Banaue while you are assigned, here in Baguio," she said to Leandro.

"I'll be very glad to visit it, ma'am, when I can take a break from work."

"Try to find the time," Samuel said. "It is beautiful; so are the other rice terraces in Central Cordillera. They are not as grand and extensive, though, as those in Banaue."

"Mister Tyler is doing a lot of research work there. A foundation in the United States is providing the funds for his work there. You can see in the bookshelf there, the result of his work in the manuscripts, magazine and newspaper articles written about him, or which he himself had written about those people living in Central Cordillera. They help promote a better understanding and appreciation of their life and culture."

"Fascinating people, fascinating place," Samuel said as he then told Leandro about the mountain tribes in Central Cordillera and their rice terraces in Banaue, Hungduan, Kiangan and Mayoyao.

Chapter forty-five

Leandro was, a few weeks later, allowed a few days' break from work. He went with Samuel to Banaue.

They first went by truck to Bontoc where they spent the night. They took their breakfast and then started out, early morning of the following day, in a hired horse-drawn rig. It took them as far as it could on the trail to Banaue which, not long after, was built into a road by Pacific & Gulf. They walked, the rest of the way to Banaue..

He was, by late morning, tired and hungry. The knapsack on his back and the canvas bags of provisions, he was carrying, seemed to be heavier now than when they started out in Baguio. But he was encouraged by what Samuel said to him that they were now approaching Banaue.

He was, not long after, rewarded with a grand view of the rice terraces in Banaue. They were carved out of the mountainsides there. They rose, layer by layer, from the base to the top of the mountains, the water in the lower layers mirror-like in reflection of the sunlight.

"It is worth the hike, we took, is it not?" Samuel said to Leandro.

"It is, sir."

"Can you see the Ifugao village there?" Samuel said at a cluster of huts there. Some of them were partly hidden by the trees while others were near a stream running at the base of a mountain, carved into layers of rice terraces.

"I can see it, sir."

"The Ifugaos started building their rice terraces in those mountains, some two thousand years ago. I have never ceased to be amazed at how they built that engineering marvel with their bare hands and simple tools, like picks and shovels.

"They made, in changing the face of those mountains, serve their purpose of drawing food from them, for all time. Rice, to them, the product of those terraces, is life itself."

He was so impressed by their beauty and magnificence, he overlooked one, very important point that Samuel had said about them. Without the Ifugaos who carved out those rice terraces, those mountains would have remained, just as ordinary mountains, untouched and undeveloped by creative human minds and hands.

He was not surprised, though, by what Samuel had said about the Ifugaos and their rice terraces. He is, after all, an anthropologist and he saw, what someone like him, had failed to see, a balanced view of the Ifugaos, the creators, and the rice terraces, their magnificent creations.

His attention was next drawn to a chapel with a small building beside it. They stood in an open ground, a short distance from the Ifugao village. Samuel saw him, looking at them.

"That is Father O'Farrell's chapel and rectory," he said. "He is an Irish-American missionary. We are staying there for the simple reason that it has accommodations for visitors like us."

They walked down toward the chapel and the rectory.

A young man tending a vegetable plot there saw them coming.

"Good morning, Mister. Tyler," he said to Samuel, "I'm so glad to see you again."

"How are you, Basilio?" Samuel said to him.

"I'm fine, sir."

"This is Basilio Basneg," Samuel said to Leandro. "He is Father O'Farrell's acolyte, cook, gardener and all-around handyman."

"I'm Leandro Sumaka," he said as he and Basilio were waving a friendly greeting at each other.

Basilio made a move to take their bags.

"Thank you, Basilio," Samuel said as he and Leandro were passing on to him, some of the canvas bags, they were carrying.

"Is Father O'Farrell around?" Samuel asked Basilio.

"He is in the rectory, sir."

They proceeded there. Samuel knocked at the door. It opened to Father O'Farrell, a wide grin on his timeworn face, exclaiming to Samuel, "Am I so glad to see you again!"

"So am I, Father," Samuel said as he shook hands with Fr. O'Farrell. They stepped inside the rectory with Leandro and Basilio, following behind them.

He told Father O'Farrell, as he was going over the contents of his knapsack, that Leandro is visiting Banaue for a look at the rice terraces and the Ifugaos who built them.

"Glad to see you, young man," Father O'Farrell said to Leandro. "You must have seen them on your way here. There is nothing like them in the entire world."

"They are, indeed, Father," Leandro said.

Samuel took out from his knapsack, two tin cans of pipe tobacco and gave them to Father O'Farrell.

"Thank you, Samuel. I was about to run out of pipe tobacco," Father O'Farrell said.

"We also brought you, some foodstuff, Dorothy had gathered for our visit here," Samuel said as he took out from the canvas bags, sugar, flour, oatmeal, tinned meat, coffee, smoked sausages and other foodstuff.

He gave them to Father O'Farrell who passed them on to Basilio. He in turn took them to the pantry in the kitchen.

"Thank you and Dorothy for all that nice foodstuff," Father O'Farrell said to Samuel..

"You are welcome, Father."

"We will have coffee."

Basilio left to make coffee in the kitchen.

"A good smoke will go well with it," Samuel said as he took out his pipe and tobacco pouch from his jacket and filled it with pipe tobacco.

Father O'Farrell also took out a pipe from a drawer in his desk and filled it with pipe tobacco. He was about to light it up when he glanced at Leandro. He said to him, "You don't smoke?"

"No, Father."

"Try it. Pipe-smoking can be relaxing. I have an extra pipe, Basilio's father gave me."

He took out a corncob pipe from a drawer and said as he was giving it to Leandro, "Here, take it. I've never used it."

"Thank you, Father," Leandro said as he filled the pipe with tobacco from Samuel's tobacco pouch, after which Samuel lit it up with his match.

He sucked at his pipe slowly and deeply and found it a good feeling to blow the smoke away.

He listened as Father O'Farrell said to Samuel, "We have another baptism, a boy, the fourth, we have this month. You might know the parents—Justo and Risa Lumaweg."

"I know them. We will pay them a visit when we go to the village. So, we have there, another example of the progress you are making, Father, in converting the Ifugaos to Christianity."

"A lot of work lies ahead of us. Let me show you something," Fr. O'Farrelll said to Samuel as he then spread out a piece of paper on his desk. "This is a rough plan I drew up for a school needed here badly."

It showed the school's facade, sides and interior.

"Banaue needs such a school," Samuel said. "The nearest school the Insular Government has so far built in Central Cordillera is in Kiangan. That is so many miles from here. It is hard for the young people here to walk every school day to that school. The answer to that is a school built, right here."

"I will talk to the villagers later today about this school project."

"It is right in the alley of Bill Shay. He is building schools, all over the islands, why not one, here in Banaue?'

"He has been here for a look at the road, his company, with the funding by the Insular Government, will soon build here."

"Did you talk to him about your school project?"

"It was not in my mind then."

"Would you like me to talk to him about your school project?"

"That will be perfect, if we can do it together."

Basilio returned with a tray of four steaming cups of coffee, which he then served to Father O'Farrell, Samuel and Leandro. He took the remaining cup of coffee.

Leandro smoked in his pipe, all the tobacco until it had burned out. He went out and tamped on a stone there, the ashes in his pipe. He returned to the rectory as Samuel was asking Father O'Farrell, how many children, the school will accommodate.

"It will be anywhere from forty to fifty students. It depends, though, on the number of enrollees and our resources."

"Will you do the teaching yourself?"

"I will ask our mission house in Baguio to send to us, one or two teachers, depending on the number of students, but I will handle the class in religion."

Samuel and Leandro were finished drinking their coffee. They proceeded to the guest room in the rectory. Samuel took out from his knapsack, a new towel and put it inside a canvas bag, which he then carried. Leandro also took out from his knapsack, a big paper bag full of candies, Samuel had suggested he bring with him for the children there.

They left for the village. Father O'Farrell and Basilio stayed behind. They will join them later on, at the celebration at lunchtime of the baby's baptism.

Two young Ifugao men met them as they were approaching their village.

Leandro could not understand a word of what they were telling Samuel, but he gathered from the glum look in their faces, the tone of their voices and with them pointing now and then at the rice terraces, that they had a poor harvest there. One of them swept his hand like a scythe cutting grass in showing how a typhoon had swept across the rice terraces and damaged his crop.

Samuel said something which seemed to have consoled the two young Ifugaos.

They proceeded toward an open ground, surrounded by huts in the village. Some elderly Ifugaos were seated there on logs and benches. They stood up and Leandro saw, from their warm friendly greetings, that Samuel was very much loved there.

The word spread around about their arrival there. More villagers soon came and gathered around Samuel. A stool was obtained for him. He had just sat down there when a woman came to him and said something about the baby in her arms. A stool was also obtained for her.

Samuel asked the woman a few questions while he was pressing the baby's stomach lightly with his fingers. Then he took out from his canvas bag, a bottle of medicine. He gave it to the woman and told her how she should give it to her baby. The treatment was over and the woman, looking happy and relieved, thanked Samuel and left.

Leandro all the while was watching Samuel who, he could see, was not only the villagers' friend, but also their village doctor.

"It is nothing, but simple colic," Samuel said to Leandro.

"I did not know, sir, that you are also a doctor."

"I am not. There is not a single doctor in the area. I had to fill the need, so I studied simple medical procedures in Baguio."

Some of the villagers had, by then, formed themselves in a line and waited for their turn to be treated by Samuel.

"I also have a job for the children here," Leandro said about the bag of candies in his hand.

"Go ahead, make them happy," Samuel said to Leandro.

He walked around in the village to look for the children. Some of the men he met were barefooted and dressed in nothing more than sleeveless shirts and G-strings. The women were more modestly dressed in knee-length skirts and colorful blouses.

He came to know more about the village as he was looking for the children. The villagers' most common dwellings were made of thatch and bamboo. Some of them were built near the stream, running at the base of the mountain or were clustered around the village center. Many of them were at the base of the other terraced mountains.

A group of children playing in a yard stopped in their game and looked on when, on approaching them, he took out candies from his bag.

"You want some?" he said to them, the candies held out to them.

The boldest among them, a boy, stepped forward and took a candy. He removed the wrapper and ate it.

The other children, encouraged by the boy's example, swarmed around Leandro as he handed out to them, the candies in his hand.

Word got around about the candies, he was giving away and more children came to him.

He made them form in a line, so no one will be left out in the distribution of the candies. He left them when he had given away, all the candies. He returned to the village center and saw Samuel who was finished with his own good deed for the villagers.

"So, you have made the children here, happy," Samuel said to Leandro, who nodded and smiled.

Samuel then said, "Let us pay the Lumawegs, a visit."

They arrived in the yard of Justo and Risa Lumaweg's hut, busy with them, preparing the food for the feast in celebration of their child's baptism. Two women were chopping vegetables on a table. A young man was filling a large jar with water while a young girl was tending the fire in a clay stove in the open-air kitchen. Another woman was removing from another clay stove, a steaming clay pot of cooked rice.

They looked on when Justo and Risa greeted Samuel who introduced Leandro to them.

They then went with Risa to the hut, for a look at the baby while Justo went back to work.

They did not follow Risa, inside the hut. They stayed beside the hut's bamboo stairs and looked on at the child who was lying on a blanket spread out on the hut's bamboo floor.

She told Samuel with the few English words she knew about her difficult labor with her child.

Samuel gave her a few words of advice on how to care for her child. Then he took out the towel from his bag and gave it to her. It was his gift for the baby.

Leandro was not to be outdone and he dug into his pocket and gave her, money for her child.

"We will see you later," Samuel then said to Risa.

They left the hut and proceeded toward the stream at the base of the terraced mountain.

The air there was so cool and refreshing, Leandro inhaled it deeply. He listened, pleased, as he was standing at the water's edge, to the sound of the water rushing, past the stones and boulders in the stream. He looked around, pleased even more, at the rice terraces that began right there, near the stream at the base of the mountain.

Samuel, on the other hand, had sat down at the base of a tree, its leafy branches overhanging a part of the stream.

"Enjoy the view," he said to Leandro, "while I do some work."

He took out from his canvas bag, a pencil and a notebook and began to write.

Leandro, on the other hand, was looking at a boulder in the stream as a good spot for a short rest with a nice view of the rice terraces.

He crossed the stream by stepping fast on the stones protruding in the rushing water and scaled the boulder. He said to himself, as he was now lying there and looking up at the mountain and the sky, his teacher was right, the rice terraces there were like grand stairways to the sky.

He fell asleep, pleased and satisfied, as he was looking on at the grand terraced mountain.

Samuel, later on, called out to him. It was time for the feast.

They returned to the village center where the villagers had gathered for the feast. They joined Father O'Farrell who was seated on a stool, eating with a wooden spoon, the food in the clay bowl on his lap.

"You are just on time," Father O'Farrell said to them.

They put in the clay bowls, Risa gave them, food they took from the clay vessels in a bamboo table there. There were, aside from the rice and stewed chicken, several vegetable dishes.

Leandro was so hungry, he could, he said to himself, eat everything there on the table. He sat down on a log and, like the villagers, he began to eat with his hands.

The villagers, after the baptismal feast, returned to their huts, but the village elders stayed behind to take up with Father O'Farrell and Samuel, the schoolhouse project.

They listened and asked questions about the school, drawn by Father O'Farrell, which he had spread out on the bamboo table.

Leandro was not interested in their discussion of the schoolhouse project, not a word of which, he could understand. He signaled to Samuel, his forefinger pointed in the direction of the stream, that he is going back there. Samuel nodded in reply.

He went back to the same boulder in the middle of the stream with a grand view of the rice terraces. He felt so relaxed, he closed his eyes with the pleasant sound of rushing water in his ears.

It came to him then, a feeling of kinship with the Ifugaos. He is, like them, a child of the earth. While he farmed in the lowland in Bangar and they upland in Banaue, it was the same earth in which they grew rice. They labored, planting the rice shoots, row by row, on the waterlogged soil and caring for them until, with the nourishment of water and sunlight, they grew into rice stalks, full of golden grain.

He slept, filled with admiration of the Ifugaos for what they had done with the mountains around them so that, upon waking up, moments later, he turned his eyes once again to their rice terraces.

It was time for him to go up there, for there is nothing like being up there. He crossed the stream once again by stepping quickly on the rocks and stones protruding in the rushing water. He proceeded toward the lowest terrace, he found out, with its wall of stone and packed earth, too high and too slippery for him to climb over. He looked around, his mind on how to go up there. He nodded, glad to see, a short distance away, steps carved out of the terrace wall. He proceeded there and stepped up on them.

He marveled, as he now stood at the lowest terrace, at the way the Ifugaos raised their rice crops there. They kept the water level at a certain height, just right for the rice shoots. The excess water then ran through a channel lined with stones to the stream below. It prevented the water from flooding the rice shoots and breaking the wall in the rice terrace as well. The lowest rice terrace was, at the same time, provided with the water from the higher terrace.

It was a simple, but ingenious way, the Ifugaos controlled the water level in the rice terraces, from the top to the base of the mountain.

Now that he has found the way up there, climbing the next rice terraces was quite easy. He went on climbing until he had reached the middle of the rice terraces. He looked at, down below, the Ifugao village, the stream, the chapel and the rectory.

He then looked around, as far as he could see, at the other terraced mountains with the clouds hovering over some of them. He had yet to reach the top of the terraced mountain and he already had this lofty feeling brought about by height and space, of looking at the sky and the wonderful view all around him. He stood on the terrace for quite a while, marveling at the panoramic view of those natural and man-made wonders.

He called out to Basilio when he saw him, walking near the stream.

Basilio looked up and shouted, "What are you doing there?"

"I am up here, touching the sky!"

"Be careful. It is slippery there with the recent rain."

"I will be careful. Where are you going?"

"I am going, fishing."

"Up here, in this mountain?"

"Not up there, but down here, in the stream."

"Wait for me, I will go with you."

He walked down fast but carefully until he had reached the base of the terraced mountain.

"Lead the way," he said to Basilio, who was waiting for him, a bamboo fishing rod and a wicker basket in his hands.

They walked on until they reached a still pool of water.

"My favorite fishing spot," Basilio said.

They sat down beside each other, at the edge of the pool.

Leandro looked on as Basilio then took out from the wicker basket, a string in which a weight and a fishhook were tied at one end. He tied the other end to his bamboo fishing pole. Then he took out from the wicker basket, a small tin box and took out there, an earthworm. He cut it up with a knife and thrust a part of it into the fishhook.

He is now ready to fish as he then wrapped his hand around the bamboo fishing pole and cast it toward the pool.

"Do you always catch fish here?" Leandro asked Basilio.

"I do, most of the time."

"How big are the fish you catch here?"

"They are mostly as big as my hand, although there were a few times when I caught several big ones, some of them, nearly a foot long."

"Look, a fish is taking your bait," Leandro said as he pointed at the fishing line now moving in the water.

"Take the whole thing," Basilio said as he yanked his fishing pole backward. A fish then shot out of the pool and landed on the ground, behind them.

"Let me take care of it," Leandro said to Basilio.

He grabbed the fish. Then he removed from the fish, the fishhook in its mouth and put it inside the wicker basket.

"That was one quick work, you just did," Basilio said to Leandro. "I have done some fishing myself."

"Where was that?"

"It was in the pond in my hometown in San Isidro and at sea in Zamboanga and Davao."

"You fished at sea? How big were the fish, you caught there?"

"Some were big; some were small."

"What was the biggest fish that you caught there?"

"It was a yellowfin tuna, I caught in Zamboanga. If it stood on its tail, it was taller than me."

"Wow! A fish that big, taller than you, will feed a lot of people in our village."

"It was big indeed. It fed scores of my fellow workers in Zamboanga."

He thrust an earthworm into the fishhook and Basilio, at a nod from him, cast his fishing line into the pool.

They waited for another fish to be caught in the fishhook.

"The fish you catch here will make a fine dinner," Leandro said.

"I am doing this for my family and Father O'Farrell. He is like a father to me."

"I got that impression in the rectory. So you are Father O'Farrell's acolyte. Do you want to be a priest someday?"

Basilio did not reply.

"Do you want to be a priest?" Leandro asked Basilio again.

"Yes, I want to be a priest."

"Why did you hesitate about giving an answer? Are you not sure about it?"

"More than anything else in the world, that is what I want to be. I am not sure, though, if an Ifugao like me, will be accepted in the seminary."

"Don't worry about that. It does not matter, if you are from here or anywhere else. What matters is your religious vocation and I have no doubt you have it. One more thing, you can be sure, Father O'Farrell will see to it that you will be a priest."

Leandro saw Basilio, smiling. He seemed pleased by what he said to him.

They sat quietly for a while, their thoughts kept to themselves, their eyes turned to the pool.

"Have you thought of becoming a priest, too?" Basilio, after a while, asked Leandro.

"I was also an acolyte in our town church and I have also thought about it, but that was a long time ago. I have other goals now."

The day was almost over when they decided, they had caught enough fish. Luck was with them and they had quite a catch, eight fish in all.

They passed by the hut of Basilio's family. He gave his pleased parents, four of the fish.

His parents, younger brother and two sisters were about to begin their supper.

The gruel in their low dining table showed Leandro about the hard life led by Basilio's family. Life must be hard in the rest of the village and he said to himself, so too was the life he led in Bangar.

The supper, Leandro and Basilio took later on at the rectory with Father O'Farrell and Samuel, was much more substantial. They had the fish, Basilio fried, vegetables, he picked up from the vegetable plot and the tinned meat, Samuel had brought with him from Baguio.

Leandro, after their supper, offered to help Basilio clear the table and wash the dishes. He thanked him for the offer he made, but said he could do it by himself. He joined Father O'Farrell and Samuel as they smoked and drank the coffee, prepared and served by Basilio.

"So, how do you like Banaue?" Father O'Farrell asked Leandro.

"It's a wonderful place, Father. I have never seen anything like those rice terraces. It is ingenious, how the Ifugaos carved those mountainsides into those rice terraces. They do certain things differently, though. They even look different with their narrow eyes."

"Their narrow eyes showed," Samuel said, "that they came from mainland Asia."

"They came from there?" Father O'Farrell said. "They don't look like seafaring people to me. How did they get here?"

Leandro asked himself, the same question.

He listened, very much interested, when Samuel then said to Father O'Farrell, "They crossed the land bridges, which appeared from mainland Asia to these islands toward the end of the last Ice Age when the sea level dropped by several hundred feet. "

"And they have, since then, lived here, relatively isolated."

"The Spaniards left them alone and I can understand why. It is hard to live here. There is not enough arable land here to grow crops. That is why they carved those rice terraces from those mountainsides."

"Was it good, the Spaniards left them alone?"

"It has its good and bad side. One good side is that their isolation spared them from outside influences. It gave them the freedom to keep to their ways and develop their own culture."

"What about the bad side?"

"They were left out from the blessings of modern civilization. Not until now, when the Insular Government and you and I are doing a lot for them. But, we should also remind ourselves that we, who came from supposedly advanced societies, have something to learn from them. Thanks to the untiring efforts of missionaries like you, Father, and the effective pacification work of the Insular Government, they now live in peace and harmony. They were fighting each other before. That is something, we cannot say about some of the so-called advanced, modern societies in the world that are often at war with each other."

"They should be admired for that."

"They should be, but they are not admired for what they have done with those mountains and that is just too bad—for them and their fellow countrymen in the lowlands."

"Will you elaborate on that?"

"Those living in the lowlands' distorted sense of values can be seen, right here, in Banaue. Instead of being admired and emulated for having kept their culture and identity intact and for their skill and ingenuity in carving out of the mountainsides those magnificent rice terraces that since time immemorial have been objects of beauty and means of livelihood for them, the Ifugaos, like the Ibalois and the Kalingas, are scorned and looked down upon by their fellow countrymen in the lowlands as poor, primitive people, the men, dressed in G-strings.

"What, on the other hand, do they have to show for themselves? Their nipa huts! They are nothing compared to those rice terraces. They show nonetheless their imaginary superiority to those mountain tribes with what they copied from the Spaniards and what they are now copying from us, nothing else, for they have nothing else to show about themselves."

Samuel caught Leandro looking downcast at the floor.

"I am not," he said to Leandro, "referring to you, but to your fellow countrymen in the lowlands."

Leandro nodded. He kept silent and did not take part in the conversation between Samuel and Father O'Farrell. It would be rude and presumptuous of him to do that.

"You don't approve of them," Father O'Farrell said to Samuel.

"I don't," Samuel replied. "They have no originality. They copied from the Spaniards as they are now copying from us because they consider the little of their own as inferior and even worthless.

"Just as bad, they do not or could not distinguish between what is good and what is bad in what they copy. They simply copy the whole lot. What, then, do we have there, vain imitators, people without even a national purpose."

"They are seeking independence. Is that not their national purpose?"

"That is what their political leaders want to make it appear. It is actually a self-serving goal. Those political leaders want to take over from us and rule these islands themselves."

"That is understandable. It is their country, after all. The more important point, though, is this: Are they ready for that?"

"They are not. They will only make a mess out of it. I see very little evidence of them possessing the civic spirit, the discipline, the honesty and the competence to build in these islands, a just, peaceful, orderly, democratic and progressive society."

"All of those are now obtaining here."

"They are, but only because we, who brought them here, are still around. They will mess up everything, once they are on their own."

"They might do well, out of pride."

"Their vanity cannot make up for their mediocrity. They do not have the competence, much less the strong character to run their country well."

Samuel's indictment of his fellow countrymen, particularly their political leaders, came hammering into Leandro's head. He asked to be excused when he could no longer take it and he left the rectory.

It was cold outside, the night sky lovely with a half-moon and a sprinkling of starlights, the mountains' silhouettes visible in the dark. The view of those cold heights had a salutary effect on him and he calmly went over what Samuel had said in the rectory. It hurt, what he said about their lack of competence and strength of character. Had it been another man, who made those disparaging remarks, he would have given him, a punch in the nose.

He felt neither anger nor resentment toward Samuel for what he said and it was not only out of respect for the American teacher. He knew Samuel by now as a kindhearted man who spoke frankly. He spoke, not out of contempt or condescension, but out of an objective view of his fellow countrymen. While he was hurt by what Samuel said, he agreed to what he said, for what he said was quite true.

He returned to the rectory. Samuel and Father O'Farrell's conversation had turned dreary and they had fallen silent. It was also getting late.

"I hope, what we talked about will not keep us awake tonight," Father O'Farrell said, smiling, as he said, "Good night, gentlemen."

Leandro, as he was lying down on his cot, went once again over what Samuel had said about the Filipino people, especially their political leaders, lacking in competence and strength of character. It was depressing. He could only hope that with the Americans' guiding hand, they could develop into a just, stable, peaceful, orderly and progressive nation.

As for himself, he is satisfied with his lot and could see nothing, but good things ahead of him. He is like a sailor steering his ship on a steady course in a calm, blue sea. The things he copied and acquired from the Americans were good for him and he liked them. He liked most of all, now that he is working in Baguio, the pleasant and instructive company of Samuel and Dorothy Tyler.

Chapter Forty-six

The days passed with Leandro occupied with work in the company projects in Baguio. He was, often in his free time, in the Tyler cottage, playing with Alfred in his playpen. His thoughts, at night, often turned to Crisanta. He would look at the dark sky, longing for her.

A problem with the supplies, all of them, hardware items, gave him the chance to visit her in Manila. De La Pena was on sick leave and he reported the problem directly to Fitzsimmons.

"I have sent several telegraph messages to Manila," he said, "and all I got was a reply that they are working on it."

"When did you make the requisition?"

"Two weeks ago. Some of our projects will be delayed if they will not get those hardware items on time."

Fitzsimmons said, frowning, "You will leave tomorrow for Manila and attend to this problem."

He met Esteban at the motor pool, the following day.

"So, we are traveling again, this time back to Manila," Esteban said as they were entering his truck.

He was smiling when, hours later, he saw Crisanta in her food stall as the truck was approaching the company gate in Parola. He will see her, later on. He must first attend to his job.

He put his gear in a locker in the warehouse and then went to see John Tomlinson, the warehouse manager, about the hardware supplies, he requested, two weeks ago.

"I don't have them in my inventory," Tomlinson replied.

He frowned. So, they have not even been bought yet. This is the job of Antonio Balemal, the chief purchasing officer.

"Why don't you see Balemal about them?" Tomlinson said.

"I will do that, sir."

He went to see Balemal in his office. Balemal admitted, he has not purchased those supplies needed in Baguio, for he has been busy with other things. He asked Leandro to buy them himself.

Leandro was upset. Balemal ignored the request he made because it was he, a mere employee, a Filipino like him, and not Fitzsimmons or any of their American bosses, who made the request. He agreed, although reluctantly, to make the purchases himself.

Balemal then wrote down his name and the name and address of the hardware store below the list of the hardware items where, he said to Leandro, he should buy them.

He signed a blank check, gave it to Leandro and said, "Tell the storeowner, I sent you."

Esteban drove for Leandro in his truck. They went to Gandara Street, the heart of the Chinese section in Manila. The street was lined with Chinese hardware stores, a restaurant and a junkyard. Esteban waited in the truck while he went to the said hardware store. The storeowner was very accommodating, but he was out of stock with most of the items, he needed. He could not wait for the storeowner to get those hardware items from other stores, a task that may take one whole day to accomplish, a waste of time and he is in a hurry.

He left the hardware store and looked around. A hardware store nearby might have the hardware items, he needed. He went in and showed the list to the storeowner who took a cursory look at it and said he did not have them in his store. The same thing happened in the next hardware store he went to.

He returned to the truck.

"Have you bought nothing yet?" Esteban asked him.

"Nothing yet," he replied as he was looking hard at the hardware list. There is something odd about it. He nodded as something then came to his mind. He erased on the hood of the truck, everything that Balemal wrote there.

He went to another Chinese hardware store. He showed the list to the storeowner and asked him if he has them in his store.

"They are all available here."

"How much are they?" he asked the storeowner.

The storeowner wrote down their prices from the computation he made on his abacus.

He gave the list back to Leandro who, on reading it, was stunned by the wide discrepancy between the prices quoted by the storeowner and the prices of those same hardware items, Balemal had previously purchased for the company. Balemal was overpricing his purchases in connivance with the Chinese storeowner. Balemal was cheating Pacific & Gulf.

He shook his head sadly. Balemal will soon be found out, once Fitzsimmons had seen the price discrepancy between what he and Balemal had paid for those same hardware items. How the telephone line between Baguio and Manila will then burn!

"Will you get them for me," he said to the storeowner who then told his store helper to gather and put in boxes, the hardware items in Leandro's list.

"I will pay with a check," he said to the storeowner.

"I accept only cash or a manager's check," the storeowner said, "and that will depend on the company, you are representing."

"Will this be okay with you?" he said as he showed to the storeowner, the blank Pacific & Gulf check.

"Why, of course! It is as good as a check from the governor-general himself."

He said, as Leandro was writing on the check, the amount and the name of the store, "So, you are working for Pacific and Gulf."

"I do the purchasing for our construction projects in Baguio."

"You do?" the storeowner said as he was giving Leandro the receipt. "So, you will come back here for more purchases?"

"I might just do that. We do it on a fairly regular basis."

"You buy here, everything you need," he said while looking slyly at Leandro. "I will give you a good price for everything, you buy here. I will make it, worthwhile for you."

The storeowner then mentioned the refrain, all too familiar to Leandro, that the price of anything, he will buy there will remain the same, whether or not he will accept a rebate. It is, he added, his way of sharing the benefit of doing business with his major regular customers.

Leandro had long known, way back in Davao, that accepting a rebate was not cheating the company. He just did not feel good about it. Balemal's case was entirely different. The fellow was so greedy that, not satisfied with the rebate he was getting from their suppliers, he was overpricing his purchases and was therefore cheating their company.

The storeowner opened the cash register and took out there, some bills. He put the money inside an envelope and gave it to Leandro.

He said, as he was returning it to the storeowner, "Thank you, but I cannot accept it."

"Why?"

"It is better this way, so it won't spoil, doing business with you."

He will not go along with the way the storeowner, like Yupang and the other Chinese merchants, conducted business wherein they engaged in mutual corruption with their important customers like him. He will make his purchases and pay for them, nothing more and nothing less.

Leandro then checked the hardware items he bought and loaded them with the help of Esteban into the truck. They returned to Pacific & Gulf, Leandro's mind, dwelling still on his transactions with the Chinese storeowners in Gandara.

Some of them just took a cursory look at the list while the names of Balemal and the Chinese storeowner were written there. He got what he wanted only after he had erased their names in the list.

He was jolted when he realized that the Chinese storeowners were running their stores, not in competition, but in cooperation with each other, a Chinese business fraternity where they help and protect each other. No one, outside of their group, could then compete with them. They, as a result, monopolized the retail trade in the colony.

He parted with Esteban after they had stored the hardware items in the warehouse. Then he took out from his locker, a big paper bag containing a bunch of flowers wrapped in cellophane, bottles of strawberry jam and a basket of fresh strawberries. They were his presents for Crisanta and her parents.

He arrived in their food stall as they were cleaning it up before closing it.

A young man was idling on the bench there, smoking a cigarette.

"Well, look who is here," Crisanta said when she saw Leandro coming. "When did you get here?"

"I arrived here, a while ago, but I had to attend first to some company business."

He said good afternoon to Mang Emong and Aling Pacing.

"I have something for you, from Baguio," he said to them.

He took out his presents from the bag and gave them to Crisanta and her parents. They smiled, delighted, and thanked him for the gifts.

"I can tell from the way you are looking at our empty food counter that you are hungry. Have dinner with us, at home," Crisanta said to him.

"Nothing will please me more," he replied.

The young man heard them. He stood up and walked away, a sad look on his face.

"Who is he?" he asked Crisanta, once the young man was far enough from them.

"A dockhand who has been hanging around here," Crisanta replied. "Don't mind him."

He looked on at the young man. So, he now has competition. He better work fast. He did not want to lose Crisanta to that dockhand.

They had a fine dinner. The food, Crisanta and Aling Pacing had cooked, was so delicious. It was like what they served in their food stall. They had for dessert, the strawberry jam and the fresh strawberries.

Leandro tried to help, clear the table when they were finished with their dinner. Crisanta told him to join her father instead, who was watching them, seated in the small couch.

She helped her mother clear the table and wash the dishes, a task which they finished in just a short while.

Aling Pacing then took out from a shelf, her sewing kit and began sewing in the dining table, a partly finished housedress while Crisanta joined Leandro and Mang Emong as they were talking about Baguio.

She asked Leandro as she sat down near him on the large wooden couch, "I heard it is cold in Baguio. How cold is it, there?"

"It is very cold there. You must wear a thick sweater or a jacket at all times, but you will, after a while, get used to it. Not only that. You will, as I have found out, come to like it. Its cold climate made me so energetic."

"I will have none of that," Mang Emong said. "I like it here in Manila where it is warm throughout the year."

He stood up and joined Aling Pacing at the dining table when she asked for his help with the housedress, she was working on.

She said as she was extending the hem of the dress to him, "Will you hold this for me?"

"Whose dress, is it?" Mang Emong asked Aling Pacing.

"It is your cousin Manolita's dress."

Leandro watched Mang Emong and Aling Pacing. It was just as he liked it, with them preoccupied with work at the dining table and he and Crisanta seated near each other on the wooden couch.

He wanted some intimacy with her, a risky thing to do. Her parents were but a few steps away from them. But their backs were turned to him and Crisanta and the gas lamp in a corner table gave a poor light. The flowers he gave Crisanta, now in a vase in the coffee table, also screened them partly from her parents.

She was saying how she wished she could study in the University of the Philippines when he moved closer to her and held her hand.

She became tense, her eyes turned to her parents. She tried to pull her hand away, but he held it even more tightly.

He looked at her and saw her on the verge of tears.

"Why are you doing this to me?" she whispered to him, "Why do you hold my hand every time, I'm near you?"

"I'm doing this," he whispered to her, "because you are my girl, my one and only love."

Her hand remained, held firmly by him.

He left her, later on, happy and satisfied with himself. He could now make plans.

He made, the following morning, an arrangement with Esteban for him to bring to Baguio, the hardware items, he bought in Gandara. He told him he was staying behind to attend to an important, personal matter.

Then he went to Caloocan, glad to find the vacant lot, he saw there on his way to Baguio with Esteban, was still unoccupied. Its sagging wooden gate at the corner of the two streets there of Rodriguez and General Luna that ended in the lot was closed, but unlocked.

He saw, as he went in and walked around, that it was quite big. Some thirty huts could easily fit there. It was all open ground except for a few fruit trees there. It sloped down at the back of the lot, facing the lagoon and Manila Bay.

He smiled at the thought of the house he will build there, a house with a balcony overlooking the lagoon and Manila Bay and a smaller balcony overlooking Rodriguez Street, but he must first, find the owner.

He knocked at the door of a house in General Luna Street.

A woman opened it.

He greeted her, a good morning and asked her about the owner of the vacant lot.

"Don Manolo owns it."

"Where does he live, ma'am?"

"He lives down the street, near the town hall and the town square. You won't miss it. It is the biggest house in our neighborhood."

"Is he selling it?"

"For a good price, Don Manolo will sell his own mother."

He was laughing when he left the woman. He walked, following the direction she gave him, toward Don Manolo's house near the town hall and knocked on the door.

Someone peered through a peephole in the door and asked him, who he was and what he wanted there.

He gave his name and the purpose of his visit there. The door, after a while, was opened and a man told him to wait there in the living room. It was grand, like Don Camilo's house.

Don Manolo appeared in a short while, a Spanish mestizo like Don Camilo. He said as he motioned Leandro to a chair there. "So, you are interested in my property there, at the end of our street."

"I am, sir."

"What are you going to do with it?"

He looked at Don Manolo, his eyes wide in surprise that he was asked such a question. What he did with the property, once he had acquired it, was his own business. He said instead, "I plan to build my home there."

Don Manolo nodded and said, "Good, if that is what you are planning to build there. I don't want anyone putting up shady businesses there that will turn our street into a magnet for troublemakers. This is a fine, peaceful neighborhood and I want it, kept that way."

"That is why I want to live there, sir."

Don Manolo nodded. He asked him what he did for a living.

"I am an employee in Pacific and Gulf Construction Company."

Don Manolo nodded again and said, "That is a fine American company. Mister Shay, your president, lives, not far from there."

"That is why I want to live there, close to Mister Shay."

"Now, let us get to the point. How much will you pay for it?"

"I would rather, if you will tell me how much you are selling it."

Don Manolo mentioned the price of the vacant lot.

He did some quick, mental computation. The price was reasonable. He could afford it and still have something left with which to build a house there. He had saved a big sum of money from all the years that he had been working in Pacific & Gulf. He wanted the property, but he will look overeager, if he did not haggle a bit.

"Could you lower the price, sir," he said.

"That is my final offer."

"At that price, I will not have enough money left to build, not like your grand home, but a home adequate for my needs."

"All right, for you, I will lower the price," Don Manolo said, and he mentioned the price.

"Thank you, sir. It's fine with me."

"It is settled then. I will have the deed of sale prepared. I will call you when it is ready for signing. Give me your telephone number."

He gave his office telephone number in Baguio, which Don Manolo then wrote down on a piece of paper.

"Now," Don Manolo said, "would you like to take a look at your n   ew property?"

"I have already done that, but I won't mind taking another look."

Don Manolo showed him around the lot and gave suggestions on how he could best develop it. He was not keen, though, about the backyard that sloped down to its neighbors, most of them, modest nipa huts.

"If I were you, I will leave that alone," Don Manolo said. "There is nothing, you can do about it. The rain washed away the fruit trees, I planted there. Concentrate instead on the level part."

He listened quietly, his mind on how he will develop the vacant lot. Don Manolo left after a while.

Now that he is alone, he looked around at the big lot, quite satisfied with it. He is now, the lord and master of his own domain. It will be elegant like the home of Carlos in San Miguel, but not showy like the landlords' homes in San Isidro.

As he saw it in his mind, it will be made of stone and wood and it will have two floors. It will be painted white, with its awnings and roof of galvanized iron sheets, painted green, like the American bungalows in Ermita and Malate. A wide wooden staircase will lead to the living room and the balcony overlooking the front yard and Rodriguez Street. The living room connected to four bedrooms will lead to another wider and longer balcony that will overlook the lagoon and Manila Bay. On one end of the balcony will be the master bedroom with the dining room and the kitchen at the other end. There will be a roofed staircase at the back of the house. There will be a guest room and the servants' quarters at the ground floor. The rest of it will be one large hall. The house gate will face Rodrigez Street, which leads to Mabini Street. At the back of the house gate will be the wide front yard and the garage. At the center of the garden, in front of the house, will be a circular terrace of flowering plants. As for the backyard, which had so frustrated Don Manolo, he will have it terraced, like in Banaue and it will have plenty of fruit trees, like in Bangar.

He left the vacant lot and walked back to General Luna Street, toward Don Manolo's house. He was so preoccupied with thoughts about the house, he will build there, he hardly noticed the houses there when he passed by there a while ago. He now saw, they were mostly plain simple huts and cottages except for two fairly large houses made of stone and wood. The street, he noticed now, had an abundance of trees and shrubs.

A Methodist chapel stood there, partly hidden by a tall tamarind tree beside it. He did not notice it before, his mind then preoccupied with the vacant lot. He halted and looked at it, glad at the thought that Crisanta will have her own chapel, near their future home.

He walked on, past Don Manolo's house and turned right toward the town square, lovely and luxuriant with trees and flowering plants. He crossed Mabini Street and entered the acacia tree-shaded churchyard in San Roque Catholic Church. It was deserted at that time of the day.

A side door in the church was open and he went inside. It was also deserted, but for a veiled woman, praying on a pew and another woman, lighting a votive candle at a stand of votive candles set against the wall.

He knelt down on a pew and prayed in thanksgiving to God for the many blessings that had come his way, like the home he will build for Crisanta and himself, a home that will overlook the lagoon and Manila Bay.

He was back in Parola at past noon and went straight to Crisanta's food stall. He sat down there, his eyes fastened to the food counter there.

"You look like you have not eaten in one entire week," Crisanta said, smiling. "Where did you come from?"

He ignored the question and said instead, "that looks good" at a pork dish in the food counter. It was not yet the time to tell her about the vacant lot and their home, he will build there.

Crisanta smiled and prepared his lunch.

He had dinner in Crisanta's home, later that day, after work.

She sat down beside Leandro on the wooden couch after she had cleared the table and washed the dishes.

He was pleasantly surprised when Mang Emong said he and Aling Pacing were going out to bring to Crisanta's aunt Manolita, the housedress they made for her. They always stayed around and watched over Crisanta, every time he visited her in their house.

He looked inquiringly at Crisanta as Mang Emong and Aling Pacing were stepping out of the house.

"They want to leave us alone," she said to him. "They know what is going on between us."

Chapter Forty-seven

The bells in the Catholic Church in Tondo pealed joyously, one morning, the following summer, to a crowd gathered at the churchyard there. They drew curious glances from people passing by on the sidewalk there or were taking in the morning air in the tiny square in front of the church. It was not everyday that the church had such a gathering. The men were in suits while the women were regal in gowns and elegant dresses on the special occasion of the wedding of Crisanta Mercaida and Leandro Sumaka.

The crowd parted for the bridal car as it was entering the churchyard. It was a Model T Ford decorated with flowers and ribbons, Leandro bought only a week ago. Esteban, who volunteered to be the driver, was behind the wheel.

The crowd looked on smiling when Crisanta alighted from the car with Aling Pacing and Mang Emong.

She smiled shyly, blushing from the crowd's attention, her happiness etched in her face that was never as radiant as it was this morning at her wedding. She did not look at all like the girl who served food in a food stall.

Her cheeks for the first time in her life were powdered, her lips a light pink with lipstick. Her hair was coiffured in the latest style of hairdressing so unlike before when it was simply swept back into a bun.

She was in a white silk wedding gown that trailed to the ground with sleeves that reached to her wrists. White silk gloves hid her hands made rough from cooking and scrubbing and washing dishes. Hanging down from her neck was the gold necklace with a pearl pendant, Leandro gave her as a Christmas gift to her.

The guests entered the church, once the bridal party had assembled in the churchyard. They had hardly settled themselves at the pews there when the church bells stopped ringing. The organ player in the choir loft had begun to play Mendelssohn's *Wedding March.*

The bridal procession proceeded toward the middle aisle, decked out with flowers and trains of ribbons.

Crisanta came in, her hand on Mang Emong's arm, at the rear of the bridal procession, the center of attention of everyone in the church.

Leandro was at the foot of the altar, the groom waiting for his bride, a charming lovely woman, love had made lovelier in his eyes.

He was a bit tipsy from the effect of the wine he drank last night in a bachelor's party held for him by Carlos and Esteban. He was in a daze, not so much from that, as from this momentous event in his life. He will, within an hour, no longer be a man responsible only to himself, but a man responsible to a woman. So much of that was unknown to him.

It was as if he was in a dream with his eyes wide open when he then went along with the rite performed by the parish priest. He heard himself say, "I do," when the priest asked him if he was taking Crisanta for his wife. He was only dimly aware of himself, putting the wedding ring on her finger and of her, putting the other wedding ring on his finger.

He realized the wedding rite was over when light flashed from a camera taking their wedding picture.

The church organ then broke out with a triumphant hymn. The hearty applause of the crowd, filling his ears, he walked down the aisle with her, to the churchyard awash with sunlight. They smiled at each other. They were now married to a life, full of many wonderful possibilities.

Their wedding was the latest in a train of events that came from their decision to get married. Bill Shay readily agreed when Leandro asked him if he and his wife Esperanza could be the principal sponsors at their wedding. So that he will not be working, far from his wife, Bill Shay had him transferred to Manila. Not only that, he was appointed as the company's chief purchasing officer, in place of Balemal, who was fired.

The fact that the Big Boss and his wife were the principal sponsors at their wedding was not lost to the other company executives. Philip Beldry, Mark Clavier, Jones, Tom Guernsey, Stroheim, Tomlinson, Kirkpatrick, Fitzsimmons, Lehigh and Williams came with their wives at the church and the wedding reception held in the ballroom of Columbus Club.

The wedding reception was like a reunion of sorts for Leandro's friends and relatives. Samuel and Dorothy Tyler came with their son, Alfred. So did Mayor Paulo Palanas and his wife Teresa with their sons Lukas and Demetrio. Dick McCall and his wife Nieves were there too. They were also sponsors at their wedding. Berting and Agueda were there. Candido and Maria came with their son Miguel, the ring bearer.

There was one sour note, though, at their wedding. Angela snubbed it. She looked down on Leandro even more when she learned he was getting married to a server in a food stall. Regina wanted to attend it, but Ruy would not allow her. Carlos came as Leandro's best man.

The lunch served was an array of delicious dishes, washed down with wine and liquor. It was not quite over yet when Carlos stood up and, a glass of champagne in his hand, he said, "Ladies and gentlemen! Let us offer a toast to the bride and the groom for them to have a happy, fruitful and prosperous marriage."

The guests raised their glasses in a toast to the newlyweds. The orchestra then played a waltz and everyone waited for Leandro and Crisanta to take to the dance floor. They hesitated, for they have never danced before. But dance, they must. He steeled himself for the coming ordeal by assuring himself that they could do it simply by doing it, the way he had seen dancing couples do it.

"Let us not disappoint our guests," he said to her.

He stood up, took her hand and moved toward the dance floor where they were soon dancing happily, if awkwardly. He found, to his pleasant surprise as they were dancing on, that it was easy enough in dancing the waltz. All they had to do was move and sway to the beat of the music. He found even more amazed that they had a natural grace of movement.

The guests followed suit and the dance floor was soon lively with dancing couples. The orchestra played another waltz and Leandro and Crisanta found themselves with other dancing partners. They had to accommodate the guests who had formed themselves into two lines, one for the men and another one for the women who took turns in dancing with them. It took a while. Mang Emong and Aling Pacing then told them to move from one table to another and greet the guests seated there.

The reception in Columbus Club was unusual for the presence there of a large number of Americans. While the Filipinos considered it an honor to have them as guests in their parties, fiestas and weddings, the Americans, on the other hand, held their own social affairs where Filipinos were seldom invited. They had their own clubs where Filipinos were generally kept out.

It was quite noticeable that the American guests kept to themselves and had little contact with the Filipino guests. As the party progressed and with the wine and liquor flowing liberally and the orchestra playing with hardly a pause, the drinks and the music soon had an unrestrained effect on them and they were soon mixing freely and happily with each other.

Leandro did not show it, but he was now getting impatient. They must leave now while there was still time. Baguio, where they will have their honeymoon, was quite far. But there was the wedding cake that had to be cut yet and distributed to the guests. He led Crisanta to a round table on which was placed a big three-tiered wedding cake.

She sliced a piece and gave it to him who gamely swallowed it down to the cheers of those around the table. He did the same for her.

Maria, Aling Pacing, Agueda and Manolita then took it upon themselves to cut slices of the cake and distribute them to the guests.

The guests were dancing, drinking or eating when Leandro and Crisanta slipped quietly out of the ballroom. They were going to their new home in Caloocan to get their things there and change their clothes before leaving for their honeymoon in Baguio.

The shadow, a tree cast on the club's parking lot, showed them it was already midafternoon, too late now for them to go to Baguio. They will be caught on the road at night and he did not like that. They will have to spend the night in Caloocan and leave tomorrow morning for Baguio.

A couple walking in Rodriguez Street paused and looked on at a bridal car, passing by. It stopped at the gate of the big, newly built house at the end of the street. It attracted their attention for its decoration of ribbons and flowers. They watched the man driving it and the woman beside him, the owners of that big new house. The car's decoration and what they were wearing showed them, they had just come from their wedding.

Leandro left the car and pressed the house gate bell button for Lucia, Crisanta's townmate, they hired as their domestic helper. She appeared right away and opened the gate.

She closed it after the car had passed and ran after it and opened the garage door as well.

Leandro and Crisanta left their car to Lucia congratulating them on their wedding.

"Thank you, Lucia," he said to her. "Where did you get those running legs of yours?"

"Where else," Crisanta, said, smiling, "but from playing softball in her school's playing field in Arayat."

Lucia returned to the house as they were looking around at the house and its wide grounds. Leandro brought Crisanta there only once, at the start of its construction. He purposely limited her visit there, for he wanted their home to come as a big, pleasant surprise to her.

She said as they stood there, her eyes bright with happiness, "We have a big, beautiful home."

He nodded, proud and happy. Their home is indeed beautiful. Its white paint matched its roof and awning, painted green. It cast a shadow on the garden, in the middle of which was a circular three-tiered terraced bed of flowers. Construction of the house looked finished, but the hall in the ground floor had yet to be cemented. Had this been done, they would have held their wedding reception in the house and not in Columbus Club, but there will be other parties that will be held there.

"I never imagined myself," she said, "living in such a big house."

"It is big, all right. We will call it then the Big House with wide grounds."

"It lacks something, though."

"What is it?"

"It lacks shade, trees! We will have the grounds, the garden and the corners of the gate planted to flowering and vegetable plants and fruit and palm trees. I want our home to look like we are living in an orchard and living on the fruits of the plants and trees there."

He looked tenderly at her, touched by what she said. She spoke with such enthusiasm, now that she had fulfilled her lifelong dream of a home of her own. She came, like him, from a poor, peasant family. The only piece of land she owned, she once told him with a bit of humor, was the pot of soil at the back of their house in Nicodemus Street in Tondo where she raised tomatoes during summer. The soil came from her hometown in Arayat. They did not own their house there. They were only renting it.

"Do whatever you want to do here," he said to her. "Plant and grow anything you want, flowering plants, fruit trees, even tomatoes during summer."

She laughed so hard from her sheer enjoyment of the reference he made to her pot of soil in their house in Tondo.

They entered their home. She glanced, when they reached the stairhead, at the balcony to her left. A rattan rocking chair stood there, the open shell-paned window there, looking out at the front yard, the house gate and the modest homes lining the left side of Rodriguez Street.

"So, you will be rocking yourself there," she said to him.

"Not yet. Only when I am old and have nothing else to do, will I rock myself there."

The two-paneled door to the living room was closed, but unlocked. He opened it wide enough for them to enter the living room. She looked around, nodding and smiling at what she saw there.

It was tastefully decorated and it had a cozy air about it. To their left and right were large cushioned rattan couches. They faced, across the floor, a Steinberg piano. It was set against a Cellotex board wall. The piano stood between two large vases with flowering plants on top of them. A rattan coffee table stood in front of the couches.

The wall and the ceiling lights, enclosed in frosted glass, were not switched on, the day being sunny and bright. The wooden floor gleamed from the light of the day. It was coming from the barred window to their left and another one across the living room, at the back of another couch. The window there overlooked the roofed staircase leading to the back of the house. The wooden fence, a few feet away, enclosed the grounds.

"It is so beautiful," she said. "I never imagined the living room will look like that."

He had the house furnished with furniture and appliances, he ordered through the catalogues of Sears Roebuck, Montgomery Ward and Marshall Field's.

"That will be a perfect place for our wedding picture," she said, her finger pointed to the blank wall above the piano, "but what is a piano doing there except as an expensive piece of decoration. I don't play the piano. Do you?"

"No, I don't."

"Why then did you buy it?"

"I bought it for our children. They will play it for us."

"You seem sure about the children, we will have."

"Yes, indeed, I am as sure about it as the number of bedrooms we have, here in our home."

She looked around at the closed bedroom doors in the living room and said, "So, we have four bedrooms here."

"There are actually five bedrooms. Our bedroom is at the right end of the long balcony overlooking the lagoon and the bay."

"So, you are set on a big family."

"Right," he said as he winked at her, "a big house for a big family and the earlier we work on it, the more children, we will have."

He yelled when she then pinched his thigh.

They walked on, his arm, now around her waist, and turned right toward the balcony overlooking the lagoon and Manila Bay.

"I know where I will put my copy of the Holy Bible—right there in the top shelf," she said at a glass cabinet set against a wall to their left, its shelves bare, but for the book, *The Adventures of Tom Sawyer*.

"How often do you read it?"

"I try to read a passage everyday. It has the answer to all our questions and problems especially on matters of life and death. You should read it, too. You will find it very helpful."

He smiled. She was unlike him was a Protestant and was encouraged to read the Holy Bible. Father Saludo, the parish priest in San Isidro, on the other hand, advised him to read it only when he is old enough to understand it.

He never came around to read it, for he never got hold of a copy of the Holy Bible. Now, with her copy of the Holy Bible, he can find the time to read it.

They turned their eyes to a phonograph console, standing in a corner in the living room.

"So, we have that, too," she said.

She looked on when he raised the lid of the phonograph.

He asked her, "Have you heard Enrico Caruso sing?"

"Who is he?"

"He is a great Italian singer. The first time I heard him sing was in the phonograph in Carlos' house. What a pure tenor voice! I bought this phonograph and his records, so we can listen to him, again and again. Would you like to hear him sing?"

She nodded. He placed a record on the phonograph and cranked it up. Then he lifted with his finger, the playing arm with its tulip-shaped speaker and put it down gently on the record.

The voice of Enrico Caruso came out, full and mellow, as he sang the beautiful aria *M'appari* from Flotow's opera, *Martha.*

Caruso's voice accompanied them to the balcony, its glass window running in the entire length of that side of the house that overlooked Manila Bay and the lagoon, now partly converted into fishponds, their surface of water bright in reflection of the afternoon sun.

He watched her, pleased, that she was looking at the beautiful view of Manila Bay and the lagoon. Few homes in Manila and in Caloocan have such a beautiful view.

Caruso's song had ended and he went back to the phonograph console. He removed the speaker from the record and put the record, back to the record rack at the side of the phonograph console.

He returned to her as she was looking at the dining room and the kitchen at one end of the balcony. He placed his arm around her waist as he led her to the master bedroom, at the other end of the balcony.

The two-paneled door was closed. He pulled the panels apart and they entered their bedroom. She looked around at the bedroom, fragrant from a vase of flowers on a table there. She turned to him, her face radiant, and yielded with a sigh as he then took her in his arms.

The sun was low in the horizon when he woke up and saw her seated on the bed, her back against the headboard.

"Are you happy?" she asked him, smiling.

"Yes, I am very happy."

"You will be happier on a full stomach."

"You said it right."

They were so busy and so excited at their wedding reception they hardly touched the food there. He was so hungry by now and, he could imagine, so was she.

She asked him, "Do we have anything to eat here?"

"I bought some canned goods, a few days ago. You will find them in the pantry."

"Let me see what I can cook for you."

"Let Lucia do that."

She shook her head and said,"She can help, but I will do it myself. I want no one else, but me, to cook the very first meal, I will be sharing with my husband, here in my own home."

"Wow!" he said as he reached out to her. "Let me have another one with you and much better and longer this time."

"Not, now. We have all the time for that."

She bent down and gave him instead, a peck on his cheek. Then she left their bed and crossed the room. She took out a housedress from her luggage there and put it on.

He said, as he also left their bed, "I will call Lucia."

He pulled a cord, hanging from the ceiling in a corner of the room. It was a signal for Lucia to come up in the house. The cord was connected to a bell in the servants' quarters, downstairs. It has the same function as the device in his cubicle in Pacific & Gulf.

He dressed up quickly and joined Crisanta in the kitchen. She was inspecting the pantry there.

"Can I be of some help?" he said to her.

"You can, provided you will not spoil my cooking," she said, smiling.

"I cannot guarantee that," he said, smiling as well.

He left the kitchen. He went to the living room and was soon taking a nap on a couch there. The gate bell began to ring. He looked out from the window and saw at the house gate, Candido, Maria and Miguel. They have arrived from their wedding reception. They were staying in the house while they were in Manila. He watched Lucia, who was opening the house gate for them.

"Why are you still here?" Candido asked Leandro when he saw him in the living room. "Are you not supposed to be on your way to Baguio for your honeymoon?"

He yawned as he replied, "We will leave tomorrow morning. I don't want us to leave so late and be caught on the road at night."

"You're right," Canddo said. "It's not advisable to travel at night."

"Where is Crisanta?" Maria asked Leandro.

"She is in the kitchen, preparing our dinner."

"I will help her after I have changed into my housedress," Maria said as she proceeded with Candido and Miguel to their bedroom.

They returned to the living room, a short while later. Candido sat down on another couch there while Maria proceeded toward the kitchen.

Miguel was insisting, as he held on to her dress, for her to give him a bath first. She slapped his hand away from her dress and walked on toward the kitchen.

Miguel cried and stamped his feet angrily on the floor. When he saw no one was minding him, he followed his mother quietly to the kitchen.

Leandro watched Miguel, amused with the boy who was so thrilled by the novelty of taking a shower in the bathroom where, at the mere turn of the faucet, water streamed out of the showerhead.

He was just as amused at Candido who was looking around, wide-eyed in admiration of the living room.

"If only our townmates can see you now," he said to Leandro, "you, who used to live no differrently from us in Father's hut in Bangar, now living in such a fine, big house with a car in the garage and a maid to boot, how they will envy you."

Leandro smiled, flattered by the compliment, but said nothing. How things had changed between him and his cousin. He looked up at Candido, back in Bangar. Now, four years later, here in Caloocan, it was Candido who was now looking up at him.

He felt good about it, but was sorry for his cousin who, in comparison, had remained so poor. His cousin's dire financial situation showed in the plain white shirt, he wore at his wedding. He may not want to be reminded about it, but for lack of anything else to say, he asked him, "So, how are you getting along?"

"I manage. I'm still working in the sugar mill in Santa Ignacia."

He nodded. His cousin, at least, still has his job.

"I don't know, if you know it," Candido continued, "but another election is coming up. Our townmates have asked me to make another run for the town mayor."

"Are you?"

"I have been giving it, considerable thought."

"Is Enrique running for reelection?"

"He is."

"I don't want to dampen your enthusiasm, but your chances of winning could be even less now with Enrique, running as an incumbent."

"On the contrary, it is exactly because of Enrique's very bad administration of the town that I am being asked to run again. You should see what he has done as mayor of San Isidro. It is in such a mess and the graft and corruption going on there!"

He noticed, as he was looking at Candido and listening to him, a marked change in the tone of his voice and the expression in his face. He is animated and self-assured, now that he is talking about politics. Candido is in his element there.

"How," he said, "could the Americans allow all that wrongdoing there?"

He knows the Americans are strict in the observance of the law.

"They cannot see everything, going on in the colony, just as they cannot see everything, going on in San Isidro."

"But don't they send people to check on the town?"

"They do, but if you are not from there, you will think everything is all right there, at least that is how it looks on the surface of things. The Monte Arazteas and their men have robbed the town blind. I know all the government officials there, from Enrique to the members of the town council, to the police and the other town officials. Except for the health officer, an honest man, they are all on the take."

"So, our town's government is nothing but a fraternity of thieves."

"Do you know what the doctor, once told me? He said the government is one place in the town that is so easy to rob."

"So," he said to test his cousin's intentions, "you are running again for mayor, so you will not be left out of what is going on there."

"You know me better than that. I am not running for myself. I am running for mayor so I can put to an end the abuses and the graft and corruption going on there."

"I know, you are, but you will face another tough fight. You can deal with that jellyfish Enrique, but there is his father, Don Camilo. He is the real power in San Isidro. How is he, by the way?"

"He is like a bad grass. You cannot easily get rid of him. He has been imprisoned in his wheelchair. That has not stopped him from running the town. The Monte Arazteas control, not only the government, but also the business in San Isidro. Liaolu and Angsiang get along well with them with the bribe money they are giving them. As for their tenants, their grip on them is tighter than ever."

"Well, cousin, all that you said compels you to run again. The town needs you to clean it up and put to an end the Monte Arazteas' corrupt, abusive rule. There is also the issue of land reform that needs to be addressed. You face a lot of obstacles. But this time, you will win; you must win, I will help you win."

"Thank you, cousin. With your help, I have no doubt, I will win. We will win; it is our fight."

Maria was coming.

"Dinner is ready," she said to them.

A large plate of fried pork on a bed of lettuce, another one of fish fillet cooked in spices and tomatoes, a plate of egg roll and a large plate of fried rice were laid out on the dining table. Crisanta and Maria, with Lucia's help, had prepared a veritable feast in just a short time.

"Where did all this food come from?" Leandro asked Crisanta. "I don't think we had them in the pantry or in the icebox."

"You are right," Maria said. "Your pantry and your icebox were almost empty when we arrived here yesterday. I did some hurried marketing with Lucia."

"You, men, left by yourselves, you will starve to death," Crisanta said to laughter at the table.

"There are canned goods in the pantry. We can open them without much difficulty," Leandro said. He turned to Candido and said, "Right, cousin?"

"Right," Candido replied, nodding and smiling.

"Right," Maria said. "They taste good, eaten raw."

Leandro and Candido smiled away, Maria's sarcastic remark.

They said grace after which they began their dinner. Leandro was so hungry, the food so good, that he had his fill, in no time at all. He was also tired and sleepy. He and Crisanta had a hectic day and he wanted to be, just alone with her.

Candido and Maria glanced at each other when, at the end of their dinner, Leandro stood up and said good night to them.

He and Crisanta were soon, deep in marital bliss.

He woke up a few hours later by the need to go to the bathroom. Crisanta was sleeping soundly and he moved carefully, out of their bed. He was on his way back to their bedroom when he halted at an entrancing view of the lagoon and Manila Bay.

A ship, bright with its garland of lights, was moving in the bay. There were also lights in the outriggers, used in harvesting the milkfish in the lagoon, now partly converted into fishponds. The night with its crescent moon was sprinkled with the stars' pinpricks of light.

He was so taken by the view that he stayed there for a while. To make himself more comfortable, he pulled toward the window, a chair in the balcony and sat down there with his elbows laid on the windowsill.

He watched, so many times before, the same dark sky, the same crescent moon and the same stars, his feelings then, so different now. He watched them sadly on his last night in Bangar, not sure if he will ever set foot there again. He watched the same night sky in Zamboanga and Davao, in Masakao and Baguio, lonely for friends and loved ones.

Now, here in Caloocan, the same crescent moon and the same stars appeared brightly to him, who was now so happy and so satisfied.

He dozed off, but woke up to someone brushing his hair. He looked up at Crisanta, who was looking down at him.

"What are you doing here?" she asked him. "I got worried when I woke up and did not find you in bed."

"I'm sorry. I fell asleep while I was watching the view there."

"Come to bed," she said when they returned to their bedroom.

She said the same thing to him, moments after they arrived, the afternoon of the following day in Baguio.

They had a blissful honeymoon there. He was glad to be back in Baguio, no longer alone, but with the love of his life by his side. She was so ecstatic about Baguio and its cold, bracing climate that, at her insistence, they spent most afternoons, taking a stroll or were seated close to each other on a bench in Burnham Park.

They talked, made plans, watched the pine tree-covered hills or simply waited in silence for the fog and then as it descended on them, in luxuriating in its cold, bracing feel on their cheeks.

They had dinner, one evening, with Samuel and Dorothy Tyler and their son Alfred in their cottage in Brendan School. It was only the second time, Crisanta had met the Tylers. The first was at their wedding.

She remained silent, preferring to listen to the talk at the dining table. The Tylers' friendliness helped her overcome her shyness and she was soon conversing with them despite her accent and inadequacy with the English language. She left the Tylers with Leandro, now more self-assured when socializing with the Americans.

Leandro was walking toward his car in the garage when he paused and waved at Crisanta who was smiling and also waving at him from a window in the Big House.

One week had passed since their wedding and he is going back to work in Pacific & Gulf.

He saw, on his arrival in his office, that he has a lot of catching up to do on his work load from a pile of paper in the incoming tray in his desk. He spent a big part of the day in going over them, in checking the inventory of supplies and equipment in the warehouse, in preparing invoices, in making calls and in placing orders.

The pile of paper, by the end of the day, had been reduced to just a couple of sheets. He had moved the pile to the outgoing tray or had the rest, brought to the other departments in the company.

He drove out, the following day with Esteban and picked up the orders he had placed with their suppliers—the Chinese hardware stores, the British importing firms, the American trading companies—and stored them in the warehouse.

The reclamation of the shore in Intramuros into a new port in Manila was another major project of Pacific & Gulf that required Leandro's attention. He had not been to the Port Area, as the project site was now called, since he left for Zamboanga, four years ago. Except for the breakwaters being built there, it was then all water when he saw it before leaving for Zamboanga.

He went there, the following morning, to get a feel of the work being done there and to take up with the project engineers, the materials and equipment they need from him.

He saw there Bill Shay, who was showing to Dick McCall, the work being done there by Pacific & Gulf.

"Once we are finished with our work here," Bill said to Dick, "we will have here, not only the finest seaport in the Orient, but one of the finest in the world."

"And as I often hear you say, that and all the others of your company projects will be done, 'all in good time, all good time.' "

Bill nodded and smiled.

They watched, spread out before them, the extent of the work being done there.

The two long breakwaters, a few hundred feet away from the shore, enclosed the harbor where ships could dock safely even in bad weather. The area within them was dredged, the soil dug up and used in reclaiming the shore into the Port Area.

There were several concrete finger piers there. They extended toward the bay, each one of them with a big and long warehouse.

At its landside was a wide concrete road. Lining it were office buildings under construction. Its southern end was at the back of Manila Hotel, whose frontage faced the western end of Luneta Park.

Bill said, as he and Dick were looking on at the port, "We are also building, south of here, starting in Luneta Park, a sea wall and beside it, a four-lane boulevard with a traffic island in the middle."

"I can hardly wait for that day when I will be driving with Nieves in that bayside boulevard. Where will it be built?"

"It will be built, right in front of the homes in Ermita and Malate and the church there."

"How far will it go?"

"It will run up to Vito Cruz or initially about two-and-a-half miles. It will later on be extended to the beaches in Pasay and connect it to the road in the salt beds in Paranaque and perhaps, later on, up to the mouth of Manila Bay."

"That will be changing the face of Manila at its western side, facing the bay."

"It will indeed do that. Hotels, office buildings and condominiums will then rise there. It will be like Manila's version of the seafront boulevards in Hawaii and Florida."

"Have they thought of a name for that boulevard?"

"It will be named after Admiral George Dewey as a memorial to his victory over the Spanish fleet in the naval battle in Manila Bay."

Leandro returned to his office, his mind on this new fad in Manila of giving many of its parks and streets, new American names, like the planned seaside boulevard to be named after Admiral Dewey and the streets in Ermita and Malate, named after some states in America.

His own neighborhood in Caloocan was, at least, spared from this new fad of renaming the streets. The two streets along his property retained their names of Rodriguez and General Luna. So too with Caloocan's main street, which retained its name of Mabini—"The Brains of the Philippine Revolution." The Spanish name of *Heroes del 1896* in the street along the railroad's marshaling yard and repair shops was also retained.

It did not matter to him, though, whatever were their names. What mattered to him was the quality of life in Manila and in his quiet peaceful neighborhood in Caloocan. Its abundance of trees and shrubs gave it something, he and Crisanta loved—a countryside setting.

They took a pause, one late afternoon, from the gardening they were doing in the newly terraced backyard in the Big House when they saw Candido, Maria and Miguel coming.

"Look at what we brought you," Candido said as he removed from his shoulders and put down on the ground, a big, bulging jute sack.

"What is it?" Crisanta asked Candido.

"Take a look," Candido replied as he was untying the string around the top of the jute sack. He opened it, revealing mangoes, some a ripe yellow, others, still green in color.

"How nice of you to bring me those mangoes," Crisanta said, her hands clasped in delight.

Candido learned, in an exchange of letters between her and Maria that she had been craving for the mangoes ever since she started conceiving. He gathered the sweetest mangos he could find in Bangar and brought a sack of them on their visit to Caloocan, to discuss with Leandro and Crisanta, his campaign for mayor of San Isidro.

"It is now official," Candido said to them. "I am the Nationalist Party candidate for mayor in our town."

"Good! It is just as we expected," Leandro said to Candido.

Leandro and Candido discussed that evening over dinner, Candido's campaign for the mayor of San Isidro. Crisanta and Maria listened and gave helpful suggestions while Miguel concentrated on his food. Leandro could not visit San Isidro and manage Candido's campaign for mayor. He could not even take a few days' off from his job in Pacific & Gulf. But he was raising funds for Candido. They had a few months left before the election in November.

"As I have said before, you are in for another tough fight with Enrique," Leandro said to Candido. "Enrique has the advantage of running as the incumbent mayor. He has the money and other resources. He has, most of all, Don Camilo who is running his campaign."

"He is the real power in San Isidro, not Enrique," Maria said. "The whole town knows that."

"What do you have, going for you?" Crisanta asked Candido.

"I said this before, the reason for my optimism. I have what I need—the townsfolk's support. Their votes matter more than the money of the Monte Arazteas. This time, we will watch closely, the counting of the ballots. Our people are sick of the corruption in Enrique's administration. They see in this election, the chance to remove him from office."

Leandro nodded. Dick McCall made the same observation in an article, he wrote in *The Philippines Newsmagazine:* "The townsfolk in San Isidro have found Mayor Enrique Monte Araztea wanting in accomplishments. They will express their sentiment in the coming election when he is facing, once again, his old opponent, Candido Sumaka."

Leandro hatched something novel and unexpected on the Monte Arazteas, one week before the election in San Isidro. Candido led a torch parade, the first time, one was held in the town. It will be a show of Candido's political strength and the townsfolk's support for him.

It was led by the marching band in Santa Ignacia, they hired secretly. It went around in San Isidro with the parade participants bearing torches and placards with Candido's name written there and with them shouting Candido's name as the next mayor of San Isidro. The parade grew in number when people watching it along its route, joined it.

The number of its participants had grown to more than a thousand people, a considerable number in the light of the town's small population of a few thousand people, by the time it was passing by the house of the Monte Arazteas.

Don Camilo, Dona Isabella, Enrique, Nicasio and some of their political supporters were in the living room, discussing Enrique's campaign for his reelection when their attention was drawn to the marching band music and the parade participants, shouting the name of Candido, the next mayor of San Isidro.

They went to the window, ignoring Dona Isabella who said Candido's torch parade was not worth watching.

"I want them to see me, watching them," Don Camilo growled, his right fist clenched in anger.

The sight of Candido, smiling and waving his hand while his supporters were shouting his name as the next mayor of San Isidro, sent Don Camilo boiling mad.

He stood up from his wheelchair and, his fist clenched and his eyes wide with hate and anger, he shouted obscenities at Candido.

"Sit down, please! Don't be affected by those people," Dona Isabella said to Don Camilo who then sat down on his wheelchair.

The torch parade had passed and the road in front of the Monte Araztea house was dark and quiet again. Don Camilo and the others resumed their discussion of Enrique's reelection campaign.

A line of lights, not long after, appeared in the distance, in the road that cut across the rice fields. The torch parade was now headed toward the hamlet of Bangar, Candido's bailiwick.

They heard faintly, but distinctly, the marching band music and the parade participants, shouting Candido's campaign slogan. It sent Don Camilo, boiling mad again. He rose from his wheelchair and shouted at the window, "Damn you, Candido Sumaka! Damn you!"

He had barely said that when he suddenly clutched his chest and cried out in pain. He collapsed on his wheelchair so violently it sent the wheelchair running backward in the living room. Nicasio caught up with it, only after it had slammed itself against a wall in the living room.

Enrique was so shocked he could only watch his father helplessly. Dona Isabella ran after the wheelchair. She knelt down beside Don Camilo, who was now slumped on his wheelchair. She dropped a pill in Don Camilo's mouth, Nicasio had forced open. It proved to be futile, for Don Camilo had stopped breathing, his face wracked still with pain and anger.

With Don Camilo dead and no one to run it, Enrique's reelection campaign fell apart. It lost all semblance of organization. Money that was supposed to be used in buying votes disappeared. Shocked and saddened out of his wits by his father's death, Enrique kept to himself in the house in the few days left before the election.

Its outcome was made clear by the townsfolk who showed their political sentiment by staying away from Don Camilo's burial in the town cemetery. Only the Monte Araztea family, their servants and the other town landlords attended it.

Chapter Forty-eight

The tired look in Crisanta's face gave way to an amused smile as she was watching Leandro who was trying out, name after name, for their newborn child.

He was seated on a chair beside Crisanta's bed, the hospital room fragrant with flowers, placed all over it.

Word about Leandro, having become a father, had spread around in Pacific & Gulf. Carlos, Bill Shay and Esperanza sent bouquets, so did the other executives of Pacific & Gulf.

Mang Emong and Aling Pacing and the owners of the other food stalls had visited Crisanta, although only a few of them were able to see the baby.

It was kept most of the time in the nursery of Emmanuel Hospital, where Crisanta delivered her child.

It was early evening and they were by themselves, Leandro having dropped by the hospital from work.

He said, "How about Margarita, or Roberta? They both sound nice to me."

"No, not any of those," Crisanta said, shaking her head and smiling.

"How about naming her, after you?"

"Not my name, please!" she said as she was shaking her head in disagreement. "I don't want us to be accused of so lacking in imagination, we cannot even think of another name for our baby."

Leandro sighed in disappointment and rubbed his forehead with his palm. He went over in his mind, other possible names for their baby.

Pacita, the name of Crisanta's mother, is out. He did not want his baby, named after his mother-in-law. Milagros, his mother's name, will be a nice name for their baby, but he never even knew his mother.

They turned toward a knock on the door.

"Come in," he said.

The door opened to Candido and Maria, smiling. Miguel was with them.

"Congratulations on your newborn baby," Candido and Maria said to them.

They both kissed Crisanta on the cheek and shook hands with Leandro.

"Congratulations to you, too, Mayor Sumaka," Leandro said, smiling, to Candido.

It was only a week after Candido was proclaimed the winner in the election for mayor in San Isidro.

"Thank you, cousin," Candido said. "I owe much of my victory to you and Crisanta. So, we are having, a double celebration—my victory in the election and the birth of your baby girl. What will you name her?"

"We have run through, a number of names," Leandro said, "but we have not come up with a name, both of us like."

Maria suggested, "Why don't you look for her name in a church calendar?"

Leandro and Crisanta looked at each other.

He said, "Why not? Our child, named after a saint."

"I will look for a calendar," Candido said as he stepped out of the room.

He returned, a few minutes later, with a church calendar and gave it to Leandro. He turned the pages and looked for a saint in November 15, the baby's date of birth.

"There is," he said to Crisanta, "only one saint—Albert the Great—the day our baby was born. Do you want her named Alberta?"

Crisanta winced at the mention of the name while Candido and Maria laughed.

"Okay, not Alberta, although it is a great name for a boy," Leandro said. "There are two female saints, the following day—Saints Margaret and Gertrude."

They both sounded nice to him.

"What do you think?" he asked Crisanta.

"I like both of them; they are beautiful names, but I am inclined toward Saint Gertrude."

"So am I," Leandro said. "We will call her then, Gertrude, Gertrude Mercaida Sumaka. It sounds nice, don't you think so?"

Candido nodded and glanced at Maria who was also nodding in agreement with Leandro and Crisanta's choice of the name for their baby.

They turned their gaze to the door, opened by a nurse with the baby in her arms.

"There is my Gertrude now," Leandro said as the nurse laid the baby, beside Crisanta.

They looked closely at the baby. She was pinkish, she had little hair, she was smiling with her eyes closed.

"She looks just like you," Maria said to Crisanta.

"Now, now," Leandro protested. "Look closely at my baby. Those lips and the shape and the expression in her face are all mine. Why, she looks just like me when I was a baby!"

Leandro then took his baby in his arms and was soon dancing around in the room with her.

Gertrude's eyes were now open and she was smiling when, a month later, she was baptized by Father Absedo, Caloocan's parish priest, to the pealing of the church bells in San Roque Catholic Church.

Only Candido and Maria, who were the godparents, Crisanta and Leandro were in attendance at Gertrude's baptism in the church. The guests had gone straight to the Big House for the baptismal party there, their attendance reflecting the various stages in Leandro's life.

Candido and Maria moved around the house with Miguel, in attending to the guests, their presence there, a reminder of Leandro's poor, peasant life in San Isidro. Berting and Agueda and some of their children were there, a reminder of Leandro's bad, life-threatening start in Manila.

Carlos, as usual, came alone and he moved around the house with complete familiarity, for he was considered, a part of the family. Esteban and other lower-ranked employees of Pacific & Gulf were there, too.

They kept to themselves in a corner near a mango tree in the garden, in front of the house with its lovely terraced centerpiece, blooming with flowers. They would venture inside the house only to get food at the buffet table there and drinks at a bar set up also in the hall downstairs.

They worked with Leandro when he was starting out as a janitor and messenger in Pacific & Gulf. He had, since then, left them far behind. He has gone up. This was evident in the attendance of the company executives, led by Bill Shay, his wife Esperanza and their son Michael. Dick and Nieves were there; so were Paulo and Teresa with their children, Lukas and Demetrio, Samuel and Dorothy Tyler and their son, Alfred.

Crisanta's friends and relatives came, too. They looked up to her since she married Leandro, the poor server in a food stall who now owned a big house with a domestic helper serving her and a car in the garage.

An outdoor kitchen had been set up at the back of the house, below the water tank there. It was rich with the inviting smell of pigs, chickens and fish being cooked or were roasting in hot coals. Mang Emong and Aling Pacing were cooking those various dishes with the help of the owners of the other food stalls and their helpers.

Portions of those dishes were then laid out at the long table in the hall downstairs or were brought up in the roofed staircase to the dining room upstairs.

There was dancing in the hall downstairs, the music provided by the console phonograph operated by Crisanta's cousin, Armando.

Gertrude's christening was the very first grand party held in the Big House. The celebrant herself was in her crib, completely unaware of the celebration being held in her honor. She looked lovely in her pink baptismal dress with a pink bonnet. She stirred and smiled when Leandro picked her up from her crib.

She kept on smiling when Leandro, cradling her in his arms, danced the waltz with her. The guests looked on appreciatively, now making funny remarks, now encouraging Leandro to dance on with his baby daughter until Crisanta, her brow creased with worry that all that dancing might make Gertrude dizzy, took her away from Leandro, right in the middle of the music.

"How is that for my little girl's first dance?" Leandro said to the guests there.

They were unanimous in their approval except Candido, who said to the others' laughter, "You did very well, considering that you dance with two left feet."

Leandro was so taken by what Candido said in jest, he roared with laughter so hard, he threw his head back with his eyes turned to the ceiling. Candido said that about him, one time, when he danced around in their hut in Bangar with Miguel, just a baby then.

"Be assured," he said smiling to Candido, "by the time, my little girl is grown enough to dance, I will be an expert with the waltz and maybe, even with the tango."

Leandro kept his promise. By the time Gertrude was five years old, he could move around nimbly enough in dancing the waltz, but not the tango, which he found exacting in its movement.

He showed off his new dancing skill at the children's party held on Gertrude's fifth birthday. While there were not as many guests, at each of her birthday parties, as there were at her baptismal party, it was just as merry with a lot of children around.

Gertrude, by then, could dance the waltz and dance she did with her father to the lovely *Merry Widow Waltz.*

"That is nice, dancing, with your little girl," Bill Shay said to Leandro. He was standing beside Esperanza, a glass of whisky in his hand.

Bill and the other company executives seldom missed the parties, Leandro and Crisanta held in their home. They were now in far more intimate terms than ever.

Leandro had, by then, risen even higher in rank in Pacific & Gulf. Aside from his job as chief purchasing officer, he was now also the chief supply officer and warehouse manager, in place of John Tomlinson who returned to the United States.

He was, unknown to him, eyed for those positions by his superiors in Pacific & Gulf when he became a member of their exclusive fraternal club.

It came about, one day, when he ran into Mark Clavier as he was on his way to take a snack at the cafeteria.

"So, how is your purchasing work?" Mark asked him.

"It is mostly routine work," Leandro replied, "although we have to anticipate the needs of our project managers."

"I have yet to hear of any complaint about any delay in the provision of those supplies since you started doing the purchasing for the company."

"Thank you. That is so nice to hear."

He was about to move on when Mark asked him, "Will you be free after work on Friday?"

Mark's question sounded to Leandro like an invitation to something. He was going home that day after work.

"Yes, I will be free," he said. "Why did you ask about it?"

"I'm inviting you to our club's monthly socials. You will meet a lot of interesting people there. We will go there in my car. I will take you back here afterwards."

Leandro hesitated, but then he said, "Okay."

He walked on toward the cafeteria, his mind on Mark's invitation. Mark is not on close familiar terms with him. He considered it beneath him, an American and the personnel manager, to be close to him, a Filipino of lower rank in the company.

Why, he asked himself, did Mark invite him to the monthly socials of whatever was that club of his?

He shook his head in regret. He should not have accepted Mark's invitation. He will be out of place there, a club exclusively for the Americans.

He could only blame himself for the attitude, common among the Filipinos, of taking as a command, every wish expressed to them by the Americans. But that was how he advanced in Pacific & Gulf.

Had he not done that, instead of rising to higher positions, he may have remained a lowly janitor and messenger. Mark will be offended had he refused his invitation and he could not afford to disappoint and even antagonize him.

He left that Friday with Mark for his club's monthly socials.

He said to Mark, as they were leaving Parola, "I forgot to ask you, about your club's name."

"It is called the Elk Lodge."

"First time, I heard about it. Is it some kind of a secret society?"

"It is secret only in the sense that it is an exclusive, fraternal club. We don't just take in, anybody."

"Do you want me to join your club?"

"You may, if you want to."

"What do you do there?"

"It is a fraternal club. We look after each other."

"So you believe in brotherhood; that sort of thing. Does it discriminate against any religion? I asked that because I am a Catholic."

"You need not be concerned about that. It is not against any established religion."

"So, it is purely a social club. It is neither, a religious nor an anti-religious club."

"It is religious only in the sense that its members believe in God and in the immortality of the soul."

Mark's explanation of the Elk Lodge removed whatever reservation, Leandro had about attending its monthly socials.

He was impressed to find, on their arrival at the club's social hall in Malate, men prominent in business and government. Bill Shay, the Big Boss himself, was there.

He got the impression from Bill as they were exchanging pleasantries that he is expected to join in and he readily agreed to be a member of their exclusive club. It will be to his advantage to be a member of this club whose members ran things in the colony. Even better, it will put him in close fraternal terms with the Big Boss and the other executives of Pacific & Gulf who were also there.

It was thus in a fraternal manner that Leandro entertained the Pacific & Gulf executives and their wives at the children's party on Gertrude's fifth birthday. Bill Shay was there with Esperanza and their son Michael. So were Dick and Nieves, Samuel and Dorothy Tyler and their son Alfred, Paulo Palanas, his wife Teresa and their sons, Lukas and Demetrio.

He was the amiable host, a glass of whisky in his hand, moving around, attending to the guests' needs and savoring the festive air in his oldest girl's birthday party. He came across Candido and Maria who were watching Gertrude and the other children, playing in the living room.

He watched them, pleased with himself. He now has everything, a man could aspire for: a top job in the colony's largest construction firm, wealth, social position, a loving wife and three adorable little girls.

Gertrude was yet to turn one year old when Elizabeth was born. Donita was born, eleven months later. Leandro is confident, Crisanta will bear him a son. He wanted a large family. His three cute daughters were the objects of his care and attention, especially Gertrude, the apple of his eye.

"My girls will have everything, I never had," he said to Candido. "They will have the best education. They can even study abroad, should they want to. They will be in the best society."

"They are smart kids, especially your oldest daughter," Candido said, the glass of brandy in his hand, tipped to his lips.

He smiled, pleased with Candido's complimentary remark about Gertrude, for it confiirmed his own impression of his oldest child. Gertrude, at such an early age, could already read and write and do simple arithmetic. He had seen her climb the piano stool and with her dainty little fingers, make musical sounds on the piano.

Donita had just then dropped her bottle of milk on the floor. Leandro watched, even more pleased, when Gertrude picked up the milk bottle and held it to Donita's mouth. Gertrude has not only outgrown her resentment toward her younger sisters for the attention they were getting from their elders, she has taken upon herself to look after them.

"Good girl!" he said, tapping Gertrude appreciatively on her shoulders.

"Your little girl has the makings of a public servant," Maria said.

"She could be a politician like me," Candido said.

What Candido said reminded Leandro about something, he had long wanted to take up with him. He made a sign to Candido with his finger pointed in the direction of the balcony. They left Maria and the children.

There was no one at the end of the balcony, near the master bedroom. He sat down on a couch there, his face, cheerful a while ago, now looking so serious.

He glanced at Candido who had sat down at the other end of the couch. The change in Candido's life had also changed in the way he now looked. Candido, when he was a tenant farmer, had a lean build from the backbreaking work he did in the rice fields and his sparse farmer's diet, mostly of gruel, fish and vegetables.

Now, as the mayor of San Isidro, the food he ate was the kind that he used to crave when he was a poor tenant farmer, but seldom ate: pork, beef and chicken washed down with wine or liquor.

Candido was now so stout his stomach looked so bloated despite the cover provided by the coat he was wearing. His cheeks, hollow before, were now full and fleshy. He looked smug and well-fed where before he was so thin and looked so defiant and determined.

What disturbed Leandro as he took a sip from his glass of whisky, was not so much in the change in Candido's appearance as in what he had done and failed to do as the mayor of San Isidro. Now that he was no longer a tenant farmer, he had ceased, not only to look like one, but also to think like one. He did not keep the campaign promise, he made to his fellow tenant farmers of pursuing land reform. Because he no longer stood to gain from it and will instead alienate him from the town landlords with whom, as the town mayor, he now had a cozy relationship, Candido had set aside his campaign promise of working for land reform.

He supported Candido, as much for their blood ties, as for his goals as mayor, foremost of which was land reform. He kept silent about it for four long years. He decided the time had come for him to take it up with Candido. He took out his pipe from his coat pocket. A good smoke will help him with his thoughts.

He was stopped from lighting his pipe when Candido said, "Don't you feel great, seated here with a great view of Manila Bay? Your house is the best proof that you have made it big."

Candido has given him the opening to another matter he also wanted to take up with him.

"I can say the same thing about you," he said to Candido. "Not only are you now, the mayor of San Isidro, you are also now, the new owner of the former home of the Monte Arazteas."

"It is one more instance," Candido said, smiling, "that.we got even with Don Camilo and Enrique."

He learned about it from Crisanta who picked it up from Maria. Candido bought the Monte Araztea house from another landlord in Santa Ignacia to whom Enrique and his mother sold it after his defeat to Candido in the last election. Rather than fight on, as Don Camilo would have done, Enrique, a jellyfish of a man, made a full retreat. He and his mother sold to that landlord everything that they owned in San Isidro. They were not seen there again. The talk in the town was that Enrique left with his family for Spain.

"Let us drink to my acquisition of the house of the Monte Arazteas," Candido said as he drank his glass of brandy.

He looked sharply at Candido. His cousin could not afford to buy the Monte Araztea house on his salary of the town mayor. It could not even buy the kitchen there. The money Candido used in buying it could have come only from questionable sources like the bribe money from Liaolu and Angsiang. Candido had been corrupted by political power.

"That adds up to what I heard are the questionable things you are doing as our town mayor," he said to Candido.

"You don't seem, pleased, that I now own Don Camilo's house."

"I am not. It raises questions, not only on how you got it, but also on how you are running our town."

"I did not come here to be lectured on how I should run our town."

.   "I helped you get elected as the town mayor. I have the right to know how you are running it. I have been hearing about a lot of irregularities, going on there."

"That nasty talk again. Do you want me to put it, straight to you?"

"That is how it has always been, between us."

"All right, I am only doing what everybody else will do when given the opportunity.

"Speak for yourself."

"Yes, I will. We cannot help this graft and corruption, you are talking about. We inherited it from our past Spanish rulers. It is now in our blood; in our system. That may sound incredible to you because you are on the outside, looking in. But once you are inside there, as I have found out as the mayor of our town, you will become a part of it. You cannot escape from it. You will just have to go along with it, like everybody else."

"That may be so during the Spanish time. I don't know how the Americans, who are strict on law and order, could allow that."

"They cannot see everything, going on in the colony, much less in San Isidro and that is just fine with me."

"I can imagine what will happen, once we are on our own when the Americans will no longer be around, looking over our shoulders."

The United States took the steps along with that when its Congress passed the Jones Law, a few years later. It committed the United States to the eventual independence of the Philippines. It was the first time in the world that a colonial power, on its own initiative, had formally declared its intention of granting independence to its colony.

Candido yawned. He was bored with the subject.

"Well, cousin," he said. "When that time comes, when we will be on our own, we can do whatever we want to do. It will be, free for all. If you cannot lick them and you cannot, then join them."

"I will never be a part of anything like that. It is wrong; it is bad, very bad and you are now a part of it."

"I don't like what you just said about me. I don't like it at all."

"I don't care how you take it."

"I don't think, I'm still welcome in this house," Candido said as he then stood up and left Leandro.

He watched Candido as he was walking away, sore with him and with himself, as well. He was harsh with his cousin, accusing him of graft and corruption when he himself had toyed with it and had nearly succumbed to it. Whatever those Chinese merchants called it, a rebate or goodwill, what they offered him was pure, simple bribe or kickback.

He shook his head. Candido ruled their hometown as he had seen it ruled by Enrique and the other Spanish mestizos before him, a perfect dark brown Indio copy of their Spanish mestizo town rulers. They were freed slaves, not any better than their bad, past Spanish masters

There were no set rules, much less a tradition of public service to guide Candido, now that he held the power and the authority in their hometown. Candido had, not surprisingly, succumbed to the easiest of temptations, the temptation of greed, graft and corruption.

He remained seated on the couch in the balcony, glum, wretched and far removed from the rest of the Big House that was filled with cheerful talk, laughter and music.

He and Candido parted ways that day, at the party in Gertrude's fifth birthday. Candido and Maria never set foot there again in the Big House while he vowed, he will never set foot in San Isidro for as long as Candido was its mayor.

Leandro concentrated on the only two things that mattered to him now: his family and his job.

Three more children, all boys this time, were added within a few years to his family: Adrian, the oldest boy, followed by Franklin and Albert.

He bought another car, a Buick, for Crisanta and the children's use. He hired Gonzalo, a distant relative of Crisanta, as the family driver. They also hired a nanny named Magda and a cook and housekeeper named Delia.

Weekends were special to Leandro and his family when he would drive the Buick around Manila with them and then take a stroll in Luneta Park and watch the ships and the beautiful sunset in Manila Bay, just like he used to do with Carlos and Regina. They would cap the day with dinner in any of the restaurants in San Jacinto or in Carvajal Street.

He often took Crisanta to shows in the newly opened Manila Grand Opera House and the children to the circus during carnival time where they watched the clowns' antics and the elephants perform tricks. They made it a point to spend at least one week in Baguio during summer, which was always enjoyable for its cold, bracing climate, the sights there, and the company of the Tylers whom they never failed to visit whenever they were visiting Baguio.

He continued to make progress; so did the rest of the colony. The agriculture sector was booming with its products in great demand in Europe, where war was about to take place between the Alliied powers of England, France, Italy and Russia against the Central powers of Germany, the Austro-Hungarian Empire and Turkey.

Carlos came one day to Leandro's office and said, "Can you spare me, a few minutes of your time?"

"For you, I will make it an hour," Leandro replied in jest to Carlos who was looking so serious.

"No, not here," Carlos said.

"Let us then have coffee at the cafeteria. It is my treat."

They took a table in a corner of the cafeteria. Carlos waited while Leandro was placing his order of two cups of coffee.

"I have never seen you, looking so serious, even gloomy, as you are today. What is going on?" Leandro asked Carlos as he was putting the cups of coffee on the table.

"I am thinking of resigning."

"What! Are you serious? You are not kidding?"

"I am not kidding. I have given it much serious thought, but it will help me, if you can tell me, what you think about it."

"All right, tell me, why are you resigning?"

"Menardo has been ill for sometime. He has been in and out of the hospital over some ailment, the doctors up to now could not figure out. He is going to the United States with his family for further treatment and he might decide to stay there.

"No one, in the meantime, is running our agricultural estate in Batangas. Our overseer is not up to it. My father cannot do it. He is getting old and he has slowed down considerably in his activities, including his law practice and our trading business, which he sold out.

No one in the family can take over our family business in Batangas except me."

"How about Ricardo and Sebastian? They should be old enough by now to help you run your family business."

"They are, but they are also old enough to get married and that is what they did instead of returning home after finishing their studies in the United States."

"I did not know that."

"There has been very little communication with them since they went to America and married those American girls. But I am happy to tell you that they are both doing well. Ricardo is working in a bank in New York while Sebastian is helping manage his wife's family trading business in San Francisco."

"How about Ruy, why don't you tap him for assistance?"

"There is not much that we can expect from that member of our family."

Leandro smiled sourly at the snide remark Carlos had made about Ruy. Carlos ordinarily kept his criticism of other people to himself, but it may have been getting too much for him to keep quiet about his irresponsible and dissolute brother-in-law. He was sorry for Regina. How she must rue the day, she married Ruy.

As he had learned about it from Carlos, Ruy and Regina were now living downstairs in the Yturalde house in San Miguel after they were evicted from their apartment for failure to pay the rent. They started well enough, living in the big house in Quiapo, Ruy inherited from his parents, which he lost, though, from gambling. It still pained him that Regina chose Ruy over him and all because he was from a low, social class and not of Spanish descent like her and Ruy.

He drank his coffee to distract himself from those dismal thoughts.

Carlos asked Leandro, "What do you think? Should I resign and take over our family business?"

"No, you should not. You have got a good job here in Pacific and Gulf. Why give it up? Why trade it for your family business that may or may not do well."

"I don't see it that way. Our family business will do even better with me, running it. It is a better alternative to my job here in Pacific and Gulf where I seem to be at a dead end."

"So, that is the real reason," Leandro said to himself, his eyes wide at Carlos' startling revelation of what was really making him leave Pacific & Gulf.

He was very sorry for Carlos. He has left him far behind in the company. He is now a department manager, among his other top jobs there while Carlos has remained a personnel assistant, two grades higher now, but still a personnel assistant. But he liked and admired Carlos, all the more, for never showing envy or resentment over his advancement in the company. He was a true friend.

"With the war likely to happen in Europe and America, just as likely to be drawn to it, there will be a great demand for coffee, beef, coconut and other agricultural products," Carlos said with great enthusiasm. "This is the perfect time to engage in agriculture when a lot of money could be made from those products."

"That is what I have gathered, too."

He had read Dick McCall's editorials in *The Philippines Newsmagazine* about the likelihood of the United States getting involved in Europe and what it would mean for the Philippines. Carlos was simply restating what Dick McCall had written, on how business and agriculture will then boom in the Philippines. He was, on that point, greatly supportive of Carlos' decision to leave Pacific & Gulf and attend to his family business in agriculture and the prospect of making a lot of money from it.

Carlos was so liked in Pacific & Gulf that, aside from Leandro, Mark Clavier also threw a farewell party for him.

Carlos turned out to be right. Europe, not too long after, was embroiled in a war. The United States was, later on, dragged into it.

Dick McCall then observed in his newsmagazine, "Good times will soon be upon us, here in the Philippines, even if unfortunately, there will be so much bloodshed and suffering elsewhere in the world."

Chapter Forty-nine

Leandro glanced at Crisanta as he was coming to the living room in the Big House. She was watching Elizabeth and Donita in the open door of their bedroom as they were making frenzied preparation for their return to their boarding school after a weekend at home.

He shook his head and sat down on a couch and likewise watched their two daughters. They were getting in each other's way, making critical comments at each other, at the same time that they were putting their clothes in their suitcases laid open in their beds, then removing some of them and putting them back, once again.

"You should have done that earlier," Crisanta said to them.

Her criticism made them even more frantic.

He sighed. He was resigned to wait for their two daughters. He is the indulgent father who left it to his wife to manage their children.

He saw trouble ahead when Albert appeared from the bedroom, he shared with Franklin, and walked toward Elizabeth and Donita's bedroom. His third son was always needling his two sisters and he was not surprised to hear them, yell at him to get out of their bedroom.

"Leave them alone!" Crisanta said to Albert.

"But," Albert protested, "I did not do or say anything!"

"You were making ugly faces at us!" Elizabeth shouted at Albert. Albert walked away with a sullen face, muttering, "Slowpokes!"

He nearly collided with Gertrude, who had just come out of her bedroom, her suitcase held in her hand.

"Now, be good, Albert," Gertrude said to him, "and stop annoying Donita and Elizabeth."

"I'm only hurrying them up. They are keeping us, waiting."

"Why don't you go ahead to the car and take my suitcase with you."

Albert took the suitcase from Getrude. She was walking with him to the staircase when Leandro caught her slipping a coin into Albert's hand. She was fond of Albert while Albert idolized her. He never said or did anything that might annoy her.

He said, when Gertrude was back in the living room, "Why don't you play something while we are waiting for your sisters?"

"Gladly," she said, smiling.

She sat down on the piano stool and made a practice run on the keyboard. Crisanta left Elizabeth and Donita's bedroom and sat down on another couch. Elizabeth and Donita went on with their task, their voices now kept low. Leandro listened in sheer pleasure as Gertrude then played Chopin's classic piano music, *Fantasie Impromptu,* from the introduction of the theme melody to its flourishes and variations and back to its theme melody.

It was Sunday afternoon and Leandro and Crisanta were taking their three girls, back to their boarding school, the *Instituto de Mujeres.* Every time their three girls were at home was special to them, now that they no longer see them as much as they did when they were younger.

The thought came to Leandro as he was listening to Gertrude playing the musical piece, that few men could be like him who was so happy and satisfied with his life.

He has gone far, very far from his peasant days in Bangar. He has a loving, sensible wife, wonderful children, a big beautiful home with a view of Manila Bay and the fishponds, its grounds decked out with flowers and trees, a good job that paid so well, his income made even bigger when Bill Shay allowed him to do the catering for some of their field projects.

"Play another one," he said to Gertrude when she was finished playing Chopin's beautiful piano music.

Gertrude's fingers once again moved deftly on the keyboard, the sound they gave, Beethoven's lovely *Fur Elise*.

Leandro shut his eyes as he was listening to it. It was just like the first time he heard it played many years ago, one morning on his way to Carlos' house, when he saw Regina for the first time. He listened then with the same pleasure to the music, although as Gertrude was playing it, it was now tinged with nostalgia for that time long gone. Its last notes still ringing in his ears, he opened his eyes to Crisanta, who was looking down at him.

"We are going now," she said to him.

"Are those two girls ready?"

"They are, finally."

He stood up.

Adrian suddenly appeared in the living room, all dressed up.

"Can I go with you?" he said to them.

Leandro and Crisanta glanced at each other. Adrian, their oldest son, was so quiet and inconspicuous, they sometimes failed to notice, he was at home. So was their second son, Franklin. He preferred to stay at home, reading a book in his room, than go out with them.

"Of course, son," Leandro replied to Adrian, "your mother and I will be pleased to have you, go out with us. You will sit in the front seat with me and your mother."

"Thank you, Mod, Pod. I will go ahead to the car," Adrian said as he went down quickly in the staircase.

Gertrude and her siblings coined "Mod" for Mother and "Pod" for Father. It was a part of a unique family language, they invented as part of the little world they created in the Big House. They were born to wealth and privilege and they kept to themselves in the Big House, far apart from their neighbors of modest circumstances. The children there, peeved by the snob, called them "the royalty of Caloocan."

A group of boys playing a noisy game of tag in the vacant lot between the Big House and Florinda Theater stopped in their game and looked on, their eyes wide with envy and admiration, as the Buick, the new car of the Sumaka family, was moving out of the house gate with Leandro at the wheel.

He had the car slowed down almost to a stop as it was approaching Mabini Street. The moviegoers were coming out of Florinda Theater. Some of them were waiting at the street corner for his car to pass by. He glanced at them as he was crossing Mabini Street.

Florinda Theater was a familiar sight to Leandro and his family, from the time it was built, a few years ago. It was but a stone's throw from the Big House, but neither he nor any member of his family had ever been inside the movie house and for a good reason.

He learned from their servants who have seen movies there, what Florinda Theater was like. Its roof and walls were made of corrugated, galvanized iron sheets and it could get to be sweltering hot inside the movie house. He and his family saw movies instead in the first-class, air-conditioned movie houses in Manila—the Avenue, Ideal and State theaters in Rizal Avenue and the Lyric and Capitol theaters in Escolta.

He was not taking today, his usual route from Mabini Street, southward to Manila. He was instead taking the route from Grace Park in the newly opened Rizal Avenue Extension to downtown Manila.

He will then drive around before taking his three girls back to their school. He will drive down on Dewey Boulevard, near Manila Bay for a whiff of cool sea breeze and watch the sunset there. They will afterwards take a snack at Loy's Bakeshop and Restaurant in Santa Cruz.

This was a small gesture he made to please Crisanta who was housebound the entire week. Their weekend outing was special to her.

He was driving down the avenue when a glance he took at the rice fields there reminded him of the opportunity they lost of owning there, large tracts of land.

"Why did you not take up Esperanza's invitation to buy land there?" he said to Crisanta. "Don't you want to be the proud owner of a big part of Grace Park? It will soon be developed into a suburb of Manila."

"We have enough property. Why do you want more?"

He looked ahead at the avenue and did not reply to her. He would rather keep silent than tell her that she was not being true to herself. He knew about her craving for land. It stemmed from her landless peasant roots. The Mercaida family was only renting their house in Nicodemus Street, in Tondo. But how she had since then made up for her deprived childhood.

She handled the family finances and she had been buying real estate, left and right. She held the view that land is permanent and only by one's doing, does one lose it.

She bought a corner lot in Solis Street and two other lots in Tondo, where she built apartment buildings, three lots in the outskirts of

Caloocan, a corner lot in Malabon, two lots near Samson Road and another lot in Pasay.

She bought from Candido, strictly for sentimental reason, the lot in Bangar where his father's hut used to stand; likewise the lot in the village in Arayat where she was born and grew up. She also bought a choice property in the commercial area near the church in San Isidro, where she built a commercial building.

All of those were small and insignificant compared to the acre upon acre of land she could have bought there in Grace Park with Esperanza, who bought there a lot of several acres.

To Crisanta who remained a small-time peasant at heart, Esperanza's invitation to buy land with her in Grace Park was so overwhelming, she turned it down.

He was sorry, Crisanta had missed the chance for them to be big-time urban landowners, but then he had to admit that what she had acquired with all those lots and apartments for their family were, by their standard, quite substantial.

He glanced sideward at Crisanta, pleased with her, when he saw in the rear-view mirror, Albert from behind him at the backseat, tapping Donita on her shoulders. She was seated, left of Albert with Gertrude seated at the right corner and Elizabeth at the left corner in the car's backseat.

"Do you know what the girl to your left said this morning?" Albert asked Donita. "She said, she looks like Anita Noble."

Donita giggled while Gertrude suppressed her laughter with the palm of her hand over her mouth. Adrian, who was seated between Leandro and Crisanta in the front seat, turned around and said to Elizabeth, "Did you really say that?"

Elizabeth was the homely daughter of Leandro and Crisanta. Her claim to the contrary was a standing joke among her siblings. Albert and Franklin often called her "Chita," after the chimpanzee with that name in a newspaper cartoon strip.

She glared at Adrian and Albert.

"I never said that," she said, her voice hoarse in anger. "I don't look bad compared to her. That is all that I said!"

Anita Noble, the object of their quarrel, was the beautiful "Queen of the Philippine Carnival," whose proclamation they attended, the night before in Luneta Park.

"Enough of that," Crisanta said to Albert and Elizabeth who then fell silent.

Peace and silence having been restored inside the car, Leandro now drove leisurely in Rizal Avenue, down to Santa Cruz, then across the Pasig River and on to Luneta Park. They walked around there and had, from the seawall, an uninterrupted view of the beautiful sunset in Manila Bay. They have a similar view from their house in Caloocan, but it was now partly obstructed by a mango tree in the terraced backyard.

He drove on afterwards in Dewey Boulevard, up to where it ended in Vito Cruz. He headed back to Santa Cruz, where they had snacks at Loy's Bakeshop and Restaurant.

They were, nearly an hour later, at the doorstep of Instituto de Mujeres. Gertrude, Elizabeth and Donita moved out of the car with Leandro and Crisanta. They took turns in hugging them before going inside the school building with their suitcases and boxes of pastries they bought at Loy's. They made it a point to bring with them, on their return to school, presents for their teachers and Dona Rosa Sevilla-Alvero, the school head and founder.

It was in keeping with the freethinking ways he adopted in Elk Lodge that Leandro chose Instituto de Mujeres over the girls' boarding schools in Manila, ran by nuns. Instituto de Mujeres was the first nonsectarian boarding school for women established in Manila and it attracted many of the city's prominent families.

Dona Rosa was a woman with modern views on education and society. She had, aside from her wide academic background, one other distinction in having fought with Bonifacio and the other leaders in the Philippine Revolution in 1896.

Leandro returned to their car with Crisanta. He glanced at his three girls, now waving at him and Crisanta from a window in the school building. He waved back proudly and then drove away.

His children were doing well in school, especially Gertrude. She was first in academics, first in school activities and first in just about everything else in Instituto de Mujeres.

He drove back home mildly disconcerted at this period in his family life when he was seeing less and less of his three older children. They were at home only on weekends and during summer, semestral and Christmas vacations. They will be in college, a few years hence. Then they will get married and start their own families. They were moving gradually, but surely toward the world outside.

He glanced at the rear view mirror, distracting him from those depressing thoughts. Adrian was now seated beside Albert at the car's backseat. At least there were still his younger children to keep him and Crisanta, company in the Big House.

They may make such a racket at times, but the sound of their voices and their laughter were much more welcome to him than the silence in the house when they were also away in school or were with their friends. Their weekend was always special to him and Crisanta when their children were all at home.

He stopped his car in Juan Luna Street, beside a newsstand there.

"Will you give me a copy of *The Philippines Newsmagazine?*" he said to the newsstand owner and paid him for a copy of Dick McCall's newsmagazine. The cover showed an illustration of people celebrating the boom years in the twenties.

He was, later on at home, seated in an armchair in the balcony overlooking Manila Bay and the lagoon, now fully converted into fishponds. He began to read by the glow of the sunset in the horizon, Dick McCall's article:

"Life in Manila and in the rest of the Philippines has never been as good as it is today. The problems in the economy, in food production, in sanitation and with lawlessness have all been solved.

"The Philippines is in the midst of an era of peace and prosperity. This is never more evident than in Manila itself. New suburbs have sprouted, like Grace Park in the north and Pasay in the south. The restaurants are full with families eating out, the department stores, full of shoppers. So are the parks especially on weekends. Vaudeville theaters and movie houses have sprung up, all over the place. The cabarets of an earlier time are just as popular now and are filled with people dancing there, the waltz, the tango and the foxtrot.

"A new government center will soon rise in Wallace Field, the architecture of the buildings there, neoclassic and therefore grand and magnificent. One will find in the parks in many towns, bands playing on Sunday afternoon to the delight of the townsfolk there. Business is booming in the cities while agriculture in the countryside has never been in better shape.

"Good times are upon us. Here is hoping they will last for a long, long time."

Leandro got, the following day in his office, a call from Carlos. They have not seen each other since Carlos left Pacific & Gulf. He called a few times to say hello and report to him, how he and his family were doing. That was all, but not this time.

"Angela and I are inviting you and Crisanta to dinner at home, this coming Friday," Carlos said.

The telephone receiver pressed to his ear, Leandro pondered over Carlos' invitation. He mentioned Angela in his invitation, out of courtesy to Crisanta, although he knew Angela never cared for him and Crisanta and that she would never invite them to dinner in her house. Angela snubbed them at their wedding and in all the parties they held in the Big House. If he is going to accept Carlos' dinner invitation, it will be solely out of courtesy to his friend. Friday was the end of his week of work. He could then stay out late.

"Friday will be fine," he said to Carlos. "We will be there after work."

He told Crisanta, the moment he arrived home, about Carlos and Angela's dinner invitation.

"Go there, if you like, but I am not going with you," Crisanta said.

He understood perfectly, Crisanta's feelings toward Angela and he did not mention again, their dinner invitation.

He drove out of the company compound on Friday, that week and called out, following his habit, a good day to Mang Emong and Aling Pacing who were closing up their food stall.

He dropped by a liquor store on his way to the Yturalde house and bought there, a box of pastries, a bottle of wine and a bottle of whisky, his favorite drink.

His car, not too long after, was parked in the street, in front of Carlos' house. He pressed the doorbell button in the gate, opened for him in a short while by the maidservant.

He went up in the stone staircase, his mouth hanging open in surprise, the moment he was at the sill of the door to the living room when he found himself, facing Regina. They stood so close to each other, he could almost hear her deep-drawn breathing and he could see tiny lines under and at the corner of her eyes in her drawn face. They were not there, the last time he saw her. Gone was the cheerful expression in her face, replaced by a sad look. She is not the same person with the slim figure of a schoolgirl. She now had the full body of a married woman. He mumbled a greeting to her.

"Good afternoon to you, too, Leandro," she said. "It is so nice to see you again."

So was he, glad to see her, now that she is free again. He learned from Carlos that she and Ruy had separated. They have a lot to talk about, but now that he was facing her, he found himself suddenly tongue-tied.

"Let us not just stand here," she said to him. "Do come in."

He looked around the living room as he was entering it. It looked the same as in the last time he was there. The big chandelier was still hanging over the large cushioned couches and so were the family pictures on the wall and the phonograph console there.

"Do, sit down," she said, "and make yourself comfortable while I tell Carlos and Angela, you are already here."

She was about to leave when he looked down at the paper bag of wine, liquor and pastries in his arm and said to her, "Where can I put these? These are all for you."

"You need not have bothered to bring anything. Thank you," she said. "You are so thoughtful."

Their hands, as she took the bag from him, brushed at each other. They were so close to each other, her fragrance, so sweet and inviting.

He held her hand. It was something he had long wanted to do to her. She let him, for a moment, hold her hand. He released her hand when she then turned around

He watched her as she left the living room, her hips swaying slightly to the forward movement of her feet. She had not changed the way she walked, gracefully and with her chin thrust out.

He sat down on the large couch, his thoughts on her. She is the most desirable woman he had ever met. He is sorry for her life ruined by the wrong choice she made in marriage. Ruy left her and ran away with another woman after years of living as a parasite in their house.

How she must have suffered from her marriage to that dissolute and irresponsible Ruy! She is at least now finally rid of him, but how she must now crave for a man's arms around her.

He swallowed hard at that thought, for she was just then returning to the living room with Carlos and Angela.

He stood up and, as they greeted each other, he shook hands with Carlos and Angela who, he noticed, was smiling at him. She was never like that to him before.

"Nice of you to come," Carlos said to him. "Why is Crisanta, not with you?"

"She would be here with me," he said, "but she was kept from coming here by a terrible headache."

Angela and Regina looked skeptically at him, but said nothing.

"You will then have to eat her share of the food, we prepared for the two of you," Carlos said as he and Leandro then sat down on the large couch.

"Excuse us, we will see to our dinner," Regina said as she and Angela then returned to the dining room.

"Nice of you to bring some pastries and firewater," Carlos said to Leandro.

"Don't mention it. So, how have you been doing?"

"Great! Things could not have been better for us. We could barely meet the demand for our coffee, copra and beef."

"How do you like country life?"

"I tell you, I should have taken to it earlier. The slow pace, the peace and quiet, I like it there. It is early to bed and early to rise for us and you can see the result in the number of children, Angela and I now have, three children."

"You have three only? Well, you and Angela have a lot of catching up to do with me and Crisanta. We now have six children."

"Angela and I can easily have as many children as you have, if not more."

They erupted with laughter, Carlos so heartily that tears came out of his eyes, which he then rubbed with the back of his hand. It was like the old times when they engaged in banter, in-between discussions of serious subjects like their jobs and life in general.

Leandro was completely at ease in Carlos' company. He felt now, as he felt then, like a member of his family.

"So, how are your folks?" he asked Carlos.

"They are getting on, in years, but they are fine."

"How about Menardo, how is he getting along?"

"He moved with his family to San Francisco and joined Sebastian, our youngest brother, in handling the marketing of our agricultural products in the United States."

"Things could not have been better for you and your folks."

"Except for one member in our family," Carlos said as he glanced in the direction of the dining room. "You know who, I am referring to."

Leandro nodded. Carlos is referring to no one else in their family, but Regina.

"It was her idea that we invited you to dinner, here at home," Carlos said. "She is leaving on Sunday for the United States."

His eyes wide in surprise, he asked Carlos, "Why is she leaving?"

"She wants to make a fresh start in life and she feels, she can only do that by being far away from here."

"I wish her good-luck. I hope she will be happy in America."

"I hope so, too, but don't let her know, I told you. Let her, tell you herself."

Don Alfonso and Dona Magdalena were coming in the hallway.

They greeted each other.

"You have not changed, Leandro," Don Alfonso said to him.

He nodded and smiled.

"I have been hearing a lot of good things about you."

"Thank you, sir.".

Angela announced, when she came back from the dining room, that dinner is ready. They proceeded to the dining room.

"Where are the children?" Dona Magdalena asked them when they were about to sit down at the dining table.

"They took their dinner ahead of us,"Carlos said.

"They were so tired from playing the whole day at the park that, right after taking their dinner, they went straight to bed," Angela said.

"So, we can now eat in peace," Carlos said to laughter at the dining table.

Don Alfonso sat down at the head of the table with Carlos and Leandro to his left and right, facing Dona Magdalena at the other end of the table. Regina was seated beside Leandro and Angela, beside Carlos

They prayed and then proceeded with their dinner. The maidservant served course after course of meat, fish and vegetables.

"You might be interested to know," Carlos said to Leandro, "that everything served here at the table came from our farm and ranch in Batangas."

"The fish too came from your farm?" Leandro asked no one in particular.

"The fish, too," Don Alfonso replied. "It came from the river that runs through our property, from its headwaters in Lake Taal."

"It is soft and tasty," Leandro said.

"It is a special, rare kind of fish," Carlos said to Leandro. "You can find it only in the river and in the lake."

"What is it called?"

"It is called Maliputo."

The maidservant held out to Leandro, a beef dish. He put several pieces of it on his plate and laced it with a thick sauce. He cut a piece, ate it and said, "This is tender and delicious."

"You have just tasted our supertender Batangas beef," Carlos said proudly to Leandro.

"You seem self-sufficient with food."

"We are," Dona Magdalena said. "All you need to be like us is a piece of land."

"Have you thought of likewise doing what Carlos is doing?" Don Alfonso asked Leandro. "Life in the countryside has been good to him. It should be to you, too, since you came from the countryside."

Leandro nodded, but kept silent. He will have nothing of life in the countryside again. He had nothing, but unrewarded toil there.

"Leandro by now must prefer to live in the city than in the countryside," Angela said.

"I live where I am happy."

"So it is with all of us, especially with Regina here," Don Alfonso said. "Thank you, Leandro, for sharing with us, this send-off party for Regina."

Leandro glanced at Regina, his eyes wide open in a faked look of surprise in his face.

"I'm leaving for America," she said to Leandro.

"Why?"

Carlos said before Regina could reply, "She will help out in marketing our products there. She is leaving on Sunday."

"I wish you, good luck," Leandro said to Regina. "They will gain in America what we will lose, here in the Philippines."

Regina smiled wanly and gazed downcast at the dining table. The mood at the table had turned gloomy and they finished their dinner in silence.

Don Alfonso and Dona Magdalena returned to their bedroom while Carlos, Angela and Leandro repaired to the living room.

Carlos sat down on one of the two small couches, facing Angela who sat down at the other small couch. Leandro sat down at the corner of the large couch, facing the coffee table.

Regina came a short while later, a tray of steaming cups of coffee in her hands which she then set down on the coffee table. She sat down near Leandro on the large couch and she distributed with his help, the cups of coffee.

"Now, you don't have to tell me," he said. "I am drinking pure Batangas coffee and it came from your farm."

"You got it right," Carlos said.

"We are marketing it in the United States," Angela said proudly.

"Regina will handle the marketing there," Carlos said.

"You have everything planned well," Leandro said.

They drank their coffee.

The maid then came with a tray of glasses and the bottles of wine and whisky.

"You don't have to wait on us," Carlos said to the maid who left for the servants' quarters after picking up the tray of empty cups of coffee.

The wine bottle gave a popping sound when Carlos removed the cork with his thumb. Then he twisted open, the cap in the bottle of whisky.

He said, "What will it be for you, ladies, wine or whisky?"

"Wine," Regina and Angela chorused.

Carlos poured the wine on three of the glasses and gave Angela and Regina, each a glass of the wine.

"I know what you want," he said to Leandro.

He poured whisky on the fourth glass, gave it to Leandro and picked up the remaining glass of wine on the coffee table.

"Here is to all of us," he said as he raised his glass of wine.

Unlike Leandro who was by now a habitual drinker, Carlos drank only occasionally, Regina and Angela even less so. Carlos did not control the rate they were drinking, so that as they talked about whatever came to their minds, he poured, again and again, wine and whisky on their glasses.

Carlos then began to sing:

Yes, we have no bananas.
We have no bananas today.
We have string beans and onions.
Cabbages and scallions. . .

The wine had a strong effect on Angela. She stood up and walked toward Carlos who sang on the song with her now seated on his lap.

Leandro glanced at Regina who seemed to be embarrassed by Carlos and Angela's uninhibited, drunken behavior.

"I know what they need to sober up," she said to Leandro as she stood up and went to the phonograph console.

"What are you going to play there?" he asked her.

"Something nice and fitting," she replied as she was putting a record on the phonograph. .

She returned to the couch, accompanied by the song:

I'm forever blowing bubbles,
Pretty bubbles in the air.
They fly so high
Nearly reach the sky
Then like my dreams
They fade and die.
Fortune's always hiding.
I look everywhere.
I'm forever blowing bubbles,
Pretty bubbles in the air.

Carlos and Angela were so affected by the song and they looked at each other's eyes as they then stood up from the couch.

"Well, folks," Carlos said, "that is it for us, good-night."

They walked away, his arm, around her waist.

Leandro watched them leave, his ears turned to the melancholy song, his mind turned to Regina. After tonight, just like the faded dreams in the song, she will be nothing more to him than a lovely memory.

He stood up at the end of the song and walked toward the phonograph console.

"Do you want me to play it again," he asked her.

She shook her head. He took out the record from the phonograph and returned it to the record rack..

He returned to the couch and sat down beside her.

"I suppose," he said to her, "you have no regrets about leaving us."

"I have no regrets except one."

"And what is that?"

"You, I'll miss you."

He looked at her, surprised and happy. So, she had this feeling for him, all along. She yielded when he then took her in his arms and kissed her briefly, softly, then long and hard.

She said as their lips parted, "Take me just this once, so I will have something to remember you by, for the rest of my life."

He looked into her eyes and nodded.

They stood up from the couch. They were holding hands as they went down in the stairs to her room, where she was living alone.

Chapter Fifty

The somber tone in Nancy Jamieson's voice on the telephone told Leandro, it must be over something serious that Bill Shay wanted him to go right away to his office. He hurried out of the warehouse and arrived shortly in Bill's office. He sat stunned when Bill said to him, "I learned about it only now. Samuel is dead."

"How did it happen?"

"The report from Baguio is sketchy. It seems Samuel caught the flu while he was doing research work in a remote village in Central Cordillera. He was beyond help by the time he was brought in a stretcher to Baguio."

Leandro shook his head in disbelief at the thought of Samuel, dying of a sickness as common and curable as the flu. He gave countless villagers medical assistance, but when he himself needed it, there was no one who could give it to him. He took risks to his health in conducting work among the mountain tribes—from the food he ate, to the primitive condition in some of the villages in Central Cordillera. But he died doing the work he loved, among the people he loved, second only to his family and his friends. How his death must have crushed Dorothy.

"I'm going to Baguio with Esperanza for Samuel's interment," Bill said. "So will Dick and Nieves. Would you like to go with us?"

"Yes, I'll go with you."

He left Bill's office wondering why sometimes when bad things happen, they happen like a flood.

He met Carlos, a week ago. He was looking for a job. His agricultural enterprise in Batangas had collapsed when his market in the United States dried up completely following the great crash called The Black Thursday at the New York Stock Exchange on October 24, 1929. It brought about The Great Depression in the United States. It affected the Phlippines so badly.

Carlos struggled for three more years, but finally had to give up. He asked for his help in getting a job in Pacific & Gulf, but the company was not hiring and was even cutting down on its work force. It managed to keep on with long-term government contracts like building roads, wharves and bridges and maintaining them.

He kept his job, for he was as important to the company, as he was close to Bill Shay, who now looked at him, like he was a member of his family. The only sacrifice he made, considering the hard times, was a pay cut, he took along with the other company executives. His pay remained high, though, much higher than what the ordinary workers were receiving.

The hard times were evident in the empty department stores and restaurants in Manila. People were not buying, nor eating out.

"I must have a job," Carlos said to him, "any kind of job. I must provide for my family."

"Is there no one among your folks who can help you?"

Carlos shook his head and said, "My parents died only a few days apart while they were visiting Regina in Detroit with her Irish-American husband. She is, like Menardo, Ricardo and Sebastian, in financial difficulties. They cannot do anything when I sought their help."

"I will see what I can do."

He told Bill Shay about Carlos. Bill had only a vague memory of Carlos, but he assured him that Carlos worked well in Pacific & Gulf and that he will take any job available.

"Did you say he will take any job?" Bill asked him.

"That is what he told me."

"We have no jobs available here in Manila. We have an opening in one or two of our provincial projects. Will he take any of those jobs?"

"A job is a job anywhere it is available."

"See Mark and tell him to check for any available jobs for Carlos Yturalde."

Leandro thanked Bill and left his office. He went to Mark Clavier's office. Mark went over his job listing, a quarter-page long, unlike before when times were good and it was so many pages long.

"What I have got here are only for manual work, like laying out asphalt, mixing cement and doing carpentry work. Here is one for a construction helper for the bridge, the longest in the Philippines, we are building in Pangasinan."

"Can he see you about that job?"

"Sure. Tell Carlos to see me."

Leandro called Carlos, the moment he was back in his office. He told him about the job in Pangasinan. Carlos saw Mark Clavier, the next day. He left Personnel with a job of construction helper in the bridge project in Pangasinan. It meant being far away from his family for weeks, even months, but with his job his family will have enough for at least their basic needs.

Leandro told Crisanta about the death of Samuel and that he will attend his interment with Bill and Esperanza, Dick and Nieves.

"I wish I can go with you," she said.

She was big and heavy with a child, their eighth. She was due to deliver within two months and was not allowed to do any traveling.

Leandro left the following day with Bill and Esperanza, Dick and Nieves. They arrived in Baguio shortly before Samuel's interment.

Samuel's mortal remains had lain in state in the Episcopalian school's chapel for three days. The area around the chapel was full of the mountain tribesmen who came from all over Central Cordillera to pay Samuel, their last respects. They were kept there since the chapel could accommodate only the school officials, the teachers and the guests from Manila.

Leandro, Bill and Esperanza, Dick and Nieves went straight to Samuel's casket, placed at the foot of the altar. They prayed there for the repose of his soul. Then they turned to Dorothy who was seated at the front pew with the other teachers in Brendan School.

She stood up when Bill and Esperanza, Dick and Nieves, one after the other, hugged her. Leandro did the same to Dorothy who pressed herself tightly to him. He could feel her deep-drawn breathing as if she was suppressing the urge to cry.

"He is gone, Leandro, he is gone," Dorothy said to him, her voice barely a whisper.

"He is gone," he replied, "for his just reward."

Dorothy suddenly broke down in tears. He hugged her tighter in an effort to comfort her. Then, together with Dick and Bill, they helped her sit down on the pew. Bill then gave her, his handkerchief with which she wiped the tears in her eyes.

"Be brave, be strong," Bill said to her. "Samuel wants you to pray for him as he now leaves for his just reward."

Dick had featured several times in *The Philippines Newsmagazine,* Samuel's extensive work on the mountain tribes in Central Cordillera. He said to Dorothy, "It should be of great comfort to you that Samuel lives on in the hearts and minds of the people in Central Cordillera."

The minister then came in from the side door of the chapel. The necrological service for Samuel was about to begin. Bill held Dorothy's hand tightly as he, together with Esperanza, Dick, Nieves and Leandro then proceeded to a pew reserved for them.

Leandro was not surprised to see at the burial site of Samuel, Father O'Farrell and Basilio Basneg, who was now also a priest. They were asked to give Samuel, out of consideration for their friendship, the final blessing at his burial.

Samuel and Dorothy bought, years before, for their final resting place, a piece of land, a few miles from Baguio, on a hill overlooking the valley in La Trinidad.

Samuel's casket was being lowered by rope to his grave, dug on the ground, when the fog started descending from the mountain peaks, to the hills around, to the valley below.

Not a few persons asked at the reception held later on at the school cafeteria, why Samuel and Dorothy's only son was not around at Samuel's interment. Alfred, unknown to them, was now living in Boston.

Dorothy replied, when Leandro also asked her about it, "I sent him a cable. He will be here within a couple of weeks."

He nodded as he recalled how Alfred had tried to persuade Samuel and Dorothy to live with him in Boston. They turned him down.

It was summer and he, Crisanta and their children were visiting Samuel and Dorothy in Baguio.

"Why did you turn him down?" he asked Samuel and Dorothy. "Don't you want to live with your own son in America, your homeland?"

Samuel repeated to him, what he said to Alfred, "You live where you are happy and your mom and I are happy where we are living, here in Baguio."

That was the last time, he saw Samuel alive.

Alfred that very moment was some ten thousand miles away. He had just left Boston and was on his way to Baguio. He was coming alone since his pregnant wife Rachel was not fit to travel.

He learned about his father's death when he returned home after exploring the marshlands in Florida. He inherited the love of the outdoors from his father.

He had a tearful reunion with Dorothy, her auburn hair now with flecks of gray hair in just a few days since Samuel died. They visited Samuel's grave in La Trinidad, now blooming with the same kind of flowers, Samuel grew in his flower box in their cottage in Brendan School.

Alfred could stay in Baguio for three weeks only and he used the little time he had in trying to persuade Dorothy to live with him in Boston.

Her reply was always the same: "This is my home, my dear son, and when my time has come, I want to be, beside your dad."

Leandro accompanied Dorothy to Pier 7 in Port Area where they will see Alfred leave in a ship, bound for San Francisco. The pier was swarming with people who were seeing off, the ship's passengers.

He looked away when Alfred hugged and kissed Dorothy, a few moments before he went up to the ship. He appeared in a short while in the ship's deck where he was now saying something to Dorothy.

"What is he saying?" Dorothy asked Leandro.

He shook his head. He could not also understand what Alfred was saying. The noise in the crowd and a band playing music had drowned out what Alfred was saying.

He watched Alfred when he then leaned out of the ship's railing and said something louder.

"What is he saying now?" Dorothy asked Leandro.

"He said, he is expecting you to join him, later on, in Boston."

"He is like his father," Dorothy said, smiling. "He will not take no for an answer."

"Don't you want to pay your home country, at least a visit?"

"No. Once I am in Boston, Alfred will never let me, leave him and come back here."

The ship blew its horn as it began to move out of the pier. Leandro looked on as Dorothy and Alfred then waved in good-bye at each other.

They watched the ship until it was far away in Manila Bay.

Dorothy was returning to Baguio, the next day yet and Leandro took her to dinner at home with Crisanta and their children before driving her back to Manila Hotel where she was staying for the night.

She took over the work of Samuel, once she was back in Baguio. There were researches that have to be finished and reports and articles that have to be written or edited and finished. She must also write and thank the foundation in the United States which provided the funds for Samuel's work on the mountain tribes in Central Cordillera.

Dick, in an article, he wrote in *The Philippines Newsmagazine,* commended Samuel for advancing their cause. He wrote that they should not be left out in the development efforts, once the Philippines had obtained its independence.

It was the big issue of the day and Dick was fighting for that cause. His effort and that of countless other people were rewarded with the passage by the United States Congress in 1934 of the Tydings-McDuffie Act. It will grant the Philippines its independence in 1946, after a ten-year transition period, starting in 1936. The colony called the Philippine Islands will now be called the Philippine Commonwealth. It was now a self-governing state except in foreign affairs and national defense.

An election was held in 1935. Manuel Quezon defeated Emilio Aguinaldo in the fight for the President while Sergio Osmena won as the Vice President of the Philippine Commonwealth.

Leandro and his family drove in two cars to Luneta Park that day, November 15, 1935, to attend Quezon and Osmena's inauguration.

The weather was fine, the sky a clear blue with a few cotton-like clouds, the cool morning and a feeling of anticipation in the air, a harbinger of Christmas.

The new Legislative Building in Wallace Field was the site of the inauguration ceremony. Sunken Garden, which faced the building, was full of people. The newspapers predicted that up to one-fourth of Manila's population will turn out there for the festivities along with thousands more from the provinces. So many of them came to Manila, a newspaper wag commented about Manila, rich with the stench of the provincial folks.

Leandro dropped off Crisanta and the girls in the reserved area in Sunken Garden. Gonzalo did the same with the boys in the other car. He followed Leandro to Intramuros, where they parked their cars.

They walked back to Sunken Garden. Gonzalo stayed with the crowd behind the reserved area where an usher led Leandro to the row of seats reserved for him, Crisanta and their children.

He picked up the program on the chair, sat down there and looked around.

The magnificent Legislative Building with its neoclassic design, stood some two hundred feet away, across Burgos Drive. Its balcony and driveway had been converted into a grandstand for the inauguration ceremony.

He read the program. In a short while, after the invocation, Quezon and Osmena will take their oaths of office as President and Vice President of the Philippine Commonwealth. A parade will follow in Burgos Drive after the speeches. It was the final step taken when, ten years later, the Philippine Commonwealth will be the Philippine Republic.

Leandro sat proudly on his chair. He had done his job. He had played a part, though tiny, but still a part, in developing that area into a lovely, worthy site of the Philippine Government.

That area, ten years ago, where the Legislative Building now stands, was then, all grass. Now, there it is, standing majestically in Wallace Field at the eastern end of Luneta Park, near the two equally grand neoclassic buildings of the Finance and Agriculture Departments. Farther north was the imposing Post Office building which stood at the southern bank of Pasig River.

The moat at the base of the wall in Intramuros was, thirty-five years ago, infested with snakes, the water there, malarial. It was filled with soil and is now a part of this wide beautiful lawn of verdant green grass called the Sunken Garden.

The whole area with its majestic neoclassic buildings was another testimony to the great positive changes that have taken place in the islands. Pacific & Gulf built them and so, as its warehouse manager and chief supply and purchasing officer, Leandro felt he had a hand, though tiny and insignificant, in building those grand monuments to the great American rule in the Philippines.

His children stood up from their seats as they played a game of identifying the distinguished men and women who were leaving their cars in Burgos Drive and walking up to the grandstand.

Albert shouted, when a tall and handsome American in double-breasted suit and straw hat got off from his car, "That is MacArthur!"

It was General Douglas MacArthur, all right. The general was a familiar face in Manila. MacArthur was a well-known name there. General Douglas MacArthur's father, General Arthur MacArthur, Jr. was a top Amercan general in the Philippine-American War.

The two top Filipino officials of the Philippine Commonwealth arrived, close to each other. Osmena arrived first. He looked more

Chinese than Filipino with his almond eyes and fair complexion. Quezon arrived, a bit later, looking more Spanish than Filipino with his sharp tall nose and fair complexion.

"Our two great leaders," Franklin said, "don't even look like us."

"They are at least," Albert said, "as good-looking as MacArthur."

"Be quiet, you two," Crisanta said to them.

Leandro smiled, amused. Franklin may complain about Quezon and Osmena's looks, but they are one hundred percent Filipino in spirit and sentiment. They led the movement for the Philippine independence, right at the very start of the American rule in the Philippines.

The ceremony followed with clock-like precision: the invocation, the oath-taking and Quezon's speech. He spoke about social justice and land reform as the two main goals of his administration.

Leandro was in buoyant spirit, a while ago, but now, as Quezon was speaking about land reform, he listened, depressed and with a skeptical ear. He heard that before, even when he was a young boy in Bangar. Nothing had been done about that vital, troublesome aspect of Filipino life.

The public address system then announced, to the cheers of the crowd, that the parade was about to begin. The Philippine Constabulary Band then came, playing to the delight of the crowd, *The Stars and Stripes Forever.*

The Philippine troops, newly organized by MacArthur, then came marching by, behind the band. They were followed by delegations from various government agencies, civic organizations and the cultural minorities from the highlands in the north to the islands in the south.

Led by a dozen men waving colorful banners, the Muslims, several hundred of them, were now passing by the grandstand. They were dressed in colorful native attire, the men in tight trousers and shirts, the women in blouses and tight skirts. They passed by, chanting something like a slogan in their local dialect.

Leandro watched the Muslim men worriedly as they were marching by. They had swords in their belts, just like in Panakol.

He was in the village market in Panakol with Lehigh and four American soldiers when four Muslim men, the Huramentados, ran amok and attacked them with their swords. Had the American soldiers with them been slow on the trigger, one of them might have killed him.

"What," he asked himself, "if they will ran amok now?"

He realized soon enough, as he was watching them, that he had been worrying needlessly and unfairly. Their swords maybe instruments of violence in their home islands, but here in Wallace Field, they were merely ceremonial swords. He was glad and satisfied to see them marching by, to the cheers and the applause of the crowd watching them.

The public address system next announced a delegation of Manobos from Davao. They came marching by, ten abreast on Burgos Drive, about a hundred of them. They were dressed in colorful clothing, especially the women who had necklaces on their necks and bracelets around their wrists.

He was watching them when he was surprised to see Marina there. How she had changed! How she had aged! She was not the same beautiful woman he made love to, one afternoon, so many years ago in his homestead in Mandala.

What a terrible time, he had afterwards. He would have forced himself to marry her, had she conceived a child. How differently, his life would have turned then. He would have ended up to a life of a farmer in Davao, hardly better than the life he led as a peasant in Bangar.

Marina was often glancing sideways at the crowd. She seemed to be looking for someone. His eyes shot wide when he saw her, now looking in his direction. She is looking for him.

He ducked his head, so she would not see him. He pretended to look for something in the grass at his feet, so Crisanta will notice nothing odd in his behavior.

"What are you doing?' she asked him.

"I dropped something."

"What is it?"

"It is a coin; it slipped from my fingers."

He kept on with his fake search, his hand sweeping the grass as he glanced, now and then, at the Manobos passing by in Burgos Drive.

"Here it is, I found it," he said while pretending to pick up a coin in the grass and putting it inside his coat pocket.

He raised his head and saw Marina had passed by. He could now see only the back of her head, she was now and then turning sideward toward the crowd in what seemed to him was her unceasing search for him.

They, he decided, must not see each other. No one in his family, Crisanta, most of all, should know about her. To avoid crossing paths with her, he decided to leave while the parade was still going on.

"Come on, children," he said as he stood up. "It's time to go."

"But the parade," Franklin protested, "is not over yet."

"I know," he said, "but we must avoid the rush of people when it is over."

Crisanta and the girls followed quietly while there was some grumbling from Franklin.

Leandro looked around as he was leading his family, back to their cars parked in Intramuros. There was a slight chance that he might then run into Marina. He sighed in relief when they got to their cars without him and Marina having seen each other.

His worries were not over yet. Marina might look for him.

He and Crisanta had planned to make it a festive day for their family. But now that he had seen Marina, he thought it prudent to avoid the public festivities and thus avoid the likelihood of them, seeing each other again.

He took his family to lunch at the exclusive Columbus Club. Only members like him, the rich, the prominent and the powerful men and women in Manila were allowed there with their families and their guests.

The older children were, afterwards, allowed to see a movie while he and Crisanta returned home with their two youngest children, Carolyn and Robert, who were too young to go to the movies. Led by Gertrude, they saw Shirley Temple, the popular child star, in *Curly Top*, shown in Lyric Theater. They returned home after the movie.

They went to Luneta Park that night to watch the fireworks display there. He and Crisanta watched it with Carolyn and Robert from the balcony in the exclusive Army and Navy Club. The older ones were allowed to watch the fireworks, right there in Luneta Park.

The children returned home after the show while he and Crisanta attended the inaugural ball in Santa Ana Cabaret. He was just as certain, he will not find Marina there. The inaugural ball was exclusive to the bigwigs in Manila. He belonged there, but not her. She will never dare go there. He and Crisanta had an enjoyable evening there, dancing and rubbing elbows with the high and the mighty of the Philippine Commonwealth.

And yet he still worried, Marina might decide to visit him in Pacific & Gulf. To avoid her from seeing him there, he called in sick and did not report for work for three days. He told Agrifino, his assistant, not to entertain or provide any information to any stranger, man or woman who might visit him there.

He called Agrifino on the third day of his absence and learned to his relief that no one came, looking for him.

If, he decided, Marina really wanted to see him, she could have done so by now. That she did not call nor see him in his office meant that she was not that keen about seeing him again.

He reported for work, the following day, assured that they will never see each other again.

His close brush with Marina had so worried him he vowed never again to be involved with any other woman. They only complicated his life and jeopardized his marriage as well. That meant cutting all ties as well with Angela.

She called a week ago and asked him if they could meet over some problem she was having with Carlos. She would not tell him what it was until they have met. He agreed to have lunch with her in a restaurant in Santa Cruz. Angela then told him, her marriage was on the verge of breaking up.

"What," he said to her, "made you say that?" .

"Carlos is seeing another woman in Urdaneta."

He stared unbelieving at Angela. Carlos was lodging in Urdaneta, the town in Pangasinan where the bridge was being built. Carlos may have met the woman there, but then he may just be making friends with her.

Carlos, as he knew him in all the years that they have been friends, never played around with women. Angela may have become so lonely and insecure from the long periods of time they did not see each other that she had begun to imagine things about him.

He said to her, "Whoever told you that may just be making up stories about Carlos."

"I saw them myself," she said, her voice low in repressed anger.

"Carlos may just be having a friendly chat with the woman."

"Some friendly chat they were having while they were embracing each other!" she said, her voice, now high-pitched in anger.

"It could be just a friendly hug," he said, still downplaying her accusation. "I have hugged, a few women myself."

"I can tell the difference between a friendly hug, as you call it, and a romantic embrace. That is what I saw Carlos and the woman were doing! They were kissing each other!"

Only then was he convinced that Carlos was having an affair with another woman. He did not expect that from Carlos and yet he had to admit there is always the first time when a man, perhaps without intending it, could get involved with a woman. Angela's accusation had a solid basis but he kept quiet, out of loyalty to his friend.

He could see in the angry, downcast look in Angela's face that she was taking his silence as a sign that she was not getting through to him. She started to cry. She needed sympathy. He made such a gesture with his handkerchief, he gave her.

"Cry on," he said to her, "if it will make you feel better."

He regretted immediately for having said that when she cried harder and louder. He looked around, embarrassed, at the waiter and the other restaurant patrons who were watching him and Angela. They were presuming, he and Angela were having, a lovers' quarrel.

He was relieved when she finally stopped crying.

"Thank you, for keeping me company in this very hard time, I'm going through," she said as she was wiping with his handkerchief, the tears in her eyes.

"I hope I am of some help to you," he said, smiling and tapping her hand gently.

"You are, you really are!" she said in a vehement tone of voice that took him by surprise.

He looked at her, worried that she might break out into another crying spell. He was instead stunned when suddenly she held his hand.

"I have been thinking a lot about you at night when I am alone in bed," she said, her voice now soft and soothing. "I want to make up for what I have done to you in the past."

He blinked his eyes, not sure how he should take her unexpected confession of her love for him. She could only be using him to get even with Carlos. His heart, though, was leaping for joy. She rejected him before. Now, there she is, practically begging him to take her in his arms.

He nodded when she then told him to visit her when her children will be visiting their relatives in San Isidro. She will then be all alone in the house. They will meet in the same room where, a few years before, he made love with Regina.

He sat back, stunned, in his swivel chair when he realized his tryst with Angela was set for tomorrow! But then he had sworn, after his close brush with Marina, that never again will he be involved with another woman. It also made him change his mind about his coming tryst with Angela. He will see her, not tomorrow, not the next day, not ever again.

The day of their tryst came and went. The telephone in his desk rang, early morning of the following day. He did not answer it. He knew it was Angela, calling. It rang again, a few seconds later. He did not, once again, answer the call.   He finally answered it, the third time the phone rang. He must get it over with. She was on the line. She was hurt and angry. She asked him why he did not come to their tryst.

"I'm sorry about that," he replied, "but I'll never hurt my friend."

While he will henceforth have nothing to do with Angela, he could not also let Carlos ruin his life and his marriage. He shut his eyes when something then came to his mind. He had found a way for Carlos to leave that woman of his, make up with Angela and start anew

He was, a week ago, listening while Bill Shay, Tom Guernsey and Philip Beldry were discussing a problem with the supplies and equipment coming from the United States. Their suppliers did their job, but they knew next to nothing about Pacific & Gulf's operations. They simply went by the specifications sent to them. It worked fine, but changes sometimes had to be made in the specifications, in the size of the orders, among so many other things. Only someone who knows Pacific & Gulf's operations could do that. It was a job cut out for Carlos.

He called Nancy Jamieson that very minute and asked her if he could see Bill Shay. He was, in less than a minute, in Bill's office. He had, in less than five minutes, made his case for Carlos.

Bill nodded and said, "Carlos Yturalde is perfect for that job."

Carlos showed up, smiling, two days later, in Leandro's office.

"I don't know what went on here," he said to Leandro, "but I was told yesterday to report to Personnel, my old turf. I just came from there and, you know what? Mark Clavier offered me the job of merchandiser in the United States!"

"Did you accept it?"

"Of course, I did! I cannot miss out on this opportunity of a lifetime!"

"Angela and your children will be very happy to hear about your new job. You owe it to them, to your children, most especially, this rare, golden opportunity to live and work in America."

He watched Carlos who seemed to him was weighing in his mind who between Angela and the other woman will go with him to America. He tried to influence his decision by mentioning his children, hoping that will make him favor Angela over the other woman. He waited for what Carlos would say to him.

"You are right," Carlos said to him. "My children's future comes first. I don't want them to miss this rare, golden opportunity to live and work in America."

He smiled and nodded in relief.

Carlos had two weeks to prepare everything for their departure to the United States. As the only member of the Yturalde family left in the Philippines, he attended to the disposition of their house in San Miguel and whatever was left of their agricultural estate in Batangas. Angela took care of the children's needs, like their clothes and their school records.

Carlos was in Parola everyday, conferring with the company executives, getting briefings and instructions on his new job.

He was Carlos' constant companion at lunch. They also had a couple of drinking sessions and dinner in the Big House. They were making the most of the little time they had left together.

He could not, in all this time, make up his mind on whether or not he should see Carlos and his family at the pier. He did not want to see Angela again, but then, he also felt obliged to see Carlos leave. He owed his friend, this last gesture of their friendship.

The day of Carlos and his family's departure came. He went to the pier and found it swarming with people. Carlos, Angela and their children were surrounded by their relatives who were seeing them off. He waved at Carlos, but kept himself at a distance from him and his family. He thus avoided talking to Angela.

The ship blew its horn, time for the passengers to board the ship.

He shook hands with Carlos who came hurriedly to him.

"Good luck and all for the best," he said to Carlos.

"Right, all for the best, for all of us," Carlos replied as they were bidding good-bye to each other.

He looked on when Carlos and Angela, his arm on her shoulders, then walked with their children toward the ship's gangplank.

His eyes shot wide in surprise when Angela suddenly detached herself from Carlos' arm. She rushed to him and said, as she was embracing him tightly, "Thank you for not showing up in our appointment. Good-bye."

Then, just as quickly, she returned to Carlos.

He was now smiling as he watched them, walking toward the ship with Carlos' arm once again on Angela's shoulders.

Leandro settled them with such finesse and secrecy, Crisanta never saw nor learned anything that might arouse her suspicion. She was happy and satisfied with the love and care, he lavished on her and their children. She could not ask for anything more except for one thing. He stopped going to church since he joined the Elk Lodge.

It was, she learned, a club of freethinkers. All she got, whenever she asked him about it, was an evasive answer. He was a very religious person before and she prayed for him to return to the fold. While they were of different religious persuasions, they both believed in the same God and in the same Son of God, Jesus Christ. Other than this concern, she could not be any happier despite the hard times in the rest of the country. They were still in the midst of the Great Depression.

They were now a thoroughly Americanized family. Leandro's favorite drink was either Johnny Walker, black or red, White Horse, or White Label. He smoked his pipe with the finest Virginia pipe tobacco. Crisanta did her sewing on her Singer sewing machine. Their household appliances were ordered by catalogue from Sears Roebuck, Marshall Field's and Montgomery Ward. Robert learned to bike in his Schwinn bicycle, also ordered by catalogue.

Donita tried to sing like Deanna Durbin while Elizabeth once lost her voice when she tried to imitate Jeanette MacDonald. Albert imitated Nelson Eddy and Bing Crosby. They listened, but dared not hit the high note in the arias Enrico Caruso sang in their phonograph console.

They were avid listeners of President Franklin Roosevelt's "Fireside Chats" with the American people broadcast in their Philco shortwave radio in the living room. They followed avidly Babe Ruth and Lou Gehrig in their quest of baseball's World Series title. They subscribed to the *Reader's Digest* and the *Saturday Evening Post.*

Adrian loved so much its cover of Norman Rockwell's charming illustrations of American life, he collected them in a scrapbook. The glass cabinet in the living room was now filled with books, from the Encyclopedia Americana to Modern Library books. Prominent in the top shelf were *The Adventures of Tom Sawyer* and Crisanta's copy of the Holy Bible.

The children were moving along in school. Franklin, in a show of insubordination, studied in Torres High School, a public school in Tondo. The other sons, as fitting to their family's place in the cream of society in Manila, studied in elitist schools, Albert and Adrian in a school ran by the American Jesuits, Robert in a school ran by the Benedictine monks.

Leandro wanted a doctor in the family and he picked Franklin, the brightest among his sons, to take up medicine. It took a while before Franklin agreed to take up that course, for he preferred law or engineering. Carolyn was enrolled in a school ran by nuns. Elizabeth and Donita got married ahead of Gertrude who was taking another academic course.

She finished her doctorate in pharmacy with honors, the same as with the other academic courses she took. She had taken up chemistry and education on top of the home economics and Spanish course she had finished. As her siblings, often kidded her, she now has more degrees than the thermometer.

Two more cars, a Chevrolet and a Studebaker, were added to the Buick and the Chrysler which had long replaced their first car, the very useful and venerable Model T Ford.

Although times were still hard, the Philippines was beginning to recover from the Great Depression, a tribute to its wise and effective rule by the Americans.

They continued to look over the shoulders of the Filipino political leaders in the transition of the Philippines from Commonwealth status to independence, a few years later.

It was 1938. The entire Sumaka family was in the Big House. Elizabeth was visiting with her husband Fernando and their daughter Gladys. Donita, who had her home built for her at the northern side of the property, had dropped by with her husband Isauro and their son Isauro Junior, more often called Bebong. The children were all at home.

They were in the living room to listen to Paul McNutt, the former governor-general, now the United States high commissioner, report over the radio on the situation in the Philippines.

"Will you hurry up with that," Franklin said to Albert who was fiddling with the knob of their Philco shortwave radio while Leandro, Crisanta and the rest of the family watched and waited.

The radio gave nothing, but static until Albert had found the right station—KZRH. They were, in a short while, listening to Paul McNutt make his report:

"Today, the Philippines is the only bright, prosperous spot in the Orient. Its people enjoy the highest wages and best standard of living in the Far East. The deadly tropical diseases, smallpox, cholera, bubonic plague, which long decimated the population, have been wiped out. Thousands of miles of good highways are maintained. Bridges have replaced bamboo rafts."

"Pod, Paul McNutt is talking about what you and Pacific and Gulf are doing here," Albert said.

The children cheered. Crisanta told them to be quiet, so she could hear more clearly, McNutt's radio report. The living room was quiet again and McNutt could be heard clearly:

"The budget is balanced. Taxes are the lowest in the world. The reserve behind the currency is one hundred per cent. The per capita national debt is less than $2.00. Schools and hospitals dot the jungle and plain. "We built well in the Philippines. Our work is a monument to American idealism and enterprise, a living monument of fifteen million people rescued from tyranny, rebellion, ignorance, poverty and disease, and set upon the path of free government, peace, education, prosperity and health. With all seriousness, no nation in the world can boast of so grand a monument."

Albert and Franklin gave a loud cheer.

"So, you and I are now living monuments to American idealism and enterprise," Albert said to Franklin.

They quieted down when Crisanta frowned at them while a worried look had appeared in Leandro's face to what McNutt then said:

"But a problem has arisen, and one which we alone can solve. Politically we brought the islands through progressive steps to the verge of independence. Economically we brought the islands through progressive steps to almost complete dependence upon our markets. On one hand we sought to sever ties, on the other we chained them ever closer to us.

"The events of last year have given many thoughtful Filipino leaders an object lesson and food for thought. Perhaps, suddenly but they hope not too late, many have come to realize that independence, however attractive from the spiritual viewpoint, may mean a mere trade of sovereignties. They realize that the laws—United States laws—excluding Asiatic immigration could scarcely be enforced by an independent small nation in their quarter of the globe.

"The Philippines is sparsely populated, and it is surrounded with nations whose teeming millions are spilling over their national boundaries. An independent Philippines thus faces a very real threat of racial extinction. Add to this the question of its ability to defend itself from foreign military aggression and the economic disaster attendant upon a sudden loss of the American market and you have the picture."

Leandro shook his head at the shift in McNutt's report from a glowing report to a dismal portrayal of the Philippines. McNutt was categorical about the Philippines doing very well under the Americans, but so poorly, once it will be on its own.

The depressing aspect of McNutt's report made the air in the living room, so stifling to him and he went to the balcony by the staircase for some fresh air. He sat down on the rocking chair there and pressed his feet to the floor, sending it on a forward then backward movement, relaxing him and stimulating his mind.

McNutt, he observed, was diplomatic enough, not to express doubt on the capacity of the Filipinos for self-rule. He did not have to. The evidence was everywhere. He had seen, in the example of Candido, how prone they were to graft and corruption and how they look at public office, not as a public service, but as a means for personal gain and glory. It was a small, but clear sign of the kind of government they will then have. It spoke poorly of their ability for self-rule.

He had seen, on the other hand, the benefits of American rule over the islands. He benefited from it. Why give it up now? He is for independence, but not eight years later. They need perhaps, fifty years or so, when the Philippines hopefully will be by then, economically and militarily strong and politically mature.

They faced, right now, the urgent problem of security. Japan had invaded Manchuria and China. Hitler's Germany had annexed Austria and the Sudetenland in Czechoslovakia. War was imminent. The Philippines will be drawn to it. It cannot defend itself, once Japan will send its troops rampaging down in Southeast Asia.

McNutt's voice was barely audible from where he was seated, his thoughts now turned to Mori. He was at the top of a tall ladder, trimming into a pyramidal shape, the branches of one of the two cypress trees standing at each side of the house gate.

He could not have been more pleased with the young Japanese. Mori had done, in nearly a year since he took him in as a part-time gardener, wonders with the garden and the trees and the vegetation in the grounds around the house. The garden was blooming with flowers; the grass there trimmed a verdant green. They had a bountiful harvest last summer from the mango and other fruit trees in the garden, at the side of the house and in the terraced backyard from the care and attention, Mori had lavished on them.

He was so pleased with Mori that he had him enrolled in a vocational school. A trade will help him advance in life. Tanaga, a lumberyard owner, from whom he bought some of the lumber for Pacific & Gulf, recommended Mori. He was an orphan who left Japan in a quest of a better life in Manila. He recommended Mori to Bill Shay, who took him also as a part-time gardener. Mori worked hard and was very friendly.

It did not come as a surprise to him that, with Mori's good nature, he was soon making friends with everyone, especially with Albert. Crisanta and Gertrude were smiling when they told him that Albert had been ghostwriting for Mori, love letters to a girl, he was courting and how Mori, in return, had been doing messenger work for Albert in bringing flowers and bars of chocolate to Adelita, a girl, Albert was courting.

The young doctor, Erasto Makiling, was coming from the street, a package in his arm. He waved at Mori, who waved back and then went down quickly from the ladder and opened the house gate for him. He was visiting Gertrude and the package he was carrying was a present for her.

He sighed as he was watching Erasto who was now approaching the house. Gertrude will soon be leaving him, Crisanta and their home for that young man, a good-looking doctor. Much as he and Crisanta loved Gertrude, they could not deny her, the happiness she found in Erasto who, they were certain, will make a good husband to her.

Chapter Fifty-one

It was the day of Gertrude and Erasto's wedding and Leandro was so upset. He was railing at the manager of the catering service that will provide most of the food at the wedding banquet in the Big House.

"What kind of a service, do you have there?" he shouted at the manager. "Why is the food, not here up to now?"

He frowned, skeptical of the manager's assurances that the food truck will be there, any moment now.

"It better be here or I will run you out of business," he said as he dropped the telephone receiver to its cradle.

He could not wait for the food truck, though, and he hurried out of the house and entered the Buick where Gertrude and Crisanta were waiting for him. Gonzalo drove the car to Santissimo Rosario Church in the campus of the University of Santo Tomas where Gertrude and Erasto will be married.

He was restless throughout the wedding ceremony, his mind on the food. It might not arrive on time for the wedding banquet in the Big House. He left right after the wedding ceremony to check on the food.

He was relieved to see, when he arrived in the Big House, the catering service waiters, dressed in white, long-sleeved shirts with dark blue bow ties, standing by or making last-minute touch-up work on the dining tables there.

The headwaiter came to him and said the ten courses of food, he ordered, were in a room downstairs and would he like to take a look at them?

"I will shortly," he said to the headwaiter.

He could now savor the festive atmosphere in his favorite daughter's wedding, now that the problem with the food is over.

He looked around, satisfied at the dining tables placed in the front yard, in the terraced backyard and around the terraced circle of flowering plants in the garden. Each table covered with white linen tablecloth had a fine table setting with flowers in porcelain vases.

The long head table facing the house was decorated with gardenias, Gertrude's favorite flower. He looked up, pleased as well, at the lights strung up in the front yard, in the garden, in the terraced backyard and in the two cypress trees at each side of the house gate.

Music then filled the air and he listened, pleased, as the string ensemble made up of a bass player, two violinists, a viola player and a cellist, all of them dressed in white sharkskin suits, began their practice run on *Ramona,* a top hit song of the day and one of Gertrude's favorite songs.

They placed themselves between the door to the hall downstairs and the main staircase. They could be heard from there, inside the Big House, in the front yard, in the garden and even in the terraced backyard.

He was humming the song as he was going inside the hall. Everything there was ready. The waxed tile floor gleamed from the lights in the ceiling. The chairs set against the wall stood empty now, the hall deserted, but it will be full of people later on at the dancing there that will follow the banquet.

He looked out through the window overlooking the terraced backyard and nodded in satisfaction at the tables also set up there with the lights strung up in the mango and other fruit trees there.

The headwaiter accompanied him when he entered the room where pots and dishes of the ten courses of food were placed in two long tables. He removed the cover of a pot and nodded in approval. Not only did it look good, it smelled good and must also taste good.

"We are all set here, sir," the headwaiter said to him.

"Good. I will give the signal when to serve the food."

He left the room, satisfied, and went upstairs. The living room was deserted. Everyone in the family was in the church. He is alone.

He walked on, his thoughts on Gertrude as he was opening the door to her bedroom. He looked around, at the bed, at the bookshelf, at her collection of dolls. She is leaving her bedroom, her home. She is leaving her family, her father who doted on her for the man she loves.

He closed the bedroom door and walked on toward the balcony

He fell to more musing as he was looking out at Manila Bay and the lagoon, now fully converted into fishponds. His children are, one by one, leaving him and Crisanta. The day will come when he will find himself, back at the start of their marriage when he and Crisanta will once again be solely by themselves. What will be left by then will be memories that are mostly happy of their family life.

The string ensemble broke the silence in the balcony with lively music. It is not the time for those sad thoughts.

He descended the roofed staircase at the back of the house and was halfway down there when he halted and looked around. The two young men, both of them Crisanta's distant relatives, were at work on two roast pigs. One of them, seated on a low stool, was turning slowly on its wooden posts, a pig stuck in a bamboo pole, roasting in hot coals, its skin a crisp golden brown.

The other young man was chopping on a table, the other roast pig. The roast pigs will supplement the catered food along with those

Lucia, Delia and Magda were preparing in the open-air kitchen, they set up beneath the water tank. They were putting in large bowls the food they took from the large cooking pots sitting on the clay stoves there.

Mang Emong and Aling Pacing, who used to do the cooking there and in every party they held in the house, were no longer around. They died a year ago. Mang Emong died ahead of Aling Pacing who could not live without him. She died, just a few days later.

The sound of lovely music made it only depressing to him when he left the staircase and walked on sadly in the flagstone path to the garden. Some of those dear to him are not around at his daughter's wedding.

Other than a few postcards, he had no contact with Carlos since he and his family left for America; not a single letter. They are not a letter-writing people. Candido and Maria will not be there. Esteban is ill in Baguio.

He shook off those sad thoughts and turned his gaze to the garden, now bright and festive with the light bulbs overhead or strung up in the trees, having been switched on. A light bulb there was broken

He was debating with himself on whether or not to replace it with another light bulb when he saw Crisanta, waving at him. Gertrude was beside her at the reception line, they formed near the house gate with Erasto and his parents, Macario and Maxima. They were greeting and shaking hands with the guests who had arrived there.

He walked quickly toward them. He was still catching his breath as he was now standing beside Crisanta when Bill Shay and Esperanza came, smiling at them.

"Congratulations on this, another rite of passage in your family," Bill said as they were shaking hands with Leandro and Crisanta.

"It is the third wedding in our family," he replied, smiling also.

"What a marvelous reception, you are having for Gertrude's wedding," Esperanza said as she was looking around at the front yard and the garden, bright and festive with lights and music.

Elegantly dressed men and women were moving around or were conversing or were drinking wine or liquor taken from the waiters' trays. Other guests were taking their places at the dining tables. The yard and the garden were lively with talk and laughter while the string ensemble made the evening lively and romantic with its rendition of *Ramona* and other popular songs of the day.

"If we only had this kind of grand reception at Michael's wedding," Esperanza said with a sigh.

Michael gave Bill and Esperanza, a notice so short they barely made it to his wedding, a simple, quiet one in New York.

"That is how young people sometimes do it in America," Bill said to Esperanza, "simply, spontaneously with no frills. What mattered, though, was that Michael did it so properly."

Leandro watched Bill and Esperanza as they then walked away..

He was amused at their contrary views on Michael's preference for a simple, quiet wedding reception. His own folks, like his parents and his uncle Julian and aunt Tarcila, so he was told, had simple, quiet church weddings. So was the wedding of Candido and Maria. Only close friends and immediate members of the family attended the simple reception that followed it, a practical thing they did, considering how poor they were.

A neighbor in Bangar made the mistake of holding a big wedding party with the money they borrowed from Don Camilo. The couple virtually slaved and starved themselves early in their married life as they worked hard and saved and scrimped on everything to pay back what they owed Don Camilo. But that applied to them, not to him.

He saw no reason to be frugal in Gertrude's wedding. It was grand because, he could afford it and more important, it was his favorite daughter's wedding.

He was startled, as he was thinking about it, when a man came to him and said good evening to him. He shook hands with the man who was a complete stranger to him. He asked Crisanta who the man was, once he had walked away. Crisanta in turn asked Gertrude who the man was. He heard from Gertrude that the man was Erasto's cousin, Tomas.

He nodded, satisfied, that the man was not an uninvited guest.

So many people were invited to the wedding banquet, it took a while before they were all welcomed in and had taken their seats at the dining tables there.

Gertrude and Erasto were seated in the middle of the head table with Leandro and Crisanta to their left and Maxima and Macario to their right. The sponsors and members of the bridal party occupied the rest of the head table.

Leandro nodded at the headwaiter who then told the waiters to start serving the food. Hence, for more than an hour, everyone at the wedding banquet feasted on the ten catered courses of beef, chicken, pork, seafood and vegetable dishes, supplemented by the roast pigs and other dishes prepared in the Big House. They washed the food down with wine, soda, coffee, brandy, whisky and plain water.

His head light from his second glass of whisky, Leandro turned and smiled at Albert, his sociable son, who had stood up from his seat.

"Ladies and gentlemen," Albert then said. "Let us offer a toast to the newlyweds."

The chairs were then moved back from the tables as everyone there stood up except for Gertrude, Erasto and the children in the bridal party who remained seated at the head table. They raised their glasses and said, "To Gertrude and Erasto, may they have a long, happy and fruitful marriage."

Leandro said to himself as he was looking on at Gertrude, how lovely his oldest child is. Her face, a bit thin with a small nose and thin lips, was fixed in a smile. A tiara was on her head, her hair waved in the current style of hairdressing. Her white silk wedding gown was adorned with pearly beads. Erasto, seated beside her, was in his new tuxedo.

They made, he decided, a handsome couple.

But then he frowned as he remembered how Gertrude's marriage to Erasto was for a time a contentious issue among his children.

Erasto was from Apalit, a town along the Pampanga River. He moved to the working-class district of Tondo with his father, a carpenter, his mother, a market vendor, and his two younger brothers. By dint of effort and perseverance, he finished medicine. He first met Gertrude at the pharmacy, he put up for her in Tondo after she had finished her doctorate in pharmacy at the University of Santo Tomas.

Except for Albert, who idolized Gertrude, her other siblings had, in varying degrees, objected to her choice of her husband from among the men who courted her. Two of them were also doctors, one was a lawyer, and three were businessmen, all of them from rich, prominent families in Manila.

Why Gertrude chose Erasto, who was socially and economically way below them, was something her siblings could not understand. But he and Crisanta knew why. Gertrude was in love with Erasto as he was with her and that was enough for her.

He remained frowning as he recalled how Gertrude's siblings showed their disapproval of Erasto in various ways. They avoided him and kept themselves in their rooms every time, he paid Gertrude a visit. They ignored him, the few times he was invited to dinner in the house.

None of them was as vehement in his objection to Erasto as Franklin was. He is now seated at a corner of a table, nibbling at his food, drinking wine and talking to no one. It is as if he is there at the wedding banquet only because he was ordered to be there.

He said to them, a few days before Gertrude's wedding, "I don't want you to do anything that will spoil this special day for your sister. Make it truly, a happy day for her."

He looked around. His children, in obedience to his wishes, were at their best behavior.

Albert is walking around in attending to the needs of the guests. As the oldest son, Adrian should have taken that role, but he sat quietly at one end of the head table, too shy and too withdrawn for that task. Donita and her husband Isauro are attending to the guests in the front yard while Elizabeth and her husband Fernando are with the guests in the garden.

Carolyn, his youngest daughter, who was the flower girl, and Robert, his youngest son, who was the ring bearer, are eating quietly at the head table, along with the other members of the bridal party.

His children are at their best behavior although he would like it even better if Franklin will smile and talk to the others at the table instead of drinking wine, seated there, all alone.

He sighed in regret. He could only blame himself for his children's negative attitude toward Erasto. He should have been more open to them about his and Crisanta's poor, humble start in life. Had he done that, they might have been friendly and sympathetic to Erasto. His children could not believe the little that they have picked up from their relatives about his and Crisanta's poor, humble backgrounds. They were born and raised in a life of comfort and luxury and could not imagine their parents, having been born and raised poor.

They live in the largest house in that corner in Caloocan. At a time when only one Filipino family, out of several hundred, had a car, they have four cars. One was for his own use, another one for Crisanta and the younger children's use, and one each, for Albert and Franklin. He could get a car for Adrian, but he was so scared of driving.

They spent summer in Baguio and in Los Banos, for the mineral springs there in what for them was a life they were spending like a holiday.

His children were enjoying the good life and they could not allow any interloper, even if he is a doctor, to spoil it. But he approved of Erasto because he saw something of himself in the young doctor. They were both born poor who realized their dreams in life through hard work and perseverance.

A waiter holding before him a tray of fried chicken drumsticks interrupted him in his thoughts. He waved the dish away, drank his glass of whisky and blew tobacco smoke from his pipe, he had then lit up.

He caught Crisanta glancing at him and frowning in disapproval of the smell of tobacco. She told the waiter to put on his plate, a chicken drumstick beside the still uneaten fish fillet and a vegetable dish.

"What is the matter with you?" she said to Leandro. "You have done nothing, but smoke and drink whisky, the whole evening. Why are you not eating your food?"

He looked sourly at his wife. Why must she nag him about his drinking and smoking and at their daughter's wedding, at that? He had become such a habitual drinker he is now called "Whisky," behind his back.

They might as well call him also "Smoker" from the habit of pipe smoking, he picked up from Samuel Tyler and Father O'Farrell. Crisanta had better leave him alone in indulging in these, his two remaining pleasures in life, but he also knows her well enough that it is useless to answer back at her.

The food is good. He found this out when he began to eat. He finished everything on his plate in quick order. He is about to call the waiter for another serving of the drumstick when the string ensemble began to play the lovely wedding song, *I Love You Truly*. Dancing at the wedding banquet is about to begin.

Gertrude and Erasto, to the encouragement of the guests, left the head table and went inside the hall. Some of the guests joined them there. Leandro, prodded by Crisanta, stood up also, but before leaving their table, he drank down the remaining whisky in his glass and emptied his pipe of tobacco by tamping it on an ashtray on the table.

He put his pipe inside his suit pocket and entered the hall with Crisanta where Gertrude and Erasto and other couples are now dancing to the lovely wedding song.

"You have got there, another milestone in your family," Bill Shay said to Leandro.

He is with Esperanza, watching Gertrude and Erasto dance.

"I'm still not used to it," he replied, although it is now the third wedding in our family."

"Your eyes can get misty when you see your children, leaving you to get married," Esperanza said, a sad look on her face. "I felt that way in Michael's wedding. Bill and I are back to where we started. We are, once again, solely by ourselves."

Leandro gazed sadly at Gertrude and sighed. He had the same feeling, a while ago and it came back to him now, this sense of parting as he is watching Gertrude dancing with Erasto. One after another, his children are leaving him and Crisanta. Elizabeth and Donita, though younger, had married ahead of Gertrude.

But he did not feel sad then as he felt now that his favorite child is leaving him.

How time had passed. His children had grown up as he had grown old.

He realized this with a jolt, early in the morning when, at the mirror in the closet of their bedroom, he noticed for the first time, a few strands of gray hair sticking out of his close-cropped black hair.

It is also like only yesterday when the early morning routine in the house was of his children rushing through their breakfast and into their car so they will not be late in school.

It is Gertrude, among his children, who gave him the greatest satisfaction at the countless times he went up to the school stage to pin medals on her, for her academic and extracurricular achievements. She was the most studious among his children and he had caught her so many times, studying, late into the night.

All of that is now in the past and yet every bit of it had remained vivid in his mind.

He watched Albert who was coming to him.

"Pod," he said, "you must also dance with Mod."

"Do I have to do that?" he said to Albert. "I did not do that at the weddings of Donita and Elizabeth."

"Donita and Elizabeth had nothing like this grand wedding of Gertrude," Albert said to him.

A shadow passed across his face as he then remembered how he had to quickly and quietly marry off Donita and Elizabeth with only the family and a few close friends and relatives in attendance when he found them to be several months pregnant. He did not want any of his grandchildren to be born out of wedlock.

He will not let that unpleasant thought spoil his favorite child's wedding and he turned to Crisanta and said to her, "Your son said we should dance, so dance, we will."

They began to dance, at first with awkward steps. They have not danced in a long time and were off, both in their timing and movement, but as they caught on with the rhythm of the lovely wedding song, they were soon dancing gracefully and beautifully on the tile floor.

"We should do this more often," he said to her.

"You are telling me that, only now," she replied, smiling.

Some of the guests, led by Bill and Esperanza, Paulo and Teresa, began to dance also. A glass of brandy in his hand, Dick McCall was standing in a corner of the hall, beside Nieves who was talking to Dorothy Tyler.

Nancy Jamieson was there too, along with Philip Beldry and the other executives of Pacific & Gulf who came with their wives. They were watching the dancing couples or were talking, their voices and their laughter adding to the gaiety in the hall.

He is now enjoying himself immensely in dancing with Crisanta when he felt someone tapping him on his shoulders. He looked back and saw Gertrude and Erasto, smiling at him and Crisanta.

"Time to change partners," Gertrude said to them.

"All right," he said.

Crisanta was soon dancing with Erasto and he with Gertrude to the lovely wedding song, the string ensemble had been playing continuously.

He danced on with Gertrude, the smile on his face, betraying nothing of the sadness that had then overtaken him. Gertrude, the apple of his eye, is no longer his own little girl. She is now Erasto's wife.

"Be happy in your marriage," he said to her.

"I will see to that," she replied when suddenly she said close to his ear, "I love you, Pod, I always will and I will always be, your own little girl."

Part Four

Chapter Fifty-two

Leandro was on his way to work when he saw at the sidewalk in Rosario Street, a newsboy holding high a newspaper and shouting, "Japs attack Hawaii! Japs attack Pearl Harbor!"

It was early morning on December 8, 1941 in Manila.

He stopped his car and bought a copy. His lips pressed tight in anger, he read the news report about thousands of American sailors, soldiers and airmen killed or wounded and the destruction of American warships and warplanes in the Japanese sneak attack on Pearl Harbor.

"Damn those Japs!" he shouted as he threw angrily the newspaper to the car floor.

He was mad as he sat back on his car. He shut his eyes to calm himself. He was jolted instead by the thought that then flashed in his mind: The Philippines is now at war! It is an American colony and like Hawaii, it is home to American military and naval bases. The Japanese will next attack and invade the Philippines, just as they invaded China and French Indochina.

His mind reeling at the death, violence and destruction that will come in the wake of the war, he turned his gaze, to distract himself, to Rosario Street. It was peaceful out there. It was so unlike what he had read in the newspaper. The shops and the stores there were still closed. The sidewalk was deserted except for the newsboy there.

He had stayed there long enough and he drove his car away. He turned right on Muelle de la Industria. Pasig River to his left was also peaceful, its maritime traffic, now limited to a solitary fishing boat moving toward the bay.

His car had passed through the company gate when he realized, from what he was seeing there, that it will not be an ordinary working day in Pacific & Gulf. The workers have not gone to work. They were instead milling around or were huddled in small groups and talking in excited, worried voices about the sneak attack by the Japanese on Pearl Harbor.

He did not proceed, as he always did, to his office in the warehouse. He went instead to Bill Shay's office. He should, at a time like this, be with the Big Boss so he would know what was needed to be done.

The anteroom was deserted. He knocked at the door of Bill's office. He saw, when it was opened, full of the top people in the company, the expression in their faces either worried or angry.

Philip Beldry, Tom Guernsey, Joseph Kirkpatrick, Mark Clavier and John Stroheim were seated in front of Bill's desk. Nancy Jamieson and the rest of Bill's executive staff were standing around. Bill glanced at Leandro and then turned his gaze to Stroheim.

His shoulders slightly stooped with age and his arms crossed on his chest, Stroheim asked Bill, "Now that we are at war with the Japs, do we stay open or do we close down?"

"We will stay open," Bill replied, "as long as we can."

"After Pearl Harbor," Guernsey said, "the Japs will send their warplanes and attack Manila. What do we do then?"

"The only thing we can do then is to seek cover," Philip replied.

"Do they think they can get away with it?" Guernsey said. "Our navy should attack Tokyo."

The sirens in Manila suddenly broke out with their warning sound. Everyone in the room looked out anxiously at the window there. It could mean enemy warplanes were coming or it could be just another drill. Manila had been holding such drills for several days now in anticipation of the war and the enemy attack. No Japanese warplanes appeared and the sirens' warning sound soon died down.

Leandro left Bill's office, worried that the next time of the sirens' warning sound, it will be for a real Japanese attack.

His mind, like everyone else in Pacific & Gulf, was not on his job, but on the war. He called Crisanta and told her about Pearl Harbor. She told him that Albert, Carolyn and Robert had been sent home from school. Carolyn and Robert came to the breakfast table, earlier in the morning, in their gala white uniforms for the celebration that day in their schools of the Feast of the Immaculate Conception. The religious festivity was cancelled. The schoolchildren were told to go home.

Leandro spent the day mostly in idleness, in discussions of their situation with his fellow employees and in listening to the radio in the cafeteria. Everyone there, from Bill Shay to the janitor, feared the Japanese air attacks and the invasion that will soon take place there.

He left the office, late in the afternoon, shocked to find Rosario Street completely different from what it was in the morning. It was now full of people. Some of them were running and shouting. Others were lugging bags and boxes or were pushing carts, full of probably stolen goods. Most of the stores and the shops were closed. Some had been broken into. Paper, boxes and broken goods were all over in the street. Looting was taking place in some of the stores and shops. People were shouting and pushing each other in a frenzy of panic buying in a store while a fisfight was going on in another store.

He looked on, disgusted, at the chaos, he was seeing there. The Americans instilled on them in nearly half a century of their rule there, civic spirit, discipline, law and order. All of those had vanished in just one day in an orgy of looting and panic buying in Rosario Street.

He saw similar looting and panic buying, taking place in the stores and shops in Azcarraga Avenue.

He went on driving, his mind on the enemy who will soon come. There will be fighting, death and destruction. There will be shortages of everything, particularly of food.

He could do his own panic-buying, right there in those stores, but then, it will be so unbecoming of him, a respectable company executive in white drill suit and blue tie, to jostle with other panic buyers for maybe a few cans of sardines, a sack of rice or a bag of sugar.

He will do that quietly and discreetly in some stores, once he had arrived home. Those storeowners will be accommodating to him for the past favors, he had extended to them. Those stores, though, might be looted or cleaned out before he could get there.

He dashed out of his car, the moment, he arrived home. He went up to the house and was pleasantly surprised to see, as he was entering the living room, sacks of rice, flour, sugar and beans, gallons of shortening, bars of soap, boxes and bottles of medicine.

Crisanta had done what he was yet thinking of doing.

He looked for her in the dining room and saw the balcony also stocked up with the same provisions. He found her in the kitchen. A turner in her hand, she was frying fish with Lucia assisting her.

"You must have read my mind," he said, pleased with her. "I was thinking of buying those things, once I have arrived home, but you have already done that."

"We went on a buying spree, right after you called. What a terrible thing they did to Pearl Harbor!"

"Worse things are yet to come, that is why we must be ready. We must stock up on the necessary provisions. What have we got here?"

"Everything, I think we will need."

She gave the turner to Lucia and checked with Leandro the goods in the balcony and in the living room.

He said to her, "You must have cleaned out the store you bought them."

"They all came from Jim Tan's store, but we are not done yet. Franklin, Adrian and Albert are getting more stuff in Tony Sy's grocery store. Carolyn, Robert, Gonzalo, Magda and Delia are storing in the guest room downstairs the goods we bought."

"How did you get them in Jim Tan's store? The stores I saw on my way home were closed or looted."

"Jim Tan also closed his store. He let us in by the back door of his store. We made the same arrangement with Tony Sy."

He nodded, satisfied. Those storeowners owed him a lot for giving them so much business. Bill Shay had let him do the catering for some of the company's field projects. He bought from those stores, many of the goods he needed. It was payback time for him for all the goods, he bought from those storeowners.

He turned to the sound of Gertrude's voice. She was coming up in the staircase behind Delia who was carrying a big box of elixir of paregoric.

"Be careful with that," Gertrude said to Delia. "That is the last we have of that medicine."

Gertrude paused at the stairhead and held on to the doorknob, her right hand pressed to her midriff, big and heavy with child.

"So, you are also into this," he said to Gertrude as he held her in the arm and helped her in sitting down on a couch there.

"Mod called me about the attack on Pearl Harbor. Erasto and I knew immediately what it meant. War. Aside from the fighting, there will be shortages of food and medicine. We are bringing here, all the medicine we'll need. This is our second trip from our pharmacy."

Erasto entered the living room with Gabriel in his arms. Gabriel was almost a year old. Leandro took him from Erasto.

"How is my grandson, the most handsome boy of them all," he said as he was poking playfully with his finger, the tummy of Gabriel.

"Don't say that when Genaro is around or he might get jealous," Gertrude said to Leandro.

"Where is he, by the way?" Crisanta asked Gertrude about her oldest child.

"He is in the yard, playing with his cousins," Erasto replied. He turned toward the staircase and said, "I will get more stuff in the car."

"Why don't you stay here for the night," Leandro said to Gertrude,
" so I will have more time with your children?"

"That is what we'll do. Mod and I have agreed that, for the duration of the war, we will split our time between here and our pharmacy and clinic. We work there, we sleep here."

"Good," Leandro said, delighted, which he expressed with an impromptu dance he did with Gabriel, who just then had said the first word out of his mouth, "Dada! Dada! Dada! "

Crisanta and Gertrude looked on happily as Leandro was dancing with Gabriel in his arms. He would rather that, at a time like this of the feared Japanese air attacks and invasion, his entire family is with him and Crisanta in the Big House.

The Japanese warplanes came the following day.

Leandro was taking his lunch at the cafeteria when he heard the drone of those warplanes. He rushed toward the cafeteria window and saw them flying so low, he could see on the wings and on the warplanes' bodies, their red circle markings. They were headed toward the American military bases at the outskirts of Manila.

He learned, later in the day, that Nichols Airbase had been bombed. The naval base in Sangley Point was attacked, the following day. A pillar of smoke that then rose from the naval base could be seen as far as in Parola. The Japanese will soon invade the Philippines.

Bill Shay will never allow the Japanese to lay their hands on the machineries and equipment of Pacific & Gulf. He ordered them dismantled. Agrifino, Leandro's assistant in the warehouse, volunteered to look after them. They were crated and brought for safekeeping to his orchard in Del Monte. Pacific & Gulf had ceased operations. Its compound in Parola was, for the first time in forty years, silent and deserted.   The police arrested dozens of people and clubbed a few heads in restoring peace and order during the looting and panic buying, the day Pearl Harbor was attacked. The American military command opened, a week later, their warehouses to the public. They were abandoning Manila. They were moving their forces to Bataan Peninsula and Corregidor Island.

It set off another round of looting much worse than the first. The looters took whatever they could lay their hands on, setting accidentally on fire some of the military warehouses. They spread rapidly, burning to the ground, big areas in Manila.

Gertrude and Erasto's home, pharmacy and clinic in Tondo were among those burned down. They had nowhere to stay except in the Big House. They appeared there while the fires were still raging there, tired, dirty and hungry. Gertrude was holding three-year-old Genaro's hand while Erasto was carrying Gabriel in his arms.

"It happened, so fast, we managed to save only a few of our belongings," Gertrude said to Leandro who was in the living room with Crisanta, Albert and Adrian. Elizabeth was near a bedroom door watching Gladys playing a game by herself. Robert and Carolyn were dusting the books and magazines in the glass bookshelf while Bing Crosby could be heard from the phonograph console, opened just then by Franklin.

Albert said to Gertrude, "I'll get your things in your car."

"A good thing," Gertrude said, "we have taken out most of the medicines before the fire, but not much else." .

Leandro said as he took Gabriel from Erasto, "You are all safe. That is what is important."

"It seems," Gertrude said, "everyone is here. So, it is just like the good old days,"

Leandro watched her, filled with pity and sympathy for her and her family. They lost just about everything they owned. And yet, he could not but admire her for remaining cheerful in spite of what they had been through. She liked to see the bright, good side in people, places and events.

The children stayed at home with the schools, now closed. Gertrude, Erasto and their children Genaro and Gabriel were now permanent residents in the Big House. Gertrude was due to give birth to another child within a few months. Elizabeth and her daughter Gladys were also living in the Big House ever since she was widowed, a year before. Donita and her husband Isauro and their children Bebong, Bien and Nenita were living nearby in their house in a corner of the lot.

The children spent the day, playing games in the Big House and in its wide grounds. The games they played, their cheerful voices and their laughter were a welcome relief to their elders.

The drone of the Japanese warplanes, the rattle of their machineguns, the explosions by their bombs were, on the other hand, the sounds of war now heard with increasing frequency in Manila and in its suburbs like Caloocan.

Gertrude led them in trying to lead in the Big House, a life as normal as possible. She saw to it that they kept their routine activities, be it, at work, play or study. She was strict about their religious obligations.

It was still dark, one early morning when Leandro woke up to Crisanta and Gertrude talking in the balcony, outside the master bedroom.

"Pod should attend the *Misa de Gallo* with us,￼" Gertrude said to Crisanta.

"I told your father that so many times, to no effect. Your father stopped going to church ever since he joined the Elk Lodge."

"Pod was in our church weddings."

"Those were special occasions and I suspect your father did that only for appearances."

"It will be good for Pod, if we will try again."

Leandro listened, the same question, running through in his mind as to what had made him stop going to church. Crisanta was right. It was his association with those fellows in Elk Lodge.

While no one there had asked him to be like them, who treated established religion with lofty indifference, he ended up being just like them. The Elk Lodge was a club of freethinkers who had no faith, to begin with, or who had ceased to have faith. He was in the second category, a religious backslider. He became one because it was to his advantage to get along with those fellows in Elk Lodge. That was how he advanced in life, by going along with those who mattered to him.

He sighed. How he had changed. He was, back in San Isidro, a deeply religious boy who even served as an acolyte at the Mass held in the town church. He felt good doing that, especially during Christmas.

It was the best time of the year. He would leave their hut in Bangar, early in the morning when it was still dark.

A gas lantern in his hand, he would walk sometimes with his folks and his friends, but just as often by himself in the dark road in Bangar to the town church for the *Misa de Gallo,* the nine-day series of Mass held there at dawn. It culminated with the *Misa de Aguinaldo,* the Midnight Mass held on the eve of Christmas Day.

He smiled. What a joyous time it was! The church was filled with the faithful, praying and singing hymns, the lyrics of one such hymn having been retained in his memory:

> *"Nacio, nacio pastores*
> *Jesus el nino hermoso*
> *como paso preseroso*
> *vayamos le adorar. . . ."*

He smiled even more broadly as he recalled those early morning snacks after Mass of tea and rice cakes, he took with his folks and friends at the food stalls set up in the churchyard during the Christmas season.

It would be nice, if he could do that again.

He pretended to be asleep when he heard footsteps approaching the bedroom. He gazed drowsily at Crisanta when she shook him lightly on his shoulders and said to him, "Would you like to attend the Misa de Gallo with us?"

"Do I have to?"

"Yes, about time, you did."

"Did you say, you are also going to attend the Misa de Gallo?"

"Do you have to ask me about that? You know, I have been attending the Mass with the children."

"And you know how much I appreciate that."

Crisanta had remained a Methodist. She often attended the Catholic Mass with their children who were baptized and raised as Catholics because it fostered unity and harmony in their family. She also said it is all the same to her, whether one is a Catholic or a Protestant. They all believe in the same God and in the same Son of God, Jesus Christ.

She asked him again, "Are you going to attend the Mass with us?"

"I won't mind, doing that. It is Christmas, after all."

She smiled when he rose from the bed and walked toward the closet to change into his street clothes. He will attend the Misa de Gallo.

Christmas was only three days away. Leandro was in the living room, listening with Crisanta, Gertrude and Elizabeth to the radio, playing Christmas carols when the newscaster broke in with the news that the Japanese had landed in Lingayen. The feared but expected Japanese invasion of the Philippines had begun.

The newscaster claimed American and Filipino forces will drive the Japanese invaders, back to the sea. Exactly the opposite happened.

The Japanese crashed through the American and Filipino forces in Lingayen and pushed on toward Manila and Baguio.

General MacArthur, President Roosevelt appointed as commander of the American military forces in the Far East, considered Manila indefensible. To spare it from destruction, he declared it an "open city." The Japanese continued bombing Manila.

MacArthur had by then withdrawn his forces to Bataan Peninsula and Corregidor Island. Quezon, Osmena and their families fled there and were later brought by submarine to the United States. MacArthur will make a stand there until relief will arrive from the United States.

Dorothy Tyler was preparing a simple dinner for herself in her cottage in Brendan School. She was alone. Her housemaid had left for her village to attend to her sick mother.

She agonized since the Japanese landed in Vigan and Lingayen between staying in her cottage and fleeing into the hinterlands of Central Cordillera. Father Basneg, who was now assigned in Baguio, had pleaded with her to flee. Doing either of them was fraught with danger and uncertainty.

It was inevitable, if she stayed in her cottage, that she would soon face the Japanese who now occupied Baguio. She had no way of knowing how they will treat her. They might treat her badly, send her to a prison camp and harm her. But what purpose will it serve the Japanese to harm and imprison an old woman like her? They just might leave her alone.

While she never doubted the news reports about the terrible things the Japanese had done in China, her own experience with the Japanese was not bad, at all. She looked at them as a quiet and polite people. The Uyamoto couple who tended a vegetable patch in the valley in La Trinidad were friendly and respectful. Perhaps the Japanese soldiers will likewise be polite and friendly.

While she has no doubt about the kindness and the hospitality of the mountain tribes, the mere thought of living the life of a fugitive in the hinterlands worried her. The pain and discomfort she had to bear in the few times she visited the mountain tribes with Samuel will be nothing compared to the life of a fugitive, she will then live by herself. She even fell ill, one time, she and Samuel were caught in the rain, deep inside a forest, on their way to a village. She is not up to it.

She will take her chances with the Japanese in the comfort of her cottage in Brendan School. She took her meals there, hot from the stove. She is comfortably warm in the fireplace in the living room and she slept, warm and comfortable in her bed.

She could not bear also to leave behind, Samuel's books and writings and his other personal things. Other than the memory of their wonderful life together, those were all that were left in her long and happy marriage to Samuel.

She is staying in her cottage. She will welcome with good, old American friendliness, any Japanese soldiers who may come knocking at the door in her cttage. They might then treat her in the same manner.

She was setting the dining table for her evening meal when she was startled by the banging at the cottage door. She opened it and gasped at the sight of a Japanese officer and two soldiers, their eyes fixed to her.

The Japanese officer, apelike with his chin thrust out and his arms hanging down from his shoulders was short, he stood only up to her ear. He was gaping at her, so stupefied by her patrician beauty. The many years that had passed, her gray hair and the lines at the corner of her eyes had not diminished her beauty, at all.

"You alone?" the Japanese officer asked her in a gruff, menacing tone of voice.

She nodded, scared of what it implied.

The Japanese officer then ordered the two soldiers to inspect the cottage. They came back with one of them, holding a radio.

The Japanese officer shouted at her, "You, American spy!"

"No, I am not," she said.

The Japanese officer then waved at the two soldiers to leave the cottage. He faced her, a lewd expression, now on his face.

She turned rigid with fear when the Japanese suddenly grabbed her on her waist as he tried to grope her.

She was so repelled by what the Japanese was doing to her, her fear of him vanished. She pushed him away and ran toward the back door of the cottage. She was opening it when the Japanese grabbed her again.

They struggled with the Japanese, groping her. She was so filled with disgust, she pushed the Japanese away, so hard this time, he fell down on his butt.

The Japanese rose quickly to his feet. He was growling at her as he then swung his sword at her. A thick line of blood shot out from her neck as she fell down, dead on the floor.

A smirk on his face, the Japanese looked down at Dorothy's lifeless body.

He wiped with a rag, Dorothy's blood in his sword. He threw it at Samuel's flower box as he was leaving her cottage.

An Igorot boy working nearby saw the three Japanese soldiers enter the cottage. He hid in the bush there and waited. Two of them came out of the cottage, a few minutes later. The third soldier, an officer with a sword on his side, later on also came out of the cottage.

The boy peered inside the cottage, once the Japanese were out of his sight. What he saw there sent him running to Father Basneg, whose church was near Brendan School.

Father Basneg went hurriedly to Dorothy's cottage, but the boy stayed behind. The Japanese had put Baguio on a curfew. Anyone caught outside during the curfew faced jail and it was almost curfew time.

He was on his way to Dorothy's cottage when he came across the Japanese sentry at the school gate. He bowed, as the city residents were ordered to do, when passing by a Japanese sentry.

The bow he made was not low enough to the Japanese sentry and he slapped Father Basneg.

Father Basneg looked down sadly at the ground when the siren sounded at the start of the curfew. He will be detained. The Japanese sentry was pointing, though, at his wristwatch, indicating that he wanted it.

Father Basneg hesitated. While it was only an ordinary, inexpensive wristwatch, he treasured it. The late Father O'Farrell gave it to him on his ordination as a priest. But he must avoid getting jailed, so he could attend to Dorothy. He reluctantly gave his wristwatch to the Japanese sentry.

The Japanese sentry then pulled up his sleeve, revealing his collection of three wristwatches wrapped around his arm and his wrist. He slid Father Basneg's wristwatch into his wrist.

Father Basneg hurried away when the Japanese sentry dismissed him with a curt wave of his hand.

His cheek was still burning when he entered Dorothy's cottage.

He stood there, sad and shocked, at the sight of Dorothy sprawled dead on the cottage floor. Tears were streaming down on his face as he then carried her lifeless body to her bed. He held that night a solitary vigil for her, praying with hardly a pause with his rosary for the repose of her soul.

He met, when morning came, with the school authorities on what to do with Dorothy. They deemed it prudent, not to hold a wake in the school chapel. The Japanese might consider that provocative. They decided instead on a quick, simple burial for Dorothy with only Father Basneg and some Brendan School staffmembers and teachers in attendance.

A casket was obtained for her. It was brought in a cart for her burial beside Samuel's grave on a hill overlooking the valley in La Trinidad.

Her death and burial spread fast in Baguio and in La Trinidad. She was known as the kind and lovely American teacher, the wife of Samuel Tyler, the friend and benefactor of the mountain tribes.

The city residents watched from the windows in their homes, the funeral party as it was passing by on its way to the burial site where her grave, beside that of Samuel, had been dug by an advance party of men.

The funeral party, their hands clasped in prayer, looked on when Father Basneg then whisked the holy water on the casket as it was being lowered by rope into the ground.

He then looked up at the sky and prayed, "Dear Lord, accept into thy kingdom in heaven, thy humble servant, Dorothy Dickinson Tyler."

Chapter Fifty-three

It was New Year's Day in 1942. Leandro faced the year ahead with dread and uncertainty, now that the Japanese had invaded the Philippines. It was so unlike in the past, when he would look at the new year with the expectation of an even brighter future,

He was seated on his rocking chair in the balcony, taking it easy after breakfast, when he was overtaken with fear at the sight of the Japanese troops and tanks passing by in Mabini Street. He had read about the terrible things they did in China and they might do that too in the Philippines.

He feared most especially for the Americans who will likely be treated badly by the Japanese. He sighed in relief, for he had prevailed upon Bill Shay and Dick McCall to go into hiding. It took some doing, though.

They wavered, when the Japanese landed in Lingayen, between staying at home, hoping for the best and fleeing to a safe place. They paid no attention to Nieves and Esperanza who pleaded for them to flee to Masakao, where they could hide from the Japanese.

They turned to him for help. He went to see Bill and Dick. They also paid no attention to what he said that they have better chances of surviving the war in Masakao than in Caloocan, but he was persistent.

"I must be blunt," he said to them. "The Japanese will arrest you, if not shoot you, the moment they find you here and they surely will. You cannot hide here. You should flee to Masakao, to Alkayag."

"But will we be safe there?" Bill said. "Can we hide in Alkayag, like what Paulo did there before?"

"I'm sixty-six years old," Dick said. "I'm too old to do that."

"You will not be alone there. You will be in good hands there. Paulo and the folks there will take care of you. You know that."

It was his most persuasive argument.

Bill and Dick looked at each other.

Esperanza and Nieves gave them no time to talk about it. They said to them, "We will leave, right away."

"Let me help, put your things in your cars," Leandro said.

It took them just a few minutes to do that. Nieves and Esperanza had the foresight to pack up their things when they learned that the Japanese will soon be in Manila. Esperanza told Tibo and his wife Teofila to look after their house and Nieves's house, as well, while they were away.

He waved in good-bye at Bill and Esperanza, Dick and Nieves when they drove away in their cars. That was the other day.

The rest of Leandro's household had sensed the arrival of the Japanese troops from the rumbling noise, their tanks were making as they were moving on in Mabini Street. They joined him in the balcony and watched the Japanese soldiers marching by.

"There they come, the troops of Nippon Express," Albert said.

"They look mean, sinister and ugly," Franklin said.

"Stop that kind of talk," Leandro said to them. "It will get us into trouble with them."

The house gate bell rang the following day while Leandro and his family were taking their lunch.

"I will see who is at the gate," Albert said.

He saw from the window in the living room, Gonzalo opening the house gate for Mori.

He returned quickly to the dining room and said, "It is Mori! He is in military uniform! He is on his way here!"

Leandro sat stunned on his chair at the thought of Mori, a Japanese military officer! So, he was spying on them in all the time that he was working for them. That should explain why he never showed up in the house from the day the Japanese attacked Pearl Harbor. He must find out what he wants from them.

They left the dining room and met Mori as he was entering the living room.

"You look fine in military uniform, Mori," Albert said to him.

"Stop calling me, Mori," he said as he looked sharply at Albert. "From now on, it is Lieutenant Mori Takamatsu, intelligence officer of the Imperial Japanese Army!"

Leandro looked away, smiling, at Mori's pompous manner. He showed, though, a serious, worried look when he faced Mori at the thought that this was no longer Mori, his ward and gardener, but Mori, a Japanese military officer, now an enemy. Mori did not come on a social call, but for a purpose that worried him.

He asked Mori, "What can we do for you, Lieutenant Takamatsu?"

Mori set his shoulders and said, "I am here to take over your house."

He looked on at Mori, shocked and angry, but helpless about what Mori said. The Japanese Army is taking his home. He could not refuse Mori. He is at the mercy of Mori and yet his instinct told him, he must try to save his home. But what could he do?

He looked, surprised and apprehensive, at Albert when he said to Mori, "Come now, Lieutenant Takamatsu, did we treat you badly that you are now driving us, out of our home!"

Mori blinked his eyes. He seemed to be taken aback by what Albert had said to him.

"I'm sorry, Don Leandro," Mori replied, "but I have my orders."

He nodded, surprised and relieved by the abrupt change in Mori's attitude. He even addressed him now as Don Leandro. The old respect was still there in his former gardener. Mori was even apologetic. A play on his ego might help.

He said to Mori, "I suppose you have the authority on how you can make good use of our house."

"I have the authority."

"The Imperial Japanese Army could not have picked, a better man. What are you going to do with our house?"

"I am thinking of using your house as the headquarters of my company. We are assigned here in Caloocan."

"Are you taking the entire house?"

"Yes."

"There are far bigger and better buildings in the town square that are more suitable for your company headquarters."

"You may be right about that, but I have my orders to take over your house."

He pursed his lips. It was futile to talk Mori, out of taking his home. He could at least try to strike a bargain with Mori and he said to him, "Could you at least, let us stay here in the second floor of our house? We have nowhere to go."

He looked on at Mori, who seemed to be wavering now. He had, by appealing to Mori's better nature, put him in a situation where he was now torn between his duty as a Japanese military officer and gratitude to him and his family. He had managed to break down Mori's resolve to take over the entire house.

He saw his insight confirmed when Mori turned his head slightly to his right. It was a reflex movement, Mori made with his head whenever, as their gardener, he was taking orders from him. An old habit had taken control of Mori. He had brought him to his way of thinking. What Mori needed now was a face-saving gesture, a compromise.

He said to Mori, "You can turn the hall in the ground floor into a kitchen and dining area for your company."

Mori nodded and said, seemingly satisfied, "The ground floor will do as a kitchen and dining area for our troops. I am also taking your cars. Give me the keys."

He saw in the determined look in Mori's face that by asserting himself, Mori was now trying to save face for having given in to him. It was now his turn to give in to Mori and he told Albert to get the car keys.

Albert returned in a short while with the car keys. He said, when he was about to give them to Mori, "Can you at least leave one car with us?"

"You can keep the Chevy," Mori replied. "That is it, no more haggling."

Mori took the car keys from Albert. He was about to step down to the staircase when Albert said to him, "Can we still go, courting girls like what we used to do?"

He looked sharply at Albert, who should know better, not to be intimate with Mori. He is no longer their gardener, but an officer in the Japanese army. He might take offense to any reminder of that time when he was their gardener. He was instead, very much surprised, when he saw Mori, now smiling.

"Not while this war is going on," he said to Albert. "I hope, though, if we can do that again."

He watched Mori as he was going down the stairs. So nothing has changed between him and Albert. They remained as friends. Their friendship could be useful to them.

He watched Mori when he left in the Buick, which then crossed Mabini Street. He is going to arrest Bill Shay and Dick McCall. The Japanese were now conducting a roundup of the Americans, but Mori will not find them in their homes. They left Caloocan, two days ago, with Esperanza and Nieves. They must be, by now, safe in Masakao.

He rushed downstairs with Crisanta and everyone else in the house, once Mori was out of their sight.

They removed from the guest room, the goods they kept there and brought them upstairs. It was bare when the Japanese soldiers came, nearly an hour later, with their kitchen equipment and chairs and dining tables.

Leandro and his family kept alive, their hope of deliverance from the Japanese as they settled down to the enemy occupation.

The Japanese were denied the use of Manila as a port for their offensive toward the rest of Southeast Asia and Australia for as long as the Filipino and American forces were in Bataan and Corregidor Island.

They were heartened by the talk of mile-long convoys of American troops and weapons on their way to the Philippines.

They were taking their dinner, one evening, when they saw in the dark horizon, across Manila Bay, streaks and flashes of artillery fire. American and Filipino troops were trading artillery shots with the Japanese.

"It looks like," Albert said, "the battle in Bataan has begun,"

Their dinner aside, they watched the battle from the glass window that ran in the entire length of that side of the house which faced across Manila Bay, Corregidor Island and Bataan Peninsula.

They were stunned when, a few minutes later, shock waves generated by the exchange of artillery fire swept across Manila Bay and rattled the glass window in the house.

"It looks like they are evenly matched," Franklin said at the fairly even exchange of artillery fire as indicated by the streaks and flashes of artillery fire coming from two opposite directions.

The artillery fire coming from the left was from the southern side of Bataan Peninsula. The American and Filipino troops were holding their position there. Facing them on the right side were the Japanese troops.

"That is a big load our troops just delivered there," Albert said at the streaks of artillery fire that had shot out from the left side.

Adrian, Carolyn and Robert cheered.

"Be quiet," Leandro said to them. "Watch, but say nothing. We should not let the Japs downstairs to hear us, cheering our troops."

Leandro and his family watched from then on, the battle in Bataan. They took their dinner at dusk when there was still light outside. They would repair after that to the balcony near Albert and Franklin's bedroom where there were no mango or palm trees to obstruct the view of Manila Bay and Bataan Peninsula.

They watched the battle, sometimes with the hope that their troops could hold on until the arrival of the relief convoys from the

United States, but more often with dread at the likely defeat of the American and Filipino troops in Bataan.

Leandro was sometimes so affected by the artillery firing and the following shock waves that rattled the balcony window. It was as if he, himself was taking the blows from the exchange of artillery fire from both directions in Bataan.

The Philco shortwave radio, Leandro bought years earlier, was so useful to them now. They followed the course of the battle from the Voice of Freedom, broadcast from Corregidor. They kept the radio, when it was not in use, hidden inside a hole they made in the wall below the water closet in the bathroom. The consequences will be serious, if not fatal for them, if the Japanese will find the radio, but they never found it.

One evening, early in April, following what by now was his routine after dinner, Leandro settled himself on a couch in the balcony to watch the battle in Bataan. He was joined in a short while by Franklin, Albert, Adrian and Erasto while Crisanta, Gertrude and Elizabeth helped Lucia in clearing the table and washing the dishes. The grandchildren had taken their supper, ahead of their elders. Lucia and Gonzalo were now married and were the only remaining domestic help in the Big House. Magda and Delia were sent home so they could be with their families for the duration of the war.

Leandro and the others saw nothing but darkness across the bay. Everything seemed to be quiet in Bataan, no flashes and streaks of artillery fire, no shock waves across the bay that rattled the glass window in the balcony. Something had happened there.

"It looks like they have taken a break from the fighting," Albert said.

"Get the radio," Leandro said.

They will learn from the Voice of Freedom, what was going on in Bataan.

Albert, Franklin and Adrian had agreed to take turns in listening to the radio. It was Albert's turn. He took the radio from its hiding place and went inside his bedroom with Leandro, Crisanta, Gertrude and Erasto.

Adrian and Franklin had, at the same time, posted themselves as lookouts at the front and back doors in the second floor of the house. While it was unlikely that a Japanese soldier will go up the stairs, for Mori gave the Japanese soldiers downstairs, strict orders to leave them alone, they must still be careful.

Albert turned the dial to the spot where the Voice of Freedom was broadcast. They heard nothing, but radio static.

"That is it, there is no message tonight," Albert said.

He stood up to unplug the radio.

"Let us wait for a minute more," Leandro said.

The radio, moments later, played *The Star-Spangled Banner,* the sign of a coming broadcast.

"This is the Voice of Freedom," the broadcaster said. "Bataan has fallen ..."

The rest of the announcement came garbled to Leandro's ears. His mind had blacked out everything else. All he could think of was that Bataan had fallen. The American and Filipino troops had lost the battle against the Japanese.

Leandro stood up, went to the window and looked out at Manila Bay. All that talk about the mile-long convoys of men and weapons coming to the aid of the American and Filipino troops fighting in Bataan was nothing but propaganda. He was so sad and disappointed. He was only dimly aware of Albert unplugging the radio and Crisanta, asking Gertrude, "What will happen to us now?"

It was a question the 70,000 American and Filipino troops who fought in Bataan might have asked themselves. Later known as the "Death March," they were forced to walk for sixty-six miles to San Fernando, Pampanga in the heat of the sun without food or water.

The Japanese guards shot or bayoneted to death those who faltered. A Japanese officer on horseback slashed to death with his sword every prisoner, he was passing by. 2,500 Filipino and 500 American soldiers died or were killed by the Japanese in that inhuman, forced walk.

The closed boxcars in the trains that then brought the soldiers from San Fernando to the prison camps in Camp O'Donnell and in Cabanatuan were packed so tightly, scores of them were suffocated to death. 26,000 Filipino and 1,500 American soldiers died in those prison camps from starvation and disease or were executed by the Japanese.

It will be a huge disaster for the United States if the Japanese will capture General MacArthur who was leading the fight from Corregidor. President Roosevelt ordered him to leave for Australia. He will, from there, continue the fight against the Japanese.

"I shall return," MacArthur vowed on his arrival in Australia.

Those three simple words encouraged the Filipinos to continue the fight against the Japanese. American and Filipino soldiers who escaped capture in Bataan were soon waging guerrilla warfare against the Japanese.

That was one aspect of the war from which Leandro and his family drew some comfort and satisfaction. Everything else about the war was bad. Even worse for the civilian population, aside from the brutal Japanese occupation, they were now suffering from shortages of food, fuel, medicine and other necessities. Worse things were yet to come.

Leandro Crisanta, Gertrude and Albert were in the living room, one morning, when Gonzalo and Lucia came in with the news, they picked up in the town market, about people dropping dead from malnutrition and starvation in the streets in Manila. Leandro frowned while the others met Gonzalo and Lucia's report in stunned silence.

"It cannot be that bad," he said.

"But, Pod," Albert said. "What if it is true that people are dropping dead from malnutrition and starvation in the streets in Manila?"

"We will know that soon enough."

Leandro and Albert went, a few days later, to the flea market in Carriedo Street in Manila with old clothes they will barter for something useful to them. They were in an aisle, looking around at the stalls there when Albert saw what looked like was garbage partly covered with newspapers, left on the pavement.

"They don't even collect the garbage here," he said.

They were shocked, when they came near, to find that what the newspaper covered was not garbage, but a corpse. The dead man's bloated stomach and his thin arms and legs showed, he died from malnutrition and starvation.

"Here is another one," a man walking behind them said to his companion. They avoided the corpse and walked on, apparently not concerned about it.

Other people passing by did the same thing.

"Something should be done about that dead man," Albert said.

A stall owner nearby was watching them.

"Don't worry about that corpse," he said to them. "The authorities may come and pick it up, if not today, maybe tomorrow or the next day."

"You mean it will be left there, just like that?" Albert said to the stall owner.

The stall owner nodded.

"You seem to take this thing for granted, as if it happens here everyday," Albert said.

"It happens here, almost everyday," the stall owner replied. "It is shocking, the first time you see that, but you get used to it."

Leandro and Albert walked away, sad and upset.

"Did you notice, Pod," Albert said, "how those people walked on, unconcerned, that a corpse was lying there on the pavement?"

Leandro said, as he shook his head, "The Japs and our leaders have ignored this very serious problem of food shortage that has led to so many people dying of starvation and malnutrition in the streets in Manila."

"I heard some of our leaders have abandoned us and fled to Tokyo to avoid this problem."

By then, the food still available in the markets was so expensive it took a bagful of Japanese military currency notes to buy a small, spoiled fish or an ounce of mung beans.

The currency notes were printed without gold or any other kind of monetary backing. They were so worthless, the Filipinos called them contemptuously, "Mickey Mouse money."

Leandro and his family had fortunately no problem with the food. While they were now running low in some of the foodstuff they hoarded, they could still count on a steady supply of food from the Japanese kitchen downstairs.

Albert had managed to persuade Mori to order the Japanese cooks to set aside for them, a portion enough for all of them, of every food they cooked there. This came to an abrupt end, one day, when a Japanese soldier went upstairs and told Leandro that Lieutenant Takamatsu wanted to have a word with him.

He met with Mori who then said to him, "My unit is being assigned elsewhere. We are closing the kitchen."

Leandro stared, stunned, at Mori. Now, like the others, he and his family will face starvation.

He thought quickly. They will have to go to where food was still available—in the provinces.

He said to Mori,"Can I ask you for one more favor?" .

"What is it, now?"

"We cannot stay here in the house, once you have closed down your kitchen. There is no food here in Caloocan or in Manila. We will have to move to the provinces where food is still available. We need transportation for us to do that. Can you help us?"

He waited while Mori was thinking about his request for help.

"I will provide you with two trucks," Mori then said. "But you must leave tomorrow. Those trucks must be back here, right away. We will be out of here, a week from today."

"Thank you," he said to Mori.

He had a feeling, as he was watching the Buick, passing out of the house gate, that he will not see Mori again.

He rushed upstairs. The urgency of their evacuation to the provinces now foremost in his mind, he called everyone to the living room. They all agreed to evacuate there, where food was still available. Lucia and Gonzalo will stay behind to look after the Big House and

Donita's house with the foodstuff they have hoarded, passed on to them. They will leave the Chevy, their remaining car, inside the garage.

Leandro picked, from among the places where they will evacuate, Erasto's hometown in Apalit. Aside from him and Crisanta, Erasto, Gertrude and their children Genaro, Gabriel and Lumin, the others evacuating to Apalit were Adrian, Franklin, Carolyn, Robert, Elizabeth and her daughter Gladys. Albert was newly married and he will evacuate with his wife Adelita to her hometown in Tarlac while Donita will move on with her family to her husband Isauro's hometown in Lingayen. They will all go first to Apalit. Albert and Adelita will move on from there to Tarlac while Donita and her family will move on to Lingayen.

Chapter Fifty-four

The arrival of two Japanese military trucks in the main road in Apalit sent two men, idling at the bamboo gate of a house there, running inside their house. They feared the Japanese had come to search the town for the guerrillas. They peered from the window there at the trucks that had stopped in front of the house of Lola Tinang, a town elder. They were surprised to see Erasto, a familiar face there, getting off with his family and his in-laws from one of the two trucks.

The townsfolk in Apalit knew Erasto had married into a rich family, well-connected with the Americans. There he is now with this family apparently well-connected as well with the Japanese. Gasoline by then was so hard to come by, only the Japanese and high-ranking Filipino government officials could be seen riding in cars and trucks anywhere in the islands. Everybody else went on foot.

Those living in Manila took the streetcar. The trains were still running, although irregularly. People relied more on the horse-drawn rig or cab for transportation, if they could find one. Now, there was Erasto who had arrived with his family and in-laws in two trucks of the Imperial Japanese Army and with security guards, as well.

Leandro looked around at the deserted town road and the homes there with their shuttered windows. They arrived in Japanese army trucks and were thus seen as friends of the enemy. They might not be welcome there. He could only hope, Erasto's relatives will be accommodating to them. He will know that soon enough from Erasto.

He waited while Erasto went inside the house of his grandaunt, Lola Tinang. He came out, later on, with her, who said they are welcome in her home. Since they could not all be accommodated there, Erasto went with Lola Tinang to the homes of Erasto's cousins, Tomas and Pining, who also agreed to take them in.

They followed Erasto and Gertrude's suggestion that Leandro and Crisanta will stay in the house of Tomas while Adrian, Franklin, Carolyn, and Robert will stay in Pining's house. Erasto, Gertrude and their three sons Genaro, Gabriel and Lumin will stay in the house of Lola Tinang, along with Elizabeth and her daughter Gladys.

Erasto never spoke about it, but Leandro had told him confidentially before they left Caloocan that they will not be freeloaders in whatever home will accommodate them.

Erasto passed this on, also confidentially, to Lola Tinang, Tomas and Pining who were just so glad for the money they will get from Erasto and his in-laws.

Their accommodations in Apalit now settled, Albert and Adelita, Donita and her family then left for Tarlac and Lingayen. The other truck returned to Caloocan.

Leandro and Erasto, later in the day, paid Father Agunod, the town parish priest, a visit in his rectory. The following day was a Sunday and Leandro and his family attended the Mass in the town church, officiated by Father Agunod.

The priest in his sermon welcomed the Sumakas and urged the congregation to extend their hospitality to them. No one else, aside from Lola Tinang, Tomas and Pining, could have done so well for Leandro and his family. The parish priest was the most respected and influential person in the town.

Leandro was seated beside Crisanta who was smiling.

"What did you do in the rectory yesterday," she whispered to Leandro, "that the priest is giving us, the royal treatment?"

"We paid the priest, a social call; that is all."

He and Erasto had decided, no one else will know what had transpired in their visit to the priest. He learned from Erasto that he and Father Agunod had known each other from the time Erasto was a small boy and that they trusted each other implicitly. He learned from Erasto that Father Agunod was helping the guerrillas, fighting the Japanese. Now there they were, having arrived in the town with something very useful to the priest and the guerrillas, the Philco shortwave radio.

"You are lucky, the Japanese did not find the radio or they would have shot you, right there on the spot," Father Agunod said to them. "How did you manage to take it with you, undetected by the Japanese?"

Leandro then told the priest about Mori, his gardener who turned out to be an officer in the Japanese army and how the Japanese used the hall downstairs in his house as a kitchen. Mori provided the trucks when they decided to evacuate to the provinces. Mori told the Japanese drivers and their security escort to be polite to them, as a result of which, the soldiers, fearful of incurring his ire, conducted only a cursory look at their belongings. The radio was hidden inside a bag of clothes.

"I need not tell you how useful the radio will be to the Huks," Father Agunod said to Leandro.

"The Huks, Father? Are they the guerrillas, Erasto told me that you are helping fight, the Japs?"

"Yes, they are."

"Why are they called Huks?"

"Huks is short for Hukbalahap or *Hukbo ng Bayan Laban sa Hapon* or army of the people fighting the Japanese. It is a loosely bound peasant organization agitating for the return to them of the land estates. They found a new cause of fighting the Japanese when the war came."

"Where I came from in San Isidro, land reform is also an important issue there, but for now, the tenant farmers' preoccupation there may also be in fighting the Japs."

Erasto, later that night, took the radio to the rectory. Mang Tonio, the priest's trusted assistant, found for it, a safe hiding place in a locked cabinet in the choir loft of the church.

Mang Tonio went up to the church roof, the following day on the pretext of doing some repair work there. He was actually putting up the wire between the church dome and one of the two belfries that will serve as the antenna for the radio. The town had no electricity, but Mang Tonio found a car battery to run it.

No one else knew about the radio, other than Leandro, Erasto, Father Agunod and Mang Tonio, who also served as their courier to the Huk guerrillas.

Because the parish priest welcomed them, the townsfolk were soon lavishing their hospitality to Leandro and his family. Because he was a doctor, Erasto was so valuable to his townmates. The town had two other doctors, but unlike them, he treated patients even in the remote villages. Medicine was nonexistent in the town and what they brought with them from Gertrude's pharmacy was likewise so valuable to them. All of those endeared them even more to the townsfolk.

The attitude of Gertrude's siblings toward Erasto had changed as well. They became very friendly, even deferential to him, now that they depended on him for their shelter and the food they ate.

But for a slight bay window, he developed from his mostly desk job as a manager in Pacific & Gulf, Leandro had kept himself relatively lean with physical activity, like gardening at home.

He noticed, now that he was physically inactive, that, a year since their arrival in the town, he had gained so much weight, his shirts were now tight in his arms and in his midriff. He was a boarder in Apalit with no garden and orchard to attend to that could make him even slightly physically active.

The hours passed by him while he was seated on a chair, watching from the window there, young boys swimming, diving for clams, or fishing in the river. Even better, he now had all the time to read books, like those he borrowed from the public school library. Best of all, he finally had the time to read *The Adventures of Tom Sawyer,* from start to finish. It was, for him then, like getting an education again, four decades after he quit school in San Isidro.

He also learned from Father Agunod that the Huks were operating, far from the town, in the swamps in Candaba and in the deserted bayside areas in Manila Bay. They were careful not to operate in Apalit to protect the townsfolk from Japanese reprisal. Apalit, in all the time Leandro and his family were living there, was like a peaceful island in a stormy sea. The townsfolk were so peaceful and cooperative, the Japanese thought it unnecessary to conduct patrols, much less set up a garrison in the town.

The radio informed Leandro and the others about the American forces leapfrogging across Southwest Pacific, isolating in the process Japanese island strongholds and leaving them "to wither on the vine," as the radio reports put it. American forces were moving steadily toward the liberation of the Philippines from the Japanese occupation.

One evening, in September, 1944, as Father Agunod, Leandro, Erasto and Mang Tonio were in the rectory, drinking tea made from dried papaya leaves, Mang Tonio asked them why nothing was being reported about the guerrilla activities in other countries in Southeast Asia. They had just finished listening to the radio broadcast from Australia. The broadcaster commended the Filipinos for waging guerrilla warfare against the Japanese. No mention was made about the other Southeast Asian countries, the Japanese had also conquered and occupied.

"There is nothing to report about them, that is why," Father Agunod said. "Things are so quiet in those countries because, unlike us, the people there have not resisted the Japanese occupation. We are the only ones in Southeast Asia waging guerrilla warfare against the Japanese. The others are simply, sitting the war out."

Mang Tonio asked Father Agunod, "Why are we fighting the Japanese when the safe thing to do, as the others are doing, is to just sit the war out."

Leandro listened quietly, his mind on his own experience with the Americans. He got his job in an American company and with it, the means to advance in life. This American company was instrumental in literally changing the Philippine landscape with the schools, homes, roads, bridges, hospitals, wharves, dams and ports, it built there.

"I can say nothing about our Asian neighbors," he said. "As for us, I suppose, we are fighting the Japs in a show of our loyalty and gratitude to the Americans. They have been good to us."

A month later, on October 20, 1944, Leandro, Erasto, Father Agunod and Mang Tonio were in the choir loft when they heard on the radio, a report they have been waiting for: American forces have landed in Leyte, an island province in the central region in the Philippines.

They listened as General MacArthur then announced on a beach in Leyte: "People of the Philippines, I have returned. By the grace of almighty God, our forces stand again on Philippine soil—soil consecrated in the blood of our two peoples."

Leandro and the others smiled, but kept themselves from cheering by the need for silence in the choir loft. They shook hands instead and hugged each other, their eyes blurry with tears of joy.

"It will not be long now when the Americans will be here in Apalit," Father Agunod said.

True enough American forces landed in Lingayen on January 9, 1944 where, three years before, the Japanese had landed.

The Japanese fought a delaying action on the beaches in Lingayen, in other coastal towns in Pangasinan, but not in Central Plain. It was not, being so flat, suitable for defense. The Japanese, like what the Americans did before in Bataan in 1942, brought instead the bulk of their forces to mountainous terrain—to Central Cordillera and the mountains in Zambales. They brought the rest of their forces to Manila and the provinces, south of it.

Apalit lay open to the Americans.

Robert was with his friends in San Vicente, Apalit's commercial area, when he saw in the provincial highway, a seemingly endless column of American jeeps, trucks and tanks while American warplanes were flying above them in the sky.

He mounted his bicycle and, pumping his feet hard and fast on the bike pedal, he rushed toward Lola Tinang's house.

He shouted, as he was passing through the house gate, "The Americans are coming! The Americans are here!"

The news about the Americans spread quickly in the town. The townsfolk came out of their homes and hailed the Americans when they arrived there. Many of them young, some of them very young, they smiled at the townsfolk who were cheering them and waving with their fingers, the V-sign for victory.

A number of jeeps, trucks and tanks peeled off from the column and proceeded toward the center of the town. The officer in the lead jeep ordered his driver to stop in front of Lola Tinang's house when he saw there, Lumin perched on the shoulders of Erasto.

He was waving with his fingers, the V-sign for victory, at the same time that he was shouting, "Victory, Joe!, Victory, Joe!, Victory Joe!"

With him were Gertrude and his brothers Genaro and Gabriel who were likewise cheering and waving the V-sign for victory.

Erasto's youngest son, all three years of him, and his two brothers had attracted the attention of the American officer. He left the jeep and ordered his troops following behind him to park, right there at the side of the road, their jeeps, trucks and tanks.

He said, as he was approaching Erasto and Gertrude, "That is a great cheering squad, you have there!"

"They sure are," Erasto said. "I'm Doctor Makiling and this is my wife, Gertrude. This cheerleader on my shoulders and these two boys beside us, are our sons Lumin, Genaro and Gabriel."

"I'm Major Thompson," the officer said as he shook hands with Erasto and Gertrude.

Then he gave the three boys several sticks of bubble gum, he took out from his breast pocket.

"What will you say to the nice officer?" Gertrude asked them.

"Thank you, sir. This is very nice."

Leandro and Crisanta were coming. Erasto introduced them as well to Major Thompson.

"We are so glad to see you, major," Leandro said to Major Thompson. "We have been waiting for you, for three years."

"I'm also glad to be here. Other than our troops, you are the first persons since we left New Guinea that I am talking to in English."

"We know quite well our English," Gertrude said, smiling. "How long will you be in town, major?"

"We will be here for an hour or two. My men need to rest. We have been on the move since we landed in Lingayen."

"So, you have time to have dinner with us."

"Thank you, but you need not put yourselves into any trouble on my account."

"It is no trouble, at all."

"We are pleased to have you for dinner with us," Leandro said.

"I don't think I can say no to that. I have had nothing, but C rations since we left the United States. Home cooking! Why, that is superb!"

"We will be glad if your officers can also come," Erasto said.

"That is great," Major Thompson said. "I will round them up."

Erasto and Leandro waited at the gate while Gertrude and Crisanta went inside the house with the children to prepare their dinner.

Leandro also told Robert, who was standing nearby, to tell the others to take their dinner with the Americans.

They all came, Franklin, Adrian, Carolyn, Tomas, Pining and their families, Albert and his wife Adelita who had moved to Apalit.

Leandro was surprised, when Major Thompson came back with the other officers, to find them so young. Except for Major Thompson, who could be in his early thirties, the other officers, five lieutenants and two captains, looked like they were only in their twenties with the two youngest-looking in their late teens. They were practically boys sent to war. Major Thompson introduced them by their rank.

"And this," Major Thompson said about the youngest-looking officer, "is our baby officer from Idaho, Lieutenant Ronald Yturalde."

His eyes wide in utter surprise, Leandro looked closely at the young lieutenant. He is an exact copy of Carlos! He raised his palm in a sign for the young lieutenant to stay with him while the other officers, led by Erasto and Major Thompson, proceeded to Lola Tinang's house.

"I have a friend," Leandro said to the young lieutenant, "his name is Carlos Yturalde. You might be related."

"You could be referring to my father."

"How is Carlos?"

"Dad is fine, sir."

"How about, Angela, how is she?"

"She is fine, too."

Lieutenant Yturralde then spoke of what they did in America. His father bought a small farm in Idaho when Pacific & Gulf ceased operations. They raised cattle and planted potatoes there. Everything they produced there went to a canning factory which produced the C rations for America's fighting men.

"How about your aunt Regina, how is she doing?"

"She is living in Detroit. She is working as a riveter in a Ford plant producing tanks and warplanes."

"I am glad to hear you are all giving your share to the war effort."

They walked toward the house and joined the others in the living room. Gertrude, not too long after, announced that dinner is ready.

Leandro, as the family patriarch, sat at the head of the table. The Americans occupied the rest of it while the other men ate, standing up. The Americans were quiet at the start of their dinner except Major Thompson who, by reason of his rank, carried the talk at the dining table.

"Lieutenant Yturalde was right when he told us about the beautiful Philippine countryside. He was born here," Major Thompson said.

"I know," Leandro said. "His father is a good friend of mine."

"What a small world!" Major Thompson said.

Leandro saw Crisanta looking wide-eyed at Lieutenant Yturalde. He will tell her about Carlos, Angela and Regina after the Americans had left.

They took their simple, but filling dinner of fried rice, chicken stew, pork marinated in garlic, soy sauce and vinegar and fish, fried and then sauteed in garlic, onion and tomatoes.

They became, as their dinner progressed, lavish in their appreciation of what they said was their first real home-cooked meal in almost two years, including the few weeks they spent in the boot camps before they were sent overseas.

"Let me tell you, ma'am," a captain said to Gertrude who was serving their guests, along with Crisanta, Adelita, Lola Tinang, Pining and Elizabeth, "the food on this dining table is as good and tasty as the food served in St. Francis Hotel in San Francisco."

"Same thing with our top restaurant in Westchester, Illinois," a lieutenant said.

"I take it from what is on the table here, that dining is a fine art in these islands. You must have quite a number of fine eating places here," Major Thompson said to Leandro.

"We had a few before the war," he replied.

"What were you doing before the war?" a captain asked Leandro.

"I was with the Pacific and Gulf," he replied. "It is the largest construction company in the islands. It is an American-owned company. Lieutenant Yturalde's father had worked there, too. Its president is Bill Shay. I last saw him when he fled when the Japs were coming. As for the other American executives, I have not heard from them, as well. They could be confined in the University of Santo Tomas, we heard the Japs are using as an internment camp, but I have no way of confirming that."

"We have intelligence reports on that internment camp," a captain said. "The executives in your company, like the other American civilians, could be confined there. Do you know what it is like?"

"Gertrude and Erasto can tell you more about it," Leandro said. "They studied there."

As the Americans ate and listened, Gertrude and Erasto spoke about the university, its layout, the buildings there, the streets around it.

"Thank you," Major Thompson said at the end of their report on the internment camp. "What you have just told us will be of great help in taking the internees, out of there."

"Is it one of your targets in Manila?" Erasto asked Major Thompson.

"The whole of Manila is our target."

"Would it be all right, major, if I can hitch a ride, in one of your trucks?" Albert said. "While you found us here in Apalit, we actually live in Caloocan. It is a town near Manila. We want to know what happened to our house there."

"We don't allow that," Major Thompson said. "You can follow, provided you will stay back at some distance, so you will not interfere with our movement and only when it is safe enough for you to do so. You have a car, I suppose?"

"We had four cars before," Albert said, "but the Japs took them all except the Chevy. We cannot drive it, though."

"Why," a captain asked him, "can you not drive it?"

"We have no gasoline," Albert said, which sent Major Thompson shaking his head. "But I really would like to follow your troops, so I can see something about the war."

"That son of mine is so eager to see the war," Leandro said to Major Thompson. "He was with the ROTC. His unit was set to move to Bataan, but there was a change in the orders at the last minute. His unit was disbanded instead."

The Americans groaned in regret at Albert having missed out on the war.

"Don't worry about it," Major Thompson said. "There is a lot of fighting left yet."

A short while later, when they were finished with their dinner, Major Thompson said to the women who served them, "We have not had such a fine dinner in a long time. Thank you very much."

Leandro then led the Americans in repairing to the living room. The women stayed behind in the dining room to clear the table and wash the dishes, after which they took their dinner.

It was early to bed yet for the children who had their dinner ahead of their elders. They were allowed to stay in the living room. They watched and listened, seated on the wooden floor while their elders and the Americans were talking about the war and what they did before the war.

The Americans brought with them, packs of Camel, Chesterfield, Piedmont and Lucky Strike cigarettes. They gave them to their hosts. The house was soon filled with the fine smell of Virginia tobacco.

Getrude, Elizabeth, Pining and Adelita came, a short while later, to the living room with trays containing cups and a coffeepot.

"It is not much of a coffee, but it is the best that we have here," Gertrude said to the Americans.

The coffee, she and the other women were serving, was actually ground corn, toasted black.

The cups were filled and passed around. The Americans drank their "coffee" and complimented the women at how nice and different it tasted.

"Now, for a song to go with our coffee," Major Thompson said. He turned to a lieutenant and said, "How about it, Teddy?"

The officer referred to, nodded. He was pulling out his harmonica from his breast pocket when Major Thompson said, "Lieutenant Garfield is our company musician. He used to play in jam sessions and school programs in his hometown in South Carolina before he was drafted into the army."

His face in an eager smile from Major Thompson's testimonial, Lieutenant Garfield blew into his harmonica, its brassy sound encouraging the other officers to sing along, *You Are My Sunshine,* a song sung and heard for the first time in Apalit:

You are my sunshine, my only sunshine.
You make me happy, when skies are gray.
You'll never know, dear, how much I love you.
Please don't take my sunshine away.

The children cheered and applauded at the end of the song while their elders looked on happily.

Major Thompson then said, "How about another beautiful song? Something nostalgic,"

Lieutenant Garfield blew into his harmonica, another song, *Home on the Range,* its lyrics and melody as sung by the Americans and the sociable Albert evoking life in the prairies in America:

Oh, give me a home, where the buffalo roam,
Where the deer and the antelope play.
Where seldom is heard a discouraging word
And the skies are not cloudy all day.
Home, home on the range,

Where the deer and the antelope play.
Where seldom is heard a discouraging word
And the skies are not cloudy all day.

Leandro looked around. The women were finished with their dinner and they had joined them in the living room to listen to the music. The rapt expression in their faces showed the song had so touched them.

Some of the words were strange to their ears, for there were no deer, antelope or buffalo in Apalit. And yet the image of home in the open and of cloudless skies was familiar to them and they were as affected as the Americans were by the song. They, at that moment, might be thinking of the meadows and the prairies in America as they sang on like the cowboys and the ranchers gathered around a campfire in a Western movie.

Leandro saw in Lieutenant Ronald Yturalde's face that he might then be thinking of his family in Idaho. He was touched as memories then came to his mind about those good times he had with Carlos and Regina and of those early evenings in Bangar when young men sang love songs to their loved ones.

The singing ended to the applause by everyone there, the loudest, punctuated by cheers, coming from Gladys and Gertrude's three young boys.

Major Thompson then stood up from his seat and said, "Thank you for your hospitality. We have not had such an enjoyable time in a long time, but we must get going."

The women groaned in protest to Major Thompson having broken off just as they were listening in rapture to the music.

"Is it not too early for you to leave, major?" Gertrude said to Major Thompson.

"We cannot, much as we would like to, stay longer" Major Thompson replied. "There is this serious, urgent business that requires our attention."

He and the other officers shook hands with everyone there, tapped the children playfully on the head as they stepped out of the living room.

They were going down the stairs when they saw a Christmas Star, glowing in the dark, hanging at a window in the house. Inside the Christmas Star was a candle, Robert had lit up while the Americans were taking their dinner. Other Christmas Stars were glowing in the windows in the homes across the road.

The townsfolk were celebrating the Feast of The Three Kings in January 6, the last day of the Christmas season. It was so joyful and meaningful to them, now that the Americans were back and the feared and hated Japanese were gone.

"It is still Christmas here," Major Thompson said.

"Yes, indeed. It is still Christmas here and Merry Christmas to all of you," Leandro said as he stood with Crisanta, Lola Tinang, Gertrude and Erasto in the balcony of the house while the rest of them were looking on from the windows in the living room.

"Merry Christmas to you, too!" the Americans chorused

They waved in good-bye and walked out of the yard, to the town road lined on both sides with their jeeps, trucks and tanks.

It was so unlike in the past evenings in the town when the windows in the homes there were shuttered and the road was dark and deserted. They simply observed, not celebrated Christmas with its spirit of peace and good will when the town was under the fearful Japanese occupation.

The town had no electricity, but enough could be seen from the glow of the Christmas Stars of the holiday spirit, now obtaining there.

The townsfolk were taking a stroll in the town road, savoring the festive spirit there. Some of them, by what they were saying and their laughter, were making friends with the American soldiers. Many of them looked so young they could still be in their teens. They were standing or were seated on the ground, their backs against the tires of their jeeps and trucks and the caterpillar treads of their tanks, the lighted ends of the cigarettes they were smoking, making reddish marks in the dark.

It was a touching scene. The presence there of the Americans meant the town was now free of the feared and hated Japanese. The townsfolk were celebrating on the last day of the Christmas season, the Christmas spirit of joy, hope, peace and good will.

Erasto woke up, later in the night, to a knock on the door of the house. He lit up a gas lamp and opened it to three American soldiers, looking at him. Their leader, a sergeant, apologized for waking him up.

"Major Thompson told us to bring these to you," the sergeant said as he trained his flashlight to a jerry can of gasoline and large boxes of C rations, blankets and cartons of cigarettes piled shoulder-high, beside them in the balcony.

"Thank you," Erasto said to the sergeant. "Please tell Major Thompson, how much we appreciate these gifts from him."

He waited until the soldiers had left in their truck. Then he brought them inside the house.

He heard, on waking up, early in the following morning excited voices in the living room. He went there, pleased and excited as well, and watched Gertrude as she, Lola Tinang, Elizabeth and the children were going over the gifts from Major Thompson.

"Where did all these come from?" Gertrude asked Erasto.

"Major Thompson gave them to us."

"That is so nice of him."

"Look at what is inside this box," Genaro said when he and Gladys, with Gabriel and Lumin helping them, took out the contents of the box. They cried out in delight and passed around, tinned ham, potted meat and luncheon meat, rice pudding, biscuits, bars of chocolate, candies, a tin can of instant coffee, a bag of sugar, powdered milk and powdered eggs. The C ration was a veritable feast to them.

"Go and tell your grandparents, your uncles and your aunts to come here for breakfast," Gertrude said to Genaro and Gladys. "Tell them what the Americans gave us."

Leandro and Crisanta arrived in a short while with Tomas and his family. So did Franklin, Adrian, Carolyn, Robert, Albert and Adelita, Pining and her family.

Word about the gifts from the Americans spread quickly in the neighborhood and their friends and relatives also came, filling the house.

The kitchen was soon rich with the mouth-watering smell of cooked ham and luncheon meat, coffee and fried fish, rice and powdered eggs.

Those who came waited in the living room while they were having real coffee. The children were fed first. Gertrude called everyone in the living room for breakfast after the children had finished eating and the table had been cleared and the food spread out there,

They prayed before starting their breakfast. Not everyone could be accommodated at the dining table and only Lola Tinang, Leandro and Crisanta sat down there. The rest of them ate, standing up.

"How do you like this, Pod?" Albert said to Leandro, "nothing like a good American breakfast to start our day."

Leandro sipped his coffee, its aroma and the plates of ham and eggs there, reminding him of the food like that, which he used to eat at the cafeteria in Pacific & Gulf with Bill Shay and the other Pacific & Gulf executives.

Bill Shay had the same thought although he was in a far different situation from Leandro. He was confined in the University of Santo Tomas., most of which, except for the church and the residence of the Dominican priests, the Japanese had converted into an internment camp.

He was confined there, along with Dick McCall, the other executives of Pacific & Gulf, three thousand, five hundred American civilians and military nurses, a hundred British, Canadian and Australian internees, and a few of other nationalities like a Russian and a Burmese.

He cast aside the thought about food, for it only made worse the pain on his back and the grumbling in his stomach. He took instead a sip from the cup of tea in his hand and then put it down on the writing arm of the school chair where he was seated. He sighed and shook his head.

All that he had for breakfast this morning was his cup of tea. It was made from dry, crushed guava and papaya leaves and sprinkled over a pot of hot water. The leaves came from the pharmacy garden, he could see through the barred window in a room in the university main building. The trees and the plants in the pharmacy garden were cast in the subdued sunlight, now that it was early in January, right in the midst of the winter solstice.

The winter sunlight was like that as he remembered it in his boyhood in Iowa. The autumn leaves scattered on the ground made the cornfields there seemed carpeted with gold until, a few weeks later, at the height of winter, when they would then be white with the snow.

But he is not a young boy anymore having fun, playing in the snow in Iowa. He is now an old man suffering, like the others, from the brutal treatment by the Japanese guards in their internment camp.

The gym, the main and other buildings where the internees were confined, along with the shanties they built there, were scrubbed regularly to keep out the lice, insects and even rats to prevent there, an outbreak of disease. It could not remove, though, the reality of despair and harsh treatment by their Japanese guards.

They kept whatever privacy they could in their shanties and in their assigned rooms in the university gym, in the main and other buildings with the soiled sheets they placed around their wooden bunks.

It was the third year of their internment and more and more of them were dying or falling sick from disease, malnutrition, starvation and the brutal treatment by their Japanese guards.

Bill, as the chairman of the council of internees, looked after the welfare of the internees. He will meet with the other council members—James Miller, Tom Richards and Bob Smith—to discuss those problems.

Dick McCall was formerly a member of the council, but he contracted tuberculosis. He was confined, along with the others suffering from that disease, in an isolated area in the university compound.

Bill greeted the other council members, the moment they came in and sat down on the chairs arranged in a circle in a corner in the classroom. They were, like him, all skin and bones. Their hollow cheeks and the dull expression in their eyes showed their hunger and suffering.

But it will not be long now when they will have their deliverance. They know from the radio, they smuggled there, that American troops will soon be coming to their rescue. They were worried, though, that before they could be rescued, many more of them might be dead by then.

The Japanese at the start of the war, when it was going well for them, were benign in their treatment of the internees. All of them received, early in their confinement, food and medicine packages from the Red Cross.

That was the only time they received packages like those from the Red Cross in the three years, they were confined there.

The Japanese also allowed limited trading between the internees and the residents in the vicinity of the university. They stopped all of those when the tide of the war turned against them. Their treatment of the internees then turned from benign to bad, to very bad.

They became brutal as, unable to stop the American warplanes from bombing and hitting their camps and installations in Manila, they vented their anger and frustration on the internees. Their food rations were recently taken away from them by their guards for their own food. The internees resorted to eating the leaves of the trees and plants in the university campus. Medicine was nonexistent. So many of them had fallen sick, they might soon join the four hundred of them, or one-tenth of the number of internees there, who died from sickness, disease and starvation and malnutrition.

Only one man could remedy their dreadful situation: Captain Toyo, as they called the new camp commandant behind his back. Toyo was the Tagalog word for soy sauce. Captain Toyo liked so much his food laced with it, he kept a jug of soy sauce in his office at the top floor of the university main building.

"We must see Captain Toyo," Bill said. "More internees will die if our food rations, his guards took away from us, will not be returned to us and the sick are given medical treatment."

"What about his temper?" Tom Richards said to Bill.

Bill wore a grim face, but said nothing. His back was still hurting. He met Captain Toyo, a few days ago, in a corridor in the main building. He asked Captain Toyo to return to the internees, their food rations his guards recently took away from them.

The irascible Japanese commandant took Bill's request as an affront to the way he was running the internment camp. He screamed at Bill and then shouted an order to the guard with him. The guard then hit Bill on his back with the butt of the guard's rifle.

The following day, instead of returning the internees' food rations, Captain Toyo ordered the internees to stop picking the leaves of the plants and trees there, which they were taking for their food.

"We have no choice. We must make another appeal to Captain Toyo," Tom Richards said. "If we don't, more internees will die."

"The others are looking at us, to do something," Bob Smith said.

"What do you think?" James Miller asked Bill.

Bill pondered over what they said. The internees pin their hope for a good Japanese treatment on him and the other council members.

"You know what Captain Toyo did to me when I made an appeal to him," he said. "I'll do that again, if that is what is needed to be done."

"We will go with you," Bob Smith said.

"That way, we can be more persuasive," James Miller said.

"And there is safety in numbers," Tom Richards said.

"It may look provocative," Bill said, "but then we could be more persuasive if all of us will see Captain Toyo."

Bill and the others risked getting hurt in seeking an audience with Captain Toyo. They proceeded nonetheless to his office.

"What do you want?" Captain Toyo shouted at Bill and the others when the guards ushered them into his office.

"We are here, Captain, to make one more appeal," Bill said. "Many of the internees are in a very bad shape. They need food and medicine."

"You are prisoners here! You make no demands!"

"Please, Captain," Bill said, "We know you are a kindhearted man who cares for people, whether they are Japanese or Americans."

Captain Toyo nodded, flattered by what Bill had said about him.

He was considering Bill's request when the room was suddenly filled with the drone of American warplanes flying by, right above them. They were on their way to destroy the Japanese military camps in Manila. They have been doing that for so many days now,

Captain Toyo saw Bill and the others looking up at the ceiling, the expression in their faces, one of relief and satisfaction.

It sent Captain Toyo boiling mad, he shouted at them, "You want to see your airplanes? You want to see them?"

He then ordered the guards to take them out of his office.

That was the last time, Bill and the others were seen alive in the internment camp. Their bodies were later found in a remote corner there.

They were executed as Captain Toyo had ordered.

Chapter Fifty-five

Leandro decided, it was time to check on the Big House when he learned that the Americans had liberated the northern side of Manila.

American military engineers had the trains running again and going to Caloocan posed no difficulty for him, Adrian, Franklin and Albert who accompanied him. They saw no trace of the fighting in the towns, the train was passing by.

They arrived in Caloocan, relieved to find the Big House and the neighborhood have been spared from the fighting. Adrian and Franklin stood by when Albert then pressed the button of the house gate bell.

Leandro looked around at the Big House and its wide grounds while he was waiting for Lucia or Gonzalo to open the house gate for them. The windows and the doors to the staircase and the hall downstairs were closed. The roof, green in color before, was beginning to turn brown with rust. The white paint in the house looked faded into a dirty gray.

The Big House now looked to him as like an aging symbol of a gracious time, the brutal Japanese occupation had put to an abrupt end.

He looked on at the house, a lump on his throat, at the good times they had there. He knew, right from the very first time he walked around there, that he would be happy to live there.

They celebrated with food and music whatever was the occasion: someone in the family winning a medal in school, someone's birthday, someone getting married, a child born and baptized, the town fiesta, the changes in the seasons as in summer when the fruit trees were full of fruits. Best of all was Christmas. The windows were then decked out with Christmas Stars, the air filled with Christmas carols, the dining table, laden with food in their celebration of the *Noche Buena,* the midnight feast before Christmas Day.

Gonzalo was coming. Leandro noticed as Gonzalo was opening the house gate that he too had aged. His hair entirely black then, now had a few strands of gray hair.

He shook his head sadly. He is the aging owner returning to his aging house, being met by his aging caretaker. The war and the brutal Japanese occupation had aged them all.

"How are you and Lucia?" Albert asked Gonzalo, who replied, "We have somehow survived the Jap occupation."

Lucia came and likewise greeted Leandro and the others. Albert and Franklin proceeded to the garage with the jerry can of gasoline to check on the Chevy while Adrian went inside the house.

"I will first take a look around," Leandro said to Gonzalo.

"We'll keep you, company," Gonzalo said.

Leandro nodded, pleased, as they were walking in the terraced backyard to find the mango trees there blooming with yellow buds, promising a bountiful harvest of mangoes in the coming summer.

He saw also in the terraced backyard, rows of vegetable plots and the guava, tamarind, palm and other fruit trees there, blooming with fruits. He was pleasantly surprised to see the Japanese had left, near the flagstone path to the garden, two cast-iron vats, they used in cooking food.

"The water supply is now erratic," Gonzalo said, "but with the water tank and those two large vats, we have stored enough water for the plants, the trees and our own personal needs."

They went inside the hall at the ground floor of the house, the Japanese had used as their kitchen.

Leandro nodded, relieved to find the damage done there to be minimal. The soot in the ceiling and the burned spots on the tile floor, the only signs the hall was once used as a kitchen.

"Mori ordered the hall, cleaned up before they left," Gonzalo said.

They went up in the stairs to the second floor of the house where Gonzalo and Lucia were soon busy in removing the sheet covers on the couches in the living room.

Leandro looked around, pleased. The wooden floor gleamed. Everything there was in order. It was just as he left it, two years ago.

They brought with them, aside from the jerry can of gasoline, several boxes of C ration. Leandro left it to Lucia and Gonzalo to choose the food they will cook from a box of C ration.

Lucia, just the same, asked them, "What would you like me to cook for you?"

"The meat loaf and the powdered eggs will make a fine lunch," Albert said.

"Do you like some vegetables, too?" Gonzalo asked them.

"They will be fine, too," Leandro replied.

They had a fine lunch. They spent time afterwards, listening to Gonzalo and Lucia report on what happened in Caloocan and in Manila while they were in Apalit.

"You left, just on time," Gonzalo said. "Things got much worse then. Food in the market disappeared completely. A good thing you left us with the rice and other foodstuff. We survived on them and the fruits and the vegetables in the backyard. Things improved for us only when the Americans came. They gave us food."

"I heard in the train, the Japanese are still in the southern side of Manila," Leandro said to Gonzalo.

"A big battle is going on there. You can see it from here."

They watched that night, from the kitchen window, the battle at the southern side of Manila. They could not see much, though, with the trees and the roofs in the neighbors' houses obstructing the view.

"We can have a better view of the battle there," Albert said as he looked up at the water tank there. It stood beside the house, its view deck at the same level as the roof of the house.

"Let us give it a try," Franklin said. "How about you, Pod? Can you go up there?"

"Show the way," he said to Franklin, more amused than annoyed with Franklin for doubting his ability to climb to the water tank.

His children never knew, for he never told them, about the great amount of time, he spent in climbing, in removing and in eating the fruits in the mango and other fruit trees in Bangar.

He did that to fill himself with food and earn money as well in selling the fruits in the town market.

"I will go up, first," Albert said.

Leandro looked on as Albert then went up to the water tank. Franklin and Adrian followed Albert.

He used, when it was his turn to go up there, a chair in stepping up to the windowsill. He then held on to a post in the water tank at the same time that he was moving up to the view deck.

He may be an old man now, but he found, pleased and satisfied, that climbing the water tank was just like climbing the fruit trees in Bangar.

He shook his head in refusal when Albert tried to help him in climbing the water tank. He reached the view deck entirely on his own.

He looked around, the moment he was in the view deck, pleased with the great wide view there of the fishponds, Manila Bay, Bataan, Manila, Caloocan and the towns of Malabon and Navotas.

They were barely a minute in the view deck when they saw, south of them, in the dark horizon, the sky in Manila suddenly lit up with flashes and streaks of artillery fire.

It was like watching the battle in Bataan in 1942, with the situation, now in reverse. Where they watched the battle in Bataan with dread at the likely defeat of the American and Filipino troops, they were now watching the battle in Manila with the Japanese making a last desperate stand there, their defeat, the only outcome in the battle.

They soon realized, they were too far back to see nothing more than the flashes and streaks of artillery fire.

"We can see the battle there, a lot better, if we will watch it, right there in Manila," Franklin said.

"Good idea," Albert said. "I want to see closely the Americans beat the hell out of the Japs."

"Can we go there, tomorrow?" Albert asked Leandro.

"You can, but you must be careful."

Albert asked Leandro, the following morning, as he and Franklin were about to drive to Manila, if he would like to go with them.

"I am going to see Bill and Esperanza, Dick and Nieves," he replied. "They might be back from Masakao."

"How about you, Adrian," Franklin asked Adrian.

"Go ahead. I have things to do here."

They dropped off Leandro in front of Bill Shay's house before proceeding to Manila.

It looked deserted, but the grass in the lawn there was well-trimmed. Someone was looking after it.

He pressed the gate bell button and looked at the house. It seemed to have aged like his house. Its paint was also peeling off.

He walked away when, after a while of waiting, no one came. He turned back when he heard Esperanza calling out to him.

"I'm sorry," she said as she let him in. "I was in the bathroom when you rang the gate bell and I could not come out, right away."

"No problem," he said, smiling, to her.

The smile in his face vanished, replaced by shock, when he saw, how she had aged. Not only that. There was a haunted look in her eyes, a deep sense of sadness there.

"How are you?" he asked her.

She replied with a shrug of her shoulders.

"Is the Big Boss around?" he asked her.

It took her, a moment to reply.

"Bill is dead," she said.

"What!"

"Bill is dead," she repeated when suddenly, she burst into tears.

He watched her cry, at a loss of what to say, and all he could say was, "I'm sorry to hear that."

She kept on crying. What he said had no effect on her and he felt, she needed more than words. He laid his arm on her shoulders and led her inside the house.

He helped her in sitting down on a couch there. He took out his handkerchief from his pocket and gave it to her as he sat down beside her. She stopped crying as she was wiping with it, the tears in her eyes.

He saw her, now composed and he asked her, "How did he die? Was it from some illness?"

"The Japs killed Bill at the internment camp in Santo Tomas."

"But, I thought, all along, you were in Masakao!"

"We fled there, remember? The Japs had advanced so rapidly, they caught us and arrested Bill and Dick when we were only a mile or so away from the town. Only a mile more and we would have been safe!"

The sight of her, crying again, was beginning to affect him, too.

He drew a deep breath. He must dam up, his own grief over Bill's death so he could give her the help and comfort she needed. He held her hand and said to her, "Be strong, pray for him. He is now up there for his just reward."

She nodded but kept on crying.

He realized then that what he said and did had no effect on the pain and sorrow she was feeling so deeply over Bill's death.

The sheer futility of what he was doing for her left him drained of will and strength. He looked down at the floor, his eyes, now blurry with tears as he too had succumbed to his own grief over the death of Bill.

They kept to themselves as if the grief they were feeling over Bill's death was now so deep and so personal for them to share it with each other. The point then came when both of them were drained of their grief and sadness over Bill's death.

They were roused from this state of calm and apathy by the arrival from the market of Tibo and Teofila who looked after the house when she and Bill fled to Masakao. They proceeded to the kitchen where they were soon busy in preparing their lunch.

"Did you see him again after the Japs took him away?" Leandro asked Esperanza.

"I never saw him again after that."

He saw her catch her breath. She might break down into another crying spell.

He asked her to divert her mind, "What did you do after the Japs took him away

"I did the only thing, I could do. I prayed for Bill's safety."

"How did you know, he was interned in Santo Tomas?"

"Nieves told me. I learned from her that Dick was also imprisoned there. We did not see each other all throughout the Jap occupation. I was so scared to come here and I stayed in Masakao, all that time, while Nieves returned to their house nearby. She came to see me, the day I returned here when the Americans had liberated the northern side of Manila.

"We went to Santo Tomas right after the Americans had liberated it. I learned from Dick that Bill was killed by the Japs, the day following the Feast of The Three Kings."

Leandro shook his head. They were celebrating with a feast that day in Apalit, the C rations Major Thompson gave them.

"Why," he asked her, "did the Japs kill him?"

"I learned from Dick that Bill and three other internees came to see the Jap camp commandmant to ask him to return to the internees their food rations, the Japs took away from them and provide them as well with medical treatment. The Jap commandant had them executed instead."

"They killed Bill and the others for that?"

"Are you surprised by that? The Japs are worse than wild animals!"   He said to comfort her, "Bill died for helping others."

"He was that kind of a man," she said as she wiped the tears in her eyes. "He thought more about the others than about himself."

"He is blessed for what he did. That should relieve us of the sadness we feel over his death."

"Thank you, for your kindness. You are such, a good friend."

"He was such a good man. I want to pay him, my respects."

"His body is kept temporarily in the hospital morgue in Santo Tomas. We will have him a proper burial in a few weeks, in our plot in North Cemetery."

"Let me know about it, so Crisanta and I can attend it."

He knew about the cemetery plot, Esperanza and Crisanta bought, years before, two plots beside each other in North Cemetery.

"What a terrible time, we have been through," he said and sighed.

"I know of no one who did not suffer at the hands of the Japs. Teresa was also widowed by the Japs."

"Paulo is dead, too?"

"He could not just stand by and watch the Japs as they did terrible things to us. He joined, despite his old age, the guerrillas and fought the Japs."

"Paulo died, fighting for our country."

"He will still be alive today had he not been betrayed by those who collaborated with the Japs. They killed him in the town fort jail."

Another friend who suffered and died at the hands of the Japanese soldiers sent him frowning and shaking his head in anger and sadness.

He stayed, following her invitation, to have lunch with her.

He left her afterwards, sad over the death of Bill and Paulo, but was somehow relieved of it by the comfort and sympathy, he had given her.

He was walking out on the road when he was nagged by what she said about everyone having suffered at the hands of the Japanese. He and his family, in comparison to her and Teresa, have not suffered, at all. Fear and anxiety, some inconvenience and a few losses like his cars, were all that they suffered and endured in the war and in the brutal Japanese occupation.

Albert and Franklin returned home, later in the day.

"We finally got even with the Japs, compliments of the Americans," Albert said to Leandro and Adrian. "They are now beating the hell out of the Japs in Intramuros."

They listened as Albert and Franklin then told them what they saw and learned about the battle in southern Manila.

"We were with a big crowd," Franklin said, "watching the battle at a safe distance, behind the American troops there. They were positioned near the riverbank, at the western end of Escolta, near the northern foot of the collapsed Jones Bridge."

"That is where the old Puente de Espana Bridge once stood," Leandro said.

"The Japs," Albert then said, "were holed up in the building of the College of Saint John of Lateran. It stood behind the thick stonewall of Intramuros. They prevented, from the school building, which overlooked Plaza Lawton and Pasig River, the Americans from crossing the river to Plaza Lawton and mounting an infantry attack on Intramuros."

"So, the Americans were not able to cross the river," Leandro said.

"They did, after a while."

"How did they do it?"

"Franklin and I were looking at the school building when I saw a Jap soldier at a top floor window there. I pointed him out to Franklin.

"The American soldiers, directing the shooting from their tanks, saw the Jap, too. The tanks' machine guns were in an instant shooting the Jap at the window. We cheered when we saw the Jap, hit by gunfire, drop dead on the windowsill. More Jap soldiers appeared at the other windows. They fired back at the Americans, prompting us and the rest of the crowd to seek cover behind a building there."

"We heard but saw nothing of the fighting in the next few minutes."

"We could hear, though, the intense machinegun and cannon firing by the American tanks. The firing ceased momentarily and we looked out and saw the windows in the school building's top floor, now completely unrecognizable. The tanks resumed firing their machineguns, now directed at the building's lower floors. They, in just a short while, were now also, so unrecognizable. No Jap soldier holed up there could have survived all that machinegun and cannon shooting by the American tanks."

"It was now safe enough for the American infantrymen to cross the river. Some of them had been waiting behind the protective cover of their tanks, others, behind the buildings. A number of soldiers then rushed toward the riverbank, rubber assault boats on their shoulders. They put them down into the river. The infantrymen then boarded the assault boats. They crossed the river and arrived in the southern bank in just a short while."

"We watched them when they crossed Plaza Lawton and moved on toward Intramuros. The assault boats, in the meantime, had returned to our side of the river to pick up more infantrymen.

"Someone in the crowd of onlookers suggested that we join the American soldiers and likewise board those assault boats. We could then have a much closer view of the battle there. Franklin and I needed no prompting and we joined the crowd, now rushing toward the riverbank. We were about to board an assault boat there when an American officer came, rushing to us."

"Get back! Get back!" he shouted. He was ignored and he pulled out his gun and fired at the sky.

"We moved back then. We could only look on when more American soldiers then crossed the river on the assault boats and rushed across Plaza Lawton to the Puerta Isabel Gate and the Rampart of San Gabriel, in front of Lateran. Fighting was now going on, inside Intramuros. We could see nothing, though, but the smoke and flashes of artillery fire, coming from the Jap side of the wall."

"That is just too bad," Leandro said with a shake of his head. "All the trouble you took and you could see nothing of the battle in Intramuros."

"We will try again, tomorrow," Albert said.

They came back, the following day, to the same spot, hoping that this time they will be allowed to cross the river. The three bridges, not far from each other, have been destroyed and the only way to the other side in the river was by the only available watercraft—the Americans' assault and supply boats, but civilians still were not allowed to board them.

They stopped going there, since they could see nothing there of the battle now going on inside Intramuros. They resumed their nightly routine of watching from the Big House, the battle in southern Manila.

A few days passed. They watched the battle there from the view deck, but saw no sign of fighting there.

"The battle seems to be over and the Americans won," Albert said.

"How can you say that?" Leandro asked Albert

Albert then told Leandro, what he and Franklin had picked up in Manila, about the powerful American forces that moved southward across Pasig River, eastward from Santa Ana and northward from Batangas and converged on Intramuros and the southern side Manila.

Leandro and his children were taking their breakfast, the following morning, when Gonzalo told them about the great news, he picked up in the town market. The Americans were now in full control of Intramuros and the rest of southern Manila. The battle there was over and the Americans won, as they expected.

Albert, Adrian and Franklin cheered.

"I have got something to celebrate it with," Albert said.

He went to his old bedroom and came back with a bottle of brandy.

"I kept this, for this occasion," he said.

Adrian found some wine glasses and Albert filled them with the liquor. They offered each other, a toast to the liberation of Manila by the Americans. It was a euphoric moment. Leandro agreed when Albert said, they could really savor the American victory in Intramuros with a close look at how the battle went there.

They were on their way to Manila, a short while later. Leandro, who was driving, parked the Chevy on a side street in Escolta. They walked the rest of the way to the northern bank of Pasig River.

A pontoon bridge was now spanning the river. The Americans put it there for the use by their troops, but with the battle over, it was now open to the public. Adrian, though, was reluctant to step on it.

"There is nothing to be afraid of," Albert said to Adrian as he was stepping down confidently into the pontoon bridge.

Adrian was encouraged by what Albert did and he stepped down too into the pontoon bridge.

Leandro followed them. He watched every step he took on the pontoon bridge's wooden planks. It was swaying slightly from the push of the water on the sealed empty steel drums which kept it afloat. A slight misstep and he might fall into the river. He raised his eyes only when his feet were on solid ground again. He recoiled at what he saw there.

"What happened there?" he asked his sons.

Plaza Lawton was so unrecognizable at the destruction brought about there in the battle. There was not a single building within Leandro's view that was not damaged or destroyed in the fighting. The Post Office Building was burned out. The Insular Ice Plant, the Metropolitan Theater, and the building in Saint John of Lateran were so badly damaged.

The trees in Plaza Lawton had been stripped bare of their leaves by the fighting there. They now stood there, grotesque and skeletal.

The City Hall, the Finance and the Agriculture buildings and other buildings there were severely damaged.

He watched, ten years ago, with Crisanta and their children, the inauguration of the Philippine Commonwealth in the balcony and driveway of the Legislative Building. It now stood there, completely ruined.

It took years for the Insular Government, with Pacific & Gulf as the principal contractor, to build and develop it into a lovely section of Manila. It was destroyed in just a few weeks of fighting.

Intramuros suffered an even worse fate. It took decades of work to build the wall and the homes, schools, churches and government buildings within that wall, a protection for centuries for its residents, made into a death trap by the Japanese soldiers.

It survived earthquakes, the British invasion in the 18th century, fires and the course of time only to be reduced within a few weeks of fighting to burned-out shells by the Japanese soldiers who set them on fire or to heaps of rubble by American bombing and artillery shelling.

Only San Agustin Church was left relatively untouched. Its dome looked in the distance like a shrouded woman's head bowed with grief at the death and destruction brought about there.

Leandro walked on toward Intramuros with his sons. They were about to enter Fort Santiago when a gust of wind, heavy with the stench of burned and decomposed human remains, blew across them.

"This is terrible!" Adrian shouted. "Let us get out of here!"

"Get out of here, if that is what you want to do," Franklin said irritably to Adrian, "but I am moving on with Albert. We want to see what happened here."

Leandro resolved the conflict between the two with a slight push he made on Adrian's back. They walked on.

They saw, ahead of them, in the open ground there, gray patches of ashes. They discovered to their horror when they came near them, that those were not the ashes of burned wood, paper, or clothing, but the burned or decomposed remains of people. They were all over the fort.

They stood still for a moment, stunned by the horrible sight and smell there. They looked around when, after a while, they had somewhat recovered from shock.

A young man standing there was poking with a stick, a mound of bones and ashes. Something he saw there caught his eyes and he picked up there, a belt buckle. He was examining it when suddenly he broke into a piercing, mournful cry.

They approached the young man.

"What happened?" Leandro asked him. "Are you hurt?"

The young man seemed not to hear him as he went on crying and cursing the Japanese for what they had done to his brother.

Leandro asked the young man when he had somewhat calmed down, what had so troubled him. He listened and drew from the young man's narrative and what Franklin and Albert had told him, a mental picture of what happened in Intramuros and in southern Manila:

American troops, right after they had liberated northern Manila, moved southward across Pasig River, westward from Santa Ana and northward from Batangas. They converged in Intramuros and in the rest of southern Manila.

The sixteen thousand, six hundred Japanese troops there were trapped by the American forces. But, rather than surrender, they fought to the last man and brought with them to their death, most of the residents there.

The Japanese went on an orgy of burning down and destroying homes, schools, hospitals, churches and government buildings, of killing the men and raping the women before many of them were then killed. The bellies of pregnant women were cut open with the babies thrown up into the air and then pierced with their bayonets.

San Agustin Church was one of the few buildings left standing in Intramuros. The Americans, with their firepower, could have reduced it into rubble in less than a minute of artillery shelling. They spared it from destruction when they learned that hundreds of Intramuros residents had sought refuge there.

They were the few lucky ones, unlike the more than one hundred thousand, or one-tenth the population of Manila, who died or were killed by the Japanese in the battle in southern Manila, most severely in Intramuros.

The Japanese herded in Fort Santiago, thousands of the men living in Intramuros, including the young man, his father and his younger brother. They were to be used as a human protective shield from

American artillery and warplanes. It did not work out that way for the Japanese. The Americans dropped their bombs and fired their artillery shells, not in a selective manner, but in a general way the battle took place there.

The Japanese, having failed with their tactic of blackmailing the Americans, took it out on their hostages in Fort Santiago. The Japanese massacred them, either with machine guns fired at them or by dousing them with gasoline, sending them burning with hand grenades thrown at them.

The hostages broke into a stampede. The young man got separated from his father and his brother. He managed to escape, along with no more than fifty men, out of the thousands of hostages, the Japanese killed there.

He came back after the battle to look for his father and his brother. What he found there was his brother's college belt buckle, he was now holding, close to his heart.

The young man had been through a terrible time and Leandro tapped him lightly on his shoulders and said how sorry he was. The young man thanked him for his sympathy and kindness.

He looked back as he was walking away and saw the young man looking down sadly at what could be his father and his brother's bones and ashes scattered at his feet.

He saw in the grimace in Adrian's face that everything they saw, smelled and heard there had been too much for him to bear. Albert and Franklin were walking on, though. They seemed to be not so badly affected by the horrible sight there.

"Go on, look around," he said to them. "Adrian and I are going back to the car. We will wait for you there."

He was assailed, the moment he was inside their car with Adrian, by the stench of burned human flesh, the very smell of death, clinging to his skin, hair and clothes. Soap and water will remove the stench, but not what was embedded, deep in his mind, of that unspeakable horror, he saw in southern Manila, most of all, in Intramuros.

Chapter Fifty-six

The rest of Leandro's family returned to Caloocan, a few days later, but Erasto and Gertrude stayed behind in Apalit with their children. Gertrude had just then given birth to a girl, they named Flora.

Erasto was having a lucrative medical practice in the town. Gertrude, with the medicines they took out from their pharmacy, was of great help to his medical practice. He had more patients than the town's two other physicians, Doctors Salvador and de Guzman, combined. He was popular with the townsfolk, for he treated for free those who had no money. He also accepted payment in kind, whether it was fish, fowl or produce from the poor farmers who had no money.

Erasto, unlike the two other doctors, had peasant roots and he had no second thought about treating patients even in the remote farming villages in Apalit. It was a risky thing to do, for the Huks, by then, had risen in rebellion against the Philippine government.

They rose in rebellion, following the government's refusal to recognize them as a legitimate guerrilla group because of their Communist leanings.

They were also angry that those who sat the war out, but had bribed their way to the necessary documents, were recognized by the government as genuine guerrillas entitled to government benefits like free college education for some of their children.

Tenancy, though, lay at the root of the Huk insurgency. Nothing had been done about land reform. The Huks then decided that since they could not obtain it through government action and legislation, they will obtain it by force, at the point of their guns.

An evacuation in reverse was now taking place in the country. Manila residents fled to the provinces during the Japanese occupation to avoid starvation. Now, it was the provincial folks fleeing to Manila to avoid the fighting between the military and the Huk insurgents.

Fighting between the Huks and the military had broken out in the remote villages in Apalit and in the swamps in Candaba.

Erasto knew some of his patients in those remote villages who farmed during the day and fought the military at night.

He thought himself as above the conflict. He is a doctor doing his sole job of fighting disease and healing the sick, nothing more and nothing less.

He would proceed to a remote village, often accompanied by Genaro, Gabriel and Lumin, and treat the sick people there while his children played games with the children there.

The treatment was usually over by lunchtime. After a lunch of whatever the villagers had managed to prepare, the men would then engage Erasto in a talk about the huge tracts of land around them that they tilled as tenants, which they claim, should be theirs.

He was sympathetic, but also objective about it.

He said to them, "I can see the ground around this hut, lying idle—no vegetable plots, no pig pen and no poultry house. Before you try to get those huge tracts of land, why don't you attend first to what you have here?"

An army captain came, one morning, and met Erasto in his clinic at the ground floor of Lola Tinang's house.

"We have received reports that you are treating the Huks," the captain said to Erasto. "They are enemies of our government. You are, by treating them, making yourself our enemy, as well. Stop treating them, so you will not get into any trouble with us."

Erasto was not to be intimidated, though.

He said, "with all due respect, captain, I do not ask my patients, when I treat them, if they are Huks or Huk sympathizers or whatever is their political belief and affiliation. I treat them solely because they need medical help. You have your duty of fighting the enemies of our government while I have my duty of fighting sickness and disease. Do yours and let me do mine."

The captain left. The military never bothered Erasto again. He stopped, just the same, on Gertrude's advice, in treating patients in the remote villages. If they needed his medical help, they willl now have to see him in his clinic.

Erasto and Gertrude felt this precautionary measure they took was enough until one day when Doctor Salvador's body was found floating in the river. Police investigation showed that a group of men, several nights before, knocked on the door of Doctor Salvador's house. The servant opened it, to guns pointed at him. The men took Doctor Salvador away. It was the last time, he was seen alive.

His murder sent the townsfolk into panic. Now they know the Huks were roaming the town freely at night and could kidnap and kill anyone.

The town did not have enough policemen to protect the townsfolk. As for the military, its resources were stretched so thinly, all that it could assign in the town were one corporal and two privates. They were clearly not enough to keep the town safe from the Huks.

Father Agunod helped the Huks during the war, when they were fighting the Japanese. He continued to believe in the Huks as peasants fighting for their rights.

He felt betrayed when he learned that Communist ideologues, godless enemies of the Christian faith, had infiltrated and taken over the leadership of the Huks.

He conferred with the town mayor who welcomed his offer to make the church, a sanctuary for the townsfolk. The mayor then gave the order for the town residents to leave their homes at dusk and spend the night safely in the church. Its thick stonewall will make the church impregnable to any Huk attack.

The soldiers and the police, in defending the church from the Huk attack, mounted machineguns in the rectory and in the two belfries.

Erasto and Gertrude were among those who followed the mayor's order. Time passed quietly and uneventfully, the first week they and their children spent in the church. Erasto passed the time by engaging in small talk with the men while Gertrude nursed Flora. Genaro, Gabriel and Lumin played with the other children. They explored the choir loft, gathered molten wax from the burning candles there and watched Mang Tonio make from wafers or unleavened bread, the Sacred Host taken at the Holy Mass.

Bedtime was instructive to the three boys. They plied Erasto and Gertrude, as they were lying down on the two pews, they pushed together to make a long bed, with questions about the paintings in the ceiling and in the dome. They depicted scenes and characters in the Holy Bible. They explained what they meant until, moments later, the three boys had fallen asleep.

Things were not the same in the church, a week later. Genaro, Gabriel and Lumin were already asleep when they woke up to the frightening sound of gunfire echoing inside the church. The Huks were attacking. The soldiers and the police fired back. The three boys were huddled in a corner of the pew, their eyes wide from shock and fear.

"Are we going to die, Father?" Genaro asked Erasto.

"No, we are not. There is nothing to be afraid of," he said reassuringly to his children.

"What about all that firing?" Gabriel asked Erasto.

"It will pass."

True enough, the firing ceased after a while. The Huks had withdrawn. The children went back to sleep.

Erasto and Gertrude discussed their situation, the following morning.

"We cannot go on, like this," she said. "The longer we stay here in Apalit, the more we are putting ourselves in danger and all that shooting will have a bad effect on the children."

"What would you suggest then?"

"We should go back to Caloocan."

"What about my medical practice here?"

"What good is your medical practice here if you will end up dead, like Doctor Salvador?"

"So, you want us to move to the Big House."

"Only for the time being while we are building a new home where you will have your clinic and I will have my pharmacy."

Erasto, Gertrude and their children left Apalit, a few days later. Their arrival in the Big House so pleased Leandro and Crisanta. It was just as they liked it, now that their entire family was starting all over again in the Big House or nearby in the case of Donita. The country was also starting all over again, now that it had been granted its independence.

Leandro's main concern now is in getting his old job in Pacific & Gulf. But with Bill Shay's death, he lost not only his boss, but also his benefactor. He got the managerial job which was normally given only to the Americans, on Bill's order. Whoever is now in charge of the company may not be as kindly disposed as Bill was to him.

But he has, going for him, his fine work record and his long association with the company. Whoever is now in charge will call him, once Pacific & Gulf is ready to reopen.

He decided to do the calling when, after a few days of waiting, no one called.

He called Pacific & Gulf's office in Parola, but found all the telephones there, dead. He called Philip Beldry and Mark Clavier and was told they were not at home. Then he called Joseph Kirkpatrick and Tom Guernsey in their homes in Malate, but found their telephones dead.

He was puzzled, but then he remembered that Malate, like most of southern Manila, was destroyed during the war. He had no other recourse but to go to Pacific & Gulf's office in Parola.

The main gate, he found out, was closed when he drove there, the afternoon of the following day. He parked the Chevy outside in the street. He went in through the partially open, pedestrian side gate.

He was shocked, once he was inside the company compound, to find it completely unrecognizable. The warehouse and the buildings there were reduced to ashes or to rubble by bombing or artillery fire.

The compound was full of squatters' shanties, everyone there, a complete stranger to him. The stench there was so offensive, he winced as he ccovered his nose. Everyone there seemed to be used to the stench, though.

The women were doing their laundry with the lone faucet there while the children, most of them half-naked, were playing in the marshaling yard, now just an open ground. The men seated on long benches were passing the time away with idle talk. That they were there, loafing on a working day, meant they were jobless.

He stood near the gate, undecided on whether he should leave or talk to the squatters. He had read about them in the newspapers. They were migrants from the provinces who fled from the fighting in the countryside between the military and the Huks.

Those provincial migrants now occupied every available space in Manila, like the ruined compound of Pacific & Gulf. They were poor, jobless and desperate, their future, uncertain and bleak.

The men showed, by the hostile expression in their faces, that he is not welcome there. It reminded him of that time, long ago in Palomar, when he was newly arrived in Manila. He faced danger then in Palomar as he now faced danger there in Parola.

He hurried out, back to his car, sad and angry. The compound of Pacific & Gulf, a second home to him for forty years, was ruined by the war and was now occupied by squatters. He left it sadly.

He was on his way home when he saw a magazine displayed in a newsstand in Rosario Street. He stopped his car. Just as he had thought, it was *The Philippines Newsmagazine.* Dick McCall was back in business.

He bought a copy and drove home. Crisanta met him in the balcony, near their bedroom.

"How is Pacific and Gulf?" she asked him, "Was it damaged by the war?"

"It is worse than that. It is totally ruined and it is now completely occupied by squatters."

She looked at him, her mouth hanging open from shock.

He dropped the newsmagazine on the couch in the balcony and entered their bedroom.

She asked him as she tagged along, "Does it mean, Pacific and Gulf will not reopen anymore?"

"How will it reopen with the squatters, now occupying its compound in Parola?"

"There could be something, we do not know. Is there no one who can give you some information about it?"

"I called Philip Beldry and Mark Clavier. They were both, not at home. I also called Joseph Kirkpatrick and Tom Guernsey. Their telephones were dead. Their homes may have been destroyed in the fighting in Malate. For all I know, they could both be dead, like Bill."

"We can have the information about the company at Bill's interment."

They both knew about Bill's interment in North Cemetery in a few days or weeks.

She left for the kitchen to prepare their dinner while he changed his clothes. Then he picked up the newsmagazine and sat down on the couch there.

He frowned as he was looking at its cover. It was a composite illustration of what ailed the young Philippine Republic: the destruction brought about by the war, the fake guerrilla racket, the prostitution dens, the squatters, fraud in the elections, graft and corruption in the government, the Huk insurgency and the poverty in the cities and in the countryside.   The cover caption read: "A Country in a Mess."

He leafed through its pages and stopped at the editorial page and began to read Dick McCall's editorial with the same title as in the cover caption.

"Quezon once made a vain, bombastic statement that turned out to be true: 'I prefer a government run like hell by the Filipinos to a government run like heaven by the Americans.'

"The Filipino people may now be eating those words, he said, for what they now have is a Philippine government and the rest of the Philippines, they are now running like hell.

"Now that they are on their own, the lack of competence, integrity and other ills and shortcomings that have long plagued them, which were cured by the antidote of a wise and effective American administration, have burst forth like the pus of a virulent disease. It has affected every aspect of the nation's life, from government, to business and industry, down to the smallest detail of everyday life.

"Other countries have been rebuilding from the ashes of the war, but not the Philippines: the scars of the war remain everywhere in the country: the ruined buildings, roads and ports, the squatter colonies. The root cause of the nation's problems lies as much in its corrupt and ineffective government as in its leaders and people wanting in integrity, industry and competence.

"Take, for instance, the problem of graft and corruption in the government. Filipinos address it with the cynicism that echoes a Filipino politician's classic statement: "What are we in power for?"

"Then there is the matter of nation-building. How can the Filipinos rebuild their country when they cannot even make the streetcars run again? The Americans established this modern, reliable means of mass transportation in Manila, long ago, early this century. The streetcars went on running, right through the last few months of the Japanese occupation. They disappeared after the war. The streetcars were sold as scrap while the rail tracks were covered with asphalt. They do not know, nor care to learn how to run that very efficient mass transportation system by themselves.

"They replaced the streetcars with the Jeepney, which they never cease to brag as a prime example of their so-called skill and ingenuity. The Jeepney is not even an original Filipino creation, but a gaudy remodeling of surplus American military jeeps, they picked up from the junkyards in Guam, Saipan and in other islands in Southwest Pacific.

"The American military jeep did well for rugged use in wartime. Converted into public transport and renamed the Jeepney, it is uncomfortable, uneconomical, inefficient and plain ugly. A temporary measure in transportation after the war has become a permanent fixture in the city streets and in the town roads in the country.

"The Jeepney is a good example of the Filipinos' knack for improvisation while its driver embodies many of the Filipino traits of character. The Jeepney driver drives the way Filipinos in general conduct themselves, that is, in an arbitrary, self-centered manner with little or no regard for others and a cynical regard for law and order. This kind of attitude accounts, not only for the chaos in city streets, but also for the disorder, violence, corruption and lack of progress in the Philippines."

Leandro stopped reading, Dick's article and gazed sadly at Manila Bay. How he missed those days when they had peace and order, progress and prosperity in the country. What happened since then, he asked himself, that all they now have are chaos, violence, poverty, graft and corruption?

It was, he answered himself, the American rule in the Philippines. That made all the difference between then and now. Those happy, peaceful days of plenty and progress in the Philippines came about only because they were then under the Americans.

They brought law and order, good government, immense economic resources, among other things. They were sorely lacking when the Philippines became an independent country. It was devastated by the war, its moral values put askew by the brutal Japanese occupation. They were granted independence when they were not ready for it. They descended then into this mess, they could not get out of. All of that confirmed what Samuel Tyler said, a long time ago, about the Filipinos lacking in the character and the competence to run their country well.

As he saw it in his mind, worse times are ahead of them. If his generation, now at the helm of the government, which the Americans had imbued with honesty, civic spirit, discipline and respect for law and order, was now making such a mess, the next generation and the generation after that, raised without those values, will fare even worse.

He had been worrying too much, a fact made obvious to him by a headache. He laid his elbow on the armrest and rubbed his forehead to ease the pain.

Gladys and Genaro were coming from the dining room.

"Are you all right, Grandpa?" Gladys asked Leandro when she and Genaro were right beside him.

"I have a slight headache. I'm otherwise all right."

"You are just hungry, Grandpa," Genaro said. "Take something and your headache will go away. Dinner is ready."

Genaro's smile and the look of concern in Gladys' face had eased up immediately, Leandro of his headache. He asked them what they were having for dinner.

"We have fish," Gladys said, "cooked the way you like it, fried and then sautéed in garlic, onion and tomatoes."

"Don't forget the meat and the vegetables," Genaro said to Gladys.

Leandro smiled at the fine dinner waiting for them. Even better, his headache was gone as they were proceeding toward the dining room.

Bill Shay's interment in North Cemetry was a kind of a reunion, tempered by sadness and a deep sense of loss, by his friends and associates in Pacific & Gulf who survived the war and the Japanese occupation.

Philip Beldry was there, so were Anthony Fitzsimmons, Mark Clavier, Teddy Williams and Joseph Kirkpatrick. Nancy Jamieson was there. So was Dick McCall who came with Nieves and Teresa. So were some American military officers and Pacific & Gulf workers. Tom Guernsey and John Stroheim were not there. They also died at the internment camp in Santo Tomas.

To Leandro, who came with Crisanta, Gertrude, Elizabeth, and Donita, it was the time to pay homage to Bill Shay, the one man who meant so much to him and his family.

Michael, who came from the United States with his wife Ann and their children Beth and William, watched Leandro as he was looking at the casket, draped with an American flag, a medal laid on the flag.

"The United States government," he said to Leandro, "in recognition of what dad and his three companions did for the internees, awarded them posthumously, the Presidential Medal of Freedom. It is the highest award given to American civilians."

Leandro nodded. Bill and his companions were honored for the sacrifice they made with their lives for the sake of their fellow internees.

Michael then spoke for Esperanza. He thanked those gathered there at the interment of his father. The medal and the flag were then removed from the casket and given to Esperanza.

Father Domingo, a priest in the university, said at the interment rite, "We are here to honor this man who is blessed for the sacrifice he made with his life for the sake of his fellowmen."

The priest then whisked holy water on the casket. He followed it, along with those gathered there, with the Lord's Prayer and concluded it with the prayer for the dead.

The American military officers saluted as Bill's casket was then interred in a tomb of black marble.

A snack of soda and sandwiches was then served to everyone there.

"We can now eat as much as we want to," Kirkpatrick said, "That goes especially for you, Dick, on how you survived in that hell-hole."

"I owe it to the troops in the First Cavalry. They came just in time with the medicine for my ailment."

Philip said as he shook his head, "If Bill did not take issue with the Jap commandant over the internees' needs, he would still be alive today."

"Bill did a noble thing for his fellowmen," Dick said. "I consider it a privilege to be his friend."

His comment was met with a nod by the others.

He turned to Leandro and said, "Well, old boy, extend a glad hand to Philip. He is the new president of Pacific and Gulf."

Leandro smiled, his eyes turned wide, when Philip said to him, "You will handle, as before, the warehousing and the purchasing."

"I have been raring to go to work," he said, "but how do we start operation with the company compound in Parola, ruined by the war and is now completely occupied by the squatters? I saw them when I went there, a few weeks ago. I don't think we can drive them out."

"I know," Philip replied. "We cannot have them evicted from Parola with the politicians coddling them for their votes. Bill had the foresight, though, of acquiring a property in San Juan before the war. We will start there."

"From scratch," Mark Clavier said.

"Why from scratch?" Leandro asked Mark, "What about the equipment and machineries kept for us by Agrifino?"

"That guy Agrifino," Fitzsimmons said, "who is supposed to look after them, sold them to a group of Jap businessmen who then shipped them to Japan."

He turned to Leandro and said, "He was your assistant in the warehouse, was he not? Was it not on your recommendation that those machineries and equipment were put under his care?"

"He volunteered to look after them. I did not recommend him for that job."

Philip intervened to prevent spoiling Bill Shay's interment.

"Any finger-pointing," he said, "will not bring back to us, those machineries and equipment. We should not let their loss stop us from starting, all over again."

"That is the spirit," Dick said. "Never mind if you have to start from scratch. I also started that way. The Japs took away my printing press, my linotype machine and everything else in my office. But that did not stop me from starting all over again."

"I know, you are back, tilting at the windmills and you have got a lot to take issue with," Philip said.

"I have been doing that," Dick said, "for some forty years now and I will continue to do that."

He drew Leandro aside when he saw, he was finished eating his sandwich.

"Have you a got a minute?" he said to Leandro. "I have got something, I think you should know."

He led Leandro away from the others.

"What is it about?" he asked Dick, once they were far enough from them.

"I came across a news story yesterday in the teletypewriter of National Press Agency, my office neighbor. The Huks killed in an ambush, former Mayor Candido Sumaka and his son, Councilor Miguel Sumaka of San Isidro. They are your cousin and your nephew, are they not?"

Leandro looked wide-eyed from shock at Dick who then said how sorry he was about it as he then joined the others.

Leandro stayed rooted there, shocked by the news about the death of Candido and Miguel.

Crisanta asked Leandro, as he was driving their car on their way home from the interment service for Bill Shay, "What did you and Dick talk about? Was it something so confidential, you had to walk away while you were talking about it?"

He drove on as he weighed in his mind whether he should tell her now about the death of Candido and Miguel. It might dampen her enthusiasm over his return to work in Pacific & Gulf. But then, he could not keep the sad news from her and their children.

"Candido and Miguel are dead," he said to them. "The Huks ambushed and killed them in San Isidro. That is what Dick told me."

Crisanta and the others were so shocked by what he said, they broke down in tears.

He tried to remain calm, but then he too was overcome with grief, his eyes now blurry with tears. It was affecting his driving and he stopped the car at a side of the road.

They cried on until they were spent of their tears. They settled down into a complete calm.

He resumed driving while Crisanta and the others sat quietly in the car, the rest of their way home.

Adrian was in the garden, watering the flowering plants in front of the house when he saw them coming. He opened the house gate and followed the car and opened the garage door as well.

He asked Crisanta, "How was Mister Shay's interment?"

"It was solemn and very touching."

They went up to the house. Gladys was playing on the piano, the lively song, *Mary Had A Little Lamb.*

Albert, Adelita, Erasto and Franklin were in the living room, listening to Gladys. The rest of the household were elsewhere in the house.

Gladys stopped playing the song when she saw the other grandchildren rushing toward Leandro and Crisanta. They jostled each other in taking their hands and touching them to their foreheads, the way they accorded respect to their elders. Albert, Adelita, Robert, Carolyn, Erasto and Franklin did the same gesture of respect to Leandro and Crisanta.

The satisfaction, Leandro felt at their show of respect to him and Crisanta, combined with the sadness that lingered in his mind over the death of those dear to him, left him dazed and confused.

Albert asked them, "Were there many people who attended Mister Shay's interment?"

"They were mostly familiar faces," Crisanta replied. "Michael and his family were there, so were some American military officers, but most of those who came were from Pacific and Gulf."

"Are they going to reopen the company?" Franklin asked Crisanta.

"They are," she replied, "and you will be glad to know that your father is going to work there again."

The grandchildren cheered.

"This calls for a celebration. I have a bottle of whisky, I kept for this occasion," Albert said as he proceeded to his old bedroom.

"Albert never runs out of a stiff drink to celebrate with," Franklin said to the others' laughter.

"I will get the glasses," Adrian and Robert said.

"And we will see to our lunch, a special one," Gertrude said as she then left for the kitchen with Elizabeth, Adelita and Donita.

They took from there and put in the dining table, various dishes, they cooked beforehand with Lucia's help.

They knew in advance that Pacific & Gulf will reopen and that Leandro will be retained there.

They learned about it, a couple of days ago from Esperanza when they brought to her, fruits and vegetables, they gathered from the terraced backyard. She told them to keep the news to themselves, for the time being. She wanted Philip Beldry himself to make the announcement at Bill's interment.

Albert returned with his bottle of whisky and filled the glasses with the stiff drink.

No one noticed it, but as they were talking and drinking the whisky, Leandro had not said a word. Neither did he drink, even a drop from his glass of whisky.

He kept it to himself, but something strange and disturbing had happened to him. His memory had suddenly gone blank.

He knew he had just attended the interment of someone, whose name he could not remember now. Neither could he remember the names of two other persons, he was told, had also died.

The men had started another round of whisky when Gertrude called them to lunch. The grandchildren had taken their lunch earlier.

"Pod, time for lunch," Franklin said as they then proceeded to the dining room.

"So, it is back to the good, old days, Pod," Albert said as he was helping Leandro in taking the seat at the head of the table.

They prayed, after which Albert stood up and said, "Let us offer Pod, a toast on his return to work in Pacific and Gulf."

"Cheers!" they said, their glasses, raised in a toast to Leandro who was staring blankly at them, his glass of whisky remaning on the table.

"Drink up, Pod," Franklin said to him.

He picked up the glass when suddenly he felt pain, shooting inside his head. He collapsed on the chair, the glass, he dropped on the floor.

Albert, Erasto and Franklin rushed to Leandro's side while Crisanta, Gertrude and the others looked on, their eyes wide from shock.

"Quick, let us massage Pod's chest," Franklin said to Albert.

"You will be all right, Pod," Albert said as he and Franklin were massaging Leandro's chest.

"It is my head. It seems to be breaking apart," he said as he then passed out.

They carried him to the master bedroom. He came to, nearly an hour later and saw Crisanta seated at the side of their bed and holding his hand.

She smiled and said, "Come quickly, your father is awake!"

He watched them, somewhat relieved, when they came to the room, smiling also in relief. He looked around at the room. A shaft of sunlight on the wall showed him, it was now midafternoon. He had passed through a crisis, what it was, he did not know.

"You are, all right now, Pod," Franklin said to him.

"What happened?" he said in a slurred manner. "I seem to have passed out."

"Do you remember," Franklin asked Leandro, "anything unusual before you passed out?"

"Nothing except that, all of a sudden, I could not remember the names of some people, I know or what happened to them."

Erasto and Franklin looked at each other. The sudden loss of memory and the slurred speech were signs of a stroke.

"You had a stroke, Pod," Franklin said, "but it is a mild one."

He met the bad news with silence. He may not go back to work anymore. He glanced at Crisanta, who said, "I told them what happened to Candido and Miguel."

Leandro was not fit to travel. Crisanta, Albert, Adelita and Adrian attended Candido and Miguel's burial in San Isidro.

He called Philip Beldry when he felt strong enough and told him he had a stroke. Philip was sympathetic.

"Get a full rest," he said. "That is the best cure for a stroke. Go to Baguio. You can start working anytime, you are ready and able."

Philip's assurances that he is going to work in Pacific & Gulf had a strong, positive effect on Leandro. To further improve his condition, he went, after resting for a week in the Big House, with Crisanta, Franklin and Adrian to Baguio. Its cold climate will be good for him.

He also wanted to see Dorothy Tyler. He has not heard from her since the Japanese invasion and occupation of the country. He called Brendan School before leaving Caloocan, but found the line there, dead.

They checked in at Vallemar Hotel.

"I called from Manila," he said to the hotel desk clerk, "but I could not get any connection to Brendan School."

"The telephone service here was cut off during the war," the desk clerk replied, "It was restored only recently and is, for now, within Baguio only."

Leandro frowned in disappointment. He went with Crisanta to their room, accompanied by Franklin and Adrian.

He called Brendan School and asked for Dorothy. The telephone operator replied that she knows no Dorothy Tyler in the school.

"How come," he said, "you don't know her when she has been teaching there for the past forty years?"

The telephone operator was apologetic, but remained positive that there was no Dorothy Tyler, teaching in the school.

"That is strange," he said as he hung up the telephone.

"Dorothy may have returned to the United States," Crisanta said.

"She will not leave without letting us know about it," he said.

"Why don't we just visit her in her cottage?" Franklin suggested.

It was, Leandro thought, a good suggestion, but unlike them, the Americans observe protocol. One does not just go visiting someone without writing or calling up first, but then he tried calling Dorothy and was not able to talk to her.

"We'll do that," he said. "But I will make one more phone call."

He called Father Basneg on a hunch that he might know Dorothy's whereabouts. He smiled, pleased and satisfied, when he heard Father Basneg's familiar voice.

"I called Brendan School, just now," he said, "the telephone operator told me, she knows of no Dorothy Tyler there. Do you know where I can reach her?"

It took Father Basneg, a moment to reply.

"Dorothy Tyler is dead," he said. "A Japanese military officer killed her."

Leandro was so shocked by what he heard from Father Basneg, his legs buckled, the telephone dropped by his hands. Franklin caught it while Adrian held him in the arm and helped him, sit down on a chair.

"Hello, who is this?" Franklin said angrily on the telephone. "What did you tell my father that had so upset him?"

He apologized for his outburst when Father Basneg identified himself and repeated what he said to Leandro. He asked Father Basneg where Mrs. Tyler was buried. He replied that she is buried, beside the grave of her husband, Samuel Tyler, in La Trinidad.

Franklin told Leandro where Dorothy is buried.

"I know where it is located. Take me there."

"We will go there, right away," Franklin said to Father Basneg, who said, "I will meet you there."

Leandro's legs were so weak Adrian and Franklin held him in the arm when they went to their car.

He was seated in the front seat, his head bent down sadly at the thought of his former teacher. She was the kindest person, he had ever met.   He was suddenly in a rage as he asked himself why someone like her, a good person, died in the hands of an evil person.

They arrived at the burial site in La Trinidad and saw Father Basneg waiting for them. Adrian and Franklin helped Leandro walk toward the priest.

"It is so nice to see you again," he said to Leandro. "We should meet more often, but under cheerful circumstances."

He nodded and smiled. The last time they saw each other was in Baguio before the war, in Dorothy's cottage. Father Basneg was then newly assigned there. That was a cheerful time, unlike now when he is there to pay respect to Samuel and Dorothy Tyler.

He shook his head sadly at the thought of their generation, now on the wane. They are going, one by one, with Bill Shay, Paulo Palanas and Dorothy Tyler having met death at the hands of evil Japanese soldiers.

He looked on at the graves of Samuel and Dorothy as he stood there with Father Basneg.

Their gravesite looked so different now, when it was then, just a plot of ground at Samuel's burial. There is now, a concrete cross at the head of each grave, each of them with their names, dates of birth and death. Wildflowers were at the side of their graves.

Placed between their graves was an epitaph for both of them: "Rest in peace for Samuel and Dorothy Tyler, whose lives were full of love and kindness."

Father Basneg said to Leandro, as he was looking on at the graves, "Dorothy had Samuel's grave, set in concrete. Father O'Farrell, as she requested, wrote the epitaph for Samuel. I had Dorothy's grave, set also in concrete, but I had Samuel's epitaph changed for both of them."

Crisanta brought with her, two bouquets, she bought in the hotel's gift shop.

"Someone must have been here," she said when she saw a couple of bouquets, the flowers wilting, in Samuel and Dorothy's graves. She then put her bouquets, beside the bouquets laid there.

"Alfred and his wife Donna put those bouquets there. They were here, last week," Father Basneg said.

"Are they still here?" Leandro asked Father Basneg.

"They left, four days ago. They could not stay long. They were going to Australia. They made a detour here, so they could visit the graves of Alfred's parents. It was the second time that they did that."

Leandro shook his head. He missed, by just a few days, what could have been a chance for him to see Alfred. He asked himself, why those dear to him were either dead or were far away.

Father Basneg then began to whisk the holy water on the graves.

Leandro said to himself, as he was looking on at the graves of Samuel and Dorothy Tyler, what mattered in the end were the lives they led that were marked with love and kindness, their mortal remains laid there, in this land, they loved.

He nodded as he was looking on at their graves. They could not have made a better choice for their final resting place.

It lay in the shadow of the mountain peaks, near other hills dotted as well with pine trees and overlooking the valley below

It looked lonely now in the gathering darkness at dusk, the sky, now heavy and gray.

The fog then began descending from the mountain peaks, down to the hills around and the valley below.

They were soon enveloped as well with the fog as Father Basneg continued to pray for the souls of Samuel and Dorothy Tyler.

Chapter Fifty-seven

Leandro passed the time, now that he is confined at home, mostly in solitary activity. He would start the day after breakfast, seated on his rocking chair in the balcony, near the staircase. He will read, later on, the morning paper, lying on the table beside his rocking chair. He preferred, for now, to watch a couple walking toward Mabini Street.

His health had hardly improved since he had a stroke.

Erasto and Franklin could prescribe only an anticoagulant, complete rest and controlled diet to keep the blood flowing freely and his blood pressure, stable. Alcohol was completely prohibited. Meat was also curtailed and so were salty and fatty foods. Those measures did little to improve his health.

He turned in desperation to Timoteo, a barber who doubled as a healer over Franklin's objection to the quack doctor. Timoteo had limited, formal education, but voracious reading had made him a well-informed man. He was known in their neighborhood as "the barbershop historian."

Timoteo was coming. He watched him when he passed through the house gate opened for him by Gonzalo and entered the house.

"How are you today, Don Leandro?" Timoteo said to him as he was walking up to him in the balcony.

"I'm sick, of course, or you won't be here today and stop calling me, Don Leandro."

He hated the honorific title.

"I'm sorry, I forgot it again," Timoteo said.

He waved aside, Timoteo's apology, his eyes turned to the healer's timeworn face and close-cropped, gray hair. Cradled in his arm was a big bottle containing leeches.

"Let us get on with the treatment," he said to Timoteo.

He pulled up the sleeve in his shirt and laid his exposed arm on the arm of his rocking chair.

Timoteo then took out from the bottle, a leech twisting in his fingers. It became still when he pressed it to Leandro's arm as it then went to work. It was, within a short time, bloated with the blood it had sucked from Leandro's arm.

Timoteo performed this procedure, four times, each time with a different leech.

"That should do it for today," he then said. "You will now feel much better with all that excess blood I drew out from your body."

He pulled down his sleeve, back to his wrist. It was time for the big talk. He liked this incidental part of Timoteo's treatment. He seldom had company now, other than his family, and he liked talking to Timoteo.

Timoteo sat down on the chair at the other side of the table while he resumed rocking his chair.

"The newspaper carries nothing, but bad news," Timoteo said, his eyes turned to the newspaper on the table. "Not a good start for us, now that we are on our own. Roxas spoke about nothing good in our country."

Manuel Roxas, the first President of the Philippine Republic spoke in his inaugural address about the devastation brought about by the war in the Philippines.

"Our country would not have been devastated if Macarthur did not return here," Timoteo said.

"You don't seem to approve of what MacArthur did in liberating our country from the Japs."

"I don't."

"Why?"

"The Philippines was turned into a battlefield and it resulted in our country's devastation especially in southern Manila and Intramuros."

"We were at war then. It was unavoidable."

"It was avoidable."

"Explain that to me."

"Very few people know this. President Roosevelt one time held a meeting with MacArthur and Admiral Nimitz on the strategy for the defeat of Japan. Nimitz wanted Formosa as the jump-off point for the invasion of Japan. MacArthur argued for the Philippines, for at the same time, he will then be keeping his pledge to us contained in those three words, 'I shall return.'

"MacArthur won in the argument. We all know the dreadful consequences of that. The fighting led to the destruction of Intramuros and the rest of southern Manila."

"The Japs, not the Americans, did that. I have an eyewitness to all of that. The Japs began their occupation of our country with the Death March in Bataan and ended it with mass rape and murder and the destruction of the southern side of Manila, most severely in Intramuros. I saw with my own eyes, what happened there."

Timoteo was not to be outtalked. He said, "Our leaders do not even have the common sense to seek the postponement of our country's independence by twenty, even by fifty years, so that, with the Americans' generosity and economic might, we could then rebuild our country. We are now instead in a mess and the politicians have made it worse."

"They have been doing that, for as long as I can remember."

He said it as a joke, but Timoteo took it seriously.

"Quezon," as he then said, "is a good example. He declared social justice and land reform as his two primary goals as the President of the Philippine Commonwealth. What did he do about land tenancy, our most serious problem of social injustice in our country? He paid it simply with lip serice, not much else, for he did not want to offend the landowners and some religious orders who owned those vast tracts of land. Land tenancy has remained to this day, a very serious social problem in our country.

"Quezon did nothing, as well, to make our country economically strong for the day when we will be independent, at that time when we could have taken advantage of America's generosity and industrial might.

"During the Jap occupation, to make repairs in my house, I had to chisel and make into nails, the door of a truck, I picked up in a junkyard in Gandara. Nails were then completely unavailable. We did not have then and will never have an integrated steel industry. An example is the iron ore mine in Alkayag. Those who bought it, never went beyond exporting the iron ore mined there. We'll never be a producer of industrial goods."

Timoteo was not finished in his tirade against Quezon as he then said, "I also question his gratitude and loyalty to the United States from whom he had benefited so much. What did he do when the Jap invasion was imminent? He called for a neutral Philippines that would put us apart from America, the beneficiary turning his back to his benefactor.

"What about Aguinaldo, who swore allegiance to America? He collaborated with the Japs. He wrote articles, delivered speeches and radio addresses calling on us to support the Japs and fight the Americans. Aguinaldo even had the nerve to tell MacArthur to surrender to the Japs during the battle in Bataan."

Leandro frowned as he then said, "It is not just the politicians who should be blamed for the bad things that happened to us. We all share in the blame. It is only a short time since we became an independent country. We need time to get used to running things by ourselves."

"Winston Churchill once said that it took the English people, a hundred years to change themselves from a nation of thieves to a nation of shopkeepers. Can we do that, too? The way we are doing it, it will take us, not a hundred years, but forever to get us out of this mess."

"Good leadership will get us out of it."

"And where will that good leadership come from?"

"We have good people who can provide that kind of leadership."

"Those so-called good people become corrupt and abusive once they get the power and the authority."

Leandro shook his head. It was about Candido and others like him that Timoteo was talking about the corrupt and abusive politicians.

"We are caught in a vicious circle," Timoteo said. "As a generation wanes, another one rises doing the same wrong, bad things. We are, I'm, sorry to say, a vain people with twisted minds and morals."

"I am not giving up on our country, though. Who knows? We may one day find the men and the women who are exceptionally strong, wise and morally straight whose only concern is the welfare of our country. Together with the people who in turn must regain the civic spirit and the discipline when we were under the Americans, we could yet get out of this mess. I'm hopeful about all of that."

"So am I," Timoteo said as he then stood up. "Hope keeps us going, although I have yet to see the basis for that."

Leandro smiled sourly. That was it for the leeching and the big talk. He dug into his pocket and paid Timoteo for his services.

"Have a good day," he said as Timoteo was going down the stairs.

He resumed rocking his chair as he was watching Timoteo pass out of the house gate. The barber-historian had given him an earful about their country's bad situation, he saw as having been brought about by their leaders, the politicians and the government officials. He could see the reason for Timoteo's prejudiced viewpoint. He was a sharp observer who saw the vast problems plaguing their country as problems brought about by their corrupt, incompetent leaders and by the people themselves.

The front page in the newspaper lying on the table sent him frowning. It carried nothing, but bad news. He shook his head and turned his eyes toward the more pleasant sight of the front yard, the cypress trees by the house gate and Rodriguez Street, deserted but for a young man, biking there toward Mabini Street.

His grandchildren were talking and laughing as they were coming out of the living room. They fell silent, the moment they had passed through the door in the living room and started descending on the staircase, their eyes averted from him. He smiled, amused. They were in the presence of their grandfather and should not make any noise that might annoy him.

He remained smiling when, once they were out in the front yard, they picked up from where they left off in their conversation. Genaro and Gladys were arguing with Gabriel and Lumin on whether they should play a game or climb the fruit trees in the terraced backyard.

Their cousins Bebong, Bien and Nenita were coming from their house. They added to the argument in the front yard.

It was summer in Caloocan. They were on vacation and they filled the time with whatever fun-filled activity that came to their minds. This morning, though, they preferred to tell each other stories and were not yet inclined to play games or climb the fruit trees in the terraced backyard and eat the fruits they will get there.

He frowned when he turned his eyes to the newspaper on the table and the bad news it carried in the front page: A racket uncovered in the dollar allocation for the country's imports. A fake guerrilla group exposed. A police captain charged for running a prostitution den. The politicians accusing each other of graft and corruption. A governor killed in a Huk ambush. Mandala ravaged by a flood.

The Mandala flood story sent his mind, back to his old homestead there. He shook his head sadly as he read how wanton, indiscriminate logging and slash-and-burn farming had denuded the hills and the mountains in Mandala. Without the forest cover, there was nothing to hold the rainwater from inundating the plain. It was, the news report concluded, but one small part of the mess the country was in.

He frowned. That never happened during the prewar years, although even then, what was now taking place in the country had been anticipated by those with prescient minds like Candido and Samuel

Tyler. Samuel warned about the mess they will make, once they are on their own while Candido said it will be free for all, by then. Their prophetic words were now coming to pass.

The news stories in the front page were so depressing he turned the pages, but stopped himself abruptly in the business section, at its shocking top story about a group of Filipino and Chinese businessmen who have taken over the control of Pacific & Gulf.

He looked hard at the newspaper, his lips pressed tight at the thought that he might lose his job there because of the takeover. The newspaper, though, could have misinterpreted an investment into a buyout of Pacific & Gulf. Philip Beldry could tell him the real story. He called him about the newspaper report.

"I'm sorry, you were not told beforehand," Philip replied. "We were forced to sell out for lack of jobs. We have been losing out in the bidding for government contracts."

"But we have always offered the best quotes and done the best jobs with the government contracts."

"That was before, during the prewar years. Things are so different now. We cannot compete with those who are favored with the bribes they are giving the government officials. We cannot go any lower than those who offer very low bids and then, in connivance with those officials, they build, way below minimum engineering standards. Examples are those asphalt and concrete roads, they built that were soon full of cracks and potholes.

"Bill never resorted to such questionable practices, neither did I. We have no other choice. We have to sell out or go bankrupt for lack of government work contracts."

"Will I still work in Pacific and Gulf?"

"No, you will not. I'm very sorry about that."

He nearly dropped tne telephone in his hand, so shocked he was by what Philip said.

He asked Philip, "Are they going to keep you?"

"No, they will not keep us. They want only their own people to run the company."

"What will you do now?"

"I'm going back to the United States. So will Fitzsimmons, Mark Clavier, Kirkpatrick, Williams and Nancy Jamieson. So too will Dick McCall. He took it so badly when he learned what happened in Pacific and Gulf. He decided it is also time for him to leave the Philippines and go back to America. He is leaving his magazine in the hands of his staff. Much as we love it here, our time here is over."

He looked down sadly at the floor, crushed by the sellout of Pacific & Gulf, the loss of his job and Philip and the others' departure from the country. He worked with them for forty years. They were like a family to him. As for Dick, like Bill, he was like an older brother, he never had.

"When are you leaving?" he asked Philip.

"In about a month, after we have settled all of our affairs here."

"Crisanta and I will hold a send-off party for you, Dick and the others. We will tell the others about it."

He returned to his rocking chair, terribly sad at the loss of his job, the sell-out of Pacific & Gulf and the departure of his friends.

Other than his health, his family is Leandro's only concern now. Gertrude and Erasto are building in their new home in Tondo, her pharmacy and his clinic. Donita's husband Isauro is looking for a job. Elizabeth is teaching English in a high school. Albert got a job in a bank. He and Adelita are now living in a house that he built for them in a lot in Caloocan, Crisanta bought, long ago.

He stopped rocking his chair at the thought of his other children. Franklin finished medicine. He even placed among the top ten in the medical board examinations, but he refused to practice medicine in a show of protest against that course, he was forced to take over his preference for law or engineering. Adrian has not dared fill a cavity or pull out a decayed tooth since he finished dentistry. Carolyn has finished home economics, but has not bothered to apply for a job where she could make use of her skill in cooking. Robert is in college.

He shook his head at the thought that it was his fault for the way, he raised them. He spoiled them. He did not teach them, the value of money, the necessity of working or how to earn a living. Unlike him, they never worked for the food they ate and the clothes they wore. How will they manage, once he and Crisanta were no longer around to guide them and provide for their needs? They will not go hungry, though, or homeless. They can always live in the Big House and they can live on the rent from the apartments, he and Crisanta had built before the war.

There is also his legacy from Bill Shay. Bill, in his last will, gave him substantial shares of stock in Pacific & Gulf. He converted this legacy into cash, which he then put in a time deposit in Albert's bank. The interest, which he could withdraw every quarter, is quite substantial.

He nodded at the thought of Bill Shay, whose kindness and generosity went beyond his grave. But while his children will not go hungry nor homeless, what they now have is just enough for their needs. Life for them will not be like during the prewar years when they were under America.

He could do more if he were still young, but at his age, in his condition and without a job, there is nothing that he could now do except to pass the days idly.

Carolyn is coming from the living room.

"Lunch is ready," she said.

He stood up from his rocking chair and proceeded with Carolyn to the dining room. His grandchildren were already seated at the dining table with Crisanta and Adrian. He sat down at the head of the table, his attention drawn to them. They were having an argument.

Crisanta pressed her finger to her lips in a sign for them to be quiet. They prayed. They resumed their argument, once they were finished praying.

"What," he asked them, "are you arguing about?"

"Do you remember, Grandpa," Genaro replied, "the drawing of a mosquito, I once saw in your magazine?"

"What about it?" he said, although he could not recall, a drawing of a mosquito in *The Philippines Newsmagazine.* He was searching in his mind for a clue when Genaro said, "It is so big it could swallow me."

"There are no mosquitoes that big," Gladys said.

"If they are that big, how come, I cannot see them?" Lumin said, to Gladys' laughter.

The mosquito's huge size, Leandro now remembered, is the clue. It is the editorial cartoon in *The Philippines Newsmagazine.* The mosquito, he then explained to his grandchildren, symbolized the bad ones, sucking the people of their lifeblood.

"But, Grandpa," Gabriel said. "They don't have to be that big to do that. They bite people all the time and never get bigger than they are."

He gazed, amused, at Gabriel. There are no easy answers for him, the sharpest among his grandchildren. They are supposed to be eating, though, not discussing a disgusting insect like the mosquito.

"It is good," he said to them, "they don't grow that big, or they will bite and then swallow children like you. Now, finish your lunch."

His grandchildren, in obedience to him, concentrated on their lunch. They ate quietly and quickly and asked to be excused and left, right after they had finished their lunch.

He hardly noticed their departure, his attention now turned to Carolyn.

She said, frowning, "You cannot walk around in Manila anymore without being accosted by a beggar. They are everywhere. But that is nothing compared to what happened to a friend of mine yesterday. She was walking in Ermita when a man propositioned her. Imagine that!

She was mistaken for a whore, all because she had strayed in that area of bars and nightclubs."

"Ermita was not like that before the war," Adrian said. "It was then a nice, quiet residential community."

"Some of Pacific and Gulf's American executives used to live there," Crisanta said. "Your father and I visited Joseph Kirkpatrick, who lived there, and Tom Guernsey, who was living nearby in Malate."

"Kirkpatrick, Philip Beldry, Mark Clavier, Nancy Jamieson, even Dick McCall will soon be gone," Leandro said, "They are going back to the United States."

"Why," Crisanta asked him, "are they leaving?"

"Pacific and Gulf has been sold to a group of Filipino and Chinese businessmen."

"Will that," Crisanta asked him, "affect your job?"

"I am not going to work in Pacific and Gulf. The group which bought it will take over its management."

He spoke softly to soften the impact of what he said.

Crisanta, Adrian and Carolyn were nonetheless stunned by what it meant for them. They faced, without his job in Pacific & Gulf, a bleak, uncertain future.

He was so depressed, he lost his appetite. He said, as he stood up from his chair, "I'm going to take a nap."

The terraced backyard, unlike the gloom in the Big House, was lively with Genaro, Gabriel, Lumin and Gladys who were now arguing, now telling each other stories. They talked as children do, at random, from one subject to another.

They were soon joined there by their cousins Bebong, Bien and Nenita. They just had their lunch and were likewise not yet inclined to play games.

They turned instead their attention to the fruit trees in the terraced backyard whose branches were full of fruits.

Nenita, at the others' urging, agreed to climb a palm tree there, some twenty feet high, near the edge of the backyard and remove some of the fruits there. She is only eight years old, but she could, like a monkey, easily climb a tree. Gladys had a new wristwatch and she timed her.

She was, the instant Gladys shouted, "Go," climbing the palm tree on all fours while the boys cheered her on. Gladys shouted, "thirty seconds," the moment she had reached the treetop. It was her best time yet.

She began removing from the palm tree, a mature fruit, the size of a small basketball, by twisting its stem around until it broke. She then threw it down to Bien who, they conceded, is their best fruit catcher.

An old man in a house nearby threw a fit when he saw Nenita at the treetop.

"Hey, you!" the old man shouted at her, "Go down from that tree! I'll have a heart attack for what you are doing there!"

The old man then came out of the house, shouting still at Nenita to go down that instant from the palm tree.

Nenita got so scared she slid down quickly from the palm tree.

Gabriel looked, frowning, at the old man who was so rough with Nenita. He shouted at the old man, "Don't look, sir, if you cannot stand what she is doing! What she is doing is none of your business! It is not your tree! It is our tree!"

Lumin, Nenita and Gladys looked coldly at the old man.

Bien, Bebong and Genaro were not to be outdone by Gabriel, they also shouted, "It is not your tree! It is our tree!"

They were making so much noise that Adrian, from the balcony in the Big House, called out to them to be quiet, for their grandfather was taking a nap.

Leandro, though, had just then woke up, disturbed by a dream.

It began with a walk he took with Gabriel in General Luna Street, something he has not done for so many years. The changes he saw there made him painfully aware that he now belonged, more to the past than to the present and the future.

It pained him to see, when they came near the Big House, how it had aged like him. The green roof was now brown with rust. The paint in some parts of the house had peeled off.

He halted when they were about to enter the house. He said to his grandson, "Run along, Gabriel, and thank you for keeping me company."

"Are you sure, Grandpa, you don't need help in going up to the house?"

"I'm sure. Go and play with your brothers and your cousins."

Gabriel ran toward his brothers and his cousins who were perched on the mango and guava trees in the terraced backyard. They were eating the fruits they were removing from those trees.

They are not, he thought, as he was watching them, going through what he went through when he was their age. It was all work for him, nothing of the fun-filled life for him.

He entered the house and went up in the staircase. He was halfway there when he suddenly felt dizzy. He held on to the staircase railing to keep his balance as he continued to climb the stairs slowly, laboriously. He paused to catch his breath when he reached the stairhead.

His body suddenly turned stiff as he was sitting down on his rocking chair, he could not even move his fingers. He cried out for help, but not a sound, came out of his lips.

The house gate, the cypress trees, the moviehouse, the sky above, everything within his sight seemed to be spinning around until he blacked out.

He saw himself, when he came to, slumped on his rocking chair. A force like a strong wind then sent him soaring away in the sky. Caloocan lay below, so did Manila and the bay and the towns, near and far.

He shut is eyes as he then began to descend, so he won't see himself, crashing down to earth.

He saw himself, when he opened his eyes, now standing beside Crisanta.

She was in the balcony, watching their grandchildren. They were perched on the mango and guava trees there and were picking and eating the fruits there.

She was not aware of his presence there, for she could not see him, but then, she twitched her nose as she often did at the smell of whisky and pipe tobacco in his breath. She looked around, mystified.

He could be with her only for a moment, no longer than that. He bade her good-bye as a force like a strong wind then sent him soaring away again. Down below were images of his past life.

There he was in San Isidro, in the pond with Candido, inside the hut in Bangar with his uncle Julian and aunt Tarcila, at the foot of his mother's grave.

There he was in a sailboat in the sea in Zamboanga, in his homestead in Davao with Marina, in a rise in the ground overlooking Masakao.

There he was with Carlos and Regina, watching the sunset in Manila Bay, shaking hands with Bill Shay and Esperanza, with Dorothy and Samuel in their cottage in Baguio, with Nieves and Dick McCall. There he was, dancing with Gertrude, the night of her wedding.

Other images were now flitting by as he soared farther away on his journey out of the world.

He left for the bathroom, now that he was fully awake, and glanced from the balcony at his grandchildren who were now in a huddle in the terraced backyard. He glanced at Crisanta's copy of the Holy Bible as he was passing by the glass cabinet. He walked on toward the bathroom.

He was bent over the faucet in the bathroom sink when the cold water, he splashed on his face, caused him to start. Crisanta once told him that the Holy Bible has the answer to all questions, especially on matters of life and death. It could have the answer to what he had dreamt, a while ago.

The thought had so excited him, he dried his face quickly with a towel, left the bathroom and took out the Holy Bible from the glass cabinet.

He went to the balcony near the staircase and sat down on his rocking chair there.

He was about to open the Holy Bible when he was jolted by the screams and laughter of his grandchildren who were now playing tag in the front yard.

Nenita was daring Lumin to run past her while Bien and Gabriel were giving them contrary instructions. Genaro, Gladys and Bebong added to the confusion there with their cheers and laughter.

He ignored the disturbance made by his grandchildren and turned his eyes to the Holy Bible, his mind on what it would tell him about what he had dreamt a while ago.

He turned the pages and found himself, stopping at the Gospel of Saint Mathew. He was stunned by what Jesus Christ said there:

"What does it profit a man if he gains the whole world and loses his own soul?"

It struck him like a blow on his head. Everything he did in what he had dreamt has a meaning on what, as a consequence, he will face in the afterlife.

His aim, all his life, was in getting ahead and he had gone far, but at the expense of his Christian faith. He had achieved what few men had achieved. He will have to leave all of that behind him. He will in the end be nothing, but his soul. Where will it go: up in heaven or down in hell?

He trembled at the thought that, with the kind of life he led, his soul might be headed down, not up; that instead of reward in heaven, he faced punishment in hell.

There was only one thing that he could do. He must make a clean breast of everything he had done and put himself in the right with God. He must go to confession even if, not having done that for so many years, he might find it hard to do. But it was time for him to do that, so that, if his time had come, he will leave, pure in heart and clear in conscience.

He closed the Holy Bible, put it on the table beside his rocking chair and went to their bedroom. He had dressed up in street clothes when Crisanta appeared in their bedroom door.

"Why?" she asked him, "are you, all dressed up?"

"I am going to take a walk to the town square."

He was only going to pass by the town square. The church confessional is his real destination. Male pride had kept him from telling her that, for he would then be admitting to her that he was not, in all those years, living in a state of grace and was in great need of penance and repentance.

"Let Franklin drive you there," she said.

"He is not even here."

"He will soon be here."

"I said, I am going out for a walk, not for a ride in the car."

"You cannot do that, not after your stroke."

"It is only a mild stroke."

"Mild or not, a stroke is a stroke. You cannot go out by yourself."

He frowned in dismissal of her objection and left the bedroom.

She tagged along.

"Wait here," she said to him when they reached the stairhead.

She went to the window overlooking the front yard and said to their grandchildren, playing tag there, "Who is the good child who will take a walk with your grandfather?"

They pointed at each other.

She said to them, "I want the most obedient child to come here."

No one made any move, but then, at a nod by Bebong, Gladys and Genaro suddenly grabbed Gabriel in the arm.

They had him, despite his loud objection, moving toward the house.

Gladys shouted, once they were at the foot of the staircase, "Here is Gabriel, Grandma!"

Gabriel went up reluctantly in the staircase.

"Now, here is a good boy," Crisanta said to Gabriel when he reached the stairhead. "You will take a walk with your Grandpa."

Gabriel nodded and looked on when Crisanta took out, a coin from her purse and put it in his hand.

"I gave you that," she said to Gabriel, "for being such a good boy."

"Thank you, Grandma," Gabriel said, smiling, to Crisanta.

"Are you ready, boy?" Leandro said to him.

They went down in the staircase. The other children stopped in their game and watched them when they came out of the house. Their faces fell when Gabriel waved the coin in his hand and said to them, "Grandma gave me money for going out with Grandpa!"

"Where are we going, Grandpa?" Gabriel asked Leandro as they were passing out of the house gate.

"We are going to the church."

"Why are we going there?"

"I am going to see the priest, but don't tell anyone about it."

"I will not, Grandpa, but what are you going to see him about?"

He will not answer anymore questions from his inquisitive grandson and he tapped Gabriel's shoulders in answer to his question.

He looked around at the neighborhood as they were walking on. It had changed a lot. The nipa huts had given way to wooden houses. Only the Methodist chapel had remained the same in his old neighborhood.

So, too, did the town square look so different now. The garden there with its palm and fruit trees and flowering plants had been replaced by a tennis court, a basketball court and a concrete stage.

He smiled and nodded as they were now crossing Mabini Street and walking on toward the San Roque Catholic Church. Nothing had changed there. The church remained the same: a stone structure, its lone belfry thrust against the sky, the churchyard partly screened from the sunlight by the leaves and branches of the acacia trees there. Like the Methodist chapel in his neighborhood, the Catholic Church had remained the same in the town square, both which had undergone so many changes.

He walked on with Gabriel in the churchyard and went up to the rectory—an old stone, tile-roofed building, at the right side of the church.

He told the matron there that he would like to see Father Absedo. The parish priest baptized all of his children.

"Let me check if he is already awake from his afternoon nap," the matron said to Leandro.

He told Gabriel, while he was waiting for the priest, to play in the churchyard and wait for him there.

Father Absedo appeared there in a short while.

The priest had aged. He saw that in Father Absedo's deeply lined face, his gray, thinning hair and by the way he was walking as if he was burdened by a heavy load on his shoulders.

The priest said to him, as they were shaking hands, "It is so nice to see you again, Don Leandro."

He ignored the honorific title and said to the priest, "Same here, Father. It is so nice to see you again."

"What," the priest asked him, "can I do for you? Are you here for another baptism?"

"I'm a long way past that," he replied, smiling. "I am here for something I have not done for so many years. I would like you to hear my confession."

The priest then led him to a room where he made his confession. He had a lot to confess, it took him quite a while in doing it.

The priest then spoke about the wages of sin and how he welcomed his return to the fold. He said he must pray for his penance, the Lord's Prayer and three Hail Mary's. The priest's voice was but a murmur when he gave him his absolution. He then stood up and left the room.

He sat for a while on the chair, puzzled by the light penance, Father Absedo gave him, not until it came to him that the priest gave it, not as a punishment for his sins, but in the spirit of forgiveness and reconciliation. What mattered to Father Absedo was his repentance, not the amount of penance that he deserved. There came to him, as he then prayed his penance, a feeling of beatific peace. He has made a clean breast of himself and he now felt, in the right with God.

He was humming the song, *Home on the Range,* .as he and Gabriel were walking back to the Big House. He was happy as he sang it in Mandala as he is happy now in Caloocan.

He said to his grandson as they were passing through the house gate, "Run along, Gabriel. It is so good of you to go out with me."

"Don't you need help, Grandpa, in going up to the house?"

"No, I don't need your help. Thank you, just the same. Go now and play with your brothers and your cousins."

He went up in the staircase and sat down on his rocking chair. He watched, smiling in amusement, his grandchildren who were now engaged in a lively discussion in the front yard of the money, Crisanta gave Gabriel.

"How much did Grandma give you?" Genaro asked Gabriel.

"Grandma gave me one peso."

"What will you do with your money?" Lumin asked Gabriel.

"I have not thought about it yet."

"We can help you,' Bien said, "on how you can best spend it."

"That is what we are here for," Bebong said.

"With your money," Gladys said, "we can all see a movie."

"It is too late now," Gabriel said, "to see a movie."

"Your money," Nenita said, "can buy us all, enough ice cream."

"That is what I like to do," Gabriel said as the others cheered.

He watched them as they then drew up in a huddle at the house gate. An argument between Lumin and Nenita on the flavor of the ice cream they will order told him they were going to the ice cream parlor in Mabini Street. Genaro and Bien settled their argument with their suggestion that Lumin and Nenita could order whatever flavor they like and leave to them, their own choice of flavor for their ice cream.

A beautiful song, aired from the radio in a neighbor's house, filled him with gladness as he was watching his grandchildren.

When the sun in the morning peeps over the hill
And kisses the roses on my windowsill
And my heart filled with laughter
When I hear the trill of the birds
In the treetops on Mockingbird Hill.
Tra-la-la tweedle-deedee
It gives me a thrill to wake up in the morning
To the mockingbirds' trill
Tra-la-la tweedle-deedee
There's peace and goodwill
You're welcome as the flowers on Mockingbird Hill.

It is, like the lovely song, early morning in the lives of his grandchildren while it is now, late at night, for him.

He watched them, happy and satisfied, as they were now approaching Mabini Street. They came to a unanimous decision on the single resource they had in the money, Crisanta gave Gabriel.

If that is how young people like them will do things when it is their turn to take the lead, there is then something to be hopeful about in the future of their country.

He was rocking his chair when suddenly, a sharp pain shot across his chest. He had a heart attack. He rubbed his chest to ease the pain as he reflected on what it meant to him. His time had come. He is, unlike a while ago, now ready to go, full of hope on where he is going.

The Holy Bible was where he left it on the table, beside his rocking chair. Crisanta must have seen it there a while ago. She left it there with the hope that he will read it.

He nodded, grateful to his helpmate who shared his thoughts and concerns, for that is what he will now do. He picked up the Holy Bible and turned the pages to where he had left off in the Gospel of Saint

Matthew.   As he began to read it again, the same words of Jesus Christ that had then so troubled him, now gave him, hope and peace.

He looked up at the sky, a beatific smile, now on his face, as he then set forth on his final journey, out of the world and into the eternity.

Dick McCall, a month later, was at the deck of a ship, docked in Port Area's Pier 7. Philip Beldry, Nancy Jamieson and the other former American executives and technicians of Pacific & Gulf were nearby.

The pier was swarming with a big crowd seeing off the ship's passengers. Among them were Teresa, Esperanza and Crisanta. So were the Pacific & Gulf workers and the staff members of Dick's newsmagazine. The ship was bound for San Francisco.

He was looking around, his elbows on the ship's railing, at what he was seeing there now and what he saw there, so many years ago. What is now the Port Area was then except for the wall in Intramuros, all seashore lapped by the seawater in Manila Bay. Instead of the steamships docked at the finger piers in Port Area, sailing ships were then docked at the port in Pasig River. The Insular Government decided then to build out of that seashore, the finest harbor in the Orient.

Bill Shay had the satisfaction of building with his company, the Port Area, among the many construction projects that he had done there. They were all done, "all in good time, all in good time," as Bill often said about what he had done there. Everything that Bill and their fellow Americans had set out to do in the Philippines had been done and done so well.

He nodded, satisfied with *The Philippines Newsmagazine,* he left to his Filipino staff members. He had done well too with his newsmagazine. It was the chronicler of just about everything important and significant that had taken place in the Philippines, particularly in the exceptional work done there by the United States in nearly half a century of its rule there.

He was even more pleased as he recalled what Paul McNutt, the American high commissioner, once said: "Today the Philippines is the only bright, prosperous spot in the Orient. Its people enjoy the highest wages and the best standard of living in the Far East. The deadly tropical diseases, smallpox, cholera, bubonic plague, which long decimated the population, have been wiped out. Thousands of miles of good highways are maintained. Bridges have replaced bamboo rafts.

"We built well in the Philippines. Our work is a monument to American idealism and enterprise, a living monument of fifteen million people rescued from tyranny, rebellion, ignorance, poverty and disease, and set upon the path of free government, peace, education, prosperity and health. With all seriousness, no nation in the world can boast of so grand a monument."

He smiled, happy and satisfied as well with his own special relationship with that grand monument, built by the United States of America. It took so long, nearly half a century long.

But much, as he loves that grand monument of the Philippines and the Filipino people, he knows, he ultimately does not belong there.

He is going away like Bill, Samuel and Dorothy, Paulo and Leandro who have gone ahead. Where their souls are now, a certainty to him for the good lives they led while they were here in the world.

Nieves is coming, his jacket in her hand, which she then draped on his shoulders. She is leaving her homeland while he is going home after having been away for such a long time.

"Thank you, my dear," he said, smiling at her in appreciation of the love and care, she lavished on him in all the years that they were married.

He knows, as she then smiled at him, that she will be happy too where they are going and he said to her, "You will love San Francisco."

"I certainly will and I can hardly wait to be there with you and see, from the pictures in a book you gave me, a cable car passing by in Union Square, the Fisherman's Wharf, the Coit Tower, the ascending and descending streets, the Golden Gate Bridge partly shrouded by a fog, the great view from Twin Peaks of San Francisco.

"I want to see, most of all, the fingertip-size garden and vineyard at the back of your house."

"The flowers and the grapes there must be in full bloom by now."

The ship blew its horn.

Their elbows on the ship's railing, they turned their eyes with Nancy, Philip, the other American executives and technicians of Pacific & Gulf toward Intramuros, Pasig River, Luneta Park and Dewey Boulevard for one last look with their families at Manila.

They then waved in good-bye at Teresa, Esperanza, Crisanta and a big crowd in Pier 7 as a brass band there began to play the *Auld Lang Syne* at their sad departure from the Philippines.

The ship then began to move out slowly toward Manila Bay cast in the glow of a glorious sunset.